BRIEF CONTENTS

Deadweight Loss

By Joseph Stenard

Evaluating a Tax Policy

Economics includes cost/benefit analysis of various options to arrive at better decisions. The realm of tax policy provides us with an opportunity to balance the benefits of a particular tax (the Tax Revenue) against the costs of a tax (the Deadweight Loss)

Definition of 'Deadweight Loss'

The costs to society created by market inefficiency. Mainly used in economics, deadweight loss can be applied to any deficiency caused by an inefficient allocation of resources. Price ceilings (such as price controls and rent controls), price floors (such as minimum wage and living wage laws) and taxation are all said to create deadweight losses. Deadweight loss occurs when supply and demand are not in equilibrium. (Princeton)

Investopedia explains 'Deadweight Loss'

Minimum wage and living wage laws can create a deadweight loss by causing employers to overpay for employees and preventing low-skilled workers from securing jobs. Price ceilings and rent controls can also create deadweight losses by discouraging production and decreasing the supply of goods, services or housing below what consumers truly demand. Consumers experience shortages and producers earn less than they would otherwise. Taxes are also said to create a deadweight loss because they prevent people from engaging in purchases they would otherwise make because the final price of the product will be above the equilibrium market price.

FIGURE 1

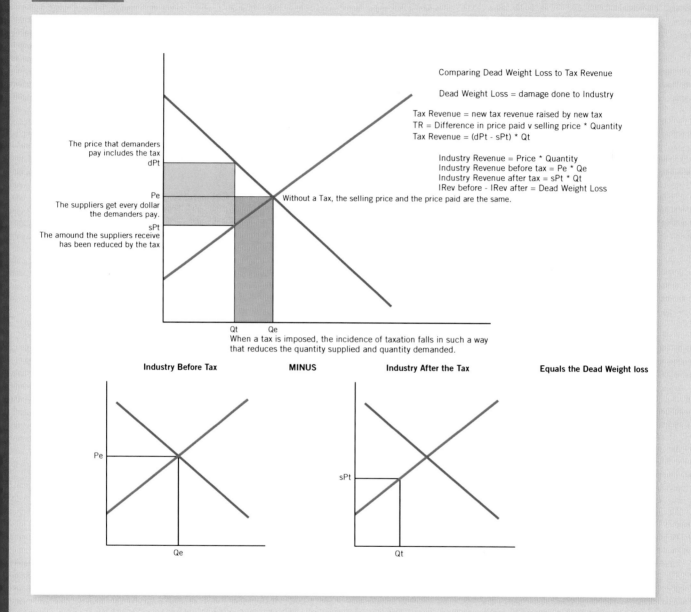

Comparing Dead Weight Loss to Tax Revenue

Dead Weight Loss = damage done to Industry

Tax Revenue = new tax revenue raised by new tax
TR = Difference in price paid v selling price * Quantity
Tax Revenue = (dPt - sPt) * Qt

Industry Revenue = Price * Quantity
Industry Revenue before tax = Pe * Qe
Industry Revenue after tax = sPt * Qt
IRev before - IRev after = Dead Weight Loss

Without a Tax, the selling price and the price paid are the same.

The price that demanders pay includes the tax
dPt

Pe
The suppliers get every dollar the demanders pay.

sPt
The amound the suppliers receive has been reduced by the tax

Qt   Qe
When a tax is imposed, the incidence of taxation falls in such a way that reduces the quantity supplied and quantity demanded.

Industry Before Tax   **MINUS**   **Industry After the Tax**   **Equals the Dead Weight loss**

Pe

Qe

sPt

Qt

Dead Weight Loss

- The damage to the market which is caused by taxation
- The loss of sales
- The loss of production
- The loss of jobs
- The loss of revenue
- The loss of the benefit of the product or service

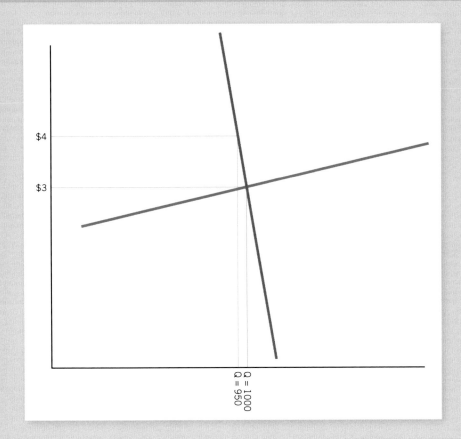

FIGURE 2

Compare Tax Revenue to Dead Weight Loss

Before the tax was passed this market enjoyed $3 prices and 1000 units were produced and consumed each month. After the $1.05 tax was passed the price jumped to $4 and the number of units decreased to 950. The Tax Revenue is $997.50 ($1.05 * 950) and the deadweight loss is $197.50

Incidence of taxation

- The ultimate payer of a tax
- The group who actually bears the burden of a tax
- Incidence of taxation tends to fall on those who have the least power and options – the group who has the most inelastic curve
- Example: Who really pays the Yacht Tax?
- What about a luxury tax, cigarette tax, salt,

The following schedule indicates the Quantity Demanded and Quantity Supplied at various prices in the market for lemonade. Use the schedule to answer the following questions.

Price	Qs	Qd
55¢	850	1250
62¢	875	1240
70¢	900	1210
78¢	925	1190
85¢	950	1180
92¢	980	1080
$0.93	984	1070
$0.94	988	1060
$0.95	992	1050
$0.96	995	1040
$0.97	997	1030
$0.98	998	1020
$0.99	999	1010
$1.00	1000	1000
$1.01	1001	990
$1.02	1011	980
$1.03	1021	970
$1.04	1031	960
$1.05	1041	950
$1.06	1050	940
$1.07	1060	930
$1.08	1070	920
$1.09	1080	910
$1.10	1090	900
$1.11	1100	891
$1.12	1110	883
$1.13	1120	875
$1.14	1130	862
$1.15	1140	850

1. What is the current Equilibrium Price and Quantity? (No Taxation Initially)

   a. How much do buyers pay?
   b. How much do sellers receive?
   c. How many units are bought and sold?
   d. What is the total revenue? (Size of the lemonade market)

2. Which is relatively more elastic, supply or demand, in this market?
3. To whom would you expect the incidence of taxation to fall?

   a. Completely absorbed by seller
   b. Completely paid for by buyer
   c. Shared equally between buyers and sellers
   d. Shared, but majority of the tax would be paid by sellers
   e. Shared, but majority of the tax would be paid by buyers

4. Now suppose the government imposes a 10¢ per unit tax on this lemonade market. The tax will prevent the market from reaching equilibrium. What are the answers to these questions now?

    a. How much do buyers pay?
    b. How much do sellers receive?
    c. How many units are bought and sold?
    d. What is the total revenue? (Size of the taxed lemonade market)

5. Compare the total revenue of the lemonade industry before and after the tax. What is the deadweight loss of the tax?
6. What is the total tax revenue raised by the 10¢ tax?
7. Which is greater, the tax revenue or the deadweight loss?
8. Do you support this tax? What might be more efficient?

Consider the graphs for the four markets below. Which market would you predict will suffer the greatest deadweight loss due to taxation? Which market(s) appear to generate a greater tax revenue compared to the associated deadweight loss?

FIGURE 3

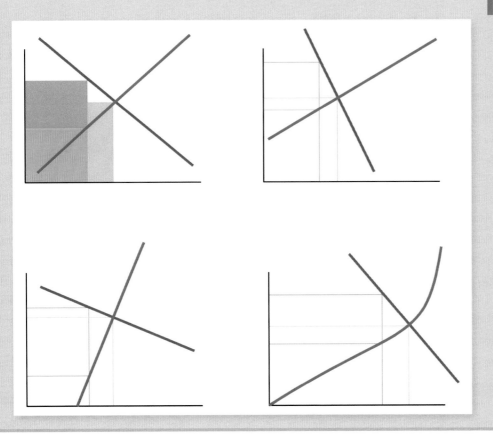

TKKNOK – An Allegory

By Sam Stenard

Far across the blue ocean whose bottom is sand,
Where the sigglethrush hunt for fine places to land,
By the Mishler still fishing for figs in the deep,
And cacophonous caves where the Caterwall sleeps . . .

Far beyond all these places there exists a fine spot,
Where the sun's always shining quite bright and quite hot,
It's the land of the Neetches! The fine land of Knox!
All surrounded by mountains with glass on their tops.

Now these Knobbly-Kneed Neetches (as most know them best)
Are famous for the feathers on their wings and their breasts,
Very useful for catching a mid-morning breeze,
And the envy of those without knobs on their knees.

Also existing in this country of Knox,
Stands the Cliffs of Much Tallness, a pile of rocks
That reach their way upward, past the day's glow,
And casts a long shadow on things far below.

On the face of that cliff grows a plant that's quite rare:
The fresh Ju-Ju Fruit that is found only there.

The juice of this fruit turns Neetch feathers bright,
Makes them grow large and allows them their flight.
On these fine feathers they soar to great heights,
Eating the Ju-Jus with great beaky bites.

Searching the sky on one sunny day,
The Neetches in Charge were rather dismayed
To see their fellows in flight for so long;
They decided right there it mustn't go on.

So they came up with a plan,
A method, a way,
To keep Neetches on land
All through the day.

"We'll make a device, a great big machine!
That will fly up the rocks and pick the cliffs clean!"

"No need for Neetches flying about,
Exhausting themselves day in and day out;
All we need is a feather or two,
From each of the Neetches
To see our plan through."

The Neetches freely obeyed without fuss.
But faced a dilemma really quite rough:
That despite all their giving . . .
                                    There wasn't enough!

When the Neetches in Charge again begged their fellows,
They found that their feathers had withered and yellowed.
For fewer feathers on the wings of the Neetches
Meant trouble ascending to the Cliff's highest reaches.

Yet it was here that the finest fruit could be found,
And without they must settle for the fruit on the ground.
But the juice of this fruit didn't make feathers so bright,
It actually did nothing but inhibit their flight.

So with feathers smaller than ever they'd seen,
It'd take two times the number to complete the machine!
Yet again they gave as the leaders implored,
Only to find that they still needed more.

But they had picked all the feathers, every last one.
And still the machine wasn't done.

From *Zombie Economics: A Guide to Personal Finance*

By Lisa Desjardins and Rick Emerson

Types of Zombies

Can we be blunt? If you smoke, you're doing the zombies' job for them. If you abuse yourself with drugs or alcohol, or stuff yourself full of fattening foods, with no regard for your poor body's increasingly futile attempts to keep itself alive . . . you will die. It might be fast, or it might take a long, long time.[1]

Your body is an amazing machine—the most elaborate, complex mechanism on Earth. It needs to be—everything that walks, swims, crawls, flies, or lurches is fighting for the apex position on the food chain.

Your body needs every trick it's got, because nothing else out there will cut it an inch of slack. In issues of fitness, as in issues of economy, one immutable fact remains: No one is coming to save you.

Your finances and your health are intertwined, to put it mildly. Your health allows you to work and, hopefully, to prosper. The rewards of that prosperity allow you to take better care of yourself and your loved ones as the inevitable ravages of aging, environment, and bad luck take their toll. Lose or damage your health, and your financial stability can soon follow. It's easy to find yourself in a spiraling nightmare of medical bills, diminished income, and physical deterioration—each of them exacerbating the others.

Let's be clear: the world is a dangerous place. Any number of people are stricken—sometimes at birth—with debilitating, excruciating diseases. Every day, scores of those who made the right choices are victims of chance, heredity, or the passing of years.

There are lots of things out there waiting for the chance to hurt you—whether you deserve it or not. Putting yourself in danger by willfully mistreating your body is selfish, disrespectful, and unacceptably stupid.

It's also bad business.

Why Your Health Is a Financial Issue

Preventable chronic diseases are costly. Let us count the ways:

At the Hospital

- Medication
- Stopgap or "temp" cures (such as heart stents, which must be replaced overtime)
- Maintenance treatments (such as dialysis)

---

[1] As a special bonus to your loved ones, your slow death means they'll get to worry, and cry, and take care of your mangled, overworked, mistreated body while it gradually falls apart. If you've really managed to make a spectacular wreck of things, the person who shares your bed might get to tend to your bathroom needs.

On the Job
- Income lost due to illness
- Sick days also scream "weakness" and/or "liability" to many employers.

In Your Personal Economy
- Someone who is chronically ill doesn't have the same energy to manage their finances or career because they are weakened by the sickness itself. Additionally, time spent managing the disease is time not spent managing their job/money.
- Medical bills are the single largest reason for personal bankruptcies. The single largest reason for medical bills? Preventable Chronic Disease.

Still Not Convinced?

We're going to take a wild guess here: You probably don't want to end up in a nursing home. Most hospital stays and most nursing home admissions are related to preventable chronic diseases.

Remember that fact.

Write it on your refrigerator or in the drawer where you keep your cigarettes: "I don't want to spend the last ten years of my life in a nursing home."

When Congress passed health reform in 2010, it allowed employers to lower your premiums 30 to 50 percent if you enter a wellness program and meet certain goals for health factors such as weight and cholesterol level.

Check to see if your company is doing this now or is even considering this. It could be a rare double zombie kill: saving money and making you stronger.

It works both ways, of course: not meeting these goals could cost workers/families thousands of dollars a year.

Traveling through the zombie apocalypse, one encounters ghouls in numerous forms, each of them dangerous in its own way, each requiring a specific kind of defense:

Zombies trapped inside a building, howling and moaning at survivors who pass nearby. The key: keep moving. Don't enter the building, and don't linger nearby.

Damaged or severely decomposed zombies, unable even to crawl, remaining shrouded by an overgrown field or in a pile of rubble. The key: such areas must be searched carefully and, when possible, avoided altogether.

Zombies who have lost their windpipes and voice boxes to injury or decay. Lacking the physical capability to produce a zombie's telltale moan, these specimens give little audible warning of their approach, emitting only a ragged, wet gasp. Beyond an inadvertent stealth, this condition carries another danger: because such creatures are unable to vocalize—and thus, unable to attract other zombies to their location—they are often alone, rather than traveling in an easily spotted swarm. The key: pure and simple vigilance. Check your surroundings constantly. Make as little noise as possible. Always give yourself an escape route.

In a similar fashion, the three most common chronic diseases can, to a large extent, be avoided by changes in your behavior. These are things you can control, things you have the power to alter, and doing so will save your health—and a ton of money. Protect yourself. If you give these monsters the upper hand, they'll take your whole body.

Type 2 Diabetes

Arguably the most common of all preventable chronic diseases.

What it will do to you—It decreases wound healing. It can destroy feeling in your extremities. If it goes unchecked, it can lead to multiple amputations. It will lead to multiple hospitalizations. Oh . . . and it can also cause you incredible, permanent pain as it destroys your nerves. What it will cost you— Diabetics have to check their blood sugar levels regularly to monitor fluctuations, or risk lapsing into a diabetic coma. Testing involves pricking your finger with a small blade, putting the blood on a testing strip, then inserting the testing strip into a small machine. The machine is a onetime expense, but the testing strips and blades have an ongoing price tag that some insurance won't cover . . . and diabetics need as many as four strips and blades a day. Additionally, diabetics must pay for medications such as insulin,[2] oral blood sugar regulators, and high-glucose tabs (to raise blood sugar should it fall below normal).

People with diagnosed diabetes incur average medical costs nearly 150 percent higher than those without diabetes. Remember: This cost won't show up immediately . . . and neither will the savings. Both accrue over time, like bad (or good) credit scores.

Why you? You're at great risk for diabetes if:

- You have relatives with diabetes.
- You're over forty-five.
- And most important, if you're overweight.

While the first two factors are unalterable, the third is preventable and crucial. Obesity is a large enough factor that if you get your weight under control even after being diagnosed with diabetes, it's possible to reverse it altogether, and go off all medications.

Prevention—Don't get fat. This means avoiding processed sugars and processed carbs. Eat large amounts of vegetables, fruits, lean proteins, and legumes (such as lentils, beans, and peas). When you eat grains (e.g., bread, pasta, cereal), eat whole grains—those that haven't been bleached, fried, or doused with suspicious chemicals.[3]

Also: exercise. But you knew that. (For tips on foods that maximize the effect of your workout, go to ZombieEconomics.com.)

You can reduce your risk of developing Type 2 diabetes by 58 percent by eating healthfully and exercising at moderate intensity for thirty minutes each day. Likewise, calorie restriction can reduce body weight by 5 to 7 percent, yielding a 60 percent reduction in risk.

Heart Disease

Heart disease is the alpha zombie of illnesses. It's incredibly costly . . . if it doesn't kill you first. The Centers for Disease Control list heart disease as the number-one cause of death in the United States. (Contrary to widespread belief, heart disease is the number-one killer of women, surpassing breast cancer.)

---

[2] **Chronic Disease** (noun): A disease that is recurring or long-lasting (defined as a minimum of three months, though these are often lifelong ailments). Nearly one in ten Americans has a chronic disease.

[3] And the razor-sharp needles with which it's injected.

What it will do to you—Heart disease can mean a horde of ailments, including: high blood pressure, high cholesterol, chronic heart failure, and coronary artery disease . . . all of which can lead to a heart attack and/or a stroke (leaving you, in turn, with severe speech, memory, and/or mobility problems).

What it will cost you—If you let heart disease into your life, the costs are enormous and grow as the disease progresses. Cholesterol medication, blood pressure pills, doctors' visits, blood tests, echocardiograms, electrocardiograms, stress tests, MRIs and other image scans. Strokes are the single biggest cause of long-term disability, forcing some victims to depend on others for their care.

Why you? You're at great risk for heart disease if:

- You eat a diet heavy in fats and/or processed foods.
- You are obese.
- You smoke.
- You suffer from high blood pressure (which is, in turn, caused by and/or aggravated by the above three).

Prevention—Similar to diabetes prevention: diet and exercise. Don't overwhelm your heart with a poor diet or a huge body to lug around, and voilà—your heart endures less strain.

Lung Disease
For those of you who prefer to spend your last years (and perhaps decades) rasping for breath, carting around an oxygen tank, growing fistfuls of revolting tumors inside your lungs, and, for a finale, feeling like you're drowning—all the time—nothing beats cigarettes.[4] If you feel like these are things you'd rather avoid, don't smoke, and minimize the time you spend around those who are smoking.

Eat to Live . . . or Live to Be Eaten
We're not going to spend a lot of time on this point for one simple reason: you already know.

Eat sensibly and in moderation.
Allow yourself to indulge from time to time.
Exercise.
Repeat.

If you ignore this, or stray from it for long periods of time, you will gain weight. Maybe a lot of it. The more weight you gain, the greater your chance of dying and/or going broke keeping yourself alive.

Diet Is Crucial.
Diets are Crap. Let's be crystal clear on this point:

Good for You
- Fruits and vegetables
- Whole grains (not white bread painted brown; things such as oats or whole wheat)

---

[4] This is true regardless of whatever insane diet craze is sweeping the populace. More on this later in the chapter.

- Legumes
- Low- or no-fat dairy (with cheese, this means tending toward white varieties, such as mozzarella)

And, for you carnivores, some lean meats:

- Ground turkey
- Lean pork chops or pork tenderloin
- Chicken, especially in thin cutlets
- Beef; leaner cuts include strip steak, T-bone steak, and tenderloin; the leanest cuts include top sirloin and top round.

Will Make You Fat and Weak

- Processed sugars (read: 99 percent of candies/sodas)
- Large amounts of fatty meats (primarily red meat)
- Trans fats (found in most sweet or salty vending-machine type snacks)
- Alcohol
- Large amounts of salt/sodium
- Large servings of dairy

Any diet that contradicts the above is definitely deceptive, possibly dangerous, and will not lead to long-term weight loss. There is, however, an industry built on reinterpreting this information in confusing and terrifying ways.

Areas of Particular Danger

- Any diet that focuses on eating only—or mostly—one specific food. The cabbage soup diet will only last as long as your willpower . . . and your willpower sucks, or you wouldn't be fishing around for a quick-fix weight solution.
- Any diet based on one kind of food. Similar to the above, but centered on a particular "category," such as protein. These are often targeted at men, because they offer the chance to overindulge. (You know the sort of thing we're talking about: the all-sausage-and-big-slabs-of-cheese diet.) This approach will work well as long as you are on it, but unless you can tolerate meat and eggs for life (and you can't . . . just ask your heart), you will soon have to learn how to deal with a piece of toast or an apple, and that tends to go poorly if your tongue has been in a sensory-deprivation tank for six months.

We are meant to consume a wide variety of real foods, and if any diet preaches against this, you are being lied to.

- Any diet that sells you the food involved, or recommends a certain brand of food. Run for the door. And check your wallet on the way out.
- Any diet based overwhelmingly on shakes, bars, powders, pills. These are often the most expensive diets on Earth because you rely on one business to provide your basic nutritional needs. They will charge you infinitely more for their trademarked, powdered concoction than the real foods it is meant to replicate.

If you feel you need more information regarding diet and nutrition, or if you have specific dietary needs (such as a vegan regimen), read health books . . . not diet books. When in doubt, ask a librarian, and be specific: say you want a book (preferably a textbook) on nutrition.

Remember: All weight loss comes down to calorie reduction—burning more calories than you consume. There are no exceptions to this. At all.

Do not:

Buy any large piece of exercise equipment. There are too many treadmills-turned-clothing hangers in the world to justify even one more purchase.

Buy any exercise equipment until you establish a routine . . . and have stuck to that routine for at least two months.

Immediately join a gym or health spa. Investigate pay-per-play options. Give yourself a trial period to see if you will actually get your money's worth. If you are sure you will use a gym, it is a great investment. But only if you use it. If a gym doesn't offer or won't consider a pay-as-you-go membership, that tells you something: not even they seriously expect you'll stick with the plan; that's why they want their money up front.

Regarding Health Insurance

If you do not have insurance, your life—both literally and figuratively—is on a rickety platform. You know this. So do we.

Do not throw things further off balance by living dangerously.

We're not your mom, your dad, your guidance counselor, or your priest. We're not here to pass moral judgment or make your life less interesting. We're here to make sure you live long enough to have a shot at prosperity.

If you behave recklessly, it will cost you. You do not have the nine lives afforded to folks with health care. You get one strike, if you're lucky. Screw up more than that, and you'll spend the rest of your life in a paper hat, serving orange soda to teenagers and living paycheck to paycheck.

You cannot take chances with your health if you are uninsured.

Bitter? Angry? Jealous of those who can afford (or were given) health care? You won't prove anything by dying young or dying broke.

Treat yourself like a survivor, because no one else will.

If you have insurance, congratulations. Use it. Don't delay or postpone, because that coverage—especially if it's a function of your job—could vanish overnight.

Get your teeth cleaned, filled, or whatever else they need.

Get a physical and any annual/regular checkups. If you have a family history of some particular ailment, make sure to ask the doctor about age of onset and possible symptoms . . . and when you need to start watching out for them.

And, though it should go without saying . . . keep your job.

If you do not have insurance, it is even more important that you:

Take your vitamins. This doesn't require joining a club or going to some freak-filled vitamin store. Just buy a massive bottle of multivitamins – generics are fine – and take one every day. If you're vegan/vegetarian, add some additional B vitamins to the mix.

Sleep. There is no magic number, but you probably need more than you're getting. Too little will make you sick and dull your decision-making capability.

Take care of your teeth. Brush at least twice a day. Yes, flossing sucks. Do it anyway. Tip: do it while watching TV at night. Don't wait until you're asleep on the couch and drooling, or it won't get done.

Do your own self-screenings. Many hospitals and clinics offer free lessons/ information about self-checks for breast cancer, testicular cancer, skin cancers, etc. Women should talk to a local nonprofit clinic or women's health organization for information on free or reduced-cost yearly checkups. (For more information, go to Zombie Economics.com.)

Drink water. Guess what? If you feel dehydrated, you've probably been that way for some time. Drink small amounts throughout the day. Do not buy bottled water. Get a permanent bottle, fill it, and keep it with you.

Limit fast food. Limit to as close as none as possible.

Control your vices. If you are a recreational drug user or drinker, keep a close eye on your intake; don't let it get the upper hand.

If you are struggling with addiction, or have a tendency to binge, it's time to get a handle on things. Seek help, or it will cost you a great deal of money, productivity and health.

Wear protection. Use your seat belt. Your motorcycle helmet. Your bike helmet. Your condom (see next point). Your sunscreen. All these things were created to save you from health risks and hardships. Not using any of them just once could be a life-altering, financially devastating event.

Have safe sex, or don't have sex at all. There are no other options. And the truth is: The only guaranteed way of avoiding sexually transmitted disease and unwanted pregnancy is to not have sex.

If you are struggling financially and don't have children . . . don't have children. Again, either use birth control or don't have sex. Having kids while in dire fiscal straits is stress-inducing for the parent(s), damaging to the child, and risks permanent doom for everyone involved.

Is it Crucial to Get Health Insurance?

If you can get health insurance, you absolutely should. But if you are so tight on cash that this would come at the expense of other necessities, consider these questions to help you prioritize:

1. How old are you? (Younger people are less prone to illness; their use of insurance is often for major, unexpected health concerns.)
2. Do children or others depend on you?
3. What would you have to give up to afford health insurance? Consider different levels of insurance, from full coverage to basic-catastrophic coverage.

If at all possible, try to have at least catastrophic coverage.

Physical concerns—like financial concerns—are an unavoidable fact of life, and are something for which you must prepare.

The zombies are coming for your money. Misfortune and time are coming for your health. Surrender either of these things . . . and you will lose them both.

From *How to Lie with Statistics*

By Darrell Huff and Irving Geis

Post Hoc Rides Again

There are two clocks which keep perfect time. When "a" points to the hour "b" strikes. Did "a" cause "b" to strike?

Somebody once went to a good deal of trouble to find out if cigarette smokers make lower college grades than non-smokers. It turned out that they did. This pleased a good many people and they have been making much of it ever since. The road to good grades, it would appear, lies in giving up smoking; and, to carry the conclusion one reasonable step further, smoking makes dull minds.

This particular study was, I believe, properly done: sample big enough and honestly and carefully chosen, correlation having a high significance, and so on.

The fallacy is an ancient one that, however, has a powerful tendency to crop up in statistical material, where it is disguised by a welter of impressive figures. It is the one that says that if B follows A, then A has caused B. An unwarranted assumption is being made that since smoking and low grades go together, smoking causes low grades. Couldn't it just as well be the other way around? Perhaps low marks drive students not to drink but to tobacco. When it comes right down to it, this conclusion is about as likely as the other and just as well supported by the evidence. But it is not nearly so satisfactory to propagandists.

It seems a good deal more probable, however, that neither of these things has produced the other, but both are a product of some third factor. Can it be that the sociable sort of fellow who takes his books less than seriously is also likely to smoke more? Or is there a clue in the fact that somebody once established a correlation between extroversion and low grades—a closer relationship apparently than the one between grades and intelligence? Maybe extroverts smoke more than introverts. The point is that when there are many reasonable explanations you are hardly entitled to pick one that suits your taste and insist on it. But many people do.

To avoid falling for the post hoc fallacy and thus wind up believing many things that are not so, you need to put any statement of relationship through a sharp inspection. The correlation, that convincingly precise figure that seems to prove that something is because of something, can actually be any of several types.

One is the correlation produced by chance. You may be able to get together a set of figures to prove some unlikely thing in this way, but if you try again, your next set may not prove it at all. As with the manufacturer of the toothpaste that appeared to reduce decay, you simply throw away the results you don't want and publish widely those you do. Given a small sample, you are likely to find some substantial correlation between any pair of characteristics or events that you can think of.

A common kind of covariation is one in which the relationship is real but it is not possible to be sure which of the variables is the cause and which the effect. In some of these instances cause and effect may change places from time to time or indeed both may be cause and effect at the same time. A correlation between income and ownership of stocks might be of that kind. The more money you make, the more stock you buy, and the more stock you buy, the more income you get; it is not accurate to say simply that one has produced the other.

Perhaps the trickiest of them all is the very common instance in which neither of the variables has any effect at all on the other, yet there is a real correlation. A good deal of dirty work has been done with this one. The poor grades among cigarette smokers is in this category, as are all too many medical statistics that are quoted without the qualification that although the relationship has been shown to be real, the cause-and-effect nature of it is only a matter of speculation. As an instance of the nonsense or spurious correlation that is a real statistical fact, someone has gleefully pointed to this: There is a close relationship between the salaries of Presbyterian ministers in Massachusetts and the price of rum in Havana.

Which is the cause and which is the effect? In other words, are the ministers benefiting from the run trade or supporting it? All right. That's so farfetched that it is ridiculous at a glance. But watch out for other applications of post hoc logic that differ from this one only in being more subtle. In the case of the ministers and the rum it is easy to see that both figures are growing because of the influence of a third factor: the historic and worldwide rise in the price level of practically everything.

And take the figures that show the suicide rate to be at its maximum in June. Do suicides produce June brides—or do June weddings precipitate suicides of the jilted? A somewhat more convincing (though equally unproved) explanation is that the fellow who licks his depression all through the winter with the thought that things will look rosier in the spring gives up when June comes and he still feels terrible.

Another thing to watch out for is a conclusion in which a correlation has been inferred to continue beyond the data with which it has been demonstrated. It is easy to show that the more it rains in an area, the taller the corn grows or even the greater the crop. Rain, it seems, is a blessing. But a season of very heavy rainfall may damage or even ruin the crop. The positive correlation holds up to a point and then quickly becomes a negative one. Above so-may inches, the more it rains the less corn you get.

We're going to pay a little attention to the evidence on the money value of education in a minute. But for now let's assume it has been proved that high-school graduates make more money than those who drop out, that each year of undergraduate work in college adds some more income. Watch out for the general conclusion that the more you go to school the more money you'll make. Note that this has not been shown to be true for the years beyond an undergraduate degree, and it may very well not apply to them either. People with Ph.D.s quite often become college teachers and so do not become members of the highest income groups.

A correlation of course shows a tendency that is not often the ideal relationship described as one-to-one. Tall boys weigh more than short boys on the average, so this is a positive correlation. But you can easily find a six-footer who weighs less than some five-footers, so the correlation is less than 1. A negative correlation is simply a statement that as one variable increases the other tends to decrease. In physics this becomes an inverse ratio: The farther you get from a lightbulb the less light there is on your book; as distance increases light intensity decreases. These physical relationships often have the kindness to produce perfect correlations, but figures from business or sociology or medicine seldom work out so neatly. Even if education generally increases incomes it may easily turn out to be the financial ruination of Joe over there. Keep in mind that a correlation may be real and based on real cause and effect—and still be almost worthless in determining action in any single case.

Reams of pages of figures have been collected to show the value in dollars of a college education, and stacks of pamphlets have been published to bring these figures—and conclusions more or less based on them—to the attention of potential students. I am not quarreling with the intention. I am in favor of education myself, particularly if it includes a course in elementary statistics. Now these figures have pretty conclusively demonstrated that people who have gone to college make more money than people who have not. The exceptions are numerous, of course, but the tendency is strong and clear.

The only thing wrong is that along with the figures and facts goes a totally unwarranted conclusion. This is the post hoc fallacy at its best. It says that these figures show that if *you* (your son, your daughter) attend college you will probably earn more money than if you decide to spend the next four years in some other manner. This unwarranted conclusion has for its basis the equally unwarranted assumption that since college-trained folks make more money, they make it because they went to college. Actually we don't know but that these are the people who would have made more money even if they had not gone to college. There are a couple of things that indicate rather strongly that this is so. Colleges get a disproportionate number of two groups of kids: the bright and the rich. The bright might show good earning power without college knowledge. And as for the rich ones . . . well, money breeds money in several obvious ways. Few sons of rich men are found in low-income brackets whether they go to college or not.

The following passage is taken from an article in question-and-answer form that appeared in *This Week* magazine, a Sunday supplement of enormous circulation. Maybe you will find it amusing, as I do, that the same writer once produce a piece called "Popular Notions: True or False?"

Q: What effect does going to college have on your chances of remaining unmarried?

A: If you're a woman, it skyrockets your chances of becoming an old maid. But if you're a man, it has the opposite effect—it minimizes your chances of staying a bachelor.

Cornell University made a study of 1,500 typical middle-aged college graduates. Of the men, 93 percent were married (compared to 83 percent for the general population).

But of the middle-aged women graduates only 65 percent were married. Spinsters were relatively three times as numerous among college graduates as among women of the general population.

When Susie Brown, age seventeen, reads this she learns that if she goes to college she will be less likely to get a man than if she doesn't. That is what the article says, and there are statistics from a reputable source to go with it. They go with it, but they don't back it up; and note also that while the statistics are Cornell's the conclusions are not, although a hasty reader may come away with the idea that they are.

Here again a real correlation has been used to bolster up an unproved cause-and-effect relationship. Perhaps it all works the other way around and those women would have remained unmarried even if they had not gone to college. Possibly even more would have failed to marry. If these possibilities are no better than the one the writer insists upon, they are perhaps just as valid conclusions: that is, guesses.

Indeed there is one piece of evidence suggesting that a propensity for old-maidhood may lead to going to college. Dr. Kinsey seems to have found some correlation between sexuality and education, with traits perhaps being fixed at pre-college age. That makes it all the more questionable to say that going to college gets in the way of marrying.

Note to Susie Brown: It ain't necessarily so.

A medical article once pointed with great alarm to an increase in cancer among milk drinkers. Cancer, it seems, was becoming increasingly frequent in New England, Minnesota, Wisconsin, and Switzerland, where a lot of milk is produced and consumed, while remaining rare in Ceylon, where milk is scarce. For further evidence it was pointed out that cancer was less frequent in some Southern states where less milk was consumed. Also, it was pointed out, milk-drinking English women get some kinds of cancer eighteen times as frequently as Japanese women who seldom drink milk.

A little digging might uncover quite a number of ways to account for these figures, but one factor is enough by itself to show them up. Cancer is predominantly a disease that strikes in middle life or after. Switzerland and the states mentioned first are alike in having populations with relatively long spans of life. English women at the time the study was made were living an average of twelve years longer than Japanese women.

Professor Helen M. Walker has worked out an amusing illustration of the folly in assuming there must be cause and effect whenever two things vary together. In investigating the relationship between age and some physical characteristics of women, begin by measuring the angle of the feet in walking. You will find that the angle tends to be greater among older women. You might first consider whether this indicates that women grow older because they toe out, and you can see immediately that this is ridiculous. So it appears that age increases the angle between the feet, and most women must come to toe out more as they grow older.

Any such conclusion is probably false and certainly unwarranted. You could only reach it legitimately by studying the same women—or possibly equivalent groups—over a period of time. That would eliminate the factor responsible here. Which is that the older women grew up at a time when a young lady was taught to toe out in walking, while the members of the younger group were learning posture in a day when that was discouraged.

When you find somebody—usually an interested party—making a fuss about a correlation, look first of all to see if it is not one of this type, produced by the stream of events, the trend of the times. In our time it is easy to show a positive correlation between any pair of things like these: number of students in college, number of inmates in mental institutions, consumption of cigarettes, incidence of heart disease, use of X-ray machines, production of false teeth, salaries of California schoolteachers, profits of Nevada gambling halls. To call some one of these the cause of some other is manifestly silly. But it is done every day.

Permitting statistical treatment and the hypnotic presence of numbers and decimal points to befog causal relationships is little better than superstition. And it is often more seriously misleading. It is rather like the conviction among the people of the New Hebrides that body lice produce good health. Observation over the centuries had taught them that people in good health usually had lice and sick people very often did not. The observation itself was accurate and sound, as observations made informally over the years surprisingly often are. Not so much can be said for the conclusion to which these primitive people came from their evidence: Lice make a man healthy. Everybody should have them.

As we have already noted, scantier evidence than this—treated in the statistical mill until common sense could no longer penetrate to it—has made many a medical fortune and many a medical article in magazines, including professional ones. More sophisticated observers finally got things straightened out in the New Hebrides. As it turned out, almost everybody in those circles had lice most of the time. It was, you might say, the normal condition of man. When, however, anyone took a fever (quite possibly carried to him by those same lice) and his body became too hot for comfortable habitation, the lice left. There you have cause and effect altogether confusingly distorted, reversed, and intermingled.

From *Game-Changer: Game Theory and the Art of Transforming Strategic Situations*

By David McAdams

Introduction

The wise win before they fight, while the ignorant fight to win.
—*Zhuge Liang, regent of the Shu kingdom, lived AD 181–234*

"The wise win before they fight." So wrote Zhuge Liang, the great statesman, scholar, and military commander of China's Three Kingdoms period.[1] That may sound like an empty platitude, but it captures an essential truth. The wise win before they fight by recognizing all the games that could be played, steering the strategic environment in their favor, and then fighting with confidence in their ultimate victory. By contrast, the ignorant just play the game that lies before them, their victory or defeat largely out of their control, a matter of luck and fortune.

I refer to the wisdom of Zhuge Liang as game awareness, the ability to see the strategic world around you with open eyes. Game-awareness helps protect you from the many dangers of not knowing what games you are really playing. Moreover, once you are truly aware of the games in your life, you can take steps to change them to your strategic advantage. That's why, in addition to cultivating your game-awareness, my focus throughout this book is on how the lessons of game theory inform the art of changing games. Mastering this art will allow you to recognize and seize strategic opportunities that others do not see, giving you a significant advantage over your peers.

Over the past forty years, the science of game theory has risen from a fairly obscure branch of applied mathematics to the engine driving many of the most important intellectual advances in the social sciences. In the classroom, game theory is now a mainstay in a wide variety of fields, from economics and political science to business strategy, and is making inroads in disciplines such as law, corporate finance, managerial accounting, and social entrepreneurship, even biology and epidemiology.

Even if you've never heard of game theory, its lingo and concepts are in the air you breathe. What does America's planned troop withdrawal "signal" to the Afghan Taliban? Will a Greek debt default lead to "contagion" and financial crises elsewhere? Did Sprint's early investment in 4G WiMAX technology give them a "first-mover advantage"? These game-theoretic questions were all in the news in recent years.

---

[1] Zhuge Liang is widely viewed as the greatest strategist of China's Three Kingdoms period, distinguishing himself as a brilliant scholar (writing military classics such as Thirty-Six Statagems and Mastering the Art of War), inventor (credited with the world's first land mine and with mantou, a steamed bun still enjoyed today, military commander, and statesman.

Game Theory in Business

In 2005, Fast Company magazine made a splash with an article claiming that no one uses game theory in business.[2] In their reporting, however, Fast Company doesn't appear to have spoken with any actual business leaders. Those people tell a different story: how game theory can and does give them and their businesses a strategic advantage.

First, game theory helps businesses plot tactics. The most obvious games in business are those played at the tactical level—how to set prices, how to launch a new product, and so on. Management consultants the world over use game theory when formulating tactical strategic advice on how to win such games.[3]

US military planners long ago learned the value of game theory for tactics. Before any major mission, they routinely play "war games," in which one group of officers is tasked with playing the enemy and achieving the enemy's objectives. War gaming is essential, as it exposes weaknesses in one's initial strategy and leads to a more robust final plan. On the other hand, a McKinsey global survey of over 1,800 business leaders found that about half don't even consider more than one of their own options when making important business decisions, much less how the competition might respond.[4] Of course, that just gives your firm a leg up if you can deploy game theory in a more meaningful way.

Second, game theory provides actionable insights. We are surrounded by games whose outcomes affect us, including many over which we have little control. Game theory provides conceptual insights that allow one to understand and predict, before others, what is likely to happen in such games. For example, according to Tom Copeland, chairman emeritus of corporate finance at Monitor, a leading strategy consulting firm: "Game theory can explain why oligopolies tend to be unprofitable, the cycle of overcapacity and overbuilding, and the tendency to execute real options earlier than optimal."[5]

Finally and most importantly, game theory can transform the culture of an organization. Firms are not simply players in games. They are also the milieu in which many games are played: among divisions, between workers and managers, between ownership and management, among stockholders and bondholders, and so on. Game theory realizes its greatest business potential when leaders of a firm create the culture and organizational structures needed for everyone to thrive together.

Raymond Smith's key insight, as stated at the start of the prologue, was that the process of planning business strategy is itself a game played within the firm. This game can often be dysfunctional and unproductive, as employees fear to openly question the status quo and managers defend the parochial interests of their divisions. To change this game for the better, it's essential

---

[2] Martin Kihn, "You Got Game Theory!", Fast Company, February 1, 2005.

[3] See www.gametheory.net/links/consulting.html for a partial list of business strategy consulting firms that use game theory. (Unless mentioned otherwise, this and all other links in the notes were successfully accessed on April 30, 2013).

[4] "How Companies Respond to Competitors: A McKinsey Global Survey," MicKinsey Quarterly, May 2008.

[5] Tom Copeland is the author, with Vladimir Antikarov, of Real Options: A Practitioners's Guide (Cheshire, UK: Texere, 2001).

to attract and/ or cultivate a different sort of player ("flexible, intellectually rigorous, and highly tolerant of ambiguity") and to motivate everyone to contribute meaningfully to the planning process (by creating "a climate of open, frank, and relentlessly objective discussion . . . without political repercussions"). That's true, but planning is just the tip of the iceberg. A game-aware management team can transform everything from how employees are motivated to how buyer and supplier relationships are nurtured, and much more.

Perhaps the best example of what game-awareness can accomplish in business is provided by Alfred Sloan, the legendary leader of General Motors (GM). Sloan is the paragon of game-awareness at the highest levels of modern management. As his brilliant autobiography My Years with General Motors (1963) makes abundantly clear, Sloan's ability to deeply understand the games of the automobile market profoundly transformed not only GM but the entire industry. For instance, Sloan's appreciation of the importance to consumers of fashion and aspiration led GM to introduce the annual model (a new design each year) and to encourage trade-ins of used cars for new. Similarly, Sloan's understanding of dealers' incentives and strategic (un) sophistication led GM to be the first manufacturer to offer to buy back unsold inventory, as well as to pioneer an integrated accounting system. Most importantly, Sloan recognized how each of his divisional managers had a competitive incentive to advance only his own division's interests. Transforming this game among his subordinates led Sloan to invent a new organizational form for the modern firm, as a confederacy of divisions, with a profound and enduring impact on American business.

Game Theory for Strategic Advantage

Most people who have learned a little game theory can't imagine how they might use it in real life. Real world strategic interactions are never as simple as the examples typically given in books or classes on game theory. It's often even unclear what game is really being played. In this book, we won't run from such complications or pretend they don't exist. Instead, we will embrace complexity and ambiguity as creating additional opportunities and avenues by which to change games to our advantage.

For instance, consider the notion that players are "rational." Rationality requires (i) a coherent view of the world and what one wants in life and (ii) consistent pursuit of that self-interest. But who among us can pass such a stringent test? Who among us knows what we really want—all the time, in every situation—and never succumbs to temptation or self-destruction? All in all, it's fairly obvious that no one is truly rational. Fortunately, game theory does not require rationality.[6] Indeed , game theory is perfectly suited

---

[6] In fact, game theory predicts irrational-seeming behavior in some contexts. In the financial world, for instance, "asset bubbles" occur, in which an asset persistently trades at a price above its inherent value. Recently, economists have shown how such bubbles can arise from a game played among investors and endure even after all investors know that the asset is overpriced. See, e.g., Dilip Abreu and Markus Brunnermeier, "Bubbles and Crashes," Econometrica, 2003.

to provide guidance on how to strategize in settings with potentially irrational players—including whether to act crazy yourself.

Several years ago, while a young professor at the MIT Sloan School of Management, I created a new type of business school course based on this deeper and more applicable vision of game theory. The course attracted just thirty students in its first year, 2004, as few were willing to take a chance on an untried class taught by a little-known professor. But those first thirty students experienced something unexpected. They emerged with eyes wide open to the world of games around them, ready to transform those games to their strategic advantage, and eager to spread the word to friends and colleagues. Sixty students enrolled in 2005, then 120 in 2006, after which "Game Theory for Strategic Advantage" became one of the most popular courses in the school. Student comments in spring 2008 included: "the best class at MIT Sloan," "fun, challenging, and useful," "incredibly effective," and "we will apply this in real life."

The best part of this course is a final project in which student teams (i) identify someone (real or imagined) who faces a strategic challenge of vital importance, and then (ii) provide wise advice in a persuasive, jargon-free memo. These projects run the gamut, including:

- *business strategy*: e.g., the future of Google Wallet, the auto industry's response to TrueCar.com
- *public policy*: e.g., how best to direct resources to encourage New Orleanians to return after Hurricane Katrina
- *foreign policy*: e.g., how to tame the scourge of Somali piracy
- *sports*: e.g., how to spice up the NBA Slam Dunk Contest
- *home life*: e.g., how to get a toddler to sleep in her own bed
- *historical fiction*: e.g., how Pontius Pilate should deal with the troublesome case of Jesus the Nazarene
- *just plain silly*: e.g., how Elaine Benes can procure a fabulous Nicole Miller dress in episode 129 of the TV show *Seinfeld*

These student projects, as much as anything else, have converted me fully to the view that game theory—when used properly, with wisdom and humility—can be a powerful and positive transformative force. My goal in writing this book is nothing less than to spread this good news, to convert you too into a game-theory disciple, and to equip and empower you to employ game theory to maximum positive effect—not just to win the games you play, but to change those games and the strategic ecosystems in which they reside, to transform your life and our lives together for the better.

When used with wisdom and humility, game theory can be a powerful and positive transformative force.

Of course, we face many intractable problems that game theory alone cannot solve: close to home, in our families and workplaces; on the national stage, in our politics and public policy; and even as a species, striving to survive against disease and hateful ideology. However, even in these cases, clear-eyed strategic thinking can help identify key factors that cause or contribute to these problems. A proper application of game theory can then point the way to practical solutions, while also highlighting (before it's too late) unintended consequences that could make the cure worse than the disease.

That said , game theory is one of those tools that can cause trouble when used improperly. The process of modeling a game has a tendency to lull one into uncritical acceptance of the assumptions implicit in that model, false confidence in the predictions and recommendations that it generates, and intellectual blindness to changing conditions. Combating this modeler's malaise requires discipline, energy, and the rigorously flexible mind-set of a game theorist. Without such a mind-set and the game-awareness that it provides, game theory is worse than useless, even dangerous, to those who wield it.

The Danger of Mathematical Theories

A little knowledge is a dangerous thing. So is a lot.

—*Albert Einstein*

According to a 2012 Gallup poll, 45 percent of Americans have a gun in their home.[7] Guns offer protection, but they also create new dangers. Fortunately, these dangers can be mitigated by training (e.g., learning to shoot safely and accurately) and by adopting best practices (e.g., storing your weapon out of children's reach). Mathematical theories are different, often only becoming truly dangerous in the hands of those with the most training and expertise.

Example: Newton's Folly

I can calculate the motions of heavenly bodies, but not the madness of people.

—*Isaac Newton, 1720*

Sir Isaac Newton was the genius of his age. The inventor of Newtonian physics and co-inventor of calculus, Newton understandably believed that he could leverage his analytical skills to make money in stocks. After all, Newton knew more about the laws of motion than anyone else alive in his time. Certainly he could apply that knowledge to outperform the average broker or blacksmith speculator. And 1720 was an excellent year to make a lot of money trading in Britain's fledgling stock market. Prices were extremely volatile, and someone who could predict future price movements could make a killing.

Stock in the South Sea Company especially caught Newton's eye. Founded in 1711, the South Sea Company was granted a monopoly to trade in Spain's South American colonies.[8] Nothing excited early eighteenth-century investors more than the prospect of untold riches from trade with the New World. In 1720, this fervor led South Sea Company stock to rise tenfold, from £100 a share in January to nearly £1,000 a share in July, before it fell back down again to about £100 a share in December. Countless fortunes were made in the "South Sea Bubble" by those who rode the wave up and got off before the crash.[9] But for every big winner, there was an equally big loser.

---

[7] http://www.gallup.com/poll/1645/guns.aspx.

[8] Spain granted this concession in the Treaty of Utretch as a condition for Britain joining the victorious alliance that opposed French-Spanish unification in the War of Spanish Succession.

[9] See Peter Temin and Hans-Joachim Voth, "Riding the South Sea Bubble," American Economic Review, 2004, for a fascinating case study of one winner, C. Hoare and Co., a fledgling West End bank that made a profit of over £28,000.

Newton was one of the biggest losers, down £10,000 at a time when £200 was a comfortable annual income for a middle-class family. Newton complained in his diary that he was unable to fathom the "madness of people," as if his losses were their fault for not behaving as Newton had predicted. In fact, Newton had no one to blame but himself for his overconfidence in his own analysis.

Newton's laws of gravity and momentum apply to inanimate objects like planets and other heavenly bodies only because inanimate objects lack the will to pursue their own objectives. When NASA sends a new probe up to Mars, there are many complications and variables to consider, but there's one thing NASA doesn't need to worry about—that Mars will see them coming and get out of the way. But that's exactly what happens in games, including the stock market,[10] from Newton's time to our own.

Example: Options and the Black–Scholes Formula

It ain't what you don't know that gets you into trouble. It's what you know for sure that just ain't so.

—*Mark Twain*

In 1973, Fischer Black, Myron Scholes, and Merton Miller published a pair of academic papers developing the theory of how to price options, an esoteric sort of financial contract that was rarely traded at the time. These papers transformed finance and would earn Scholes a Nobel Prize in Economics in 1997.[11] The crowning glory of this work is the Black–Scholes formula, which allows traders to identify when options are "mispriced" according to the theory. A new breed of "risk arbitrageurs" was born, all of them trading options on the basis of the Black–Scholes formula and making money hand over fist, at least for a while.

But then, in 1998, it all came crashing down with the fall of the hedge fund Long-Term Capital Management (LTCM) and the subsequent crisis in the financial markets. You see, there was one little problem. Just about every sophisticated, deep-pocketed financial investor was betting on the basis of the Black–Scholes formula, often with huge, dramatically leveraged bets that could themselves move markets. When one of those bets went bad in mid -1998 and everyone needed to sell to satisfy creditors, no one was available on the other side of the market to buy. This created a so-called "liquidity crisis" that . . . not only destroyed LTCM but nearly brought down the entire market.[12]

Ironically, the Black–Scholes formula lost its accuracy and validity— thereby becoming dangerous knowledge—only when it became well known

---

[10] For instance, traders who can forecast another trader's need to sell routinely engage in "predatory trading," forcing one in need to accept greater losses than he would otherwise suffer. See Markus Brunnermeier and Lasse Pederson, "Predatory trading," Journal of Finance, 2005. Predatory trading may help explain why J.P. Morgan's $2 billion trading loss on credit default swaps in May 2012 was revised upward to $5.8 billion in July.

[11] Miller received the Nobel Prize in 1990 for other pioneering work. Black died before receiving his prize.

[12] This is not hyperbole. William J. McDonough, president of the New York Federal Reserve, was quoted as saying that, absent intervention, "Markets would . . . probably cease to function" due to the LTCM crisis.

and widely adopted. As Nobelist Merton Miller himself noted after the fact: "The question . . . is whether the LTCM disaster was merely a unique and isolated event, a bad drawing from Nature's urn [i.e., just bad luck]; or whether such disasters are the inevitable consequence of the Black–Scholes formula itself and the illusion it may give that all market participants can hedge away all their risk at the same time."[13] More game-awareness might have allowed traders to avert this crisis, by helping them to realize how their investment decisions were strategically intertwined.

Isaac Newton and the architects of LTCM were brilliant and creative mathematicians. How could they have failed to appreciate the limitations of their own analyses and the risks inherent in their investment strategies? Part of the problem may have been their reliance on mathematics itself. Mathematics is built on logic and proof, often creating the perception that mathematical arguments have authority over intuition and even empirical observation. However, the "proof" that mathematics offers is conditional on the assumptions that one brings to the table. It's therefore essential that anyone who uses mathematics to make real-world decisions complements analysis with awareness of how the world really works, including what games are really being played.

A deeper issue is how mathematics can change the way that we view a situation. In one famous study,[14] college students were asked to put themselves in a manager's shoes and decide how many workers to fire during a hypothetical business slump. When the problem was presented mathematically, with profits described by a formula rather than shown in a table, students fired far more workers than otherwise. Even philosophy majors transformed into heartless suits once their firing decision was framed in terms of a formula.

Presenting the problem mathematically caused students to think about layoffs differently, focusing more on the bottom line than on the people involved. Some business leaders might say that's a good thing, that emotions and fellow feeling have no place in business. But that's plainly wrong. Long-term profits depend on having a motivated workforce, a loyal customer base, and a trusted supplier network, none of which can be properly cultivated if one just focuses on next quarter's number.

Successful business leaders must invest in relationships, but how? Will a salary increase motivate employees to work smarter? Can cut-rate prices buy customer loyalty? We know that's not the whole story either, since the most energized and devoted workers often demand the lowest wage (e.g., volunteers for a charity) and the most loyal customers often pay the highest price (e.g., Mac and iPhone lovers). Charities and businesses like Apple have learned how to stoke and harness the passions of their workers and customers, to achieve lower labor costs and greater profit.

The same principle applies to all businesses, even boring ones. Stronger relationships translate into greater profits, but nurturing such relationships requires game-awareness to understand others' true motivations. More than that, game-awareness allows us to avoid the pitfalls and needless blunders

---

[13] This quote is taken from Roger Loewenstein, *When Genius Failed: The Rise and Fall of Long-Term Capital Management* (New York: Random House, 2000).

[14] Ariel Rubinstein, "A Sceptic's Comment on the Study of Economics," Economic Journal, 2006.

that can come when we fail to anticipate the hidden players, hidden options, and hidden connections in games. In business, game-awareness failures can cost millions and embarrass a firm, while in war, game unawareness can cost thousands of lives and even shape the destiny of nations.

Clearly, we need game-awareness in our boardrooms and among our military brass. More broadly, we need game-awareness in all avenues of life where a nexus of strategic interactions creates the possibility for dramatic failure or fantastic success. Perhaps most of all, we need more game-awareness in our schools and in our homes, so we can strengthen our families and prepare our children for a future that will be rich in strategic opportunities but rife with strategic dangers—a future where Game-Changers will thrive best.

The greatest power of game theory is to build your awareness of what games are being played and to illuminate ways in which those games can be changed for the better. The goal of this book is to introduce you to game theory at this deeper level, to set you on the path to becominga Game-Changer in your own right, so that you can win *before* you fight, in business and in life, by actively shaping the games you play.

Leaders of all stripes—lawmakers and policymakers in government, CEOs and managers in business, mavens and trendsetters in society, professors and administrators in academia—face countless decisions that shape the games played by themselves and others.

Chapter 1

Commit

> *Oh my warriors, whither would you flee? Behind you is the sea, before you, the enemy. You have left now only the hope of your courage and your constancy.*
> —*Tariq ibn Ziyad, general of the Umayyad caliphate, after burning the fleet that carried his troops to Spain in AD 711*

In AD 711, Tariq ibn Ziyad led the Muslim army that would conquer the Iberian Peninsula. After crossing the Strait of Gibraltar (which is named after him),[15] Tariq famously burned his fleet, just before facing—and routing—the vastly more numerous forces of King Roderick of the Visigoths. In fact, Tariq probably did not burn his ships.[16] His men were recent converts to Islam, fierce Berber warriors eager for a fight, so there was little need to steel their resolve. Furthermore, Tariq had already sown the seeds of near-certain victory, by cultivating secret allies within Roderick's ranks who would turn on their king at a decisive moment during the battle.

Even though Tariq the man probably didn't burn his fleet, Tariq the legend did, and Spaniards repeated the tale for centuries. Certainly, that legend was well known to the Spanish conquistador Hernán Cortés when, in 1519, he took a page from Tariq's book and scuttled all but one of his ships near Veracruz, Mexico, just before facing—and routing—the vastly more numerous forces of King Moctezuma of the Aztecs. Indeed, the parallels between

---

[15] "Gibraltar" is a Spanish derivation of Jabal Tariq ("The Mountain of Tariq").

[16] Another reason Tariq probably didn't burn the fleet: it was the gift of an African ally. Burning the fleet would therefore have been an uncharacteristically impolitic move for Tariq, especially since he could have achieved the same effect by simply sending the ships back across the strait.

Tariq and Cortés are so complete that it's hard to imagine Cortés did not make the connection.

Both men rose from humble origins (Tariq started as a slave, Cortés came from a family of "lesser nobility") to positions of great authority based on merit alone, during long campaigns of imperial conquest. Both led expeditions that wound up conquering a new land (Spain for Tariq, Mexico for Cortés), against a vastly more numerous native force (Visigoths for Tariq, Aztecs for Cortés). Both succeeded by recognizing and exploiting preexisting divisions among those natives. But neither had been given a mandate for their conquest. Indeed, both set forth in direct defiance of jealous superiors (North African governor Musa for Tariq, Cuban governor Velázquez for Cortés) who ordered them to abandon their expeditions, and both were chastised afterward (Tariq being briefly imprisoned, Cortés being named only 1st Marquis of the Valley of Oaxaca, a minor honor) despite their fabulous successes.

Cortés may have mimicked many aspects of Tariq's Iberian conquest, but there was one key difference: Cortés left one boat untouched. As Cortés told his men:

> As for me, I have chosen my part. I will remain here, while there is one to bear me company. If there be any so craven, as to shrink from sharing the dangers of our glorious enterprise, let them go home, in God's name. There is still one vessel left. Let them take that and return to Cuba. They can tell there how they deserted their commander and their comrades, and patiently wait till we return loaded with the spoils of the Aztecs.

Leaving one boat was a stroke of genius, as it forced each of Cortés's men to choose whether to remain, while also creating an intense social pressure not to be one of the craven few to return to Cuba. Having chosen to remain, his men were then psychologically committed to the mission in a way that wouldn't have been possible if Cortés had just sunk the whole fleet and held them hostage.

Cortés's decision to scuttle his ships is often described as an example of commitment. However, this decision didn't commit Cortés himself in any meaningful way, since he planned to remain in Mexico for some time and had little need for the fleet. Rather, it committed his men not to return to Cuba, by making it impossible for all of them to leave and by creating a new incentive (not to appear craven) to remain.

Committing others to do what you want has an obvious appeal. If you are able to change what strategies others can play and/ or change their payoffs, as Cortés did, then you can gain a strategic advantage by inducing them to take actions that benefit you. This idea applies even to games that we play with ourselves, such as when we make commitments so as to be able to resist self-destructive impulses.

Example: Resisting Temptation

It is a man's own mind, not his enemy or foe, that lures him into evil ways.
—Buddha

Take me and bind me to the crosspiece half way up the mast; bind me as I stand upright, with a bond so fast that I cannot possibly break away. . . . If I beg and pray you to set me free, then bind me more tightly still.
—Odysseus to his men as they approached the Sirens, in Homer's Odyssey

Like me, you may spend your days mostly chained to a desk. Have you ever noticed that you tend to eat and snack *more* in the office than when you are up and about and, presumably, might really need the extra energy? One obvious reason is the easy availability of snacks. More subtle, but just as real, is the effect of sedentary work on our ability to resist temptation.

The scientific journal *Appetite* recently featured a research report on chocolate consumption by those engaged in a computer task.[17] During breaks in that task, subjects were free to take as many chocolates as they wanted from a bowl that was prominently displayed. First, though, each subject was asked to engage in either fifteen minutes of brisk walking or fifteen minutes of quiet contemplation. Besides the obvious effect of burning calories, exercise is generally regarded as a virtuous act. It's natural then to expect that subjects who exercised would allow themselves a little more vice and consume extra chocolate. In fact, those who exercised actually consumed less chocolate on average, 15.6 grams, compared to the 28.8 grams consumed by those who engaged in quiet contemplation.

How could this be? The leading theory appears to be that exercising affects the mix of chemicals in your brain, suppressing your appetite and cravings for things like chocolate. When you choose to exercise, then, you are playing a game with your "future self,"[18] by changing your future self's desire to eat chocolate. In my own case, for example, the only time I can go running most days is in the morning, while most of my snacking opportunities come in the afternoon. "Morning David" never wants to run, but is willing to do so if that will stop "Afternoon David" from snacking so much. As long as Afternoon David prefers not to snack after a run, my snacking problem is no big deal. Anticipating that Afternoon David will snack *unless* I exercise, Morning David hits the trails.

Sometimes the solution is not so easy. Consider the problem of losing weight. How can you (i.e., your present self) incentivize yourself (i.e., your future self) to make a real effort to lose weight? Just eating less today won't be enough, since your future self may then just splurge and gain all the weight back again. In a 2006 *Forbes* magazine article[19], 5 economists Ian Ayres and Barry Nalebuff envisioned a new sort of business offering a novel solution to this problem: "weight-loss bonds." Dieters would pay $1,000 for a weight-loss

---

[17] Hwajung Oh and Adrian Taylor, "Brisk Walking Reduces Ad Libitum Snacking in Regular Chocolate Eaters During a Workplace Simulation," *Appetite*, 2012.

[18] Believe it or not, this business of having "two selves" is fairly standard economics. For decades, economists have grappled with the fact that people routinely make commitments whose only real effect is so restrict their own options. One of our leading theories is now the "dual self model." According to this model, motivated and supported by psychological and neurological evidence, each of us is really two selves: (i) an impulsive self who has default control over moment-by-moment actions and (ii) a cooler self who can step forward and take control on an as-needed basis. The impulsive self is easily swayed by the temptation, while the cooler self is more able to resist. However, exercising control is tiring for the cooler self, so that it actually becomes harder to control oneself the longer that one most exercise control. This model helps to explain many diverse phenomena. For example, why do alcoholics pour their drink down the drain? If they can muster the willpower to do that, surely they must have enough strength to resist taking a little sip? No—not if willpower is "like a muscle." When tired, in a moment of weakness, they will drink. Anticipating this, it makes sense for alcoholics to commit not to drink, or at least force themselves to take the extra step of going to buy more alcohol. See, e.g., Drew Fudenberg and David K. Levine, "Timing and Self-Control," *Econometrica*, 2012, presented as the Fisher-Schultz Lecture at the 2010 World Congress of the Econometric Society.

[19] Ian Ayres and Barry Nalebuff, "Skin in the Game," *Forbes*, November 13, 2006.

bond and then, as long as they met prespecified dieting goals, would receive an above-market rate of return. Ayres and Nalebuff's business would make money as some dieters "defaulted," while dieters would benefit by having more of an incentive to keep off the pounds.

A weight -loss bond is a way for your present self to incentivize your future self to stick to a diet. In this sense, buying a weight-loss bond is very much like Cortés's decision to sink his fleet, a way for one player (Cortés, your present self) to commit another player (Cortés's men, your future self) to do what it wants.

How Is Commitment Related to "Moving First"?

Commitments are only effective when made early enough (and visibly enough) to have an impact on what others choose to do. Thus, anyone who commits needs to "move first," in the sense of committing before others make their decisions. But what people typically mean when they speak of "moving first" is the notion of moving earlier or more quickly. The rest of this chapter (and the Game-Theory Focus section that follows) explores what moving first really means, from a strategic point of view.

Influence the Timing of Moves

Git thar fust with the most men.
> —*General Nathan Bedford Forrest, legendary Confederate cavalry commander, on the key to his battlefield success*

"The early bird gets the worm." That may be true for birds but, in business , there isn't always an advantage to being first into a new market space. As marketing professors Gerard Tellis and Peter Golder note in *Will and Vision: How Latecomers Grow to Dominate Markets* (2001): "Market pioneering is neither necessary nor sufficient for long-term success." Indeed, many companies that are widely believed to be pioneers were in fact late arrivals to their categories: Kodak in cameras (their 1888 entry was preceded by the daguerrotype in 1839), Procter & Gamble in diapers (their Pampers launch in 1961 was preceded by Johnson & Johnson's Chux in 1934), Xerox in photocopiers (it faced a crowded field of about thirty copying machine manufacturers when it entered in 1959), and Apple in personal computers (its 1976 launch came eighteen months after the MITS Altair).

These firms dominated their markets for years not because they did things first, but because they did things best. Consider Apple. The first affordable personal computer wasn't the Apple I but the Altair from Micro Instrumentation and Telemetry Systems (MITS). In July 1976, the very month that Apple I launched, *BusinessWeek* magazine ran a story titled "Microcomputers Catch on Fast,"[20] in which it referred to MITS as the "IBM of home computers" and reported that MITS's "early lead has made its design the de facto industry standard." Indeed, the Altair had a clear lead both in hardware (its method of transferring data within the computer, the S-100 bus, quickly became the industry standard) and in software (its operating system, Altair BASIC, was Microsoft's first ever product). But few have ever heard of the Altair because

---

[20] "Microcomputers Catch on Fast," *BusinessWeek*, July 12, 1976.

MITS pursued a losing business strategy. The Altair was sold unassembled, as a hobbyist kit, and the user interface was extremely limited, essentially just a bunch of switches and lights. This left the door open for Apple to enter with a pre-assembled personal computer featuring an easy-to-use video display. Indeed, being "late to the game" may actually have been to Apple's advantage, since it could learn from the Altair's flaws when designing the Apple I.

Other times, being first is absolutely essential. Nowhere is this more true than in military battle, where the side that positions itself first (on more advantageous ground) often enjoys a decisive advantage. Of course, moving an army quickly is also quite hazardous, as it can strain supply lines and force a commander to drive blind. This may help explain why only the rarest commander seems capable of translating the need for speed in battle into a sustained strategic advantage. When one of these rare commanders comes along, however, he can alter the course of an entire war. Nazi Field Marshal Erwin Rommel, master of the art of tank warfare during World War II, is one example of such a Game-Changer.

Even better may be Confederate General Nathan Bedford Forrest. Civil War historians Shelby Foote and Bruce Catton have said of Forrest: "The Civil War illuminated only two men of military genius. One was Abraham Lincoln. The other was Nathan Bedford Forrest"; and, "Forrest used his horsemen as a modern general [does] motorized infantry. . . . Not for nothing did Forrest say the essence of strategy was 'to git thar fust with the most men.'"

Forrest entered the war as an uneducated private but left as the Confederacy's most feared general. Union General William Tecumseh Sherman once wrote to his commander, General Ulysses S. Grant: "I will order them to go out and follow Forrest to the death, even if it costs ten thousand lives and breaks the Treasury. There will never be peace in Tennessee until Forrest is dead!" Certainly, the man was fierce. During the war, he purportedly had thirty horses shot out from under him but personally killed thirty-one Union soldiers. "I was a horse ahead at the end," he said.

FIGURE 1

Game-Changers Erwin Rommel and Nathan Bedford Forrest

Forrest's ability to position and reposition his cavalry forces quickly (and fearlessly) was key to his ability to defeat superior Union forces time and time again throughout the war. In 1864, for instance, Union General Samuel Sturgis descended on Forrest at Brice's Crossroads in northern Mississippi with a force nearly twice as large. Uncowed, Forrest advanced aggressively while Sturgis was still on the move, engaging and defeating Sturgis's cavalry before the rest of his army could arrive. Unhorsed, the Union forces were then blind to Forrest's moves. When he assaulted a bridge near the back of their position, Union troops feared the worst, that Forrest had found a way to attack them from behind. Sturgis ordered a general retreat which quickly descended into a chaotic, panicky rout. The ensuing chase stretched through six counties, until finally Forrest's men grew too tired to ride down any more fleeing Union troops, more than 1,500 of whom were taken prisoner.

In any battle, whether in business or in war, the combatants' desire to win creates an adversarial dynamic that spills even into the question of who moves first. In a military battle, generals like Nathan Bedford Forrest may race to be the first to claim the high ground, while in business, savvy firms may wait in hopes of prompting someone else to pioneer a new market. Not all games are like that. Sometimes, as in the following example, everyone agrees who ought to move first.

Example: Vacation Rental By Owner (VRBO)

HomeAway Inc. is the giant of the vacation rental by owner (VRBO) market, with many popular websites including HomeAway.com, VRBO.com, VacationRentals.com, and BedandBreakfast.com. HomeAway.com alone offers "more than 325,000 vacation rentals to choose from." With so many properties, however, it is difficult to ensure the accuracy of every listing. Not surprisingly, some owners slip through the cracks with deceptive descriptions of their rental properties. There is even a term for this phenomenon: "SNAD" ("significantly not as described").

HomeAway.com user "vixen25" described her own SNAD experience on HomeAway's community discussion board:

> Everything in the ad turned out to be grossly exaggerated. The house was not within walking distance to the beach (it was a 15 minute drive at best). There were no large sauce pans to cook with (despite the house being rented for 14 guests). The dishwasher was broken. And on and on.[21]

---

[21] This is a heavily condensed version of vixen25's actual statement, available at http://community
.homeaway.com/thread/3381. As it turns out, vixen25's real problems began after the vacation ended, when the owner refused to return her $500 security deposit and played a dirty trick to get HomeAway to remove vixen25's complaint from their site. (According to vixen25, the owner offered to give back the deposit if vixen25 removed her complaint and, when she agreed, asked her to put that in writing. When vixen25 sent an email stating "I will remove my negative feedback once you return my deposit," the owner forwarded it to HomeAway, claiming that vixen25 was trying to extort her. HomeAway removed the complaint and the owner never returned the deposit.)

At least vixen25 had a place to stay. In a November 2011 piece titled "Vacation rental scams are a growing problem,"[22] consumer advocate Christopher Elliott told the even more unfortunate story of Tania Rieben. Ms. Rieben had wired $4,300 for a six-week Maui condo rental to an owner she found through VRBO.com, only to discover that that person's VRBO.com account had been hacked and her money had been lost to a scam. Worse yet, neither the owner nor VRBO.com took any responsibility for her loss, leaving her with no money . . . and no vacation.

From a game-theory perspective, the fundamental problem here relates to the timing of moves: renters must pay to reserve a property before they can verify whether it has been described accurately. This gives unscrupulous property owners an incentive to post deceptive listings. Fortunately, a new site called Airbnb.com has burst onto the scene with a radical new business model that solves this problem. Under Airbnb's approach, renters are not charged until twenty-four hours after their stay begins. This gives renters a chance to inspect the property and ensure that deceptive property owners aren't paid.[23] Anticipating this, owners have an incentive to describe their properties truthfully, while scammers have nothing to gain from hacking into property owners' accounts.

Everyone wins in a system like this, in which renters don't need to worry about scams or SNADs. The only potential loser is HomeAway, whose system fails to engender the same level of automatic trust and whose market is therefore potentially vulnerable to invasion by the Airbnb model. Perhaps this explains why upstart Airbnb already had a $1 billion valuation in July 2011.[24] HomeAway's CEO, Brian Sharples, recently told the Wall Street Journal that he isn't worried ("Those guys are really good, [but] not as good as we are"),[25] but perhaps he should be. Even better, perhaps he should learn from what works at Airbnb and find a way to let HomeAway property owners "move first," so that vacationers can be even more confident in the quality of HomeAway rentals.

Sometimes, Moving First Isn't Possible

In October 2000, Sony launched the Playstation 2 (PS2), the best-selling videogame console of all time. (As of January 2011, 150 million PS2 devices had been sold, along with 1.5 billion games.) A year later, Microsoft and Nintendo launched their own highly anticipated "sixth-generation" consoles, known as the Xbox and GameCube. Each of these competitors faced a fundamental

---

[22] http://www.elliott.org/blog/vacation-rental-scams-are-a-growing-problem.

[23] Airbnb's system also protects property owners from unscrupulous renters. First, Airbnb's reputation system allows property owners to offer feedback on renters, helping owners to identify (and not rent to) freeloaders who might try to stay one night and then make a false complaint. Second, Airbnb mediates all payments between owners and renters. This allows Airbnb to limit owners' flexibility to renegotiate the price. This stops unscrupulous renters from threatening payment cancellation or negative feedback to pressure the property owner to accept a lower price. Such "buyer extortion" is a problem on other sites, such as eBay, that bring buyers and sellers together but do not mediate the payment process. (For more on eBay, see Game-Changer File 5, "eBay Reputation.")

[24] Geoffrey Fowler, "Airbnb Is Latest Start-Up to Secure $1 Billion Valuation," Wall Street Journal, July 26, 2011. By September 2012, Airbnb had a valuation of $2 billion; see Alyson Shontell, "Airbnb Raising $100 Million at a $2 Billion+ Valuation," SFGate.com, September 27, 2012.

[25] Ty McMahan, "HomeAway's CEO Talks IPOs & Airbnb's Valuation," *Wall Street Journal*, October 13, 2011.

FIGURE 2

Game tree for the Xbox Entry Game

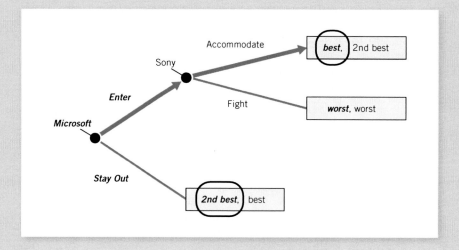

decision: whether to pursue a "me-too" strategy and attempt to match or better the PS2 in terms of graphics and immersive experience, or to design a device with different strengths that would compete less directly with Sony. In effect, Microsoft and Nintendo had to decide whether to enter the same computation-intensive niche that Sony had already carved out, or strike out in their own directions.

Whether it's a good move for (say) Microsoft to enter Sony's turf depends on how Sony is likely to respond. Will Sony launch an all-out price war, selling the PS2 at a loss to ensure that Microsoft also loses money? Or will Sony be more accommodating and set a profitable price at which both can peacefully coexist? It's not worth entering Sony's territory if doing so will trigger a price war, but otherwise there is room enough for both Sony and Microsoft to make plenty of money sharing the hardcore gamer market. Figure 2 describes this Xbox Entry Game in the form of a game tree, where Sony naturally decides whether to launch a price war after Microsoft decides whether to enter with a similar device.

How to Read a Game Tree
A game tree provides a convenient way to summarize each player's strategic options in games in which players move sequentially. For instance, figure 2 illustrates how (i) Microsoft moves first, deciding whether or not to enter the hardcore gamer market, and (ii) if Microsoft enters, Sony must then decide whether or not to fight. The game tree also shows how each player ranks the possible outcomes of the game, from best to worst, under the convention that the first-mover's payoff is listed first. For instance, "Microsoft Enter + Sony Accommodate" is the best possible outcome for Microsoft but only the second-best outcome for Sony, while "Microsoft Enter + Sony Fight" is the worst possible outcome for both.

Returning to our discussion of the Xbox Entry Game, Sony could have potentially deterred Microsoft from entering its market by committing, ahead of time, to fight any entry with an all-out price war. Such a commitment would effectively allow Sony to move first, from a strategic point of view, and induce Microsoft to stay out. Unfortunately for Sony, there was no way to *credibly* commit to such a threat. Why not? Once the Xbox launches, there is no hope of inducing Microsoft to take it off store shelves.[26] Thus, the only possible future benefit of fighting a price war would be if Microsoft were sufficiently punished that it decided to stay away from Sony's turf in the *next* generation of videogame consoles. But that's several years away, a "lifetime" in Sony's business. Moreover, without the ability to harvest sufficient profits now to plow into next-generation R & D, Sony could find itself in a risky and vulnerable position in the next product generation.

Thus, Sony really had no way to move first and deter Microsoft's introduction of the Xbox.[27] Sony remained profitable, but not nearly as profitable as it would have been if only Microsoft had chosen to stay out of the console business, or launched a different sort of console that didn't compete so directly with the PS2.

In all of the games that we've considered so far, it matters who moves first. But there are other situations in which the likely outcome of the game doesn't depend on the timing of moves. The most famous such game is the Prisoners' Dilemma.

The Prisoners' Dilemma

The police have arrested two criminals on charges that carry a prison term of up to five years, but strongly suspect that they also committed a worse crime (say, armed robbery) that carries a term of up to twenty years. The police interrogator puts them in separate cells and says to each, "It's time for you to confess to the armed robbery. How long you stay in prison will depend on who confesses. If you're the only one to confess, I will let you walk free today because of your cooperation. Otherwise, you'll spend five years behind bars if neither of you confesses, ten years if both of you confess, and twenty years if you're the only one not to confess."

Figure 3 illustrates the players' payoffs (in terms of jail time) in each possible outcome of the game, using a so-called payoff matrix. These diagrams will be used throughout the book so, before proceeding, let me describe how to read them. (While potentially confusing at first, payoff matrices will become easy to read and understand once you get used to them.)

HOW TO READ A PAYOFF MATRIX

A payoff matrix is a quick and easy way to summarize players' incentives in a game, as well as to draw strategic connections between games that may at first glance seem to have little in common. Every payoff matrix shows

---

[26] Videogame console makers incur huge R&D costs in developing new gaming systems. Once these costs are "sunk," console makers have an incentive to keep their systems on the market, even at prices too low for them to recover all their costs.

[27] Nintendo also launched a me-too console in 2001, but the GameCube was a resounding failure, with only about 21 million units sold worldwide. In 2006, Nintendo changed course and carved out its own niche with the Wii, a console that doesn't even attempt to appeal to hardcore gamers. Despite conceding that market to the PS2 and Xbox, Nintendo's Wii led both Sony and Microsoft in cumulative sales as of the first quarter of 2012.

FIGURE 3

Payoff matrix for the Prisoners' Dilemma

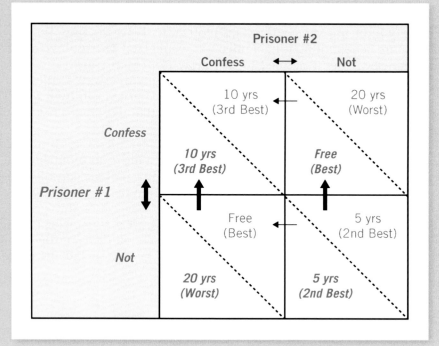

FIGURE 4

Generic payoff matrix (without incentive arrows)

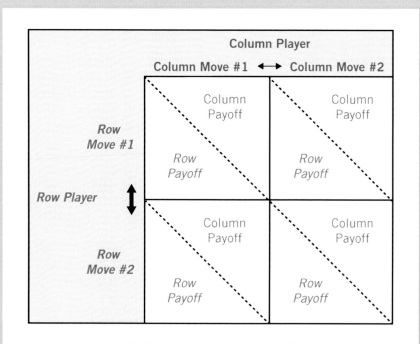

(i) who the players are, (ii) each player's available moves, (iii) the possible outcomes depending on players' chosen moves, and (iv) how players rank these possible outcomes, i.e., players' payoffs. In addition, I will often use "incentive arrows" to illustrate whether and how players' incentives depend on what others do.

1. *Players*: Payoff matrices are typically used to describe two-player games. One player is called "Row player" while the other is called "Column player." Their names appear, respectively, on the left and at the top of the diagram. For further clarity, all terms relating to Row player are ***italicized and bolded***, while all terms relating to Column player are in regular print.
2. *Moves*: Each row of the matrix corresponds to a possible move of Row player, while each column corresponds to a possible move of Column player.
3. *Outcomes*: Each box of the matrix corresponds to a possible outcome of the game. In the 2 x 2 example shown in figure 4, there are four possible outcomes.
4. *Payoffs*: Depending on players' chosen moves, each player will get a payoff. By definition, a player's payoff captures everything that he/ she cares about vis-à-vis the outcome of the game.24 This allows us to rankall of the possible outcomes from each player's point of view. Each box of the payoff matrix shows how both players rank the outcome corresponding to that box, with Row player's ranking in the bottom left triangle and Column player's ranking in the upper right triangle within the box.
5. *Incentive arrows*: A payoff matrix can be helpful for visualizing each player's incentives in the game, i.e., how each player's preferred move (a.k.a. "best response") depends on the other player's move. To illustrate such incentives, I use up–down arrows to show Row player's incentives and left–right arrows to show Column player's incentives.

Returning to the Prisoners ' Dilemma, whose payoff matrix is shown in figure 3, note that each prisoner has a unilateral incentive to confess, regardless of the other's move. (If the other prisoner confesses, confessing reduces your own sentence from twenty to ten years. If the other prisoner does not confess, confessing allows you to avoid prison entirely.) That is, each prisoner has a "dominant strategy" to confess. However, if both confess, both get a longer sentence (ten years, the third-best outcome) than if neither confessed (five years, the second-best outcome).[28]

A "dominant strategy" is a move that maximizes a player's own payoff, regardless of others' moves, holding others' moves fixed.

Princeton mathematician Albert W. Tucker[29] created the story of the Prisoners' Dilemma in 1950 as an example for a lecture on game theory to psychology students. Since then, others have generalized the game to apply

---

[28] The fact that both players get their third-best outcome instead of their second-best outcome is a general feature of all of the Prisoners' Dilemma games that we will see throughout the book.

[29] Tucker (1905–95) stood out for his generous spirit, passion for mathematics education (he helped found the AP Calculus exam), and outstanding PhD advisees. In 1950, the same year that Tucker coined the term "Prisoners' Dilemma," one of those students—John Nash—submitted a PhD thesis that would later earn the Nobel Prize in Economics.

to situations with many players. In its most general form, the Prisoners' Dilemma is defined as any game having the following two features:

1. Each player has a dominant strategy, a move that maximizes that player's own payoff regardless of others' moves. (Each prisoner has a dominant strategy to confess.)
2. All players are worse off when they all play their dominant strategies, compared to when each plays some other strategy. (Both prisoners are worse off when both confess, compared to when neither confesses.)

COMMUNICATING AND/ OR MOVING FIRST DOESN'T HELP

A key feature of Tucker's classic tale is that the prisoners are isolated in separate cells, unable to communicate or observe whether the other has confessed. But these features aren't essential to the dilemma. To see why, consider a variation of Tucker's original story in which the police interrogator brings both prisoners to the same cell and makes a slightly different speech: "It's time for you both to confess to the armed robbery. I'm going to leave you alone for ten minutes. Talk it over. When I come back, you will each have just one chance to confess. First, I'll ask you [Prisoner #1] whether you confess, then you'll leave the room. Then, I'll ask you [Prisoner #2] whether you confess."

It's easy to imagine what the prisoners will talk about during their ten minutes. Prisoner #2, especially, needs to convince Prisoner #1 that he won't confess once Prisoner #1 has left the room, if only Prisoner #1 also doesn't confess. But whatever Prisoner #2 may promise, Prisoner #1 knows that "words are wind" and that Prisoner #2 will prefer to confess once the time comes. Anticipating this, Prisoner #1 will also confess when given the chance. They'll still both go to jail for ten years, notwithstanding their chance to communicate and Prisoner #1' s chance to move first.

The Greater Significance of the Prisoners' Dilemma

In competition, individual ambition serves the common good. —Russell Crowe (as John Nash) in *A Beautiful Mind* (2001), completely missing the point of the Prisoners' Dilemma

The Prisoners' Dilemma is, without a doubt, the most studied and widely cited of all games. Yet some feel that the Prisoners' Dilemma has received more than its fair share of attention. Richard H. McAdams (no relation to the author), the Bernard D. Meltzer Professor of Law at the University of Chicago, made this point in the context of game theory and the law:

> Legal scholars are nearly obsessed with the Prisoners' Dilemma, mentioning the game in a staggering number of law review articles (over 3,000), but virtually ignoring other equally simple games that offer equally sharp insights into legal problems. . . . In particular, the need for coordination is as pervasive and important to law as the Prisoners ' Dilemma, such as in constitutional law, international law, property disputes, traffic, culture, gender roles, and many other topics. Further, the profession's over-focus on the Prisoners' Dilemma unnecessarily contributes

to the divide between Law & Economics and Law & Society scholars, all of whom might find some common ground in exploring coordination games.[30]

The "coordination games" that Professor McAdams mentions here are those, naturally enough, in which players have an incentive to coordinate their moves. For instance, in traffic, we all benefit when everyone drives on the same side of the road. I agree that coordination games are important but, nonetheless, the Prisoners' Dilemma has earned its pride of place.

First of all, many important and vexing real-world games are Prisoners' Dilemmas. In business, for instance, competition itself can be a Prisoners' Dilemma (see chapter 3). Indeed, even the most basic aspect of business, the transaction, can be viewed as a Prisoners' Dilemma (see chapter 5). Fortunately for business, firms long ago found ways to escape the Prisoners' Dilemma of competition, reducing or even eliminating their incentive to compete, while trusted institutions have arisen to facilitate transactions.

Perhaps the most important aspect of the Prisoners' Dilemma is that it presents an eminently solvable strategic problem. Indeed, game theory provides five distinct "escape routes" from the Prisoners' Dilemma,[31] each of which is broadly relevant in many other games as well:

1. Regulation (chapter 2)
2. Cartelization (chapter 3)
3. Retaliation (chapter 4)
4. Trust (chapter 5)
5. Relationships (chapter 6)

A deeper understanding of the Prisoners' Dilemma can also enrich the ongoing philosophical and political debate, sometimes caricatured as "capitalism vs. socialism," over the proper scope of individual freedom, personal responsibility, and collective action. The Prisoners' Dilemma encompasses any situation in which individual incentives conflict with the greater good, so much so that everyone is worse off when everyone pursues their own self-interest.[32]

In this way, the Prisoners' Dilemma embodies the fundamental distinction between license and liberty and highlights the need, in some situations, to restrict our ability to make certain choices and/ or to increase our personal responsibility for the consequences of our actions. After all, even the most ardent defender of personal liberty can appreciate the damage and chaos of "freedom" run amok, and the importance of institutions that protect our liberty to make a good life for ourselves while ensuring that we don't deny others that same opportunity.

---

[30] This quote is a lightly edited combination of text from the abstract and introduction to Richard H. McAdams, "Beyond the Prisoners' Dilemma: Coordination, Game Theory, and Law," *Southern California Law Review,* 2009.

[31] These escape routes from the Prisoners' Dilemma naturally combine and reinforce one another, e.g., the success of a cartel may hinge on its members' ability to retaliate, you and I may trust each other because we have a relationship and/or we may have a relationship because we trust each other, and so on. However, each escape route is conceptually distinct.

[32] When competition takes the form of a Prisoners' Dilemma, it is not true that "individual ambition serves the common good." Russell Crowe was wrong.

Game-Theory Focus 1: the Timing of Moves

The way that games are likely to play out depends critically on what game theorists refer to as the timing of moves. This terminology is a bit misleading, since the player who moves first from a chronological point of view need not be the "first-mover" from a strategic perspective. The chronological order in which players make their moves matters, but so does their observability and capability to pre-commit to how they will play the game. For the sake of clarity, I will focus here on the simplest sort of game, in which two players each make a single irreversible move. There are three possibilities for the timing of moves in such games:

- Simultaneous moves
- Sequential moves
- Commitment moves

SIMULTANEOUS MOVES

A game has simultaneous moves if each player must decide what to do without observing the other player's choice, i.e., if the players make their choices in mutual ignorance. The term "simultaneous moves" comes from the fact that mutual ignorance is automatic if both players make their moves at exactly the same moment. However, chronological simultaneity is not necessary for a game to have simultaneous moves in the strategic sense, as illustrated by the following example.

A game has "simultaneous moves" if each player does not observe the other player's move prior to choosing its own move, i.e., if players make their moves in mutual ignorance.

Example: The Battle of the Bismarck Sea

Our losses for this single battle were fantastic. Not during the entire savage fighting at Guadalcanal did we suffer a single comparable blow. —Masatake Okumiya, Japanese staff officer at Rabaul, 1943

In January 1943, just a year after the attack on Pearl Harbor, Japan's imperial forces were on the defensive. They had just lost Guadalcanal and, after the brutal battle of Buna-Gona, the Allies had landed forces on New Guinea that might soon threaten the important Japanese base at Lae. Desperate to turn the tide, Imperial General Headquarters dispatched Major General Toru Okabe's 51st Infantry Division to convoy to Lae from nearby Rabaul and drive the Allies off the island. Allied aircraft intercepted Okabe's convoy and decimated the fleet of Japanese aircraft that was protecting it, along with a few vessels carrying critical supplies, but most of the convoy made it through. It soon became clear, however, that Okabe's forces could not successfully drive out the Allies without reinforcements and supplies. And so one of the most critical decisions of the Pacific War was made, to send two more Japanese divisions in a make-or-break gamble to retake New Guinea.

These new troops arrived in Rabaul and, like those before them, faced the prospect of a treacherous passage through waters within reach of Allied bombers. Worse yet, because of Japanese aircraft losses during the first convoy, the second convoy had little air protection. Indeed, it wasn't a question

FIGURE 5

The second Rabaul-Lae Convoy, march 1943

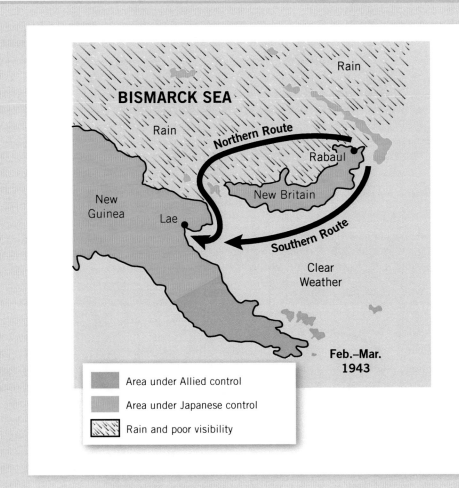

of whether the second convoy would be bombed on the way to Lae, but of how long they would suffer such attacks. The answer would depend on whether the Japanese convoy took the northern or southern route to Lae, and over which of these routes the Allies sent most of their limited reconnaissance craft.

Retired US Air Force Colonel O. G. Haywood considered this game—a decisive episode in the Battle of the Bismarck Sea—in his 1954 classic article, "Military Decision and Game Theory."[33] As he explained it, the Japanese would face from one to three days of bombing, depending on which route they took and which route the Allies patrolled. See figure 6, which can be interpreted as an (unlabeled) payoff matrix, with the Allies (under General George Kenney) as the Row player.

---

[33] O. G. Haywood, Jr., "Military Decision and Game Theory," *Journal of Operations Research Society of America, 1954*. Figures 5 and 6 are taken from Haywood's article.

FIGURE 6

Possible outcomes of the second Rabaul-Lae Convey

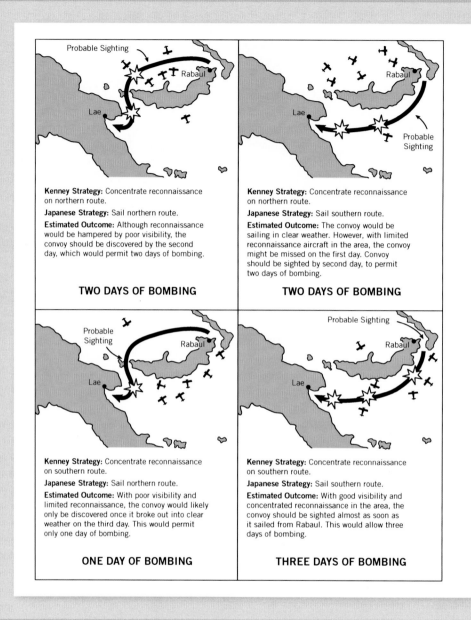

Kenney Strategy: Concentrate reconnaissance on northern route.

Japanese Strategy: Sail northern route.

Estimated Outcome: Although reconnaissance would be hampered by poor visibility, the convoy should be discovered by the second day, which would permit two days of bombing.

TWO DAYS OF BOMBING

Kenney Strategy: Concentrate reconnaissance on northern route.

Japanese Strategy: Sail southern route.

Estimated Outcome: The convoy would be sailing in clear weather. However, with limited reconnaissance aircraft in the area, the convoy might be missed on the first day. Convoy should be sighted by second day, to permit two days of bombing.

TWO DAYS OF BOMBING

Kenney Strategy: Concentrate reconnaissance on southern route.

Japanese Strategy: Sail northern route.

Estimated Outcome: With poor visibility and limited reconnaissance, the convoy would likely only be discovered once it broke out into clear weather on the third day. This would permit only one day of bombing.

ONE DAY OF BOMBING

Kenney Strategy: Concentrate reconnaissance on southern route.

Japanese Strategy: Sail southern route.

Estimated Outcome: With good visibility and concentrated reconnaissance in the area, the convoy should be sighted almost as soon as it sailed from Rabaul. This would allow three days of bombing.

THREE DAYS OF BOMBING

In the end, the Japanese took the cloud-covered northern route and the Allies also focused their patrols there. The Japanese suffered two decimating days of Allied bombing runs. All eight Japanese transports were lost, along with four destroyer escorts and nearly 3,000 troops. This crushing defeat marked a decisive moment in the Pacific War. Never again did the Japanese attempt to reinforce Lae by sea, and without that option they were unable to stem the Allied tide. Less than a year later, Lae had fallen, Rabaul lay crippled and broken, and the Japanese themselves were crouched in a purely defensive posture. In a real sense, the Battle of the Bismarck Sea marked the beginning of the end of the Pacific War.

The Battle of the Bismarck Sea was a game on many levels, but I've focused here on just one: the Japanese decision whether to send their convoy to the north or south of New Britain, and the Allied decision where to send their reconnaissance aircraft. What was the timing of moves in this game? Obviously, the Allies didn't know exactly when the Japanese convoy would depart, so their reconnaissance began before the Japanese put to sea. Since the Japanese couldn't detect Allied reconnaissance craft from their port at Rabaul, however, it didn't matter that the Allies made their decision first from a chronological point of view. The Japanese still had to choose their own route in ignorance of the Allies' move. Since the Allies and the Japanese made their decisions in mutual ignorance, the game therefore had "simultaneous moves" from a strategic point of view.

Sequential Moves vs. Commitment Moves

A stealthy meeting Thursday night between former presidential rivals Barack Obama and Hillary Clinton is no longer a secret, but what they discussed—and whether they said the words "vice president"—remains a mystery. —ABC News report, June 6, 2008[34]

In August 2008, John McCain was in a tough spot. Rumors were swirling that conservative elements within the Republican Party had pressured the presidential candidate to drop his good friend, Senator Joe Lieberman, from his short list for vice president. Making matters worse, the possibility of an Obama–Clinton ticket seemed quite real. Barack Obama and Hillary Clinton, fierce adversaries in the Democratic presidential primaries, had snuck off to a secret meeting in June where, Senator Dianne Feinstein reported to ABC, "They both left laughing." Senator Chuck Schumer, a close friend and ally of Clinton, was also quoted in mid-June as saying, "She has said if Senator Obama should want her to be vice president and thinks it would be best for the ticket, she will serve, she will accept that."

McCain's camp had been hoping for Obama and Clinton's relationship to remain frosty, since that might mean many of Clinton's female supporters would sit out the election. Indeed, were Obama not to choose Clinton, McCain might hope to attract some of those female votes himself, especially if he were to pick a female running mate such as Kay Bailey Hutchison (Texas senator), Carly Fiorina (businesswoman), Sarah Palin (Alaska governor), or Condoleezza Rice (former secretary of state). So, in choosing his own running mate, McCain desperately needed to know: would Obama pick Clinton, or not?

Fortunately for McCain, the Democrats held their national convention a week before the Republicans that year, forcing Obama to reveal his choice (Senator Joe Biden) before McCain had to finalize his own. Furthermore, given all the lead time between when McCain secured the Republican nomination and his own convention, there was no inherent reason why McCain

34 Kate Snow, "Obama, Clinton Ditch Press for Secret Meeting," ABC News, June 6, 2008

couldn't have multiple vice presidential candidates fully vetted and ready to go, some best suited if Obama chose Clinton and others best suited if he did not.[35] Since McCain was capable of observing and responding to Obama's choice, their game of choosing vice presidential nominees did not have simultaneous moves. Rather, Obama was the first-mover and McCain was the last-mover.

How games with a first-mover and a last-mover are likely to play out depends critically on one more factor: whether the last-mover is able to commit ahead of time to how it will respond to the first-mover's choice. To emphasize this, I will use different terminology for the timing of moves when the last-mover is capable or incapable of committing to how it will respond. In particular, a game has "sequential moves" if the last-mover cannot commit ahead of time to how it will respond, while it has "commitment moves" if the last-mover can so commit.

A game has "sequential moves" if (i) some player ("last-mover") can observe and respond to the other player ("first-mover")'s move and (ii) the last-mover cannot commit ahead of time to how it will respond to what the first-mover does.

A game has "commitment moves" if (i) some player ("last-mover") can observe and respond to the other player ("first-mover")'s move and (ii) the last-mover can commit ahead of time to how it will respond to what the first-mover does.

In 2008, McCain had an overriding incentive to pick whichever running mate would maximize his chance of winning the presidency. In other words, McCain's response to Obama's choice was dictated by McCain's own desire to win. Consequently, while McCain moved last, he did not have last-mover commitment power, so the game itself had sequential moves. McCain might have changed the timing of moves by announcing and credibly committing to his intended candidate ahead of the Democrats' national convention. Since Obama could observe and respond to such an announcement, McCain would then have been the "first-mover" from a strategic perspective. However, this is not the same as making a commitment move.

For a game to have commitment moves, the last-mover must be able to commit to any response, even one that hurts. Consider the threat of corporal punishment of naughty children, mostly out of favor nowadays but widely used by generations of loving parents. "This is going to hurt me more than it hurts you" was the dreaded refrain just before a spanking or whipping. The threat of corporal punishment by a loving parent is a commitment move, since (i) the parent can observe and respond to the child's behavior (parent is "last-mover") and (ii) the parent can commit to respond to the child's behavior by doing things that s/ he doesn't want to do (parent has "last-mover commitment power").

What's essential here is that the parent commits to how s/ he will respond, which is very different from tying one's hands. Knowing that they will be spared a spanking if only they behave, children have an incentive to stay

---

out of trouble. Tying your hands in this context would mean committing always to beat your children, no matter how they behave. Unlike the threat of punishment for misbehavior, such a cruel commitment would have no deterrent effect on the child. Recognizing this, law enforcement authorities arrest parents who beat their children without reason (as first-movers), but grant some latitude to parents who beat their children after misbehavior (as last-movers).

Changing the Timing of Moves

Since game outcomes depend on the timing of moves, it should come as no surprise that players routinely take steps to change the timing of moves to their advantage. There are three basic ways to do so.

1. Change Observability   One way to make your move observable is to cultivate third parties (e.g., rating agencies, auditors, consumers on feedback forums) who can credibly report on what you do. Or, to keep your move secret, "signal jam"[36] by making statements and taking steps that could be consistent with more than one course of action. For instance, one way for a politician to keep her intentions secret would be to quietly deputize friends and associates to speculate about a wide variety of possible plans. That way, even if someone should leak the truth, the media and her opposition may not even notice.

2. Change Chronological Timing   One way to move first is to impose an *artificial deadline* on yourself. Another way to move first is to grant the other player *"inspection rights"*—the ability to verify your move before they make their own choice. For instance, offering a money-back guarantee gives customers the right to return a product that they do not enjoy, in effect allowing them to move last. Or, to move last yourself, acquire the *flexibility* to change your move until the bitter end, by taking preparatory steps that keep all your options open. For instance, a supplier who is bidding for a contract could commit to beat any competitor's offer. If so, the buyer will be sure to give the supplier a chance to observe and respond to any competing bid. Similarly, on eBay, "sniping" software allows bidders to submit offers at the very last moment. As such, sniping software allows bidders to observe as much as possible about others' bids before committing to their own.

3. Cultivate the Last-Mover's Commitment   One way to make a commitment credible is to tie the outcome of the current game to something else that's bigger and more important, for instance, by invoking personal honor and/ or committing to a future relationship. If you renege on your commitment today, you will tarnish your honor and/ or lose all future benefits from the relationship. As long as your incentive to cheat

---

[36] Signal jamming is the (usually deliberate) transmission of signals that disrupt communications by decreasing the signal-to-noise ratio. For instance, totalitarian regimes routinely censor foreign radio broadcasts by sending out strong signals of their own over the same wavelengths, drowning out the undesired message in a great wash of noise.

today is small enough, such steps can allow you to credibly commit not to cheat. Absent honor or relational concerns, you could also sign an enforceable contract that specifies damages should you renege on your commitment.

Summary
How to Escape the Prisoner's Dilemma

Before proceeding to the applications of Part Two, let's pause for a moment and review the various ways we have seen to escape the Prisoners' Dilemma. The flow diagram of figure 22 summarizes which (if any) escape routes are open to players, depending on the details of the situation.

FIGURE 7

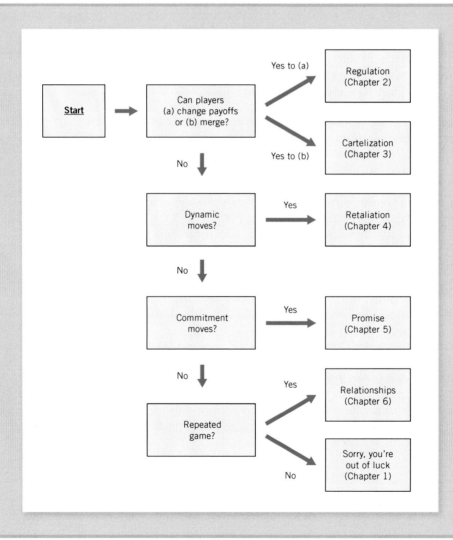

First, are the players capable of *changing their payoffs*, either directly themselves or indirectly via the intervention of some third party? If so, obviously, they can change the payoffs so that the game is no longer a Prisoners' Dilemma. For example, colleges formed the NCAA to institute new rules to eliminate their incentive for extreme violence on the football field. See chapter 2.

Second, are the players capable of *merging or forming a "cartel"*? If so, again obviously, they can merge so as to look after their collective interest. For example, the Big Four in barbed wire merged to form the American Steel and Wire Company. See chapter 3.

Third, does the game have *dynamic moves*? (Recall that a game has dynamic moves if it occurs in real time and both players can observe and quickly react to changes in each other's moves.) If so, amutual threat to retaliate is enough to escape the Prisoners' Dilemma. For example, in the Dynamic Pricing Game seen earlier (and to be reprised in Game-Changer File 1), the airlines keep posted prices high by each threatening to immediately match any discount. See chapter 4.

Fourth, does the game have *commitment moves*? (Recall that a game has commitment moves if the players move in sequence and the last-mover can commit ahead of time to how it will respond to whatever the first-mover does.) If so, a promise by the last-mover is enough to escape the Prisoners' Dilemma. For example, I get my kids to eat a healthy dinner by promising to serve dessert if they eat their vegetables. See chapter 5.

Fifth and finally, is this a *repeated game*? (Recall that a game is "repeated" if the same players interact repeatedly in the context of a relationship, or, more broadly, if the outcome of the current game can be strategically linked to the outcomes of other games.) For example, the Mafia leveraged their "family ties" to avoid confessing to the police for decades. See chapter 6.

When any of these five conditions holds, there is a way out of the Prisoners' Dilemma. When none of them holds, however, there is no hope of escape. One such hopeless situation is Albert Tucker's classic version of the Prisoners' Dilemma, in which the prisoners are isolated in different cells and asked whether they confess to the crime. This game is clearly not repeated and, since each prisoner is unable to observe the other's decision, the game has simultaneous moves.[37] Consequently, it is not possible to enable retaliation (chapter 4), make a promise (chapter 5), or leverage relationships (chapter 6). If the prisoners could bribe the judge and influence sentences that way, then perhaps it would be possible to invite regulation (chapter 2) to change the payoffs. Absent that, however, it's clearly impossible to form a cartel (chapter 3) to merge their interests, since each much serve out his own sentence in jail. So, all five escape routes are closed to the prisoners in the classic Prisoners' Dilemma.

Fortunately, these hopeless situations are more the exception than the rule.

---

[37] In a more realistic setting, the prisoners and/or their associates will likely interact again, either inside or outside of prison. If so, the game would have repeated moves, in the sense that the prisoners can potentially link what happens in this game to what will happen in future games.

Buddhist Economics

By E. F. Schumacher

"Right Livelihood" is one of the requirements of the Buddha's Noble Eight-fold Path. It is clear, therefore, that there must be such a thing as Buddhist economics. Buddhist countries have often stated that they wish to remain faithful to their heritage. So Burma: "The New Burma sees no conflict between religious values and economic progress. Spiritual health and material well-being are not enemies: they are natural allies." Or: "We can blend success-fully the religious and spiritual values of our heritage with the benefits of modern technology." Or: "We Burmans have a sacred duty to conform both our dreams and our acts to our faith. This we shall ever do."

All the same, such countries invariably assume that they can model their economic development plans in accordance with modern economics, and they call upon modern economists from so-called advanced countries to advise them, to formulate the policies to be pursued, and to construct the grand design for development, the Five-Year Plan or whatever it may be called. No one seems to think that a Buddhist way of life would call for Buddhist economics, just as the modern materialist way of life has brought forth modern economics.

Economists themselves, like most specialists, normally suffer from a kind of metaphysical blindness, assuming that theirs is a science of absolute and invariable truths, without any presuppositions. Some go as far as to claim that economic laws are as free from "metaphysics" or "values" as the law of gravitation. We need not, however, get involved in arguments of methodology. Instead, let us take some fundamentals and see what they look like when viewed by a modern economist and a Buddhist economist.

There is universal agreement that a fundamental source of wealth is human labour. Now, the modern economist has been brought up to consider "labour" or work as little more than a necessary evil. From the point of view of the employer, it is in any case simply an item of cost, to be reduced to a minimum if it cannot be eliminated altogether, say, by automation. From the point of view of the workman, it is a "disutility"; to work is to make a sacrifice of one's leisure and comfort, and wages are a kind of compensation for the sacrifice. Hence the ideal from the point of view of the employer is to have output without employees, and the ideal from the point of view of the employee is to have income without employment.

The consequences of these attitudes both in theory and in practice are, of course, extremely far-reaching. If the ideal with regard to work is to get rid of it, every method that "reduces the work load" is a good thing. The most potent method, short of automation, is the so-called "division of labour" and the classical example is the pin factory eulogised in Adam Smith's *Wealth of Nations*. Here it is not a matter of ordinary specialisation, which mankind has practiced from time immemorial, but of dividing up every complete process of production into minute parts, so that the final product can be produced at great speed without anyone having had to contribute more than a totally insignificant and, in most cases, unskilled movement of his limbs.

The Buddhist point of view takes the function of work to be at least threefold: to give man a chance to utilise and develop his faculties; to enable him to overcome his ego-centredness by joining with other people in a common task; and to bring forth the goods and services needed for a becoming existence. Again, the consequences that flow from this view are endless. To organize work in such a manner that it becomes meaningless, boring, stultifying, or nerve-racking for the worker would be little short of criminal; it would indicate a greater concern with goods than with people, an evil lack of compassion and a soul-destroying degree of attachment to the most primitive side of this worldly existence. Equally, to strive for leisure as an alternative to work would be considered a complete misunderstanding of one of the basic truths of human existence, namely that work and leisure are complementary parts of the same living process and cannot be separated without destroying the joy of work and the bliss of leisure.

From the Buddhist point of view, there are therefore two types of mechanisation which must be clearly distinguished: one that enhances a man's skill and power and one that turns the work of man over to a mechanical slave, leaving man in a position of having to serve the slave. How to tell the one from the other? "The craftsman himself," says Ananda Coomaraswamy, a man equally competent to talk about the modern West as the ancient East, "can always, if allowed to, draw the delicate distinction between the machine and the tool. The carpet loom is a tool, a contrivance for holding warp threads at a stretch for the pile to be woven round them by the craftsmen's fingers; but the power loom is a machine, and its significance as a destroyer of culture lies in the fact that it does the essentially human part of the work." It is clear, therefore, that Buddhist economics must be very different from the economics of modern materialism, since the Buddhist sees the essence of civilisation not in a multiplication of wants but in the purification of human character. Character, at the same time, is formed primarily by a man's work. And work, properly conducted in conditions of human dignity and freedom, blesses those who do it and equally their products. The Indian philosopher and economist J. C. Kumarappa sums the matter up as follows:

If the nature of the work is properly appreciated and applied, it will stand in the same relation to the higher faculties as food is to the physical body. It nourishes and enlivens the higher man and urges him to produce the best he is capable of. It directs his free will along the proper course and disciplines the animal in him into progressive channels. It furnishes an excellent background for man to display his scale of values and develop his personality.

If a man has no chance of obtaining work he is in a desperate position, not simply because he lacks an income but because he lacks this nourishing and enlivening factor of disciplined work which nothing can replace. A modern economist may engage in highly sophisticated calculations on whether full employment "pays" or whether it might be more "economic" to run an economy at less than full employment so as to insure a greater mobility of labour, a better stability of wages, and so forth. His fundamental criterion of success is simply the total quantity of goods produced during a given period of time. "If the marginal urgency of goods is low," says Professor Galbraith in *The Affluent Society*, "then so is the urgency of employing the last man or the last million men in the labour force." And again: "If . . . we can afford some unemployment in the interest of stability—a proposition, incidentally, of impeccably conservative antecedents—then we can afford to give those who are unemployed the goods that enable them to sustain their accustomed standard of living."

From a Buddhist point of view, this is standing the truth on its head by considering goods as more important than people and consumption as more important than creative activity. It means shifting the emphasis from the worker to the product of work, that is, from the human to the subhuman, a surrender to the forces of evil. The very start of Buddhist economic planning would be a planning for full employment, and the primary purpose of this would in fact be employment for everyone who needs an "outside" job: it would not be the maximisation of employment nor the maximisation of production. Women, on the whole, do not need an "outside" job, and the large-scale employment of women in offices or factories would be considered a sign of serious economic failure. In particular, to let mothers of young children work in factories while the children run wild would be as uneconomic in the eyes of a Buddhist economist as the employment of a skilled worker as a soldier in the eyes of a modern economist.

While the materialist is mainly interested in goods, the Buddhist is mainly interested in liberation. But Buddhism is "The Middle Way" and therefore in no way antagonistic to physical well-being. It is not wealth that stands in the way of liberation but the attachment to wealth; not the enjoyment of pleasurable things but the craving for them. The keynote of Buddhist economics, therefore, is simplicity and non-violence. From an economist's point of view, the marvel of the Buddhist way of life is the utter rationality of its pattern—amazingly small means leading to extraordinarily satisfactory results.

For the modern economist this is very difficult to understand. He is used to measuring the "standard of living" by the amount of annual consumption, assuming all the time that a man who consumes more is "better off" than a man who consumes less. A Buddhist economist would consider this approach excessively irrational: since consumption is merely a means to human well-being, the aim should be to obtain the maximum of well-being with the minimum of consumption. Thus, if the purpose of clothing is a certain amount of temperature comfort and an attractive appearance, the task is to attain this purpose with the smallest possible effort, that is, with the smallest annual destruction of cloth and with the help of designs that involve the smallest possible input of toil. The less toil there is, the more time and strength is left for artistic creativity. It would be highly uneconomic, for instance, to go in for complicated tailoring, like the modern West, when a much more beautiful effect can be achieved by the skillful draping of uncut material. It would be the height of folly to make material so that it should wear out quickly and the height of barbarity to make anything ugly, shabby, or mean. What has just been said about clothing applies equally to all other human requirements. The ownership and the consumption of goods is a means to an end, and Buddhist economics is the systematic study of how to attain given ends with the minimum means.

Modern economics, on the other hand, considers consumption to be the sole end and purpose of all economic activity, taking the factors of production—and, labour, and capital—as the means. The former, in short, tries to maximise human satisfactions by the optimal pattern of consumption, while the latter tries to maximise consumption by the optimal pattern of productive effort. It is easy to see that the effort needed to sustain a way of life which seeks to attain the optimal pattern of consumption is likely to be much smaller than the effort needed to sustain a drive for maximum consumption. We need not be surprised, therefore, that the pressure and strain of living is very much less in say, Burma, than it is in the United States, in spite of the fact that the amount of labour-saving machinery used in the former country is only a minute fraction of the amount used in the latter.

Simplicity and non-violence are obviously closely related. The optimal pattern of consumption, producing a high degree of human satisfaction by means of a relatively low rate of consumption, allows people to live without great pressure and strain and to fulfill the primary injunction of Buddhist teaching: "Cease to do evil; try to do good." As physical resources are everywhere limited, people satisfying their needs by means of a modest use of resources are obviously less likely to be at each other's throats than people depending upon a high rate of use. Equally, people who live in highly self-sufficient local communities are less likely to get involved in large-scale violence than people whose existence depends on world-wide systems of trade.

From the point of view of Buddhist economics, therefore, production from local resources for local needs is the most rational way of economic life, while dependence on imports from afar and the consequent need to produce for export to unknown and distant peoples is highly uneconomic and justifiable only in exceptional cases and on a small scale. Just as the modern economist would admit that a high rate of consumption of transport services between a man's home and his place of work signifies a misfortune and not a high standard of life, so the Buddhist would hold that to satisfy human wants from faraway sources rather than from sources nearby signifies failure rather than success. The former tends to take statistics showing an increase in the number of ton/miles per head of the population carried by a country's transport system as proof of economic progress, while to the latter—the Buddhist economist—the same statistics would indicate a highly undesirable deterioration in the pattern of consumption.

Another striking difference between modern economics and Buddhist economics arises over the use of natural resources. Bertrand de Jouvenel, the eminent French political philosopher, has characterised "Western man" in words which may be taken as a fair description of the modern economist:

He tends to count nothing as an expenditure, other than human effort; he does not seem to mind how much mineral matter he wastes and, far worse, how much living matter he destroys. He does not seem to realize at all that human life is a dependent part of an ecosystem of many different forms of life. As the world is ruled from towns where men are cut off from any form of life other than human, the feeling of belonging to an ecosystem is not revived. This results in a harsh and improvident treatment of things upon which we ultimately depend, such as water and trees.

The teaching of the Buddha, on the other hand, enjoins a reverent and non-violent attitude not only to all sentient beings but also, with great emphasis, to trees. Every follower of the Buddha ought to plant a tree every few years and look after it until it is safely established, and the Buddhist economist can demonstrate without difficulty that the universal observation of this rule would result in a high rate of genuine economic development independent of any foreign aid. Much of the economic decay of southeast Asia (as of many other parts of the world) is undoubtedly due to a heedless and shameful neglect of trees.

Modern economics does not distinguish between renewable and non-renewable materials, as its very method is to equalise and quantify everything by means of a money price. Thus, taking various alternative fuels, like coal, oil, wood, or water-power: the only difference between them recognised by modern economics is relative cost per equivalent unit. The cheapest is automatically the one to be preferred, as to do otherwise would be irrational and "uneconomic." From a Buddhist point of view, of course, this will not do; the essential difference between nonrenewable fuels like coal and oil on the one hand and renewable fuels like wood and water-power on the other cannot be simply overlooked. Non-renewable goods must be used only if they are indispensable, and then only with the greatest care and the most meticulous concern for conservation. To use them heedlessly or extravagantly is an act of violence, and while complete non-violence may not be attainable on this earth, there is nonetheless an ineluctable duty on man to aim at the ideal of non-violence in all he does.

Just as a modern European economist would not consider it a great achievement if all European art treasures were sold to America at attractive prices, so the Buddhist economist would insist that a population basing its economic life on non-renewable fuels is living parasitically, on capital instead of income. Such a way of life could have no permanence and could therefore be justified only as a purely temporary expedient. As the world's resources of non-renewable fuels—coal, oil, and natural gas—are exceedingly unevenly distributed over the globe and undoubtedly limited in quantity, it is clear that their exploitation at an ever-increasing rate is an act of violence against nature which must almost inevitably lead to violence between men.

This fact alone might give food for thought even to those people in Buddhist countries who care nothing for the religious and spiritual values of their heritage and ardently desire to embrace the materialism of modern economics at the fastest possible speed. Before they dismiss Buddhist economics as nothing better than a nostalgic dream, they might wish to consider whether the path of economic development outlined by modern economics is likely to lead them to places where they really want to be. Towards the end of his courageous book The Challenge of Man's Future, Professor Harrison Brown of the California Institute of Technology gives the following appraisal:

Thus we see that, just as industrial society is fundamentally unstable and subject to reversion to agrarian existence, so within it the conditions which offer individual freedom are unstable in their ability to avoid the conditions which impose rigid organisation and totalitarian control. Indeed, when we examine all the foreseeable difficulties which threaten the survival of industrial civilisation, it is difficult to see how the achievement of stability and the maintenance of individual liberty can be made compatible.

Even if this were dismissed as a long-term view there is the immediate question of whether "modernisation," as currently practised without regard to religious and spiritual values, is actually producing agreeable results. As far as the masses are concerned, the results appear to be disastrous—a collapse of the rural economy, a rising tide of unemployment in town and country, and the growth of a city proletariat without nourishment for either body or soul.

It is in the light of both immediate experience and long term prospects that the study of Buddhist economics could be recommended even to those who believe that economic growth is more important than any spiritual or religious values. For it is not a question of choosing between "modern growth" and "traditional stagnation." It is a question of finding the right path of development, the Middle Way between materialist heedlessness and traditionalist immobility, in short, of finding "Right Livelihood."

Applying Microeconomic Theory: The Case of Milk and Dairy Products

By Edwin Mansfield

Introduction

The milk and dairy products industry is big and economically (and politically) important. In recent years, cash receipts from U.S. milk and dairy products have been about $20 billion, well over 10 percent of the cash receipts from all farm commodities. While milk is produced and processed in every state, over half the country's milk production has occurred in Wisconsin, California, New York, Minnesota, and Pennsylvania.[1] Furthermore, the milk industry is unconcentrated, there being over 100,000 dairy farms in the United States. If the government did not intervene in the milk market, which it does, this market might be reasonably close to perfectly competitive, as there are very large numbers of buyers and sellers and the product is reasonably standardized.[2]

At present, the milk industry is in a state of turmoil and faces fundamental problems and opportunities in the future. In particular, recent decades have seen massive revisions in consumers' perceptions of the desirability and dietary safety of some milk products, bold new technologies that have stirred enormous controversies within and outside the industry itself, keen economic and cultural rivalries between the traditional farmers of Wisconsin and New York and the comparative newcomers of California and Texas, and continual arguments over the role of the federal government in regulating the price of milk and other dairy products.

In this chapter, we present ten multipart problems, which analyze selected aspects of many of these trends and issues. To provide the background information required to understand and do these problems, we begin with a thumbnail sketch of the costs, returns to scale, demand, regulation, and prospective changes in technology of dairy farms. Our principal focus is on Dennis and Sue McGraw, owners of an actual Wisconsin dairy farm.

The Costs of Producing Milk

Dennis and Sue McGraw have a dairy farm with 60 cows on the outskirts of Dodgeville, Wisconsin, a town of about 3,500 people. They live in a farmhouse built in 1929, close to a large white barn. In the summer, "the sweet smell of blossoms mingles with fresh-cut grass, manure, and sour molasses-smelling silage."[3] All members of the McGraw family—Dennis, Sue, and their

---

[1] R. Fallert, D. Blayney, and J. Miller, *Dairy: Background for 1990 Farm Legislation* (Washington, D.C.: U.S. Department of Agriculture, 1990), part of which is reprinted in E. Mansfield, *Study Guide and Casebook in Applied Microeconomics, 2d ed.* (New York: Norton, 1997).

[2] Dairy farming has been the least concentrated of all animal products enterprises. A. Manchester, *The Public Role in the Dairy Economy* (Boulder, Colo.: Westview, 1983).

[3] *Philadelphia Inquirer*, June 14, 1992, p. C2.

children, as well as Dennis's father, who has grown the cows' feed—have worked on the 370-acre farm. Even their two dogs have earned their keep by rounding up the cows.

Dairy farmers like the McGraws use many types of labor, materials, services, capital, and land as inputs. For the country as a whole, the breakdown of the average total cost of producing a pound of milk in 1989 is given in Table 1. As you can see, the average total cost was 14.03 cents, of which 6.55 cents (or almost 50 percent) went for feed for the cows. Another 2.92 cents went for hired labor, milk hauling and marketing, and miscellaneous items; and 2.98 cents went for general farm overhead, taxes, insurance, and capital replacement. Finally, 1.58 cents were the estimated costs of using the owner's capital and labor, as well as the cost of unpaid labor (like that of the McGraw family).

Take a close look at the last two cost items in Table 1. Are they the ordinary sorts of costs on which any accountant focuses? No, they are implicit costs. Specifically, they are the estimated alternative cost (or opportunity cost) of the capital and land owned by the farmer and used on his or her farm, and the estimated alternative cost (or opportunity cost) of the unpaid labor of the people who work on the farm. The U.S. Department of Agriculture, which gathers and publishes these cost figures, is sophisticated enough to recognize the distinction between explicit and implicit costs and the importance of including both.

TABLE 1

Average Cost of Producing a Pound of Milk, United States, 1989[a]

	Cents per pound
Feed	6.55
Hired labor	1.05
Milk hauling and marketing	0.61
Miscellaneous[b]	1.26
General farm overhead	0.87
Taxes and insurance	0.40
Capital replacement[c]	1.71
Return to owner's capital and land	1.00
Unpaid labor	0.58
	14.03

[a] Besides milk, dairy farms sell breeding or culled livestock, which in 1989 brought in receipts of 1.26 cents per pound of milk.

[b] Includes artificial insemination (0.13); veterinary and medicine (0.21); livestock hauling (0.03); fuel, lube, and electricity (0.25); repairs (0.38); fees (0.06); and supplies (0.20).

[c] Replacement costs are an imputed charge sufficient to maintain average equipment, machinery, and purchased breeding livestock investment and production capacity through time. They are based on current prices of capital assets.

Source: Fallert, Blayney, and Miller, *Dairy: Background for 1990 Legislation.*

Returns to Scale in Milk Production

Whereas the farm operated by Dennis and Sue McGraw is representative of the traditional type of farm that has been the bulwark of the great dairy states like Wisconsin, Minnesota, New York, and Pennsylvania, there is considerable evidence that the nature of dairy farming is changing. Between 1980 and 1989, the share of United States milk production in the Pacific, Mountain, and Southern Plains states increased by 6.1 percentage points, while the share of the long-time dairy regions fell. In the early 1990s, California produced more milk than Wisconsin.[4] (For changes in national milk production from 1971 to 1994, see Table 2.)

One reason why California has overtaken Wisconsin is that it has lower costs. In 1988, the average total cost of a pound of milk in the Pacific states was 11.17 cents, as contrasted with 13.89 cents in the Upper Midwest. This cost differential is due in part to economies of scale. Dairy farms on the Pacific coast and in Florida lead the country with herd sizes typically in the range of 500 to 1,500 cows. In traditional milk producing areas of the Upper Midwest and Northeast, dairy farms generally have 50 to 150 cows. The big dairy farms in California and elsewhere are essentially milk factories where herds of about

TABLE 2

Milk Production, United States, 1971–1994

Year	Billions of pounds	Year	Billions of pounds
1994	154	1982	136
1993	151	1981	133
1992	151	1980	128
1991	148	1979	123
1990	148	1978	121
1989	144	1977	122
1988	145	1976	120
1987	143	1975	115
1986	143	1974	116
1985	143	1973	115
1984	135	1972	120
1983	140	1971	119

Sources: U.S. Bureau of the Census, *Statistical Abstract of the United States* (Washington, D.C.: Government Printing Office, 1987, 1991), Economic Research Service, U.S. Department of Agriculture, *Dairy Situation and Outlook Yearbook*, August 1991, and National Agricultural Statistics Service, Washington, D.C., February 1995.

[4] U.S. Congress, Office of Technology Assessment, *U.S. Dairy Industry At a Crossroad* (Washington, D.C.: U.S. Government Printing Office, May 1991), *Philadelphia Inquirer*, June 14, 1991, p. C2, and U.S. Department of Agriculture, *Milk Production*, February 16, 1995.

1,000 cows (or more) are constantly being fed and milked, with their output being monitored by computers.[5]

To illustrate, consider the Ron Quinn dairy of Tulare County, California, the leading county for milk production in the United States. This dairy hires a work force of 22 people, and cows are milked 18 hours a day. The dairy's 1,200 cows, protected by sunshades, live in corrals and are fed eight times a day by machines that push high-protein feed toward them. During the summer, they are sprayed with water by misters. Because exercise cuts their milk production, they never walk more than 200 yards to be milked. The farm contains 1,200 acres on which alfalfa is grown year-round for the cows. Computers on the dairy's feed trucks enable its managers to get the best available price on the feed that the dairy purchases.[6]

The Enormous Controversy over bST

The McGraws, like other dairy farmers, are currently enmeshed in a nation-wide controversy over the application of biotechnology. Based on research conducted at Cornell University, the National Institute for Research in Dairying in England, and elsewhere, it was found that somatotropin, sometimes called growth hormone, could increase the amount of milk produced by cows. Somatotropin is produced by the anterior pituitary gland, a small gland located at the base of the brain. Artificially introduced somatotropin must be injected to be biologically active.

According to the U.S. Office of Technology Assessment,

> The impact of bST [bovine somatotropin] on milk production will vary according to the quality of management on individual farms, but a reasonable expectation is that successful adopters would experience, on average, a 12 percent boost in production. However, the increase in output per cow tends to be absolute (in number of pounds) rather than proportional to normal production. Thus, approximately the same increase in pounds of milk produced might be expected (in comparably managed herds) from all cows. . . . Because bST is rapidly cleared from the bloodstream and is not stored in the body, . . . bST is needed every day to sustain the increase in milk yield. This requires daily injections or use of a prolonged release formulation of bST.[7]

In November 1993, the Food and Drug Administration (FDA) approved the marketing of bST. In its view, milk produced with the genetically engineered hormone is indistinguishable from milk that is not. Nonetheless, a variety of concerns have been raised about the safety of bST for humans and animals, as well as its economic effects. Critics claim that bST increases the incidence of udder infections in treated cows and taints the milk supply with pus and bacteria.[8] During its first year on the market, Monsanto, the firm which developed and marketed it, reported that about 11 percent of the country's dairy farmers were using it, a figure that critics challenged.[9]

---

[5] U.S. Congress, Office of Technology Assessment, *U.S. Dairy Industry At a Crossroad.*

[6] *Philadelphia Inquirer*, June 14, 1992, p. C2.

[7] U.S. Congress, Office of Technology Assessment, *U.S. Dairy Industry At a Crossroad*, p. 4.

[8] *Science*, October 21, 1994, and *New York Times*, October 30, 1994.

[9] *New York Times*, February 1, 1995, and March 12, 1995.

The Demand for Milk and Dairy Products

Dairy farmers like the McGraws know that changes in consumer tastes, as well as new techniques like bST, can affect their industry significantly. Table 3 shows the per capita consumption of milk from 1960 to 1990. As you can see, the consumption of plain whole milk fell during this period by over 50 percent, while the consumption of low-fat milk increased markedly, and the consumption of skim milk more than doubled. Adding all types of milk together, per capita milk consumption declined by about 20 percent. Turning to products made from milk, the average U.S. consumer purchased more and more cheese and yogurt, but less butter and condensed milk, as shown in Table 3. (Ice cream consumption has remained fairly steady.)

These dramatic changes have been due in part to the altered views of what is a healthy diet. Consumers have become much more concerned about calories, fat, and cholesterol intake. Gone are the days when mothers encouraged their families to slather butter on their toast and drink plenty of whole milk. Instead, the emphasis now is on few calories and the avoidance of fats and cholesterol. However, not all is gloom on the nation's dairy farms: the big bright spot is the increase in the per capita consumption of cheese, shown in Table 3.

Government Regulation of Milk Prices

The McGraws and other milk suppliers have been subject to a host of regulations. In part, this reflects people's concerns about health hazards. Early in this century, the U.S. Public Health Service became interested in the problem of milk-borne diseases; in 1924, it developed a model regulation—the Standard Milk Ordinance—which was adopted by many states and municipalities. But in recent years, much of the controversy over milk regulation has been concerned with pricing, not health hazards. Federal and state regulations put floors under the price of milk. As pointed out in Chapter 1, these price floors

TABLE 3

Per Capita Consumption of Milk and Dairy Products, United States, 1960–1990 (pounds per year)

Year	Plain whole milk	Low-fat milk	Skim milk	Yogurt	Cream	Condensed and evaporated milk	Butter	Cheese	Ice cream
1990	88	98	23	4	5	3	4	25	16
1985	120	83	13	4	4	4	5	22	18
1980	141	72	12	3	3	4	4	18	18
1975	175	55	12	2	3	5	5	14	19
1970	207	31	12	1	4	7	5	11	18
1960	251	2	11	a	b	14	8	8	18

[a] Less than 0.5 pound per year.
[b] Published figures include specialties as well.
Source: See Table 2.

have been established to bolster the incomes of farmers, who benefit from higher prices. Consumers, in contrast, have been hurt by them.[10]

For milk eligible for fluid consumption, milk processors have paid minimum prices based on how the milk is used. The lowest prices have been for milk used to make butter, cheese, and nonfat dry milk; a somewhat higher price has had to be paid for milk used to make ice cream and yogurt; a still higher price has had to be paid for milk used for fluid consumption. For the last type of milk, the minimum price has gone up with increasing distance from Eau Claire, Wisconsin. In other words, the price floor has gotten higher as one moves away from Eau Claire—a facet of the regulations that has angered dairy farmers in Wisconsin and Minnesota. (This regulation dates back to the 1930s when Eau Claire had a great deal of surplus milk, and the federal government established higher minimum prices elsewhere to reimburse Wisconsin farmers for their shipping costs.) In addition, the federal government has bought butter, cheese, and nonfat dry milk in whatever quantities have been needed to keep their market price from falling below the floors which the government itself has set.[11] (Prices of milk and cheese in recent years are shown in Table 4.)

These price floors for milk and dairy products have aroused widespread and intense controversy for many years. Editorials in urban newspapers have regularly attacked government milk programs as complex devices enabling dairy farmers to perform legal economic muggings on consumers. In response,

TABLE 4

Price of Milk and Cheese, 1970–1990 (cents per pound)		
	Price received by farmers for whole milk	Wholesale price of American cheese (Wisconsin assembly points)
1990	13.73	137
1988	12.26	124
1986	12.51	127
1984	13.46	138
1982	13.61	138
1980	13.05	133
1975	8.75	87
1970	5.71	55

Source: See Table 2.

---

[10] Manchester, *The Public Role in the Dairy Economy*.

[11] U.S. Congress, Office of Technology Assessment, *U.S. Dairy Industry At a Crossroad*. Also, see U.S. General Accounting Office, *Milk Pricing* (Washington, D.C.: Government Printing Office, November 1989), and U.S. General Accounting Office, *Milk Marketing Orders: Options for Change* (Washington, D.C.: Government Printing Office, March 1988).

politicians from dairy states portray the farmers as deserving and unappreciated; for example, William Proxmire, former senator from Wisconsin, has said, "The No. 1 victim of economic injustice in this country today is the farmer and especially the dairy farmer."[12] In 1996, Congress phased out price supports for butter, powdered milk, and cheese over four years, and reduced the number of regional price supports for milk.

Milk Production: Can You Apply the Theory?

The following four problems take up various aspects of a dairy farm's market, technology, and costs, now and in the past.

PROBLEM **1**   George and Gloria Wilber owned a dairy farm in Colebrook, Connecticut. They were the last dairy farmers in this town where there were more than a dozen a generation ago. They owned 60 Brown Swiss cows, which they said were worth about $2,000 apiece, and they sold their milk to Agri-Mark, a marketing cooperative. In early 1992, they received about $4,500 per month for their milk which, after deducting other expenses, did not cover half their $3,000-a-month feed bill. After five years of losing money, the Wilbers were trying in 1992 to sell their herd and leave dairy farming.

(a) According to Mr. Wilber, one of the principal reasons for his losses was that fuel and labor costs, as well as taxes, were relatively high in Connecticut. Some dairy farmers believe that Connecticut's state government should support the price of milk at a higher level than in other states in order to offset these disadvantages, which they regard as unfair. Evaluate this proposal.

(b) Mr. Wilber has said, "In the town of Colebrook, our soil is very stony. You're not going to be able to set strawberry beds or plant sweet corn."[13] Does this imply that the alternative (or opportunity) cost of using Mr. Wilber's land for dairy farming is low? Why or why not?

(c) The area surrounding the Wilber farm, once dotted with many grazing cows, now contains the weekend homes of many New Yorkers. Do you think that the alternative (or opportunity) cost of using Mr. Wilber's land for dairy farming has increased over the past 20 years? Why or why not? What signals does the price system use to inform the Wilbers whether their land can be used more efficiently for purposes other than dairy farming?

(d) Did the fact that the Wilbers' land was used for dairy farming bring satisfaction and enjoyment to other people in the area? (Hint: Were there environmental effects?)

PROBLEM **2**   Many years ago, the U.S. Department of Agriculture carried out experiments to determine how a cow's milk production during a particular period was related to how much she was fed.[14]

---

[12] J. Grant, "Milk and Honey," *Barron's*, May 30, 1977, p. 7.

[13] *New York Times*, June 2, 1992, p. B6.

[14] See L. Weiss, *Case Studies in American Industry* (2d ed.; New York: Wiley, 1971)

A cow must be fed a certain amount just to maintain herself; beyond that point, more feed resulted in more milk, as shown below:

Pounds of feed consumed by a cow	Pounds of milk produced by a cow
5,700	7,600
6,100	8,200
6,600	8,800
7,100	9,400
7,500	9,800
7,900	10,000

(a) What is the marginal product of a pound of feed if between 5,700 and 6,100 pounds of feed are consumed? If between 7,500 and 7,900 pounds of feed are consumed?

(b) What is the average product of a pound of feed if 5,700 pounds of feed are consumed? If 7,900 pounds of feed are consumed?

(c) Does milk production seem to conform to the law of diminishing marginal returns? Why or why not?

(d) If a farmer increases the quantity of feed consumed from 5,700 pounds to 6,100 pounds, does this raise the average product of a pound of feed? If so, would you expect the marginal product of a pound of feed to be more than the average product? Why or why not?

(e) At which of the above quantities of feed consumed is the average product of a pound of feed greatest?

(f) A dairy farmer hires you as a consultant to determine whether the optimal amount to feed a cow is the amount at which the average product of feed is highest. The farmer says that he has been told that the smart thing to do is maximize the amount of milk produced per pound of feed, and that this seems reasonable to him. Is he right? Why or why not?

PROBLEM 3   At the Cox Dairy Farm, which has 50 cows, suppose that the relationship between the milk output of a cow and the amount she is fed is as shown in Problem 2. For simplicity, suppose that this farm's only variable cost is the amount it spends for feed, which costs 6¢ per pound, and that its fixed costs total $40,000 during the relevant period. The farmer, Robert Cox, and his family do all the work on this farm, and hold no other jobs. Their time is fully occupied (dawn to dusk) by the farm work, regardless of how much milk their cows produce.

(a) Why is the cost of labor on this farm a fixed cost, not a variable cost?

(b) Since all of the labor is performed by family members, how can one attach a monetary value to the farm's labor cost?

(c) What is the farm's total cost if each of its cows produces 7,600 pounds of milk during this period? If each cow produces 10,000 pounds of milk?

(d) What is the farm's average variable cost if each cow produces 7,600 pounds of milk during this period? If each cow produces 10,000 pounds of milk?

(e) What is the farm's average fixed cost if each cow produces 7,600 pounds of milk during this period? If each cow produces 10,000 pounds of milk?

(f) What is the farm's marginal cost if each cow produces between 9,800 and 10,000 pounds of milk during this period?

(g) Robert Cox asks his accountant how much he should feed his cows. His accountant replies that he should choose the amount of feed per cow that minimizes the farm's average total cost. According to his accountant, if each cow consumes 7,500 pounds of feed, the farm's average total cost is 13.0¢ per pound of milk, and this is the minimum value of the farm's average total cost. Is this really the amount of feed (according to Problem 2) that would minimize the farm's average total cost? Is this really the optimal amount to feed each cow? Why or why not?

PROBLEM 4   According to an early study conducted by the U.S. Department of Agriculture, 8,500 pounds of milk can be produced during a specified time period by a cow fed the following combinations of hay and grain:[15]

Quantity of hay (pounds)	Quantity of grain (pounds)
5,000	6,154
5,500	5,454
6,000	4,892
6,500	4,423
7,000	4,029
7,500	3,694

(a) Plot these data as an isoquant. Is this isoquant convex?

(b) What is the marginal rate of technical substitution when between 5,000 and 5,500 pounds of hay are used? What is it when between 5,500 and 6,000 pounds of hay are used?

(c) If the price of a pound of hay equals the price of a pound of grain, should a cow be fed 5,000 pounds of hay and 6,154 pounds of grain? Why or why not?

(d) If the price of a pound of hay equals 1.05 times the price of a pound of grain, what is the least-cost combination of inputs to produce 8,500 pounds of milk?

(e) Dairy farms produce both milk and cows. If the cost of producing 100,000 pounds of milk and 4 cows is 60 percent of the cost of producing them separately, what is the degree of economies of scope?

Economies of Scale: Can You Apply the Theory?

The following two problems pertain to economies of scale, a very important topic to dairy farmers.

---

[15] For further discussion, see E. Heady's classic work, *Economics of Agricultural Production and Resource Use* (New York: Prentice-Hall, 1952).

PROBLEM 5   According to the U.S. Office of Technology Assessment, the relationship between the long-run average cost of milk production and the size of a dairy farm (as measured by its number of cows) in California and New York in 1985 were as shown below:[16]

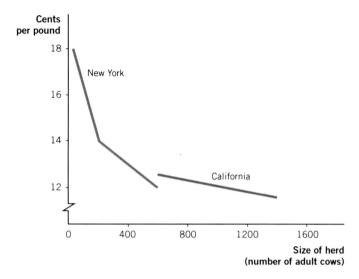

(a) What is the average total cost of a pound of milk produced by a New York farm with 50 cows? By a New York farm with 400 cows? Based on these data, do there appear to be economies of scale in milk production in New York?

(b) What is the average total cost of a pound of milk produced by a California farm with 600 cows? By a California farm with 1,200 cows? Based on these data, do there appear to be economies of scale in milk production in California?

(c) The climate is much milder in California than in New York or Wisconsin. Thus, as Kent Cheeseborough, manager of the Ron Quinn dairy in Tulare County, California, has pointed out, "We get 9 or 10 cuttings [of alfalfa, which is fed to cows] a year. In Wisconsin, they're lucky if they can get three."[17] A consultant prepares a study for the dairy industry in which he assumes that the production function for milk is the same in California as in Wisconsin. He attributes California's lower costs to the availability of relatively inexpensive immigrant labor. Evaluate the assumptions and findings of this study.

(d) When asked whether he was planning to expand his Wisconsin farm to match the size of those in California, Dennis McGraw said, "Right now I have no desire to get that big. Why should we? We're making a go of it right now."[18] One reason why Mr. McGraw is reluctant to expand his farm is that it would mean becoming a full-time manager. As he put it, "I'd fall asleep sitting behind a desk."[19] Does it appear that Mr. McGraw wants to maximize profit? How would you characterize his objectives?

---

[16] U.S. Congress, Office of Technology Assessment, *U.S. Dairy Industry At a Crossroad.*

[17] *Philadelphia Inquirer*, June 14, 1992, p. C2.

[18] Ibid.

[19] Ibid.

PROBLEM 6   Agricultural economists have estimated the production functions for dairy farms. Suppose that a study came up with the following result for a particular type of Minnesota dairy farm:

$$Q = KA^{.05}L^{.05}E^{.10}N^{.80}F^{.60},$$

where Q is the output of milk per period, A is the amount of land used, L is the amount of labor used, E is the amount of equipment used, N is the number of cows on the farm, F is the amount of feed used, and K is a constant.[20]

The owner of a Minnesota dairy farm of this type is concerned that her farm may be too small to compete effectively with larger dairy farms. Her farm is of below-average size, and she is troubled by the possibility that larger farms may be more efficient than farms like hers. She is considering the merger of her farm with a neighboring farm that is essentially the same (in size and other characteristics) as her own.

(a) If the amount of every input is doubled, in accord with the merger under consideration, what will be the percentage change in output, according to the above equation?
(b) Are there economies of scale, according to this equation?
(c) For many years, there has been considerable technological change in dairy farming. For example, whereas milking used to be largely a hand operation, milking machines are now found almost everywhere, and with the general use of artificial insemination, bulls have become as rare on dairy farms as calls to the Maytag repairman. Does the above equation recognize that technological change of this sort occurs? If so, how? Can a merger influence how rapidly new technologies are adopted?

Effects of bst: Can You Apply the Theory?

The following two problems take up some of the economic effects of bST from the points of view of both an individual farm and the industry as a whole.

PROBLEM 7   If the Cox Dairy Farm, discussed in Problem 3, were to adopt bST, output per cow would increase by 1,200 pounds during the relevant period. For simplicity, suppose that this increase would be the same (that is, 1,200 pounds) regardless of how much feed a cow consumes.

(a) Would the marginal product of a pound of feed (when between 5,700 and 6,100 pounds of feed are consumed) be increased by the use of bST? Why or why not? Would the marginal product curve for feed shift to the right? Why or why not?
(b) After the adoption of bST, what would be the average product of a pound of feed when 7,500 pounds of feed are consumed per cow? Would it be higher than before bST was used? (Use the data in Problems 2 and 3 to answer this and subsequent parts of this problem.)
(c) If this farm adopts bST, what would be the total cost of producing 10,000 pounds of milk per cow? (Assume that the cost of using bST is $60 per cow during the relevant period.) Would it be lower than if bST is not adopted? If so, how much lower?

---

[20] The formula shown above is illustrative, not the result of a careful statistical study. But for present purposes, this makes no real difference.

(d) After the adoption of bST, what would be the average total cost, average variable cost, and average fixed cost of producing 10,000 pounds of milk per cow? Would all of them be lower than before the introduction of bST? Why or why not?

(e) If bST is adopted, what would be the marginal cost of a pound of milk if each of this farm's cows is producing between 11,000 and 11,200 pounds of milk? Would the adoption of bST result in the movement of the farm's marginal cost curve to the right by 50 times 1,200 pounds? Why or why not?

(f) If the price of a pound of milk was 12.132 cents, what would be the break-even point for this farm after the adoption of bST? Should you assume that the total cost function is linear as in Figure 8.14?

(g) If you were asked to provide Mr. Cox with advice as to whether he should use bST, what would your advice to him be?

PROBLEM **8**   In the early 1990s, there was a bitter battle waged over the acceptance of bST. On the one side, the National Farmers Union (with 300,000 members) and other farm groups fought hard to convince state legislators and other organizations to ban its use, even though the Food and Drug Administration had decided that it posed no health hazard to people. On the other side, farmers like William Morris of Chatham, Pennsylvania, who has 500 cows on 1,000 acres, believe that, "The question is do consumers want high-quality milk for less money, or do they want us to produce it

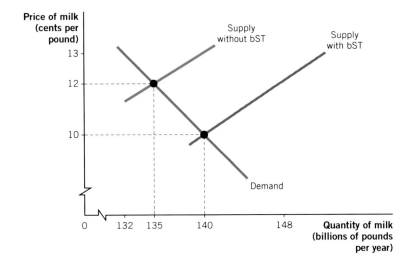

the way we always have?"[21] Of course, the firms that developed and produced bST—American Cyanamid, Eli Lilly, Monsanto, and Upjohn—fought hard to get it approved and marketed.[22]

(a) If the situation is as shown in the graph on the preceding page, how big an effect would the adoption of bST have on the price of milk if the government did not intervene in the milk market?

---

[21] *West Chester Daily Local News*, August 11, 1992, p. C5.

[22] "Market Sours on Milk Hormones," *Science*, November 17, 1989.

(b) Why would the adoption of bST shift the supply curve for milk to the right?

(c) In dollar terms, how large would the benefits to consumers be if bST were adopted (and if the government did not intervene)?

(d) If consumers can be convinced by those fighting against bST that milk from bST-supplemented cows is dangerous, what will be the effect on the demand curve for such milk?

(e) According to the *New York Times*, "Lower milk prices will . . . benefit consumers . . . [But as] many as 10 percent of the country's dairy farmers might be forced out of business."[23] Why might they be forced out of business?

(f) Some states, like Wisconsin and Minnesota, have banned the use of bST, although these bans were later rescinded. Do you think that its use should be banned by the states? Why or why not?

(g) In April 1996, *Business Week* said that bST had not caught on. "Monsanto has had difficulty persuading farmers to use the product, which requires complicated training. Continued consumer resistance has also hurt. Analysts estimate that bST is losing about $10 million annually."[24] If you were president of Monsanto, what factors would you consider in determining whether to continue marketing this product?

The Demand for Dairy Products: Can You Apply the Theory?

The following problem pertains to what we previously singled out as a bright spot in the dairy industry: the big increase in the consumption of cheese.

PROBLEM 9   Between 1980 and 1990, the per capita consumption of cheese rose from 18 to 25 pounds per year, a big boost for the milk and dairy products industry. Suppose that you were an analyst of this industry, and that a client asked you to explain why this increase in cheese consumption occurred. Looking at publications of the U.S. Department of Agriculture, you find that the price elasticity of demand for cheese is about 0.30, and the income elasticity of demand for cheese is about 0.45.[25]

(a) Between 1980 and 1990, the retail price of cheese increased by about 48 percent, but it is important to correct for inflation when comparing prices at various points in time. During this same period, the Consumer Price Index rose by about 59 percent. When corrected for inflation, did the price of cheese go up or down between 1980 and 1990? When the price of cheese in both 1990 and 1980 is measured in 1980 dollars, what was the percentage change in the price of cheese during this period?

(b) Based on the change in its price alone, how big a percentage change would have been expected in the quantity of cheese demanded between 1980 and 1990?

(c) Per capita disposable personal income went up by 18 percent (adjusted for inflation) during 1980 to 1990. Based on this fact, how big a

---

23 "Hiding Behind Hormones in Milk," *New York Times*, May 15, 1989.

24 "So Shall Monsanto Reap?" *Business Week*, April 1, 1996.

25 See Economic Research Service, U.S. Department of Agriculture, *Dairy Situation and Outlook Yearbook*, August 1991, and R. Haidacher, J. Blaylock, and L. Myers, *Consumer Demand for Dairy Products* (Washington, D.C.: U.S. Department of Agriculture, 1988). The income elasticity of demand for cheese in Table 5.5 is somewhat different from the figure given by the Department of Agriculture because it pertains to a different time and area.

percentage change in the quantity of cheese demanded would have been expected between 1980 and 1990?

(d) Taken together, do changes in price and income account for the entire growth from 1980 to 1990 in the quantity of cheese demanded? If not, how much of this growth is unaccounted for?

(e) The per capita consumption of Italian-style cheese more than doubled between 1980 and 1990. Why did this occur? Does this suggest one of the factors explaining the growth in cheese consumption unaccounted for by price and income changes?

(f) Recent studies show that the cross elasticity of demand for cheese with respect to the price of beef is about –0.30.[26] Can you think of any reason why this cross elasticity is negative?

(g) George Lee's indifference curves and price-consumption curve for cheese are as shown below:

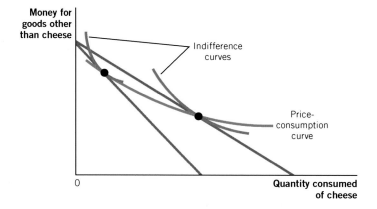

Is he a typical consumer, on the basis of the data given in this problem? If not, in what respect is he atypical, and why?

Government Regulation: Can You Apply the Theory?

The remaining problem is concerned with the price floors established by the federal government; much more will be said on this score in Chapter 10.

PROBLEM **10**   In 1983, a new federal milk program was established. According to *Business Week*, "Agriculture Secretary John R. Block struck a secret deal with the powerful dairy lobby. He agreed to support a new milk program proposed by the dairy industry. . . . In return, the dairy lobby agreed to throw its weight behind a bill that would cut subsidies to grain and cotton farmers."[27] But this strategy didn't work, since Congress rejected the cuts in other farm programs but adopted the dairy bill and President Ronald Reagan signed it.

(a) The problem that the new program was designed to solve was a mounting oversupply of milk. U.S. output rose in 1983 to a record 140 billion pounds, and as shown in Table 5, the Agriculture Department's Commodity Credit Corporation, which was obligated by law to purchase surplus dairy products so as to maintain the price floor set by the government,

26 Ibid.

27 "Why the New Milk Law Won't Cure the Dairy Glut," *Business Week*, December 12, 1983.

TABLE 5

Dairy Products Removed from the Commercial Market by the U.S. Department of Agriculture, 1970–1990

		Removals		Percent of amount marketed
Year	Butter	Cheese	Nonfat dry milk	
		(millions of pounds)		
1990	400	22	118	1.1
1988	313	238	268	3.8
1986	288	468	827	10.1
1984	202	447	678	9.4
1982	382	642	948	13.1
1980	257	350	634	8.6
1975	63	68	395	4.7
1970	246	49	452	5.1

Source: Dairy Situation and Outlook Yearbook.

accumulated a huge amount of butter, cheese, and nonfat dry milk—about 10 percent of annual consumption. (And this was after the federal government made massive donations of these products to the poor.) Some critics of the new program within the Reagan administration claimed that, if the price floor of about 13 cents per pound had been reduced, the dairy industry would have been healthier. But according to Irvin Elkin, president of the Associated Milk Producers, Inc., "Major cuts in support prices run the risk of driving many dairy farm families out of business, which would mean higher milk prices."[28] If the situation was as shown in the graph on page 294, is this true? (Warning: To provide some variety, the situation in the graph above differs from that in the graph in Problem 8.)

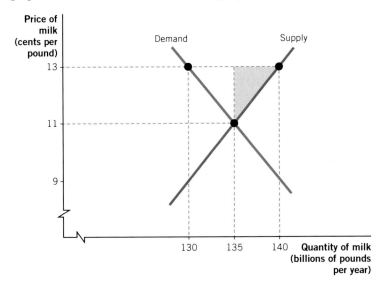

(b) In dollar terms, how big was the reduction in consumer surplus because the government supported the milk price at 13 cents per pound? (Your answers to this and subsequent parts of this problem should be based on the graph above.)

(c) Farmers would have produced 135 billion pounds of milk per year if the government had abandoned its price support. Without the price support, how much less would the farmers' profits have been from these 135 billion pounds of milk?

(d) If the price support had been abandoned, farmers would have produced 135 billion pounds of milk; with the price support, they produced 140 billion pounds of milk. In Chapter 10, we shall see that their profit from the extra 5 billion pounds of milk equals the shaded area in the graph above.[29] Adding this area to your answer to part (c), you can obtain the total amount of extra profit farmers received because of the government price support. What is this amount?

(e) How much did taxpayers pay farmers for the milk bought up by the Department of Agriculture?

(f) Because taxpayers are consumers in another guise, if you add your answer to part (b) to your answer to part (e), you can obtain the total losses to consumers because of this government price support. What is this amount? Does it exceed the farmers' gains?

(g) If the aim of the price support program was to bolster farmers' incomes, can you think of a less costly (to consumers) way of increasing farmers' profits by the amount they receive from this price support program? (Hint: What if direct payments were made by consumers to producers, but the milk price supports were abolished?)

Conclusion

It is time now to return from the dairy farms of Dennis and Sue McGraw, Ron Quinn, and George and Gloria Wilber to the classroom. Clearly, their industry is in a state of dramatic change, both because of alterations in consumer tastes and because of regional shifts and technological upheavals. Also, government price regulation (which will be discussed further in Chapter 10) is a major issue affecting the general public as well as the milk industry. But the most important point for present purposes is that the microeconomic concepts and models you learned in previous chapters are essential to understand how to manage a dairy farm, or how the milk industry is evolving. Such simple concepts as alternative (or opportunity) cost, production function, average and marginal cost, and returns to scale are enormously useful, and help sophisticated managers and investors (and sometimes even observers) to earn their bread and butter. As you can see from this case, it would be hopeless to try to understand what is going on in this industry without them.

---

[29] More accurately, this is the increase in producer surplus due to the production of the extra 5 billion pounds of milk. Producer surplus includes both the aggregate profits of the farmers and the amount that owners of inputs (used to make milk) are compensated above and beyond the minimum they would insist on. The concept of producer surplus is taken up in Chapter 10. For now, we assume that the increase in producer surplus in this case equals the increased profits of the farmers.

Selected Supplementary Readings

1. U.S. Congress, Office of Technology Assessment, *U.S. Dairy Industry at a Crossroad* (Washington, D.C.: U.S. Government Printing Office, May 1991).
2. J. Grant, "Milk and Honey," *Barron's*, May 30, 1977.
3. R. Haidacher, J. Blaylock, and L. Myers, *Consumer Demand for Dairy Products* (Washington, D.C.: U.S. Department of Agriculture, 1988).
4. "Milking Consumers," *New York Times*, July 22, 1995.
5. "Monsanto Has Its Wonder Hormone. Can It Sell It?" *New York Times*, March 12, 1995.
6. "Analysis Questions BST's Safety to Cows," *Science*, October 21, 1994.
7. "So Shall Monsanto Reap?" *Business Week*, April 1, 1996.
8. "House-Senate Committee Agrees on Overhaul of Farm Programs," *New York Times*, March 22, 1996.

Principles of Microeconomics

Principles of Microeconomics

Dirk Mateer
University of Kentucky

Lee Coppock
University of Virginia

W·W·NORTON

NEW YORK · LONDON

W. W. Norton & Company has been independent since its founding in 1923, when William Warder Norton and Mary D. Herter Norton first published lectures delivered at the People's Institute, the adult education division of New York City's Cooper Union. The firm soon expanded its program beyond the Institute, publishing books by celebrated academics from America and abroad. By midcentury, the two major pillars of Norton's publishing program—trade books and college texts—were firmly established. In the 1950s, the Norton family transferred control of the company to its employees, and today—with a staff of four hundred and a comparable number of trade, college, and professional titles published each year—W. W. Norton & Company stands as the largest and oldest publishing house owned wholly by its employees.

Editor: Jack Repcheck

Developmental Editor: Rebecca Kohn

Manuscript Editor: Alice Vigliani

Project Editor: Jack Borrebach

Media Editor: Cassie del Pilar

Associate Media Editors: Nicole Sawa, Carson Russell

Assistant Editor: Hannah Bachman

Marketing Manager, Economics: John Kresse

Production Manager: Eric Pier-Hocking

Photo Editor: Nelson Colón

Photo Researcher: Dena Digilio Betz

Permissions Manager: Megan Jackson

Text Design: Lisa Buckley

Art Director: Rubina Yeh

Cover Design and "Snapshot" Infographics: Kiss Me I'm Polish

Composition: Jouve

Manufacturing: Courier Kendallville

A catalogue record is available from the Library of Congress
ISBN 978-0-393-27728-9

W. W. Norton & Company, Inc., 500 Fifth Avenue, New York, NY 10110-0017
wwnorton.com

W. W. Norton & Company Ltd., Castle House, 75/76 Wells Street, London W1T 3QT
1 2 3 4 5 6 7 8 9 0

BRIEF CONTENTS

CONTENTS

PART I   Introduction

1 The Five Foundations of Economics   4

PART II The Role of Markets

5 Price Controls   146

PART III The Theory of the Firm

13 Oligopoly and Strategic Behavior 382

PART IV Labor Markets and Earnings

PART V Special Topics in Microeconomics

17 Behavioral Economics and Risk Taking   526

PART X International Economics

Preface to the First Edition

We are teachers of principles of economics. That is what we do. We each teach principles of microeconomics and macroeconomics to over a thousand students a semester, every single semester, at the University of Kentucky and the University of Virginia.

We decided to write our own text for one big reason. We simply were not satisfied with the available texts and felt strongly that we could write an innovative book to which dedicated instructors like us would respond. It's not that the already available texts are bad or inaccurate—it's that they lack an understanding of what we, as teachers, have learned through fielding the thousands of questions that our students have asked us over the years. We do not advise policy makers, but we do advise students, and we know how their minds work.

For instance, there really is no text that shows an understanding for where students consistently trip up (for example, cost curves) and therefore provides an additional example, or better yet, a worked exercise. There really is no text that is careful to reinforce new terminology and difficult sticking points with explanations in everyday language. There really is no text that leverages the fact that today's students are key participants in the twenty-first-century economy, and that uses examples and cases from markets in which they interact all the time (for example, the markets for cell phones, social networking sites, computing devices, online book sellers, etc.).

What our years in the classroom have brought home to us is the importance of meeting students where they are. This means knowing their cultural touchstones and trying to tell the story of economics with those touchstones in mind. In our text we meet students where they are through resonance and reinforcement. In fact, these two words are our mantra—we strive to make each topic resonate and then make it stick through reinforcement.

Whenever possible, we use student-centered examples that resonate with students. For instance, many of our examples refer to jobs that students often hold and businesses that often employ them. If the examples resonate, students are much more likely to dig into the material wholeheartedly and internalize key concepts.

When we teach, we try to create a rhythm of reinforcement in our lectures that begins with the presentation of new material, followed by a concrete example, followed by a reinforcing device, and then closes with a "make it stick" moment. We do this over and over again. We have tried to bring that rhythm to the book. We believe strongly that this commitment to reinforcement works. To give just one example, in our chapter "Oligopoly and Strategic Behavior," while presenting the crucial-yet-difficult subject of game theory, we work through the concept of the prisoner's dilemma at least six different ways.

No educator is happy with the challenge we all face to motivate our students to read the assigned text. No matter how effective our lectures are, if our students are not reinforcing those lectures by reading the assigned text chapters, they are only partially absorbing the key takeaways that properly trained citizens need to thrive in today's world. A second key motivation for us to undertake this ambitious project was the desire to create a text that students would read, week in and week out, for the entire course. By following our commitment to resonance and reinforcement, we are confident that we have written a text that's a good read for today's students. So good, in fact, that we believe students will read entire chapters and actually enjoy them. Certainly the reports from our dozens of class testers indicate that this is the case.

What do we all want? We want our students to leave our courses having internalized fundamentals that they will remember for life. The fundamentals (understanding incentives, opportunity cost, thinking at the margin, etc.) will allow them to make better choices in the workplace, their personal investments, their long-term planning, their voting, and all their critical choices. The bottom line is that they will live more fulfilled and satisfying lives if we succeed. The purpose of this text is to help you succeed in your quest.

What does this classroom-inspired, student-centered text look like?

A Simple Narrative

First and foremost, we keep the narrative simple. We always bear in mind all those office-hour conversations with students where we searched for some way to make sense of this foreign language—for them—that is economics. It is incredibly satisfying when you find the right expression, explanation, or example that creates the "Oh, now I get it . . ." moment with your student. We have filled the narrative with those successful "now I get it" passages.

The Ice Cream Float, a cool idea on a hot day at the lake.

stores often close by 9 p.m. because operating overnight would not generate enough revenue to cover the costs of remaining open. Or consider the Ice Cream Float, which crisscrosses Smith Mountain Lake in Virginia during the summer months. You can hear the music announcing its arrival at the public beach from over a mile away. By the time the float arrives, there is usually a long line of eager customers waiting for the float to dock. This is a very profitable business on hot and sunny summer days. However, during the late spring and early fall the float operates on weekends only. Eventually, colder weather forces the business to shut down until the crowds return the following season. This shutdown decision is a short-run calculation. If the float were to operate during the winter, it would need to pay for employees and fuel. Incurring these variable costs when there are so few customers would result in greater total costs than simply dry-docking the boat. When the float is dry-docked over the winter, only the fixed cost of storing the boat remains.

Fortunately, a firm can use a simple, intuitive rule to decide whether to operate or shut down in the short run: if the firm would lose less by shutting down than by staying open, it should shut down. Recall that costs are broken into two parts—fixed and variable. Fixed costs must be paid whether the business is open or not. Since variable costs are only incurred when the business is op[en] employee will choo

Prices act to ration scarce resources. When the demand for generators or other necessities is high, the price rises to ensure that the available units are distributed to those who value them the most. More important, the ability to charge a higher price provides sellers with an incentive to make more units available. If there is limited ability for the price to change when demand increases, there will be a shortage. Therefore, price gouging legislation means that devastated communities must rely exclusively on the goodwill of others and the slow-moving machinery of government relief efforts. This closes off a third avenue, entrepreneurial activity, as a means to alleviate poor conditions.

Incentives

Large generator: $900 after Hurricane Wilma hit.

Figure 5.5 shows how price gouging laws work and the shortage they create. If the demand for gas generators increases immediately after a disaster (D_{after}), the market price rises from $530 to $900. But since $900 is considered excessive, sales at that price are illegal. This creates a binding price ceiling for as long as a state of emergency is in effect. Whenever a price ceiling is binding, it creates a shortage. You can see this in Figure 5.5 in the difference between quantity demanded and quantity supplied at the price ceiling level mandated by the law. In this case, the normal ability of supply and demand to ration the available generators is short-circuited. Since more people demand generators after the disaster than before it, those who do not get to the store soon enough are out of luck. When the emergency is lifted and the market returns to normal, the temporary shortage created by legislation against price gouging is eliminated.

Examples and Cases That Resonate and Therefore Stick

Nothing makes this material stick for students like good examples and cases that they relate to, and we have peppered our book with them. They are not in boxed inserts. They are part of the narrative, set off with an Economics in the Real World heading.

---

132 / CHAPTER 4 Elasticity

ECONOMICS IN THE REAL WORLD

The Wii Rollout and Changes in the Video Game Industry

When Nintendo launched the Wii console in late 2006, it fundamentally changed the gaming industry. The Wii uses motion-sensing technology. Despite relatively poor graphics, it provided a completely different gaming experience from its competitors, Playstation 3 (PS3) and the Xbox 360. Yet the PS3 and Xbox 360 had larger storage capacities and better graphics, in theory making them more attractive to gamers than the Wii.

During the 2006 holiday shopping season, the three systems had three distinct price points:

Wii = $249
Xbox = $399

The Wii rollout generated long waiting lines.

Wii and X
ply in stor
had hope
360 outso
ing, a mo
the deteri

ECONOMICS IN THE REAL WORLD

Blockbuster and the Dynamic Nature of Change

What happens if your customers do not return? What if you simply had a bad idea to begin with, and the customers never arrived in the first place?

When the long-run profit outlook is bleak, the firm is better off shutting down. This is a normal part of the ebb and flow of business. For example, once there were thousands of buggy whip companies. Today, as technology has improved and we no longer rely on horse-drawn carriages, few buggy whip makers remain. However, many companies now manufacture automobile parts.

Similarly, a succession of technological advances has transformed the music industry. Records were replaced by 8-track tapes, and then by cassettes. Already, the CD is on its way to being replaced by better technology as iPods, iPhones, and MP3 players make music more portable and as web sites such as Pandora and Spotify allow live streaming of almost any selection a listener wants to hear. However, there was a time when innovation meant playing music on the original Sony Walkman. What was cool in the early 1980s is antiquated today. Any business engaged in distributing music has had to adapt or close.

Similar changes are taking place in the video rental industry. Blockbuster was founded in 1982 and experienced explosive growth, becoming the nation's largest video store chain by 1988. The chain's growth was fueled by its large selection and use of a computerized tracking system that made the checkout process faster than the one at competing video stores. However, by the early 2000s Blockbuster faced stiff competition from online providers like Netflix and in-store dispensers like Redbox. Today, the chain has one-quarter the number of employees it once had and its future is very uncertain.

In addition to changes in technology, other factors such as downturns in the economy, changes in tastes, demographic factors, and migration can all force businesses to close. These examples remind us that the long-run decision to go out of business has nothing to do with the short-term profit outlook. ✳

Blockbuster's best days are long gone.

So far, we have examined the firm's decision-making process in the short run in the context of revenues versus costs. This has enabled us to determine the profits each firm makes. But now we pause to consider *sunk costs*, a special type of cost that all firms, in every industry, must consider when making decisions.

Reinforcers

Practice What You Know boxes are in-chapter exercises that allow students to self-assess while reading and provide a bit more hand-holding than usual. While other books have in-chapter questions, no other book consistently frames these exercises within real-world situations that students relate to.

PRACTICE WHAT YOU KNOW

Income Elasticity

Question: A college student eats ramen noodles twice a week and earns $300/week working part-time. After graduating, the student earns $1,000/week and eats ramen noodles every other week. What is the student's income elasticity?

Yummy, or all you can afford?

Answer: The income elasticity of demand using the midpoint method is

$$\frac{(Q_2 - Q_1) \div [(Q_1 + Q_2) \div 2]}{(I_2 - I_1) \div [(I_1 + I_2) \div 2]}$$

$$\frac{(\ldots 5 - 2.0) \div [(2.0 + 0.5) \div 2]}{(\ldots - \$300) \div [(\$300 + \$1000) \div 2]}$$

$$E_I = \frac{-1.5 \div 1.25}{\$700 \div \$650}$$

emand is positive for normal goods and negative he negative coefficient indicates that ramen noo- he range of income—in this example, between should confirm your intuition. The higher post- e student to substitute away from ramen noodles rovide more nourishment and enjoyment.

PRACTICE WHAT YOU KNOW

Shift or Slide?

Cheap pizza or . . .

. . . cheap drinks?

Suppose that a local pizza place likes to run a "late-night special" after 11 p.m. The owners have contacted you for some advice. One of the owners tells you, "We want to increase the demand for our pizza." He proposes two marketing ideas to accomplish this:

1. Reduce the price of large pizzas.
2. Reduce the price of a complementary good—for example, offer two half-priced bottles or cans of soda with every large pizza ordered.

Question: What will you recommend?

Answer: First, consider why "late-night specials" exist in the first place. Since most people prefer to eat dinner early in the evening, the store has to encourage late-night patrons to buy pizzas by stimulating demand. "Specials" of all sorts are used during periods of low demand when regular prices would leave the establishment largely empty.

Next, look at what the question asks. The owners want to know which option would "increase demand" more. The question is very specific; it is looking for something that will increase (or shift) demand.

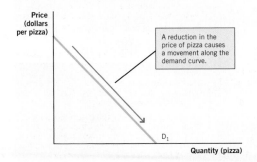

Price (dollars per pizza)

A reduction in the price of pizza causes a movement along the demand curve.

D₁

Quantity (pizza)

(CONTINUED)

Additional Reinforcers

Another notable reinforcement device is the Snapshot that appears in each chapter. We have used the innovation of modern infographics to create a memorable story that reinforces a particularly important topic.

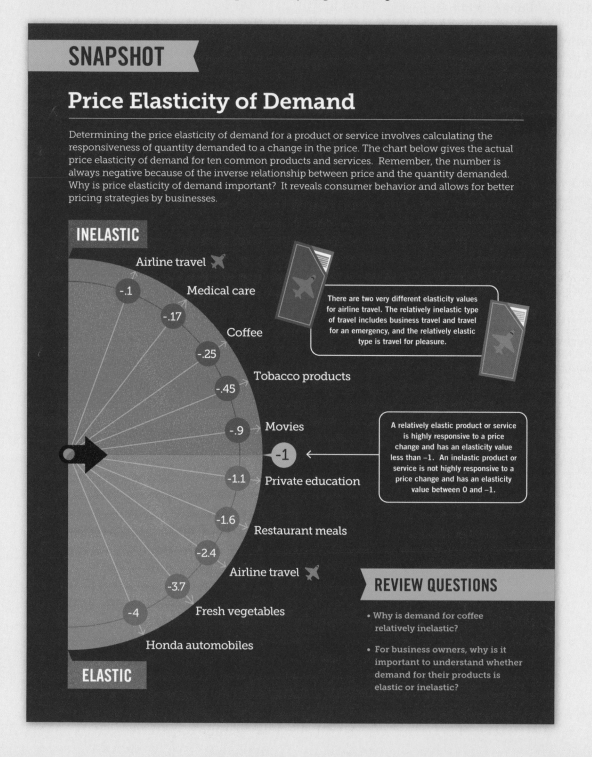

SNAPSHOT

Price Elasticity of Demand

Determining the price elasticity of demand for a product or service involves calculating the responsiveness of quantity demanded to a change in the price. The chart below gives the actual price elasticity of demand for ten common products and services. Remember, the number is always negative because of the inverse relationship between price and the quantity demanded. Why is price elasticity of demand important? It reveals consumer behavior and allows for better pricing strategies by businesses.

INELASTIC

Airline travel −.1

Medical care −.17

Coffee −.25

Tobacco products −.45

Movies −.9

−1

Private education −1.1

Restaurant meals −1.6

Airline travel −2.4

Fresh vegetables −3.7

Honda automobiles −4

ELASTIC

There are two very different elasticity values for airline travel. The relatively inelastic type of travel includes business travel and travel for an emergency, and the relatively elastic type is travel for pleasure.

A relatively elastic product or service is highly responsive to a price change and has an elasticity value less than −1. An inelastic product or service is not highly responsive to a price change and has an elasticity value between 0 and −1.

REVIEW QUESTIONS

- Why is demand for coffee relatively inelastic?

- For business owners, why is it important to understand whether demand for their products is elastic or inelastic?

We have two additional elements that may seem trivial to you as a fellow instructor, but we are confident that they will help to reinforce the material with your students. The first appears near the end of each chapter, and is called Economics for Life. The goal of this insert is to apply economic reasoning to important decisions that your students will face early in their post-student lives, such as buying or leasing a car. And the second is Economics in the Media. These boxes refer to classic scenes from movies and TV shows that deal directly with economics. One of us has written the book (literally!) on economics in the movies, and and we have used these clips year after year to make economics stick with students.

Costs in the Short Run

The Office

The popular TV series *The Office* had an amusing episode devoted to the discussion of costs. The character Michael Scott establishes his own paper company to compete with both Staples and his former company, Dunder Mifflin. He then outcompetes his rivals by keeping his fixed and variable costs low.

In one inspired scene, we see the Michael Scott Paper Company operating out of a single room and using an old church van to deliver paper. This means the company has very low *fixed costs*, which enables it to charge unusually low prices. In addition, Michael Scott keeps *variable costs* to a minimum by hiring only essential employees and not paying any benefits, such as health insurance. But this is a problem, since Michael Scott does not fully account for the cost of the paper he is selling. In fact, he is selling below unit cost!

As we will discover in upcoming chapters, firms with lower costs have many advantages in the market. Such firms can keep their prices lower to attract additional customers. Cost matters because price matters.

ECONOMICS IN THE MEDIA

Price Elasticity of Supply and Demand: Buying Your First Car

When you buy a car, your knowledge of price elasticity can help you negotiate the best possible deal.

Recall that the three determinants of price elasticity of demand are (1) the share of the budget, (2) the number of available substitutes, and (3) the time you have to make a decision.

Let's start with your budget. You should have one in mind, but don't tell the salesperson what you are willing to spend; that is a vital piece of personal information you want to keep to yourself. If the salesperson suggests that you look at a model that is too expensive, just say that you are not interested. You might reply, "Buying a car is a stretch for me; I've got to stay within my budget." If the salesperson asks indirectly about your budget by inquiring whether you have a particular monthly payment in mind, reply that you want to negotiate over the invoice price once you decide on a vehicle. Never negotiate on the sticker price, which is the price you see in the car window, because it includes thousands of dollars in markup. You want to make it clear to the salesperson that the price you pay matters to you—that is, your demand is elastic.

Next, make it clear that you are gathering information and visiting other dealers. That is, reinforce that you have many available substitutes. Even if you really want a Honda, do not voice that desire to the Honda salesperson. Perhaps mention that you are also visiting the Toyota, Hyundai, and Ford showrooms. Compare what you've seen on one lot versus another. Each salesperson you meet should hear that you are seriously considering other options. This indicates to each dealership that your demand is elastic and that getting your business will require that they offer you a better price.

Taking your time to decide is also important. Never buy a car the first time you walk onto a lot. If you convey the message that you want a car immediately, you are saying that your demand is inelastic. If the dealership thinks that you have no flexibility, the staff will not give you their best offer. Instead, tell the salesperson that you appreciate their help and that you will be deciding over the next few weeks.

A good salesperson will know you are serious and will ask for your phone number or email address and contact you. The salesperson will sweeten the deal if you indicate you are narrowing down your choices and they are in the running. You wait. You win.

Also know that salespeople and dealerships have times when they want to move inventory. August is an especially good month to purchase. In other words, the price elasticity of supply is at work here as well. A good time to buy is when the dealer is trying to move inventory to make room for new models, because prices fall for end-of-the-model-year closeouts. Likewise, many sales promotions and sales bonuses are tied to the end of the month, so salespeople will be more eager to sell at that time.

Watch out for shady negotiation practices!

ECONOMICS FOR LIFE

Big-Picture Pedagogy

Chapter-Opening Misconceptions

When we first started teaching we assumed that most of our students were taking economics for the first time and were therefore blank slates that we could draw on. Boy, were we wrong. We now realize that students come to our classes with a number of strongly held misconceptions about economics and the economy, so we begin each chapter recognizing that fact and then establishing what we will do to clarify that subject area.

Big Questions

After the opening misconception, we present the learning goals for the chapter in the form of Big Questions. We come back to the Big Questions in the conclusion to the chapter with Answering the Big Questions.

CHAPTER 12 | Monopolistic Competition and Advertising

Advertising increases the price of products without adding value for the consumer.

MISCONCEPTION

If you drive down a busy street, you will find many competing businesses, often right next to one another. For example, in most places a consumer in search of a quick bite has many choices, and more fast-food restaurants appear all the time. These competing firms advertise heavily. The temptation is to see advertising as driving up the price of a product, without any benefit to the consumer. However, this misconception doesn't account for why firms advertise. In markets where competitors sell slightly differentiated products, advertising enables firms to inform their customers about new products and services; yes, costs rise, but consumers also gain information to help make purchase decisions.

In this chapter, we look at *monopolistic competition*, a widespread market structure that has features of both competitive markets and monopoly. We also explore the benefits and disadvantages of advertising, which is prevalent in markets with monopolistic competition.

BIG QUESTIONS

* What is monopolistic competition?
* What are the differences among monopolistic competition, compe[...] and monopoly?
* Why is advertising prevalent in monopolistic competition?

ANSWERING THE BIG QUESTIONS

What is monopolistic competition?

* Monopolistic competition is a market characterized by free entry and many firms selling differentiated products.
* Differentiation of products takes three forms: differentiation by style or type, location, and quality.

What are the differences among monopolistic competition, competitive markets, and monopoly?

* Monopolistic competitors, like monopolists, are price makers who have downward-sloping demand curves. Whenever the demand curve is downward sloping, the firm is able to mark up the price above marginal cost. This leads to excess capacity and an inefficient level of output.
* In the long run, barriers to entry enable a monopoly to earn an economic profit. This is not the case for monopolistic competition or competitive markets.

Why is advertising prevalent in monopolistic competition?

* Advertising performs useful functions under monopolistic competition: it conveys information about the price of the goods offered for sale, the location of products, and new products. It also signals differences in quality. However, advertising also encourages brand loyalty, which makes it harder for other businesses to successfully enter the market. Advertising can be manipulative and misleading.

Solved Problems

Last but certainly not least, we conclude each chapter with two fully solved problems that appear in the end-of-chapter material.

SOLVED PROBLEMS

5.

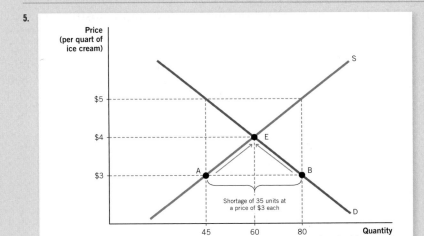

a. The equilibrium price is $4 and quantity is 60 units (quarts). The next step is to graph the curves. This is done above.

b. A shortage of 35 units of ice cream exists at $3; therefore, there is excess demand. Ice cream sellers will raise their price as long as excess demand exists. That is, as long as the price is below $4. It is not until $4 that the equilibrium point is reached and the shortage is resolved.

8. a. The first step is to set $Q_D = Q_S$. Doing so gives us $90 - 2P = P$. Solving for price, we find that $90 = 3P$, or $P = 30$. Once we know that $P = 30$, we can plug this value back into either of the original equations, $Q_D = 90 - 2P$ or $Q_S = P$. Beginning with Q_D, we get $90 - (30) = 90 - 60 = 30$, or we can plug it into $Q_S = P$, so $Q_S = 30$. Since we get a quantity of 30 for both Q_D and Q_S, we know that the price of $30 is correct.

b. In this part, we plug $20 into Q_D. This yields $90 - 2(20) = 50$. Now we plug $20 into Q_S. This yields 20.

c. Since $Q_D = 50$ and $Q_S = 20$, there is a shortage of 30 units.

d. Whenever there is a shortage of a good, the price will rise in order to find the equilibrium point.

Specifics about *Principles of Microeconomics*

Principles of Microeconomics follows the traditional structure found in most texts. Why? Because it works! One difference is the separate chapter on price discrimination. We have done this because the digital economy has made price discrimination much more common than it ever was before, so what was once a fun but somewhat marginal topic is no longer marginal. Plus, students really relate to it because they are subject to it in many of the markets in which they participate—for example, college sporting events.

The consumer theory chapter has been placed toward the end of the volume, but that does not mean that we consider it an optional chapter. We have learned that there is tremendous variation among instructors for when to present this material in the course, and we wanted to allow for maximum flexibility.

Though every chapter is critical, in our opinion, supply and demand, elasticity, and production costs are the *most* fundamental, since so many other insights and takeaways build off of them. We tried triply hard to reinforce these chapters with extra examples and opportunities for self-assessment.

Specifics about *Principles of Macroeconomics*

Principles of Macroeconomics follows the traditional structure found in most texts, but it contains several chapters on new topics that reflect the latest thinking and priorities in macroeconomics. First, at the end of the unit on macroeconomic basics, we have an entire chapter on financial markets, including coverage of securitization and mortgage-backed securities. The economic crisis of 2008–2009 made everyone aware of the importance of financial markets for the worldwide economy, and students want to know more about this fascinating subject.

Economic growth is presented before the short run, and we have two chapters devoted to the topic. The first focuses on the facts of economic growth. It discusses in largely qualitative terms how nations like South Korea and Singapore can be so wealthy, and nations like North Korea and Liberia can be so impoverished. The second chapter presents the Solow model in very simple terms. We've included this chapter to highlight the importance of growth and modeling. That said, it is optional and can be skipped by those instructors who have time for only one chapter on growth.

Coverage of the short run includes a fully developed chapter on the aggregate demand–aggregate supply model, and a second chapter that uses this key model to analyze—essentially side by side—the Great Depression and the Great Recession. We feel that this is a very effective way of presenting several of the key debates within economics.

Finally, we've written a unique chapter on the federal budget, which has allowed us to discuss at length the controversial topics of entitlements and the foreign ownership of U.S. national debt.

Supplements and Media

Norton Coursepack

Bring tutorial videos, assessment, and other online teaching resources directly into your new or existing online course with the Norton Coursepack. It's easily customizable and available for all major learning management systems including Blackboard, Desire2Learn, Angel, Moodle, and Canvas.

The Norton Coursepack for *Principles of Economics* includes:

* Concept Check quizzes
* A limited set of adapted Norton SmartWork questions
* Infographic quizzes
* Office Hours video tutorials
* Flashcards
* Links to the e-book
* Test bank

The Ultimate Guide to Teaching Economics

The Ultimate Guide to Teaching Economics isn't just a guide to using *Principles of Economics,* it's a guide to becoming a better teacher. Combining more than 50 years of teaching experience, authors Dirk Mateer, Lee Coppock, Wayne Geerling (Penn State University), and Kim Holder (University of West Georgia) have compiled hundreds of teaching tips into one essential teaching resource. The *Ultimate Guide* is thoughtfully designed, making it easy for new instructors to incorporate best teaching practices into their courses and for veteran teachers to find new inspiration to enliven their lectures.

The hundreds of tips in *The Ultimate Guide to Teaching Microeconomics* and *The Ultimate Guide to Teaching Macroeconomics* include:

* Think-pair-share activities to promote small-group discussion and active learning
* "Recipes" for in-class activities and demonstrations that include descriptions of the activity, required materials, estimated length of time, estimated difficulty, recommended class size, and instructions. Ready-to-use worksheets are also available for select activities.
* Descriptions of movie clips, TV shows, commercials, and other videos that can be used in class to illustrate economic concepts
* Clicker questions
* Ideas for music examples that can be used as lecture starters
* Suggestions for additional real-world examples to engage students

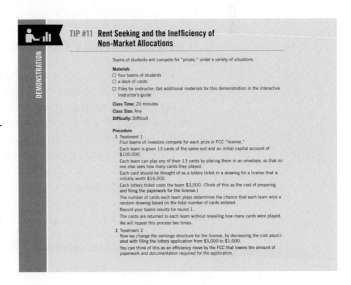

In addition to the teaching tips, each chapter begins with an introduction by Dirk Mateer, highlighting important concepts to teach in the chapter and pointing out his favorite tips. Each chapter ends with solutions to the unsolved end-of-chapter problems in the textbook.

Interactive Instructor's Guide

The Interactive Instructor's Guide brings all the great content from *The Ultimate Guide to Teaching Economics* into a searchable online database that can be filtered by topic and resource type. Subscribing instructors will be alerted by email as new resources are made available.

In order to make it quick and easy for instructors to incorporate the tips from *The Ultimate Guide to Teaching Economics,* the IIG will include:

* Links for video tips when an online video is available
* Links to news articles for real-world examples when an article is available
* Downloadable versions of student worksheets for activities and demonstrations
* Downloadable PowerPoint slides for clicker questions
* Additional teaching resources from dirkmateer.com and leecoppock.com

Office Hours Video Tutorials

This collection of more than 45 videos brings the office-hour experience online. Each video explains a fundamental concept and was conceived by and filmed with authors Dirk Mateer and Lee Coppock.

Perfect for online courses, each Office Hours video tutorial is succinct (90 seconds to two minutes in length) and mimics the office-hour experience. The videos focus on topics that are typically difficult to explain just in writing (or over email), such as shifting supply and demand curves.

The Office Hours videos have been incorporated throughout the Norton SmartWork online homework system as video feedback for questions, integrated into the e-book, included in the Norton Coursepack, and available in the instructor resource folder.

Test Bank

Every question in the *Principles of Economics* test bank has been author reviewed and approved. Each chapter (except Chapter 1) includes between 100 and 150 questions and incorporates graphs and images where appropriate.

The test bank has been developed using the Norton Assessment Guidelines. Each chapter of the test bank consists of three question types classified according to Bloom's taxonomy of knowledge types (Remembering, Understanding Applying, Analyzing Evaluating, and Creating). Questions are further classified by section and difficulty, making it easy to construct tests and quizzes that are meaningful and diagnostic.

Presentation Tools

Norton offers a variety of presentation tools so new instructors and veteran instructors alike can find the resources that are best suited for their teaching style.

Enhanced Lecture Powerpoint Slides

These comprehensive, "lecture-ready" slides are perfect for new instructors and instructors who have limited time to prepare for lecture. In addition to lecture slides, the slides also include images from the book, stepped-out versions of in-text graphs, additional examples not included in the chapter, and clicker questions.

Art Slides and Art JPEGs

For instructors who simply want to incorporate in-text art into their existing slides, all art from the book (tables, graphs, photos, and Snapshot infographics) will be available in both PowerPoint and .jpeg formats. Stepped-out versions of in-text graphs and Snapshot infographics will also be provided and will be optimized for screen projection.

Instructor Resource Folder

The Instructor Resource Folder includes the following resources in an all-in-one folder:

＊ The test bank in ExamView format on a CD
＊ Instructor's Resource Disc: PDFs of *The Ultimate Guide to Teaching Economics*, PowerPoints (enhanced lecture slides, active teaching slides, Snapshot slides, art slides, art .jpegs)
＊ Office Hours video tutorial DVD

dirkmateer.com

Visit dirkmateer.com to find a library of over 100 recommended movie and TV clips, and links to online video sources to use in class.

Coming for Fall 2014: Norton SmartWork for *Principles of Economics*

Norton SmartWork is a complete learning environment and online home-work course designed to (1) support and encourage the development of problem-solving skills, and (2) deliver a suite of innovative tutorials, learning tools, and assessment woven together in a pedagogically effective way. Highlights include:

* Pre-created assignments to help instructors get started quickly and easily
* Guided learning tutorials to help students review each chapter objective
* Answer-specific feedback for every question to help students become better problem solvers
* An intuitive, easy-to-use graphing tool consistent with the coloration and notation of in-text graphs and art

ACKNOWLEDGMENTS

We would like to thank the literally hundreds of fellow instructors who have helped us refine both our vision and the actual words on the page for this text. Without your help, we would never have gotten to the finish line. We hope that the result is the economics teacher's text that we set out to write.

Our class testers:

Jennifer Bailly, California State University, Long Beach
Mihajlo Balic, Harrisburg Community College
Erol Balkan, Hamilton College
Susan Bell, Seminole State College
Scott Benson, Idaho State University
Joe DaBoll-Lavoie, Nazareth College
Michael Dowell, California State University, Sacramento
Abdelaziz Farah, State University of New York, Orange
J. Brian O'Roark, Robert Morris University
Shelby Frost, Georgia State University
Karl Geisler, University of Nevada, Reno
Nancy Griffin, Tyler Junior College
Lauren Heller, Berry College
John Hilston, Brevard Community College
Kim Holder, University of West Georgia
Todd Knoop, Cornell College
Katharine W. Kontak, Bowling Green State University

Daniel Kuester, Kansas State University
Herman Li, University of Nevada, Las Vegas
Gary Lyn, University of Massachusetts, Lowell
Kyle Mangum, Georgia State University
Shah Mehrabi, Montgomery College
Sean Mulholland, Stonehill College
Vincent Odock, State University of New York, Orange
Michael Price, Georgia State University
Matthew Rousu, Susquehanna University
Tom Scales, Southside Virginia Community College
Tom Scheiding, University of Wisconsin, Stout
Clair Smith, St. John Fisher College
Tesa Stegner, Idaho State University
James Tierney, State University of New York, Plattsburgh
Nora Underwood, University of Central Florida
Michael Urbancic, University of Oregon
Marlon Williams, Lock Haven University

Our reviewers and advisors from focus groups:

Mark Abajian, California State University, San Marcos
Teshome Abebe, Eastern Illinois University
Rebecca Achee Thornton, University of Houston
Mehdi Afiat, College of Southern Nevada
Seemi Ahmad, State University of New York, Dutchess
Abdullah Al-Bahrani, Bloomsburg University
Frank Albritton, Seminole State College
Rashid Al-Hmoud, Texas Tech University
Tom Andrews, West Chester University

Becca Arnold, San Diego Mesa College
Lisa Augustyniak, Lake Michigan College
Dennis Avola, Bentley University
Roberto Ayala, California State University, Fullerton
Ron Baker, Millersville University
Kuntal Banerjee, Florida Atlantic University
Jude Bayham, Washington State University
Mary Beal-Hodges, University of North Florida
Stacie Beck, University of Delaware
Jodi Beggs, Northeastern University

Richard Beil, Auburn University
Doris Bennett, Jacksonville State University
Karen Bernhardt-Walther, The Ohio State University
Prasun Bhattacharjee, East Tennessee State University
Richard Bilas, College of Charleston
Kelly Blanchard, Purdue University
Inácio Bo, Boston College
Michael Bognanno, Temple University
Donald Boudreaux, George Mason University
Austin Boyle, Penn State
Elissa Braunstein, Colorado State University
Kristie Briggs, Creighton University
Stacey Brook, University of Iowa
Bruce Brown, California State Polytechnic University, Pomona
John Brown, Clark University
Vera Brusentsev, Swarthmore College
Laura Maria Bucila, Texas Christian University
Richard Burkhauser, Cornell University
W. Jennings Byrd, Troy University
Joseph Calhoun, Florida State University
Charles Callahan, State University of New York, Brockport
Douglas Campbell, University of Memphis
Giorgio Canarella, University of Nevada, Las Vegas
Semih Cekin, Texas Tech University
Sanjukta Chaudhuri, University of Wisconsin, Eau Claire
Shuo Chen, State University of New York, Geneseo
Monica Cherry, State University of New York, Buffalo
Larry Chisesi, University of San Diego
Steve Cobb, University of North Texas
Rhonda Collier, Portland Community College
Glynice Crow, Wallace State Community College
Chad D. Cotti, University of Wisconsin, Oshkosh
Damian Damianov, University of Texas, Pan American
Ribhi Daoud, Sinclair Community College
Kacey Douglas, Mississippi State University
William Dupor, The Ohio State University
Harold W. Elder, University of Alabama
Diantha Ellis, Abraham Baldwin Agricultural College
Tisha Emerson, Baylor University
Lucas Englehardt, Kent State University

Erwin Erhardt, University of Cincinnati
Molly Espey, Clemson University
Patricia Euzent, University of Central Florida
Brent Evans, Mississippi State University
Carolyn Fabian Stumph, Indiana University–Purdue University, Fort Wayne
Leila Farivar, The Ohio State University
Roger Frantz, San Diego State University
Gnel Gabrielyan, Washington State University
Craig Gallet, California State University, Sacramento
Wayne Geerling, Pennsylvania State University
Elisabetta Gentile, University of Houston
Menelik Geremew, Texas Tech University
Dipak Ghosh, Emporia State University
J. Robert Gillette, University of Kentucky
Rajeev Goel, Illinois State University
Bill Goffe, State University of New York, Oswego
Michael Gootzeit, University of Memphis
Paul Graf, Indiana University, Bloomington
Jeremy Groves, Northern Illinois University
Dan Hamermesh, University of Texas, Austin
Mehdi Haririan, Bloomsburg University
Oskar Harmon, University of Connecticut
David Harrington, The Ohio State University
Darcy Hartman, The Ohio State University
John Hayfron, Western Washington University
Jill Hayter, East Tennessee State University
Marc Hellman, Oregon State University
Wayne Hickenbottom, University of Texas, Austin
Mike Hilmer, San Diego State University
Lora Holcombe, Florida State University
Charles Holt, University of Virginia
James Hornsten, Northwestern University
Yu-Mong Hsiao, Campbell University
Alice Hsiaw, College of the Holy Cross
Yu Hsing, Southeastern Louisiana University
Paul Johnson, University of Alaska, Anchorage
David Kalist, Shippensburg University of Pennsylvania
Ara Khanjian, Ventura College
Frank Kim, University of San Diego
Colin Knapp, University of Florida
Mary Knudson, University of Iowa
Ermelinda Laho, LaGuardia Community College
Carsten Lange, California State Polytechnic University, Pomona
Tony Laramie, Merrimack College
Paul Larson, University of Delaware

Teresa Laughlin, Palomar College

Eric Levy, Florida Atlantic University

Charles Link, University of Delaware

Delores Linton, Tarrant County College

Xuepeng Liu, Kennesaw State University

Monika Lopez-Anuarbe, Connecticut College

Bruce Madariaga, Montgomery College

Brinda Mahalingam, University of California, Riverside

Chowdhury Mahmoud, Concordia University

Mark Maier, Glendale Community College

Daniel Marburger, Arkansas State University

Cara McDaniel, Arizona State University

Scott McGann, Grossmont College

Christopher McIntosh, University of Minnesota, Duluth

Evelina Mengova, California State University, Fullerton

William G. Mertens, University of Colorado, Boulder

Ida Mirzaie, The Ohio State University

Michael A. Mogavero, University of Notre Dame

Moon Moon Haque, University of Memphis

Mike Nelson, Oregon State University

Boris Nikolaev, University of South Florida

Caroline Noblet, University of Maine

Fola Odebunmi, Cypress College

Paul Okello, Tarrant County College

Stephanie Owings, Fort Lewis College

Caroline Padgett, Francis Marion University

Kerry Pannell, DePauw University

R. Scott Pearson, Charleston Southern University

Andrew Perumal, University of Massachusetts, Boston

Rinaldo Pietrantonio, West Virginia University

Irina Pritchett, North Carolina State University

Sarah Quintanar, University of Arkansas at Little Rock

Ranajoy Ray-Chaudhuri, The Ohio State University

Mitchell Redlo, Monroe Community College

Debasis Rooj, Northern Illinois University

Jason Rudbeck, University of Georgia

Naveen Sarna, Northern Virginia Community College

Noriaki Sasaki, McHenry County College

Jessica Schuring, Central College

Robert Schwab, University of Maryland

James Self, Indiana University, Bloomington

Gina Shamshak, Goucher College

Neil Sheflin, Rutgers University

Brandon Sheridan, North Central College

Joe Silverman, Mira Costa College

Brian Sloboda, University of Phoenix

Todd Sorensen, University of California, Riverside

Liliana Stern, Auburn University

Joshua Stillwagon, University of New Hampshire

Burak Sungu, Miami University

Vera Tabakova, East Carolina University

Yuan Emily Tang, University of California, San Diego

Anna Terzyan, Loyola Marymount University

Henry Thompson, Auburn University

Mehmet Tosun, University of Nevada, Reno

Robert Van Horn, University of Rhode Island

Adel Varghese, Texas A&M University

Marieta Velikova, Belmont University

Will Walsh, Samford University

Ken Woodward, Saddleback College

Jadrian Wooten, Washington State University

Anne York, Meredith College

Arindra Zainal, Oregon State University

Erik Zemljic, Kent State University

Kent Zirlott, University of Alabama

All of the individuals listed above helped us to improve the text and ancillaries, but a smaller group of them offered us extraordinary insight and support. They went above and beyond, and we would like them to know just how much we appreciate it. In particular, we want to recognize Alicia Baik (University of Virginia), Jodi Beggs (Northeastern University), Dave Brown (Penn State University), Jennings Byrd (Troy University), Douglas Campbell (University of Memphis), Shelby Frost (Georgia State University), Wayne Geerling (Penn State University), Paul Graf (Indiana University), Oskar Harmon (University of Connecticut), Jill Hayter (East Tennessee State University), John Hilston (Brevard Community College), Kim Holder (University of West Georgia), Todd Knoop (Cornell College), Katie Kontak (Bowling Green State

University), Brendan LaCerda (University of Virginia), Paul Larson (University of Delaware), Ida Mirzaie (Ohio State University), Charles Newton (Houston Community College), Boris Nikolaev (University of South Florida), J. Brian O'Roark (Robert Morris University), Andrew Perumal (University of Massachusetts, Boston), Irina Pritchett (North Carolina State University), Matt Rousu (Susquehanna College), Tom Scheiding (Cardinal Stritch University), Brandon Sheridan (North Central College), Clair Smith (Saint John Fisher College), James Tierney (SUNY Plattsburgh), Nora Underwood (University of Central Florida), Joseph Whitman (University of Florida), Erik Zemljic (Kent State University), and Zhou Zhang (University of Virginia).

We would also like to thank our partners at W. W. Norton & Company, who have been as committed to this text as we've been. They have been a pleasure to work with and we hope that we get to work together for many years. We like to call them Team Econ: Hannah Bachman, Jack Borrebach, Cassie del Pilar, Dan Jost, Lorraine Klimowich, John Kresse, Pete Lesser, Sasha Levitt, Jack Repcheck, Spencer Richardson-Jones, Carson Russell, and Nicole Sawa. Our development editor, Becky Kohn, was a big help, as was our copy editor, Alice Vigliani. The visual appeal of the book is the result of our photo researchers, Dena Digilio Betz and Nelson Colón, and the team at Kiss Me I'm Polish who created the front cover and the Snapshot infographics: Agnieszka Gasparska, Andrew Janik, and Annie Song. Thanks to all—it's been a wonderful adventure.

Finally, from Dirk: I'd like to thank my colleagues at Penn State—especially Dave Brown and Wayne Geerling—for their hard work on the supplements, my friends from around the country for the encouragement to write a textbook, and my family for their patience as the process unfolded. In addition, I want to thank the thousands of former students who provided comments, suggestions, and other insights that helped shape the book.

Finally, from Lee: First, I'd like to acknowledge Krista, my excellent wife, who consistently sacrificed to enable me to write this book. I'd also like to thank Jack Repcheck, who had the vision and the will to make this project a reality; we can't thank him enough. Finally, I'd also like to acknowledge Ken Elzinga, Charlie Holt, and Mike Shaub: three great professors who are my role models in the academy and beyond.

Dirk Mateer

is Senior Lecturer at the University of Kentucky. He is the author of *Economics in the Movies*. He is also nationally recognized for his teaching. While at Penn State, he received the George W. Atherton Award, the university's highest teaching award (2011), and was voted the best overall teacher in the Smeal College of Business by the readers of *Critique* magazine (2010). He was profiled in the "Great Teachers in Economics" series of the Gus A. Stavros Center for the Advancement of Free Enterprise and Economic Education at Florida State University.

Lee Coppock

is Associate Professor in the Economics Department at the University of Virginia. He has been teaching principles of economics for over twenty years, specializing in principles of macroeconomics. Before moving to UVA, he spent 9 years at Hillsdale College, where he learned how to reach college students. At UVA, Lee teaches two large sections (500+) of macro principles each spring. He has received teaching awards at both Hillsdale College and UVA. Lee lives in Charlottesville with his wife Krista and their four children: Bethany, Lee III, Kara, and Jackson.

Principles of Economics

PART

1

INTRODUCTION

The Five Foundations of Economics

Economics is the dismal science.

Perhaps you have heard of the "dismal science"? This derogatory term was first used by historian and essayist Thomas Carlyle in the nineteenth

century. He called economics the dismal science after he read a prediction from economist Thomas Malthus stating that because our planet had limited resources, continued population growth would ultimately lead to widespread starvation.

Malthus was a respected thinker, but he was unduly pessimistic. The world population was one billion in 1800, and it is seven billion today. One of the things that Malthus did not take into account was increases in technology and productivity. Today, the efficiency of agricultural production enables seven billion people to live on this planet. Far from being the dismal science, economics in the twenty-first century is a vital social science that helps world leaders improve the lives of their citizens.

This textbook will provide the tools you need to be able to make your own assessments about the economy. What other discipline helps you discover how the world works, how to be an informed citizen, and how to live your life to the fullest? Economics can improve your understanding of the stock market and help you make better personal finance decisions. If you are concerned about Social Security, this textbook explains how it works. If you are interested in learning more about health care, the answers are here. Economics provides answers to all of these questions and much more.

In this chapter, you will learn about the five foundations of economics—incentives, trade-offs, opportunity cost, marginal thinking, and the principle that trade creates value. You will find that many of the more complex problems presented later in the text are derived from one of

Predicting the future is a tough business.

these foundations. Once you have mastered these five concepts, even the most complex processes can be reduced to combinations of these foundations. Think of this chapter as a road map that provides a broad overview of your journey into economics. Let's get started!

BIG QUESTIONS

* **What is economics?**
* **What are the five foundations of economics?**

What Is Economics?

Economists study how decisions are made. Examples of economic decisions include whether or not you should buy or lease a car, sublet your apartment, and buy that Gibson guitar you've been eyeing. And, just as individuals must choose what to buy within the limits of the income they possess, society as a whole must determine what to produce from its limited set of resources.

Of course, life would be a lot easier if we could have whatever we wanted whenever we wanted it. Unfortunately, life does not work that way. Our wants and needs are nearly unlimited, but the resources available to satisfy these wants and needs are always limited. The term used to describe the limited nature of society's resources is **scarcity**. Even the most abundant resources, like the water we drink and the air we breathe, are not always abundant enough everywhere to meet the wants and needs of every person. So, how do individuals and societies make decisions about scarce resources? This is the basic question economists seek to answer. **Economics** is the study of how people allocate their limited resources to satisfy their nearly unlimited wants.

Scarcity
refers to the limited nature of society's resources, given society's unlimited wants and needs.

Economics
is the study of how people allocate their limited resources to satisfy their nearly unlimited wants.

Water is scarce . . .

. . . and so are diamonds!

Microeconomics and Macroeconomics

The study of economics is divided into two subfields: *microeconomics* and *macroeconomics*. **Microeconomics** is the study of the individual units that make up the economy. **Macroeconomics** is the study of the overall aspects and workings of an economy, such as inflation, growth, employment, interest rates, and the productivity of the economy as a whole. To see if you understand the difference, consider a worker who gets laid off and becomes unemployed. Is this an issue that would be addressed in microeconomics or macroeconomics? The question seems to fit parts of both definitions. The worker is an individual, which is micro, but employment is one of the broad areas of concern for economists, which is macro. Don't let this confuse you. Since only one worker is laid off, this is a micro issue. If many workers had been laid off and this led to a higher unemployment rate across the entire economy, it would be an issue broad enough to be studied by macroeconomists.

Microeconomics
is the study of the individual units that make up the economy.

Macroeconomics
is the study of the overall aspects and workings of an economy.

What Are the Five Foundations of Economics?

The study of economics can be complicated, but we can make it very accessible by breaking down the specific economic process that you are exploring into a set of component parts. The five foundations that are presented here are the key component parts of economics. They are a bit like the natural laws of physics or chemistry. Almost every economic subject can be analyzed through the prism of one of these foundations. By mastering the five foundations, you will be on your way to succeeding in this course and thinking like an economist.

The five foundations of economics are: incentives; trade-offs; opportunity cost; marginal thinking; and the principle that trade creates value. Each of the five foundation concepts developed in this chapter will reappear throughout the book and enable you to solve complex problems.

Every time we encounter one of the five concepts, you will see an icon of a house to remind you of what you have learned. As you become more adept at economic analysis, it will not be uncommon to use two or more of these foundational ideas to explain the economic world around us.

Incentives
Trade-offs
Opportunity cost
Marginal thinking
Trade creates value

Incentives

When you are faced with making a decision, you usually make the choice that you think will most improve your situation. In making your decision, you respond to **incentives**—factors that motivate you to act or to exert effort. For example, the choice to study for an exam you have tomorrow instead of spending the evening with your friends is based on the belief that doing well on the exam will provide a greater benefit. You are incentivized to study because you know that an A in the course will raise your grade-point average and make you a more attractive candidate on the job market when you are finished with school. We can further divide incentives into two paired categories: *positive and negative*, and *direct and indirect*.

Incentives

Incentives
are factors that motivate a person to act or exert effort.

Positive and Negative Incentives

Positive incentives are those that encourage action. For example, end-of-the-year bonuses motivate employees to work hard throughout the year, higher oil prices cause suppliers to extract more oil, and tax rebates encourage citizens to spend more money. Negative incentives also encourage action. For instance, the fear of receiving a speeding ticket keeps motorists from driving too fast, and the dread of a trip to the dentist motivates people to brush their teeth regularly. In each case, a potential negative consequence spurs individuals to action.

PRACTICE WHAT YOU KNOW

This mosaic of the flag illustrates the difference between micro and macro.

Microeconomics and Macroeconomics: The Big Picture

Identify whether each of the following statements identifies a microeconomic or a macroeconomic issue.

The national savings rate is less than 2% of disposable income.

Answer: The national savings rate is a statistic based on the average amount each household saves as a percentage of income. As such, this is a broad measure of savings and something that describes a macroeconomic issue.

Jim was laid off from his last job and is currently unemployed.

Answer: Jim's personal financial circumstances constitute a microeconomic issue.

Apple decides to open up 100 new stores.

Answer: Even though Apple is a very large corporation and 100 new stores will create many new jobs, Apple's decision is a microeconomic issue because the basis for its decision is best understood as part of the firm's competitive strategy.

The government passes a jobs bill designed to stabilize the economy during a recession.

Answer: You might be tempted to ask how many jobs are created before deciding, but that is not relevant to this question. The key part of the statement refers to "stabiliz[ing] the economy during a recession." This is an example of a *fiscal policy*, in which the government takes an active role in managing the economy. Therefore, it is a macroeconomic issue.

Conventional wisdom tells us that "learning is its own reward," but try telling that to most students. Teachers are aware that incentives, both positive and negative, create additional interest among their students to learn the course material. Positive incentives include bonus points, gold stars, public praise, and extra credit. Many students respond to these encouragements by studying more. However, positive incentives are not enough. Suppose that your instructor never gave any grade lower than an A. Your incentive to participate actively in the course, do assignments, or earn bonus points would be small. For positive incentives to work, they generally need to be coupled with negative incentives. This is why instructors require students to complete assignments, take exams, and write papers. Students know that if they do not complete these requirements they will get a lower grade, perhaps even fail the class.

Direct and Indirect Incentives

In addition to being positive and negative, incentives can also be direct and indirect. For instance, if one gas station lowers its prices, it most likely will get business from customers who would not usually stop there. This is a direct incentive. Lower gasoline prices also work as an indirect incentive, since lower prices might encourage consumers to use more gas.

Direct incentives are easy to recognize. "Cut my grass and I'll pay you $30" is an example of a direct incentive. Indirect incentives are much harder to recognize. But learning to recognize them is one of the keys to mastering economics. For instance, consider the indirect incentives at work in welfare programs. Almost everyone agrees that societies should provide a safety net for those without employment or whose income isn't enough to meet basic needs. Thus, a society has a direct incentive to alleviate suffering caused by poverty. But how does a society provide this safety net without taking away the incentive to work? In other words, if the amount of welfare a person receives is higher than the amount that person can hope to make from a job, the welfare recipient might decide to stay on welfare rather than go to work. The indirect incentive to stay on welfare creates an *unintended consequence*—people who were supposed to use government assistance as a safety net until they can find a job use it instead as a permanent source of income.

Policymakers have the tough task of deciding how to balance such conflicting incentives. To decrease the likelihood that a person will stay on welfare, policymakers could cut benefits. But this might leave some people without enough to live on. For this reason, many government programs specify limits on the amount of time people can receive benefits. Ideally, this allows the welfare programs to continue to meet basic needs while creating incentives that encourage recipients to search for jobs and acquire skills that will enable them to do better in the workforce. We'll learn more about the issues of welfare in Chapter 15.

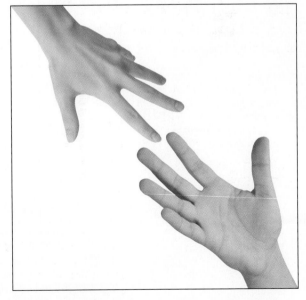

Public assistance: a hand in time of need or an incentive not to work?

ECONOMICS IN THE REAL WORLD

How Incentives Create Unintended Consequences

Let's look at an example of how incentives operate in the real world and how they can lead to consequences no one envisioned when implementing them. Two Australian researchers noted a large spike in births on July 1, 2004, shown in Figure 1.1. The sudden spike was not an accident. Australia, like many other developed countries, has seen the fertility rate fall below replacement levels, which is the birthrate necessary to keep the population from declining. In response to falling birthrates, the Australian government decided to enact a "baby bonus" of $3,000 for all babies born on or after July 1, 2004. (One Australian dollar equals roughly one U.S. dollar.)

The policy was designed to provide a direct incentive for couples to have children and, in part, to compensate them for lost pay and the added costs of raising a newborn. However, this direct incentive had an indirect incentive attached to it, too—the couples found a way to delay the birth of their children until after July 1, perhaps jeopardizing the health of both the infants and the mothers. This was clearly an unintended consequence. Despite reassurances from the government that would-be parents would not put financial gain over the welfare of their newborns, over 1,000 births were switched from late June to early July through a combination of additional bed rest and push-

FIGURE 1.1

Australian Births by Week in 2004

The plunge and spike in births are evidence of an unintended consequence.

Source: See Joshua S. Gans and Andrew Leigh, "Born on the First of July: An (un)natural experiment in birth timing," *Journal of Public Economics* 93 (2009): 246–263.

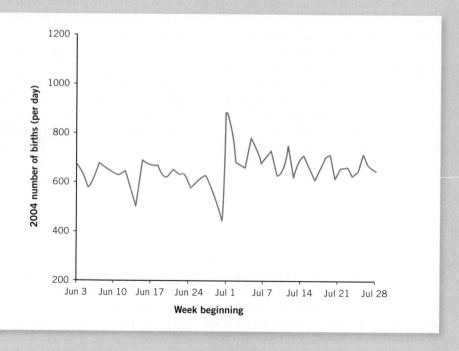

ing scheduled caesarian sections back a few days. This behavior is testament to the power of incentives.

On a much smaller scale, the same dynamic exists in the United States around January 1 each year. Parents can claim a tax credit for the entire year, whether the child is born in January or in December. This gives parents an incentive to ask for labor to be induced or for a caesarian section to be performed late in December so they can have their child before January 1 and thereby capitalize on the tax advantages. Ironically, hospitals and newspapers often celebrate the arrival of the first baby of the new year even though his or her parents might actually be financially worse off because of the infant's January 1 birthday. ✳

Incentives and Innovation

Incentives also play a vital role in innovation, the engine of economic growth. There is no better example than Steve Jobs and Apple: between them, he and the company he founded held over 300 patents at the time of his death in 2011.

In the United States, the patent system and copyright laws guarantee inventors a specific period of time in which they can exclusively sell their work. This system encourages innovation by creating a powerful financial reward for creativity. Without patents and copyright laws, inventors would bear all the costs, and almost none of the rewards, for their efforts. Why would firms invest in research and development or artists create new music if others could immediately copy and sell their work? To reward the perspiration and inspiration required for innovation, society needs patents and copyrights to create the right incentives for economic growth.

In recent years, new forms of technology have made the illegal sharing of copyrighted material quite easy. As a result, illegal downloads of music and movies are widespread. When musicians, actors, and studios cannot effectively protect what they have created, they earn less. So illegal downloads reduce the incentive to produce new content. Will the next John Lennon or Jay-Z work so hard? Will the next Dan Brown or J. K. Rowling hone their writing craft so diligently if there is so much less financial reward for success? Is the "I want it for free" culture causing the truly gifted to be less committed to their craft, thus depriving society of excellence? Maintaining the right rewards, or incentives, for hard work and innovation is essential for advancing our society.

Incentives Are Everywhere

There are many sides to incentives. However, financial gain almost always plays a prominent role. In the film *All the President's Men*, the story of the Watergate scandal that led to the unraveling of the Nixon administration in the early 1970s, a secret source called "Deep Throat" tells Bob Woodward, an investigative reporter at the *Washington Post*, to "follow the money." Woodward responds, "What do you mean? Where?" Deep Throat responds, "Just . . . follow the money." That is exactly what Woodward did. He eventually pieced everything together and followed the "money" trail all the way to President Nixon.

Incentives

Ferris Bueller's Day Off

Many people believe that the study of economics is boring. In *Ferris Bueller's Day Off* (1986), Ben Stein plays a high school economics teacher who sedates his class with a monotone voice while referring to many abstract economic theories and uttering the unforgettable "Anyone, anyone?" while trying to engage his students. The scene is iconic because it is a boring economics lecture that inspires Ferris and his friends to skip school, which leads to his wild adventures. In fact, the movie is really about incentives and trade-offs.

Was this your first impression of economics?

Understanding the incentives that caused the participants in the Watergate scandal to do what they did led Bob Woodward to the truth. Economists use the same process to explain how people make decisions, how firms operate, and how the economy functions. In fact, understanding incentives, from positive to negative and direct to indirect, is the key to understanding economics. If you remember only one concept from this course, it should be that incentives matter!

Trade-offs

Trade-offs

In a world of scarcity, each and every decision incurs a cost. Even time is a scarce resource; after all, there are only 24 hours in a day. So deciding to read one of the Harry Potter books now means that you won't be able to read one of the Twilight books until later. More generally, doing one thing often means that you will not have the time, resources, or energy to do something else. Similarly, paying for a college education can require spending tens of thousands of dollars that might be used elsewhere instead.

Trade-offs are an important part of policy decisions. For instance, one decision that some governments face is the trade-off between a clean environment and a higher level of income for its citizens. Transportation and industry cause air pollution. Developed nations can afford expensive technology that reduces pollution-causing emissions. But developing nations, like China, generally have to focus their resources elsewhere. In the months leading up to the 2008 Olympics, China temporarily shut down many factories and discouraged the use of automobiles in order to reduce smog in Beijing. The air improved, and the Olympics showcased China's remarkable growth into a global economic powerhouse. However, the cost of keeping the air clean—shutting down factories and restricting transportation—was not a trade-off China is willing to make for longer than a few weeks. The Chinese people, like the rest of us, want clean air *and* a high standard of living, but for the time being most Chinese seem willing to accept increased pollution if it means the potential for a higher level of income. In more developed countries, higher standards of living already exist, and the cost of pollution control will not cause the economy's growth to slow down to unacceptable levels. People in these countries are much less likely to accept more pollution in order to raise the level of income even further.

Would you choose clean air or economic prosperity?

Opportunity Cost

The existence of trade-offs requires making hard decisions. Choosing one thing means giving up something else. Suppose that you receive two invitations—the first to spend the day hiking, and the second to go to a concert—and both events occur at the same time. No matter which event you choose, you will have to sacrifice the other option. In this example, you can think of the cost of going to the concert as the lost opportunity to be on the hike. Likewise, the cost of going hiking is the lost opportunity to go to the concert. No matter what choice you make, there is an *opportunity cost*, or next-best alternative, that must be sacrificed. **Opportunity cost** is the highest-valued alternative that must be sacrificed in order to get something else.

Opportunity cost

Opportunity cost
is the highest-valued alternative that must be sacrificed in order to get something else.

Every time we make a choice, we experience an opportunity cost. The key to making the best possible decision is to minimize your opportunity cost by selecting the option that gives you the largest benefit. If you prefer going to a concert, you should go to the concert. What you give up, the hike, has less value to you than the concert; so it has a lower opportunity cost.

The hiking/concert choice is a simple and clear example of opportunity cost. Usually, it takes deliberate effort to see the world through the opportunity-cost prism. But it is a worthwhile practice because it will help you make better decisions. For example, imagine you are a small-business owner. Your financial officer informs you that you have had a successful year and made a sizable profit. So everything is good, right? Not so fast. An economist will tell you to ask yourself, "Could I have made *more* profit doing something differently?" Good economic thinkers ask this question of themselves all the time. "Could I be using my time, talents, or energy on another activity that would be even more profitable for me?"

Do you have the moves like Jagger?

Profits on an income statement are only part of the story, because they only measure how well a business does relative to the bottom line. Accountants cannot measure what *might* have been better. For example, suppose that your business had decided against an opportunity to open a new store. A few months later, a rival opened a very successful store in the same location you had considered. Your profits were good for the year, but if you had made the investment in the new store, your profits could have been even better. So when economists mention opportunity cost, they are assessing whether the alternatives are better than what you are currently doing, which considers a larger set of possible outcomes.

Mick Jagger did just that. Before joining the Rolling Stones, he had been attending the London School of Economics. For Mick, the opportunity cost of becoming a musician was forgoing a degree in economics. Given the success of the Rolling Stones, it is hard to fault his decision!

PRACTICE WHAT YOU KNOW

The Opportunity Cost of Attending College

Question: What is the opportunity cost of attending college?

Answer: When people think about the cost of attending college, they usually think of tuition, room and board, textbooks, and travel-related expenses. While those expenses are indeed a part of going to college, they are not its full opportunity cost. The opportunity cost is the next-best alternative that is sacrificed. This means that the opportunity cost—or what you potentially could have done if you were not in college—includes the lost income you could have earned working a full-time job. If you take the cost of attending college plus the forgone income lost while in college, it is a very expensive proposition. Setting aside the question of how much more you might have to pay for room and board at college rather than elsewhere, consider the costs of tuition and books. Those fees can be $40,000 or more at many of the nation's most expensive colleges. Add those out-of-pocket expenses to the forgone income from a full-time job that might pay $40,000, and your four years in college can easily cost over a quarter of a million dollars.

Spending thousands on college expenses? You could be working instead!

ECONOMICS IN THE REAL WORLD

Breaking the Curse of the Bambino: How Opportunity Cost Causes a Drop in Hospital Visits While the Red Sox Play

If you are injured or severely ill, you head straight to the emergency room, right? Not so fast! A 2005 study published in the *Annals of Emergency Medicine* found that visits to the ER in the Boston area fell by as much as 15% when the Red Sox were playing games in the 2004 playoffs. Part of the decline is attributable to more people sitting inside at home—presumably watching the ballgame—instead of engaging in activities that might get them hurt. But the study was able to determine that this did not explain the entire decline in emergency room visits. It turns out that a surprising number of people are willing to put off seeking medical attention for a few hours. Apparently, for some people the opportunity cost of seeking medical attention is high enough to postpone care until after the Red Sox game. ✳

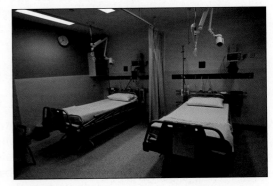

Emergency room beds are empty. Are the Sox playing?

Marginal Thinking

The process of systematically evaluating a course of action is referred to as *economic thinking*. **Economic thinking** involves a purposeful evaluation of the available opportunities to make the best decision possible. In this context, economic thinkers use a process called *marginal analysis* to break down decisions into smaller parts. Often, the choice is not between doing and not doing something, but between doing more or less of something. For instance, if you take on a part-time job while in school, you probably wrestle with the question of how many hours to work. If you work a little more, you can earn additional income. If you work a little less, you have more time to study. Working more has a tangible benefit (more money) and a tangible cost (poor grades). All of this should sound familiar from our earlier discussion about trade-offs. The work-study trade-off affects how much money you have and what kind of grades you make.

An economist would say that your decision—weighing how much money you want against the grades you want—is a decision at the *margin*. What exactly does the word "margin" mean? There are many different definitions. To a reader, the margin is the blank space bordering a page. A "margin" can also be thought of as the size of a victory. In economics, **marginal thinking** requires decision-makers to evaluate whether the benefit of one more unit of something is greater than its cost. This can be quite challenging, but understanding how to analyze decisions at the margin is essential to becoming a good economist.

For example, have you ever wondered why people straighten their places, vacuum, dust, scrub the bathrooms, clean out their garages, and wash their windows, but leave the dust bunnies under the refrigerator? The answer lies in thinking at the margin. Moving the refrigerator out from the wall to clean requires a significant effort for a small benefit. Guests who enter the kitchen can't see under the refrigerator. So most of us ignore the dust bunnies and just clean the visible areas of our homes. In other words, when economists say that

Marginal thinking

Economic thinking
requires a purposeful evaluation of the available opportunities to make the best decision possible.

Marginal thinking
requires decision-makers to evaluate whether the benefit of one more unit of something is greater than its cost.

you should think at the margin, what they really mean is that people weigh the costs and benefits of their actions and choose to do the things with the greatest payoff. For most of us, that means being willing to live with dust bunnies. The *marginal cost* of cleaning under the refrigerator (or on top of the cabinets, or even behind the sofa cushions) is too high and the added value of making the effort, or the *marginal benefit*, is too low to justify the additional cleaning.

ECONOMICS IN THE REAL WORLD

Why Buying and Selling Your Textbooks Benefits You at the Margin

New textbooks are expensive. The typical textbook purchasing pattern works as follows: you buy a textbook at the start of the term, often at full price, and sell it back at the end of the term for half the price you paid. Ouch. Nobody likes to make a bad investment, and textbooks depreciate the moment that students buy them. Even non-economists know not to buy high and sell low—but that is the textbook cycle for most students.

One solution would be to avoid buying textbooks in the first place. But that is not practical, nor is it a good decision. To understand why, let's use marginal analysis to break the decision into two separate components: the decision to buy and the decision to resell.

Let's start with the decision to buy. A rational buyer will only purchase a textbook if the expected value of the information included in the book is greater than the cost. For instance, say the book contains mandatory assignments or information that is useful for your major and you decide that it is worth $200 to you. If you are able to purchase the book for $100, the gain from buying the textbook would be $100. But what if the book is supplemental reading and you think it is worth only $50? If you value the book at $50 and it costs $100, purchasing the book would entail a $50 loss. If students only buy the books from which they receive gains, every textbook bought will increase the welfare of someone.

A similar logic applies to the resale of textbooks. At the end of the course, once you have learned the information inside the book, the value of hanging on to it is low. You might think it is worth $20 to keep the textbook for future reference, but if you can sell it for $50, the difference represents a gain of $30. In this case, you would decide to sell.

We have seen that buying and selling are two separate decisions made at the margin. If you combine these two decisions and argue that the purchase price ($100) and resale price ($50) are related, as most students typi-

Why do students buy and sell textbooks?

cally think they are, you will arrive at a faulty conclusion that you have made a poor decision. That is simply not true.

Textbooks may not be cheap, but they create value twice—once when bought and again when sold. This is a win-win outcome. Since we assume that decision-makers will not make choices that leave them worse off, the only way to explain why students buy textbooks and sell them again later is because the students benefit at the margin from both sides of the transaction. ✳

Trade

Imagine trying to find food in a world without grocery stores. The task of getting what you need to eat each day would require visiting many separate locations. Traditionally, this need to bring buyers and sellers together was met by weekly markets, or bazaars, in central locations like town squares. **Markets** bring buyers and sellers together to exchange goods and services. As commerce spread throughout the ancient world, trade routes developed. Markets grew from infrequent gatherings, where exchange involved trading goods and services for other goods and services, into more sophisticated systems that use cash, credit, and other financial instruments. Today, when we think of markets we often think of eBay or Craigslist, where goods can be transferred from one person to another with the click of a mouse. For instance, if you want to find a rare DVD of season 1 of *Entourage*, there is no better place to look than eBay, which allows users to search for just about any product, bid on it, and then have it sent directly to their homes.

Trade is the voluntary exchange of goods and services between two or more parties. Voluntary trade among rational individuals creates value for everyone involved. Imagine you are on your way home from class and you want to pick up a gallon of milk. You know that milk will be more expensive at a convenience store than it will be at the grocery store five miles away, but you are in a hurry to study for your economics exam and are willing to pay up to $5.00 for the convenience of getting it quickly. At the store, you find that the price is $4.00 and you happily purchase the milk. This ability to buy for less than the price you are willing to pay provides a positive incentive to make the purchase. But what about the seller? If the store owner paid $3.00 to buy the milk from a supplier, and you are willing to pay the $4.00 price that he has set in order to make a profit, the store owner has an incentive to sell. This simple voluntary transaction has made both sides better off.

By fostering the exchange of goods, trade helps to create additional growth through specialization. **Comparative advantage** refers to the situation in which an individual, business, or country can produce at a lower opportunity cost than a competitor can. Comparative advantage harnesses the power of specialization. As a result, it is possible to be a physician, teacher, or plumber and not worry about how to do everything yourself. The physician becomes proficient at dispensing medical advice, the teacher at helping students, and the plumber at fixing leaks. The physician and the teacher call the plumber when they need work on their plumbing. The teacher and the plumber see the doctor when they are sick. The physician and the plumber send their children to school to learn from the teacher. On a broader scale, this type of trading of services increases the welfare of everyone in society. Trade creates gains for everyone involved.

Trade creates value

Markets bring buyers and sellers together to exchange goods and services.

Trade is the voluntary exchange of goods and services between two or more parties.

Comparative advantage refers to the situation where an individual, business, or country can produce at a lower opportunity cost than a competitor can.

Our economy depends on specialization.

The same process is at work among businesses. For instance, Starbucks specializes in making coffee and Honda makes automobiles. You would not want to get your morning cup of joe at Honda any more than you would want to buy a car from Starbucks!

Specialization exists at the country level as well. Some countries have highly developed workforces capable of managing and solving complex processes. Other countries have large pools of relatively unskilled labor. As a result, businesses that need skilled labor gravitate to countries where they can easily find the workers they need. Likewise, firms with production processes that rely on unskilled labor look for employees in less-developed countries. By harnessing the power of increased specialization, global companies and economies create value through increased production and growth.

However, globalized trade is not without controversy. When goods and jobs are free to move across borders, not everyone benefits equally. Consider the case of an American worker who loses her job when her position is outsourced to a call center in India. The jobless worker now has to find new employment—a process that will require significant time and energy. In contrast, the new position in the call center in India provides a job and an income that improve the life of another worker. Also, the American firm enjoys the advantage of being able to hire lower-cost labor elsewhere. The firm's lower costs often translate into lower prices for domestic consumers. None of those advantages make the outsourcing of jobs any less painful for affected workers, but it is an important component of economic growth in the long run.

Conclusion

Is economics the dismal science?

We began this chapter by discussing this misconception. Now that you have begun your exploration of economics, you know that this is not true. Economists ask, and answer, big questions about life. This is what makes the study of economics so fascinating. Understanding how an entire economy operates and functions may seem like a daunting task, but it is not nearly as hard as it sounds. If you remember the first time you drove a car, the process is similar. When you are learning to drive, everything seems difficult and unfamiliar. Learning economics is the same way. However, once you learn a few key principles, and practice them, you can become a good driver quite quickly. In the next chapter, we will use the ideas developed here to explore the issue of trade in greater depth.

The Foundations of Economics

There are five foundations of economics—incentives, trade-offs, opportunity cost, marginal thinking, and the principle that trade creates value. Once you have mastered these five concepts, even complex economic processes can be reduced to smaller, more easily understood parts. If you keep these foundations in mind, you'll find that understanding economics is rewarding and fun.

OPPORTUNITY COST

INCENTIVES

In making a decision, you respond to incentives—factors that motivate you to act or to exert effort. Incentives also play a vital role in innovation, the engine of economic growth.

TRADE-OFFS

TRADE CREATES VALUE

+1

MARGINAL THINKING

REVIEW QUESTIONS

- Which of the five foundations explains what you give up when you choose to buy a new pair of shoes instead of attending a concert?

- What are four types of incentives discussed in the chapter? Why do incentives sometimes create unintended consequences?

Marginal thinking is the hallmark of economic analysis. It requires forward thinking that compares the extra benefits of each activity with the extra costs.

Midcareer Earnings by Selected Majors

A 2012 study by PayScale surveyed full-time employees across the United States who possessed a bachelor's degree but no advanced degree. Twenty popular subjects are listed in the graph below.

Not all majors are created equal. However, the majors that produce more income initially do not necessarily keep their advantage a decade or two later. That means that today's newly minted economics majors, with a median starting salary of $48,500, will likely surpass those who majored in civil engineering in earnings by the time they reach midcareer. The same holds true for political science majors, who have a lower starting salary than business majors but eventually surpass them. In the long run, pay growth matters to income level as much as, if not more than, starting salary. In terms of salary, any decision about what to major in that only looks at starting pay is misleading. How much you make over your whole career is what matters!

Will you make more by majoring in economics or finance?

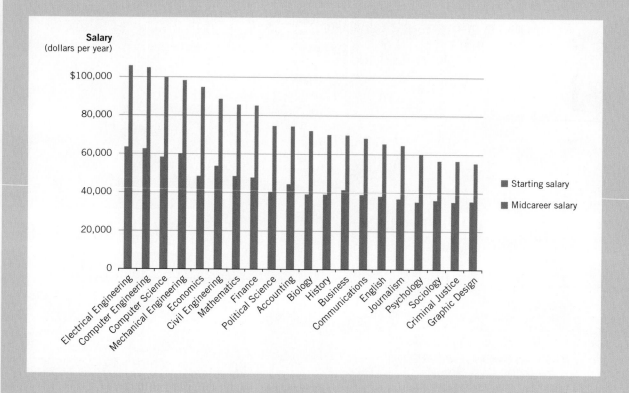

Salary
(dollars per year)

Legend:
- ■ Starting salary
- ■ Midcareer salary

ANSWERING THE BIG QUESTIONS

What is economics?

✳ Economics is the study of how people allocate their limited resources to satisfy their nearly unlimited wants. Because of the limited nature of society's resources, even the most abundant resources are not always plentiful enough everywhere to meet the wants and needs of every person. So how do individuals and societies make decisions about how to use the scarce resources at our disposal? This is the basic question economists seek to answer.

What are the five foundations of economics?

The five foundations of economics are: incentives; trade-offs; opportunity cost; marginal thinking; and the principle that trade creates value.

✳ Incentives matter because they help economists explain how decisions are made.

✳ Trade-offs exist when a decision-maker has to choose a course of action.

✳ Each time we make a choice, we experience an opportunity cost, or a lost chance to do something else.

✳ Marginal thinking requires a decision-maker to weigh the extra benefits against the extra costs.

✳ Trade creates value because participants in markets are able to specialize in the production of goods and services that they have a comparative advantage in making.

CONCEPTS YOU SHOULD KNOW

comparative advantage (p. 17)
economics (p. 6)
economic thinking (p. 15)
incentives (p. 7)

macroeconomics (p. 7)
marginal thinking (p. 15)
markets (p. 17)
microeconomics (p. 7)

opportunity cost (p. 13)
scarcity (p. 6)
trade (p. 17)

QUESTIONS FOR REVIEW

1. How would you respond if your instructor gave daily quizzes on the course readings? Is this a positive or a negative incentive?

2. Explain why many seniors often earn lower grades in their last semester before graduation. Hint: this is an incentive problem.

3. What is the opportunity cost of reading this textbook?

4. Evaluate the following statement: "Trade is like football: one team wins and the other loses."

5. Give a personal example of how pursuing your self-interest has made society better off.

STUDY PROBLEMS (*solved at the end of the section)

* 1. What role do incentives play in each of the following situations?
   a. You learn that you can resell a ticket to next week's homecoming game for twice what you paid.
   b. A state government announces a "sales tax holiday" for back-to-school shopping during one week each August.

2. Compare your standard of living with that of your parents when they were the same age as you are now. Ask them or somebody you know around their age to recall where they were living and what they owned. What has happened to the average standard of living over the last 25 years? Explain your answer.

3. By referencing events in the news or something from your personal experiences, describe one example of each of the five foundations of economics.

* 4. Suppose that Colombia is good at growing coffee but not very good at making computer software, and that Canada is good at making computer software but not very good at growing coffee. If Colombia decided to grow only coffee and Canada only made computer software, would both countries be better or worse off? Can you think of a similar example from your life?

5. After some consideration, you decide to hire someone to help you move. Wouldn't it be cheaper to move yourself? Do you think this is a rational choice? Explain your response.

* 6. The website ultrinsic.com has developed an "*ult*erior motive that causes the person to have an in*trinsic* love of knowledge." At Ultrinsic, students pay a small entry fee to compete in grades-based contests for cash prizes. Suppose that 20 students from your economics class each pay $20 to enter a grades-based contest. This would create a $400 prize pool. An equal share of the $400 pot is awarded at the end of the term to each contestant who earns an A in the course. If four students earn A's, they each receive $100. If only one student earns an A, that person gets the entire $400 pot. What economic concept is Ultrinsic harnessing in order to encourage participants to learn more?

SOLVED PROBLEMS

1.a. Since your tickets are worth more than you paid for them, you have a direct positive incentive to resell them.

b. The "sales tax holiday" is a direct positive incentive to buy more clothes during the back-to-school period. An unintended consequence of this policy is that fewer purchases are likely to be made both before and after the tax holiday.

4. If Colombia decided to specialize in the production of coffee, it could trade coffee to Canada in exchange for computer software. This process illustrates gains from specialization and trade. Both countries have a comparative advantage in producing one particular good. Colombia has ideal coffee-growing conditions, and Canada has a workforce that is more adept at writing software. Since each country specializes in what it does best, they are able to produce more value than what they could produce by trying to make both products on their own.

6. Ultrinsic is using the power of incentives to motivate learning. Earning a letter grade is a positive motivation to do well, or a penalty—or negative incentive—when you do poorly. Ultrinsic takes this one step further, as the student who earns an A also receives a small cash payment—a positive incentive. This provides extra motivation to study hard and achieve an A, since it pays, as opposed to earning a B or lower.

Model Building and Gains from Trade

Trade always results in winners and losers.

When most people think of trade, they think of it as a zero-sum game. For instance, suppose that you and your friends are playing Magic. Players

collect cards with special powers in order to assemble decks to play the game. Magic players love to trade their cards, and it is often the case that novice players do not know which cards are the most powerful or rare. When someone swaps one of the desirable cards, the other player is probably getting a much better deal. In other words, there is a winner and a loser. Now think of international trade. Many people believe that rich countries exploit the natural resources of poor countries and even steal their most talented workers. In this view, the rich countries are winners and the poor countries are losers. Still others think of trade as the redistribution of goods. If you trade your kayak for a friend's bicycle, no new goods are created; so how can this possibly create value? After all, someone must have come out ahead in the trade.

In this chapter, we will see that trade is not an imbalanced equation of winners and losers. To help us understand trade, the discussion will make a number of simplifying assumptions. We will also consider how economists use the scientific method to help explain the world we live in. These foundations will serve as the tools we need to explore the more nuanced reasons why trade creates value.

Jace, Memory Adept — 3🔵🔵

Planeshwalker — Jace · M13

+1: Draw a card. Target player puts the top card of his or her library into his or her graveyard.

0: Target player puts the top ten cards of his or her library into his or her graveyard.

-7: Any number of target players each draw twenty cards.

D. Alexander Gregory

TM & © 1993–2012 Wizards of the Coast LLC 56/249 · 4

Chandra, the Firebrand — 3🔴

Planeshwalker — Chandra · M13

+1: Chandra, the Firebrand deals 1 damage to target creature or player.

-2: When you cast your next instant or sorcery spell this turn, copy that spell. You may choose new targets for the copy.

-6: Chandra, the Firebrand deals 6 damage to each of up to six target creatures and/or players.

D. Alexander Gregory

TM & © 1993–2012 Wizards of the Coast LLC 123/249 · 3

Garruk, Primal Hunter — 2🟢🟢🟢

Planeshwalker — Garruk · M13

+1: Put a 3/3 green Beast creature token onto the battlefield.

-3: Draw cards equal to the greatest power among creatures you control.

-6: Put a 6/6 green Wurm creature token onto the battlefield for each land you control.

D. Alexander Gregory

TM & © 1993–2012 Wizards of the Coast LLC 174/249 · 3

Ajani, Caller of the Pride — 1⚪⚪

Planeshwalker — Ajani · M13

+1: Put a +1/+1 counter on up to one target creature.

-3: Target creature gains flying and double strike until end of turn.

-8: Put X 2/2 white Cat creature tokens onto the battlefield, where X is your life total.

D. Alexander Gregory

TM & © 1993–2012 Wizards of the Coast LLC 1/249 · 4

Trade is vital to Magic players, and vital to the economy.

BIG QUESTIONS

* How do economists study the economy?
* What is a production possibilities frontier?
* What are the benefits of specialization and trade?
* What is the trade-off between having more now and having more later?

How Do Economists Study the Economy?

Economics is a social science that uses the scientific method. This is accomplished by the use of economic models that focus on specific relationships in the economy. In order to create these models, economists make many simplifying assumptions. This approach helps identify the key relationships that drive the economic decisions that we are interested in exploring. In this section, you will begin to learn about how economists approach their discipline and the tools they use.

The Scientific Method in Economics

On the television show *MythBusters*, popular myths are put to the test by Jamie Hyneman and Adam Savage. In Savage's words, "We replicate the circumstances, then duplicate the results." The entire show is dedicated to scientifically testing the myths. At the end of each episode, the myth is confirmed, labeled plausible, or busted. For instance, during a memorable episode Hyneman and Savage explored the reasons behind the *Hindenburg* disaster. The *Hindenburg* was a German passenger airship, or zeppelin, that caught fire and was destroyed as it attempted to dock in New Jersey on May 6, 1937. Thirty-six people died during the disaster.

Some people have hypothesized that the painted fabric used to wrap the zeppelin sparked the fire. Others have claimed that the hydrogen used to give the airship lift was the primary cause of the disaster. To test the hypothesis that the potentially incendiary paint used on the fabric was to blame, Hyneman and Savage built two small-scale models. The first model was filled with hydrogen and had a nonflammable skin; the second model used a replica of the original fabric for the skin but did not contain any hydrogen. Hyneman and Savage then compared the burn times of their models with the original footage of the disaster.

After examining the results, they determined that the myth of the incendiary paint was "busted"; the model containing the hydrogen burned twice as fast as the one with just the painted fabric skin.

Economists work in much the same way: they use the scientific method to answer questions about observable phenomena and to explain how the world works. The scientific method consists of several steps. First, researchers observe a phenomenon that interests them. Based on these observations, they develop a hypothesis, which is an explanation for the phenomenon. Then, they construct a model to test the hypothesis. Finally, they design experiments to test how well the model (which is based on the hypothesis) works. After collecting the data from the experiments, they can verify, revise, or refute the hypothesis. After many tests, they may agree that the hypothesis is well supported enough to qualify as a theory. Or, they may determine that it is not supported by the evidence and that they must continue searching for a theory to explain the phenomenon.

The scientific method was used to discover why the *Hindenburg* caught fire.

The economist's laboratory is the world around us, and it ranges from the economy as a whole to the decisions made by firms and individuals. As a result, economists cannot always design experiments to test their hypotheses. Often, they must gather historical data or wait for real-world events to take place—for example, the Great Recession of 2008–2009—in order to better understand the economy.

Positive and Normative Analysis

As scientists, economists strive to approach their subject with objectivity. This means that they rigorously avoid letting personal beliefs and values influence the outcome of their analysis. In order to be as objective as possible, economists deploy positive analysis. A **positive statement** can be tested and validated. Each positive statement can be thought of as a description of "what is." For instance, the statement "the unemployment rate is 7.0%" is a positive statement because it can be tested by gathering data. In contrast, a **normative statement** cannot be tested or validated; it is about "what ought to be." For instance, the statement "an unemployed worker should receive financial assistance to help make ends meet" is a matter of opinion. One can reasonably argue that financial assistance to the unemployed is beneficial for society as a whole because it helps eliminate poverty. However, many would argue that financial assistance to the unemployed provides the wrong incentives. If the financial assistance provides enough to meet basic needs, workers may end up spending more time remaining unemployed than they otherwise would. Neither opinion is right or wrong; they are differing viewpoints based on values, beliefs, and opinions.

A **positive statement** can be tested and validated; it describes "what is."

A **normative statement** is an opinion that cannot be tested or validated; it describes "what ought to be."

Economists are concerned with positive analysis. In contrast, normative statements are the realm of policy-makers, voters, and philosophers. For example, if the unemployment rate rises, economists try to understand the conditions that created the situation. Economics does not attempt to determine who should receive unemployment assistance, which involves normative analysis. Economics, done properly, is confined to positive analysis.

Economic Models

Thinking like an economist means learning how to analyze complex issues and problems. Many economic topics, such as international trade, Social Security, job loss, and inflation, are complicated. To analyze these phenomena and to determine the effect of various policy options related to them, economists use models, or simplified versions of reality. Models help us analyze the component parts of the economy.

The Wright brothers' wind tunnel

A good model should be simple to understand, flexible in design, and able to make powerful predictions. Let's consider one of the most famous models in history, designed by Wilbur and Orville Wright. Before the Wright brothers made their famous first flight in 1903, they built a small wind tunnel out of a six-foot-long wooden box. Inside the box they placed an aerodynamic measuring device, and at one end they attached a small fan to supply the wind. The brothers then tested over 200 different wing configurations to determine the lifting properties of each design. Using the data on aerodynamics they collected, the Wright brothers were able to determine the best type of wing to use on their aircraft.

Similarly, economic models provide frameworks that enable us to predict the effect that changes in prices, production processes, and government policies have on real-life behavior.

Ceteris Paribus

Ceteris paribus
is the concept under which economists examine a change in one variable while holding everything else constant.

Using a controlled setting that held many other variables constant enabled the Wright brothers to experiment with different wing designs. By altering only a single element—for example, the angle of the wing—they could test whether the change in design was advantageous. The process of examining a change in one variable while holding everything else constant involves a concept known as *ceteris paribus*, from the Latin meaning "other things being equal." This idea is central to model building. If the Wright brothers had changed many variables simultaneously and found that the wing worked better, they would have had no way of knowing which change was responsible for the improved performance. For this reason, engineers generally modify only one element at a time and test only that one element before moving on to test additional elements.

Like the Wright brothers, economists start with a simplified version of reality. Economists build models, change one variable at a time, and ask whether the change in the variable had a positive or negative impact on performance. Perhaps the best-known economic model is supply and demand, which economists use to explain how markets function. We'll get to supply and demand in Chapter 3.

Endogenous versus Exogenous Factors

Models must account for factors that we can control and factors that we can't. The Wright brothers' wind tunnel was critical to their success because it enabled them to control for as many *endogenous factors* as possible before attempting to fly. Factors that we know about and can control are **endogenous factors**. For example, the wind tunnel enabled the Wright brothers to see how well each wing design—an important part of the model—performed under controlled conditions.

Once the Wright brothers had determined the best wing design, they built the full-scale airplane that took flight at Kitty Hawk, North Carolina. At that point the plane, known as the "Flyer," was no longer in a controlled environment. It was subject to the gusting wind and other *exogenous factors* that made the first flight so challenging. Factors beyond our control—outside the model—are known as **exogenous factors**.

Building an economic model is very similar to the process Wilbur and Orville used. We need to be mindful of three factors: (1) what we include in the model, (2) the assumptions we make when choosing what to include in the model, and (3) the outside conditions that can affect our model's performance. In the case of the first airplane, the design was an endogenous factor because it was within the Wright brothers' control. In contrast, the weather (wind, air pressure, and other atmospheric conditions) was an exogenous factor because it was something that the Wright brothers could not control. Because the world is a complex place, an airplane model that flies perfectly in a wind tunnel may not fly reliably once it is exposed to the elements. Therefore, if we add more exogenous variables, or factors we cannot control—for example, wind and rain—to test our model's performance, the test becomes more realistic.

Endogenous factors are the variables that can be controlled for in a model.

Exogenous factors are the variables that cannot be controlled for in a model.

The Danger of Faulty Assumptions

In every model, we make certain choices about which variables to include and how to model them. Ideally, we would like to include all the important variables inside the model and exclude all the variables that should be ignored.

However, no matter what we include, using a model that contains faulty assumptions can lead to spectacular policy failures. There is no better example than the financial crisis and Great Recession that began in December 2007.

In the years leading up to the crisis, banks sold and repackaged mortgage-backed securities under the faulty assumption that real estate prices would always rise. (Mortgage-backed securities are investments that are backed by the underlying value of a bundle of mortgages.) In fact, the computer models used by many of the banks did not even have a variable for declining real estate prices. Investors around the globe bought these securities because they thought they were safe. This sounded perfectly reasonable in a world where real estate prices were rising on an annual basis. Unfortunately, that assumption turned out to be false. From 2006 to 2008, real estate prices fell. Because of one faulty assumption, the entire financial market teetered on the edge of collapse. This vividly illustrates the danger of poor modeling.

Models can be useful, but as the financial crisis shows, they are also potentially dangerous. Because a model is always a simplification, decision-makers must be careful about assuming that a model can present a solution for complex problems.

In the late 1990s and early 2000s, some investors believed that real estate prices could only rise.

PRACTICE WHAT YOU KNOW

Positive versus Normative Statements

Question: Which of the following statements are positive and which ones are normative?

1. Winters in Arkansas are too cold.
2. Everyone should work at a bank to see the true value of money.
3. The current exchange rate is 0.7 British pounds per U.S. dollar.
4. On average, people save 15% when they switch to Geico.
5. Everyone ought to have a life insurance policy.
6. University of Virginia graduates earn more than Duke University graduates.
7. Harvard University is the top education institution in the country.
8. The average temperature in Fargo, North Dakota, in January is 56 degrees Fahrenheit.

You should eat five servings of fruit or vegetables each day. Is that a positive or a normative statement?

Answers

1. The word "too" is a matter of opinion. This is a normative statement.
2. While working at a bank might give someone an appreciation for the value of money, the word "should" is an opinion. This is a normative statement.
3. You can look up the current exchange rate and verify if this statement is true or false. This is a positive statement.
4. This was a claim made by the insurance company Geico in one of its commercials. Don't let that fool you. It is still a testable claim. If you had the data from Geico, you could see if the statement is correct or not. This is a positive statement.
5. It sounds like a true statement, or at least a very sensible one. However, the word "ought" makes it an opinion. This is a normative statement.
6. You can look up the data and see which university's graduates earn more. This is a positive statement.
7. Many national rankings indicate that this is true, but others do not. Since different rankings are based on different assumptions, it is not possible to identify a definitive "top" school. This is a normative statement.
8. The statement is wrong. North Dakota is much colder than that in January. However, the statement can be verified by looking at climatological data. This is a positive statement.

What Is a Production Possibilities Frontier?

Now it's time for our first economic model. However, before you go on, you might want to review the appendix on graphing at the end of this chapter. It covers graph-reading skills that are used in this section. Graphs are one of the key tools in economics because they provide a visual display of the relationship between two variables over time. Your ability to read a graph and understand the model it represents is crucial to learning economics.

In Chapter 1, we learned that economics is about the trade-offs individuals and societies face every day. For instance, you may frequently have to decide between spending more time studying to get better grades or going to a party with your friends. The more time you study, the less time you have for your friends. Similarly, a society has to determine how to allocate its resources. The decision to build new roads will mean there is less money available for new schools, and vice versa.

Trade-offs

A **production possibilities frontier** is a model that illustrates the combinations of outputs that a society can produce if all of its resources are being used efficiently. In order to preserve *ceteris paribus*, we assume that the technology available for production and the quantity of resources remain constant. These assumptions allow us to model trade-offs more clearly.

A **production possibilities frontier** is a model that illustrates the combinations of outputs that a society can produce if all of its resources are being used efficiently.

Let's begin by imagining a society that produces only two goods—pizzas and chicken wings. This may not seem very realistic, since a real economy comprises millions of different goods and services, but the benefit of this approach is that it enables us to understand the trade-offs in the production process without making the analysis too complicated.

Figure 2.1 shows the production possibilities frontier for our two-product society. Remember that the number of people and the total resources in this two-product society are fixed. Later, we will relax these assumptions and make our model more realistic. If the economy uses all of its resources to produce pizzas, it can produce 100 pizzas and 0 wings. If it uses all of its resources to produce wings, it can make 300 wings and 0 pizzas. These outcomes are represented by points A and B on the production possibilities frontier. It is unlikely that the society will choose either of these extreme outcomes because it is human nature to enjoy variety.

If our theoretical society decides to spend some of its resources producing pizzas and some of its resources making wings, its economy will end up with a combination of pizzas and wings that can be placed somewhere along the production possibilities frontier (PPF) between points A and B. At point C, for example, the society would deploy its resources to produce 70 pizzas and 90 wings. At point D, the combination would be 50 pizzas and 150 wings. Each point along the production possibilities frontier represents a possible set of outcomes that the society can choose if it uses all of its resources efficiently.

Notice that some combinations of pizza and wings cannot be produced. This is because resources within the society are scarce. Our theoretical society would enjoy point E, but given the available resources, it cannot produce at that output level. Points beyond the production possibilities frontier are desirable but not feasible, given the resources and technology that the society has available.

FIGURE 2.1

The Production Possibilities Frontier for Pizza and Wings

The production possibilities frontier shows the trade-off between producing pizzas and producing wings. Any combination of pizzas and wings is possible along, or inside, the line. Combinations of pizza and wings beyond the production possibilities frontier—for example, at point E—are not possible with the current set of resources. Point F and any other points located in the shaded region are inefficient.

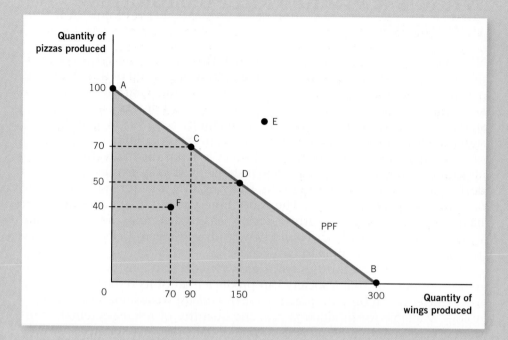

At any combination of wings and pizzas along the production possibilities frontier, the society is using all of its resources in the most productive way possible. But what about point F and any other points that might be located in the shaded region? These points represent outcomes inside the production possibilities frontier, which indicate an inefficient use of the society's resources. Consider, for example, the resource of labor. If employees spend many hours at work surfing the Web instead of doing their jobs, the output of pizzas and wings will drop and will no longer be efficient. As long as the workers use all of their time efficiently, they will produce the maximum amount of pizza and wings.

Whenever society is producing on the production possibilities frontier, the only way to get more of one good is to accept less of another. Since an economy operating along the frontier will be efficient at any point, economists do not favor one point over another. But a society may favor one particular point over another because it prefers that combination of goods. For example, in our theoretical two-good society, if wings suddenly become more popular, the movement from point C to point D will represent a desirable trade-off. The society will have 20 fewer pizzas (from 70 to 50) but 60 additional wings (from 90 to 150).

The Production Possibilities Frontier and Opportunity Cost

Trade-offs

Since our two-good society produces only pizzas and wings, the trade-offs that occur along the production possibilities frontier represent the opportunity cost of producing one good instead of the other. As we noted in Chapter 1, an opportunity cost is the highest-valued alternative given up to pursue another course of action. As Figure 2.1 shows, when society moves from point C to point D, it gives up 20 pizzas; this is the opportunity cost of producing more wings. The movement from D to C has an opportunity cost of 60 wings.

Opportunity cost

Until now, we have assumed that there would be a constant trade-off between the number of pizzas and the number of wings produced. However, that is not typically the case. Not all resources in our theoretical society are perfectly adaptable for use in making pizzas and wings. Some workers are good at making pizzas, and others are not so good. When the society tries to make as many pizzas as possible, it will be using both types of workers. That is, to get more pizzas, the society will have to use workers who are increasingly less skilled at making them. This means that pizza production will not expand at a constant rate. You can see this in the new production possibilities frontier in Figure 2.2; it is bowed outward rather than a straight line.

Since resources are not perfectly adaptable, production does not expand at a constant rate. For example, in order to produce 20 extra pizzas, the society can move from point D (30 pizzas) to point C (50 pizzas). But moving from

FIGURE 2.2

The Law of Increasing Relative Cost

To make more pizzas, the society will have to use workers who are increasingly less skilled at making them. As a result, as we move up along the PPF, the opportunity cost of producing an extra 20 pizzas rises from 30 wings between points D and C to 80 wings between points B and A.

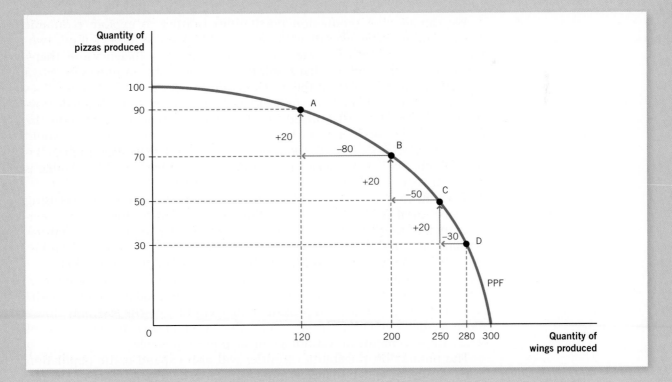

point D (280 wings) to point C (250 wings) means giving up 30 wings. So moving from D to C has an opportunity cost of 30 wings. Suppose that the society decides it wants even more pizza and moves from point C (50 pizzas) to point B (70 pizzas). Now the opportunity cost of more pizza is 50 wings, since wing production declines from 250 to 200. If the society decides that 70 pizzas are not enough, it can expand pizza production from point B (70 pizzas) to point A (90 pizzas). Now the society gives up 80 wings. Notice that as we move up along the PPF, the opportunity cost of producing an extra 20 pizzas rises from 30 wings to 80 wings. This reflects the increased trade-off necessary to produce more pizzas.

A bowed-out production possibilities frontier reflects the increasing opportunity cost of production. This is described by the **law of increasing relative cost**, which states that the opportunity cost of producing a good rises as a society produces more of it. Changes in relative cost mean that a society faces a significant trade-off if it tries to produce an extremely large amount of a single good.

> The **law of increasing relative cost** states that the opportunity cost of producing a good rises as a society produces more of it.

The Production Possibilities Frontier and Economic Growth

So far, we have modeled the location of the production possibilities frontier as a function of the resources available to society at a particular moment in time. However, most societies hope to create economic growth. Economic growth is the process that enables a society to produce more output in the future.

We can use the production possibilities frontier to explore economic growth. For example, we can ask what would happen to the PPF if our two-good society developed a new technology that increases efficiency and, therefore, productivity. Suppose that a new pizza assembly line improves the pizza production process and that the development of the new assembly line does not require the use of more of the society's resources—it is simply a redeployment of the resources that already exist. This development would allow the society to make more pizza with the same number of workers. Or it would allow the same amount of pizza to be made with fewer workers than previously. Either way, the society has expanded its resource base. The change is shown in Figure 2.3.

With the new technology, it becomes possible to produce 120 pizzas using the same number of workers and in the same amount of time that it previously took to produce 100 pizzas. Although the ability to produce wings has not changed, the new pizza-making technology causes the production possibilities frontier to expand outward from PPF_1 to PPF_2. It is now possible for the society to move from point A to point B, where it can produce more of both (80 pizzas and 220 wings). Why can the society produce more of both? Because the improvement in pizza-making technology—the assembly line—allows a redeployment of the labor force that also increases the production of wings. Improvements in technology make point B possible.

The production possibilities frontier will also expand if the population grows. A larger population means more workers to help make pizza and wings. Figure 2.4 illustrates what happens when the society adds a worker to help

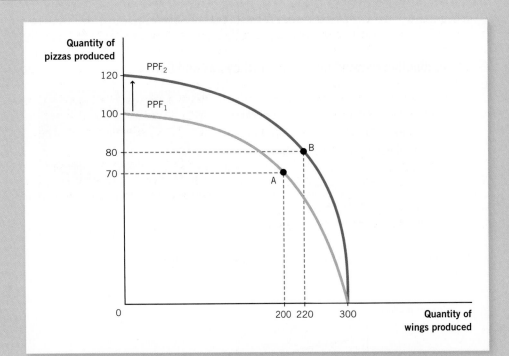

FIGURE 2.3

A Shift in the Production Possibilities Frontier

A new pizza assembly line that improves the productive capacity of pizza-makers shifts the PPF upward from PPF_1 to PPF_2. Not surprisingly, more pizzas can be produced. Comparing points A and B, you can see that the enhanced pizza-making capacity also makes it possible to produce more wings at the same time.

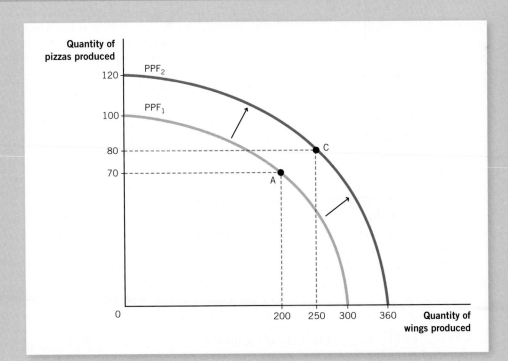

FIGURE 2.4

More Resources and the Production Possibilities Frontier

When more resources are available for the production of either pizza or wings, the entire PPF shifts upward and outward. This makes a point like C, along PPF_2, possible.

PRACTICE WHAT YOU KNOW

The Production Possibilities Frontier: Bicycles and Cars

Question: Are the following statements true or false? Base your answers on the PPF shown below.

There is a trade-off between making bicycles and cars.

1. Point A represents a possible amount of cars and bicycles that can be sold.

2. The movement along the curve from point A to point B shows the opportunity cost of producing more bicycles.

3. If we have high unemployment, the PPF shifts inward.

4. If an improved process for manufacturing cars is introduced, the *entire* PPF will shift outward.

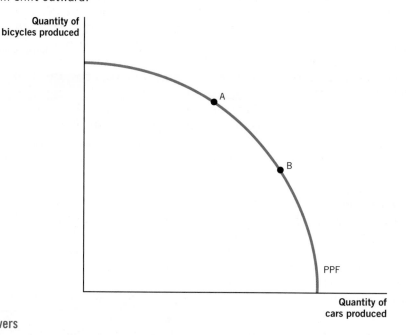

Answers

1. False. Point A represents a number of cars and bicycles that can be *produced*, not sold.

2. False. Moving from point A to point B shows the opportunity cost of producing more cars, not more bicycles.

3. False. Unemployment does not shift the curve inward, since the PPF is the maximum that can be produced when all resources are being used. More unemployment would locate society at a point inside the PPF, since some people who could help produce more cars or bicycles would not be working.

4. False. The PPF will shift outward along the car axis, but it will not shift upward along the bicycle axis.

produce pizza and wings. With more workers, the society is able to produce more pizzas and wings than before. This causes the curve to shift from PPF_1 to PPF_2, expanding up along the y axis and out along the x axis. Like improvements in technology, additional resources expand the frontier and enable the society to reach a point—in this case, C—that was not possible before. The extra workers have pushed the entire frontier out, not just one end, as the pizza assembly line did.

What Are the Benefits of Specialization and Trade?

We have seen that improving technology and adding resources make an economy more productive. A third way to create gains for society is through specialization and trade. Determining what to specialize in is an important part of this process. Every worker, business, or country is relatively good at producing certain products or services. Suppose that you decide to learn about information technology. You earn a certificate or degree and find an employer who hires you for your specialized skills. Your information technology skills determine your salary. As a result, you can use your salary to purchase other goods and services that you desire and that you are not so skilled at making yourself.

In the next section, we will explore why specializing and exchanging your skilled expertise with others makes gains from trade possible.

Gains from Trade

Let's return to our two-good economy. Now we'll make the further assumption that this economy has only two people. One person is better at making pizzas, and the other is better at making wings. When this is the case, the potential gains from trade are clear. Each person will specialize in what he or she is better at producing and then will trade in order to acquire some of the good that the other person produces.

Trade creates value

Figure 2.5 shows the production potential of the two people in our economy, Debra Winger and Mike Piazza. From the table, we see that if Debra Winger devotes all of her work time to making pizzas, she can produce 60 pizzas. If she does not spend any time on pizzas, she can make 120 wings. In contrast, Mike Piazza can spend all his time on pizzas and produce 24 pizzas, or all his time on wings and produce 72 wings.

The graphs show an illustration of the amount of pizza and wings that each person produces daily. Wing production is plotted on the x axis, and pizza production is on the y axis. Each of the production possibilities frontiers is drawn from data in the table at the top of the figure.

Debra and Mike each face a constant trade-off between producing pizza and producing wings. Debra produces 60 pizzas for every 120 wings; this means her trade-off between producing pizza and wings is fixed at 1:2. Mike produces 24 pizzas for every 72 wings. His trade-off between producing pizzas and wings is fixed at 1:3. Since Debra and Mike can choose to produce at

FIGURE 2.5

The Production Possibilities Frontier with No Trade

Debra Winger (a) can produce more pizza and more wings than Mike Piazza (b). Since Debra is more productive in general, she produces more of each food. If Debra and Mike each want to produce an equal number of pizzas and wings on their own, Debra makes 40 units of each and Mike makes 18 units of each.

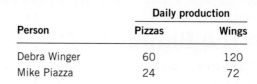

	Daily production	
Person	Pizzas	Wings
Debra Winger	60	120
Mike Piazza	24	72

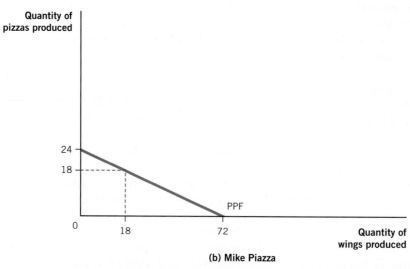

(a) Debra Winger

(b) Mike Piazza

any point along their production possibilities frontiers, let's assume that they each want to produce an equal number of pizzas and wings. When this is the case, Debra produces 40 pizzas and 40 wings, while Mike produces 18 pizzas and 18 wings. Since Debra is more productive in general, she produces more of each food. We say that Debra has an **absolute advantage**, meaning that she has the ability to produce more with the same quantity of resources than Mike can produce.

Absolute advantage refers to the ability of one producer to make more than another producer with the same quantity of resources.

At first glance, it would appear that Debra should continue to work alone. But consider what happens if they each specialize and then trade. Table 2.1 compares production with and without specialization and trade. Without trade, Debra and Mike have a combined production of 58 units of pizza and wings (Debra's 40 + Mike's 18). But when Debra specializes and produces only pizza, her production is 60 units. In this case, her individual pizza output is greater than the combined output of 58 pizzas (Debra's 40 + Mike's 18). Similarly, if Mike specializes in wings, he is able to make 72 units. His individual wing output is greater than their combined output of 58 wings (Debra's 40 + Mike's 18). Specialization has resulted in the production of 2 additional pizzas and 14 additional wings.

Trade creates value

Specialization leads to greater productivity. But Debra and Mike would like to eat both pizza and wings. So if they specialize and then trade with each other, they will benefit. If Debra gives Mike 19 pizzas in exchange for 47 wings, they are each better off by 1 pizza and 7 wings. This result is evident in the final column of Table 2.1 and in Figure 2.6.

In Figure 2.6a, we see that at point A Debra produces 60 pizzas and 0 wings. If she does not specialize, she produces 40 pizzas and 40 wings, represented at B. If she specializes and then trades with Mike, she can have 41 pizzas and 47 wings, shown at C. Her value gained from trade is 1 pizza and 7 wings. In Figure 2.6b, we see a similar benefit for Mike. If he produces only wings, he will have 72 wings, shown at A. If he does not specialize, he produces 18 pizzas and 18 wings. If he specializes and trades with Debra, he can have 19 pizzas and 25 wings, shown at C. His value gained from trade is 1 pizza and 7 wings. In spite of Debra's absolute advantage in making both pizzas and wings, she is still better off trading with Mike. This amazing result occurs because of specialization. When they spend their time on what they do best, they are able to produce more collectively and then divide the gain.

TABLE 2.1

The Gains from Trade

Person	Good	Without trade		With specialization and trade		Gains from trade
		Production	Consumption	Production	Consumption	
Debra	Pizza	40	40	60	41 (keeps)	+ 1
	Wings	40	40	0	47 (from Mike)	+ 7
Mike	Pizza	18	18	0	19 (from Debra)	+ 1
	Wings	18	18	72	25 (keeps)	+ 7

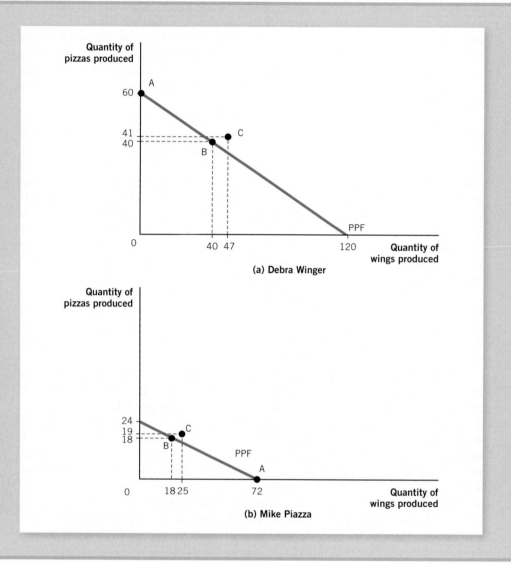

The Production Possibilities Frontier with Trade

(a) If Debra produces only pizza, she will have 60 pizzas, shown at point A. If she does not specialize, she will produce 40 pizzas and 40 wings (B). If she specializes and trades with Mike, she will have 41 pizzas and 47 wings (C).

(b) If Mike produces only wings, he will have 72 wings (A). If he does not specialize, he will produce 18 pizzas and 18 wings (B). If he specializes and trades with Debra, he can have 19 pizzas and 25 wings (C).

Comparative Advantage

We have seen that specialization enables workers to enjoy gains from trade. The concept of opportunity cost provides us with a second way of validating the principle that trade creates value. Recall that opportunity cost is the highest-valued alternative that is sacrificed to pursue something else. Looking at Table 2.2, you can see that in order to produce 1 more pizza Debra must give up producing 2 wings. We can say that the opportunity cost of 1 pizza is 2 wings. We can also reverse the observation and say that the opportunity cost of one wing is $\frac{1}{2}$ pizza. In Mike's case, each pizza he produces means giving up the production of 3 wings. In other words, the opportunity cost for him to produce 1 pizza is 3 wings. In reverse, we can say that when he produces 1 wing, he gives up $\frac{1}{3}$ pizza.

Recall from Chapter 1 that comparative advantage is the ability to make a good at a lower cost than another producer. Looking at Table 2.2, you can see

TABLE 2.2		
The Opportunity Cost of Pizza and Wings		
	Opportunity cost	
Person	**1 Pizza**	**1 Wing**
Debra Winger	2 wings	$\frac{1}{2}$ pizza
Mike Piazza	3 wings	$\frac{1}{3}$ pizza

that Debra has a lower opportunity cost of producing pizzas than Mike—she gives up 2 wings for each pizza she produces, while he gives up 3 wings for each pizza he produces. In other words, Debra has a comparative advantage in producing pizzas. However, Debra does not have a comparative advantage in producing wings. For Debra to produce 1 wing, she would have to give up production of $\frac{1}{2}$ pizza. Mike, in contrast, gives up $\frac{1}{3}$ pizza each time he produces 1 wing. So Debra's opportunity cost for producing wings is higher than Mike's. Because Mike is the low-opportunity-cost producer of wings, he has a comparative advantage in producing them. Recall that Debra has an absolute advantage in the production of both pizzas and wings; she is better at making both. However, from this example we see that she cannot have a comparative advantage in making both goods.

Opportunity cost

Applying the concept of opportunity cost helps us to see why specialization enables people to produce more. Debra's opportunity cost of producing pizzas (she gives up making 2 wings for every pizza) is less than Mike's opportunity cost of producing pizzas (he gives up 3 wings for every pizza). Therefore, Debra should specialize in producing pizzas. If you want to double-check this result, consider who should produce wings. Debra's opportunity cost of producing wings (she gives up $\frac{1}{2}$ pizza for every wing she makes) is more than Mike's opportunity cost of producing wings (he gives up $\frac{1}{3}$ pizza for every wing he makes). Therefore, Mike should specialize in producing wings. When Debra produces only pizzas and Mike produces only wings, their combined output is 60 pizzas and 72 wings.

Finding the Right Price to Facilitate Trade

We have seen that Debra and Mike will do better if they specialize and then trade. But how many wings should it cost to buy a pizza? How many pizzas for a wing? In other words, what trading price will benefit both parties? To answer this question, we need to return to opportunity cost. This process is similar to the trading of lunch food that you might recall from grade school. Perhaps you wanted a friend's apple and he wanted a few of your Oreos. If you agreed to trade three Oreos for the apple, the exchange benefited both parties because you valued your three cookies less than your friend's apple and your friend valued your three cookies more than his apple.

In our example, Debra and Mike will benefit from exchanging a good at a price that is lower than the opportunity cost of producing it. Recall that Debra's opportunity cost is 1 pizza per 2 wings. We can express this as a ratio of 1:2. This means that any exchange with a value lower than 1:2 (0.50) will be beneficial to her since she ends up with more pizza and wings than she

Opportunity cost

TABLE 2.3

Gaining from Trade

Person	Opportunity cost	Ratio
Debra Winger	1 pizza equals 2 wings	1:2 = 0.50
Terms of trade	19 pizzas for 47 wings	19:47 = 0.40
Mike Piazza	1 pizza equals 3 wings	1:3 = 0.33

had without trade. Mike's opportunity cost is 1 pizza per 3 wings, or a ratio of 1:3 (0.33). For trade to be mutually beneficial, the ratio of the amount exchanged must fall between the ratio of Debra's opportunity cost of 1:2 and the ratio of Mike's opportunity cost of 1:3. If the ratio falls outside of that range, Debra and Mike will be better off without trade, since the price of trading, which is the ratio in this case, will not be attractive to both parties. In the example shown in Table 2.3, Debra trades 19 pizzas for 47 wings. The ratio of 19:47 (0.40) falls between Debra's and Mike's opportunity costs.

Trade creates value

As long as the terms of trade fall between the opportunity costs of the trading partners, the trade benefits both sides. But if Mike insists on a trading ratio of 1 wing for 1 pizza, which would be a good deal for him, Debra will refuse to trade because she will be better off producing both goods on her own. Likewise, if Debra insists on receiving 4 wings for every pizza she gives to Mike, he will refuse to trade with her because he will be better off producing both goods on his own.

ECONOMICS IN THE REAL WORLD

Why Shaquille O'Neal Has Someone Else Help Him Move

Shaquille O'Neal is a mountain of a man—7'1" tall and over 300 pounds. At times during his Hall of Fame basketball career, he was traded from one team to another. Whenever he was traded, he had to relocate to a new city. Given his size and strength, you might think that Shaquille would have moved his household himself. But despite the fact that he could replace two or more ordinary movers, he kept playing basketball and hired movers. Let's examine the situation to see if this was a wise decision.

During his career, Shaquille had an absolute advantage in both playing basketball and moving furniture. But, as we have seen, an absolute advantage doesn't mean that Shaquille should do both tasks himself. When he was traded to a new team, he could have asked for a few days to pack up and move, but each day spent moving would have been one less day he was able to work with his new team. When you are paid millions of dollars to play a game, the time spent moving is time lost practicing or playing basketball, which incurs a substantial opportunity cost. The movers, with a much lower opportunity cost of their time, have a comparative advantage in moving—so Shaq made a smart decision to hire them!

However, since Shaquille is now retired, the value of his time is lower. If the opportunity cost of his time becomes low enough, it is conceivable that next time he will move himself rather than pay movers. ✳

Shaq and Comparative Advantage

If you ever saw Shaquille O'Neal use his size and strength on the basketball court, you might wonder how someone could have any kind of advantage over him. But when it comes to comparative advantage, opportunity costs tell the tale. Let's take a look at the numbers.

Shaq was a basketball star, but he also would have been a star mover. Experienced movers can earn $20 an hour. With Shaq's strength, he might have been worth $40 an hour. He had an absolute advantage in basketball AND moving.

But Shaq made an average of $15 million a year playing basketball! That's over $40,000 a day. Giving up basketball for moving would have meant a huge opportunity cost. When it comes to moving, the movers had a comparative advantage. It was a no-brainer for Shaq to hire them and devote his time to hoops!

REVIEW QUESTIONS

- If you are better than your roommate at both cooking dinner and cleaning the apartment, does that mean you should be responsible for both tasks? Use comparative advantage to explain.

- If you have a comparative advantage in doing something, do you experience a high or low opportunity cost?

PRACTICE WHAT YOU KNOW

Opportunity Cost

Question: Imagine that you are traveling to visit your family in Chicago. You can take a train or a plane. The plane ticket costs $300, and it takes 2 hours each way. The train ticket costs $200, and it takes 12 hours each way. Which form of transportation should you choose?

Answer: The key to answering the question is learning to value time. The simplest way to do this is to calculate the financial cost savings of taking the train and compare that to the value of the time you would save if you took the plane.

Will you travel by plane or train?

Cost savings with train	Round-trip time saved with plane
$300 − $200 = $100	24 hours − 4 hours = 20 hours
(plane) − (train)	(train) − (plane)

A person who takes the train can save $100, but it will cost 20 hours to do so. At an hourly rate, the savings would be $100/20 hours = $5/hour. If you value your time at exactly $5 an hour, you will be indifferent between plane and train travel. If your time is worth more than $5 an hour, you should take the plane, and if your time is worth less than $5 an hour, you should take the train.

It is important to note that this approach gives us a more realistic answer than simply observing ticket prices. The train has a lower ticket price, but very few people ride the train instead of flying because the opportunity cost of their time is worth more to them than the difference in the ticket prices. This is why most business travelers fly—it saves valuable time. Good economists learn to examine the full opportunity cost of their decisions, which must include both the financials and the cost of time.

We have examined this question by holding everything else constant, or applying the principle of *ceteris paribus*. In other words, at no point did we discuss possible side issues such as the fear of flying, sleeping arrangements on the train, or anything else that might be relevant to someone making the decision.

Opportunity
cost

Opportunity Cost

Saving Private Ryan

In most war movies, the calculus of battle is quite apparent. One side wins if it loses fewer airplanes, tanks, or soldiers during the course of the conflict or attains a strategic objective worth the cost. These casualties of war are the trade-off that is necessary to achieve victory. The movie *Saving Private Ryan* (1998) is different because in its plot the calculus of war does not add up: the mission is to save a single man. Private Ryan is one of four brothers who are all fighting on D-Day—June 6, 1944—the day the Allies landed in Normandy, France, to liberate Europe from Nazi occupation. In a twist of fate, all three of Ryan's brothers are killed. As a result, the general in charge believes that the family has sacrificed enough and sends orders to find Ryan and return him home.

The catch is that in order to save Private Ryan the army needs to send a small group of soldiers to find him. A patrol led by Captain Miller loses many good men in the process, and those who remain begin to doubt the mission. Captain Miller says to the sergeant, "This Ryan better be worth it. He better go

Saving one life means sacrificing another.

home and cure a disease, or invent a longer-lasting light bulb." Captain Miller hopes that saving Private Ryan will be worth the sacrifices they are making. That is how he rationalizes the decision to try to save him.

The opportunity cost of saving Private Ryan ends up being the lives that the patrol loses—lives that otherwise could have been pursuing a strategic military objective. In that sense, the entire film is about opportunity cost.

What Is the Trade-off between Having More Now and Having More Later?

So far, we have examined short-run trade-offs. In looking at our wings-pizza trade-off, we were essentially living in the moment. But both individuals and society as a whole must weigh the benefits available today with those available tomorrow.

Many of life's important decisions are about the long run. We must decide where to live, whether and whom to marry, whether and where to go to college, and what type of career to pursue. Getting these decisions right is far more important than simply deciding how many wings and pizzas to produce. For instance, the decision to save money requires giving up something you want to buy today for the benefit of having more money available in the future. Similarly, if you decide to go to a party tonight, you benefit today, while staying home to study creates a larger benefit at exam time. We are constantly making decisions that reflect this tension between today and

Study now . . .

. . . enjoy life later.

Trade-offs

tomorrow—eating a large piece of cake or a healthy snack, taking a nap or exercising at the gym, buying a jet ski or investing in the stock market. Each of these decisions is a trade-off between the present and the future.

Consumer Goods, Capital Goods, and Investment

Consumer goods
are produced for present consumption.

Capital goods
help produce other valuable goods and services in the future.

Investment
is the process of using resources to create or buy new capital.

Opportunity cost

We have seen that the trade-off between the present and the future is evident in the tension between what we consume now and what we plan to consume later. Any good that is produced for present consumption is a **consumer good**. These goods help to satisfy our wants now. Food, entertainment, and clothing are all examples of consumer goods. **Capital goods** help in the production of other valuable goods and services in the future. Capital goods are everywhere. Roads, factories, trucks, and computers are all capital goods.

For households, education is also a form of capital. The time you spend earning a college degree makes you more attractive to future employers. Even though education is not a durable good, like a house, it can be utilized in the future to earn more income. When you decide to go to college instead of working, you are making an *investment* in your human capital. **Investment** is the process of using resources to create or buy new capital.

Since we live in a world with scarce resources, every investment in capital goods has an opportunity cost of forgone consumer goods. For example, if you decide to buy a new laptop to take notes in class, you cannot use the money you spent to travel over spring break. Similarly, a firm that decides to invest in a new factory to expand future production is unable to use that money to hire more workers now.

The decision between whether to consume or to invest has a significant impact on economic growth in the future, or the long run. What happens when society makes a choice to produce many more consumer goods than capital goods? Figure 2.7a shows the result. When relatively few resources

FIGURE 2.7

Investing in Capital Goods and Promoting Growth

(a) When a society chooses point A in the short run, very few capital goods are created. Since capital goods are needed to enhance future growth, the long-run PPF_2 expands, but only slightly.

(b) When a society chooses point B in the short run, many capital goods are created, and the long-run PPF_2 expands significantly.

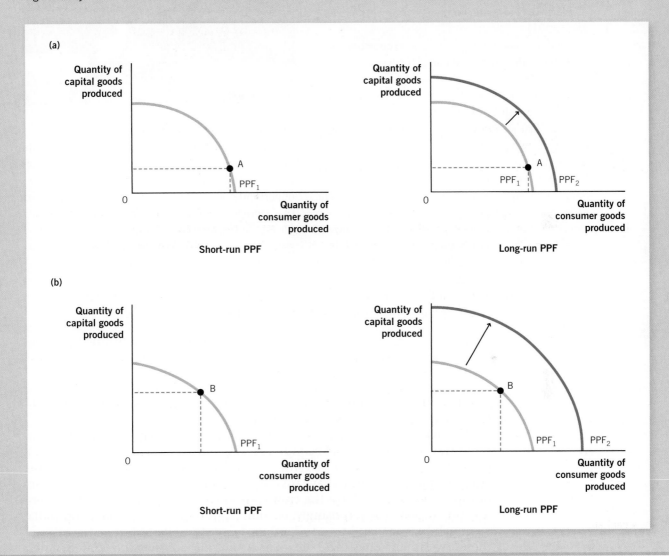

are invested in producing capital goods in the short run, not very much new capital is created. Since new capital is a necessary ingredient for economic growth in the future, the long-run production possibilities curve only expands a small amount.

What happens when society makes a choice to plan for the future by producing more capital goods than consumer goods? Figure 2.7b shows the

The Trade-off between the Present and the Future

A Knight's Tale

Before the late Heath Ledger starred in *Brokeback Mountain*, or played the Joker in *The Dark Knight*, he played an entrepreneurial peasant in *A Knight's Tale* (2001).

In the movie, three peasants unexpectedly win a jousting tournament and earn 15 silver coins. Then they face a choice about what to do next. Two of the three want to return to England and live the high life for a while, but the third (played by Ledger) suggests that they take 13 of the coins and reinvest them in training for the next tournament. He offers to put in all 5 of his coins and asks the other two for 4 coins each. His partners are skeptical about the plan because Ledger's character is good with the sword and not very good with the lance. For them to win additional tournaments, they will have to invest considerable resources in training and preparation.

The movie illustrates the trade-off between enjoying consumer goods in the short run and investing in capital goods in the long run. The peasants' choice to forgo spending their winnings

Learning to joust is a long-term skill.

to enjoy themselves now in order to prepare for the next tournament is not easy. None of the three has ever had any money. Five silver coins represent an opportunity, at least for a few days, to live the good life. However, the plan will elevate the three out of poverty in the long term if they can learn to compete at the highest level. Therefore, investing the 13 coins is like choosing point B in Figure 2.8b. Investing now will allow their production possibilities frontier to grow over time, affording each of them a better life in the long run.

result. With investment in new capital, the long-run production possibilities curve expands outward much more.

All societies face the trade-off between spending today and investing for tomorrow. Emerging global economic powers like China and India are good examples of the benefit of investing in the future. Over the last 20 years, the citizens of these countries have invested significantly more on the formation of capital goods than have the citizens in wealthier nations in North America and Europe. Not surprisingly, economic growth rates in China and India are much higher than in more developed countries. Part of the difference in these investment rates can be explained by the fact that the United States and Europe already have larger capital stocks per capita and have less to gain than developing countries from operating at point B in Figure 2.7b. China clearly prefers point B at this stage of its economic development, but point B is not necessarily better than point A. Developing nations, like China, are sacrificing the present for a better future, while many developed countries, like the United States, take a more balanced approach to weighing current needs against future growth. For Chinese workers, this trade-off typically means longer work hours and higher savings rates than their American counterparts

Trade-offs

PRACTICE WHAT YOU KNOW

Trade-offs

Question: Your friend is fond of saying he will study later. He eventually does study, but he often doesn't get quite the grades he had hoped for because he doesn't study enough. Every time this happens, he says, "It's only one exam." What advice would you give?

No pain, no gain.

Answer: Your friend doesn't understand long-term trade-offs. You could start by reminding him that each decision has a consequence at the margin and also later in life. The marginal cost of not studying enough is a lower exam grade. To some extent, your friend's reasoning is correct. How well he does on one exam over four years of college is almost irrelevant. The problem is that many poor exam scores have a cumulative effect over the semesters. If your friend graduates with a 2.5 GPA instead of a 3.5 GPA because he did not study enough, his employment prospects will be significantly diminished.

Marginal thinking

can claim, despite far lower average salaries. In contrast, American workers have much more leisure time and more disposable income, a combination that leads to far greater rates of consumption.

Conclusion

Does trade create winners and losers? After reading this chapter, you should know the answer: trade creates value. We have dispelled the misconception that many first-time learners of economics begin with—that every trade results in a winner and a loser. The simple, yet powerful, idea that trade creates value has far-reaching consequences for how we should organize our society. Voluntary trades will maximize society's wealth by redistributing goods and services to people who value them the most.

Trade creates value

We have also developed our first model, the production possibilities frontier. This model illustrates the benefits of trade and also enables us to describe ways to grow the economy. Trade and growth rest on a more fundamental idea—specialization. When producers specialize, they focus their efforts on those goods and services for which they have the lowest opportunity cost and trade with others who are good at making something else. In order to have something valuable to trade, each producer, in effect, must find its comparative advantage. As a result, trade creates value and contributes to an improved standard of living in society.

In the next chapter, we examine the supply-and-demand model to illustrate how markets work. While the model is different, the fundamental result we learned here—that trade creates value—still holds.

Failing to Account for Exogenous Factors When Making Predictions

Predictions are often based on past experiences and current observations. Many of the least accurate predictions fail to take into account how much technological change influences the economy. Here, we repeat a few predictions as a cautionary reminder that technology doesn't remain constant.

PREDICTION: "There is no reason anyone would want a computer in their home." Said in 1977 by Ken Olson, founder of Digital Equipment Corp. (DEC), a maker of mainframe computers.

FAIL: Over 80% of all American households have a computer today.

PREDICTION: "There will never be a bigger plane built." Said in 1933 by a Boeing engineer referring to the 247, a twin-engine plane that holds 10 people.

FAIL: Today, the Airbus A380 can hold more than 800 people.

PREDICTION: "The wireless music box has no imaginable commercial value. Who would pay for a message sent to no one in particular?" Said by people in the communications industry when David Sarnoff (founder of NBC) wanted to invest in the radio.

Source: Listverse.com, "Top 30 Failed Technology Predictions"

FAIL: Radio programs quickly captured the public's imagination.

PREDICTION: "The world potential market for copying machines is five thousand at most." Said in 1959 by executives of IBM to the people who founded Xerox.

FAIL: Today, a combination printer, fax machine, and copier costs less than $100. There are tens of millions of copiers in use throughout the United States.

PREDICTION: "The Americans have need of the telephone, but we do not. We have plenty of messenger boys." Said in 1878 by Sir William Preece, chief engineer, British Post Office.

FAIL: Today, almost everyone in Britain has a telephone.

These predictions may seem funny to us today, but note the common feature: they did not account for how the new technology would affect consumer demand and behavior. Nor do these predictions anticipate how improvements in technology through time make future versions of new products substantially better. The lesson: don't count on the status quo. Adapt with the times to take advantage of opportunities.

Epic fail: planes have continued to get larger despite predictions to the contrary.

ANSWERING THE BIG QUESTIONS

How do economists study the economy?

* Economists design theories and then test them by collecting real data. The economist's laboratory is the world around us; it ranges from the economy as a whole to the decisions that firms and individuals make. A good model should be simple to understand, flexible in design, and able to make powerful predictions. A model is both more realistic and harder to understand when it involves many variables. Maintaining a positive framework is crucial for economic analysis because it allows decision-makers to observe the facts objectively.

What is a production possibilities frontier?

* A production possibilities frontier is a model that illustrates the combinations of outputs that a society can produce if all of its resources are being used efficiently. Economists use this model to illustrate trade-offs and to explain opportunity costs and the role of additional resources and technology in creating economic growth.

What are the benefits of specialization and trade?

* Society is better off if individuals and firms specialize and trade on the basis of the principle of comparative advantage.
* Parties that are better at producing goods and services than their potential trading partners, or hold an absolute advantage, still benefit from trade because this allows them to specialize and trade what they produce for other goods and services that they are not as skilled at making.
* As long as the terms of trade fall between the opportunity costs of the trading partners, the trade benefits both sides.

What is the trade-off between having more now and having more later?

* All societies face a crucial trade-off between consumption in the short run and greater productivity in the long run. Investments in capital goods today help to spur economic growth in the future. However, since capital goods are not consumed in the short run, this means that society must be willing to sacrifice how well it lives today in order to have more later.

CONCEPTS YOU SHOULD KNOW

absolute advantage (p. 39)
capital goods (p. 46)
ceteris paribus (p. 28)
consumer goods (p. 46)
endogenous factors (p. 29)

exogenous factors (p. 29)
investment (p. 46)
law of increasing relative
   cost (p. 34)
normative statement (p. 27)

positive statement (p. 27)
production possibilities
   frontier (p. 31)

QUESTIONS FOR REVIEW

1. What is a positive economic statement? What is a normative economic statement? Provide an example of each.

2. Is it important to build completely realistic economic models? Explain your response.

3. Draw a production possibilities frontier curve. Illustrate the set of points that is feasible, the set of points that is efficient, and the set of points that is infeasible.

4. Why does the production possibilities frontier bow out? Give an example of two goods for which this would be the case.

5. Does having an absolute advantage mean that you should undertake everything on your own? Why or why not?

6. What criteria would you use to determine which of two workers has a comparative advantage in performing a task?

7. Why does comparative advantage matter more than absolute advantage for trade?

8. What factors are most important for economic growth?

STUDY PROBLEMS (✳ *solved at the end of the section*)

✳ 1. Michael and Angelo live in a small town in Italy. They work as artists. Michael is the more productive artist. He can produce 10 small sculptures each day but only 5 paintings. Angelo can produce 6 sculptures each day but only 2 paintings.

	Output per day	
	Sculptures	Paintings
Michael	10	5
Angelo	6	2

a. What is the opportunity cost of a painting for each artist?

b. Based on your answer in part a, who has a comparative advantage in producing paintings?

c. If the two men decide to specialize, who should produce the sculptures and who should produce the paintings?

✳ 2. The following table shows scores that a student can earn on two upcoming exams according to the amount of time devoted to study:

Hours spent studying for economics	Economics score	Hours spent studying for history	History score
10	100	0	40
8	96	2	60
6	88	4	76
4	76	6	88
2	60	8	96
0	40	10	100

a. Plot the production possibilities frontier.

b. Does the production possibilities frontier exhibit the law of increasing relative cost?

c. If the student wishes to move from a grade of 60 to a grade of 88 in economics, what is the opportunity cost?

3. Think about comparative advantage when answering this question: Should your professor, who has highly specialized training in economics, take time out of his teaching schedule to mow his lawn? Defend your answer.

❋ 4. Are the following statements positive or normative?
   a. My dog weighs 75 pounds.
   b. Dogs are required by law to have rabies shots.
   c. You should take your dog to the veterinarian once a year for a check-up.
   d. Chihuahuas are cuter than bulldogs.
   e. Leash laws for dogs are a good idea because they reduce injuries.

5. How does your decision to invest in a college degree add to your capital stock? Show this on your projected production possibilities frontier for 10 years from now compared to your production possibilities frontier without a degree.

❋ 6. Suppose that an amazing new fertilizer doubles the production of potatoes. How would this discovery affect the production possibilities frontier between potatoes and carrots? Would it now be possible to produce more potatoes *and* more carrots, or only more potatoes?

7. Suppose that a politician tells you about a plan to create two expensive but necessary programs to build more production facilities for solar power and wind power. At the same time, the politician is unwilling to cut any other programs. Use the production possibilities frontier graph below to explain if this is possible.

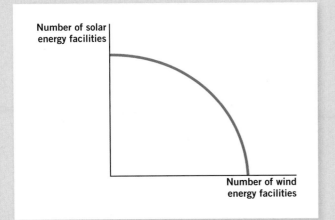

❋ 8. Two friends, Rachel and Joey, enjoy baking bread and making apple pies. Rachel takes 2 hours to bake a loaf of bread and 1 hour to make a pie. Joey takes 4 hours to bake a loaf and 4 hours to make a pie.
   a. What are Joey's and Rachel's opportunity costs of baking bread?
   b. Who has the absolute advantage in making bread?
   c. Who has a comparative advantage in making bread?
   d. If Joey and Rachel each decides to specialize in order to increase their joint production, what should Joey produce? What should Rachel produce?
   e. The price of a loaf of bread can be expressed in terms of an apple pie. If Joey and Rachel are specializing in production and decide to trade with each other, what range of ratios of bread and apple pie would allow both parties to benefit from trade?

9. Where would you plot unemployment on a production possibilities frontier? Where would you plot full employment on a production possibilities frontier? Now suppose that in a time of crisis everyone pitches in and works much harder than usual. What happens to the production possibilities frontier?

SOLVED PROBLEMS

1.a. Michael's opportunity cost is 2 sculptures for each painting he produces. How do we know this? If he devotes all of his time to sculptures, he can produce 10. If he devotes all of his time to paintings, he can produce 5. The ratio 10:5 is the same as 2:1. Michael is therefore twice as fast at producing sculptures as he is at producing paintings. Angelo's opportunity cost is 3 sculptures for each painting he produces. If he devotes all of his time to sculptures, he can produce 6. If he devotes all of his time to paintings, he can produce 2. The ratio 6:2 is the same as 3:1.

b. For this question, we need to compare Michael's and Angelo's relative strengths. Michael produces 2 sculptures for every painting, and Angelo produces 3 sculptures for every painting. Since Michael is only twice as good at producing sculptures, his opportunity cost of producing each painting is 2 sculptures instead 3. Therefore, Michael is the low-opportunity-cost producer of paintings.

c. If they specialize, Michael should paint and Angelo should do the sculptures. You might be tempted to argue that Michael should just work alone, but if Angelo does the sculptures, it frees up Michael to concentrate on the paintings. This is what comparative advantage is all about.

b. Yes, since it is not a straight line.

c. The opportunity cost is that the student's grade falls from 96 to 76 in history.

4.a. Positive.
b. Positive.
c. Normative.
d. Normative.
e. Normative.

6. A new fertilizer that doubles potato production will shift the entire PPF out along the potato axis but not along the carrot axis. Nevertheless, the added ability to produce more potatoes means that less acreage will have to be planted in potatoes and more land can be used to produce carrots. This makes it possible to produce more potatoes and carrots at many points along the production possibilities frontier. Figure 2.3 has a nice illustration if you are unsure how this works.

8.a. Rachel gives up 2 pies for every loaf she makes. Joey gives up 1 pie for every loaf he makes.
b. Rachel.
c. Joey.
d. Joey should make the bread and Rachel the pies.
e. Rachel makes 2 pies per loaf and Joey makes 1 pie per loaf. So any trade between 2:1 and 1:1 would benefit them both.

2.a.

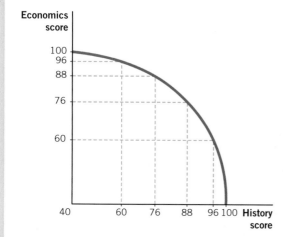

Graphs in Economics

Many beginning students try to understand economics without taking the time to learn the meaning and importance of graphs. This is shortsighted. You can "think" your way to a correct answer in a few cases, but the models we build and illustrate with graphs are designed to help analyze the tough questions, where your intuition can lead you astray.

Economics is fundamentally a quantitative science. That is, in many cases economists solve problems by finding a numerical answer. For instance, economists determine the unemployment rate, the rate of inflation, the growth rate of the economy, prices, costs, and much more. Economists also like to compare present-day numbers to numbers from the immediate past and historical data. Throughout your study of economics, you will find that many data-driven topics—for example, financial trends, transactions, the stock market, and other business-related variables—naturally lend themselves to graphic display. You will also find that many theoretical concepts are easier to understand when depicted visually in graphs and charts.

Economists also find that graphing can be a powerful tool when attempting to find relationships between different sets of observations. For example, the production possibilities frontier model we presented earlier in this chapter involved the relationship between the production of pizzas and wings. The graphical presentations made this relationship, the trade-off between pizzas and wings, much more vivid.

In this appendix, we begin with simple graphs, or visuals, involving a single variable and then move to graphs that consist of two variables. Taking a few moments to read this material will help you learn economics with less effort and with greater understanding.

Graphs That Consist of One Variable

There are two common ways to display data with one variable: bar graphs and pie charts. A **variable** is a quantity that can take on more than one value. Let's look at the market share of the largest carbonated beverage companies. Figure 2A.1 shows the data in a bar graph. On the vertical axis is the market share held by each firm. On the horizontal axis are the three largest firms (Coca-Cola, Pepsi, and Dr. Pepper Snapple) and the separate category for the remaining firms, called "Others." Coca-Cola Co. has the largest market share at 42%, followed by PepsiCo Inc. at 30% and Dr. Pepper Snapple at 16%. The height of each firm's bar represents its market share percentage. The combined market share of the other firms in the market is 12%.

A **variable** is a quantity that can take on more than one value.

We illustrate the same data from the beverage industry on a pie chart in Figure 2A.2. Now the market share is expressed as the size of the pie slice for each firm.

The information in a bar graph and a pie chart is the same, so does it matter which visualization you use? Bar graphs are particularly good for comparing sizes or quantities, while pie charts are generally better for illustrating proportions. But it doesn't really matter which visualization you use; what matters is how the audience sees your graph or chart.

FIGURE 2A.1

Bar Graphs

Each firm's market share in the beverage industry is represented by the height of the bar.

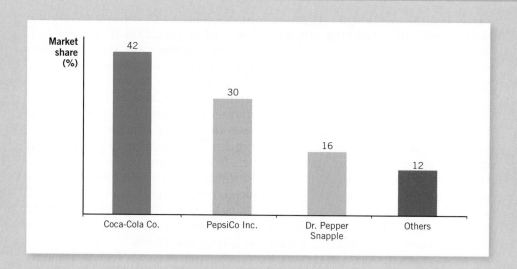

FIGURE 2A.2

Pie Chart

Each firm's market share in the beverage industry is represented by the size of the pie slice.

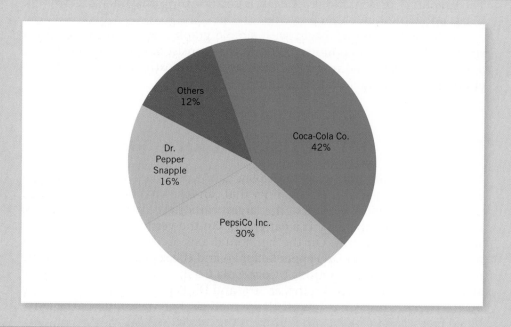

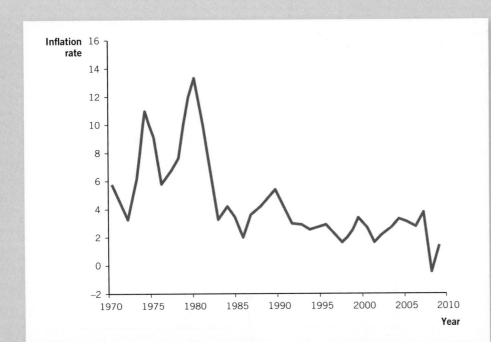

Time-Series Graph
In a time-series graph, you immediately get a sense of when the inflation rate was highest and lowest, the trend through time, and the amount of volatility in the data.

Time-Series Graphs

A time-series graph displays information about a single variable across time. For instance, if you want to show how the rate of inflation has varied over a certain period of time, you could list the annual inflation rates in a lengthy table, or you could illustrate each point as part of a time series in a graph. Graphing the points makes it possible to quickly determine when inflation was at its highest and lowest without having to scan through the entire table. Figure 2A.3 illustrates this point.

Graphs That Consist of Two Variables

Sometimes, understanding graphs requires you to visualize relationships between two economic variables. Each variable is plotted on a coordinate system, or two-dimensional grid. The coordinate system allows us to map a series of ordered pairs that show how the two variables relate to each other. For instance, suppose that we examine the relationship between the amount of lemonade sold and the air temperature, as shown in Figure 2A.4.

The air temperature is graphed on the x axis (horizontal) and cups of lemonade sold on the y axis (vertical). Within each ordered pair (x,y), the first value, x, represents the value along the x axis and the second value, y, represents the value along the y axis. For example, at point A, the value of x, or the

FIGURE 2A.4

Plotting Points in a Coordinate System

Within each ordered pair (x,y), the first value, x, represents the value along the x axis and the second value, y, represents the value along the y axis. The combination of all the (x,y) pairs is known as a scatterplot.

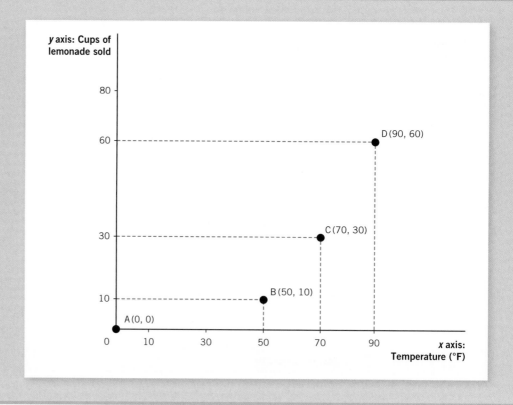

temperature, is 0 and the value of y, or the amount of lemonade sold, is also 0. No one would want to buy lemonade when the temperature is that low. At point B, the value of x, the air temperature, is 50 degrees and y, the number of cups of lemonade sold, is 10. By the time we reach point C, the temperature is 70 degrees and the amount of lemonade sold is 30 cups. Finally, at point D, the temperature has reached 90 degrees and 60 cups of lemonade are sold.

A **scatterplot** is a graph that shows individual (x,y) points.

Positive correlation occurs when two variables move in the same direction.

Negative correlation occurs when two variables move in the opposite direction.

The type of graph you see in Figure 2A.4 is known as a **scatterplot**; it shows the individual (x,y) points in a coordinate system. Note that in this example the amount of lemonade sold rises as the temperature increases. When the two variables move together in the same direction, we say that there is a **positive correlation** between them. Conversely, if we graph the relationship between hot chocolate sales and temperature, we find that they move in opposite directions; as the temperature rises, hot chocolate consumption goes down (see Figure 2A.5). This data reveals a **negative correlation**; it occurs when two variables, such as hot chocolate and temperature, move in opposite directions. Since economists are ultimately interested in using models and graphs to make predictions and test theories, the coordinate system makes both positive and negative correlations easy to observe.

Figure 2A.5 illustrates the difference between a positive correlation and a negative correlation. Figure 2A.5a uses the same information as Figure 2A.4. When the temperature increases, the quantity of lemonade sold increases as well. However, in 2A.5b we have a very different set of ordered pairs. Now, as the temperature increases, the quantity of hot chocolate sold falls. This

FIGURE 2A.5

Positive and Negative Correlations
Panel (a) displays the positive relationship, or correlation, between lemonade consumption and higher temperatures.
Panel (b) displays the negative relationship, or correlation, between hot chocolate consumption and higher temperatures.

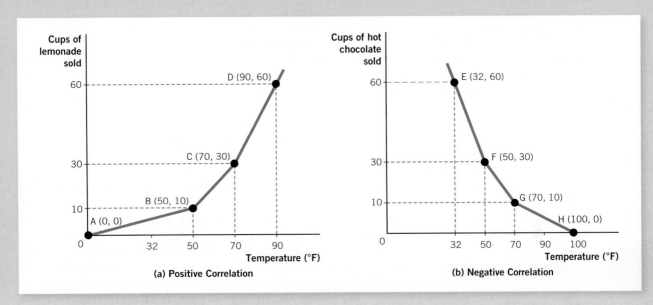

(a) Positive Correlation

(b) Negative Correlation

can be seen by starting with point E, where the temperature is 32 degrees and hot chocolate consumption is 60 cups. At point F, the temperature rises to 50 degrees, but hot chocolate consumption falls to 30 cups. Finally, at point G the temperature is 70 degrees and hot chocolate consumption is down to 10 cups. The green line connecting points E–G illustrates the negative correlation between hot chocolate consumption and temperature, since the line is downward sloping. This contrasts with the positive correlation in Figure 2A.5a, where lemonade consumption rises from point B to point D and the line is upward sloping.

The Slope of a Curve

A key element in any graph is the **slope**, or the rise along the *y* axis (vertical) divided by the run along the *x* axis (horizontal). The *rise* is the amount that the vertical distance changes. The *run* is the amount that the horizontal distance changes.

Slope
refers to the change in the rise along the *y* axis (vertical) divided by the change in the run along the *x* axis (horizontal).

$$\text{slope} = \frac{\text{change in } y}{\text{change in } x}$$

A slope can take on a positive, negative, or zero value. A slope of zero—a straight horizontal line—indicates that there is no change in *y* for a given change in *x*. However, that result is not very interesting. The slope can be positive, as it is in Figure 2A.5a, or negative, as it is in 2A.5b. Figure 2A.6 highlights the changes in x and y between the points on Figure 2A.5. (The change in a variable is often notated with a Greek delta symbol, Δ.)

In Figure 2A.6a, the slope from point B to point C is

$$\text{slope} = \frac{\text{change in } y}{\text{change in } x} = \frac{(30 - 10) \text{ or } 20}{(70 - 50) \text{ or } 20} = 1$$

All of the slopes in Figure 2A.6 are tabulated in Table 2A.1.

Each of the slopes in Figure 2A.6a is positive, and the values slowly increase from 0.2 to 1.5 as you move along the curve from point A to point D. However, in Figure 2A.6b, the slopes are negative as you move along the curve from E to H. An upward, or positive, slope indicates a positive correlation, while a downward, or negative, slope indicates a negative correlation.

Notice that in both panels of Figure 2A.6 the slope changes values from point to point. Because of this, we say that the relationships are *nonlinear*. The slope tells us something about how responsive consumers are to changes in temperature. Consider the movement from point A to point B in Figure 2A.6a. The change in y is 10, while the change in x is 50 and the slope (10/50) is 0.2. Since zero indicates no change and 0.2 is close to zero, we can say that lemonade customers are not very responsive as the temperature rises from 0 to 50 degrees. However, they are much more responsive from point C to point D, when the temperature rises from 70 to 90 degrees. At this point, lemonade consumption—the change in y—rises from 30 to 60 cups and the slope is now 1.5. The strength of the positive relationship is much stronger, and as a result the curve is much steeper, or more vertical. This contrasts with the movement from point A to point B, where the curve is flatter, or more horizontal.

The same analysis can be applied to Figure 2A.6b. Consider the movement from point E to point F. The change in y is -30, the change in x is 18, and the slope is -1.7. This value represents a strong negative relationship, so we would say that hot chocolate customers were quite responsive; as the temperature rose from 32 to 50 degrees, they cut their consumption of hot chocolate by 30 cups. However, hot chocolate customers are not very responsive from point G to point H, where the temperature rises from 70 to 100 degrees. In this case, consumption falls from 10 to 0 cups and the slope is -0.3. The strength of the negative relationship is much weaker (closer to zero) and, as a result, the line is much flatter, or more horizontal. This contrasts with the movement from point E to point F, where the curve was steeper, or more vertical.

TABLE 2A.1

Positive and Negative Slopes

(a)		(b)	
Points	**Slope**	**Points**	**Slope**
A to B	0.2	E to F	−1.7
B to C	1.0	F to G	−1.0
C to D	1.5	G to H	−0.3

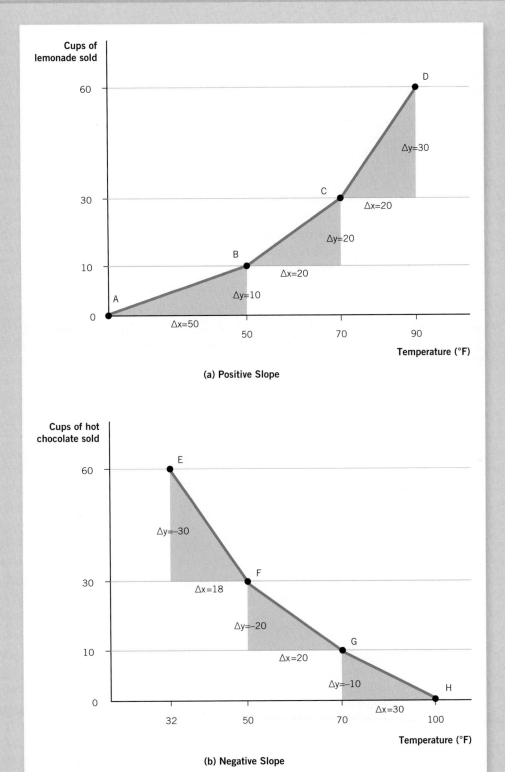

(a) Positive Slope

(b) Negative Slope

FIGURE 2A.6

Positive and Negative Slopes

Notice that in both panels the slope changes value from point to point. Because of this we say that the relationships are non-linear. In (a), as you move along the curve from point A to point D, the slopes are positive. However, in (b) the slopes are negative as you move along the curve from E to H. An upward, or positive, slope indicates a positive correlation, while a negative slope indicates a negative correlation.

Formulas for the Area of a Rectangle and a Triangle

Sometimes, economists interpret graphs by examining the area of different sections below a curve. Consider the demand for Bruegger's bagels shown in Figure 2A.7. The demand curve has a downward slope, which tells us that when the price of bagels falls, consumers will buy more bagels. But this curve also can tell us about the revenue the seller receives—one of the most important considerations for the firm. In this case, the sale price of each bagel is $0.60 and Bruegger's sells 4,000 bagels each week. We can illustrate the total amount Bruegger's takes in by shading the area bounded by the number of sales and the price—the green rectangle in the figure. In addition, we can identify the benefit consumers receive from purchasing bagels. This is shown by the blue triangle. Since many buyers are willing to pay more than $0.60 per bagel, we can visualize the "surplus" that consumers get from Bruegger's Bagels by highlighting the blue triangular area under the blue line and above $0.60.

To calculate the area of a rectangle, we use the formula:

$$\text{Area of a rectangle} = \text{height} \times \text{base}$$

In Figure 2A.7, the green rectangle is the amount of revenue that Bruegger's Bagels receives when it charges $0.60. The total revenue is $0.60 × 4,000, or $2,400.

To calculate the area of a triangle, we use the formula:

$$\text{Area of a triangle} = \tfrac{1}{2} \times \text{height} \times \text{base}$$

FIGURE 2A.7

Working with Rectangles and Triangles

We can determine the area of the green rectangle by multiplying the height by the base. This gives us $0.60 × 4,000, or $2,400 for the total revenue earned by Bruegger's Bagels. We can determine the area of a triangle by using the formula $\frac{1}{2}$ × height × base. This gives us $\frac{1}{2}$ × $0.60 × 4,000, or $1,200 for the area of consumer surplus.

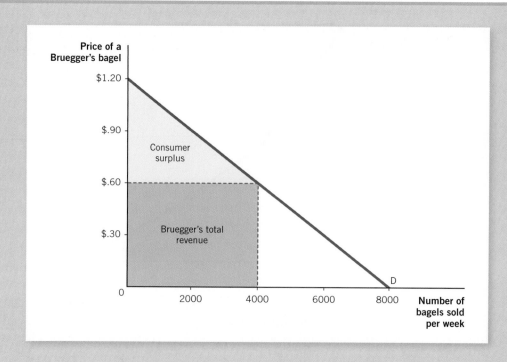

In Figure 2A.7, the blue triangle represents the amount of surplus consumers get from buying bagels. The amount of consumer surplus is $\frac{1}{2} \times \$0.60 \times \$4,000$, or $1,200.

Cautions in Interpreting Numerical Graphs

In Chapter 2, we utilized *ceteris paribus*, or the condition of holding everything else around us constant while analyzing a specific relationship. Suppose that you omitted an important part of the relationship. What effect would this have on your ability to use graphs as an illustrative tool? Consider the relationship between lemonade consumption and bottles of suntan lotion. The graph of the two variables would look something like Figure 2A.8.

Looking at Figure 2A.8, you would not necessarily know that something is misleading. However, when you stop to think about the relationship, you quickly recognize that the result is deceptive. Since the slope is positive, the graph indicates that there is a positive correlation between the number of bottles of suntan lotion used and the amount of lemonade people drink. At first glance this seems reasonable, since we associate suntan lotion and lemonade with summer activities. But the association is not **causal**, occurring when one variable influences the other. Using more suntan lotion does not cause people to drink more lemonade. It just so happens that when it is hot outside, more suntan lotion is used and more lemonade is consumed. In

Causality
occurs when one variable influences the other.

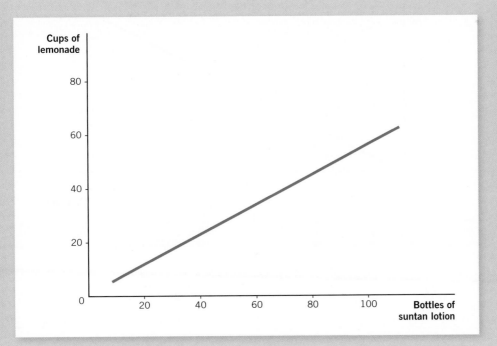

FIGURE 2A.8

Graph with an Omitted Variable
What looks like a strongly positive correlation is misleading. The demand for both lemonade and suntan lotion rises because the temperature rises, so the correlation between lemonade and suntan lotion use is deceptive, not informative.

this case, the causal factor is heat! The graph makes it look like the number of people using suntan lotion affects the amount of lemonade being consumed, when in fact they are not directly related.

Reverse causation
occurs when causation is incorrectly assigned among associated events.

Another possible mistake is known as **reverse causation**, which occurs when causation is incorrectly assigned among associated events. Suppose that in an effort to fight the AIDS epidemic in Africa, a research organization notes the correlation shown in Figure 2A.9.

After looking at the data, it is clear that as the number of doctors per 1,000 people goes up, so do rates of death from AIDS. The research organization puts out a press release claiming that doctors are responsible for increasing AIDS deaths, and the media hypes the discovery. But hold on! Maybe there happen to be more doctors in areas with high incidences of AIDS because that's where they are most needed. Coming to the correct conclusion about the data requires that we do more than simply look at the correlation.

FIGURE 2A.9

Reverse Causation and an Omitted Variable

At a quick glance, this figure should strike you as odd. AIDS deaths are associated with having more doctors in the area. But the doctors are there to help and treat people, not harm them. This is an example of reverse causation.

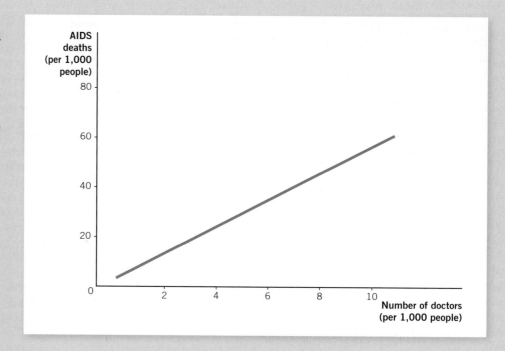

CONCEPTS YOU SHOULD KNOW

causality (p. 63)
negative correlation (p. 58)
positive correlation (p. 58)

reverse causation (p. 64)
scatterplot (p. 58)
slope (p. 59)

variable (p. 55)

STUDY PROBLEMS

1. The following table provides the price and the quantity demanded of apples (per week).

Price per Apple	Quantity Demanded
$0.25	10
$0.50	7
$0.75	4
$1.00	2
$1.25	1
$1.50	0

a. Plot the data provided in the table into a graph.
b. Is the relationship between the price of apples and the quantity demanded negative or positive?

✳ 2. In the following graph, calculate the value of the slope if the price rises from $20 to $40.

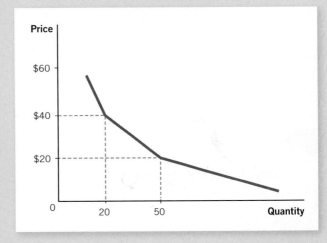

3. Explain the logical error in the following sentence: "As ice cream sales increase, the number of people who drown increases sharply. Therefore, ice cream causes drowning."

SOLVED PROBLEMS

2. The slope is calculated by using the formula:

$$\text{slope} = \frac{\text{change in } y}{\text{change in } x} = \frac{\$40 - \$20}{20 - 50} = \frac{\$20}{-30} = -0.6667$$

The Role of
MARKETS

PART 2

The Market at Work
Supply and Demand

Demand matters more than supply.

What do Starbucks, Nordstrom, and Microsoft have in common? If you guessed that they all have headquarters in Seattle, that's true. But even

more interesting is that each company supplies a product much in demand by consumers. Starbucks supplies coffee from coast to coast and seems to be everywhere someone wants a cup of coffee. Nordstrom, a giant retailer with hundreds of department stores, supplies fashion apparel to meet a broad spectrum of individual demand, from the basics to designer collections. Microsoft supplies software for customers all over the world. Demand for Microsoft products has made large fortunes for founder Bill Gates and the other investors in the company.

Notice the two recurring words in the previous paragraph: "supply" and "demand." These words are consistently used by economists when describing how an economy functions. Many people think that demand matters more than supply. This occurs because most people have much more experience as buyers than as sellers. Often our first instinct is to wonder how much something costs to buy rather than how much it costs to produce. This one-sided impression of the market undermines our ability to fully appreciate how prices are determined. To help correct this misconception, this chapter describes how markets work and the nature of competition. To shed light on the process, we will introduce the formal model of demand and supply. We will begin by looking at demand and supply separately. Then we will combine them to see how they interact to establish the market price and determine how much is produced.

Black Friday crush at Target.

BIG QUESTIONS

* **What are the fundamentals of markets?**
* **What determines demand?**
* **What determines supply?**
* **How do supply and demand shifts affect a market?**

What Are the Fundamentals of Markets?

Markets bring trading partners together to create order out of chaos. Companies supply goods and services, and customers want to obtain the goods and services that companies supply. In a **market economy**, resources are allocated among households and firms with little or no government interference. Adam Smith, the founder of modern economics, described the dynamic best: "It is not from the benevolence of the butcher, the brewer, or the baker, that we expect our dinner, but from their regard to their own interest." In other words, producers earn a living by selling the products that consumers want. Consumers are also motivated by self-interest; they must decide how to use their money to select the goods that they need or want the most. This process, which Adam Smith called the *invisible hand*, guides resources to their highest-valued use.

In a **market economy**, resources are allocated among households and firms with little or no government interference.

The exchange of goods and services in a market economy happens through prices that are established in markets. Those prices change according to the level of demand for a product and how much is supplied. For instance, hotel rates near Disney World are reduced in the fall when demand is low, and they peak in March near the week of Easter when spring break occurs. If spring break takes you to a ski resort instead, you will find lots of company and high prices. But if you are looking for an outdoor adventure during the summer, ski resorts have plenty of lodging available at great rates.

Peak season is expensive . . .

Similarly, many parents know how hard it is to find a reasonably priced hotel room in a college town on graduation weekend. Likewise, a pipeline break or unsettled political conditions in the Middle East can disrupt the supply of oil and cause the price of gasoline to spike overnight. When higher gas prices continue over a period of time, consumers respond by changing their driving habits or buying more fuel-efficient cars.

Why does all of this happen? Supply and demand tell the story. We will begin our exploration of supply and demand by looking at where they interact—in markets. The degree of control over the market price is the distinguishing feature between *competitive markets* and *imperfect markets*.

Competitive Markets

Buyers and sellers of a specific good or service come together to form a market. Formally, a market is a collection of buyers and sellers of a particular product or service. The buyers create the demand for the product, while the sellers produce the supply. It is the interaction of

. . . but off-season is a bargain.

the buyers and sellers in a market that establishes the price and the quantity produced of a particular good or the amount of a service offered.

Markets exist whenever goods and services are exchanged. Some markets are online, and others operate in traditional "brick and mortar" stores. Pike Place Market in Seattle is a collection of markets spread across nine acres. For over a hundred years, it has brought together buyers and sellers of fresh, organic, and specialty foods. Since there are a number of buyers and sellers for each type of product, we say that the markets at Pike Place are *competitive*. A **competitive market** is one in which there are so many buyers and sellers that each has only a small impact on the market price and output. In fact, the impact is so small that it is negligible.

At Pike Place Market, like other local produce markets, the goods sold are similar from vendor to vendor. Because each buyer and seller is small relative

> A **competitive market** exists when there are so many buyers and sellers that each has only a small impact on the market price and output.

to the whole market, no single buyer or seller has any influence over the market price. These two characteristics—similar goods and many participants—create a highly competitive market in which the price and quantity sold are determined by the market rather than by any one person or business.

To understand how this works, let's take a look at sales of salmon at Pike Place Market. On any given day, dozens of vendors sell salmon at this market. So, if a single vendor is absent or runs out of salmon, the quantity supplied that day will not be significantly altered—the remaining sellers will have no trouble filling the void. The same is true for those buying salmon—customers will have no trouble finding

One of many vendors at Pike Place Market

salmon at the remaining vendors. Whether a particular salmon buyer decides to show up on a given day makes little difference when hundreds of buyers visit the market each day. No single buyer or seller has any appreciable influence over the price that prevails in the salmon market. As a result, the market for salmon at Pike Place Market is a competitive one.

An **imperfect market** is one in which either the buyer or the seller has an influence on the market price.

A **monopoly** exists when a single company supplies the entire market for a particular good or service.

The **quantity demanded** is the amount of a good or service that buyers are willing and able to purchase at the current price.

The Empire State Building has the best view in New York City.

Imperfect Markets

Markets are not always competitive, though. An **imperfect market** is one in which either the buyer or the seller has an influence on the market price. For example, the Empire State Building affords a unique view of Manhattan. Not surprisingly, the cost of taking the elevator to the top of the building is not cheap. But many customers buy the tickets anyway because they have decided that the view is worth the price. The managers of the Empire State Building can set a high price for tickets because there is no other place in New York City with such a great view. From this, we see that when sellers produce goods and services that are different from their competitors', they gain some control, or leverage, over the price that they charge. The more unusual the product being sold, the more control the seller has over the price. When a seller has some control over the price, we say that the market is imperfect. Specialized products, such as popular video games, front-row concert tickets, or dinner reservations at a trendy restaurant, give the seller substantial pricing power.

In between the highly competitive environment at the Pike Place Market and markets characterized by a lack of competition, such as the Empire State Building with its iconic view, there are many other varieties of markets. Some, like the market for fast-food restaurants, are highly competitive but sell products that are not identical. Other businesses—for example, Comcast cable—function like *monopolies*. A **monopoly** exists when a single company supplies the entire market for a particular good or service. We'll talk a lot more about different market structures such as monopoly in later chapters. But even in imperfect markets, the forces of supply and demand have a significant influence on producer and consumer behavior. For the time being, we'll keep our analysis focused on supply and demand in competitive markets.

What Determines Demand?

Demand exists when an individual or a group wants something badly enough to pay or trade for it. How much an individual or a group actually buys will depend on the price. In economics, the amount of a good or service purchased at the current price is known as the **quantity demanded**.

The Invisible Hand

Why is the fish you want for dinner available in the store? It is because at each point in the economy's supply chain, the participants are concerned with their own profit. The process starts with the boat that catches the fish, then moves to the processing facility, to the truck, and finally to the store where the clerk sells the fish to you and me. At each step, the participant works to deliver the fish because they are acting in their own self-interest—matching supply to demand as if guided by an invisible hand.

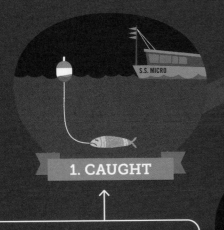

1. CAUGHT

2. PROCESSED

4. DISPLAYED

The fishing boat captain trolls the waters to earn an income. She doesn't care what happens to the fish so long as she gets paid when the boat offloads at the dock.

The trucker cares only about getting paid once the delivery is made. What's in the back of the rig is not important.

3. SHIPPED

5. PURCHASED

6. EATEN

The consumers care about freshness and price. They don't care to know the name of the fishing captain or trucker that brought the fish to the store for them to enjoy.

REVIEW QUESTIONS

- What if someone in the supply chain is not allowed to earn a profit? How will this affect their actions and the supply chain as a whole?

- If fewer Alaskan salmon are caught, what will happen the price of salmon?

PRACTICE WHAT YOU KNOW

Markets and the Nature of Competition

Question: Which of the following are competitive markets?

1. Gas stations at a busy interstate exit
2. A furniture store in an isolated small town
3. A fresh produce stand at a farmer's market

Is this a competitive market?

Answers

1. Because each gas station sells the same product and competes for the same customers, they often charge the same price. This is a competitive market. However, gas stations also differentiate themselves by offering many conveniences such as fast food, clean restrooms, ATM machines, and so forth. The result is that individual stations have some market power.

2. Residents would have to travel a significant distance to find another store. This allows the small-town store to charge more than other furniture stores. The furniture store has some monopoly power. This is not a competitive market.

3. Since consumers can buy fresh produce in season from many stands at a farmer's market, individual vendors have very little market pricing power. They must charge the same price as other vendors in order to attract customers. This is a competitive market.

When the price of a good increases, consumers often respond by purchasing less of the good or buying something else. For instance, many consumers who would buy salmon at $5.00 per pound would likely buy something else if the price rose to $20.00 per pound. Therefore, as price goes up, quantity demanded goes down. Similarly, as price goes down, quantity demanded goes up. This inverse relationship between the price and the quantity demanded is referred to as the *law of demand*. The **law of demand** states that, all other things being equal, the quantity demanded falls when the price rises, and the quantity demanded rises when the price falls. This holds true over a wide range of goods and settings.

The **law of demand** states that, all other things being equal, quantity demanded falls when prices rise, and rises when prices fall.

The Demand Curve

A table that shows the relationship between the price of a good and the quantity demanded is known as a **demand schedule**. Table 3.1 shows Meredith Grey's hypothetical demand schedule for salmon. When the price is $20.00 or more per pound, Meredith will not purchase any salmon. However, below $20.00 the amount that Meredith purchases is inversely related to the price. For instance, at a price of $10.00, Meredith's quantity demanded is 4 pounds per month. If the price rises to $12.50 per pound, she demands 3 pounds. Every time the price increases, Meredith buys less salmon. In contrast, every time the price falls, she buys more. If the price falls to zero, Meredith would demand 8 pounds. That is, even if the salmon is free, there is a limit to her demand because she would grow tired of eating the same thing.

A **demand schedule** is a table that shows the relationship between the price of a good and the quantity demanded.

The numbers in Meredith's demand schedule from Table 3.1 are plotted on a graph in Figure 3.1, known as a *demand curve*. A **demand curve** is a graph of the relationship between the prices in the demand schedule and the quantity demanded at those prices. For simplicity, the demand "curve" is often drawn as a straight line. Economists always place the independent variable, which is the price, on the *y* axis, and the dependent variable, which is the quantity demanded, on the *x* axis. The relationship between the price and the quantity demanded produces a downward-sloping curve. In Figure 3.1, we see that as the price rises from $0.00 to $20.00 along the *y* axis, the quantity demanded decreases from 8 to 0 pounds along the *x* axis.

A **demand curve** is a graph of the relationship between the prices in the demand schedule and the quantity demanded at those prices.

Market Demand

So far, we have studied individual demand, but markets comprise many different buyers. In this section, we will examine the collective demand of all of the buyers in a given market.

TABLE 3.1

Meredith's Demand Schedule for Salmon

Price of salmon (per pound)	Pounds of salmon demanded (per month)
$20.00	0
$17.50	1
$15.00	2
$12.50	3
$10.00	4
$ 7.50	5
$ 5.00	6
$ 2.50	7
$ 0.00	8

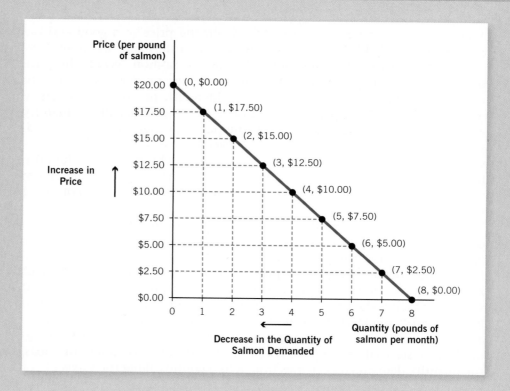

FIGURE 3.1

Meredith's Demand Curve for Salmon

Meredith's demand curve for salmon plots the data from Table 3.1. When the price of salmon is $10.00 per pound, she buys 4 pounds. If the price rises to $12.50 per pound, Meredith reduces the quantity that she buys to 3 pounds. The figure illustrates the law of demand by showing a negative relationship between price and the quantity demanded.

Market demand is the sum of all the individual quantities demanded by each buyer in the market at each price.

The **market demand** is the sum of all the individual quantities demanded by each buyer in a market at each price. During a typical day at Pike Place Market, over 100 individuals buy salmon. However, to make our analysis simpler, let's assume that our market consists of only two buyers, Derek and Meredith, each of whom enjoys eating salmon. Figure 3.2 shows individual demand schedules for the two people in this market, a combined market demand schedule, and the corresponding graphs. At a price of $10.00 per pound, Derek buys 2 pounds a month, while Meredith buys 4 pounds. To determine the market demand curve, we add Derek's 2 pounds to Meredith's 4 for a total of 6. As you can see in the table within Figure 3.2, by adding Derek and Meredith's demand we arrive at the total (that is, combined) market demand. The law of demand is shown on any demand curve with movements up or down the curve that reflect the effect of a change in price on the quantity demanded for the good or service. Only a change in price can cause a movement along a demand curve.

Shifts in the Demand Curve

We have examined the relationship between price and quantity demanded. This relationship, described by the law of demand, shows us that when price changes, consumers respond by altering the amount they purchase. But in addition to price, many other variables influence how much of a good or service is purchased. For instance, news about the possible risks or benefits associated with the consumption of a good or service can change overall demand.

FIGURE 3.2

Calculating Market Demand

To calculate the market demand for salmon, we add Derek's demand and Meredith's demand.

Price of salmon (per pound)	Derek's demand (per month)	Meredith's demand (per month)	Combined market demand
$20.00	0	0	0
$17.50	0	1	1
$15.00	1	2	3
$12.50	1	3	4
$10.00	2	4	6
$ 7.50	2	5	7
$ 5.00	3	6	9
$ 2.50	3	7	10
$ 0.00	4	8	12

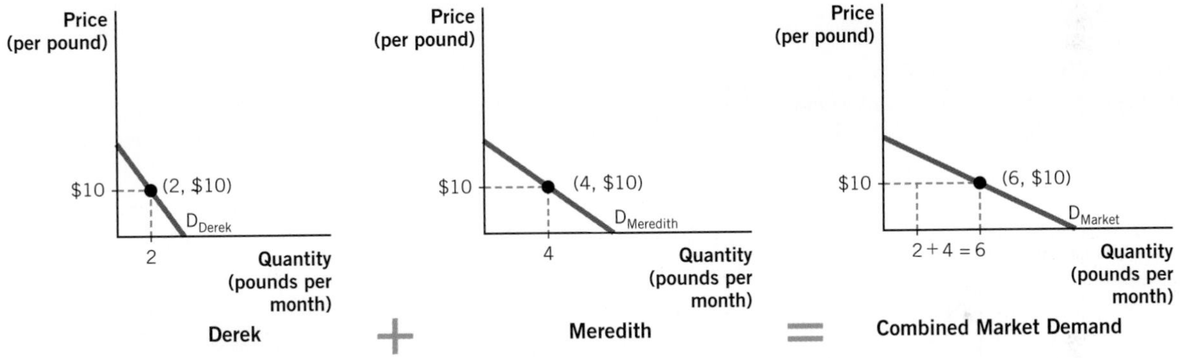

Price (per pound) — Quantity (pounds per month)

$10 — (2, $10) — D_{Derek} — 2

Derek

+

Price (per pound) — Quantity (pounds per month)

$10 — (4, $10) — $D_{Meredith}$ — 4

Meredith

=

Price (per pound) — Quantity (pounds per month)

$10 — (6, $10) — D_{Market} — $2+4=6$

Combined Market Demand

Suppose that the government issues a nationwide safety warning that cautions against eating cantaloupe because of a recent discovery of the *Listeria* bacteria in some melons. The government warning would cause consumers to buy fewer cantaloupes at any given price, and overall demand would decline. Looking at Figure 3.3, we see that an overall decline in demand will cause the entire demand curve to shift to the left of the original curve (which represents 6 cantaloupes), from D_1 to D_2. Note that though the price remains at $5 per cantaloupe, demand has moved from 6 melons to 3. Figure 3.3 also shows what does *not* cause a shift in demand curve: the price. The orange arrow along D_1 indicates that the quantity demanded will rise or fall in response to a price change. *A price change causes a movement along a given demand curve, but it cannot cause a shift in the demand curve.*

A decrease in overall demand causes the demand curve to shift to the left. What about when a variable causes overall demand to increase? Suppose that

If a new medical study indicates that eating more cantaloupe lowers cholesterol, would this finding cause a shift in demand or a slide along the demand curve?

the press has just announced the results of a medical study indicating that cantaloupe contains a natural substance that lowers cholesterol. Because of the newly discovered health benefits of cantaloupe, overall demand for it would increase. This increase in demand would shift the demand curve to the right, from D_1 to D_3, as Figure 3.3 shows.

In the example above, we saw that demand shifted because of changes in consumers' tastes and preferences. However, there are many different variables that can shift demand. These include changes in buyers' income, the price of related goods, changes in buyers' taste and preferences, expectations regarding the future price, and the number of buyers.

Figure 3.4 provides an overview of the variables or factors that can shift demand. The easiest way to keep all of these elements straight is to ask yourself a simple question: *Would this change cause me to buy more or less of the good?* If the change lowers your demand for the good, you shift the demand curve to the left. If the change increases your demand for the good, you shift the curve to the right.

FIGURE 3.3

A Shift in the Demand Curve

When the price changes, the quantity demanded changes along the existing demand curve in the direction of the orange arrow. A shift in the demand curve, indicated by the black arrows, occurs when something other than price changes.

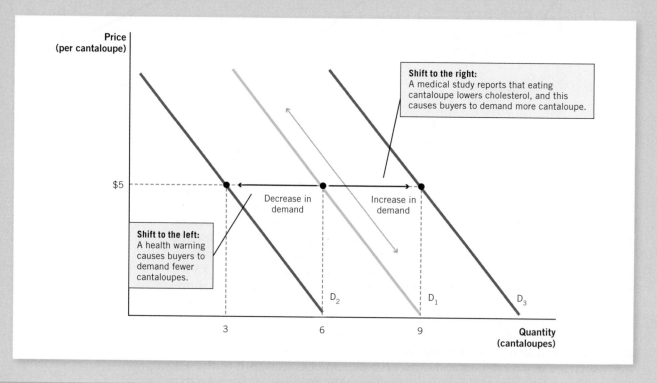

FIGURE 3.4

Factors That Shift the Demand Curve

The demand curve shifts to the left when a factor adversely affects—decreases—demand. The demand curve shifts to the right when a factor positively affects—increases—demand. (*Note*: a change in price does not cause a shift. Price changes cause slides along the demand curve.)

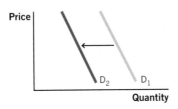

Factors That Shift Demand to the Left (Decrease Demand)

- Income falls (demand for a normal good).
- Income rises (demand for an inferior good).
- The price of a substitute good falls.
- The price of a complementary good rises.
- The good falls out of style.
- There is a belief that the future price of the good will decline.
- The number of buyers in the market falls.

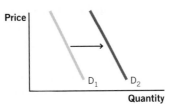

Factors That Shift Demand to the Right (Increase Demand)

- Income rises (demand for a normal good).
- Income falls (demand for an inferior good).
- The price of a substitute good rises.
- The price of a complementary good falls.
- The good is currently in style.
- There is a belief that the future price of the good will rise.
- The number of buyers in the market increases.

Changes in Income

When your income goes up, you have more to spend. Assuming that prices don't change, individuals with higher incomes are able to buy more of what they want. Similarly, when your income declines, your purchasing power, or how much you can afford, falls. In either case, the amount of income you make affects your overall demand.

When economists look at how consumers spend, they often differentiate between two types of goods: *normal* and *inferior*. A consumer will buy more of a **normal good** as his or her income goes up (assuming all other factors remain constant). An example of a normal good is a meal at a restaurant. When income goes up, the demand for restaurant meals increases and the demand curve shifts to the right. Similarly, if income falls and the demand for restaurant meals goes down, the demand curve shifts to the left.

While a consumer with an increase in income may purchase more of some things, the additional purchasing power will mean that he or she purchases less of other things, such as *inferior goods*. An **inferior good** is purchased out of necessity rather than choice. Examples include used cars as opposed to new cars, rooms in boarding houses as opposed to one's own apartment or house, and hamburger as opposed to filet mignon. As income goes up, consumers

Consumers buy more of a **normal good** as income rises, holding other things constant.

An **inferior good** is purchased out of necessity rather than choice.

buy less of an inferior good because they can afford something better. Within a specific product market, you can often find examples of inferior and normal goods in the form of different brands.

The Price of Related Goods

Complements
are two goods that are used together. When the price of a complementary good rises, the demand for the related good goes down.

Substitutes
are two goods that are used in place of each other. When the price of a substitute good rises, the quantity demanded falls and the demand for the related good goes up.

Another factor that can shift the demand curve is the price of related goods. Certain goods directly influence the demand for other goods. These goods are known as *complements* and *substitutes*. **Complements** are two goods that are used together. **Substitutes** are two goods that are used in place of each other.

Consider this pair of complements: color ink cartridges and photo paper. You need both to print a photo in color. What happens when the price of one— say, color ink cartridges—rises? As you would expect, the quantity demanded of ink cartridges goes down. But demand for its complement, photo paper, also goes down. This is because people are not likely to use one without the other.

Substitute goods work the opposite way. When the price of a substitute good increases, the quantity demanded declines and the demand for the alternative good increases. For example, if the price of the Nintendo Wii goes up and the price of Microsoft's Xbox remains unchanged, the demand for Xbox will increase while the quantity demanded of the Wii will decline.

Changes in Tastes and Preferences

In fashion, types of apparel go in and out of style quickly. Walk into Nordstrom or another clothing retailer, and you will see that fashion changes from season to season and year to year. For instance, what do you think of Madras shorts? They were popular 20 years ago and they may be popular again now, but it is safe to assume that in a few years Madras shorts will once again go out of style. While something is popular, demand increases. As soon as it falls out of favor, you can expect demand for it to return to its former level. Tastes and preferences can change quickly, and this fluctuation alters the demand for a particular good.

Though changes in fashion trends are usually purely subjective, other changes in preferences are often the result of new information about the goods and services that we buy. Recall our example of shifting demand for cantaloupe as the result of either the *Listeria* infection or new positive medical findings. This is one example of how information can influence consumers' preferences. Contamination would cause a decrease in demand because people would no longer care to eat cantaloupe. In contrast, if people learn that eating cantaloupe lowers cholesterol, their demand for the melon will go up.

Fashion faux pas, or *c'est magnifique?*

Expectations Regarding the Future Price

Have you ever waited to purchase a sweater because warm weather was right around the corner and you expected the price to come down? Conversely, have you ever purchased an airline ticket well in advance because you figured that the price would rise as the flight filled up? In both cases, expectations about the future influenced your current demand. If we expect a price to be higher tomorrow, we are likely to buy more today to beat the price increase. This leads to an increase in current demand. Likewise, if you expect a price to decline soon, you might delay your purchases to try to capitalize on a lower price in the future. An expectation of a lower price in the future will therefore decrease current demand.

PRACTICE WHAT YOU KNOW

Shift or Slide?

Cheap pizza or . . .

. . . cheap drinks?

Suppose that a local pizza place likes to run a "late-night special" after 11 p.m. The owners have contacted you for some advice. One of the owners tells you, "We want to increase the demand for our pizza." He proposes two marketing ideas to accomplish this:

1. Reduce the price of large pizzas.
2. Reduce the price of a complementary good—for example, offer two half-priced bottles or cans of soda with every large pizza ordered.

Question: What will you recommend?

Answer: First, consider why "late-night specials" exist in the first place. Since most people prefer to eat dinner early in the evening, the store has to encourage late-night patrons to buy pizzas by stimulating demand. "Specials" of all sorts are used during periods of low demand when regular prices would leave the establishment largely empty.

Next, look at what the question asks. The owners want to know which option would "increase demand" more. The question is very specific; it is looking for something that will increase (or shift) demand.

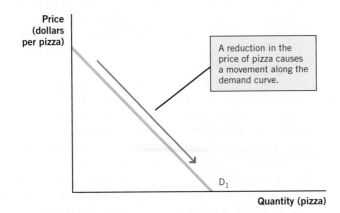

A reduction in the price of pizza causes a movement along the demand curve.

(CONTINUED)

(CONTINUED)

Consider the first option, a reduction in the price of pizzas. Let's look at this graphically (see above). A reduction in the price of a large pizza causes a movement along the demand curve, or a change in the quantity demanded.

Now consider the second option, a reduction in the price of a complementary good. Let's look at this graphically (see below). A reduction in the price of a complementary good (like soda) causes the entire demand curve to shift. This is the correct answer, since the question asks which marketing idea would increase (or shift) demand more.

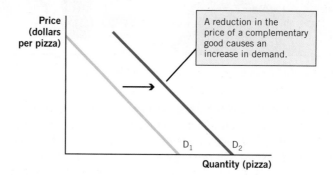

Recall that a reduction in the price of a complementary good shifts the demand curve to the right. This is the correct answer by definition! The other answer, cutting the price of pizzas, will cause an increase in the quantity demanded, or a movement along the existing demand curve.

If you move along a curve instead of shifting it, you will analyze the problem incorrectly.

The Number of Buyers

Recall that the market demand curve is the sum of all individual demand curves. Therefore, another way for the market demand to increase is for more individual buyers to enter the market. In the United States, we add 3 million people each year to our population through immigration and births. All those new people have needs and wants like the 300 million of us who are already here. Collectively, they add about 1% to the overall size of many existing markets on an annual basis.

The number of buyers also varies by age. Consider two markets—one for baby equipment, such as diapers, high chairs, and strollers, and the other for health care, including medicine, cancer treatments, hip replacement surgery, and nursing facilities. In countries with aging populations—for example, in Italy, where the birthrate has plummeted over several generations—the demand for baby equipment will decline and the demand for health care will expand. Therefore, demographic changes in society are another source of shifts in demand. In many markets, ranging from movie theater attendance to home ownership, population trends play an important role in determining whether the market is expanding or contracting.

Shifting the Demand Curve

The Hudsucker Proxy

This 1994 film chronicles the introduction of the hula hoop, a toy that set off one of the greatest fads in U.S. history. According to Wham-O, the manufacturer of the hoop, when the toy was first introduced in the late 1950s over 25 million were sold in four months.

One scene from the movie clearly illustrates the difference between movements along the demand curve and a shift of the entire demand curve.

The Hudsucker Corporation has decided to sell the hula hoop for $1.79. We see the toy-store owner leaning next to the front door waiting for customers to enter. But business is slow. The movie cuts to the president of the company, played by Tim Robbins, sitting behind a big desk waiting to hear about sales of the new toy. It is not doing well. So the store lowers the price, first to $1.59, then to $1.49, and so on, until finally the hula hoop is "free with any purchase." But even this is not enough to attract consumers, so the toy-store owner throws the unwanted hula hoops into the alley behind the store.

One of the unwanted toys rolls across the street and around the block before landing at the foot of a boy who is skipping school. He picks up the hula hoop and tries it out. He is a natural. When school lets out, a throng of students rounds the corner and sees him playing with the hula hoop. Suddenly, everyone wants a hula hoop and there is a run on the toy store. Now preferences have changed, and the overall demand has increased. The hula hoop craze is born. In economic terms, we can say that the increased demand has shifted the entire demand curve to the right. The toy store responds by ordering new hula hoops and raising the price to $3.99—the new market price after the increase, or shift, in demand.

This scene reminds us that changes in price cannot shift

How did the hula hoop craze start?

the demand curve. Shifts in demand can only happen when an outside event influences human behavior. The graph below uses demand curves to show us the effect.

First part of the scene: The price drops from $1.79 to "free with any purchase." Demand does not change—we only slide downward along the demand curve (D_1), resulting in a negligible increase in the quantity demanded.

Second part of the scene: The hula hoop craze begins and kids run to the toy store. The sudden change in behavior is evidence of a change in tastes, which shifts the demand curve to the right (D_2).

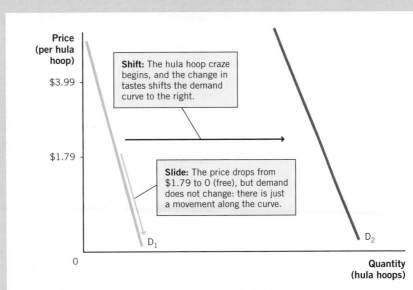

What Determines Supply?

Even though we have learned a great deal about demand, our understanding of markets is incomplete without also analyzing supply. Let's start by focusing on the behavior of producers interested in selling fresh salmon at Pike Place Market.

We have seen that with demand, price and output are negatively related. With supply, however, the price level and quantity supplied are positively related. For instance, few producers would sell salmon if the market price was $2.50 per pound, but many would sell it if the price was $20.00. (At $20.00, producers earn more profit than when the price they receive is $2.50.) The **quantity supplied** is the amount of a good or service that producers are willing and able to sell at the current price. Higher prices cause the quantity supplied to increase. Conversely, lower prices cause the quantity supplied to decrease.

The **quantity supplied** is the amount of a good or service that producers are willing and able to sell at the current price.

When price increases, producers often respond by offering more for sale. As price goes down, quantity supplied also goes down. This direct relationship between price and quantity supplied is referred to as the *law of supply*. The **law of supply** states that, all other things being equal, the quantity supplied increases when the price rises, and the quantity supplied falls when the price falls. This law holds true over a wide range of goods and settings.

The **law of supply** states that, all other things being equal, the quantity supplied of a good rises when the price of the good rises, and falls when the price of the good falls.

The Supply Curve

A **supply schedule** is a table that shows the relationship between the price of a good and the quantity supplied.

A **supply schedule** is a table that shows the relationship between the price of a good and the quantity supplied. The supply schedule for salmon in Table 3.2 shows how many pounds of salmon Sol Amon, owner of Pure Food Fish, would sell each month at different prices (Pure Food Fish is a fish stand that sells all kinds of freshly caught seafood). When the market price is $20.00 per pound, Sol is willing to sell 800 pounds. At $12.50, Sol's quantity offered is 500 pounds. If the price falls to $10.00, he offers 100 fewer pounds, or 400. Every time the price falls, Sol offers less salmon. This means he is constantly adjusting the amount he offers. As the price of salmon falls, so does Sol's profit from selling it. Since Sol's livelihood depends on selling seafood, he has to find a way to compensate for the lost income. So he might offer more cod instead.

Sol and the other seafood vendors must respond to price changes by adjusting what they offer for sale in the market. This is why Sol offers more salmon when the price rises, and less salmon when the price declines.

A **supply curve** is a graph of the relationship between the prices in the supply schedule and the quantity supplied at those prices.

When we plot the supply schedule in Table 3.2, we get the *supply curve* shown in Figure 3.5. A **supply curve** is a graph of the relationship between the prices in the supply schedule and the quantity supplied at those prices. As you can see in Figure 3.5, this relationship produces an upward-sloping curve. Sellers are more willing to supply the market when prices are high, since this generates more profits for the business. The upward-sloping curve means that the slope of the supply curve is positive, which illustrates a direct relationship between the price and the quantity offered for sale. For instance, when the price of salmon increases from $10.00 to $12.50 per pound, Pure Food Fish will increase the quantity it supplies to the market from 400 to 500 pounds.

TABLE 3.2

Pure Food Fish's Supply Schedule for Salmon

Price of salmon (per pound)	Pounds of salmon supplied (per month)
$20.00	800
$17.50	700
$15.00	600
$12.50	500
$10.00	400
$ 7.50	300
$ 5.00	200
$ 2.50	100
$ 0.00	0

FIGURE 3.5

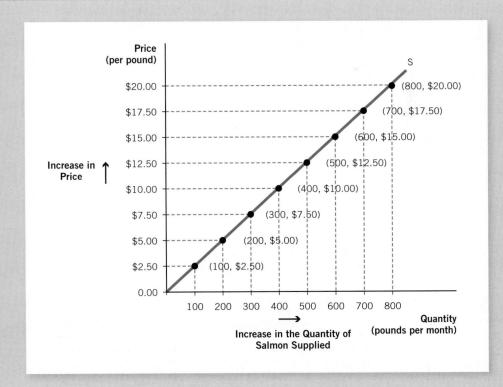

Pure Food Fish's Supply Curve for Salmon

Pure Food Fish's supply curve for salmon plots the data from Table 3.2. When the price of salmon is $10.00 per pound, Pure Food Fish supplies 400 pounds. If the price rises to $12.50 per pound, Pure Food Fish increases the quantity that it supplies to 500 pounds. The figure illustrates the law of supply by showing a positive relationship between price and the quantity supplied.

Market Supply

Market supply
is the sum of the quantities supplied by each seller in the market at each price.

Sol Amon is not the only vendor selling fish at the Pike Place Market. The **market supply** is the sum of the quantities supplied by each seller in the market at each price. However, to make our analysis simpler, let's assume that our market consists of just two sellers, City Fish and Pure Food Fish, each of which sells salmon. Figure 3.6 shows supply schedules for those two fish sellers and the combined, total-market supply schedule and the corresponding graphs.

Looking at the supply schedule (the table within the figure), you can see that at a price of $10.00 per pound, City Fish supplies 100 pounds of salmon, while Pure Food Fish supplies 400. To determine the total market supply, we add City Fish's 100 pounds to Pure Food Fish's 400 for a total market supply of 500.

FIGURE 3.6

Calculating Market Supply

Market supply is calculated by adding together the amount supplied by individual vendors. Each vendor's supply, listed in the second and third columns of the table, is illustrated graphically below. The total supply, shown in the last column of the table, is illustrated in the Combined Market Supply graph below.

Price of salmon (per pound)	City Fish's supply (per month)	Pure Food Fish's supply (per month)	Combined Market supply (pounds of salmon)
$20.00	200	800	1000
$17.50	175	700	875
$15.00	150	600	750
$12.50	125	500	625
$10.00	100	400	500
$ 7.50	75	300	375
$ 5.00	50	200	250
$ 2.50	25	100	125
$ 0.00	0	0	0

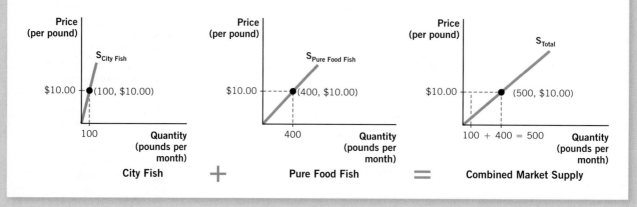

Shifts in the Supply Curve

When a variable other than the price changes, the entire supply curve shifts. For instance, suppose that beverage scientists at Starbucks discover a new way to brew a richer coffee at half the cost. The new process would increase the company's profits because its costs of supplying a cup of coffee would go down. The increased profits as a result of lower costs motivate Starbucks to sell more coffee and open new stores. Therefore, overall supply increases. Looking at Figure 3.7, we see that the supply curve shifts to the right of the original curve, from S_1 to S_2. Note that the retail price of coffee ($3 per cup) has not changed.

The first Starbucks opened in 1971 in Pike Place Market.

When we shift the curve, we assume that price is constant and that something else has changed. In this case, the new brewing process, which has reduced the cost of producing coffee, has stimulated additional supply.

FIGURE 3.7

A Shift in the Supply Curve

When price changes, the quantity supplied changes along the existing supply curve, illustrated here by the orange arrow. A shift in supply occurs when something other than price changes, illustrated by the black arrows.

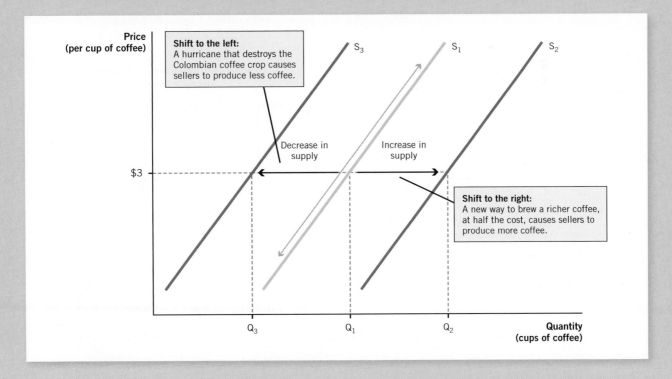

We have just seen that an increase in supply causes the supply curve to shift to the right. But what happens when a variable causes supply to decrease? Suppose that a hurricane devastates the coffee crop in Colombia and reduces world supply by 10% for that year. There is no way to make up for the destroyed coffee crop, and for the rest of the year at least, the quantity of coffee supplied will be less than the previous year. This decrease in supply shifts the supply curve in Figure 3.7 to the left, from S_1 to S_3.

Many variables can shift supply, but Figure 3.7 also reminds us of what does *not* cause a shift in supply: the price. Recall that price is the variable that causes the supply curve to slope upward. The orange arrow along S_1 indicates that the quantity supplied will rise or fall in response to a price change. *A price change causes a movement along the supply curve, not a shift in the curve.*

Factors that shift the supply curve include the cost of inputs, changes in technology and the production process, taxes and subsidies, the number of firms in the industry, and price expectations. Figure 3.8 provides an overview of these variables that shift the supply curve. The easiest way to keep them all straight is to ask yourself a simple question: *Would the change cause a*

FIGURE 3.8

Factors That Shift the Supply Curve

The supply curve shifts to the left when a factor negatively affects—decreases—supply. The supply curve shifts to the right when a factor positively affects—increases—supply. (*Note*: a change in price does not cause a shift. Price changes cause slides along the supply curve.)

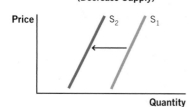

Factors That Shift Supply to the Left (Decrease Supply)

- The cost of an input rises.

- Business taxes increase or subsidies decrease.

- The number of sellers decreases.

- The price of the product is anticipated to rise in the future.

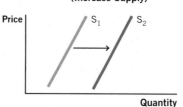

Factors That Shift Supply to the Right (Increase Supply)

- The cost of an input falls.

- Business taxes decrease or subsidies increase.

- The number of sellers increases.

- The price of the product is expected to fall in the future.

- The business deploys more efficient technology.

business to produce more or less of the good? If the change would lower the business's willingness to supply the good or service, the supply curve shifts to the left. If the change would increase the business's willingness to supply the good or service, the supply curve shifts to the right.

The Cost of Inputs

Inputs are resources used in the production process. Inputs can take a number of forms and may include workers, equipment, raw materials, buildings, and capital. Each of these resources is critical to the production process. When the prices of inputs change, so does the seller's profit margin. If the cost of inputs declines, profit margins improve. Improved profit margins make the firm more willing to supply the good. So, for example, if Starbucks is able to purchase coffee beans at a significantly reduced price, it will want to supply more coffee. Conversely, higher input costs reduce profits. For instance, at Starbucks, the salaries of store employees, or baristas as they are commonly called, are a large part of the production cost. An increase in the minimum wage would require Starbucks to pay its workers more. This would raise the cost of making coffee, cut into Starbucks' profits, and make Starbucks less willing to supply coffee at the same price.

Inputs
are resources used in the production process.

Changes in Technology or the Production Process

Technology encompasses knowledge that producers use to make their products. An improvement in technology enables a producer to increase output with the same resources or to produce a given level of output with fewer resources. For example, if a new espresso machine works twice as fast as the old technology, Starbucks could serve its customers more quickly, reduce long lines, and increase the number of sales it makes. As a result, Starbucks would be willing to produce and sell more espressos at each price in its established menu. In other words, if the producers of a good discover a new and improved technology or a better production process, there will be an increase in supply; the supply curve for the good will shift to the right.

Baristas' wages make up a large share of the cost of selling coffee.

Taxes and Subsidies

Taxes placed on suppliers are an added cost of doing business. For example, if property taxes are increased, this raises the cost of doing business. A firm may attempt to pass along the tax to consumers through higher prices, but this will discourage sales. In other cases, the firm will simply have to accept the taxes as an added cost of doing business. Either way, a tax makes the firm less profitable. Lower profits make the firm less willing to supply the product and, thus, shift the supply curve to the left. As a result, the overall supply declines.

The reverse is true for a subsidy, which is a payment made by the government to encourage the consumption or production of a good or service. Consider a hypothetical example where the government wants to promote flu shots for high-risk cohorts like the young and elderly. One approach would be to offer large subsidies to producers such as clinics and hospitals, offsetting the production costs of immunizing the targeted groups. The supply curve of immunizations greatly shifts to the right under the subsidy, so the price falls. As a result, vaccination rates increase over what they would be in a market where the price was determined solely by the intersection of the market demand and supply curves.

The Number of Firms in the Industry

We saw that when there were more total buyers, the demand curve shifted to the right. A similar dynamic happens with an increase in the number of sellers in an industry. Each additional firm that enters the market increases the available supply of a good. In graphic form, the supply curve shifts to the right to reflect the increased production. By the same reasoning, if the number of firms in the industry decreases, the supply curve will shift to the left.

Changes in the number of firms in a market are a regular part of business. For example, if a new pizza joint opens up nearby, more pizzas can be produced and supply expands. Conversely, if a pizza shop closes, the number of pizzas produced falls and supply contracts.

Price Expectations

A seller who expects a higher price for a product in the future may wish to delay sales until a time when it will bring a higher price. For instance, florists know that the demand for roses spikes on Valentine's Day and Mother's Day. Because of higher demand, they can charge higher prices. In order to be able to sell more flowers during the times of peak demand, many florists work longer hours and hire temporary employees. This allows them to make more deliveries and therefore increase their ability to supply flowers while the price is high.

Likewise, the expectation of lower prices in the future will cause sellers to offer more while prices are still relatively high. This is particularly noticeable in the electronics sector where newer—and much better—products are constantly being developed and released. Sellers know that their current offerings will soon be replaced by something better and that consumer demand for the existing technology will then plummet. This means that prices typically fall when a product has been on the market for a time. Since producers know that the price will fall, they supply as many of the new models as possible before the next wave of innovation cuts the price that they can charge.

ECONOMICS IN THE REAL WORLD

Why Do the Prices of New Electronics Always Drop?

The first personal computers released in the 1980s cost as much as $10,000. Today, a laptop computer can be purchased for less than $500. When a new technology emerges, prices are initially very high and then tend to fall rapidly. The first PCs created a profound change in the way people could work with information. Prior to the advent of the PC, complex programming could be done only on large mainframe computers that often took up as much space as a whole room. But at first only a few people could afford a PC. What makes emerging technology so expensive when it is first introduced and so inexpensive later in its life cycle? Supply and demand tell the story.

In the case of PCs and other recent technologies, both demand and supply increase through time. Demand increases as consumers find more uses for the new technology. An increase in demand, by itself, would ordinarily drive the price up. However, producers are eager to supply this new market and ramp up production quickly. Since the supply expands more rapidly than the demand, there is both an increase in the quantity sold and a lower price.

Differences in expectations account for some of the difference between the increase in supply and demand. Both parties expect the price to fall, and they react accordingly. Suppliers try to get their new products to market as quickly as possible—before the price starts to fall appreciably. Therefore, the willingness to supply the product expands quickly. Consumer demand is slower to pick up because consumers expect the price to fall. This expectation tempers their desire to buy the new technology immediately. The longer they wait, the lower the price will be. Therefore, demand does not increase as fast as the supply. ✳

Why did consumers pay $5,000 for this?

PRACTICE WHAT YOU KNOW

The Supply and Demand of Ice Cream

Question: Which of the following will increase the demand for ice cream?

a. A decrease in the price of the butterfat used to make ice cream

b. A decrease in the price of ice cream

c. An increase in the price of the milk used to make ice cream

d. An increase in the price of frozen yogurt, a substitute for ice cream

I scream, you scream, we all scream for ice cream.

Answer: If you answered b, you made a common mistake. A change in the price of a good cannot change overall market demand; it can only cause a movement along an existing curve. So, as important as price changes are, they are not the right answer. First, you need to look for an event that shifts the entire curve.

Answers a and c refer to the prices of butterfat and milk. Since these are the inputs of production for ice cream, a change in prices will shift the supply curve. That leaves answer d as the only possibility. Answer d is correct since the increase in the price of frozen yogurt will cause the consumer to look elsewhere. Consumers will substitute away from frozen yogurt and toward ice cream. This shift in consumer behavior will result in an increase in the demand for ice cream even though its price remains the same.

Question: Which of the following will decrease the supply of chocolate ice cream?

a. A medical report finding that consuming chocolate prevents cancer

b. A decrease in the price of chocolate ice cream

c. An increase in the price of chocolate, an ingredient used to make ice cream

d. An increase in the price of whipped cream, a complementary good

Answer: We have already seen that b cannot be the answer because a change in the price of the good cannot change supply; it can only cause a movement along an existing curve. Answers a and d would both cause a change in demand without affecting the supply curve. That leaves answer c as the only possibility. Chocolate is a necessary ingredient used in the production process. Whenever the price of an input rises, it squeezes profit margins, and this results in a decrease in supply at the existing price.

How Do Supply and Demand Shifts Affect a Market?

We have examined supply and demand separately. Now it is time to see how the two interact. The real power and potential of supply and demand analysis is in how well it predicts prices and output in the entire market.

Supply, Demand, and Equilibrium

Let's consider the market for salmon again. This example meets the conditions for a competitive market because the salmon sold by one vendor is essentially the same as the salmon sold by another, and there are many individual buyers.

In Figure 3.9, we see that when the price of salmon fillets is $10 per pound, consumers demand 500 pounds and producers supply 500. This is represented graphically at point E, known as the point of **equilibrium**, where the demand curve and the supply curve intersect. At this point, the two opposing forces of supply and demand are perfectly balanced.

Notice that at $10.00 per fillet, the quantity demanded equals the quantity supplied. At this price, and only this price, the entire supply of salmon in the market is sold. Moreover, every buyer who wants salmon is able to find some and every producer is able to sell his or her entire stock. We say that $10.00 is the **equilibrium price** because the quantity supplied equals the quantity demanded. The equilibrium price is also called the *market-clearing*

Equilibrium
occurs at the point where the demand curve and the supply curve intersect.

The **equilibrium price** is the price at which the quantity supplied is equal to the quantity demanded. This is also known as the *market-clearing price.*

FIGURE 3.9

The Salmon Market
At the equilibrium point, E, supply and demand are perfectly balanced. At prices above the equilibrium price, a surplus of goods exists, while at prices below the equilibrium price, a shortage of goods exists.

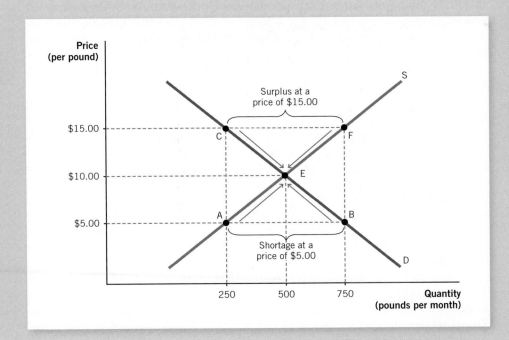

The **equilibrium quantity** is the amount at which the quantity supplied is equal to the quantity demanded.

The **law of supply and demand** states that the market price of any good will adjust to bring the quantity supplied and the quantity demanded into balance.

price, since this is the only price at which no surplus or shortage of the good exists. Similarly, there is also an **equilibrium quantity,** of 500 pounds, at which the quantity supplied equals the quantity demanded. When the market is in equilibrium, we sometimes say that *the market clears* or that *the price clears the market.* The equilibrium point has a special place in economics because movements away from that point throw the market out of balance. The equilibrium process is so powerful that it is often referred to as the *law of supply and demand.* According to the **law of supply and demand,** market prices adjust to bring the quantity supplied and the quantity demanded into balance.

Shortages and Surpluses

How does the market respond when it is not in equilibrium? Let's look at two other prices for salmon shown on the *y* axis in Figure 3.9: $5.00 and $15.00 per pound.

At a price of $5.00 per pound, salmon is quite attractive to buyers but not very profitable to sellers—the quantity demanded is 750 pounds, represented by point B on the demand curve (D). However, the quantity supplied, which is represented by point A on the supply curve (S), is only 250. So at $5.00 per pound there is an excess quantity of 500 pounds demanded. This excess demand creates disequilibrium in the market.

A **shortage** occurs whenever the quantity supplied is less than the quantity demanded.

When there is more demand for a product than sellers are willing or able to supply, we say there is a *shortage.* A **shortage** occurs whenever the quantity supplied is less than the quantity demanded. In our case, at a price of $5.00 there are three buyers for each pound of salmon. New shipments of salmon fly out the door. This is a strong signal for sellers to raise the price. As the market price increases in response to the shortage, sellers continue to increase the quantity that they offer. You can see this on the graph in Figure 3.9 by following the upward-sloping arrow from point A to point E. At the same time, as the price rises, buyers will demand an increasingly smaller quantity, represented by the upward-sloping arrow from point B to point E along the demand curve. Eventually, when the price reaches $10.00, the quantity supplied and the quantity demanded will be equal. The market will be in equilibrium.

What happens when the price is set above the equilibrium point—say, at $15.00 per pound? At this price, salmon is quite profitable for sellers but not very attractive to buyers. The quantity demanded, represented by point C on the demand curve, is 250 pounds. However, the quantity supplied, represented by point F on the supply curve, is 750. In other words, sellers provide 500 pounds more than buyers wish to purchase. This excess supply creates disequilibrium in the market. Any buyer who is willing to pay $15.00 for a pound of salmon can find some since there are three pounds available for every customer. This situation is known as a *surplus.* A **surplus,** or excess supply, occurs whenever the quantity supplied is greater than the quantity demanded.

A **surplus** occurs whenever the quantity supplied is greater than the quantity demanded.

When there is a surplus, sellers realize that salmon has been oversupplied. This is a strong signal to lower the price. As the market price decreases in response to the surplus, more buyers enter the market and purchase salmon. This is represented on the graph in Figure 3.9 by the downward-sloping arrow moving from point C to point E along the demand curve. At the same time, sellers reduce output, represented by the downward-sloping arrow moving

from point F to point E on the supply curve. As long as the surplus persists, the price will continue to fall. Eventually, the price will reach $10.00 per pound. At this point, the quantity supplied and the quantity demanded will be equal and the market will be in equilibrium again.

In competitive markets, surpluses and shortages are resolved through the process of price adjustment. Buyers who are unable to find enough salmon at $5.00 per pound compete to find the available stocks; this drives the price up. Likewise, businesses that cannot sell their product at $15.00 per pound must lower their prices to reduce inventories; this drives the price down.

Every seller and buyer has a vital role to play in the market. Venues like the Pike Place Market bring buyers and sellers together. Amazingly, all of this happens spontaneously, without the need for government planning to ensure an adequate supply of the goods that consumers need. You might think that a decentralized system would create chaos, but nothing could be further from the truth. Markets work because buyers and sellers can rapidly adjust to changes in prices. These adjustments bring balance. When markets were suppressed in communist command economies during the twentieth century, shortages were commonplace, in part because there was no market price system to signal that additional production was needed. (A command economy is one in which supply and price are regulated by the government rather than by market forces.) This led to the creation of many black markets (see Chapter 5).

How do markets respond to additional demand? In the case of the bowling cartoon shown above, the increase in demand comes from an unseen customer who wants to use a bowling lane already favored by another patron. An increase in the number of buyers causes an increase in demand. The lane is valued by two buyers, instead of just one, so the owner is contemplating a price increase! This is how markets work. Price is a mechanism to determine which buyer wants the good or service the most.

In summary, Figure 3.10 provides four examples of what happens when either the supply or the demand curve shifts. As you study these, you should develop a sense for how price and quantity are affected by changes in supply and demand. When one curve shifts, we can make a definitive statement about how price and quantity will change. In the chapter appendix that follows, we consider what happens when supply and demand change at the same time. There you will discover the challenges in simultaneously determining price and quantity when more than one variable changes.

FIGURE 3.10

Price and Quantity When Either Supply or Demand Changes

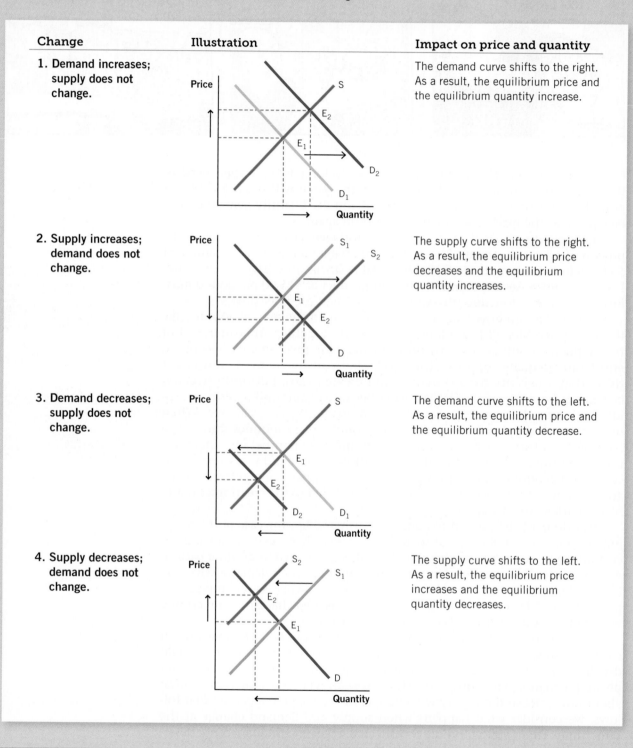

Change	Illustration	Impact on price and quantity
1. Demand increases; supply does not change.		The demand curve shifts to the right. As a result, the equilibrium price and the equilibrium quantity increase.
2. Supply increases; demand does not change.		The supply curve shifts to the right. As a result, the equilibrium price decreases and the equilibrium quantity increases.
3. Demand decreases; supply does not change.		The demand curve shifts to the left. As a result, the equilibrium price and the equilibrium quantity decrease.
4. Supply decreases; demand does not change.		The supply curve shifts to the left. As a result, the equilibrium price increases and the equilibrium quantity decreases.

Bringing Supply and Demand Together: Advice for Buying Your First Place

There is an old adage in real estate, "location, location, location." Why does location matter so much? Simple. Supply and demand. There are only so many places to live in any given location—that is the supply. The most desirable locations have many buyers who'd like to purchase in that area—that is the demand.

Consider for a moment all of the variables that can influence where you want to live. As you're shopping for your new home, you may want to consider proximity to where you work, your favorite restaurants, public transportation, and the best schools. You'll also want to pay attention to the crime rate, differences in local tax rates, traffic concerns, noise issues, and nearby zoning restrictions. In addition, many communities have restrictive covenants that limit how owners can use their property. Smart buyers determine how the covenants work and whether they would be happy to give up some freedom in order to maintain an attractive neighborhood. Finally, it is always a good idea to visit the neighborhood in the evening or on the weekend to meet your future neighbors before you buy. All of these variables determine the demand for any given property.

Once you've done your homework and settled on a neighborhood, you will find that property values can vary tremendously across very short distances. A home along a busy street may sell for half the price of a similar property that backs up to a quiet park a few blocks away. Properties near a subway line command a premium, as do properties with views or close access to major employers and amenities (such as parks, shopping centers, and places to eat). Here is the main point to remember, even if some of these things aren't important to you: when it comes time to sell, the location of the home will always matter. The number of potential buyers depends on the characteristics of your neighborhood and the size and condition of your property. If you want to be able to sell your place easily, you'll have to consider not only where you want to live now but who might want to live there later.

All of this discussion brings us back to supply and demand. The best locations are in short supply and high demand. The combination of low supply and high demand causes property values in those areas to rise. Likewise, less desirable locations have lower property values because demand is relatively low and the supply is relatively high. Since first-time buyers often have wish lists that far exceed their budgets, considering the costs and benefits will help you find the best available property.

There is a popular HGTV show called *Property Virgins* that follows first-time buyers through the process of buying their first home. If you have never seen the show, watching an episode is one of the best lessons in economics you'll ever get. Check it out, and remember that even though you may be new to buying property, you still can get a good deal if you use some basic economics to guide your decision.

Where you buy is more important than *what* you buy.

Conclusion

Does demand matter more than supply? As you have learned in this chapter, the answer is no. Demand and supply contribute equally to the functioning of markets. Five years from now, if someone asks you what you remember about your first course in economics, you will probably respond with two words, "supply" and "demand." These two opposing forces enable economists to model market behavior through prices. Prices help establish the market equilibrium, or the price at which supply and demand are in balance. At the equilibrium point, every good and service produced has a corresponding buyer who wants to purchase it. When the market is out of equilibrium, it causes a shortage or surplus. These conditions persist until buyers and sellers have a chance to adjust the quantity they demand and the quantity they supply, respectively. This refutes the misconception we noted at the beginning of the chapter.

In the next chapter, we will extend our understanding of supply and demand by examining how sensitive, or responsive, consumers and producers are to price changes. This will allow us to determine whether price changes have a big effect on behavior or not.

ANSWERING THE BIG QUESTIONS

What are the fundamentals of markets?

* A market consists of a group of buyers and sellers for a particular product or service.
* When competition is present, markets produce low prices.
* Not all markets are competitive. When suppliers have market power, markets are imperfect and prices are higher.

What determines demand?

* The law of demand states that there is an inverse relationship between the price and the amount that the consumer wishes to purchase.
* As a result of the law of demand, the demand curve is downward sloping.
* A price change causes a movement along the demand curve, not a shift in the curve.
* Changes in something other than price cause the demand curve to shift.

What determines supply?

* The law of supply states that there is a direct relationship between the price and the amount that is offered for sale.
* The supply curve is upward sloping.
* A price change causes a movement along the supply curve, not a shift in the curve.
* Changes in the prices of inputs, new technologies, taxes, subsidies, the number of sellers, and expectations about the future price all influence the location of the new supply curve and cause the original supply curve to shift.

How do supply and demand shifts affect a market?

* Supply and demand interact through the process of market coordination.
* Together, supply and demand create a process that leads to equilibrium, the balancing point between the two opposing forces. The market-clearing price and output are determined at the equilibrium point.
* When the price is above the equilibrium point, a surplus exists and inventories build up. This will cause suppliers to lower their price in an effort to sell the unwanted goods. The process continues until the equilibrium price is reached.
* When the price is below the equilibrium point, a shortage exists and inventories are depleted. This will cause suppliers to raise their price in order to ration the good. The price rises until the equilibrium point is reached.

CONCEPTS YOU SHOULD KNOW

competitive market (p. 71)
complements (p. 80)
demand curve (p. 75)
demand schedule (p. 75)
equilibrium (p. 93)
equilibrium price (p. 93)
equilibrium quantity (p. 94)
imperfect market (p. 72)
inferior good (p. 79)

inputs (p. 89)
law of demand (p. 74)
law of supply (p. 84)
law of supply and demand (p. 94)
market demand (p. 76)
market economy (p. 70)
market supply (p. 86)
monopoly (p. 72)
normal good (p. 79)

quantity demanded (p. 72)
quantity supplied (p. 84)
shortage (p. 94)
substitutes (p. 80)
supply curve (p. 84)
supply schedule (p. 84)
surplus (p. 94)

QUESTIONS FOR REVIEW

1. What is a competitive market, and how does it depend on the existence of many buyers and sellers?

2. Why does the demand curve slope downward?

3. Does a price change cause a movement along a demand curve or a shift of the entire curve? What factors cause the entire demand curve to shift?

4. Describe the difference between inferior and normal goods.

5. Why does the supply curve slope upward?

6. Does a price change cause a movement along a supply curve or a shift of the entire curve? What factors cause the entire supply curve to shift?

7. Describe the process that leads the market toward equilibrium.

8. What happens in a competitive market when the price is above or below the equilibrium price?

9. What roles do shortages and surpluses play in the market?

STUDY PROBLEMS (*solved at the end of the section)

1. In the song "Money, Money, Money" by ABBA, the lead singer, Anni-Frid Lyngstad, is tired of the hard work life requires and plans to marry a wealthy man. If she is successful, how would this marriage change the artist's demand for goods? How would it change her supply of labor? Illustrate both changes with supply and demand curves. Be sure to explain what is happening in the diagrams. (Note: the full lyrics for the song can be found by Googling the song title and ABBA. For inspiration, try listening to the song while you solve the problem!)

2. For each of the following scenarios, determine if there is an increase, a decrease, or neither an increase nor a decrease in demand for the good in *italics*.

   a. The price of *oranges* increases.
   b. The cost of producing *tires* increases.

   c. Samantha Brown, who is crazy about *air travel*, gets fired from her job.
   d. A local community has an unusually wet spring and a subsequent problem with mosquitos, which can be deterred with *citronella*.
   e. Many motorcycle enthusiasts enjoy riding without *helmets* (in states where this is permitted by law). The price of new motorcycles rises.

3. For each of the following scenarios, determine if there is an increase, a decrease, or neither an increase nor a decrease in supply for the good in *italics*.

   a. The price of *silver* increases.
   b. Growers of *tomatoes* experience an unusually good growing season.

c. New medical evidence reports that consumption of *organic products* reduces the incidence of cancer.

d. The wages of low-skill workers, a resource used to help produce *clothing*, increase.

e. The price of movie tickets, a substitute for *video rentals*, goes up.

4. Are laser pointers and cats complements or substitutes? (Not sure? Search for videos of cats and laser pointers online.) Discuss.

✳ 5. The market for ice cream has the following demand and supply schedules:

Price (per quart)	Quantity demanded (quarts)	Quantity supplied (quarts)
$2	100	30
$3	80	45
$4	60	60
$5	40	75
$6	20	90

a. What are the equilibrium price and equilibrium quantity in the ice cream market? Confirm your answer by graphing the demand and supply curves.

b. If the actual price was $3 per quart, what would drive the market toward equilibrium?

6. Starbucks Entertainment announced in a 2007 news release that Dave Matthews Band's *Live Trax* CD was available only at the company's coffee shops in the United States and Canada. The compilation features recordings of the band's performances dating back to 1995. Why would Starbucks and Dave Matthews have agreed to partner in this way? To come up with an answer, think about the nature of complementary goods and how both sides can benefit from this arrangement.

7. The Seattle Mariners wish to determine the equilibrium price for seats for each of the next two seasons. The supply of seats at the ballpark is fixed at 45,000.

Price (per seat)	Quantity demanded in year 1	Quantity demanded in year 2	Quantity supplied
$25	75,000	60,000	45,000
$30	60,000	55,000	45,000
$35	45,000	50,000	45,000
$40	30,000	45,000	45,000
$45	15,000	40,000	45,000

Draw the supply curve and each of the demand curves for years 1 and 2.

✳ 8. Demand and supply curves can also be represented with equations. Suppose that the quantity demanded, Q_D, is represented by the following equation:

$$Q_D = 90 - 2P$$

The quantity supplied, Q_S, is represented by the equation:

$$Q_S = P$$

a. Find the equilibrium price and quantity. Hint: Set $Q_D = Q_S$ and solve for the price, P, and then plug your result back into either of the original equations to find Q.

b. Suppose that the price is $20. Determine Q_D and Q_S.

c. At a price of $20, is there a surplus or a shortage in the market?

d. Given your answer in part c, will the price rise or fall in order to find the equilibrium point?

SOLVED PROBLEMS

5.

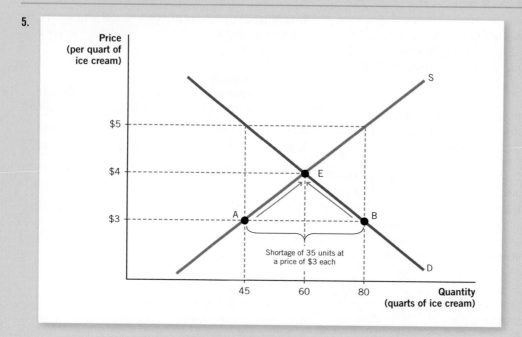

a. The equilibrium price is $4 and quantity is 60 units (quarts). The next step is to graph the curves. This is done above.

b. A shortage of 35 units of ice cream exists at $3; therefore, there is excess demand. Ice cream sellers will raise their price as long as excess demand exists. That is, as long as the price is below $4. It is not until $4 that the equilibrium point is reached and the shortage is resolved.

8. a. The first step is to set $Q_D = Q_S$. Doing so gives us $90 - 2P = P$. Solving for price, we find that $90 = 3P$, or $P = 30$. Once we know that $P = 30$, we can plug this value back into either of the original equations, $Q_D = 90 - 2P$ or $Q_S = P$. Beginning with Q_D, we get $90 - (30) = 90 - 60 = 30$, or we can plug it into $Q_S = P$, so $Q_S = 30$. Since we get a quantity of 30 for both Q_D and Q_S, we know that the price of $30 is correct.

b. In this part, we plug $20 into Q_D. This yields $90 - 2(20) = 50$. Now we plug $20 into Q_S. This yields 20.

c. Since $Q_D = 50$ and $Q_S = 20$, there is a shortage of 30 units.

d. Whenever there is a shortage of a good, the price will rise in order to find the equilibrium point.

Changes in Both Demand and Supply

We have considered what would happen if supply *or* demand changed. But life is often more complex than that. To provide a more realistic analysis, we need to examine what happens when supply and demand both shift at the same time. Doing this adds considerable uncertainty to the analysis.

Suppose that a major drought hits the northwest United States. The water shortage reduces both the amount of farmed salmon and the ability of wild salmon to spawn in streams and rivers. Figure 3A.1a shows the ensuing decline in the salmon supply, from point S progressively leftward, represented by the dotted supply curves. At the same time, a medical journal reports that people who consume at least four pounds of salmon a month live five years longer than those who consume an equal amount of cod. Figure 3A.1b shows the ensuing rise in the demand for salmon, from point D progressively rightward, represented by the dotted demand curves. This scenario leads to a two-fold change. Because of the water shortage, the supply of salmon shrinks. At the same time, new information about the health benefits of eating salmon causes demand for salmon to increase.

It is impossible to predict exactly what happens to the equilibrium point when both supply and demand are shifting. We can, however, determine a region where the resulting equilibrium point must reside.

In this situation, we have a simultaneous decrease in supply and increase in demand. Since we do not know the magnitude of the supply reduction or the demand increase, the overall effect on the equilibrium quantity cannot be determined. This result is evident in Figure 3A.1c, as illustrated by the purple region. The points where supply and demand cross within this area represent the set of possible new market equilibriums. Since each of the possible points of intersection in the purple region occurs at prices greater than $10.00 per pound, we know that the price must rise. However, the left half of the purple region produces equilibrium quantities less than 500 pounds of salmon, while the right half of the purple region results in equilibrium quantities greater than 500. Therefore, the equilibrium quantity may rise or fall.

The world we live in is complex, and often more than one variable will change simultaneously. When this occurs, it is not possible to be as definitive as when only one variable—supply or demand—changes. You should think of the new equilibrium, E_2, not as a single point but as a range of outcomes represented by the shaded purple area in Figure 3A.1c. Therefore, we cannot be exactly sure at what point the new price *and* quantity will settle. For a closer look at four possibilities, see Figure 3A.2.

FIGURE 3A.1

A Shift in Supply and Demand

When supply and demand both shift, the resulting equilibrium can no longer be identified as an exact point. This is seen in (c), which combines the supply shift in (a) with the demand shift in (b). When supply decreases and demand increases, the result is that the price must rise, but the equilibrium quantity can either rise or fall.

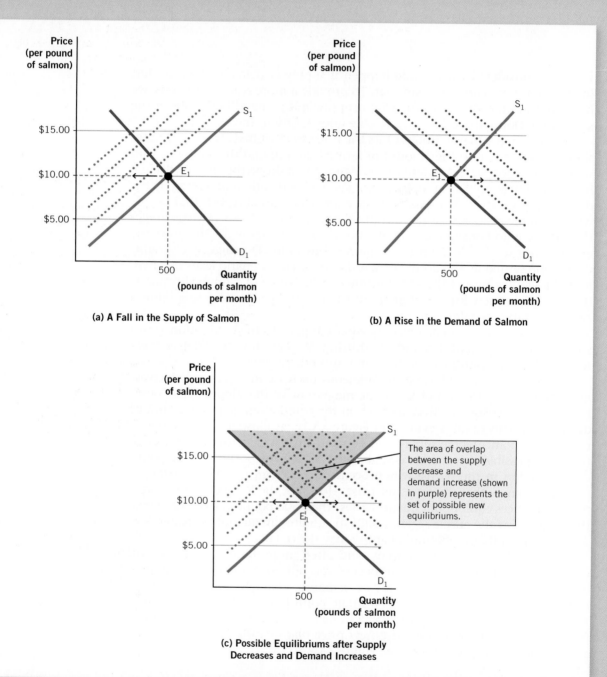

(a) A Fall in the Supply of Salmon

(b) A Rise in the Demand of Salmon

The area of overlap between the supply decrease and demand increase (shown in purple) represents the set of possible new equilibriums.

(c) Possible Equilibriums after Supply Decreases and Demand Increases

FIGURE 3A.2

Price and Quantity When Demand and Supply Both Change

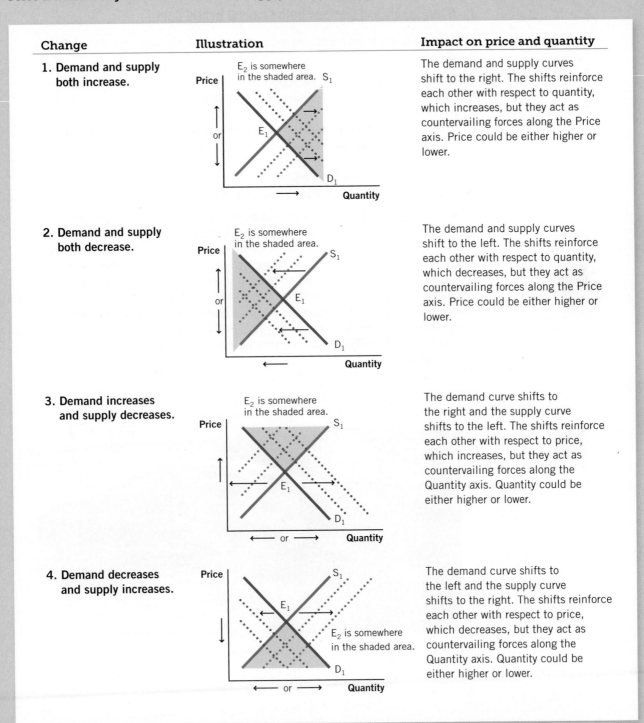

Change	Illustration	Impact on price and quantity
1. Demand and supply both increase.	E_2 is somewhere in the shaded area.	The demand and supply curves shift to the right. The shifts reinforce each other with respect to quantity, which increases, but they act as countervailing forces along the Price axis. Price could be either higher or lower.
2. Demand and supply both decrease.	E_2 is somewhere in the shaded area.	The demand and supply curves shift to the left. The shifts reinforce each other with respect to quantity, which decreases, but they act as countervailing forces along the Price axis. Price could be either higher or lower.
3. Demand increases and supply decreases.	E_2 is somewhere in the shaded area.	The demand curve shifts to the right and the supply curve shifts to the left. The shifts reinforce each other with respect to price, which increases, but they act as countervailing forces along the Quantity axis. Quantity could be either higher or lower.
4. Demand decreases and supply increases.	E_2 is somewhere in the shaded area.	The demand curve shifts to the left and the supply curve shifts to the right. The shifts reinforce each other with respect to price, which decreases, but they act as countervailing forces along the Quantity axis. Quantity could be either higher or lower.

PRACTICE WHAT YOU KNOW

When Supply and Demand Both Change: Hybrid Cars

Question: At lunch, two friends are engaged in a heated argument. Their exchange goes like this:

The first friend begins, "The supply of hybrid cars and the demand for hybrid cars will both increase, I'm sure of it. I'm also sure the price of hybrids will go down."

The second friend interrupts, "I agree with the first part of your statement, but I'm not sure about the price. In fact, I'm pretty sure that hybrid prices will rise."

They go back and forth endlessly, each unable to convince the other, so they turn to you for advice. What do you say to them?

Answer: Either of your friends could be correct. In this case, supply and demand both shift out to the right, so we know the quantity bought and sold will increase. However, an increase in supply would normally lower the price and an increase in demand would typically raise the price. Without knowing which of these two effects on price is stronger, you can't predict how it will change. The overall price will rise if the increase in demand is larger than the increase in supply. However, if the increase in supply is larger than the increase in demand, prices will fall. But your two friends don't know which condition will be true—so they're locked in an argument that no one can win!

Hybrid cars are becoming increasingly common.

QUESTIONS FOR REVIEW

1. What happens to price and quantity when supply and demand change at the same time?

2. Is there more than one potential equilibrium point when supply and demand change at the same time?

STUDY PROBLEM

1. Check out the short video at forbes .com called "Behind Rising Oil Prices," from 2008. (Search online for "behind rising oil prices forbes video.") Using your understanding of the market forces of supply and demand, explain how the market works. In your explanation, be sure to illustrate how increasing global demand for oil has impacted the equilibrium price.

Elasticity

Sellers charge the highest price possible.

Many students believe that sellers charge the highest price possible for their product or service—that if they can get one more penny from a customer, they will, even if it makes the customer angry.

It turns out that this belief is wrong. What *is* accurate is that producers charge the highest price they can while maintaining the goodwill of most of their customers.

In the previous chapter, we learned that demand and supply help regulate economic activity by balancing the interests of buyers and sellers. We also observed how that balance is achieved through prices. Higher prices cause the quantity supplied to rise and the quantity demanded to fall. In contrast, lower prices cause the quantity supplied to fall and the quantity demanded to rise. In this chapter, we will examine how decision-makers respond to differences in price and also to changes in income.

The concept of *elasticity*, or responsiveness to a change in market conditions, is a tool that we need to master in order to fully under-stand supply and demand. By utilizing elasticity in our analysis, our understanding will become much more precise. This will enable us to determine the impact of policy measures on the economy, to vote more intelligently, and even to make wiser day-to-day decisions, like whether or not to eat out. Elasticity will also help us to understand the faulty logic behind the common misconception that sellers charge the highest possible price.

How much do high prices affect the quantity demanded?

BIG QUESTIONS

* What is the price elasticity of demand, and what are its determinants?
* How do changes in income and the prices of other goods affect elasticity?
* What is the price elasticity of supply?
* How do the price elasticity of demand and supply relate to one another?

What Is the Price Elasticity of Demand, and What Are Its Determinants?

Trade-offs

Many things in life are replaceable, or have substitutes: boyfriends come and go, people rent DVDs instead of going out to a movie, and students ride their bikes to class instead of taking the bus. Pasta fans may prefer linguini to spaghetti or angel hair, but all three taste about the same and can be substituted for one another in a pinch. In cases such as pasta, where consumers can easily purchase a substitute, we think of demand as being *responsive*. That is, a small change in price will likely cause many people to switch from one good to another.

In contrast, many things in life are irreplaceable or have few good substitutes. Examples include electricity, a hospital emergency room visit, or water for a shower. A significant rise in price for any of these items would probably not cause you to consume a smaller quantity. If the price of electricity goes up, you might try to cut your usage somewhat, but you would probably not start generating your own power. Likewise, you could try to treat a serious medical crisis without a visit to the ER—but the consequences of making a mistake would be enormous. Even something as simple as taking a shower has few good alternatives. In cases such as these, we say that consumers are *unresponsive*, or unwilling to change their behavior, even when the price of the good or service changes.

The responsiveness of buyers and sellers to changes in price or income is known as **elasticity**. Elasticity is a useful concept because it allows us to measure how much consumers and producers change their behavior when prices or income changes. In the next section, we look at the factors that determine the elasticity of demand.

Your "average"-looking boyfriend is replaceable.

Determinants of the Price Elasticity of Demand

Elasticity is a measure of the responsiveness of buyers and sellers to changes in price or income.

The law of demand tells us that as price goes up, quantity demanded goes down, and as price goes down, quantity demanded goes up. In other words, there is an inverse relationship between the price of a good and the quantity demanded. Elasticity allows us to measure how much the quantity demanded changes in response to a change in price. If the quantity demanded changes significantly as a result of a price change, then demand is *elastic*. If the quantity demanded changes a small amount as a result of a price change, then demand is *inelastic*. For instance, if the price of a sweatshirt with a college logo rises by $10 and the quantity demanded falls by half, we'd say that the price elasticity of demand for those sweatshirts is elastic. But if the $10 rise in price results in very little or no change in the quantity demanded, the price elasticity of demand for the sweatshirts is inelastic. The **price elasticity of demand** measures the responsiveness of quantity demanded to a change in price.

> The **price elasticity of demand** is a measure of the responsiveness of quantity demanded to a change in price.

Four determinants play a crucial role in influencing whether demand will be elastic or inelastic. These are the existence of substitutes, the share of the budget spent on a good, whether the good is a necessity or a luxury good, and time.

The Existence of Substitutes

The most important determinant of price elasticity is the number of substitutes available. When substitutes are plentiful, market forces tilt in favor of the consumer. For example, imagine that an unexpected freeze in Florida reduces the supply of oranges. As a result, the supply of orange juice shifts to the left (picture the supply curves we discussed in Chapter 3), and since demand remains unchanged, the price of orange juice rises. However, the consumer of orange juice can find many good substitutes. Since cranberries, grapes, and apple crops are unaffected by the Florida freeze, prices for juices made with those fruits remain constant. This leads to a choice: a consumer could continue to buy orange juice at a higher price or choose to pay a lower price for a fruit juice that may not be his first choice but is nonetheless acceptable. Faced with higher orange juice prices, some consumers will switch. How quickly this switch takes place, and to what extent consumers are willing to replace one product with another, determines whether demand is elastic or inelastic. Since many substitutes for orange juice exist, the price elasticity of demand for orange juice is elastic, or responsive to price changes.

What if there are no good substitutes? Let's return to the Empire State Building example from the previous chapter. Where else in New York City can you get such an amazing view? Nowhere! Since the view is unbeatable, the number of close substitutes is small; this makes demand more inelastic, or less responsive to price changes.

To some degree, the price elasticity of demand depends on consumer preferences. For instance, sports fans are often willing to shell out big bucks to follow their passions. Amateur golfers can play the same courses that professional golfers do. But the opportunity to golf where the professionals play does not come cheaply. A round of golf at the Tournament Players Club at Sawgrass, a famous course in Florida, costs close to $300. Why are some golfers willing to pay that much? For an avid golfer with the financial means, the experience of living out the same shots seen on television tournaments is worth $300. In this case, demand is inelastic—the avid golfer does not view

Beyoncé is irreplaceable.

Saving 10% on this purchase amounts to a few pennies.

other golf courses as good substitutes. However, a less enthusiastic golfer, or one without the financial resources, is happy to golf on a less expensive course even if the pros don't play it on TV. When less expensive courses serve as good substitutes, the price tag makes demand elastic. Ultimately, whether demand is inelastic or elastic depends on the buyer's preferences and resources.

The Share of the Budget Spent on the Good

Despite the example above of an avid and affluent golfer willing to pay a premium fee to play at a famous golf course, in most cases fee is a critical element in determining what we can afford and what we will choose to buy. If you plan to purchase a 70-inch-screen TV, which can cost as much as $3,000, you will probably be willing to take the time to find the best deal. Because of the high cost, even a small-percentage discount in the price can cause a relatively large change in consumer demand. A "10% off sale" may not sound like much, but when purchasing a big-ticket item like a TV, it can mean hundreds of dollars in savings. In this case, the willingness to shop for the best deal indicates that the price matters, so demand is elastic.

The price elasticity of demand is much more inelastic for inexpensive items on sale. For example, if a candy bar is discounted 10%, the price falls by pennies. The savings from switching candy bars is not enough to make a difference in what you can afford elsewhere. Therefore, the incentive to switch is small. Most consumers still buy their favorite candy since the price difference is so insignificant. In this case, demand is inelastic because the savings gained by purchasing a less desirable candy bar are small in comparison to the consumer's budget.

Incentives

Necessities versus Luxury Goods

A big-screen TV and a candy bar are both luxury goods. You don't need to have either one. But some goods are necessities. For example, you have to pay your rent and water bill, purchase gasoline for your car, and eat. When a consumer purchases a necessity, he or she is generally thinking about the need, not the price. When the need trumps the price, we expect demand to be relatively inelastic. Therefore, the demand for things like soap, toothpaste, and heating oil all tend to have inelastic demand.

Time and the Adjustment Process

When the market price changes, consumers and sellers respond. But that response does not remain the same over time. As time passes, both consumers and sellers are able to find substitutes. To understand these different market responses, economists consider time in three distinct periods: the *immediate run*, the *short run*, and the *long run*.

Saving 10% on this purchase adds up to hundreds of dollars.

In the **immediate run**, there is no time for consumers to adjust their behavior. Consider the demand for gasoline. When the gas tank is empty, you have to stop at the nearest gas station and pay the posted price. Filling up as soon as possible is more important than driving around searching for the lowest price. Inelastic demand exists whenever price is secondary to the desire to attain a certain amount of the good. So in the case of an empty tank, the demand for gasoline is inelastic.

But what if your tank is not empty? The **short run** is a period of time when consumers can partially adjust their behavior (and, in this case, can search for a good deal on gas). When consumers have some time to make a purchase, they gain flexibility. This allows them to shop for lower prices at the pump, carpool to save gas, or even change how often they drive. In the short run, flexibility reduces the demand for expensive gasoline and makes consumer demand more elastic.

This is *not* the time to try and find cheap gas.

Finally, if we relax the time constraint completely, it is possible to use even less gasoline. The **long run** is a period of time when consumers have time to fully adjust to market conditions. If gasoline prices are high in the long run, consumers can relocate closer to work and purchase fuel-efficient cars. These changes further reduce the demand for gasoline. As a result of the flexibility that additional time gives the consumer, the demand for gasoline becomes more elastic.

In the **immediate run**, there is no time for consumers to adjust their behavior.

The **short run** is a period of time when consumers can partially adjust their behavior.

We have looked at four determinants of elasticity—substitutes, the share of the budget spent on the good, necessities versus luxury goods, and time. Each is significant, but the number of substitutes tends to be the most influential factor and dominates the others. Table 4.1 will help you develop your intuition about how different market situations influence the overall elasticity of demand.

The **long run** is a period of time when consumers have time to fully adjust to market conditions.

Computing the Price Elasticity of Demand

Until this point, our discussion of elasticity has been descriptive. However, to apply the concept of elasticity in decision-making, we need to be able to view it in a more quantitative way. For example, if the owner of a business is trying to decide whether to put a good on sale, he or she needs to be able to estimate how many new customers would purchase it at the sale price. Or if a government is considering a new tax, it needs to know how much revenue that tax would generate. These are questions about elasticity that we can evaluate by using a mathematical formula.

The Price Elasticity of Demand Formula

Let's begin with an example of a pizza shop. Consider an owner who is trying to attract more customers. For one month, he lowers the price by 10% and is pleased to find that sales jump by 30%.

Here is the formula for the price elasticity of demand (E_D):

$$\text{Price Elasticity of Demand} = E_D = \frac{\text{percentage change in the quantity demanded}}{\text{percentage change in price}} \quad \text{(Equation 4.1)}$$

TABLE 4.1		

Developing Intuition for the Price Elasticity of Demand

Example	Discussion	Overall elasticity
Football tickets for a true fan	Being able to watch a game live and go to pre- and post-game tailgates is a unique experience. For many fans, the experience of going to the game has few close substitutes; therefore, the demand is relatively inelastic.	Tends to be relatively inelastic
Assigned textbooks for a class	The information inside a textbook is valuable. Substitutes such as older editions and free online resources are not exactly the same. As a result, most students buy the required course materials. Acquiring the textbook is more important than the price paid; therefore, the demand is inelastic. The fact that a textbook is needed in the short run (for a few months while taking a class) also tends to make the demand inelastic.	Tends to be inelastic
A slice of pizza from Domino's	In most locations, many pizza competitors exist, so there are many close substitutes. This tends to make the demand for a particular brand of pizza elastic.	Tends to be elastic
A Silver Ford Escape	There are many styles, makes, and colors of cars to choose from. With large purchases, consumers are sensitive to smaller percentages of savings. Moreover, people typically plan their car purchases many months or years in advance. The combination of all these factors makes the demand for any particular model and color relatively elastic.	Tends to be relatively elastic

Using the data from the example, we can calculate the price elasticity of demand as follows:

$$\text{Price Elasticity of Demand} = E_D = \frac{30\%}{-10\%} = -3$$

What does that mean? The price elasticity of demand, −3 in this case, is expressed as a coefficient (3) with a specific sign (it has a minus in front of it). The coefficient, 3, tells us how much the quantity demanded changed (30%) compared to the price change (10%). In this case, the percentage change in the quantity demanded is three times the percentage change in the price. Whenever the percentage change in the quantity demanded is larger than the percentage change in price, we say that demand was elastic. In other words, the price drop made a big difference in how much pizza consumers purchased from the pizza shop. If the opposite occurs and a price drop makes a small difference in the quantity that consumers purchase, we say that demand was inelastic.

The negative (minus) sign in front of the coefficient is equally important. Recall that the law of demand describes an inverse relationship between the

Price Elasticity of Demand

Jingle All the Way

This amusing comedy from 1996 features two fathers who procrastinate until Christmas Eve to try to buy a Turbo Man action figure for their children for Christmas morning. It's the only present that their kids truly want from Santa. The problem is that almost every child in America feels the same way—demand has been so unexpectedly strong that the stock of toys has almost completely sold out, creating a short-term shortage. However, related items, like Turbo Man's pet, Booster, are readily available.

The two dads wind up at the Mall of America, where a toy store has received a last-minute shipment of Turbo Man, attracting a crowd of desperate shoppers. The store manager announces that the list price has doubled and institutes a lottery system to determine which customers will be able to buy the toy. The bedlam that this creates is evidence that the higher price did not decrease the demand for Turbo Man.

Based on this description, what can we say about the price elasticity of demand for Turbo Man and Booster?

Turbo Man: The toy is needed immediately, and because kids are clamoring for it specifically, no good substitutes exist. Also, because the cost of the toy is relatively small (as a share of a shopper's budget), people are not as concerned about getting a good deal. Demand is, therefore, relatively inelastic.

Is the demand for Turbo Man elastic or inelastic?

Booster: Without Turbo Man, Booster is just another toy. Therefore, the demand for Booster is much more elastic than for Turbo Man, since there are many good substitutes. We see this in the movie when the toy store manager informs the crowd that the store has plenty of Boosters available, and the throng yells back, "We don't want it!"

price of a good and the quantity demanded; when prices rise, the quantity demanded falls. The E_D coefficient reflects this inverse relationship with a negative sign. In other words, the pizza shop drops its price and consumers buy more pizza. Since pizza prices and consumer purchases of pizza generally move in opposite directions, the sign of the price elasticity of demand is almost always negative.

The Midpoint Method

The calculation above was simple because we looked at the change in price and the change in the quantity demanded from only one direction—that is, from a high price to a lower price. However, the complete—and proper—way to calculate elasticity is from both directions. Consider the following demand schedule (it doesn't matter what the product is):

Price	Quantity demanded
$12	20
$ 6	30

Let's calculate the elasticity of demand. If the price drops from $12 to $6—a drop of 50%—the quantity demanded increases from 20 to 30—a rise of 50%. Plugging the percentage changes into E_D yields

$$\text{Price Elasticity of Demand} = E_D = \frac{50\%}{-50\%} = -1.0$$

But if the price rises from $6 to $12—an increase of 100%—the quantity demanded falls from 30 to 20, or decreases by 33%. Plugging the percentage changes into E_D yields

$$\text{Price Elasticity of Demand} = E_D = \frac{-33\%}{100\%} = -0.33$$

This result occurs because percentage changes are usually calculated by using the initial value as the base, or reference point. In this example, we worked the problem two ways: by using $12 as the starting point and dropping the price to $6, and by using $6 as the starting point and increasing the price to $12. Even though we are measuring elasticity over the same range of values, the percentage changes are different.

To avoid this problem, economists use the *midpoint method*, which gives the same answer for the elasticity no matter what point you begin with. Equation 4.2 uses the midpoint method to express the price elasticity of demand. While this equation looks more complicated than Equation 4.1, it is not. The midpoint method merely specifies how to plug in the initial and ending values for price and the quantity to determine the percentage changes. Q_1 and P_1 are the initial values, and Q_2 and P_2 are the ending values.

(Equation 4.2)

$$E_D = \frac{\text{change in Q} \div \text{average value of Q}}{\text{change in P} \div \text{average value of P}}$$

$$= \frac{(Q_2 - Q_1) \div [(Q_1 + Q_2) \div 2]}{(P_2 - P_1) \div [(P_1 + P_2) \div 2]}$$

The change in the quantity demanded, $(Q_2 - Q_1)$, and the change in price, $(P_2 - P_1)$, are each divided by the average of the initial and ending values, or $[(Q_1 + Q_2) \div 2]$ and $[(P_1 + P_2) \div 2]$, to provide a way of calculating elasticity.

The midpoint method is the preferred method for solving elasticity problems. To see why this is the case, let's return to our pizza demand example.

If the price rises from $6 to $12, the quantity demanded falls from 30 to 20. Here the initial values are $P_1 = \$6$ and $Q_1 = 30$. The ending values are $P_2 = \$12$ and $Q_2 = 20$. Using the midpoint method:

$$E_D = \frac{(20 - 30) \div [(30 + 20) \div 2]}{(\$12 - \$6) \div [(\$12 + \$6) \div 2]} = \frac{-10 \div 25}{\$6 \div \$9} = -0.58$$

If the price falls from $12 to $6, quantity rises from 20 to 30. This time, the initial values are $P_1 = \$12$ and $Q_1 = 20$. The ending values are $P_2 = \$6$ and $Q_2 = 30$. Using the midpoint method:

$$E_D = \frac{(30 - 20) \div [(20 + 30) \div 2]}{(\$6 - \$12) \div [(\$6 + \$12) \div 2]} = \frac{10 \div 25}{-\$6 \div \$9} = -0.58$$

When we calculated the price elasticity of demand from $6 to $12 using $6 as the initial point, $E_D = -0.33$. Moving in the opposite direction, from $12 to $6, made $12 the initial reference point and $E_D = -1.0$. The midpoint method shown above splits the difference and uses $9 and 25 pizzas as the midpoints. This approach makes the calculation of the elasticity coefficient the same, -0.58, no matter what direction the price moves. Therefore, economists use the midpoint method to standardize the results. So, using the midpoint method, we arrived at an elasticity coefficient of -0.58, which is between 0 and -1. What does that mean? In this case, the percentage change in the quantity demanded is less than the percentage change in the price. Whenever the percentage change in the quantity demanded is smaller than the percentage change in price, we say that demand is inelastic. In other words, the price drop does not make a big difference in how much pizza consumers purchased from the pizza shop. When the elasticity coefficient is less than -1, the opposite is true, and we say that demand is elastic.

Graphing the Price Elasticity of Demand

Visualizing elasticity graphically helps us understand the relationship between elastic and inelastic demand. Figure 4.1 shows elasticity graphically. As demand becomes increasingly elastic, or responsive to price changes, the demand curve flattens.

Figure 4.1a depicts the price elasticity for pet care. Many pet owners report that they would pay any amount of money to help their sick or injured pet get better. (Of course, pet care is not perfectly inelastic, because there is certainly a price beyond which some pet owners would not or could not pay; but for illustrative purposes, let's say that pet care *is* perfectly elastic.) For these pet owners, the demand curve is a vertical line. If you look along the Quantity axis, you will see that the quantity of pet care demanded (Q_D) remains constant no matter what it costs. At

For many pet owners, the demand for veterinary care is perfectly inelastic.

FIGURE 4.1

Elasticity and the Demand Curve

For any given price change across two demand curves, demand will be more elastic on the flatter demand curve than on the steeper demand curve. In (a), the demand is perfectly inelastic, so the price does not matter. In (b), the demand is relatively inelastic, so the price is less important than the quantity purchased. In (c), the demand is relatively elastic, so the price matters more than quantity. In (d), the demand is perfectly elastic, so price is all that matters.

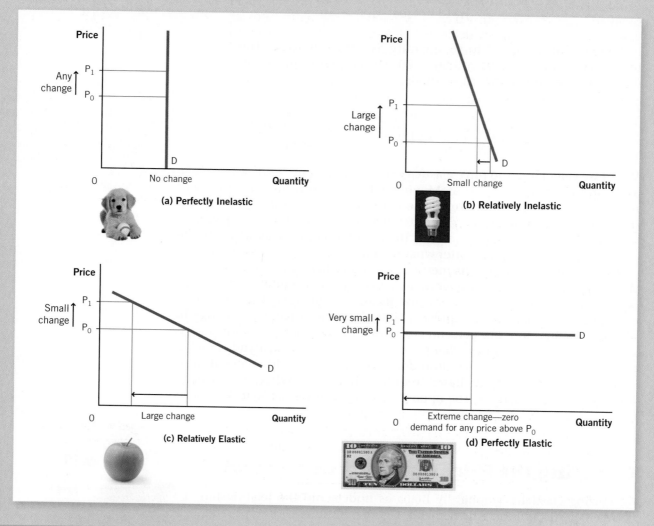

(a) Perfectly Inelastic

(b) Relatively Inelastic

(c) Relatively Elastic

(d) Perfectly Elastic

the same time, the price increases from P_0 to P_1. We can calculate the price elasticity coefficient as follows:

$$E_{\text{pet care}} = \frac{\text{percentage change in } Q_D}{\text{percentage change in P}} = \frac{0}{\text{percentage change in P}} = 0$$

When zero is in the numerator, we know that the answer will be zero no matter what we find in the denominator. This makes sense. Many pet owners will try to help their pet feel better no matter what the cost, so we can say that their demand is *perfectly inelastic*. This means that value of E_D will always be zero.

Moving on to Figure 4.1b, we consider the demand for electricity. Whereas many pet owners will not change their consumption of health care for their pet no matter what the cost, consumers of electricity will modify their use of electricity in response to price changes. When the price of electricity goes up, they will use less, and when it goes down, they will use more. But since living without electricity is not practical, using less is a matter of making relatively small lifestyle adjustments—buying energy-efficient light bulbs or turning down the thermostat a few degrees. As a result, the demand curve in 4.1b is relatively steep, but not completely vertical as it was in 4.1a.

When the variation on the Quantity axis is small compared to the variation on the Price axis, the price elasticity is *relatively inelastic*. Plugging these changes into the elasticity formula, we get

$$E_{electricity} = \frac{\text{percentage change in } Q_D}{\text{percentage change in P}} = \frac{\text{small change}}{\text{large change}}$$

The demand for electricity is relatively inelastic.

Recall that the law of demand describes an inverse relationship between price and output. Therefore, the changes along the Price and Quantity axes will always be in the opposite direction. A price elasticity of zero tells us there is no change in the quantity demanded when price changes. So when demand is relatively inelastic, the price elasticity of demand must be relatively close to zero. The easiest way to think about this is to consider how a 10% increase in electric rates works for most households. How much less electricity would you use? The answer for most people would be a little less, but not 10% less. You can adjust your thermostat, but you still need electricity to run your appliances and lights. When the price changes more than quantity changes, there is a larger change in the denominator. Therefore, the price elasticity of demand is between 0 and −1 when demand is relatively inelastic.

In Figure 4.1c, we consider an apple. Since there are many good substitutes for an apple, the demand for an apple is *relatively elastic*. The flexibility of consumer demand for apples is illustrated by the degree of responsiveness we see along the Quantity axis relative to the change exhibited along the Price axis. We can observe this by noting that a relatively elastic demand curve is flatter than an inelastic demand curve. So, whereas perfectly inelastic demand shows no change in demand with an increase in price, and relatively inelastic demand shows a small change in demand with an increase in price, relatively elastic demand shows a large change. Placing this information into the elasticity formula gives us

The demand for an apple is relatively elastic.

$$E_{apples} = \frac{\text{percentage change in } Q_D}{\text{percentage change in P}} = \frac{\text{large change}}{\text{small change}}$$

Now the numerator—the percentage change in Q_D—is large, and the denominator—the percentage change in P—is small. E_D is less than −1. Recall that the sign must be negative, since there is an inverse relationship between price and the quantity demanded. As the price elasticity of demand moves farther away from zero, the consumer becomes more responsive to price change. Since many other

The demand for a $10 bill is perfectly elastic.

fruits are good substitutes for apples, a small change in the price of apples will have a large change in the quantity demanded.

Figure 4.1d provides an interesting example: the demand for a $10 bill. Would you pay $11.00 to get a $10 bill? No. Would you pay $10.01 for a $10 bill? Still no. However, when the price drops to $10.00, you will probably become indifferent. Most of us would exchange a $10 bill for two $5 bills. The real magic here occurs when the price drops to $9.99. How many $10 bills would you buy if you could buy them for $9.99 or less? The answer: as many as possible! This is exactly what happens in currency markets, where small differences among currency prices around the globe motivate traders to buy and sell large quantities of currency and clear a small profit on the difference in exchange rates. This extreme form of price sensitivity is illustrated by a perfectly horizontal demand curve, which means that demand is *perfectly elastic*. Solving for the elasticity yields

$$E_{\$10\ bill} = \frac{\text{percentage change in Q}_D}{\text{percentage change in P}} = \frac{\text{nearly infinite change}}{\text{very small (\$0.01) change}}$$

We can think of this very small price change, from $10.00 to $9.99, as having essentially an unlimited effect on the quantity of $10 bills demanded. Traders go from being uninterested in trading at $10.00 to seeking to buy as many $10 bills as possible when the price drops to $9.99. As a result, the price elasticity of demand approaches negative infinity ($-\infty$).

There is a fifth type of elasticity, not depicted in Figure 4.1. *Unitary elasticity* is the special name that describes the situation in which elasticity is neither elastic nor inelastic. This occurs when the E_D is exactly -1, and it happens when the percentage change in price is exactly equal to the percentage change in quantity demanded. This characteristic of unitary elasticity will be important when we discuss the connection between elasticity and total revenue later in this chapter. You're probably wondering what an example of a unitary good would be. Relax. It is impossible to find a good that has a price elasticity of exactly -1 at all price points. It is enough to know that unitary demand represents the crossover from elastic to inelastic demand.

Now that you have had a chance to look at all four panels in Figure 4.1, here is a handy mnemonic that you can use to keep the difference between inelastic and elastic demand straight.

$$\text{I} = \text{inelastic and } \text{E} = \text{elastic}$$

The "I" in the word "inelastic" is vertical, just like the inelastic relationships we examined in Figure 4.1. Likewise, the letter "E" has three horizontal lines to remind us that elastic demand is flat.

Finally, it is possible to pair the elasticity coefficients with an interpretation of how much price matters. You can see this in Table 4.2. When price does not matter, demand is perfectly inelastic (denoted by the coefficient of zero). Conversely, when price is the only thing that matters, demand becomes

TABLE 4.2

The Relationship between Price Elasticity of Demand and Price

Elasticity	E_D coefficient	Interpretation	Example in Figure 4.1
Perfectly inelastic	$E_D = 0$	Price does not matter.	Saving your pet
Relatively inelastic	$0 > E_D > -1$	Price is less important than the quantity purchased.	Electricity
Unitary	$E_D = -1$	Price and quantity are equally important.	
Relatively elastic	$-1 > E_D > -\infty$	Price is more important than the quantity purchased.	An apple
Perfectly elastic	$E_D \rightarrow -\infty$	Price is everything.	A $10 bill

perfectly elastic (denoted by $-\infty$). In between these two extremes, the extent to which price matters determines whether demand is relatively inelastic, unitary, or relatively elastic.

Time, Elasticity, and the Demand Curve

We have already seen that increased time makes demand more elastic. Figure 4.2 shows this graphically. When the price rises from P_1 to P_2, consumers cannot immediately avoid the price increase. For example, if your gas tank is almost empty, you must purchase gas at the new price. Over a slightly longer time horizon—the short run—consumers are more flexible and are able to drive less in order to avoid higher-priced gasoline. This means that in the short run, consumption declines to Q_2. In the long run, when consumers have time to purchase a more fuel-efficient vehicle or move closer to work, purchases fall even further. As a result, the demand curve continues to flatten and the quantity demanded falls to Q_3.

Slope and Elasticity

In this section, we pause to make sure that you understand what you are observing in the figures. The demand curves shown in Figures 4.1 and 4.2 are straight lines, and therefore they have a constant slope, or steepness. (A refresher on slope is part of the appendix to Chapter 2.) So, looking at

Figures 4.1 and 4.2, you might think that slope is the same as the price elasticity. But slope does not equal elasticity.

Consider, for example, a trip to Starbucks. Would you buy a tall skinny latte if it cost $10? How about $7? What about $5? Say you decide to buy the skinny latte because the price drops from $5 to $4. In this case, a small price change, a drop from $5 to $4, causes you to make the purchase. You can say the demand for skinny lattes is relatively elastic. Now look at Figure 4.3, which shows a demand curve for skinny lattes. At $5 the consumer purchases 0 lattes, at $4 she purchases 1 latte, at $3 she purchases 2, and she continues to buy one additional latte with each $1 drop in price. As you progress downward along the demand curve, price becomes less of an inhibiting factor and, as a result, the price elasticity of demand slowly becomes more inelastic. Notice that the slope of a linear demand curve is constant. However, when we calculate the price elasticity of demand between the various points in Figure 4.3, it becomes clear that demand is increasingly inelastic as we move down the demand curve. You can see this in the change in E_D from -9.1 to -0.1.

FIGURE 4.2

Elasticity and the Demand Curve over Time

Increased time acts to make demand more elastic. When the price rises from P_1 to P_2, consumers are unable to avoid the price increase in the immediate run (D_1). In the short run (D_2), consumers become more flexible and consumption declines to Q_2. Eventually, in the long run (D_3), there is time to make lifestyle changes that further reduce consumption. As a result, the demand curve continues to flatten and the quantity demanded falls to Q_3 in response to higher prices.

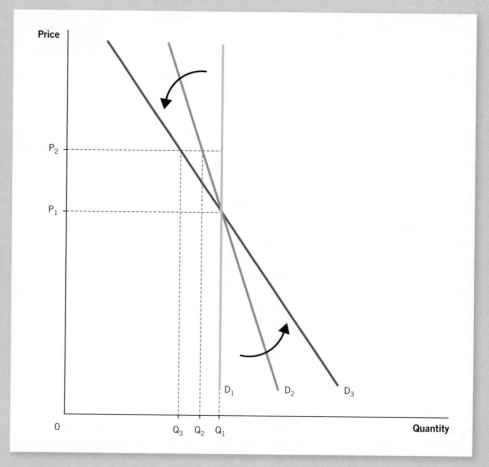

Perfectly inelastic demand would exist if the elasticity coefficient reached zero. Recall that a value of zero means that there is no change in the quantity demanded as a result of a price change. Therefore, values close to zero reflect inelastic demand, while those farther away reflect more elastic demand.

Price Elasticity of Demand and Total Revenue

Understanding the price elasticity of demand for the product you sell is important when running a business. The responsiveness of consumers to price changes determines whether a firm would be better off raising or lowering its price for a given product. In this section, we explore the relationship between the price elasticity of demand and a firm's total revenue.

But first we need to understand the concept of *total revenue*. **Total revenue** is the amount that consumers pay and sellers receive for a good. It is calculated by multiplying the price of the good by the quantity of the good that

> **Total revenue** is the amount that consumers pay and sellers receive for a good.

FIGURE 4.3

The Difference between Slope and Elasticity

Along any straight demand curve, the price elasticity of demand (E_D) is not constant. You can see this by noting how the price elasticity of demand changes from highly elastic near the top of the demand curve to highly inelastic near the bottom of the curve.

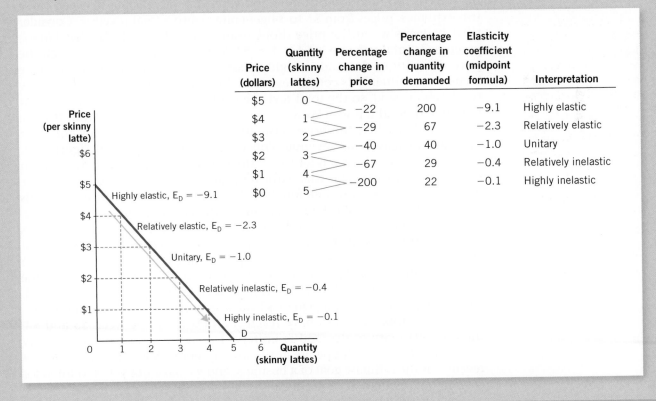

Price (dollars)	Quantity (skinny lattes)	Percentage change in price	Percentage change in quantity demanded	Elasticity coefficient (midpoint formula)	Interpretation
$5	0				
		−22	200	−9.1	Highly elastic
$4	1				
		−29	67	−2.3	Relatively elastic
$3	2				
		−40	40	−1.0	Unitary
$2	3				
		−67	29	−0.4	Relatively inelastic
$1	4				
		−200	22	−0.1	Highly inelastic
$0	5				

TABLE 4.3

The Price Elasticity of Demand and Total Revenue

Price (P) (per skinny latte)	Quantity (Q) (skinny lattes)	Total revenue P × Q	Percentage change in price	Percentage change in quantity	Elasticity coefficient	Interpretation
$5	0	$0				
			−22	200	−9.1	Highly elastic
$4	1	$4				
			−29	67	−2.3	Relatively elastic
$3	2	$6				
			−40	40	−1.0	Unitary
$2	3	$6				
			−67	29	−0.4	Relatively inelastic
$1	4	$4				
			−200	22	−0.1	Highly inelastic
$0	5	$0				

Trade-offs

is sold. Table 4.3 reproduces the table from Figure 4.3 and adds a column for the total revenue. We find the total revenue by multiplying the price of a tall skinny latte by the quantity purchased.

After calculating total revenue at each price, we can look at the column of elasticity coefficients for a possible relationship. When we link revenues with the price elasticity of demand, a trade-off emerges. (This occurs because total revenue and elasticity relate to price differently. Total revenue involves multiplying the price times the quantity, while elasticity involves dividing the change in quantity demanded by the price.) Total revenue is zero when the price is too high ($5 or more) and when the price is $0. Between these two extremes, prices from $1 to $4 generate positive total revenue. Consider what happens when the price drops from $5 to $4. At $4, the first latte is purchased. Total revenue is $4 × 1 = $4. This is also the range at which the price elasticity of demand is highly elastic. As a result, lowering the price increases revenue. This continues when the price drops from $4 to $3. Now two lattes are sold, so the total revenue continues to rise to $3 × 2 = $6. At the same time, the price elasticity of demand remains elastic. From this we conclude that when the price elasticity of demand is elastic, lowering the price will increase total revenue. This relationship is shown in Figure 4.4a. By lowering the price from $4 to $3, the business has generated $2 more in revenue. But to generate this extra revenue, the business has lowered the price from $4 to $3 and therefore has given up $1 for each unit it sells. This is represented by the red-shaded area under the demand curve in Figure 4.4a.

When the price drops from $3 to $2, the total revenue stays at $6. This result occurs because demand is unitary, as shown in Figure 4.4b. This special condition exists when the percentage price change is exactly offset by an equal percentage change in the quantity demanded. In this situation, revenue remains constant. At $2, three lattes are purchased, so the total revenue is $2 × 3, which is the same as it was when $3 was the purchase price. As a result, we can see that total revenues have reached a maximum. Between $3 and $2, the price elasticity of demand is unitary. This finding does not necessarily mean that the firm will operate at the unitary point. Maximizing profit, not revenue, is the ultimate goal of a business, and we have not yet accounted for costs in our calculation of profits.

Once we reach a price below unitary demand, we move into the realm of inelastic demand, shown in Figure 4.4c. When the price falls to $1, total

FIGURE 4.4

(a) The Total Revenue Trade-off When Demand Is Elastic

In the elastic region of the demand curve, lowering the price will increase total revenue. The gains from increased purchases, shown in the blue-shaded area, are greater than the losses from a lower purchase price, shown in the red-shaded area.

(b) ... When Demand Is Unitary

When demand is unitary, lowering the price will no longer increase total revenue. The gains from increased purchases, shown in the blue-shaded area, are equal to the losses from a lower purchase price, shown in the red-shaded area.

(c) ... When Demand Is Inelastic

In the inelastic region of the demand curve, lowering the price will decrease total revenue. The gains from increased purchases, shown in the blue-shaded area, are smaller than the losses from a lower purchase price, shown in the red-shaded area.

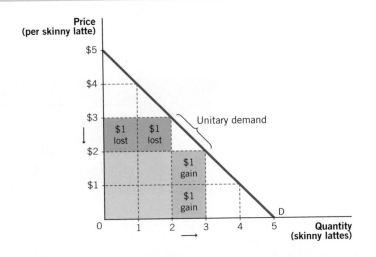

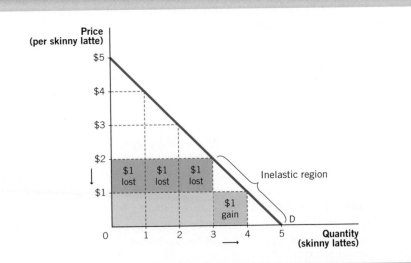

revenue declines to $4. This result occurs because the price elasticity of demand is now relatively inelastic, or price insensitive. In other words, latte consumers adding a fourth drink will not gain as much benefit as they did when they purchased the first. Even though the price is declining by $1, price is increasingly unimportant; as you can see by the blue square, it does not spur a large increase in consumption.

As we see in Figure 4.4c, at a price of $2, three units are sold and total revenue is $2 × 3 = $6. When the price falls to $1, four units are sold, so the total revenue is now $4 × 1 = $4. By lowering the price from $2 to $1, the business has lost $2 in extra revenue. This occurs because the business does not generate enough extra revenue from the lower price. Lowering the price from $2 to $1 causes a loss of $3 in existing sales revenue (the red boxes). At the same time, it generates only $1 in new sales (the blue box).

In this analysis, we see that once the demand curve enters the inelastic area, lowering the price decreases total revenue. This is an unambiguously bad

ECONOMICS IN THE MEDIA

Elasticity and Total Revenue

D'oh! The Simpsons and Total Revenue

In the episode "Bart Gets an Elephant," the Simpsons find that their pet elephant, Stampy, is eating them out of house and home. So Bart devises a plan to charge admission for people to see the elephant. He begins by charging $1. However, the revenue collected is not enough to cover Stampy's food bill. When Homer discovers that they are not covering their costs, he raises the cost to see the elephant to $100. However, Homer is not the smartest businessman in the world, and all of the customers who would have paid Bart's $1 admission stay away. We can use our understanding of elasticity to explain why Homer's plan backfires.

Homer's plan is to increase the price. This would work if the demand to see the elephant were inelastic, but it is not. For $100 you could see a concert, attend a major sporting event, or eat out at a very nice restaurant! You'd have to really want to see the elephant to be willing to pay $100. It doesn't help that you can also go to any of the best zoos in the country, and see hundreds of other animals as well, for much less money. Homer's plan is doomed to fail because no one is willing to pay $100. Remember that total revenue = price × quantity purchased. If

The Simpsons cannot afford Stampy. What should they do?

the quantity demanded falls to zero, zero times anything is still zero. So Homer's plan does not generate any revenue.

In contrast, Bart's admission price of $1 brings in $58 in revenue. This is a good start, but not enough to cover Stampy's $300 food bill. Homer actually had the right idea here. Raising the price above $1 would generate more revenue up to a point. Would most of the customers pay $2 to see the elephant? Most likely. $5? Possibly. $10? Maybe. $100? Definitely not. Why not? There is a trade-off dictated by the law of demand. Higher prices will reduce the quantity demanded and vice versa. Therefore, the trick to maximizing total revenue is to balance increases in price against decreases in the quantity purchased.

outcome for a business. The lower price brings in less revenue and requires the business to produce more goods. Since making goods is costly, it does not make sense to lower prices into the region where revenues decline. We can be sure that no business will intentionally operate in the inelastic region of the demand curve.

How Do Changes in Income and the Prices of Other Goods Affect Elasticity?

We have seen how consumer demand responds to changes in the price of a single good. In this section, we will examine how responsive demand is to changes in income and to price changes in other goods.

Income Elasticity

Changes in personal income can have a large effect on consumer spending. After all, the money in your pocket influences not only how much you buy, but also the types of purchases you make. A consumer who is low on money may opt to buy a cheap generic product, while someone with a little extra cash can afford to upgrade. The grocery store aisle reflects this. Store brands and name products compete for shelf space. Lower-income shoppers can choose the store brand to save money, while more affluent shoppers can choose their favorite brand-name product without worrying about the purchase price. The **income elasticity of demand** (E_I) measures how a change in income affects spending. It is calculated by dividing the change in the quantity demanded by the change in personal income:

The **income elasticity of demand** measures how a change in income affects spending.

$$E_I = \frac{\text{percentage change in the quantity demanded}}{\text{percentage change in income}}$$

(Equation 4.3)

Unlike the price elasticity of demand, which is negative, the income elasticity of demand can be either positive or negative. When higher levels of income enable the consumer to purchase more, the goods that are purchased are *normal goods*, a term we learned about in Chapter 3. Since the demand for normal goods goes up with income, they have a positive income elasticity—a rise in income will cause a rise in the quantity demanded. For instance, if you receive a 20% pay raise and you decide to pay an extra 10% on your cable TV bill to add HBO, the resulting income elasticity is positive, since 10% divided by 20% is 0.5. Whenever the good is normal, the result is a positive income elasticity of demand, and purchases of the good rise as income expands.

Normal goods fall into two categories: *necessities* and *luxuries*. Goods that people consider to be necessities generally

Clothing purchases expand with income.

PRACTICE WHAT YOU KNOW

The Price Elasticity of Demand

In this section, there are two questions to give you practice computing the price elasticity of demand. Before we do the math, ask yourself whether you think the price elasticity of demand for either subs or the antibiotic amoxicillin is elastic.

Question: A store manager decides to lower the price of a featured sandwich from $3 to $2, and she finds that sales during the week increase from 240 to 480 sandwiches. Is demand elastic?

Answer: Consumers were flexible and bought significantly more sandwiches in response to the price drop. Let's calculate the price elasticity of demand (E_D) using Equation 4.2. Recall that

$$E_D = \frac{(Q_2 - Q_1) \div [(Q_1 + Q_2) \div 2]}{(P_2 - P_1) \div [(P_1 + P_2) \div 2]}$$

Plugging in the values from above yields

$$E_D = \frac{(480 - 240) \div [(240 + 480) \div 2]}{(\$2 - \$3) \div [(\$2 + \$3) \div 2]} = \frac{240 \div 360}{-\$1 \div \$2.50}$$

Therefore, $E_D = -1.67$.

Whenever the price elasticity of demand is less than -1, demand is considered elastic: the percentage change in the quantity demanded is greater than the percentage change in price. This outcome is exactly what the store manager expected. But subs are just one option for a meal; there are many other choices, such as salads, burgers, and chicken—all of which cost more than the now-reduced sandwich. Therefore, we should not be surprised that there is a relatively large percentage increase in sub purchases by price-conscious customers.

Question: A local pharmacy manager decides to raise the price of a 50-pill prescription of amoxicillin from $8 to $10. The pharmacy tracks the sales of amoxicillin over the next month and finds that sales decline from 1,500 to 1,480 boxes. Is the price elasticity of demand elastic?

Answer: First, let's consider the potential substitutes for amoxicillin. To be sure, it's possible to substitute other drugs, but they might not be as effective. Therefore, most patients prefer to use the drug prescribed by their doctor. Also, in this case the cost of the drug is relatively small. Finally, patients' need for amoxicillin is a short-run consideration. They want the medicine now so they will get better! All three factors would lead us to believe that the demand for amoxicillin is relatively inelastic. Let's find out if that intuition is confirmed in the data.

Is the demand for a sub elastic or inelastic?

Is the demand for amoxicillin elastic or inelastic?

(CONTINUED)

(CONTINUED)

The price elasticity of demand using the midpoint method is

$$E_D = \frac{(Q_2 - Q_1) \div [(Q_1 + Q_2) \div 2]}{(P_2 - P_1) \div [(P_1 + P_2) \div 2]}$$

Plugging in the values from the example yields

$$E_D = \frac{(1480 - 1500) \div [(1480 + 1500) \div 2]}{(\$10 - \$8) \div [(\$8 + \$10) \div 2]}$$

Simplifying produces this:

$$E_D = \frac{-20 \div 1490}{\$2 \div \$9}$$

Therefore, $E_D = -0.06$. Recall that an E_D near zero indicates that the price elasticity of demand is highly inelastic, which is what we suspected. The price increase does not cause consumption to fall very much. If the store manager had been hoping to bring in a little extra revenue from the sales of amoxicillin, his plan was successful. Before the price increase, the business sold 1,500 units at \$8, so revenues were \$12,000. After the price increase, sales decreased to 1,480 units, but the new price is \$10, so revenues now are \$14,800. Raising the price of amoxicillin helped the pharmacy make an additional \$2,800 in revenue.

have income elasticities between 0 and 1. For example, expenditures on items such as milk, clothing, electricity, and gasoline are unavoidable, and consumers at any income level must buy them no matter what. Although purchases of necessities will increase as income rises, they do not rise as fast as the increase in income does. Therefore, as income increases, spending on necessities will expand at a slower rate than the increase in income.

Air travel is a luxury good.

Rising income enables consumers to enjoy significantly more luxuries. This produces an income elasticity of demand greater than 1. For instance, a family of modest means may travel almost exclusively by car. However, as the family's income rises, they can afford air travel. A relatively small jump in income can cause the family to fly instead of drive.

In Chapter 3, we saw that *inferior goods* are those that people will choose not to purchase when their income goes up. Inferior goods have a negative income elasticity, because as income expands, the demand for the good declines. We see this in Table 4.4 with the example of macaroni and cheese, an inexpensive meal. As a household's income rises, it is able to afford healthier food and more variety in the meals it enjoys. Consequently, the number of times that mac and cheese is served declines. The decline in consumption indicates that mac and cheese is an inferior good, and this is reflected in the negative sign of the income elasticity.

TABLE 4.4			
Income Elasticity			
Type of good	**Subcategory**	**E_I coefficient**	**Example**
Inferior		$E_I < 0$	Macaroni and cheese
Normal	Necessity	$0 < E_I < 1$	Milk
Normal	Luxury	$E_I > 1$	Diamond ring

Cross-Price Elasticity

The **cross-price elasticity of demand** measures the responsiveness of the quantity demanded of one good to a change in the price of a related good.

Now we will look at how a price change in one good can affect the demand for a related good. For instance, if you enjoy pizza, the choice between ordering from Domino's or Pizza Hut is influenced by the price of both goods. The **cross-price elasticity of demand** (E_C) measures the responsiveness of the quantity demanded of one good to a change in the price of a related good.

(Equation 4.4)

$$E_C = \frac{\text{percentage change in the quantity demanded of one good}}{\text{percentage change in the price of a related good}}$$

Consider how two goods are related to each other. If the goods are substitutes, a price rise in one good will cause the quantity demanded of that good to decline. At the same time, since consumers can purchase the substitute good for the same price as before, demand for the substitute good will increase. When the price of Domino's pizza rises, consumers will buy more pizza from Pizza Hut.

The opposite is true if the goods are complements. When goods are related to each other, a price increase in one good will make the joint consumption of both goods more expensive. Therefore, the consumption of both goods will decline. For example, a price increase for turkeys will cause the quantity demanded of both turkey and gravy to decline. This means that the cross-price elasticity of demand is negative.

What if there is no relationship? For example, if the price of basketballs goes up, that probably will not affect the quantity demanded of bedroom slippers. In this case, the cross-price elasticity is neither positive nor negative; it is zero. Table 4.5 lists cross-price elasticity values according to type of good.

To learn how to calculate cross-price elasticity, let's consider an example from the skit "Lazy Sunday" on *Saturday Night Live*. The skit features Chris Parnell and Andy Samberg rapping about going to see *The Chronicles of Narnia* and eating cupcakes. In one inspired scene, they describe enjoying the soft drink Mr. Pibb with Red Vines candy and call the combination "crazy

TABLE 4.5		
Cross-Price Elasticity		
Type of good	E_I coefficient	Example
Substitutes	$E_C > 0$	Pizza Hut and Domino's
No relationship	$E_C = 0$	A basketball and bedroom slippers
Complements	$E_C < 0$	Turkey and gravy

delicious." From this, we can construct a cross-price elasticity example. Suppose that the price of a two-liter bottle of Mr. Pibb falls from $1.49 to $1.29. In the week immediately preceding the price drop, a local store sells 60 boxes of Red Vines. After the price drop, sales of Red Vines increase to 80 boxes. Let's calculate the cross-price elasticity of demand for Red Vines when the price of Mr. Pibb falls from $1.49 to $1.29.

Have you tried Mr. Pibb and Red Vines together?

The cross-price elasticity of demand using the midpoint method is

$$E_C = \frac{(Q_{RV2} - Q_{RV1}) \div [(Q_{RV1} + Q_{RV2}) \div 2]}{(P_{MP2} - P_{MP1}) \div [(P_{MP1} + P_{MP2}) \div 2]}$$

Notice that there are now additional subscripts to denote that we are measuring the percentage change in the quantity demanded of good RV (Red Vines) in response to the percentage change in the price of good MP (Mr. Pibb).

Plugging in the values from the example yields

$$E_C = \frac{(80 - 60) \div [(60 + 80) \div 2]}{(\$1.29 - \$1.49) \div [(\$1.49 + \$1.29) \div 2]}$$

Simplifying produces

$$E_C = \frac{20 \div 70}{-\$0.20 \div \$1.39}$$

Solving for E_C gives us a value of -1.01. Because the result is a negative value, this confirms our intuition that two goods that go well together ("crazy delicious") are complements, since the decrease in the price of Mr. Pibb causes consumers to buy more Red Vines.

ECONOMICS IN THE REAL WORLD

The Wii Rollout and Changes in the Video Game Industry

The Wii rollout generated long waiting lines.

When Nintendo launched the Wii console in late 2006, it fundamentally changed the gaming industry. The Wii uses motion-sensing technology. Despite relatively poor graphics, it provided a completely different gaming experience from its competitors, Playstation 3 (PS3) and the Xbox 360. Yet the PS3 and Xbox 360 had larger storage capacities and better graphics, in theory making them more attractive to gamers than the Wii.

During the 2006 holiday shopping season, the three systems had three distinct price points:

$$Wii = \$249$$
$$Xbox = \$399$$
$$Playstation\ 3 = \$599$$

Wii and Xbox sales were very strong. As a result, both units were in short supply in stores. However, PS3 sales did not fare as well as its manufacturer, Sony, had hoped. The Wii outsold the PS3 by a more than 4:1 ratio, and the Xbox 360 outsold the PS3 by more than 2:1 during the first half of 2007. More telling, a monthly breakdown of sales figures across the three platforms shows the deterioration in the PS3 and Xbox 360 sales.

Console	Units sold, January 2007	Units sold, April 2007	Percentage change
Wii	460,000	360,000	−22%
Xbox 360	249,000	174,000	−30%
PS3	244,000	82,000	−66%

Faced with quickly falling sales, Sony lowered the price of the PS3 console. The company understood that consumer demand was quite elastic and that lowering the price was the only way to retain customers. Indeed, the lower price stimulated additional interest in the PS3 and helped to increase the number of units sold in the second half of the year. Without a firm grasp of the price elasticity of demand, Sony would not have made this move.

Meanwhile, interest in the Wii continued to be strong. For Nintendo, the market demand was relatively inelastic. Nintendo could have raised the price of its console but chose not to do so. One reason is that Nintendo also makes money by selling peripherals and games. These are strong complements to the console, and a higher console price would discourage customers from purchasing the Wii. Since the cross-price elasticity of demand for peripherals and games is highly negative, this strategy makes economic sense. Nintendo had chosen not to do this, in part, because the company wanted to maximize not only the console price, but also the prices of all of the related components. Nintendo's strategy worked. The four top-selling games during 2007 were all associated with the Wii rollout. ✳

Price Elasticity of Demand

Determining the price elasticity of demand for a product or service involves calculating the responsiveness of quantity demanded to a change in the price. The chart below gives the actual price elasticity of demand for ten common products and services. Remember, the number is always negative because of the inverse relationship between price and the quantity demanded. Why is price elasticity of demand important? It reveals consumer behavior and allows for better pricing strategies by businesses.

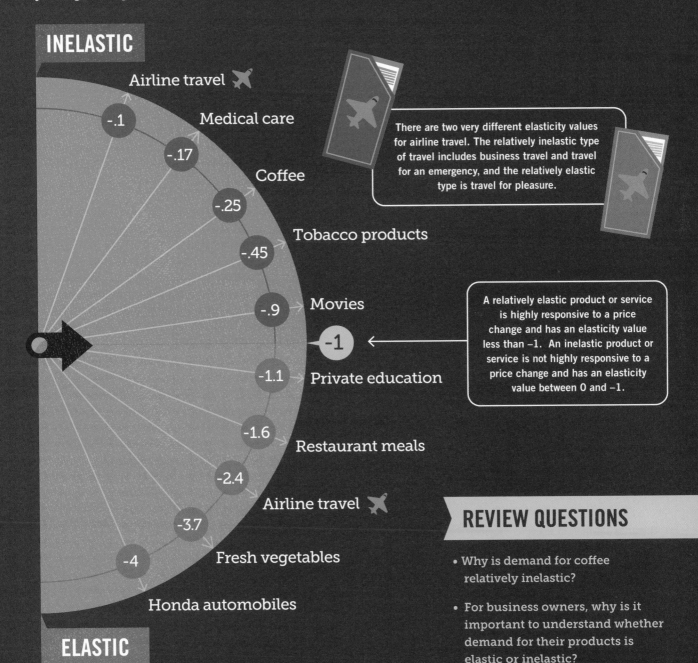

INELASTIC

Airline travel ✈ — -.1

Medical care — -.17

Coffee — -.25

Tobacco products — -.45

Movies — -.9

-1

Private education — -1.1

Restaurant meals — -1.6

Airline travel ✈ — -2.4

Fresh vegetables — -3.7

Honda automobiles — -4

ELASTIC

There are two very different elasticity values for airline travel. The relatively inelastic type of travel includes business travel and travel for an emergency, and the relatively elastic type is travel for pleasure.

A relatively elastic product or service is highly responsive to a price change and has an elasticity value less than −1. An inelastic product or service is not highly responsive to a price change and has an elasticity value between 0 and −1.

REVIEW QUESTIONS

- Why is demand for coffee relatively inelastic?

- For business owners, why is it important to understand whether demand for their products is elastic or inelastic?

PRACTICE WHAT YOU KNOW

Income Elasticity

Question: A college student eats ramen noodles twice a week and earns $300/week working part-time. After graduating, the student earns $1,000/week and eats ramen noodles every other week. What is the student's income elasticity?

Yummy, or all you can afford?

Answer: The income elasticity of demand using the midpoint method is

$$E_I = \frac{(Q_2 - Q_1) \div [(Q_1 + Q_2) \div 2]}{(I_2 - I_1) \div [(I_1 + I_2) \div 2]}$$

Plugging in yields

$$E_I = \frac{(0.5 - 2.0) \div [(2.0 + 0.5) \div 2]}{(\$1000 - \$300) \div [(\$300 + \$1000) \div 2]}$$

Simplifying yields

$$E_I = \frac{-1.5 \div 1.25}{\$700 \div \$650}$$

Therefore, $E_I = -1.1$.

The income elasticity of demand is positive for normal goods and negative for inferior goods. Therefore, the negative coefficient indicates that ramen noodles are an inferior good over the range of income—in this example, between $300 and $1,000. This result should confirm your intuition. The higher post-graduation income enables the student to substitute away from ramen noodles and toward other meals that provide more nourishment and enjoyment.

What Is the Price Elasticity of Supply?

The price elasticity of supply is a measure of the responsiveness of the quantity supplied to a change in price.

Sellers, like consumers, are sensitive to price changes. However, the determinants of the *price elasticity of supply* are substantially different from the determinants of the price elasticity of demand. The **price elasticity of supply** is a measure of the responsiveness of the quantity supplied to a change in price.

In this section, we examine how much sellers respond to price changes. For instance, if the market price of gasoline increases, how will oil companies respond? The answer depends on the elasticity of supply. Oil must be refined into gasoline. If it is difficult for oil companies to increase their output of gasoline significantly, even if the price increases a lot, the quantity of gasoline supplied will not increase much. In this case, we say that the price elasticity of supply is inelastic, or unresponsive. However, if the price increase is small and suppliers respond by offering significantly more gasoline for sale, the price elasticity of supply is elastic. We would expect to observe this outcome if it were easy to refine oil into gasoline.

When supply is not able to respond to a change in price, we say it is inelastic. Think of an oceanfront property in Southern California. The amount of land next to the ocean is fixed. If the price of oceanfront property rises, the supply of land cannot adjust to the price increase. In this case, the supply is perfectly inelastic and the elasticity is zero. Recall that a price elasticity coefficient of zero means that supply does not change as price changes.

What would it take to own a slice of paradise?

When the ability of the supplier to make quick adjustments is limited, the elasticity of supply is less than 1. For instance, when a cellular network becomes congested, it takes suppliers a long time to provide additional capacity. They have to build new cell towers, which requires the purchase of land and additional construction costs. In contrast, a local hot dog vendor can easily add another cart in relatively short order. As a result, for the hot dog vendor, supply elasticity is elastic with an elasticity coefficient that is greater than 1. Table 4.6 examines the price elasticity of supply. Recall that the law of supply states that there is a direct relationship between the price of a good and the quantity that a firm supplies. As a result, the percentage change in the quantity supplied and the percentage change in price move in the same direction. The E_S coefficient reflects this direct relationship with a positive sign.

Determinants of the Price Elasticity of Supply

When we examined the determinants of the price elasticity of demand, we saw that consumers had to consider the number of substitutes, how expensive the item was compared to their overall budget, and the amount of time they had to make a decision. Time and the adjustment process are also key elements in determining the price elasticity of supply. However, there is

TABLE 4.6

A Closer Look at the Price Elasticity of Supply

Elasticity	E_S coefficient	Example	
Perfectly inelastic	$E_S = 0$	Oceanfront land	
Relatively inelastic	$0 < E_S < 1$	Cellphone tower	
Relatively elastic	$E_S > 1$	Hot dog vendor	

a critical difference: the degree of flexibility that producers have in bringing their product to the market quickly.

The Flexibility of Producers

When a producer can quickly ramp up output, supply tends to be elastic. One way to maintain flexibility is to have spare production capacity. Extra capacity enables producers to quickly meet changing price conditions, so supply is more responsive, or elastic. The ability to store the good is another way to stay flexible. Producers who have stockpiles of their products can respond more quickly to changes in market conditions. For example, De Beers, the international diamond conglomerate, stores millions of uncut diamonds. As the price of diamonds fluctuates, De Beers can quickly change the supply of diamonds it offers to the market. Likewise, hot dog vendors can relocate quickly from one street corner to another or add carts if demand is strong. However, many businesses cannot adapt to changing market conditions quickly. For instance, a golf course cannot easily build nine new holes to meet additional demand. This limits the golf course owner's ability to adjust quickly and increase the supply of golfing opportunities as soon as the fee changes.

Time and the Adjustment Process

In the immediate run, businesses, just like consumers, are stuck with what they have on hand. For example, a pastry shop that runs out of chocolate glazed donuts cannot bake more instantly. As we move from the immediate run to the short run and a price change persists through time, supply—just like demand—becomes more elastic. For instance, a golf resort may be able to squeeze extra production out of its current facility by staying open longer hours or moving tee times closer together, but those short-run efforts will not match the production potential of adding another course in the long run.

Figure 4.5 shows how the two determinants of supply elasticity are mapped onto the supply curve. In the immediate run, the supply curve is vertical (S_1). A vertical curve tells us that there is no responsiveness when the price changes. As producers gain additional time to make adjustments, the supply curve rotates from S_1, the immediate run, to S_2, the short run, to S_3, the long run. Like the demand curve, the supply curve becomes flatter through time. The only difference is that the supply curve rotates clockwise, whereas, as we saw in Figure 4.2, the demand curve rotates counterclockwise. With both supply and demand, the most important thing to remember is that more time allows for greater adjustment, so the long run is always more elastic.

Calculating the Price Elasticity of Supply

Like the price elasticity of demand, we can calculate the price elasticity of supply. This is useful when a business owner must decide how much to produce at various prices. The elasticity of supply measures how quickly the producer is able to change production in response to changes in price. When the price elasticity of supply is elastic, producers are able to quickly adjust production. If the price elasticity of supply is inelastic, production tends to remain roughly constant, despite large swings in price.

Here is the formula for the price elasticity of supply (E_S):

(Equation 4.5)

$$E_S = \frac{\text{percentage change in the quantity supplied}}{\text{percentage change in the price}}$$

This equation is almost exactly the same as that of the price elasticity of demand. The only difference is that we are measuring the percentage change in the quantity supplied in the numerator.

Consider how the manufacturer of Solo cups might respond to an increase in demand that causes the cups' market price to rise. The company's ability to change the amount it produces depends on the flexibility of the manufacturing process and the length of time needed to ramp up production. Suppose that the price of the cups rises by 10%. The company can increase its production by 5% immediately, but it will take many months to expand production by 20%. What can we say about the price elasticity of supply in this case? Using Equation 4.5, we can take the percentage change in the quantity supplied immediately (5%) and divide that by the percentage change in price (10%). This gives us an $E_S = 0.5$, which signals that the elasticity of supply is relatively inelastic. However, with time the firm is able to increase the quantity supplied by 20%. If we divide 20% by the percentage change in the price (10%), we get $E_S = 2.0$, which indicates that the price elasticity of supply is relatively elastic in the long run.

Have you ever shopped for Solo cups?

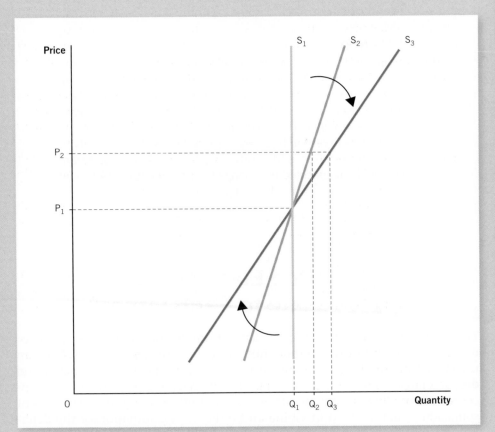

FIGURE 4.5

Elasticity and the Supply Curve

Increased flexibility and more time make supply more elastic. When price rises from P_1 to P_2, producers are unable to expand output immediately and the supply curve remains at Q_1. In the short run (S_2), the firm becomes more flexible and output expands to Q_2. Eventually, in the long run (S_3), the firm is able to produce even more, and it moves to Q_3 in response to higher prices.

PRACTICE WHAT YOU KNOW

The Price Elasticity of Supply

Question: Suppose that the price of a barrel of oil increases from $60 to $100. The new output is 2 million barrels a day, and the old output is 1.8 million barrels. What is the price elasticity of supply?

Answer: The price elasticity of supply using the midpoint method is

$$E_D = \frac{(Q_2 - Q_1) \div [(Q_1 + Q_2) \div 2]}{(P_2 - P_1) \div [(P_1 + P_2) \div 2]}$$

Plugging in the values from the example yields

$$E_S = \frac{(2.0M - 1.8M) \div [(1.8M + 2.0M) \div 2]}{(\$100 - \$60) \div [(\$60 + \$100) \div 2]}$$

Oil companies have us over a barrel.

Simplifying yields

$$E_S = \frac{0.2M \div 1.9M}{\$40 \div \$80}$$

Therefore, $E_S = 0.20$.

Recall from our discussion of the law of supply that there is a direct relationship between the price and the quantity supplied. Since E_S in this case is positive, we see that output rises as price rises. However, the magnitude of the output increase is quite small—this is reflected in the coefficient 0.20. Because oil companies cannot easily change their production process, they have a limited ability to respond quickly to rising prices. That inability is reflected in a coefficient that is relatively close to zero. A zero coefficient would mean that suppliers could not change their output at all. Here suppliers are able to respond, but only in a limited capacity.

How Do the Price Elasticity of Demand and Supply Relate to Each Other?

The interplay between the price elasticity of supply and the price elasticity of demand allows us to explain more fully how the economy operates. With an understanding of elasticity at our disposal, we can make a much richer and deeper analysis of the world around us. For instance, suppose that we are concerned about what will happen to the price of oil as economic development spurs additional demand in China and India. An examination of the determinants of the price elasticity of supply quickly confirms that oil producers have a limited ability to adjust production in response to rising prices. Oil wells can be uncapped to meet rising demand, but it takes years to bring the new capacity online. Moreover, storing oil reserves, while possible, is expensive. Therefore, the short-run supply of oil is quite inelastic. Figure 4.6 shows the combination of inelastic supply-side production constraints in the short run and the inelastic short-run demand for oil.

An increase in global demand from D_1 to D_2 will create significantly higher prices (from $60 to $90) in the short run. This occurs because increasing oil production is difficult in the short run. Therefore, the short-run supply curve (S_{SR}) is relatively inelastic. In the long run, though, oil producers are able to bring more oil to the market when prices are higher, so the supply curve rotates clockwise (S_{LR}), becoming more elastic, and the market price falls to $80.

What does this example tell us? It reminds us that the interplay between the price elasticity of demand and the price elasticity of supply determines the magnitude of the resulting price change. We cannot observe demand in isolation without also considering how supply responds. Similarly, we cannot simply think about the short-run consequences of demand and supply shifts; we also must consider how prices and quantity will vary in the long run. Armed with this knowledge, you can begin to see the power of the supply and demand model to explain the world around us.

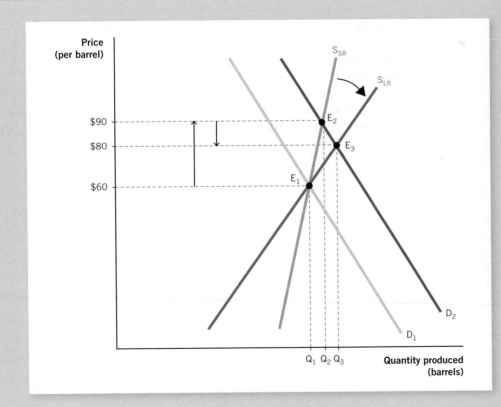

FIGURE 4.6

A Demand Shift and the Consequences for Short- and Long-Run Supply

When an increase in demand causes the price of oil to rise from $60 to $90 per barrel, initially producers are unable to expand output very much—production expands from Q_1 to Q_2. However, in the long run, as producers expand production, the price will fall back to $80.

PRACTICE WHAT YOU KNOW

Elasticity: Trick or Treat Edition

How much would you spend on a Halloween pumpkin?

Question: An unusually bad growing season leads to a small pumpkin crop. What will happen to the price of pumpkins as Halloween approaches?

Answer: The demand for pumpkins peaks in October and rapidly falls after Halloween. Purchasing a pumpkin is a short-run decision to buy a unique product that takes up a relatively small share of the consumer's budget. As a result, the price elasticity of demand for pumpkins leading up to Halloween tends to be quite inelastic. At the same time, a small crop causes the entire supply curve to shift left. This causes the market price of pumpkins to rise. Since the demand is relatively inelastic in the short run and the supply of pumpkins is fixed, we expect the price to rise significantly. After Halloween, the price of any remaining pumpkins falls, since demand declines dramatically.

Conclusion

Do sellers charge the highest price possible? We can now answer this misconception definitively: no. Sellers like higher prices in the same way consumers like lower prices, but that does not mean that they will charge the highest price possible. At very high prices, we learned that consumer demand is quite elastic. Therefore, a seller who charges too high a price will not sell much. As a result, firms learn that they must lower their price in order to attract more customers.

The ability to determine whether demand and supply are elastic or inelastic also enables economists to calculate the effects of personal, business, and policy decisions. When you combine the concept of elasticity with the supply and demand model from Chapter 3, you get a very powerful tool. As a result, we can now say much more about how the world works than we could before. In subsequent chapters, we will employ the understanding of elasticity to refine our models of economic behavior and make our results more realistic.

Price Elasticity of Supply and Demand: Buying Your First Car

When you buy a car, your knowledge of price elasticity can help you negotiate the best possible deal.

Recall that the three determinants of price elasticity of demand are (1) the share of the budget, (2) the number of available substitutes, and (3) the time you have to make a decision.

Let's start with your budget. You should have one in mind, but don't tell the salesperson what you are willing to spend; that is a vital piece of personal information you want to keep to yourself. If the salesperson suggests that you look at a model that is too expensive, just say that you are not interested. You might reply, "Buying a car is a stretch for me; I've got to stay within my budget." If the salesperson asks indirectly about your budget by inquiring whether you have a particular monthly payment in mind, reply that you want to negotiate over the invoice price once you decide on a vehicle. Never negotiate on the sticker price, which is the price you see in the car window, because it includes thousands of dollars in markup. You want to make it clear to the salesperson that the price you pay matters to you—that is, your demand is elastic.

Next, make it clear that you are gathering information and visiting other dealers. That is, reinforce that you have many available substitutes. Even if you really want a Honda, do not voice that desire to the Honda salesperson. Perhaps mention that you are also visiting the Toyota, Hyundai, and Ford showrooms. Compare what you've seen on one lot versus another. Each salesperson you meet should hear that you are seriously considering other options. This indicates to each dealership that your demand is elastic and that getting your business will require that they offer you a better price.

Taking your time to decide is also important. Never buy a car the first time you walk onto a lot. If you convey the message that you want a car immediately, you are saying that your demand is inelastic. If the dealership thinks that you have no flexibility, the staff will not give you their best offer. Instead, tell the salesperson that you appreciate their help and that you will be deciding over the next few weeks.

A good salesperson will know you are serious and will ask for your phone number or email address and contact you. The salesperson will sweeten the deal if you indicate you are narrowing down your choices and they are in the running. You wait. You win.

Also know that salespeople and dealerships have times when they want to move inventory. August is an especially good month to purchase. In other words, the price elasticity of supply is at work here as well. A good time to buy is when the dealer is trying to move inventory to make room for new models, because prices fall for end-of-the-model-year closeouts. Likewise, many sales promotions and sales bonuses are tied to the end of the month, so salespeople will be more eager to sell at that time.

Watch out for shady negotiation practices!

ANSWERING THE BIG QUESTIONS

What is the price elasticity of demand, and what are its determinants?

* The price elasticity of demand is a measure of the responsiveness of quantity demanded to a change in price.

* Demand will generally be more elastic if there are many substitutes available, if the item accounts for a large share of the consumer's budget, if the item is a luxury good, or if the consumer has plenty of time to make a decision.

* Economists categorize time in three distinct periods: the immediate run, where there is no time for consumers to adjust their behavior; the short run, where consumers can adjust, but only partially; and the long run, where consumers have time to fully adjust to market conditions.

* The price elasticity of demand can be calculated by taking the percentage change in the quantity demanded and dividing it by the percentage change in price. A value of zero indicates that the quantity demanded does not respond to a price change; if the price elasticity is zero, demand is said to be perfectly inelastic. When the price elasticity of demand is between 0 and -1, demand is inelastic. If the price elasticity of demand is less than -1, demand is elastic.

How do changes in income and the prices of other goods affect elasticity?

* The income elasticity of demand measures how a change in income affects spending. Normal goods have a positive income elasticity. Inferior goods have a negative income elasticity.

* The cross-price elasticity of demand measures the responsiveness of the quantity demanded of one good to a change in the price of a related good. Positive values for the cross-price elasticity mean that the two goods are substitutes, while negative values indicate that the two goods are complements. If the cross-price elasticity is zero, then the two goods are not correlated with each other.

What is the price elasticity of supply?

* The price elasticity of supply is a measure of the responsiveness of the quantity supplied to a change in price. Supply will generally be more elastic if producers have flexibility in the production process and ample time to adjust production.

* The price elasticity of supply is calculated by dividing the percentage change in the quantity supplied by the percentage change in price. A value of zero indicates that the quantity supplied does not respond to a price change; if the price elasticity is zero, supply is said to be perfectly inelastic. When the price elasticity of supply is between 0 and 1, demand is relatively inelastic. If the price elasticity of supply is greater than 1, supply is elastic.

How do the price elasticity of demand and supply relate to each other?

* The interplay between the price elasticity of demand and the price elasticity of supply determines the magnitude of the resulting price change.

CONCEPTS YOU SHOULD KNOW

cross-price elasticity of demand
   (p. 130)
elasticity (p. 110)
immediate run (p. 113)

income elasticity of demand
   (p. 127)
long run (p. 113)
price elasticity of demand (p. 111)

price elasticity of supply
   (p. 134)
short run (p. 113)
total revenue (p. 123)

QUESTIONS FOR REVIEW

1. Define the price elasticity of demand.

2. What are the four determinants of the price elasticity of demand?

3. Give an example of a good that has elastic demand. What is the value of the price elasticity if demand is elastic? Give an example of a good that has inelastic demand. What is the value of the price elasticity if demand is inelastic?

4. What is the connection between total revenue and the price elasticity of demand? Illustrate this relationship along a demand curve.

5. Explain why slope is different from elasticity.

6. Define the price elasticity of supply.

7. What are the two determinants of the price elasticity of supply?

8. Give an example of a good that has elastic supply. What is the value of the price elasticity if supply is elastic? Give an example of a good that has an inelastic supply. What is the value of the price elasticity if supply is inelastic?

9. Give an example of a normal good. What is the income elasticity of a normal good? Give an example of a luxury good. What is the income elasticity of a luxury good? Give an example of a necessity. What is the income elasticity of a necessity? Give an example of an inferior good. What is the income elasticity of an inferior good?

10. Define the cross-price elasticity of demand. Give an example with negative cross-price elasticity, another with zero cross-price elasticity, and a third with positive cross-price elasticity.

STUDY PROBLEMS (✳ *solved at the end of the section*)

✳ 1. If the government decided to impose a 50% tax on gray T-shirts, would this policy generate a large or small increase in revenues? Use elasticity to explain your answer.

2. College logo T-shirts priced at $15 sell at a rate of 25 per week, but when the bookstore marks them down to $10, it finds that it can sell 50 T-shirts per week. What is the price elasticity of demand for the logo T-shirts?

3. Search YouTube for the video titled "Black Friday 2006—Best Buy Line." Do the early shoppers appear to have elastic or inelastic demand on Black Friday? Explain your response.

4. If a 20% increase in price causes a 10% drop in the quantity demanded, is the price elasticity of demand for this good elastic, unitary, or inelastic?

5. Characterize each of the following goods as perfectly elastic, relatively elastic, relatively inelastic, or perfectly inelastic.
    a. a life-saving medication
    b. photocopies at a copy shop, when all competing shops charge 10 cents per copy
    c. a fast-food restaurant located in the food court of a shopping mall
    d. the water bill you pay

6. A local paintball business receives total revenue of $8,000 a month when it charges $10 per person, and $9,600 in total revenue when it charges $6 per person. Over that range of prices, does the business face elastic, unitary, or inelastic demand?

7. At a price of $200, a cellphone company manufactures 300,000 units. At a price of $150, the company produces 200,000 phones. What is the price elasticity of supply?

8. Do customers who visit convenience stores at 3 a.m. have a price elasticity of demand that is more or less elastic than those who visit at 3 p.m.?

✳ 9. A worker gets a 25% raise. As a result, he decides to eat out twice as much as before and cut back on the number of frozen lasagna dinners from once a week to once every other week. Determine the income elasticity of demand for eating out and for having frozen lasagna dinners.

10. The cross-price elasticity of demand between American Eagle and Hollister is 2.0. What does that tell us about the relationship between these two stores?

11. A local golf course is considering lowering its fees in order to increase the revenue coming in. Under what conditions is the fee reduction going to achieve its goal?

12. A private university notices that in-state and out-of-state students seem to respond differently to tuition changes.

Tuition	Quantity demanded (in-state applicants)	Quantity demanded (out-of-state applicants)
$10,000	6,000	12,000
$15,000	5,000	9,000
$20,000	4,000	6,000
$30,000	3,000	3,000

As the price of tuition rises from $15,000 to $20,000, what is the price elasticity of demand for in-state applicants and also for out-of-state applicants?

SOLVED PROBLEMS

1. To answer this question, we need to consider the price elasticity of demand. The tax is only on gray T-shirts. This means that T-shirt customers who buy other colors can avoid the tax entirely—which means that the demand for gray T-shirts is relatively elastic. Since not many gray T-shirts will be sold, the government will generate a small increase in revenues from the tax.

9. In this question a worker gets a 25% raise, so we can use this information in the denominator when determining the income elasticity of demand. We are not given the percentage change for the meals out, so we need to plug in how often the worker ate out before (once a week) and the amount he eats out after the raise (twice a week).

   Plugging into E_I gives us

   $$E_I = \frac{(2 - 1) \div [(1 + 2) \div 2]}{0.25}$$

   Simplifying yields

   $$E_I = \frac{1 \div 1.5}{0.25}$$

Therefore, $E_I = 2.67$.

The income elasticity of demand for eating out is positive for normal goods. Therefore, eating out is a normal good. This result should confirm your intuition.

Let's see what happens with frozen lasagna once the worker gets the 25% raise. Now he cuts back on the number of lasagna dinners from once a week to once every other week.

Plugging into E_I gives us

$$E_I = \frac{(0.5 - 1) \div [(1 + 0.5) \div 2]}{0.25}$$

Simplifying yields

$$E_I = \frac{-0.5 \div 0.75}{0.25}$$

Therefore, $E_I = -2.67$. The income elasticity of demand for having frozen lasagna is negative. Therefore, frozen lasagna is an inferior good. This result should confirm your intuition.

The minimum wage helps everyone earn a living wage.

You are probably familiar with the minimum wage, which is an example of a *price control*. If you have ever worked for the minimum wage, you probably think that raising it sounds like a great idea. You

MIS CONCEPTION

may support minimum wage legislation because you believe it will help struggling workers to make ends meet. After all, it seems reasonable that firms should pay workers at least enough to cover the necessities of life, or what is referred to as a living wage.

Price controls are not a new idea. The first recorded attempt to control prices was four thousand years ago in ancient Babylon, when King Hammurabi decreed how much corn a farmer could pay for a cow. Similar attempts to control prices occurred in ancient Egypt, Greece, and Rome. Each attempt ended badly. In Egypt, farmers revolted against tight price controls and intrusive inspections, eventually causing the economy to collapse. In Greece, the Athenian government set the price of grain at a very low level. Predictably, the quantity of grain supplied dried up. In 301 CE, the Roman government under Emperor Diocletian prescribed the maximum price of beef, grains, clothing, and many other articles. Almost immediately, markets for these goods disappeared.

History has shown us that price controls generally do not work. Why? Because they disrupt the normal functioning of the market. By the end of this chapter, we hope that you will understand why price controls such as minimum wage laws are rarely the win-win propositions that legislators often claim. To help you understand why price controls lead to disequilibrium in markets, this chapter focuses on the two most common types of price controls: *price ceilings* and *price floors*.

The Code of Hammurabi established the first known price controls.

BIG QUESTIONS

* ✴ When do price ceilings matter?
* ✴ What effects do price ceilings have on economic activity?
* ✴ When do price floors matter?
* ✴ What effects do price floors have on economic activity?

When Do Price Ceilings Matter?

Price controls
are an attempt to set prices through government involvement in the market.

Price ceilings
are legally established maximum prices for goods or services.

Price controls are an attempt to set prices through government involvement in the market. In most cases, and certainly in the United States, price controls are enacted to ease perceived burdens on society. A **price ceiling** creates a legally established maximum price for a good or service. In the next section, we will consider what happens when a price ceiling is in place. Price ceilings create many unintended effects that policymakers rarely acknowledge.

Understanding Price Ceilings

To understand how price ceilings work, let's try a simple thought experiment. Suppose that prices are rising because of inflation. The government is concerned that people with low incomes will not be able to afford enough to eat. To help the disadvantaged, legislators pass a law stating that no one can charge more than $0.50 for a loaf of bread. (Note that this price ceiling is about one-third the typical price of generic white bread.) Does the new law accomplish its goal? What happens?

The law of supply and demand tells us that if the price drops, the quantity that consumers demand will increase. At the same time, the quantity supplied will fall because producers will be receiving lower profits for their efforts. This twin dynamic of increased quantity demanded and reduced quantity supplied will cause a shortage of bread.

On the demand side, consumers will want more bread than is available at the legal price. There will be long lines for bread, and many people will not be able to get the bread they want. On the supply side, producers will look for ways to maintain their profits. They can reduce the size of each loaf they produce. They can also use cheaper ingredients, thereby lowering

Empty shelves signal a shortage of products.

the quality of their product, and they can stop making fancier varieties. In addition, *black markets* will develop to help supply meet demand.

Black markets are illegal markets that arise when price controls are in place. For instance, in the former Soviet Union price controls on bread and other essentials led to very long lines. In our bread example, many people who do not want to wait in line for bread, or who do not obtain it despite waiting in line, will resort to illegal means to obtain it. This means that sellers will go underground and charge higher prices to deliver customers the bread they want.

Table 5.1 summarizes the likely outcome of price controls on bread.

Black markets
are illegal markets that arise when price controls are in place.

Incentives

TABLE 5.1

A Price Ceiling on Bread

Question	Answer / Explanation	Result	
Will there be more or less bread for sale?	Consumers will want to buy more since the price is lower (the law of demand), but producers will manufacture less (the law of supply). The net result will be a shortage of bread.		Empty shelves.
Will the size of a typical loaf change?	Since the price is capped at $0.50 per loaf, manufacturers will try to maintain profits by reducing the size of each loaf.		No more giant loaves.
Will the quality change?	Since the price is capped, producers will use cheaper ingredients, and many expensive brands and varieties will no longer be profitable to produce. Thus the quality of available bread will decline.		Focaccia bread will disappear.
Will the opportunity cost of finding bread change?	The opportunity cost of finding bread will rise. This means that consumers will spend significant resources going from store to store to see if a bread shipment has arrived and waiting in line for a chance to get some.		Bread lines will become the norm.
Will people have to break the law to buy bread?	Since bread will be hard to find and people will still need it, a black market will develop. Those selling and buying on the black market will be breaking the law.		Black-market bread dealers will help reduce the shortage.

If you can touch the ceiling, you can't go any higher. A binding price ceiling stops prices from rising.

The Effect of Price Ceilings

Now that we have some understanding of how a price ceiling works, we can transfer that knowledge into the supply and demand model for a deeper analysis of how price ceilings affect the market. To explain when price ceilings matter in the short run, we will examine the outcomes of two types of price ceilings: nonbinding and binding.

Nonbinding Price Ceilings

The effect of a price ceiling depends on the level at which it is set. When a price ceiling is above the equilibrium price, we say it is *nonbinding*. Figure 5.1 shows a price ceiling of $2.00 per loaf in a market where $2.00 is above the equilibrium price (P_E). All prices at or below $2.00 (the green area) are legal. Prices above the price ceiling (the red area) are illegal. But since the market equilibrium (E) occurs in the green area, the price ceiling does not influence the market; it is nonbinding. As long as the equilibrium price remains below the price ceiling, price will continue to be regulated by supply and demand. Since there is rarely a compelling political reason to set a price ceiling above the equilibrium price, nonbinding price ceilings are unusual.

Binding Price Ceilings

When a price ceiling is below the market price, it creates a binding constraint that prevents supply and demand from clearing the market. In Figure 5.2,

FIGURE 5.1

A Nonbinding Price Ceiling

The price ceiling ($2.00) is set above the equilibrium price ($1.00). Since market prices are set by the intersection of supply (S) and demand (D), as long as the equilibrium price is below the price ceiling, the price ceiling is nonbinding and has no effect.

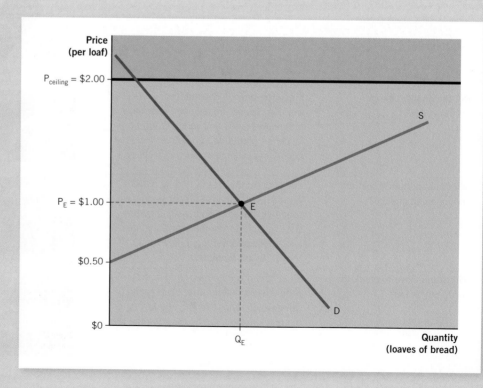

the price ceiling for bread is set at $0.50 per loaf. Since $0.50 is well below the equilibrium price of $1.00, this creates a binding price ceiling. Notice that at a price of $0.50, the quantity demanded (Q_D) is greater than the quantity supplied (Q_S)—in other words, a shortage exists. Shortages typically cause prices to rise, but the imposed price ceiling prevents that from happening. A price ceiling of $0.50 allows only the prices in the green area. The market cannot reach the equilibrium point E at $1.00 per loaf because it is located above the price ceiling, in the red area.

The black-market price is also set by supply and demand. Since prices above $0.50 are illegal, sellers are unwilling to produce more than Q_S. Once the price ceiling is in place, sellers cannot legally charge prices above the ceiling, so the incentive to produce along the original supply curve vanishes. Since a shortage still exists, an illegal market will form to resolve the shortage. At that point, purchasers can illegally resell what they have just bought at $0.50 for far more than what they just paid. Since the supply of legally produced bread is Q_S, the intersection of the vertical dashed line that reflects Q_S and the demand curve at point E$_{black\ market}$ establishes a black-market price P$_{black\ market}$, at $2.00 per loaf for illegally sold bread. Since the black-market price is substantially more than the market equilibrium price (P_E) of $1.00, illegal suppliers (underground bakers) will also enter the market in order to satisfy demand. As a result, the black-market price eliminates the shortage caused by the price ceiling. However, the price ceiling has created two unintended consequences: a smaller quantity of bread supplied (Q_S is less than Q_E), and a higher price for those who are forced to purchase it on the black market.

Incentives

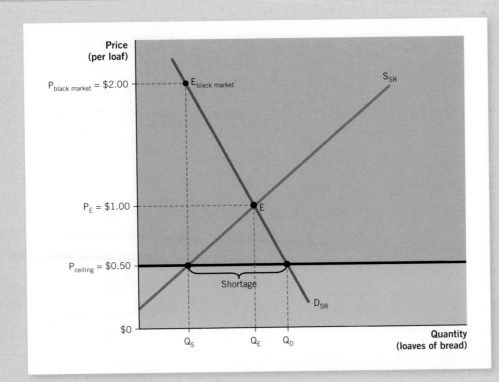

FIGURE 5.2

A Binding Price Ceiling

A binding price ceiling prevents sellers from increasing the price and causes them to reduce the quantity they offer for sale. As a consequence, prices no longer signal relative scarcity. Consumers desire to purchase the product at the price-ceiling level, and this creates a shortage in the short run; many will be unable to obtain the good. As a result, those who are shut out of the market will turn to other means to acquire the good. This establishes an illegal market for the good at the black market price.

Price Ceilings in the Long Run

In the long run, supply and demand become more elastic, or flatter. Recall from Chapter 4 that when consumers have additional time to make choices, they find more ways to avoid high-priced goods and more ways to take advantage of low prices. Additional time also gives producers the opportunity to produce more when prices are high and less when prices are low. In this section, we consider what will happen if a binding price ceiling on bread remains in effect for a long time. We have already observed that when binding price ceilings are in effect in the short run, shortages and black markets develop. Are the long-run implications of price ceilings more or less problematic than the short-run implications? Let's find out by looking at what happens to both supply and demand.

Figure 5.3 shows the result of a price ceiling that remains in place for a long time. Here the supply curve is more elastic than its short-run counterpart in Figure 5.2. The supply curve is flatter because in the long run producers respond by producing less bread and converting their facilities to make similar products that are not subject to price controls—for example, bagels and rolls—that will bring them a reasonable return on their investments. Therefore, in the long run the quantity supplied (Q_S) grows even smaller.

The demand curve is also more elastic in the long run. In the long run, more people will attempt to take advantage of the low price ceiling by changing their eating habits to consume more bread. Even though consumers will

FIGURE 5.3

The Effect of a Binding Price Ceiling in the Long Run

In the long run, increased elasticity on the part of both producers and consumers makes the shortage larger than it was in the short run. Consumers adjust their demand to the lower price and want more bread. Producers adjust their supply and make less of the unprofitable product. As a result, products become progressively harder to find.

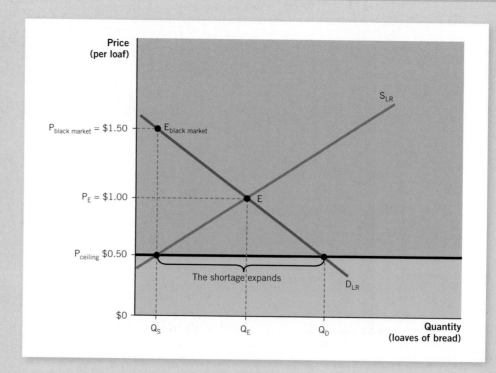

Price Ceilings

Moscow on the Hudson

This 1984 film starring Robin Williams chronicles the differences between living in the United States and the former Soviet Union. In Moscow, we see hundreds of people waiting in line to receive essentials like bread, milk, and shoes. In the Soviet Union, production was controlled and prices were not allowed to equalize supply and demand. As a result, shortages were common. Waiting in line served as a rationing mechanism in the absence of price adjustments.

This film is memorable because of the reactions that Robin Williams's character has once he immi-

Soviet-era food-rationing coupon

Soviet-era bread line

grates to the United States. In one inspired scene, he walks into a supermarket to buy coffee. He asks the manager where the coffee aisle is located, and when he sees that the aisle is not crowded, he asks the manager where the coffee line is located. The manager responds that there is no coffee line, so Williams walks down the coffee aisle slowly, naming each variety. We see his joy at being able to buy coffee without waiting and at having so many options to choose from. This scene nicely showcases the differences between the market system of the United States and the controlled economy of the former Soviet Union.

often find empty shelves in the long run, the quantity demanded of cheap bread will increase. At this point, a flatter demand curve means that consumers are more flexible. As a result, the quantity demanded (Q_D) expands and bread is hard to find at $0.50 per loaf. The shortage will become so acute that consumers will turn to bread substitutes, like bagels and rolls, that are more plentiful because they are not price controlled.

Increased elasticity on the part of both producers and consumers magnifies the unintended consequences we observed in the short run. Therefore, products subject to a price ceiling become progressively harder to find in the long run. A black market will develop. However, in the long run our bread consumers will choose substitutes for expensive black-market bread. This will cause somewhat lower black-market prices in the long run.

PRACTICE WHAT YOU KNOW

Price Ceilings: Concert Tickets

Question: Suppose that fans of Avicii persuade Congress to impose a price ceiling of $25 for every Avicii concert ticket. Would this policy affect the number of people who attend his concerts?

You've got a good feeling about this concert.

Answer: The price ceiling prevents supply and demand from reaching the equilibrium price. As a result, at $25 there is a shortage of tickets. Since Avicii controls when and where he tours, he will choose to tour less in the United States and more in countries that do not regulate the ticket prices he can charge. This will make it more difficult for his U.S. fans to see him perform live, so the answer to the question is yes: the policy will influence the number of people who attend Avicii concerts (fewer in the United States, and more abroad).

What Effects Do Price Ceilings Have on Economic Activity?

We have seen the logical repercussions of a hypothetical price ceiling on bread and the incentives it creates. Now let's use supply and demand analysis to examine two real-world price ceilings: *rent control* and *price gouging laws*.

Rent Control

Rent control
is a price ceiling that applies to the housing market.

Under **rent control**, a local government caps the price of apartment rentals to keep housing affordable. While this may be a laudable goal, rent control doesn't work. In fact, it doesn't help poor residents of a city to find affordable housing or gain access to housing at all. In addition, these policies contribute to dangerous living conditions.

Mumbai, India, provides a chilling example of what can happen when rent controls are applied over an extended period. In Mumbai, many rent-controlled buildings have become dilapidated. Every monsoon season, several of these buildings fall—often with tragic consequences. Since the rent that property owners are permitted to charge is so low, they have less income to use for maintenance. Therefore, they cannot afford to maintain the buildings properly and make a reasonable profit. As a result, rent-control policies have led to the decay of many apartment buildings. Similar controls have caused the same problem in cities worldwide.

To understand how a policy can backfire so greatly, let's look at the history of rent control in New York City. In 1943, in the midst of World War II, the federal government established the Emergency Price Control Act. The act was designed to keep inflation in check during the war, when many essential commodities were scarce. After the war, the federal government ended price controls, but the city of New York continued rent control. Today, there are approximately one million rent-controlled units in New York City. Rent controls limit the price a landlord can charge a tenant for rent. They also require that the landlord provide certain basic services; but not surprisingly, landlords keep maintenance to a minimum.

Many apartment buildings in Mumbai, India, are dilapidated as a result of rent-control laws.

Incentives

Does the presence of so many rent-controlled apartments mean that less affluent households can easily find a cheap place to rent? Hardly. When a rent-controlled unit is vacated, the property is generally no longer subject to rent control. Since most rent-controlled apartments are passed by tenants from generation to generation to remain in the program, rent control no longer even remotely serves its original purpose of helping low-income households. Clearly, the law was never intended to subsidize fancy vacation homes, but that's what it does! This has happened, in part, because some tenants who can afford to live elsewhere choose not to. Their subsidized rent enables them to save enough money to have a second or third home in places such as upstate New York, Florida, or Europe.

The attempt to make housing more affordable in New York City has, ironically, made housing harder to obtain. It has encouraged the building of upscale properties rather than low-income units, and it has created a set of behaviors among landlords that is inconsistent with the ideals of justice and affordability that rent control was designed to address. Figure 5.4 shows why rent control fails. As with any price ceiling, rent control causes a shortage since the quantity demanded in the short run ($Q_{D_{SR}}$) is greater than the quantity supplied in the short run ($Q_{S_{SR}}$). Because rent-controlled apartments are vacated slowly, the supply of rent-controlled units contracts in the long run, which causes the supply curve to become more elastic (S_{LR}). Demand also becomes more elastic in the long run (D_{LR}), which causes the quantity demanded for rent-controlled units to rise ($Q_{D_{LR}}$). The combination of fewer available units and more consumers looking for rent-controlled units leads to a larger shortage in the long run.

Price Gouging

Another kind of price control, **price gouging laws**, places a temporary ceiling on the prices that sellers can charge during times of national emergency until markets function normally again. Over 30 states in the United States

Price gouging laws
place a temporary ceiling on the prices that sellers can charge during times of emergency.

have laws against price gouging. Like all price controls, price gouging laws have unintended consequences. This became very apparent in the southern United States in 2005.

The hurricane season of 2005 was arguably the worst in U.S. history. Katrina and Rita plowed through the Gulf of Mexico with devastating effects, especially in Louisiana and Texas. Later that year, Wilma grew into the most powerful hurricane ever recorded in the Atlantic basin. When Wilma hit Fort Myers, Florida, in November, it ended a season for the record books. Florida has one of the strictest price gouging laws in the country. The statute makes it illegal to charge an "excessive" price immediately following a natural disaster. The law is designed to prevent the victims of natural disasters from being exploited in a time of need. But does it work?

Consider David Medina of Miami Beach. Immediately after Wilma hit, he drove to North Carolina, purchased 35 gas-powered generators, and returned to Florida, where he sold them from the back of his truck. He charged $900 for large generators, which he had purchased for $529.99, and $600 for small generators, which had cost him $279.99. After selling most of the units, Medina was arrested for price gouging. Under Florida law, his remaining generators were confiscated, and he was fined $1,000 for each sale. In addition, he was charged with selling without a business license. While there is no doubt that Medina intended to capitalize on the misfortune of others, it is hard to prove that he did any harm. The people who bought from him did so voluntarily, each believing that the value of the generator was greater than the price Medina was charging.

FIGURE 5.4

Rent Control in the Short Run and Long Run

Because rent-controlled apartments are vacated slowly, the supply of units contracts in the long run and the supply curve becomes more elastic. Demand also becomes more elastic in the long run, causing the quantity demanded to rise. The combination of fewer units available to rent and more consumers looking to find rent-controlled units leads to a larger shortage in the long run.

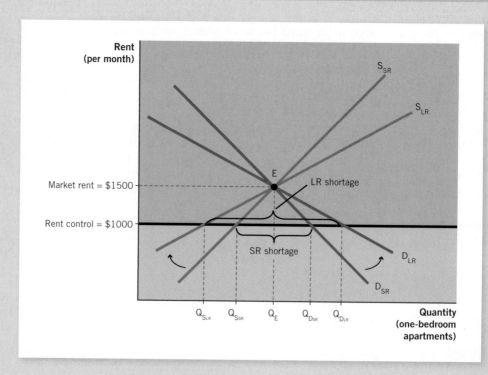

Prices act to ration scarce resources. When the demand for generators or other necessities is high, the price rises to ensure that the available units are distributed to those who value them the most. More important, the ability to charge a higher price provides sellers with an incentive to make more units available. If there is limited ability for the price to change when demand increases, there will be a shortage. Therefore, price gouging legislation means that devastated communities must rely exclusively on the goodwill of others and the slow-moving machinery of government relief efforts. This closes off a third avenue, entrepreneurial activity, as a means to alleviate poor conditions.

Incentives

Large generator: $900 after Hurricane Wilma hit.

Figure 5.5 shows how price gouging laws work and the shortage they create. If the demand for gas generators increases immediately after a disaster (D_{after}), the market price rises from $530 to $900. But since $900 is considered excessive, sales at that price are illegal. This creates a binding price ceiling for as long as a state of emergency is in effect. Whenever a price ceiling is binding, it creates a shortage. You can see this in Figure 5.5 in the difference between quantity demanded and quantity supplied at the price ceiling level mandated by the law. In this case, the normal ability of supply and demand to ration the available generators is short-circuited. Since more people demand generators after the disaster than before it, those who do not get to the store soon enough are out of luck. When the emergency is lifted and the market returns to normal, the temporary shortage created by legislation against price gouging is eliminated.

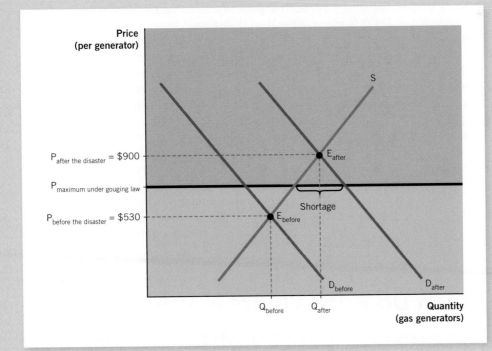

FIGURE 5.5

Price Gouging

Price gouging laws serve as a nonbinding price ceiling during normal times. However, when a natural disaster strikes, price gouging laws go into effect. In our example, this shifts the demand curve for generators to the right and causes the new equilibrium price (E_{after}) to rise above the legal limit. This creates a shortage. When the emergency is lifted, the market demand returns to normal, and the temporary shortage created by price gouging legislation is eliminated.

PRACTICE WHAT YOU KNOW

Price Ceilings: Student Rental Apartments

Here is a question that often confuses students.

Question: Imagine that a city council decides that the market price for renting student apartments is too high and passes a law that establishes a rental price ceiling of $600 per month. The result of the price ceiling is a shortage. Which of the following caused the shortage of apartments?

a. Both suppliers and demanders. Landlords will cut the supply of apartments, and the demand from renters will increase.

b. A spike in demand from many students who want to rent cheap apartments

c. The drop in supply caused by apartment owners pulling their units off the rental market and converting them into condos for sale

d. The price ceiling set by the city council

Answer: Many students think that markets are to blame when shortages (or surpluses) exist. The first reaction is to find the culpable party—either the supplier or the demander, or both.

Answer (a) is a typical response. But be careful. Supply and demand have not changed—they are exactly the same as they were before the price ceiling was implemented. What *has* changed is the quantity of apartments supplied at $600. This change in quantity would be represented by a movement along the existing supply curve. The same is true for renters. The quantity demanded at $600 is much larger than it was when the price was not controlled. Once again, there will be a movement along the demand curve.

The same logic applies to answers (b) and (c). Answer (b) argues that there is a spike in student demand caused by the lower price. But price cannot cause a shift in the demand curve; it can only cause a movement along a curve. Likewise, (c) argues that apartment owners supply fewer units for rent. Landlords cannot charge more than $600 per unit, so they convert some apartments into private residences and offer them for sale in order to make more profit. Since fewer apartments are available at $600, this would be represented by a movement along the apartment supply curve.

This brings us to (d). There is only one change in market conditions: the city council passed a new price ceiling law. A binding price ceiling disrupts the ability of the market to reach equilibrium. Therefore, we can say that the change in the price as a result of the price ceiling caused the shortage.

When Do Price Floors Matter?

In this section, we examine price floors. Like price ceilings, price floors create many unintended effects that policymakers rarely acknowledge. However, unlike price ceilings, price floors result from the political pressure of suppliers to keep prices high. Most consumers prefer lower prices when they shop, so the idea of a law that keeps prices high may sound like a bad one to you. However, if you are selling a product or service, you might think that legislation to keep prices high is a very good idea. For instance, many states establish minimum prices for milk. As a result, milk prices are higher than they would be if supply and demand set the price. **Price floors** create legally established minimum prices for goods or services. The minimum wage law is another example of a price floor. In this section, we will follow the same progression that we did with price ceilings. We begin with a simple thought experiment. Once we understand how price floors work, we will use supply and demand analysis to examine the short- and long-term implications for economic activity.

Understanding Price Floors

To understand how price floors affect the market, let's try a thought experiment. Suppose that a politician suggests we should encourage dairy farmers to produce more milk so that supplies will be plentiful and everyone will get enough calcium. In order to accomplish this, a price floor of $6 per gallon—about twice the price of a typical gallon of fat-free milk—is enacted to make production more attractive to producers. What repercussions should we expect?

First, more milk will be available for sale. We know this because the higher price will cause dairies to increase the quantity that they supply. At the same time, because consumers must pay more, the quantity demanded will fall. The result will be a surplus of milk. Since every gallon of milk that is produced but not sold hurts the dairies' bottom line, sellers will want to lower their prices enough to get as many sales as possible before the milk goes bad. But the price floor will not allow the market to respond, and sellers will be stuck with milk that goes to waste. They will be tempted to offer illegal discounts in order to recoup some of their costs.

If you're doing a handstand, you need the floor for support. A binding price floor keeps prices from falling.

Price floors
are legally established minimum prices for goods or services.

What happens next? Since the surplus cannot be resolved through lower prices, the government will try to help equalize supply and demand through other means. This can be accomplished in one of two ways: by restricting the supply of the good or by stimulating additional demand. Both solutions are problematic. If production is restricted, dairy farmers will not be able to generate a profitable amount of milk. Likewise, stimulating additional demand is not as simple as it sounds. Let's consider how this works with other crops.

In many cases, the government purchases surplus agricultural production. This occurs most notably with corn, soybeans, cotton, and rice. Once the government buys the surplus production, it often sells the surplus below cost to developing countries to avoid having the crop go to waste. This strategy has the unintended consequence of making it cheaper for consumers in these developing nations to buy excess agricultural output from developed nations like the United States than to have local farmers grow the crop. International treaties ban the practice of dumping surplus production, but it continues under the guise of humanitarian aid. This practice makes little economic sense. Table 5.2 summarizes the result of our price-floor thought experiment using milk.

The Effect of Price Floors

We have seen that price floors create unintended consequences. Now we will use the supply and demand model to analyze how price floors affect the market. We'll take a look at the short run first.

Got milk? Maybe not, if there's a price floor.

TABLE 5.2

A Price Floor on Milk

Question	Answer / Explanation		Result
Will the quantity of milk for sale change?	Consumers will purchase less since the price is higher (the law of demand), but producers will manufacture more (the law of supply). The net result will be a surplus of milk.		There will be a surplus of milk.
Would producers sell below the price floor?	Yes. A surplus of milk would give sellers a strong incentive to undercut the price floor in order to avoid having to discard leftover milk.	REDUCED MILK AHEAD	Illegal discounts will help to reduce the milk surplus.
Will dairy farmers be better off?	Not if they have trouble selling what they produce.		There might be a lot of spoiled milk.

Nonbinding Price Floors

Like price ceilings, price floors can be binding or nonbinding. Figure 5.6 illustrates a nonbinding price floor of $2 per gallon on milk. As you can see, at $2 the price floor is below the equilibrium price (P_E), so the price floor is nonbinding. Since the actual market price is above the legally established minimum price (P_{floor}), the price floor does not prevent the market from reaching equilibrium at point E. Consequently, the price floor has no impact on the market. As long as the equilibrium price remains above the price floor, price is regulated by supply and demand.

Full shelves signal a market at equilibrium.

Binding Price Floors

For a price floor to have an impact on the market, it must be set above the market equilibrium price. In that case, it is known as a binding price floor. And with a binding price floor, the quantity supplied will exceed the quantity demanded. Figure 5.7 illustrates a binding price floor in the short run. Continuing our example of milk prices, at $6 per gallon the price floor is above the equilibrium price of $3. Market forces always attempt to restore the equilibrium between supply and demand at point E. So we know that there is downward pressure on the price. At a price floor

FIGURE 5.6

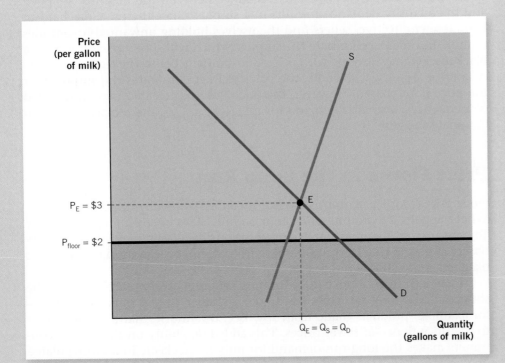

A Nonbinding Price Floor

Under a nonbinding price floor, price is regulated by supply and demand. Since the price floor ($2) is below the equilibrium price ($3), the market will voluntarily charge more than the legal minimum. Therefore, this price floor will have no effect on sales and purchases of milk.

FIGURE 5.7

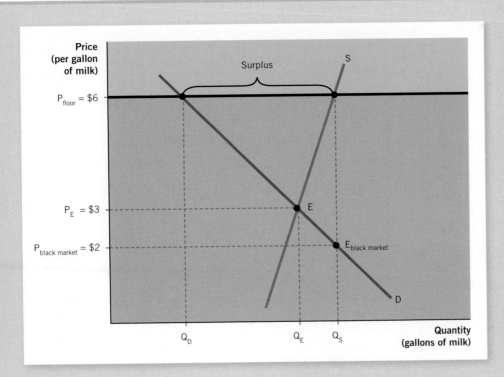

A Binding Price Floor in the Short Run

A binding price floor creates a surplus. This has two unintended consequences: a smaller demand than the equilibrium quantity ($Q_D < Q_E$), and a lower black-market price to eliminate the glut of the product.

Incentives

of $6, we see that $Q_S > Q_D$. The difference between the quantity supplied and the quantity demanded results in a surplus. Since the price mechanism is no longer effective, sellers find themselves holding unwanted inventories of milk. In order to eliminate the surplus, which will spoil unless it is sold, a black market may develop with prices substantially below the legislated price. At a price ($P_{black\ market}$) of $1, the black market eliminates the surplus that the price floor caused. However, the price floor has created two unintended consequences: a smaller demand for milk ($Q_D < Q_E$), and a black market to eliminate the glut.

Price Floors in the Long Run

Once price-floor legislation is passed, it can be politically difficult to repeal. What happens if a binding price floor on milk stays in effect for a long time? To help answer that question, we need to consider elasticity. We have already observed that in the short run binding price ceilings cause shortages and that black markets follow.

Figure 5.8 shows a price floor for milk that remains in place well past the short run. The long run gives consumers a chance to find milk substitutes—for example, products made from soy, rice, or almond that are not subject to the price floor—at lower prices. This added flexibility on the part of consumers makes the long-run demand for milk more elastic in an unregulated market. As a result, the demand curve depicted in Figure 5.8 is more elastic

FIGURE 5.8

The Effect of a Binding Price Floor in the Long Run

When a price floor is left in place over time, supply and demand each become more elastic. This leads to a larger surplus ($Q_S > Q_D$) in the long run. Since sellers are unable to sell all that they produce at $6 per gallon, a black market develops in order to eliminate the glut of milk.

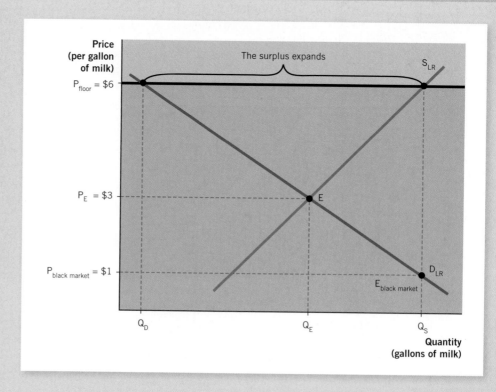

than its short-run counterpart in Figure 5.7. The supply curve also becomes flatter since firms (dairy farms) are able to produce more milk by acquiring additional land and production facilities. Therefore, a price floor ($6) that remains in place over time causes the supply and demand curves to become more elastic. This magnifies the shortage.

What happens to supply? In the long run, producers are more flexible and therefore supply is more elastic. The pool of potential milk producers rises as other closely related businesses retool their operations to supply more milk. The flatter supply curve in Figure 5.8 reflects this flexibility. As a result, Q_S expands and becomes much larger than it was in Figure 5.7. The increased elasticity on the part of both producers and consumers (1) makes the surplus larger in the long run and (2) magnifies the unintended consequences we observed in the short run.

PRACTICE WHAT YOU KNOW

Price Floors: Fair-Trade Coffee

Fair-trade coffee is sold through organizations that purchase directly from growers. The coffee is usually sold for a higher price than standard coffee. The goal is to promote more humane working conditions for the coffee pickers and growers. Fair-trade coffee has become more popular but still accounts for a small portion of all coffee sales, in large part because it is substantially more expensive to produce.

Question: Suppose that a one-pound bag of standard coffee costs $8 and that a one-pound bag of fair-trade coffee costs $12. Congress decides to impose a price floor of $10 per pound. Will this policy cause more or fewer people to buy fair-trade coffee?

Answer: Fair-trade producers typically sell their product at a higher price than mass-produced coffee brands. Therefore, a $10 price floor is binding for inexpensive brands like Folgers but nonbinding for premium coffees, which include fair-trade sellers. The price floor will reduce the price disparity between fair-trade coffee and mass-produced coffee.

To see how this works, consider a fair-trade coffee producer who charges $12 per pound and a mass-produced brand that sells for $8 per pound. A price floor of $10 reduces the difference between the price of fair-trade coffee and the inexpensive coffee brands, which now must sell for $10 instead of $8. This lowers the consumer's opportunity cost of choosing fair-trade coffee. Therefore, some consumers of the inexpensive brands will opt for fair-trade instead. As a result, fair-trade producers will benefit indirectly from the price floor. Thus the answer to the question at the top is that *more* people will buy fair-trade coffee as a result of this price-floor policy.

Would fair-trade coffee producers benefit from a price floor?

Opportunity cost

What Effects Do Price Floors Have on Economic Activity?

We have seen the logical repercussions of a hypothetical price floor on milk and the incentives it creates. Now let's use supply and demand analysis to examine two real-world price floors: *minimum wage laws* and *agricultural price supports*.

The Minimum Wage

The **minimum wage** is the lowest hourly wage rate that firms may legally pay their workers.

The **minimum wage** is the lowest hourly wage rate that firms may legally pay their workers. Minimum wage workers can be skilled or unskilled and experienced or inexperienced. The common thread is that these workers, for a variety of reasons, lack better prospects. A minimum wage functions as a price floor. Figure 5.9 shows the effect of a binding minimum wage. Note that the wage, or cost of labor, on the y axis ($10 per hour) is the price that must be paid. However, the market equilibrium wage ($7), or W_E, is below the minimum wage. The minimum wage prevents the market from reaching W_E at E (the equilibrium point) because only the wages in the green shaded area are legal. Since the demand for labor depends on how much it costs, the minimum wage raises the cost of hiring workers. Therefore, a higher minimum wage will lower the quantity of labor demanded. However, since

FIGURE 5.9

Price Floors and a Binding Minimum Wage Market in the Short and Long Run

A binding minimum wage is a price floor above the current equilibrium wage, W_E. At $10 per hour, the number of workers willing to supply their labor (S_{SR}) is greater than the demand for workers (D_{SR}). The result is a surplus of workers (which we recognize as unemployment). Since the supply of workers and demand for workers both become more elastic in the long run, unemployment expands ($S_{LR} > D_{LR}$).

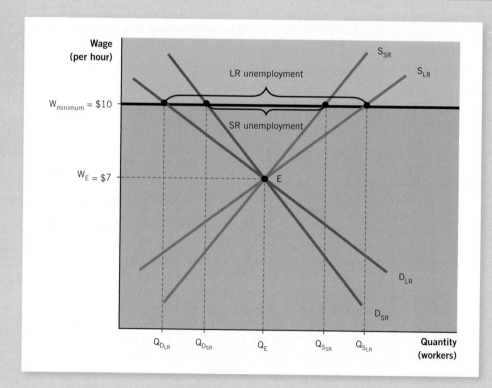

businesses still need to serve their customers, this means that labor expenses for the firm ordinarily rise in the short run. At the same time, firms will look for ways to substitute additional capital for workers. As a result, a binding minimum wage results in unemployment in the short run since $Q_{SSR} > Q_{DSR}$.

Businesses generally want to keep costs down, so in the long run they will try to reduce the amount they spend on labor. They might replace workers with machinery, shorten work hours, offer reduced customer service, or even relocate to countries that do not have minimum wage laws. As we move past the short run, more people will attempt to take advantage of higher minimum wages. Like firms, workers will adjust to the higher minimum wage over time. Some workers who might have decided to go to school full-time or remain retired, or who simply want some extra income, will enter the labor market because the minimum wage is now higher. As a result, minimum wage jobs will become progressively harder to find and unemployment will be magnified. The irony is that in the long run the minimum wage, just like any other price floor, has created two unintended consequences: a smaller demand for workers by employers (Q_{DLR} is significantly less than Q_E), and a larger supply of workers (Q_{SLR}) looking for those previously existing jobs.

Proponents of minimum wage legislation are aware that it often creates unemployment. To address this problem, they support investment in training, education, and the creation of government jobs programs to provide more work opportunities. While jobs programs increase minimum wage jobs, training and additional education enable workers to acquire skills needed for jobs that pay more than the minimum wage. Economists generally believe that education and training programs have longer-lasting benefits to society as a whole since they enable workers to obtain better-paying jobs on a permanent basis.

ECONOMICS IN THE REAL WORLD

Wage Laws Squeeze South Africa's Poor

Consider this story that appeared in the *New York Times* in 2010.[*]

NEWCASTLE, South Africa—The sheriff arrived at the factory here to shut it down, part of a national enforcement drive against clothing manufacturers who violate the minimum wage. But women working on the factory floor— the supposed beneficiaries of the crackdown—clambered atop cutting tables and ironing boards to raise anguished cries against it. Thoko Zwane, 43, who has worked in factories since she was 15, lost her job in Newcastle when a Chinese-run factory closed in 2004. More than a third of South Africans are jobless. "Why? Why?" shouted Nokuthula Masango, 25, after the authorities carted away bolts of gaily colored fabric. She made just $36 a week, $21 less than the minimum wage, but needed the meager pay to help support a large extended family that includes her five unemployed siblings and their children.

The women's spontaneous protest is just one sign of how acute South Africa's long-running unemployment crisis has become. With their own economy saddled with very high unemployment rates, the women feared being out of work more than getting stuck in poorly paid jobs.

Trade-offs

---

[*]Celia W. Dugger, "Wage Laws Squeeze South Africa's Poor," *New York Times*, September 27, 2010.

South Africans wait in line for unemployment benefits.

In the years since the end of apartheid, the South African economy has grown, but not nearly fast enough to end an intractable unemployment crisis. For over a decade, the jobless rate has been among the highest in the world, fueling crime, inequality, and social unrest in the continent's richest nation. The global economic downturn has made the problem much worse, wiping out more than a million jobs. Over a third of South Africa's workforce is now idle. And 16 years after Nelson Mandela led the country to black majority rule, more than half of blacks ages 15 to 34 are without work—triple the level for whites.

"The numbers are mind-boggling," said James Levinsohn, a Yale University economist. ✳

The Minimum Wage Is Often Nonbinding

Most people believe that raising the minimum wage is a simple step that the government can take to improve the standard of living of the working poor. However, in most places the minimum wage is often nonbinding and therefore has no impact on the market. Adjusting for inflation, the federal minimum wage was highest in 1968, so in real terms minimum wage workers are earning less today than they did almost half a century ago. Why would we have a minimum wage if it is largely nonbinding?

To help us answer this question, consider the two nonbinding minimum wage rates ($7 and $9) shown in Figure 5.10. A minimum wage of $7 per hour is far below the equilibrium wage of $10 ($W_E$), so at that point supply and demand push the equilibrium wage up to $10. Suppose that politicians decide to raise the minimum wage to $9. This new minimum wage of $9 would remain below the market wage, so there would be no impact on the labor market for workers who are willing to accept the minimum wage. Therefore, an increase in the minimum wage from $7 to $9 an hour will not create unemployment. Unemployment will occur only when the minimum wage rises above $10.

Politicians know that most voters have a poor understanding of basic economics. As a result, a politician can seek to raise the minimum wage with great fanfare. Voters would support the new rate because they do not know that it is likely to be nonbinding; they expect wages to rise. In reality, nothing will change, but the perception of a benevolent action will remain. In fact, since its inception in 1938, increases in the minimum wage in the United States have generally trailed the market wage and therefore have avoided creating unemployment. The minimum wage adjusts sporadically upward every few years but rarely rises enough to cause the market wage to fall below it. This creates the illusion that the minimum wage is lifting wages. However, it does not cause any of the adverse consequences of a binding minimum wage.

In an effort to raise the minimum wage beyond the national rate, a number of states have enacted higher minimum wage laws. Not surprisingly, some of the states with the highest minimum wage rates, like Washington, Oregon,

FIGURE 5.10

A Nonbinding Minimum Wage

An increase in the minimum wage from $7 to $9 remains nonbinding. Therefore, it will not change the demand for labor or the unemployment rate. If the minimum wage rises above the market wage, additional unemployment will occur.

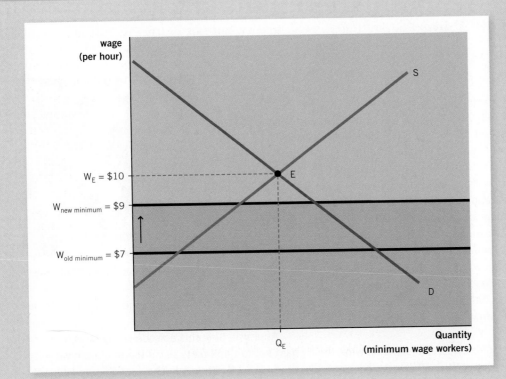

and California, also have unemployment rates that are among the highest in the country—evidence that binding minimum wage rates can have serious consequences.

ECONOMICS IN THE REAL WORLD

A Sweet Deal, If You Can Get It

Sugar is one of life's small pleasures. It can be extracted and refined from sugar cane and sugar beets, two crops that can be grown in a variety of climates around the world. Sugar is both plentiful and cheap. As a result, Americans enjoy a lot of it—an average of over 60 pounds of refined sugar per person each year!

We would consume a lot more sugar if it was not subject to price controls. After the War of 1812, struggling sugar cane producers asked the government to pass a tariff that would protect domestic production. Over the years, price supports of all kinds have served to keep domestic sugar production high. The result is an industry that depends on a high price to survive. Under the current price-support system, the price of U.S.-produced sugar is roughly two to three times the world price. This has led to a bizarre set of incentives whereby U.S. farmers grow more sugar than they should and use land that is not well suited to the crop. For instance, sugar cane requires a subtropical climate, but most of the U.S. crop is grown in Louisiana, a region that is prone to hurricanes in the summer and killing freezes in the late fall. As a result, many sugar cane crops there are completely lost.

Incentives

The Minimum Wage

30 Days

The (2005) pilot episode of this reality series focused on the minimum wage. Morgan Spurlock and his fiancée spend 30 days in a poor neighborhood of Columbus, Ohio. The couple attempt to survive by earning minimum wage (at that time, $5.15 an hour) in order to make ends meet. In addition, they are required to start off with only one week's minimum wage (about $300) in reserve. Also, they cannot use credit cards to pay their bills. They experience firsthand the struggles that many minimum wage households face when living paycheck to paycheck. *30 Days* makes it painfully clear how difficult it is for anyone to live on the minimum wage for a month, let alone for years.

A quote from Morgan Spurlock sums up what the episode tries to convey: "We don't see the people that surround us. We don't see the people who are struggling to get by that are right next to us. And I have seen how hard the struggle is. I have been here.

Could you make ends meet earning the minimum wage?

And I only did it for a month, and there's people who do this their whole lives."

After watching this episode of *30 Days*, it is hard not to think that raising the minimum wage is a good idea. Unfortunately, the economic reality is that raising the minimum wage does not guarantee that minimum wage earners will make more and also be able keep their jobs.

Which of these is the *real* thing? The Coke on the right, with high-fructose corn syrup, was made in the United States; the other, with sugar, was made in Mexico.

Why do farmers persist in growing sugar cane in Louisiana? The answer lies in the political process: sugar growers have effectively lobbied to keep prices high through tariffs on foreign imports. Since lower prices would put many U.S. growers out of business and cause the loss of many jobs, politicians have given in to their demands.

Meanwhile, the typical sugar consumer is largely oblivious to the political process that sets the price floor. It has been estimated that the sugar subsidy program costs consumers over one billion dollars a year. To make matters worse, thanks to corn subsidies high-fructose corn syrup has become a cheap alternative to sugar and is often added to processed foods and soft drinks. In 1980, Coca-Cola replaced sugar with high-fructose corn extract in the United States in order to reduce production costs. However, Coca-Cola continues to use sugar cane in many Latin American countries because it is cheaper. New research shows that high-fructose corn syrup causes a metabolic reaction that makes people who ingest it more inclined to obesity. Ouch! This is an example of an unintended consequence that few policymakers could have imagined. There is no reason why the United States must produce its own sugar cane. Ironically, sugar is cheaper in Canada primarily because Canada has no sugar growers—and thus no trade restrictions or government support programs. ✴

Minimum Wage: Always the Same?

A minimum wage is a price floor, a price control that doesn't allow prices—in this case the cost of labor—to fall below an assigned value. Although the media and politicians often discuss the minimum wage in America as if there is only one minimum wage, it turns out that there are numerous minimum wages in the USA. In states where the state minimum wage is not the same as the federal minimum wage, the higher of the two wage rates takes effect.

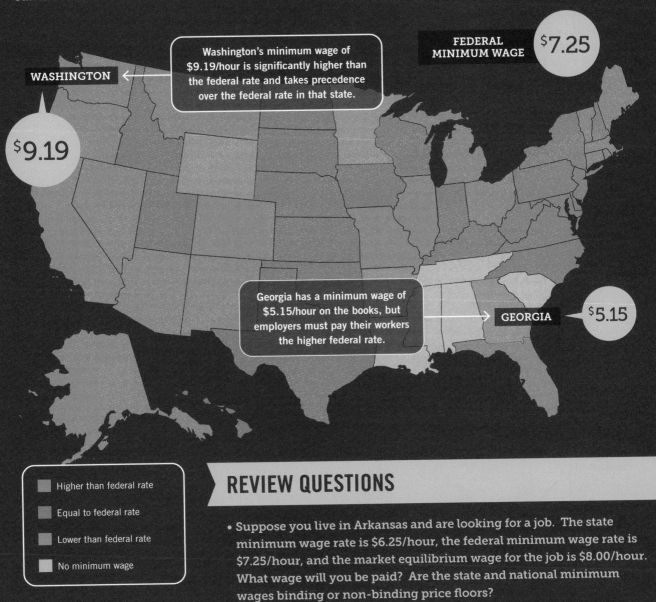

Washington's minimum wage of $9.19/hour is significantly higher than the federal rate and takes precedence over the federal rate in that state.

WASHINGTON

FEDERAL MINIMUM WAGE $7.25

$9.19

Georgia has a minimum wage of $5.15/hour on the books, but employers must pay their workers the higher federal rate.

GEORGIA $5.15

Legend:
- Higher than federal rate
- Equal to federal rate
- Lower than federal rate
- No minimum wage

REVIEW QUESTIONS

- Suppose you live in Arkansas and are looking for a job. The state minimum wage rate is $6.25/hour, the federal minimum wage rate is $7.25/hour, and the market equilibrium wage for the job is $8.00/hour. What wage will you be paid? Are the state and national minimum wages binding or non-binding price floors?

- Suppose Wisconsin increases its minimum wage from $7.25/hour, which is below the market wage for low-skill labor, to $11.00/hour, which is above the market wage. Using supply and demand curves, show how this might affect the number of employed workers.

PRACTICE WHAT YOU KNOW

In today's Internet age, four degrees of separation are all that stand between you and the rest of the world.

Price Ceilings and Price Floors: Would a Price Control on Internet Access Be Effective?

A recent study found the following demand and supply schedule for high-speed Internet access:

Price of Internet	Connections demanded (millions of units)	Connections supplied (millions of units)
$60	10.0	62.5
$50	20.0	55.0
$40	30.0	47.5
$30	40.0	40.0
$20	50.0	32.5
$10	60.0	25.0

Question: What are the equilibrium price and equilibrium quantity of Internet service?

Answer: First, look at the table to see where supply and demand are equal. At a price of $30, consumers purchase 40 million units and producers supply 40 million units. Therefore, the equilibrium price is $30 and the equilibrium quantity is 40 million. At any price above $30, the quantity supplied exceeds the quantity demanded, so there is a surplus. The surplus gives sellers an incentive to cut the price until it reaches the equilibrium point, E. At any price below $30, the quantity demanded exceeds the quantity supplied, so there is a shortage. The shortage gives sellers an incentive to raise the price until it reaches the equilibrium point, E.

Question: Suppose that providers convince the government that maintaining high-speed access to the Internet is an important element of technology infrastructure. As a result, Congress approves a price floor at $10 above the equilibrium price to help companies provide Internet service. How many people are able to connect to the Internet?

Answer: Adding $10 to the market price of $30 gives us a price floor of $40. At $40, consumers demand 30 million connections. Producers provide 47.5 million connections. This is a surplus of 17.5 million units (shown). A price floor means that producers cannot cut the price below that point to increase the quantity that consumers demand. As a result, only 30 million units are sold. So only 30 million people connect to the Internet.

(CONTINUED)

(CONTINUED)

Question: When teachers realize that fewer people are purchasing Internet access, they demand that the price floor be repealed and a price ceiling be put in its place. Congress acts immediately to remedy the problem, and a new price ceiling is set at $10 below the market price. Now how many people are able to connect to the Internet?

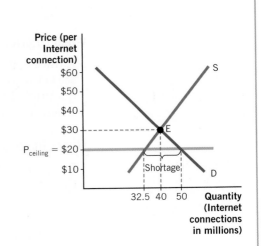

Answer: Subtracting $10 from the market price of $30 gives us a price ceiling of $20. At $20 per connection, consumers demand 50 million connections. However, producers provide only 32.5 million connections. This is a shortage of 17.5 million units (shown). A price ceiling means that producers cannot raise the price, which will cause an increase in the quantity supplied. As a result, only 32.5 million units are sold, so only 32.5 million people connect to the Internet.

Question: Which provides the greatest access to the Internet: free markets, price floors, or price ceilings?

Answer: With no government intervention, 40 million connections are sold. Once the price floor is established, there are 30 million connections. Under the price ceiling, 32.5 million connections exist. Despite legislative efforts to satisfy both producers and consumers of Internet service, the best solution is to allow free markets to regulate access to the good.

Conclusion

Does the minimum wage help everyone earn a living wage? We learned that it is possible to set the minimum wage high enough to guarantee that each worker will earn a living wage. However, the trade-off in setting the minimum wage substantially higher is that it becomes binding and many workers will no longer have jobs. In other words, setting the minimum wage high enough to earn a living wage won't raise every worker out of poverty because many of those workers will no longer have jobs.

Trade-offs

The policies presented in this chapter—rent control, price gouging laws, the minimum wage, and agricultural price controls—create unintended consequences. Attempts to control prices should be viewed cautiously. When the price signal is suppressed through a binding price floor or a binding price ceiling, the market's ability to maintain order is diminished, surpluses and shortages develop and expand through time, and obtaining goods and services becomes difficult.

The role of markets in society has many layers, and we've only just begun our analysis. In the next chapter, we will develop a technique to measure the gains that consumers and producers enjoy in unregulated markets, and we will consider the distortions created by tax policy. Then, in Chapter 7, we will consider two cases—externalities and public goods—in which the unregulated market produces an output that is not socially desirable.

ANSWERING THE BIG QUESTIONS

When do price ceilings matter?

*A price ceiling is a legally imposed maximum price. When the price is set below the equilibrium price, the quantity demanded will exceed the quantity supplied. This will result in a shortage. Price ceilings matter when they are set below the equilibrium price.

What effects do price ceilings have on economic activity?

*Price ceilings create two unintended consequences: a smaller supply of the good (Q_S) and a higher price for consumers who turn to the black market.

When do price floors matter?

*A price floor is a legally imposed minimum price. The minimum wage is an example of a price floor. If the minimum wage is set above the equilibrium wage, a surplus of labor will develop. However, if the minimum wage is nonbinding, it will have no effect on the market wage. Thus price floors matter when they are set above the equilibrium price.

What effects do price floors have on economic activity?

*Price floors lead to many unintended consequences, including surpluses, the creation of black markets, and artificial attempts to bring the market back into balance. For example, proponents of a higher minimum wage are concerned about finding ways to alleviate the resulting surplus of labor, or unemployment.

Price Gouging: Disaster Preparedness

Disasters, whether natural or human-made, usually strike quickly and without warning. You and your family may have little or no time to decide what to do. That's why it is important to plan for the possibility of disaster and not wait until it happens. Failing to plan is planning to fail. In this box, we consider a few simple things you can do now to lessen the impact of a disaster on your personal and financial well-being.

During a disaster, shortages of essential goods and services become widespread. In the 30 states where price gouging laws are on the books, they prevent merchants from charging unusually high prices. If you live in one of these states, cash alone can't save you. You will have to survive on your own for a time before help arrives and communication channels are restored.

Taking measures to prepare for a disaster reduces the likelihood of injury, loss of life, and property damage far more than anything you can do after a disaster strikes. An essential part of disaster planning should include financial planning. Let's begin with the basics. Get adequate insurance to protect your family's health, lives, and property; plan for the possibility of job loss or disability by building a cash reserve; and safeguard your financial and legal records. It is also important to set aside extra money in a long-term emergency fund. Nearly all financial experts advise saving enough money to cover your expenses for six months. Most households never come close to reaching this goal, but don't let that stop you from trying.

Preparing a simple disaster supply kit is also a must. Keep enough water, nonperishable food, sanitation supplies, batteries, medications, and cash on hand for three days. Often, the power is out after a disaster, so you cannot count on ATMs or banks to be open. These measures will help you to weather the immediate impact of a disaster.

Finally, many documents are difficult to replace. Consider investing in a home safe or safe deposit box to ensure that your important records survive. Place your passports, Social Security cards, copies of drivers' licenses, mortgage and property deeds, car titles, wills, insurance records, and birth and marriage certificates out of harm's way.

Will you be ready if disaster strikes?

CONCEPTS YOU SHOULD KNOW

black market (p. 149)
minimum wage (p. 164)
price ceiling (p. 148)

price control (p. 148)
price floor (p. 159)

price gouging laws (p. 155)
rent control (p. 154)

QUESTIONS FOR REVIEW

1. Does a binding price ceiling cause a shortage or a surplus? Provide an example to support your answer.

2. Does a nonbinding price floor cause a shortage or a surplus? Provide an example to support your answer.

3. Will a surplus or a shortage caused by a price control become smaller or larger over time?

4. Are price gouging laws an example of a price floor or a price ceiling?

5. What will happen to the market price when a price control is nonbinding?

6. Why do most economists oppose attempts to control prices? Why does the government attempt to control prices anyway, in a number of markets?

STUDY PROBLEMS (*solved at the end of the section)

1. In the song "Minimum Wage," the punk band Fenix TX comments on the inadequacy of the minimum wage to make ends meet. Using the poverty thresholds provided by the Census Bureau,* determine whether the federal minimum wage of $7.25 an hour provides enough income for a single full-time worker to escape poverty.

✳ 2. Imagine that the community you live in decides to enact a rent control of $700 per month on every one-bedroom apartment. Using the following table, determine the market price and equilibrium quantity without rent control. How many one-bedroom apartments will be rented after the rent-control law is passed?

Monthly rent	Quantity demanded	Quantity supplied
$600	700	240
$700	550	320
$800	400	400
$900	250	480
$1,000	100	560

3. Suppose that the federal government places a binding price floor on chocolate. To help support the price floor, the government purchases all of the leftover chocolate that consumers do not buy. If the price floor remains in place for a number of years, what do you expect to happen to each of the following?

a. quantity of chocolate demanded by consumers
b. quantity of chocolate supplied by producers
c. quantity of chocolate purchased by the government

4. Suppose that a group of die-hard sports fans is upset about the high price of tickets to many games. As a result of their lobbying efforts, a new law caps the maximum ticket price to any sporting event at $50. Will more people be able to attend the games? Explain your answer. Will certain teams and events be affected more than others? Provide examples.

5. Many local governments use parking meters on crowded downtown streets. However, the parking spaces along the street are typically hard to find because the metered price is often set below the market price. Explain what happens when local governments set the meter price too low. Why do you think the price is set below the market-clearing price?

*See: www.census.gov/hhes/www/poverty/data/threshld/index.html

6. Imagine that local suburban leaders decide to enact a minimum wage. Will the community lose more jobs if the nearby city votes to increase the minimum wage to the same rate? Discuss your answer.

✳ 7. Examine the following graph, showing the market for low-skill laborers.

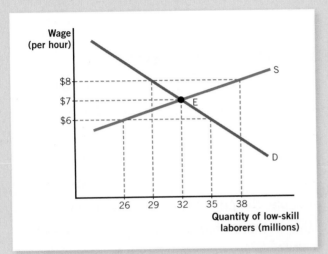

How many low-skill laborers will be unemployed when the minimum wage is $8 an hour? How many low-skill workers will be unemployed when the minimum wage is $6 an hour?

8. The demand and supply curves that we use can also be represented with equations. Suppose that the demand for low-skill labor, Q_D, is represented by the following equation, where W is the wage rate:

$$Q_D = 53{,}000{,}000 - 3{,}000{,}000\,W$$

The supply of low-skill labor, Q_S, is represented by the equation

$$Q_S = -10{,}000{,}000 + 6{,}000{,}000\,W$$

a. Find the equilibrium wage. (**Hint:** Set $Q_D = Q_S$ and solve for the wage, W.)
b. Find the equilibrium quantity of labor. (**Hint:** Now plug the value you got in part (a) back into Q_D or Q_S. You can double-check your answer by plugging the answer from part (a) into both Q_D and Q_S to see that you get the same result.)
c. What happens if the minimum wage is $8? (**Hint:** Plug W = 8 into both Q_D and Q_S.) Does this cause a surplus or a shortage?
d. What happens if the minimum wage is $6? (**Hint:** Plug W = 6 into both Q_D and Q_S.) Does this cause a surplus or a shortage?

SOLVED PROBLEMS

2. The equilibrium price occurs where the quantity demanded is equal to the quantity supplied. This occurs when $Q_D = Q_S = 400$. When the quantity is 400, the monthly rent is $800. Next, the question asks how many one-bedroom apartments will be rented after a rent-control law limits the rent to $700 a month. When the rent is $700, the quantity supplied is 320 apartments. It is also worth noting that the quantity demanded when the rent is $700 is 550 units, so there is a shortage of 550 − 320 = 230 apartments once the rent-control law goes into effect.

7. How many low-skill laborers will be unemployed when the minimum wage is $8 an hour? The quantity demanded is 29M, and the quantity supplied is 38M. This results in 38M − 29M = 9M unemployed low-skill workers.

 How many low-skill workers will be unemployed when the minimum wage is $6 an hour? Since $6 an hour is below the market-equilibrium wage of $7, it has no effect. In other words, a $6 minimum wage is nonbinding, and therefore no unemployment is caused.

The Efficiency of Markets and the Costs of Taxation

Raising tax rates always generates more tax revenue.

Many people believe that if a government needs more revenue, all it needs to do is raise tax rates. If only it were that simple. Gasoline taxes demonstrate why this is a misconception.

Most people find it painful to pay more than $3 a gallon for gas. In many places, sales and excise taxes add a significant amount to the price. For example, the price of gasoline throughout Europe is often more than double that in the United States, largely because of much higher gasoline taxes. Other countries, like Venezuela, Saudi Arabia, and Mexico, subsidize gasoline so that their citizens pay less than the market price. In countries where gasoline is subsidized, consumers drive their cars everywhere, mass transportation is largely unavailable, and there is little concern for fuel efficiency. In contrast, as you might imagine, in countries with high gasoline taxes consumers drive less, use public transportation more, and tend to purchase fuel-efficient vehicles.

How high do gasoline taxes have to rise before large numbers of people significantly cut back on their gasoline consumption? The answer to that question will help us understand the misconception that raising tax rates always generates more tax revenue.

In the previous chapter, we learned about the market distortions caused by price controls. We observed that efforts to manipulate market prices not only cause surpluses and shortages, but also lead to black markets. In this chapter, we will quantify how markets enhance the welfare of society. We begin with consumer surplus and producer surplus, two concepts that illustrate how taxation, like price controls, creates distortions in economic behavior by altering the incentives that people face when consuming and producing goods that are taxed.

How much do taxes cost the economy?

BIG QUESTIONS

* What are consumer surplus and producer surplus?
* When is a market efficient?
* Why do taxes create deadweight loss?

What Are Consumer Surplus and Producer Surplus?

Welfare economics
is the branch of economics that studies how the allocation of resources affects economic well-being.

Markets create value by bringing together buyers and sellers so that consumers and producers can mutually benefit from trade. **Welfare economics** is the branch of economics that studies how the allocation of resources affects economic well-being. In this section, we develop two concepts that will help us measure the value that markets create: *consumer surplus* and *producer surplus*. In competitive markets, the equilibrium price is simultaneously low enough to attract consumers and high enough to encourage producers. This balance between demand and supply enhances the welfare of society. That is not to say that society's welfare depends solely on markets. People also find satisfaction in many nonmarket settings, including spending time with their families and friends, and doing hobbies and charity work. We will incorporate aspects of personal happiness into our economic model in Chapter 16. For now, let's focus on how markets enhance human welfare.

Consumer Surplus

Willingness to pay
is the maximum price a consumer will pay for a good.

Consider three students: Frank, Beanie, and Mitch. Like students everywhere, each one has a maximum price he is willing to pay for a new economics textbook. Beanie owns a successful business, so for him the cost of a new textbook does not present a financial hardship. Mitch is a business major who really wants to do well in economics. Frank is not serious about his studies. Table 6.1 shows the maximum value that each student places on the textbook. This value, called the **willingness to pay**, is the maximum price a consumer will pay for a good. The willingness to pay is also known as the reservation price. In an auction or a negotiation, the willingness to pay, or reservation price, is the price beyond which the consumer decides to walk away from the transaction.

Consider what happens when the price of the book is $151. If Beanie purchases the book at $151, he pays $49 less than the $200

How much will they pay for an economics textbook?

TABLE 6.1	
Willingness to Pay for a New Economics Textbook	
Buyer	**Willingness to pay**
Beanie	$200
Mitch	$150
Frank	$100

maximum he was willing to pay. He values the textbook at $49 more than the purchase price, so buying the book will make him better off.

Consumer surplus is the difference between the willingness to pay for a good and the price that is paid to get it. While Beanie gains $49 in consumer surplus, a price of $151 is more than either Mitch or Frank is willing to pay. Since Mitch is willing to pay only $150, if he purchases the book he will experience a consumer loss of $1. Frank's willingness to pay is $100, so if he buys the book for $151 he will experience a consumer loss of $51. Whenever the price is greater than the willingness to pay, a rational consumer will decide not to buy.

Consumer surplus
is the difference between the willingness to pay for a good and the price that is paid to get it.

Using Demand Curves to Illustrate Consumer Surplus

In the previous section, we discussed consumer surplus as an amount. We can also illustrate it graphically with a demand curve. Figure 6.1 shows the demand curve drawn from the data in Table 6.1. Notice that the curve looks like a staircase with three steps—one for each additional textbook purchase. Each point on a market demand curve corresponds to one unit sold, so if we added more consumers into our example, the "steps" would become narrower and the demand curve would become smoother.

At any price above $200, none of the students wants to purchase a textbook. This relationship is evident on the *x* axis where the quantity demanded is 0. At any price between $150 and $200, Beanie is the only buyer, so the quantity demanded is 1. At prices between $100 and $150, Beanie and Mitch are each willing to buy the textbook, so the quantity demanded is 2. Finally, if the price is $100 or less, all three students are willing to buy the textbook, so the quantity demanded is 3. As the price falls, the quantity demanded increases.

We can measure the total extent of consumer surplus by examining the area under the demand curve for each of our three consumers, as shown in Figure 6.2. In Figure 6.2a the price is $175, and only Beanie decides to buy. Since his willingness to pay is $200, he is better off by $25; this is his consumer surplus. The green-shaded area under the demand curve and above the price represents the benefit Beanie receives from purchasing a textbook at a price of $175. When the price drops to $125, as shown in Figure 6.2b, Mitch also decides to buy a textbook. Now the total quantity demanded is 2 textbooks. Mitch's willingness to pay is $150, so his consumer surplus, represented by the red-shaded area, is $25. However, since Beanie's willingness to pay is $200, his consumer surplus rises from $25 to $75. So a textbook price of $125 raises the total consumer surplus to $100. In other words, lower prices create more consumer surplus in this market—and in any other.

FIGURE 6.1

Demand Curve for an Economics Textbook

The demand curve has a step for each additional textbook purchase. As the price goes down, more students buy the textbook.

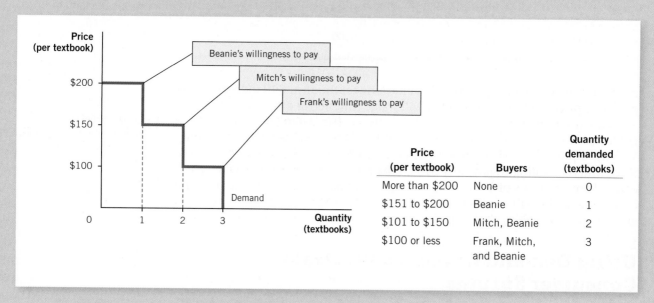

Price (per textbook)	Buyers	Quantity demanded (textbooks)
More than $200	None	0
$151 to $200	Beanie	1
$101 to $150	Mitch, Beanie	2
$100 or less	Frank, Mitch, and Beanie	3

FIGURE 6.2

Determining Consumer Surplus from a Demand Curve

(a) At a price of $175, Beanie is the only buyer, so the quantity demanded is 1. (b) At a price of $125, Beanie and Mitch are each willing to buy the textbook, so the quantity demanded is 2.

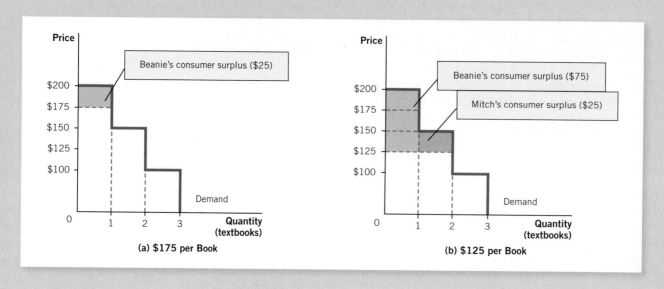

Producer Surplus

Sellers also benefit from market transactions. In this section, our three students discover that they are good at economics and decide to go into the tutoring business. They do not want to provide this service for free, but each has a different minimum price, or *willingness to sell*. The **willingness to sell** is the minimum price a seller will accept to sell a good or service. Table 6.2 shows each tutor's willingness to sell his services.

Consider what happens at a tutoring price of $25 per hour. Since Frank is willing to tutor for $10 per hour, every hour that he tutors at $25 per hour earns him $15 more than his willingness to sell. This extra $15 per hour is his *producer surplus*. **Producer surplus** is the difference between the willingness to sell a good and the price that the seller receives. Mitch is willing to tutor for $20 per hour and earns a $5 producer surplus for every hour he tutors. Finally, Beanie's willingness to tutor, at $30 per hour, is more than the market price of $25. If he tutors, he will have a producer loss of $5 per hour.

How do producers determine their willingness to sell? They must consider two factors: the direct costs of producing the good and the indirect costs, or opportunity costs. Students who are new to economics often mistakenly assume that the cost of producing an item is the only cost to consider in making the decision to produce. But producers also have opportunity costs. Beanie, Mitch, and Frank each has a unique willingness to sell because each has a different opportunity cost. Beanie owns his own business, so for him the time spent tutoring is time that he could have spent making money elsewhere. Mitch is a business student who might otherwise be studying to get better grades. Frank is neither a businessman nor a serious student, so the $10 he can earn in an hour of tutoring is not taking the place of other earning opportunities or studying more to get better grades.

Willingness to sell
is the minimum price a seller will accept to sell a good or service.

Producer surplus
is the difference between the willingness to sell a good and the price that the seller receives.

Opportunity cost

Using Supply Curves to Illustrate Producer Surplus

Continuing our example, the supply curve in Figure 6.3 shows the relationship between the price for an hour of tutoring and the quantity of tutors who are willing to work. As you can see on the supply schedule (the table within the figure), at any price less than $10 per hour no one wants to tutor. At prices between $10 and $19 per hour, Frank is the only tutor, so the

TABLE 6.2

Willingness to Sell Tutoring Services

Seller	Willingness to sell
Beanie	$30/hr
Mitch	$20/hr
Frank	$10/hr

FIGURE 6.3

Supply Curve for Economics Tutoring

The supply curve has three steps, one for each additional student who is willing to tutor. Progressively higher prices will induce more students to become tutors.

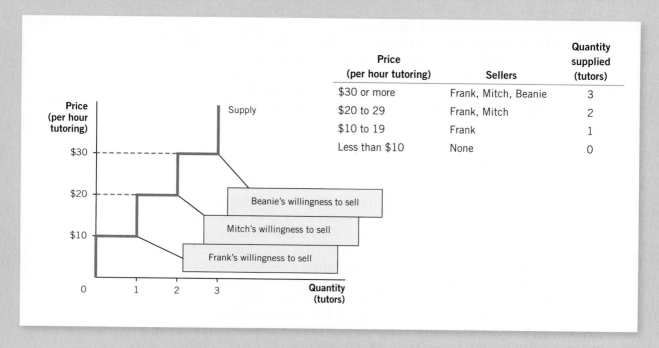

Price (per hour tutoring)	Sellers	Quantity supplied (tutors)
$30 or more	Frank, Mitch, Beanie	3
$20 to 29	Frank, Mitch	2
$10 to 19	Frank	1
Less than $10	None	0

quantity supplied is 1. Between $20 and $29 per hour, Frank and Mitch are willing to tutor, so the quantity supplied rises to 2. Finally, if the price is $30 or more, all three friends are willing to tutor, so the quantity supplied is 3. As the price they receive for tutoring rises, the number of tutors increases from 1 to 3.

What do these relationships between price and supply tell us about producer surplus? Let's turn to Figure 6.4. By examining the area above the supply curve, we can measure the extent of producer surplus. In Figure 6.4a, the price of an hour of tutoring is $15. At that price, only Frank decides to tutor. Since he would be willing to tutor even if the price were as low as $10 per hour, he is $5 better off tutoring. Frank's producer surplus is represented by the red-shaded area between the supply curve and the price of $15. Since Beanie and Mitch do not tutor when the price is $15, they do not receive any producer surplus. In Figure 6.4b, the price for tutoring is $25 per hour. At this price, Mitch also decides to tutor. His willingness to tutor is $20, so when the price is $25 per hour his producer surplus is $5, represented by the blue-shaded area. Since Frank's willingness to tutor is $10, at $25 per hour his producer surplus rises to $15. By looking at the shaded boxes in Figure 6.4b, we see that an increase in the rates for tutoring raises the combined producer surplus of Frank and Mitch to $20.

FIGURE 6.4

Determining Producer Surplus from a Supply Curve

(a) The price of an hour of tutoring is $15. At this price, only Frank decides to tutor. (b) The price for tutoring is $25 per hour. At this price, Mitch also decides to tutor.

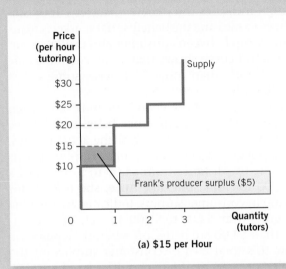

(a) $15 per Hour

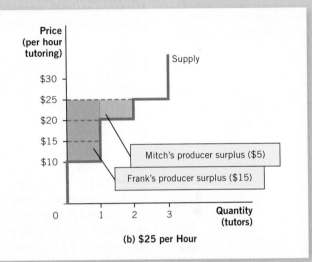

(b) $25 per Hour

PRACTICE WHAT YOU KNOW

Consumer and Producer Surplus: Trendy Fashion

Leah decides to buy a new jacket from D&G for $80. She was willing to pay $100. When her friend Becky sees the jacket, she loves it and thinks it is worth $150. So she offers Leah $125 for the jacket, and Leah accepts. Leah and Becky are both thrilled with the exchange.

Question: Determine the total surplus from the original purchase and the additional surplus generated by the resale of the jacket.

Rachel Bilson wearing a D&G jacket

Answer: Leah was willing to pay $100 and the jacket cost $80, so she keeps the difference, or $20, as consumer surplus. When Leah resells the jacket to Becky for $125, she earns $25 in producer surplus. At the same time, Becky receives $25 in consumer surplus, since she was willing to pay Leah up to $150 for the jacket but Leah sells it to her for $125. The resale generates an additional $50 in surplus.

When Is a Market Efficient?

Total surplus, also known as **social welfare,** is the sum of consumer surplus and producer surplus.

We have seen how consumers benefit from lower prices and how producers benefit from higher prices. When we combine the concepts of consumer and producer surplus, we can build a complete picture of the welfare of buyers and sellers. Adding consumer and producer surplus gives us **total surplus,** also known as **social welfare,** because it measures the welfare of society. Total surplus is the best way economists have to measure the benefits that markets create.

Figure 6.5 illustrates the relationship between consumer and producer surplus for a gallon of milk. The demand curve shows that some customers are willing to pay more for a gallon of milk than others. Likewise, some sellers (producers) are willing to sell milk for less than others.

Let's say that Alice is willing to pay $7.00 per gallon for milk, but when she gets to the store she finds it for $4.00. The difference between the price she is willing to pay, represented by point A, and the price she actually pays, represented by E (the equilibrium price), is $3.00 in consumer surplus. This is indicated by the blue arrow showing the distance from $4.00 to $7.00. Alice's friend Betty is willing to pay $5.00 for milk, but, like Alice, she finds it for $4.00. Therefore, she receives $1.00 in consumer surplus, indicated by the blue arrow at point B showing the distance from $4.00 to $5.00. In fact, all consumers who are willing to pay more than $4.00 are better off when they purchase the milk at $4.00. We can show this total area of consumer surplus on the graph as the blue-shaded triangle bordered by the demand curve, the y axis, and the equilibrium price (P$_E$). At every point in this area, the consumers who are willing to pay more than the equilibrium price for milk will be better off.

Trade creates value

FIGURE 6.5

Consumer and Producer Surplus for a Gallon of Milk

Consumer surplus is the difference between the willingness to pay along the demand curve and the equilibrium price, P$_E$. It is illustrated by the blue-shaded triangle. Producer surplus is the difference between the willingness to produce along the supply curve and the equilibrium price. It is illustrated by the red-shaded triangle.

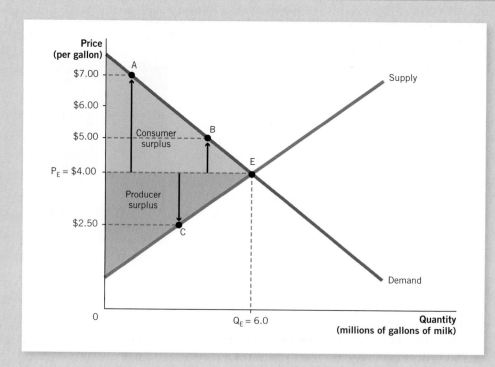

Continuing with Figure 6.5, producer surplus follows a similar process. Suppose that the Contented Cow dairy is willing to sell milk for $2.50 per gallon, represented by point C. Since the equilibrium price is $4.00, the business makes $1.50 in producer surplus. This is indicated by the red arrow at point C showing the distance from $4.00 to $2.50. If we think of the supply curve as representing the costs of many different sellers, we can calculate the total producer surplus as the red-shaded triangle bordered by the supply curve, the y axis, and the equilibrium price. The shaded blue triangle (consumer surplus) and the shaded red triangle (producer surplus) describe the increase in total surplus, or social welfare, created by the production and exchange of the good at the equilibrium price. At the equilibrium quantity of 6 million gallons of milk, output and consumption reach the largest possible combination of producer and consumer surplus. In the region of the graph beyond 6 million units, buyers and sellers will experience a loss.

The buyer and seller each benefit from this exchange.

When an allocation of resources maximizes total surplus, the result is said to be **efficient**. Efficiency occurs at point E when the market is in equilibrium. To think about why the market creates the largest possible total surplus, or social welfare, it is important to recall how the market allocates resources. Consumers who are willing to pay more than the equilibrium price will buy the good because they will enjoy the consumer surplus. Producers who are willing to sell the good for less than the market-equilibrium price will enjoy the producer surplus. In addition, consumers with a low willingness to buy (less than $4.00) and producers with a high willingness to sell (more than $4.00) do not participate in the market since they would be worse off. Therefore, the equilibrium output at point E maximizes the total surplus and is also an efficient allocation of resources.

An outcome is **efficient** when an allocation of resources maximizes total surplus.

The Efficiency-Equity Debate

When economists model behavior, we assume that participants in a market are rational decision-makers. We assume that producers will always operate in the region of the triangle that represents producer surplus and that consumers will always operate in the region of the triangle that represents consumer surplus. We do not, for example, expect Alice to pay more than $7.00 for a gallon of milk or the Contented Cow dairy to sell a gallon of milk for less than $2.50 per gallon. In other words, for the market to work efficiently, voluntary instances of consumer loss must be rare. We assume that self-interest helps to ensure that all participants will benefit from an exchange.

Efficiency only requires that the pie gets eaten. Equity is a question of who gets the biggest share.

ECONOMICS IN THE MEDIA

Efficiency

Old School

In the 2003 movie *Old School*, Frank tries to give away a bread maker he received as a wedding present. First he offers it to a friend as a housewarming gift, but it turns out that this is the friend who originally gave him the bread maker. Ouch! Later in the movie, we see Frank giving the bread maker to a small boy at a birthday party. Both efforts at re-gifting fail miserably.

From an economic perspective, giving the wrong gift makes society poorer. If you spend $50 on a gift and give it to someone who thinks it is only worth $30, you've lost $20 in value. Whenever you receive a shirt that is the wrong size or style, a fruitcake you won't eat, or something that is worth less to you than what the gift-giver spent on it, an economic inefficiency has occurred. Until now, we have thought of the market as enhancing efficiency by increasing the total surplus in society. But we can also think of the billions of dollars spent on mismatched gifts as a failure to maximize the total surplus involved in exchange. In other words, we can think of the efficiency of the gift-giving process as less than 100 percent.

Given what we have learned so far about economics, you might be tempted to argue that cash is the best gift you can give. When you give cash, it is never the wrong size or color, and the recipients can use it to buy whatever they want. However, very few people actually give cash (unless it is requested). Considering the advantages of cash, why don't more people give it instead of gifts? One reason is that cash seems impersonal. A second reason is that cash communicates exactly how much the giver spent. To avoid both problems, most people rarely give cash. Instead, they buy personalized gifts to communicate how much they care, while making it hard for the recipient to determine exactly how much they spent.

One way that society overcomes inefficiency in gifting is through the dissemination of information. For instance, wedding registries provide a convenient way for people who may not know the newlyweds very well to give them what they want. Similarly, prior to holidays many people tell each other what they would

Frank re-gifts a bread maker.

like to receive. By purchasing gifts that others want, givers can exactly match what the recipients would have purchased if they had received a cash transfer. This eliminates any potential inefficiency. At the same time, the giver conveys affection—an essential part of giving. To further reduce the potential inefficiencies associated with giving, many large families practice holiday gift exchanges. And another interesting mechanism for eliciting information involves Santa Claus. Children throughout the world send Santa Claus wish lists for Christmas, never realizing that the parents who help to write and send the lists are the primary beneficiaries.

To the economist, the strategies of providing better information, having gift exchanges, and sending wish lists to Santa Claus are just a few examples of how society tries to get the most out of the giving process—and that is something to be joyful about!

PRACTICE WHAT YOU KNOW

Total Surplus: How Would Lower Income Affect Urban Outfitters?

Question: If a drop in consumer income occurs, what will happen to the consumer surplus that customers enjoy at Urban Outfitters? What will happen to the amount of producer surplus that Urban Outfitters receives? Illustrate your answer by shifting the demand curve appropriately and labeling the new and old areas of consumer and producer surplus.

Answer: Since the items sold at Urban Outfitters are normal goods, a drop in income causes the demand curve (D) to shift to the left. The black arrow shows the leftward shift in graph (b) below. When you compare the area of consumer surplus (in blue) before and after the drop in income—that is, graphs (a) and (b)—you can see that it shrinks. The same is true when comparing the area of producer surplus (in red) before and after.

Does less income affect total surplus?

Your intuition might already confirm what the graphs tell us. Since consumers have less income, they buy fewer clothes at Urban Outfitters— so consumer surplus falls. Likewise, since fewer customers buy the store's clothes, Urban Outfitters sells less—so producer surplus falls. This is also evident in graph (b), since $Q_2 < Q_1$.

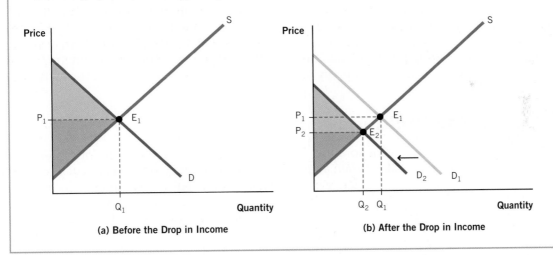

(a) Before the Drop in Income

(b) After the Drop in Income

However, the fact that both parties benefit from an exchange does not mean that each benefits equally. Economists are also interested in the distribution of the gains. **Equity** refers to the fairness of the distribution of benefits among the members of a society. In a world where no one cared about equity, only efficiency would matter and no particular division would be preferred. Another way of thinking about fairness versus efficiency is to consider a pie. If our only concern is efficiency, we will simply want to make sure that none of the pie goes to waste. However, if we care about equity, we will also want to make sure that the pie is divided equally among those present and that no one gets a larger piece than any other.

Equity
refers to the fairness of the distribution of benefits within the society.

In our first look at consumer and producer surplus, we have assumed that markets produce efficient outcomes. But in the real world, this is not always the case. Markets also fail; their efficiency can be compromised in a number of ways. We will discuss market failure in much greater detail in subsequent chapters. For now, all you need to know is that failure can occur.

Why Do Taxes Create Deadweight Loss?

Taxes provide many benefits. They also remind us that "there is no free lunch"; for example, we don't pay the police dispatcher before dialing 911, but society has to collect taxes in order for the emergency service to exist. Taxes help to pay for many of modern society's needs—public transportation, schools, police, the court system, and the military, to name just a few. Most of us take these services for granted, but without taxes it would be hard to pay for them. How much does all of this cost? When you add all the federal, state, and local government budgets in the United States, you get five trillion dollars a year!

Opportunity cost

These taxes incur opportunity costs, since the money could have been used in other ways. In this section, we will use the concepts of consumer and producer surplus to explain the effect of taxation on social welfare and market efficiency. Taxes come in many sizes and shapes. Considering there are taxes on personal income, payroll, property, corporate profits, sales, and inheritances, the complexity makes it difficult to analyze the broad impact of taxation on social welfare and market efficiency. Fortunately, we do not have to examine the entire tax code all at once. In this chapter, we will explore the impact of taxes on social welfare by looking at one of the simplest taxes, the *excise tax*.

Excise taxes
are taxes levied on a particular good or service.

Incidence
refers to the burden of taxation on the party who pays the tax through higher prices, regardless of whom the tax is actually levied on.

Tax Incidence

Economists want to know how taxes affect the choices that consumers and producers make. When a tax is imposed on an item, do buyers switch to alternative goods that are not taxed? How do producers respond when the products they sell are taxed? Since taxes cause prices to rise, they can affect how much of a good or service is bought and sold. This is especially evident with **excise taxes**, or taxes levied on one particular good or service. For example, all fifty states levy excise taxes on cigarettes, but the amount assessed varies tremendously. In New York, cigarette taxes are over $4.00 per pack, while in a handful of tobacco-producing states such as Virginia and North Carolina, the excise tax is less than $0.50. Overall, excise taxes, such as those on cigarettes, alcohol, and gasoline, account for less than 4% of all tax revenues. But because we can isolate changes in consumer behavior that result from taxes on one item, they help us understand the overall effect of a tax.

In looking at the effect of a tax, economists are also interested in the **incidence** of taxation, which refers to the burden of taxation on the party who pays the tax through

Why do we place excise taxes on cigarettes . . .   . . . and gasoline?

higher prices. To understand this idea, consider a $1.00 tax on milk purchases. Each time a consumer buys a gallon of milk, the cash register adds $1.00 in tax. This means that to purchase the milk, the consumer's willingness to pay must be greater than the price of the milk plus the $1.00 tax.

The result of the $1.00 tax on milk is shown in Figure 6.6. Because of the tax, the price of milk goes up and the demand curve shifts down (from D_1 to D_2). Why does the demand curve shift? Since consumers must pay the purchase price as well as the tax, the extra cost makes them less likely to buy milk at every price, which causes the entire demand curve to shift down. The intersection of the new demand curve (D_2) with the existing supply curve (S) creates a new equilibrium price of $3.50 ($E_2$), which is $0.50 lower than the original price of $4.00. But even though the price is lower, consumers are still worse off. Since they must also pay part of the $1.00 tax, the total price to them rises to $4.50 per gallon.

At the same time, because the new equilibrium price after the tax is $0.50 lower than it was before the tax, the producer splits the tax incidence with the buyer. The producer receives $0.50 less, and the buyer pays $0.50 more.

The tax on milk purchases also affects the amount sold in the market, which we also see in Figure 6.6. Since the after-tax equilibrium price (E_2) is lower, producers of milk reduce the quantity they sell to 750 gallons. Therefore, the market for milk becomes smaller than it was before the good was taxed.

Excise taxes paid by consumers are relatively rare because they are highly visible. If every time you bought milk you were reminded that you had to pay a $1.00 tax, it would be hard to ignore. As a result, politicians often prefer

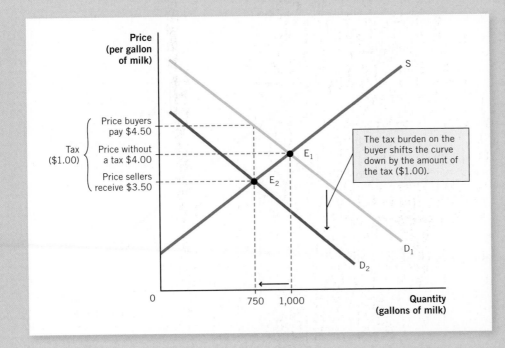

FIGURE 6.6

A Tax on Buyers

After the tax, the new equilibrium price (E_2) is $3.50, but the buyer must also pay $1.00 in tax. Therefore, despite the drop in price, the buyer still owes $4.50. A similar logic applies to the producer. Since the new equilibrium price after the tax is $0.50 lower, the producer shares the tax incidence equally with the seller in this example. The consumer pays $0.50 more, and the seller nets $0.50 less.

to place the tax on the seller. The seller will then include the tax in the sale price, and buyers will likely forget that the sale price is higher than it would be without the tax.

Let's return to the $1.00 tax on milk. This time, the tax is placed on the seller. Figure 6.7 shows the result. First, look at the shift in the supply curve. Why does it shift? The $1.00 per gallon tax on milk lowers the profits that milk producers expect to make, which causes them to produce less milk at every price level. As a result, the entire supply curve shifts to the left in response to the tax that milk producers owe the government. The intersection of the new supply curve (S_2) with the existing demand curve creates a new equilibrium price (E_2) of $4.50—which is $0.50 higher than the original equilibrium price of $4.00 ($E_1$). This occurs because the seller passes part of the tax increase along to the buyer in the form of a higher price. However, the seller is still worse off. After the tax, the new equilibrium price is $4.50, but $1.00 goes as tax to the government. Therefore, despite the rise in price, the seller nets only $3.50, which is $0.50 less than the original equilibrium price.

The tax also affects the amount of milk sold in the market. Since the new equilibrium price after the tax is higher, consumers reduce the quantity demanded from 1,000 gallons to 750 gallons.

It's important to notice that the result in Figure 6.7 looks much like that in Figure 6.6. This is because it does not matter whether a tax is levied on the buyer or the seller. The tax places a wedge of $1.00 between the price that buyers ultimately pay ($4.50) and the net price that sellers ultimately receive ($3.50), regardless of who is actually responsible for paying the tax.

FIGURE 6.7

A Tax on Sellers

After the tax, the new equilibrium price (E_2) is $4.50, but $1.00 must be paid in tax to the government. Therefore, despite the rise in price, the seller nets only $3.50. A similar logic applies to the consumer. Since the new equilibrium price after the tax is $0.50 higher, the consumer shares the $1.00/gallon tax incidence equally with the seller. The consumer pays $0.50 more, and the seller nets $0.50 less.

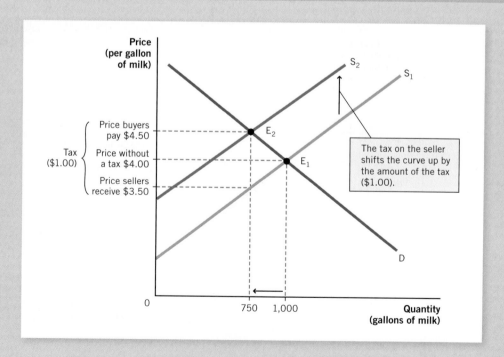

Continuing with our milk example, when the tax was levied on sellers, they were responsible for collecting the entire tax ($1.00 per gallon), but they transferred $0.50 of the tax to the consumer by raising the market price to $4.50. Similarly, when the tax was levied on consumers, they were responsible for paying the entire tax, but they essentially transferred $0.50 of it to the producer, since the market price fell to $3.50. Therefore, we can say that the incidence of a tax is independent of whether it is levied on the buyer or the seller. However, depending on the price elasticity of supply and demand, the tax incidence need not be shared equally, as we will see later. All of this means that the government doesn't get to determine whether consumers or producers bear the tax incidence—the market does!

Deadweight Loss

Recall that economists measure economic efficiency by looking at total consumer and producer surplus. We have seen that a tax raises the total price consumers pay and lowers the net price producers receive. For this reason, taxes reduce the amount of economic activity. The decrease in economic activity caused by market distortions, such as taxes, is known as **deadweight loss.**

In the previous section, we observed that the tax on milk caused the amount purchased to decline from 1,000 to 750 gallons—a reduction of 250 gallons sold in the market. In Figure 6.8, the yellow triangle represents the deadweight loss caused by the tax. When the price rises, consumers who

Deadweight loss
is the decrease in economic activity caused by market distortions.

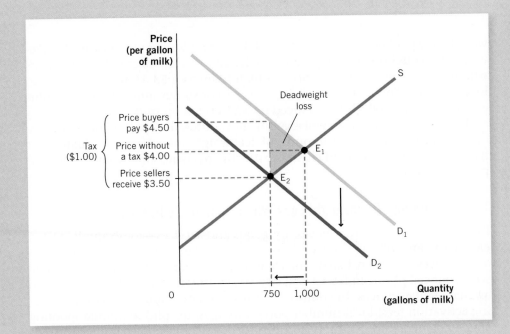

FIGURE 6.8

The Deadweight Loss from a Tax

The yellow triangle represents the deadweight loss caused by the tax. When the price rises, all consumers who would have paid between $4.00 and $4.49 no longer purchase milk. Likewise, the reduction in revenue the seller receives means that producers who were willing to sell a gallon of milk for between $3.51 and $4.00 will no longer do so.

Taxing Inelastic Goods

"Taxman" by the Beatles

"Taxman" was inspired by the theme song from the popular 1960s television series *Batman*. The Beatles—especially George Harrison, who wrote the song—had grown quite bitter about how much they were paying in taxes. In the beginning of the song, Harrison sings, "Let me tell you how it will be. There's one for you, nineteen for me." This refers to the fact that the British government taxed high-wage earners £19 out of every £20 they earned. Since the Beatles' considerable earnings placed them in the top income tax bracket in the United Kingdom, a part of the group's earnings was subject to the 95% tax introduced by the government in 1965. As a consequence, the Beatles became tax exiles living in the United States and other parts of Europe, where tax rates were lower.

The inevitability of paying taxes is a theme that runs throughout the song. The lyrics mention that when you drive a car, the government can tax the "street"; if you try to sit, the government can tax "your seat"; if you are cold, the government can tax "the

The Beatles avoided high taxes by living outside the United Kingdom.

heat"; and if you decide to take a walk, it can tax your "feet"! The only way to avoid doing and using these things is to leave the country—precisely what the Beatles did. All these examples (streets, seats, heat, and walking) are necessary activities, which makes demand highly inelastic. Anytime that is the case, the government can more easily collect the tax revenue it desires.

would have paid between $4.00 and $4.49 will no longer purchase milk. Likewise, the reduction in the price the seller can charge means that producers who were willing to sell a gallon of milk for between $3.51 and $4.00 will no longer do so. The combined reductions in consumer and producer surplus equal the deadweight loss produced by a $1.00 tax on milk.

In the next sections, we will examine how differences in the price elasticity of demand lead to varying amounts of deadweight loss. We will evaluate what happens when the demand curve is perfectly inelastic, somewhat elastic, and perfectly elastic.

Tax Revenue and Deadweight Loss When Demand Is Inelastic

In Chapter 4, we saw that necessary goods and services—for example, water, electricity, and phone service—have highly inelastic demand. These goods and services are often taxed. For example, consider all the taxes associated with your cell phone bill: sales tax, city tax, county tax, federal excise tax, and annual regulatory fees. In addition, many companies add surcharges, including activation fees, local number portability fees, telephone number pooling charges, emergency 911 service, directory assistance, telecommunications relay service surcharges, and cancellation fees. Of course, there is a way to avoid all these fees: don't use a cell phone! However, many people today feel that cell phones are a necessity. Cell phone providers and government agencies take advantage of the consumer's strongly inelastic demand by tacking on these extra charges.

Figure 6.9 shows the result of a tax on products with almost perfectly inelastic demand, such as phone service—something people feel they need to have no matter what the price. The demand for access to a phone (either a landline or a cell phone) is perfectly inelastic. Recall that whenever demand is perfectly inelastic, the demand curve is vertical. Figure 6.9a shows the market for phone service before the tax. The blue rectangle represents consumer surplus (C.S.), and the red triangle represents producer surplus (P.S.). Now imagine that a tax is levied on the seller, as shown in Figure 6.9b. The supply curve shifts from S_1 to S_2. The shift in supply causes the equilibrium point to move from E_1 to E_2 and the price to rise from P_1 to P_2, but the quantity supplied, Q_1, remains the same. We know that when demand is perfectly inelastic, a price increase does not alter how much consumers purchase. So the quantity demanded remains constant at Q_1 even after the government collects tax revenue equal to the green-shaded area.

There are two reasons why the government may favor excise taxes on goods with almost perfectly (or highly) inelastic demand. First, because these

How do phone companies get away with all the added fees per month? Answer: inelastic demand.

FIGURE 6.9

A Tax on Products with Almost Perfectly Inelastic Demand

(a) Before the tax, the consumer enjoys the consumer surplus (C.S.) noted in blue, and the producer enjoys the producer surplus (P.S.) noted in red. (b) After the tax, the incidence, or the burden of taxation, is borne entirely by the consumer. A tax on a good with almost perfectly inelastic demand, such as phone service, represents a transfer of welfare from consumers of the good to the government, reflected by the reduced size of the blue rectangle in (b) and the creation of the green tax-revenue rectangle between P_1 and P_2.

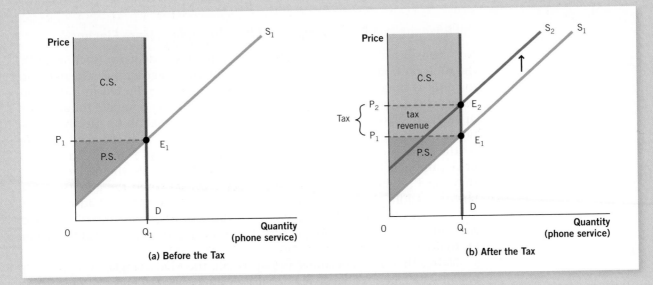

(a) Before the Tax

(b) After the Tax

goods do not have substitutes, the tax will not cause consumers to buy less. Thus, the revenue from the tax will remain steady. Second, since the number of transactions, or quantity demanded (Q_1), remains constant, there will be no deadweight loss. As a result, the yellow triangle we observed in Figure 6.8 disappears in Figure 6.9 because the tax does not alter the efficiency of the market. Looking at Figure 6.9, you can see that the same number of transactions exist in (a) and (b). This means that the total surplus, or social welfare, is equal in both panels. You can also see this by comparing the shaded areas in both panels. The sum of the blue-shaded area of consumer surplus and the red-shaded area of producer surplus in (a) is equal to the sum of the consumer surplus, producer surplus, and tax revenue in (b). The green area is subtracted entirely from the blue rectangle, which indicates that the surplus is redistributed from consumers to the government. But society overall enjoys the same total surplus. Thus, we see that when demand is perfectly inelastic, the incidence, or the burden of taxation, is borne entirely by the consumer. A tax on a good with almost perfectly inelastic demand represents a transfer of welfare from consumers of the good to the government, reflected by the reduced size of the blue rectangle in (b).

Tax Revenue and Deadweight Loss When Demand Is More Elastic

Now consider a tax on a product with more elastic demand, such as milk, the subject of our earlier discussion on calculating total surplus. The demand for milk is price sensitive, but not overly so. This is reflected in a demand curve with a typical slope as shown in Figure 6.10. Let's compare the after-tax price, P_2, in Figures 6.9b and 6.10b. When demand is almost perfectly inelastic, as it is in Figure 6.9b, the price increase from P_1 to P_2 is absorbed entirely by the consumer. But in Figure 6.10b, because demand is more sensitive to price, suppliers must absorb part of the tax, from P_1 to P_3, themselves. Thus, they net P_3, which is less than what they received when the good was not taxed. In addition, the total tax revenue generated (the green-shaded area) is not as large in Figure 6.9b as in Figure 6.10b, because as the price of the good rises some consumers no longer buy it and the quantity demanded falls from Q_1 to Q_2.

Notice that both consumer surplus (C.S.), the blue triangle, and producer surplus (P.S.), the red triangle, are smaller after the tax. Since the price rises after the tax increase (from P_1 to P_2), those consumers with a relatively low

FIGURE 6.10

A Tax on Products with More Elastic Demand

(a) Before the tax, the consumer enjoys the consumer surplus (C.S.) noted in blue, and the producer enjoys the producer surplus (P.S.) noted in red. (b) A tax on a good for which demand and supply are each somewhat elastic will cause a transfer of welfare from consumers and producers to the government, the revenue shown as the green rectangle. It will also create deadweight loss (D.W.L.), shown in yellow, since the quantity bought and sold in the market declines (from Q_1 to Q_2).

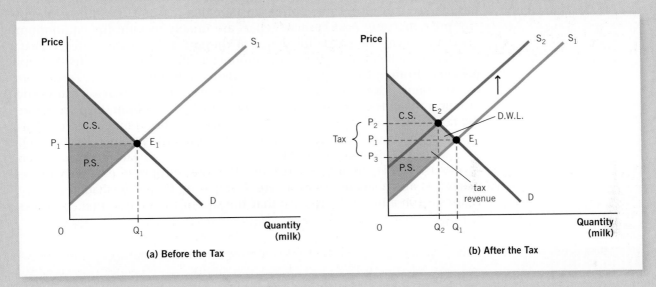

(a) Before the Tax

(b) After the Tax

willingness to pay for the good are priced out of the market. Likewise, sellers with relatively high costs of production will stop producing the good, since the price they net after paying the tax drops to P_3. The total reduction in economic activity, the change from Q_1 to Q_2, is the deadweight loss (D.W.L.) indicated by the yellow triangle.

The incidence of the tax also changes from Figure 6.9 to Figure 6.10. A tax on a good for which demand and supply are each somewhat elastic will cause a transfer of welfare from consumers and producers of the good to the government. At the same time, since the quantity bought and sold in the market declines, it also creates deadweight loss. Another way of seeing this result is to compare the red- and blue-shaded areas in Figure 6.10a with the red- and blue-shaded areas in Figure 6.10b. The sum of the consumer surplus and producer surplus in (a) is greater than the sum of the consumer surplus, tax revenue, and producer surplus in (b). Therefore, the total surplus, or efficiency of the market, is smaller. The tax is no longer a pure transfer from consumers to the government, as was the case in Figure 6.9.

Tax Revenue and Deadweight Loss When Demand Is Highly Elastic

We have seen the effect of taxation when demand is inelastic and somewhat elastic. What about when demand is highly elastic? For example, a customer who wants to buy fresh lettuce at a produce market will find many local growers charging the same price and many varieties to choose from. If one of the vendors decides to charge $1 per pound above the market price, consumers will stop buying from that vendor. They will be unwilling to pay more when they can get the same product from another grower at a lower price; this is the essence of elastic demand.

Figure 6.11 shows the result of a tax on lettuce, a good with highly elastic demand. After all, when lettuce is taxed consumers can switch to other greens such as spinach, cabbage, or endive and completely avoid the tax. In this market, consumers are so price sensitive that they are unwilling to accept any price increase. And because sellers are unable to raise the equilibrium price, they bear the entire incidence of the tax. This has two effects. First, producers are less willing to sell the product at all prices. This shifts the supply curve from S_1 to S_2. Since consumer demand is highly elastic, consumers pay the same price as before ($P_1 = P_2$). However, the tax increase causes the producer to net less, or P_3. Since P_3 is substantially lower than the price before the tax, or P_2, producers offer less for sale after the tax is implemented. This is shown in Figure 6.11b in the movement of quantity demanded from Q_1 to Q_2. Since Q_2 is smaller than Q_1, there is also more deadweight loss than we observed in Figure 6.10b. Therefore, the total surplus, or efficiency of the market, is much smaller than before. Comparing the green-shaded areas of Figures 6.10b and 6.11b, you see that the size of the tax revenue continues

FIGURE 6.11

A Tax on Products with Highly Elastic Demand

(a) Before the tax, the producer enjoys the producer surplus (P.S.) noted in red. (b) When consumer demand is highly elastic, consumers pay the same price after the tax as before. But they are worse off because less is produced and sold; the quantity produced moves from Q_1 to Q_2. The result is deadweight loss (D.W.L.), as shown by the yellow triangle in (b). The total surplus, or efficiency of the market, is much smaller than before. The size of the tax revenue (in green) is also noticeably smaller in the market with highly elastic demand.

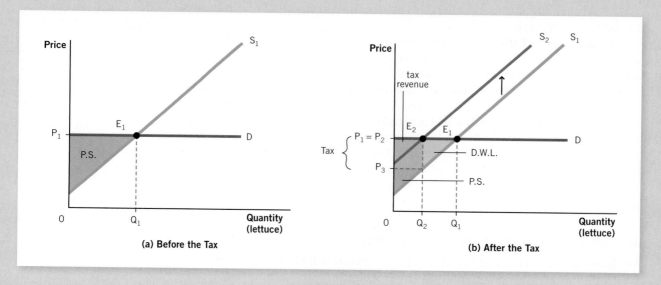

(a) Before the Tax

(b) After the Tax

to shrink. There is an important lesson here for policymakers—they should tax goods with relatively inelastic demand. Not only will this lessen the deadweight loss of taxation, but it will also generate larger tax revenues for the government.

So far, we have varied the elasticity of the demand curve while holding the elasticity of the supply curve constant. What would happen if we did the reverse and varied the elasticity of the supply curve while keeping the elasticity of the demand curve constant? It turns out that there is a simple method for determining the incidence and deadweight loss in this case. The incidence of a tax is determined by the relative steepness of the demand curve compared to the supply curve. When the demand curve is steeper (more inelastic) than the supply curve, consumers bear more of the incidence of the tax. When the supply curve is steeper (more inelastic) than the demand curve, suppliers bear more of the incidence of the tax. Also, whenever the supply and/or demand curves are relatively steep, deadweight loss is minimized.

Let's explore an example in which we consider how the elasticity of demand and elasticity of supply interact. Suppose that a $3 per pound tax is placed on shiitake mushrooms, an elastic good. Given the information in Figure 6.12, we will compute the incidence, deadweight loss, and tax revenue from the tax.

Let's start with the incidence of the tax. After the tax is implemented, the market price rises from $7 to $8 per pound. But since sellers must pay $3 to the government, they keep only $5. Tax incidence measures the share of the tax paid by buyers and sellers, so we need to compare the incidence of the tax paid by each party. Since the market price rises by $1 (from $7 to $8), buyers are paying $1 of the $3 tax, or $\frac{1}{3}$. Since the amount the seller keeps falls

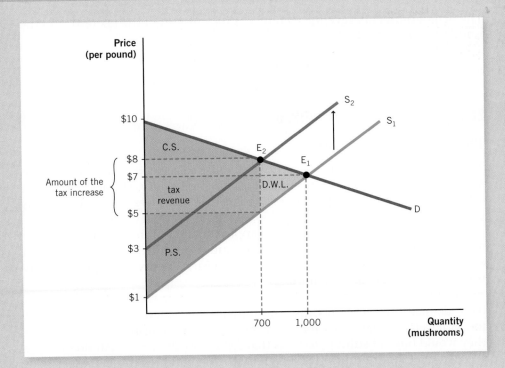

FIGURE 6.12

A Realistic Example
A $3 per pound tax is placed on mushroom suppliers. This drives the equilibrium price up from E_1 ($7) to E_2 ($8). Notice that the price only rises by $1. This means that the consumer picks up $1 of the $3 tax and the seller must pay the remaining $2. Therefore, most of the incidence is borne by the seller. Finally, neither the demand curve nor the supply curve is relatively inelastic, so the amount of deadweight loss (D.W.L.) is large.

How much would you pay per pound for these mushrooms?

by $2 (from $7 to $5), sellers are paying $2 of the $3 tax, or $\frac{2}{3}$. Notice that the demand curve is more elastic (flatter) than the supply curve; therefore, sellers have a limited ability to raise price.

Now let's determine the deadweight loss caused by the tax—that is, the decrease in economic activity. This is represented by the decrease in the total surplus found in the yellow triangle in Figure 6.12. In order to compute the amount of the deadweight loss, we need to determine the area of the triangle:

(Equation 6.1)
$$\text{The area of a triangle} = \frac{1}{2} \times \text{base} \times \text{height}$$

The triangle in Figure 6.12 is sitting on its side, so its height is $1000 - 700 = 300$, and its base is $8 - 5 = 3$.

(Equation 6.2)
$$\text{Deadweight loss} = \frac{1}{2} \times 300 \times \$3 = \$450$$

Finally, what is the tax revenue generated by the tax? In Figure 6.12, the tax revenue is represented by the green-shaded area, which is a rectangle. We can calculate the tax revenue by determining the area of the rectangle:

(Equation 6.3)
$$\text{The area of a rectangle} = \text{base} \times \text{height}$$

The height of the tax-revenue rectangle is the amount of the tax ($3), and the number of units sold after the tax is 700.

(Equation 6.4)
$$\text{Tax revenue} = \$3 \times 700 = \$2,100.$$

 ECONOMICS IN THE REAL WORLD

The Short-Lived Luxury Tax

The Budget Reconciliation Act of 1990 established a special luxury tax on the sale of new aircraft, yachts, automobiles, furs, and jewelry. The act established a 10% surcharge on new purchases as follows: aircraft over $500,000; yachts over $100,000; automobiles over $25,000; and furs and jewelry over $10,000. The taxes were expected to generate approximately $2 billion a year. However, revenue fell far below expectations, and thousands of jobs were lost in each of the affected industries. Within three years, the tax was repealed. Why was the luxury tax such a failure?

When passing the Budget Reconciliation Act, lawmakers failed to consider basic demand elasticity. Because the purchase of a new aircraft, yacht, car, fur, or jewelry is highly discretionary, many wealthy consumers decided that they would buy substitute products that fell below the tax threshold or buy a used product and refurbish it. Therefore, the demand for these luxury goods turned out to be highly elastic. We have seen that when goods with elastic demand are taxed, the resulting tax revenues are small. Moreover, in this example the resulting decrease in purchases was significant. As a result, jobs were lost in the middle of an economic downturn. The combination of low revenues and crippling job losses in these industries was enough to convince Congress to repeal the tax in 1993.

The failed luxury tax is a reminder that the populist idea of taxing the rich is far more difficult to implement than it appears. In simple terms, it is nearly impossible to tax the toys that the rich enjoy because wealthy people can spend their money in so many different ways. In other words, they have options about whether to buy or lease, as well as many good substitutes to choose from. This means that they can, in many cases, avoid paying luxury taxes. ✳

If you were rich, would this be your luxury toy?

Balancing Deadweight Loss and Tax Revenues

Up to this point, we have kept the size of the tax increase constant. This enabled us to examine the impact of the elasticity of demand and supply on deadweight loss and tax revenues. But what happens when a tax is high enough to significantly alter consumer or producer behavior? For instance, in 2002 the Republic of Ireland instituted a tax of 15 euro cents on each plastic bag in order to curb litter and encourage recycling. As a result, consumer use of plastic bags quickly fell by over 90%. Thus, the tax was a major success because the government achieved its goal of curbing litter. In this section, we will consider how consumers respond to taxes of different sizes, and we will determine the relationship among the size of a tax, the deadweight loss, and tax revenues.

Incentives

Figure 6.13 shows the market response to a variety of tax increases. The five panels in the figure begin with a reference point, panel (a), where no tax is levied, and progress toward panel (e), where the tax rate becomes so extreme that it curtails all economic activity.

As taxes rise, so do prices. You can trace this rise from (a), where there is no tax and the price is P_1, all the way to (e), where the extreme tax causes the price to rise to P_5. At the same time, deadweight loss (D.W.L.) also rises. You can see this by comparing the sizes of the yellow triangles. The trade-off is striking. Without any taxes, deadweight loss does not occur. But as soon as taxes are in place, the market-equilibrium quantity demanded begins to decline, moving from Q_1 to Q_5. As the number of transactions (quantity demanded) declines, the area of deadweight loss rapidly expands.

Trade-offs

When taxes are small, as in Figure 6.13b, the tax revenue (green rectangle) is large relative to the deadweight loss (yellow triangle). However, as we progress through the panels, this relationship slowly reverses. In (c) the size of the tax revenue remains larger than the deadweight loss. However, in (d) the magnitude of the deadweight loss is far greater than the tax revenue. This means that the size of the tax in (d) is creating a significant cost in terms of economic efficiency. Finally, (e) shows an extreme case in which all market activity ceases as a result of the tax. Since nothing is produced and sold, there is no tax revenue.

FIGURE 6.13

Examining Deadweight Loss and Tax Revenues

The panels show that increased taxes result in higher prices. Progressively higher taxes also lead to more deadweight loss (D.W.L.), but higher taxes do not always generate more revenue, as evidenced by the reduction in revenue that occurs when tax rates become too large in panels (d) and (e).

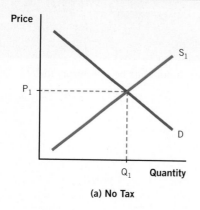

(a) No Tax

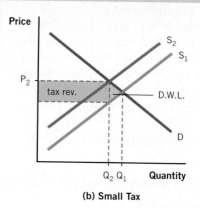

(b) Small Tax

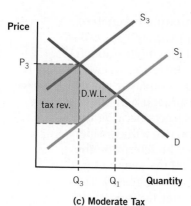

(c) Moderate Tax

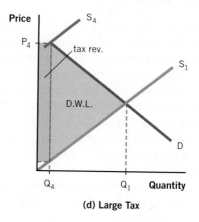

(d) Large Tax

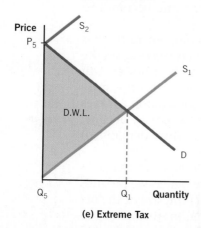

(e) Extreme Tax

Bizarre Taxes

Governments tax their citizens for a variety of reasons. Often it's to raise revenue. Sometimes, taxes are levied to influence citizens' behavior. Occasionally, both of these reasons are in play. These two motivations have led to some very bizarre tax initiatives, as seen below. Though they all seem a bit unusual, these taxes get (or got) paid every single day.

Flush Tax

Maryland's "Flush Tax," a fee added to sewer bills, went up from $2.50 to $5.00 a month in 2012. The tax is paid only by residents who live in the Chesapeake Bay Watershed, and it generates revenue for reducing pollution in Chesapeake Bay.

Bagel Tax

New Yorkers love their bagels and cream cheese from delis. In the state, any bagel that has been sliced or has any form of spread on it (like cream cheese) is subject to a 9% sales tax on prepared food. Any bagel that is purchased "unaltered" is classified as unprepared and is not taxed.

Playing Card Tax

The state of Alabama really doesn't want you playing solitaire. Buyers of playing cards are taxed ten cents per deck, while sellers must pay a $2 annual licensing fee. How much revenue does just a ten-cent tax generate? In 2011, it was almost $90,000.

Tattoo Tax

Arkansas imposes a 6% tax on tattoos and body piercings to discourage this behavior, meaning that the people of Arkansas pay extra when getting inked or pierced.

Window Tax

England passed a tax in 1696 targeting wealthy citizens—the more windows in one's house, the higher the tax. Many homeowners simply bricked over their windows. But they could not seal all of them, and the government did indeed collect revenue.

Blueberry Tax

Maine levies a penny-and-a-half tax per pound on anyone growing, handling, processing, selling, or purchasing the state's delicious wild blueberries. The tax is an effort to make sure that the blueberries are not overharvested.

Maine produces 99% of the wild blueberries consumed in the USA, meaning that blueberry lovers have few substitutes available to avoid paying the tax and that demand is therefore inelastic.

Marylanders are being taxed on a negative externality, which we'll cover in the next chapter.

REVIEW QUESTIONS

- Suppose that because of Alabama's playing card tax, fewer consumers purchase cards and fewer store owners sell them. What is this loss of economic activity called?

- Do you think the New York bagel tax is an effective tool to raise government revenue? Think about how the tax may or may not affect the purchasing behavior of New Yorkers.

PRACTICE WHAT YOU KNOW

Deadweight Loss of Taxation: The Politics of Tax Rates

Imagine that you and two friends are discussing the politics of taxation. One friend, who is fiscally conservative, argues that tax rates are too high. The other friend, who is more progressive, argues that tax rates are too low.

What is the optimal tax rate?

Question: Is it possible that both friends could be right?

Answer: Surprisingly, the answer is yes. When tax rates become extraordinarily high, the amount of deadweight loss dwarfs the amount of tax revenue collected. We observed this in the discussion of the short-lived luxury tax above. Fiscal conservatives often note that taxes inhibit economic activity. They advocate lower tax rates and limited government involvement in the market, preferring to minimize the deadweight loss on economic activity—see panel (b) in Figure 6.13. However, progressives prefer somewhat higher tax rates than fiscal conservatives, since a moderate tax rate—see panel (c)—generates more tax revenue than a small tax does. The additional revenues that moderate tax rates generate can fund more government services. Therefore, a clear trade-off exists between the size of the public sector and market activity. Depending on how you view the value created by markets versus the value added through government provision, there is ample room for disagreement about the best tax policy.

Conclusion

Let's return to the misconception we started with: raising tax rates always generates more tax revenue. That's true up to a point. At low and moderate tax rates, increases do lead to additional tax revenue. However, when tax rates become too high, tax revenues decline as more consumers and producers find ways to avoid paying the tax.

In the first part of this chapter, we learned that society benefits from unregulated markets because they generate the largest possible total surplus. However, society also needs the government to provide an infrastructure for the economy. The tension between economic activity and the amount of government services needed is reflected in tax rates. The taxation of specific goods and services gives rise to a form of market failure called deadweight loss, which causes reduced economic activity. Thus, any intervention in the market requires a deep understanding of how society will respond to the incentives created by the legislation. In addition, unintended consequences can affect the most well-intentioned tax legislation and, if the process is not well thought through, can cause inefficiencies with far-reaching consequences. Of course, this does not mean that taxes are undesirable. Rather, society must balance (1) the need for tax revenues and the programs those revenues help fund, with (2) trade-offs in the market.

Incentives

Trade-offs

ANSWERING THE BIG QUESTIONS

What are consumer surplus and producer surplus?

＊ Consumer surplus is the difference between the willingness to pay for a good and the price that is paid to get it. Producer surplus is the difference between the willingness to sell a good and the price that the seller receives.

＊ Total surplus is the sum of consumer and producer surplus that exists in a market.

When is a market efficient?

＊ Markets maximize consumer and producer surplus, provide goods and services to buyers who value them most, and reward sellers who can produce goods and services at the lowest cost. As a result, markets create the largest amount of total surplus possible.

＊ Whenever an allocation of resources maximizes total surplus, the result is said to be efficient. However, economists are also interested in the distribution of the surplus. Equity refers to the fairness of the distribution of the benefits among the members of the society.

Why do taxes create deadweight loss?

＊ Deadweight loss occurs because taxes increase the purchase price, which causes consumers to buy less and producers to supply less. Deadweight loss can be minimized by placing a tax on a good or service that has inelastic demand or supply.

＊ Economists are also concerned about the incidence of taxation. Incidence refers to the burden of taxation on the party who pays the tax through higher prices, regardless of whom the tax is actually levied on. The incidence is determined by the balance between the elasticity of supply and the elasticity of demand.

ECONOMICS FOR LIFE

Excise Taxes Are Almost Impossible to Avoid

The federal government collected $75 billion in excise taxes in 2011. Excise taxes are placed on many different products, making them almost impossible to avoid. They also have the added advantages of being easy to collect, hard for consumers to detect, and easier to enact politically than other types of taxes. You'll find excise taxes on many everyday household expenses—what you drink, the gasoline you purchase, plane tickets, and much more. Let's add them up.

1. **Gasoline.** 18.3 cents per gallon. This generates $37 billion and helps finance the interstate highway system.

2. **Cigarettes and tobacco.** $1 per pack and up to 40 cents per cigar. This generates $18 billion for the general federal budget.

3. **Air travel.** 7.5% of the base price of the ticket plus $3 per flight segment. This generates $10 billion for the Transportation Security Administration and the Federal Aviation Administration.

Data from Jill Barshay, "The $240-a-Year Bill You Don't Know You're Paying," *Fiscal Times*, Sept. 7, 2011.

4. **Alcohol.** 5 cents per can of beer, 21 cents per bottle of wine, and $2.14 for spirits. This generates $9 billion for the general federal budget.

These four categories account for $74 billion in excise taxes. You could still avoid the taxman with this simple prescription: don't drink, don't travel, and don't smoke. Where does that leave you? Way out in the country somewhere far from civilization. Since you won't be able to travel to a grocery store, you'll need to live off the land, grow your own crops, and hunt or fish.

But there is still one last federal excise tax to go.

5. **Hunting and fishing.** Taxes range from 3 cents for fishing tackle boxes to 11% for archery equipment. This generates $1 billion for fish and wildlife services.

Living off the land and avoiding taxes just got much harder, and that's the whole point. The government taxes products with relatively inelastic demand because most people will still purchase them after the tax is in place. As a result, avoiding excise taxes isn't practical. The best you can do is reduce your tax burden by altering your lifestyle or what you purchase.

Excise taxes are everywhere.

CONCEPTS YOU SHOULD KNOW

consumer surplus (p. 179)
deadweight loss (p. 191)
efficient (p. 185)
equity (p. 187)

excise taxes (p. 188)
incidence (p. 188)
producer surplus (p. 181)
social welfare (p. 184)

total surplus (p. 184)
welfare economics (p. 178)
willingness to pay (p. 178)
willingness to sell (p. 181)

QUESTIONS FOR REVIEW

1. Explain how consumer surplus is derived from the difference between the willingness to pay and the market-equilibrium price.

2. Explain how producer surplus is derived from the difference between the willingness to sell and the market-equilibrium price.

3. Why do economists focus on consumer and producer surplus and not on the possibility of consumer and producer loss? Illustrate your answer on a supply and demand graph.

4. How do economists define efficiency?

5. What type of goods should be taxed in order to minimize deadweight loss?

6. Suppose that the government taxes a good that is very elastic. Illustrate what will happen to the consumer surplus, producer surplus, tax revenue, and deadweight loss on a supply and demand graph.

7. What happens to tax revenues as tax rates increase?

STUDY PROBLEMS (✻ *solved at the end of the section*)

1. A college student enjoys eating pizza. Her willingness to pay for each slice is shown in the following table:

Number of pizza slices	Willingness to pay (per slice)
1	$6
2	$5
3	$4
4	$3
5	$2
6	$1
7	$0

a. If pizza slices cost $3 each, how many slices will she buy? How much consumer surplus will she enjoy?

b. If the price of slices falls to $2, how much consumer surplus will she enjoy?

2. A cash-starved town decides to impose a $6 excise tax on T-shirts sold. The following table shows the quantity demanded and the quantity supplied at various prices.

Price per T-shirt	Quantity demanded	Quantity supplied
$19	0	60
$16	10	50
$13	20	40
$10	30	30
$ 7	40	20
$ 4	50	10

a. What are the equilibrium quantity demanded and the quantity supplied before the tax is implemented? Determine the consumer and producer surplus before the tax.

b. What are the equilibrium quantity demanded and the quantity supplied after the tax is implemented? Determine the consumer and producer surplus after the tax.

c. How much tax revenue does the town generate from the tax?

3. Andrew paid $30 to buy a potato cannon, a cylinder that shoots potatoes hundreds of feet. He was willing to pay $45. When Andrew's friend Nick learns that Andrew bought a potato cannon, he asks Andrew if he will sell it for $60, and Andrew agrees. Nick is thrilled, since he would have paid Andrew up to $80 for the cannon. Andrew is also delighted. Determine the consumer surplus from the original purchase and the additional surplus generated by the resale of the cannon.

4. If the government wants to raise tax revenue, which of the following items are good candidates for an excise tax? Why?
   a. granola bars
   b. cigarettes
   c. toilet paper
   d. automobile tires
   e. bird feeders

* 5. If the government wants to minimize the deadweight loss of taxation, which of the following items are good candidates for an excise tax? Why?
   a. bottled water
   b. prescription drugs
   c. oranges
   d. batteries
   e. luxury cars

6. A new medical study indicates that eating blueberries helps prevent cancer. If the demand for blueberries increases, what will happen to the size of the consumer and producer surplus? Illustrate your answer by shifting the demand curve appropriately and labeling the new and old areas of consumer and producer surplus.

7. Use the graph at the top of p. 207 to answer questions a–f.
   a. What area represents consumer surplus before the tax?
   b. What area represents producer surplus before the tax?
   c. What area represents consumer surplus after the tax?
   d. What area represents producer surplus after the tax?
   e. What area represents the tax revenue after the tax?
   f. What area represents the deadweight loss after the tax?

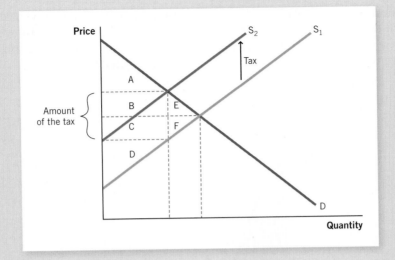

8. The cost of many electronic devices has fallen appreciably since they were first introduced. For instance, computers, cell phones, microwaves, and calculators not only provide more functions but do so at a lower cost. Illustrate the impact of lower production costs on the supply curve. What happens to the size of the consumer and producer surplus? If consumer demand for cell phones is relatively elastic, who is likely to benefit the most from the lower production costs?

9. Suppose that the demand for a concert, Q_D, is represented by the following equation, where P is the price of concert tickets and Q is the number of tickets sold:

$$Q_D = 2500 - 20P$$

The supply of tickets, Q_S, is represented by the equation:

$$Q_S = -500 + 80P$$

a. Find the equilibrium price and quantity of tickets sold. (**Hint:** Set $Q_D = Q_S$ and solve for the price, P, and then plug the result back into either of the original equations to find Q_E.)

b. Carefully graph your result in part a.

c. Calculate the consumer surplus at the equilibrium price and quantity. (**Hint:** Since the area of consumer surplus is a triangle, you will need to use the formula for the area of a triangle [$\frac{1}{2} \times$ base $\times$ height] to solve the problem.)

10. In this chapter, we have focused on the effect of taxes on social welfare. However, governments also subsidize goods, or make them cheaper to buy or sell. How would a $2,000 subsidy on the purchase of a new hybrid vehicle impact the consumer surplus and producer surplus in the hybrid market? Use a supply and demand diagram to illustrate your answer. Does the subsidy create deadweight loss?

* 11. Suppose that a new $50 tax is placed on each cell phone. From the information in the graph below, compute the incidence, deadweight loss, and tax revenue of the tax.

a. What is the incidence of the tax?
b. What is the deadweight loss of the tax?
c. What is the amount of tax revenue generated?

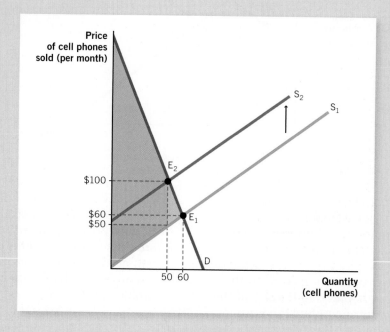

SOLVED PROBLEMS

5. **a.** Many good substitutes are available: consumers can drink tap water, filtered water, or other healthy beverages instead of bottled water. Therefore, bottled water is not a good candidate for an excise tax.

   b. Taxing prescription drugs will generate significant revenues without reducing sales much, if at all. There is almost no deadweight loss because consumers have few, if any, alternatives. Thus, prescription drugs are a good candidate for an excise tax.

   c. Consumers can select many other fruits to replace oranges. The deadweight loss will be quite large. Therefore, oranges are not a good candidate for an excise tax.

   d. Without batteries, many devices won't work. The lack of substitutes makes demand quite inelastic, so the deadweight loss will be small. Thus, batteries are an excellent candidate for an excise tax.

   e. Wealthy consumers can spend their income in many ways. They do not have to buy luxury cars. As a result, the tax will create a large amount of deadweight loss. Therefore, luxury cars are a poor candidate for an excise tax.

11. **a.** After the tax is implemented, the market price rises from $60 to $100; but since sellers must pay $50 to the government, they net only $50. Tax incidence measures the share of the tax paid by buyers and sellers. Since the market price rises by $40 (from $60 to $100), buyers are paying $40 of the $50 tax, or $\frac{4}{5}$. Since the net price falls by $10 (from $60 to $50), sellers are paying $10 of the $50 tax, or $\frac{1}{5}$.

    b. The deadweight loss is represented by the decrease in the total surplus found in the yellow triangle. In order to compute the amount of the deadweight loss, we need to determine the area inside the triangle. The area of a triangle is found by taking $\frac{1}{2} \times$ base $\times$ height. The triangle is sitting on its side, so the height of the triangle is 10 ($60 - 50$) and the base is $50 ($100 - $50). Hence the deadweight loss is $\frac{1}{2} \times 10 \times \$50 = \$250$.

    c. The tax revenue is represented by the green-shaded area. You can calculate the tax revenue by multiplying the amount of the tax ($50) by the number of units sold after the tax (50). This equals $2,500.

Market Inefficiencies
Externalities and Public Goods

Pollution should always be eliminated, no matter the cost.

We would all agree that it's important to protect the environment. So when we face pollution and other environmental degradation, should we eliminate

MIS CONCEPTION

it? If your first thought is "yes, always," you're not alone—after all, there's only one Earth, and we'd better get tough on environmental destruction wherever we find it, whatever it takes. Right?

It's tempting to think this way, but as a useful social policy, the prescription comes up short. No one wants to go back to the way it was when businesses were free to dump their waste anywhere, but it is also impractical to eliminate all pollution. Some amount of environmental damage is inevitable whenever we extract resources, manufacture goods, fertilize croplands, or power our electrical grid—all activities that are integral to modern society. But how do we figure out what the "right" level of pollution is, and how do we get there? The answer is to examine the tension between social costs and benefits, and to look carefully at markets to ensure that they are accounting for both.

In the preceding chapters, we have seen that markets provide many benefits and that they work because participants pursue their own self-interests. But sometimes markets need a helping hand. For example, some market exchanges harm innocent bystanders, and others are not efficient because the ownership of property is not clearly defined or actively enforced. To help explain why markets do not always operate efficiently, this chapter will explore two important concepts: *externalities* and the differences between *private* and *public goods*.

What is the most efficient way to deal with pollution?

BIG QUESTIONS

* What are externalities, and how do they affect markets?
* What are private goods and public goods?
* What are the challenges of providing nonexcludable goods?

What Are Externalities, and How Do They Affect Markets?

Externalities
are the costs or benefits of a market activity that affect a third party.

We have seen that buyers and sellers benefit from trade. But what about the effects that trade might have on bystanders? **Externalities**, or the costs and benefits of a market activity that affect a third party, can often lead to undesirable consequences. For example, in April 2010, an offshore oil rig in the Gulf of Mexico operated by British Petroleum (BP) exploded, causing millions of barrels of oil to spill into the water. Even though both BP and its customers benefit from the production of oil, others along the Gulf coast had their lives severely disrupted. Industries dependent on high environmental quality, like tourism and fishing, were hit particularly hard by the costs of the spill.

Internal costs
are the costs of a market activity paid by an individual participant.

External costs
are the costs of a market activity paid by people who are not participants.

Social costs
are the internal costs plus the external costs of a market activity.

For a market to work as efficiently as possible, two things must happen. First, each participant must be able to evaluate the **internal costs** of participation—the costs that only the individual participant pays. For example, when we choose to drive somewhere, we typically consider our personal costs—the time it will take to reach our destination, the amount we will pay for gasoline, and what we will pay for routine vehicle maintenance. Second, for a market to work efficiently, the *external costs* must also be paid. **External costs** are costs imposed on people who are not participants in that market. In the case of driving, the congestion and pollution that our cars create are external costs. Economists define **social costs** as a combination of the internal costs and the external costs of a market activity.

In this section, we will consider some of the mechanisms that encourage consumers and producers to account for the social costs of their actions.

The Third-Party Problem

A **third-party problem** occurs when those not directly involved in a market activity nevertheless experience negative or positive externalities.

An externality exists whenever a private cost (or benefit) diverges from a social cost (or benefit). For example, manufacturers who make vehicles and consumers who purchase them benefit from the transaction, but the making and using of those vehicles leads to externalities—including air pollution and traffic congestion—that adversely affect others. A **third-party problem** occurs when those not directly involved in a market activity experience negative or positive externalities.

If a third party is adversely affected, the externality is negative. This occurs when the volume of vehicles on the roads causes air pollution. Negative externalities present a challenge to society because it is difficult to make consumers and producers take responsibility for the full costs of their actions. For example, drivers typically consider only the internal costs (their own costs) of reaching their destination. Likewise, manufacturers would generally prefer to ignore the pollution they create, because addressing the problem would raise their costs without providing them with significant direct benefits.

In general, society would benefit if all consumers and producers considered both the internal and external costs of their actions. Since this is not a reasonable expectation, governments design policies that create incentives for firms and people to limit the amount of pollution they emit.

Incentives

An effort by the city government of Washington, D.C., shows the potential power of this approach. Like many communities throughout the United States, the city instituted a five-cent tax on every plastic bag a consumer picks up at a store. While five cents may not sound like much of a disincentive, shoppers have responded by switching to cloth bags or reusing plastic ones. In Washington, D.C., the city estimated that the number of plastic bags used every month fell from 22.5 million in 2009 to just 3 million in 2010, significantly reducing the amount of plastic waste entering landfills in the process.

Not all externalities are negative, however. Positive externalities also exist. For instance, education creates a large positive externality for society beyond the benefits to individual students, teachers, and support staff. For example, a more knowledgeable workforce benefits employers looking for qualified employees and is more efficient and productive than an uneducated workforce. And because local businesses experience a positive externality from a well-educated local community, they have a stake in the educational process. A good example of the synergy between local business and higher education is Silicon Valley in California, which is home to many high-tech companies and Stanford University. As early as the late nineteenth century, Stanford's leaders felt that the university's mission should include fostering the development of self-sufficient local industry. After World War II, Stanford encouraged faculty and graduates to start their own companies. This led to the creation of Hewlett-Packard, Varian Associates, Bell Labs, and Xerox. A generation later, this nexus of high-tech firms gave birth to leading software and Internet firms like 3Com, Adobe, and Facebook, and—more indirectly—Cisco, Apple, and Google.

Recognizing the benefits that they received, many of the most successful businesses associated with Stanford have donated large sums to the university. For

Many of the most successful businesses associated with Stanford have made large donations to the university.

When oil refineries are permitted to pollute the environment without additional costs imposed, they are likely to overproduce.

instance, the Hewlett Foundation gave $400 million to Stanford's endowment for the humanities and sciences and for undergraduate education—an act of generosity that highlights the positive externality that Stanford University had on Hewlett-Packard.

Correcting for Negative Externalities

In this section, we explore ways to correct for negative externalities. To do this, we use supply and demand analysis to understand how they affect the market. Let's begin with supply and compare the difference between what market forces produce and what is best for society in the case of an oil refinery. A refinery converts crude oil into gasoline. This complex process generates many negative externalities, including the release of pollutants into the air and the dumping of waste by-products.

The **social optimum** is the price and quantity combination that would exist if there were no externalities.

Figure 7.1 illustrates the contrast between the market equilibrium and the *social optimum* in the case of an oil refinery. The **social optimum** is the price and quantity combination that would exist if there were no externalities. These costs are indicated on the graph by the supply curve $S_{internal}$, which

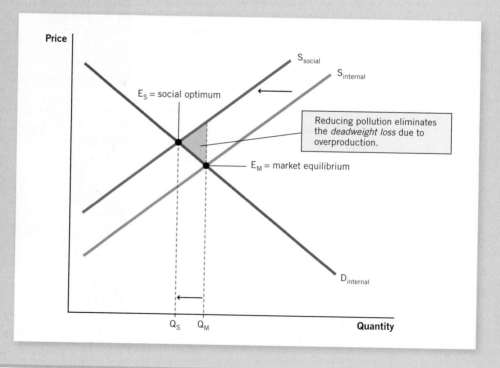

Reducing pollution eliminates the *deadweight loss* due to overproduction.

represents how much the oil refiner will produce if it does not have to pay for the negative consequences of its activity. In this situation, the market equilibrium, E_M, accounts only for the internal costs of production.

When a negative externality occurs, the government may be able to restore the social optimum by requiring externality-causing market participants to pay for the cost of their actions. In this case, there are three potential solutions. First, the refiner can be required to install pollution abatement equipment or to change production techniques to reduce emissions and waste by-products. Second, a tax can be levied as a disincentive to produce. Finally, the government can require the firm to pay for any environmental damage it causes. Each solution forces the firm to **internalize** the externality, meaning that the firm must take into account the external costs (or benefits) to society that occur as a result of its actions.

Incentives

An externality is **internalized** when a firm takes into account the external costs (or benefits) to society that occur as a result of its actions.

Having to pay the costs of imposing pollution on others reduces the amount of the pollution-causing activity. This result is evident in the shift of the supply curve to S_{social}. The new supply curve reflects a combination of the internal and external costs of producing the good. Since each corrective measure requires the refiner to spend money to correct the externality, the willingness to sell the good declines, or shifts to the left. The result is a social optimum at a lower quantity, Q_S, than at the market equilibrium quantity demanded, Q_M. The trade-off is clear. We can reduce negative externalities by requiring producers to internalize the externality. However, doing so does not occur without cost. Since the supply curve shifts to the left, the quantity produced will be lower. In the real world, there is always a cost.

Trade-offs

In addition, when an externality occurs, the market equilibrium creates deadweight loss, as shown by the yellow triangle in Figure 7.1. In Chapter 6, we considered deadweight loss in the context of governmental regulation or taxation. These measures, when imposed on efficient markets, created deadweight loss, or a less-than-desirable amount of economic activity. In the case of a negative externality, the market is not efficient because it is not fully capturing the cost of production. Once the government intervenes and requires the firm to internalize the external costs of its production, output falls to the socially optimal level, Q_S, and the deadweight loss from overproduction is eliminated.

Table 7.1 outlines the basic decision-making process that guides private and social decisions. Private decision-makers consider only their internal costs, but society as a whole experiences both internal and external costs. To align the incentives of private decision-makers with the interests of society, we must find mechanisms that encourage the internalization of externalities.

TABLE 7.1

Private and Social Decision Making

Personal decision	Social optimum	The problem	The solution
Based on internal costs	Social costs = internal costs plus external costs	To get consumers and producers to take responsibility for the externalities they create	Encourage consumers and producers to *internalize* externalities.

ECONOMICS IN THE REAL WORLD

Congestion Charges

In 2003, London instituted a congestion charge. Motorists entering the charge zone must pay a flat rate of £10 (approximately $16) between 7 a.m. and 6 p.m. Monday through Friday. A computerized scanner automatically bills the driver, so there is no wait at a toll booth. When the charge was first enacted, it had an immediate effect: the number of vehicles entering the zone fell by a third, the number of riders on public transportation increased by 15%, and bicycle use rose by 30%.

Why impose a congestion charge? The major goal is to prevent traffic-related delays in densely populated areas. Time is valuable, and when you add up all the hours that people spend stuck in traffic, it's a major loss for the economy! Heavy traffic in cities also exposes lots of people to extra pollution, with costs to health and quality of life. The congestion charge puts a price on these negative externalities and helps to restore the socially optimal level of road usage.

In 2007, Stockholm established a congestion-charge system with a new wrinkle—dynamic pricing. The pricing changes between 6:30 a.m. and 6:30 p.m. During the peak morning and evening commutes, motorists are charged 20 Swedish krona (approximately $3). At other times, the price ratchets down to 15 or even 10 krona. This pricing scheme encourages motorists to enter the city at nonpeak times.

Motorists must pay a flat-rate congestion charge to enter the central business area of London on weekdays.

Marginal thinking

Because congestion charges become part of a motorist's internal costs, they cause motorists to weigh the costs and benefits of driving into congested areas. In other words, congestion charges internalize externalities. In London, a flat £10 fee encourages motorists to avoid the zone or find alternative transportation. But once motorists have paid the fee, they do not have an incentive to avoid peak flow times. The variable pricing in Stockholm causes motorists to make marginal adjustments in terms of the time when they drive. This spreads out the traffic flow, as drivers internalize the external costs even more precisely. ✳

Correcting for Positive Externalities

Positive externalities, such as vaccines, have benefits for third parties. As with negative externalities, economists use supply and demand analysis to compare the efficiency of the market with the social optimum. This time, we will focus on the demand curve. Consider a person who gets a flu shot. When the vaccine is administered, the recipient is immunized. This creates an internal benefit. But there is also an external benefit: because the recipient likely will not come down with the flu, fewer other people will catch the flu and become contagious, which helps to protect even those who do not get flu shots. Therefore, we can say that vaccines convey a positive externality to the rest of society.

Why do positive externalities exist in the market? Using our example of flu shots, there is an incentive for people in high-risk groups to get vaccinated for the sake of their own health. In Figure 7.2, we capture this internal benefit in the demand curve labeled $D_{internal}$. However, the market equilibrium, E_M, only accounts for the internal benefits of individuals deciding whether to get vaccinated. In order to maximize the health benefits for everyone, public health officials need to find a way to encourage people to consider the external benefit of their vaccination, too. One way is to issue school vaccination laws, which require that all children entering school provide proof of vaccination against a variety of diseases. The requirement creates a direct incentive for vaccination and produces positive benefits for all members of society by internalizing the externality. The overall effect is that more people get vaccinated early in life, helping to push the market toward the socially optimal number of vaccinations.

A vaccine offers both individual and social benefits.

Government can also promote the social optimum by encouraging economic activity that helps third parties. For example, it can offer a subsidy, or price break, to encourage more people to get vaccinated. The subsidy acts as a consumption incentive. In fact, governments routinely provide free or reduced-cost vaccines to those most at risk from flu and to their caregivers.

FIGURE 7.2

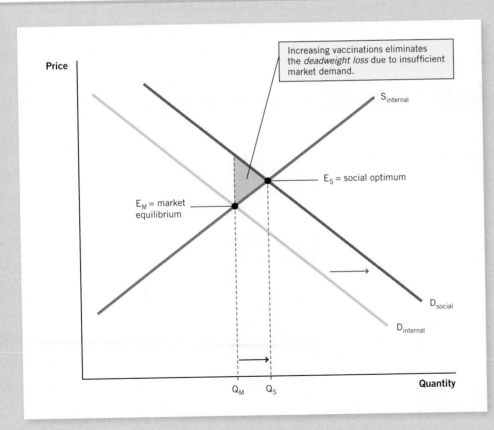

Increasing vaccinations eliminates the *deadweight loss* due to insufficient market demand.

$S_{internal}$

E_S = social optimum

E_M = market equilibrium

D_{social}

$D_{internal}$

Price

Quantity

Q_M Q_S

Positive Externalities and Social Optimum

The subsidy encourages consumers to internalize the externality. As a result, consumption moves from the market equilibrium, Q_M, to a social optimum at a higher quantity, Q_S, vaccinations increase, and the deadweight loss from insufficient market demand is eliminated.

Incentives

Since the subsidy enables the consumer to spend less money, his or her willingness to get the vaccine increases, shifting the demand curve in Figure 7.2 from $D_{internal}$ to D_{social}. The social demand curve reflects the sum of the internal and social benefits of getting the vaccination. In other words, the subsidy encourages consumers to internalize the externality. As a result, the output moves from the market equilibrium quantity demanded, Q_M, to a social optimum at a higher quantity, Q_S.

We have seen that markets do not handle externalities well. With a negative externality, the market produces too much of a good. But in the case of a positive externality, the market produces too little. In both cases, the market equilibrium creates deadweight loss. When positive externalities are present, the private market is not efficient because it is not fully capturing the social benefits. In other words, the market equilibrium does not maximize the gains for society as a whole. When positive externalities are internalized, the demand curve shifts outward and output rises to the socially optimal level, Q_S. The deadweight loss that results from insufficient market demand, and therefore underproduction, is eliminated.

Table 7.2 summarizes the key characteristics of positive and negative externalities and presents additional examples of each type.

Before moving on, it is worth noting that not all externalities warrant corrective measures. There are times when the size of the externality is negligible and does not justify the cost of increased regulations, charges, taxes, or subsidies that might achieve the social optimum. Since corrective measures also have costs, the presence of externalities does not by itself imply that the government should intervene in the market.

TABLE 7.2

A Summary of Externalities

	Negative externalities	Positive externalities
Definition	Costs borne by third parties	Benefits received by third parties
Examples	Oil refining creates air pollution.	Flu shots prevent the spread of disease.
	Traffic congestion causes all motorists to spend more time on the road waiting.	Education creates a more productive workforce and enables citizens to make more informed decisions for the betterment of society.
	Airports create noise pollution.	Restored historic buildings enable people to enjoy beautiful architectural details.
Corrective measures	Taxes or charges	Subsidies or government provision

PRACTICE WHAT YOU KNOW

Externalities: A New Theater Is Proposed

Suppose that a developer wants to build a new movie theater in your community. It submits a development proposal to the city council.

How would a new theater affect your community?

Question: What negative externalities might the theater generate?

Answer: A successful new theater will likely create traffic congestion. As a result, planning commissions often insist that developers widen nearby streets, install traffic lights, and establish new turning lanes to help traffic flows. These are all negative externalities.

Question: What positive externalities might the theater generate?

Answer: Many local businesses will indirectly benefit from increased activity in the area of the movie theater. Nearby convenience stores, gas stations, restaurants, and shopping areas will all get a boost from the people who attend the movies. Since the demand for these local services will rise, businesses in the area will earn more profits and employ more workers. These are positive externalities.

What Are Private Goods and Public Goods?

The presence of externalities reflects a divide between the way markets operate and the social optimum. Why does this happen? The answer is often related to *property rights*. **Property rights** give the owner the ability to exercise control over a resource. When property rights are not clearly defined, resources can be mistreated. For instance, since no one owns the air, manufacturing firms often emit pollutants into it.

> **Property rights**
> give the owner the ability to exercise control over a resource.

To understand why firms sometimes overlook their actions' effects on others, we need to examine the role of property rights in market efficiency. When property rights are poorly established or not enforced effectively, the wrong incentives come into play. The difference is apparent when we compare situations in which people do have property rights. Private owners have an incentive to keep their property in good repair because they bear the costs of fixing what they own when it breaks or no longer works properly. For instance, if you own a personal computer, you will probably protect your investment by treating it with care and dealing with any problems immediately. However, if you access a public computer terminal in a campus lab or library and find that it is not working properly, you will most likely ignore the problem and simply look for another computer that is working. The difference between solving the problem and ignoring it is crucial to understanding why property rights matter.

Incentives

Private Property

One way to minimize externalities is to establish well-defined *private property* rights. **Private property** provides an exclusive right of ownership that allows for the use, and especially the exchange, of property. This creates incentives to maintain, protect, and conserve property and to trade with others. Let's consider these four incentives in the context of automobile ownership.

1. *The incentive to maintain property.* Car owners have an incentive to maintain their vehicles. After all, routine maintenance, replacement of worn parts, and repairs keep the vehicle safe and reliable. In addition, a well-maintained car can be sold for more than one in poor condition.
2. *The incentive to protect property.* Owners have an incentive to protect their vehicles from theft or damage. They do this by using alarm systems, locking the doors, and parking in well-lit areas.
3. *The incentive to conserve property.* Car owners also have an incentive to extend the usable life of their automobiles by limiting the number of miles they put on their cars each year.
4. *The incentive to trade with others.* Car owners have an incentive to trade with others because they may profit from the transaction. Suppose someone offers to buy your car for $5,000 and you think it is worth only $3,000. Because you own the car, you can do whatever you want with it. If you decline to sell, you will incur an opportunity cost: you will be giving up $5,000 to keep something you value at $3,000. There is no law requiring you to sell your vehicle, so you *could* keep the car—but you probably won't. Why? Because private property gives you as the owner an incentive to trade for something better in the market.

The incentives to maintain, protect, and conserve property help to ensure that owners keep their private property in good shape. The fourth incentive, to trade with others, helps to ensure that private property is held by the person with the greatest willingness to pay for it.

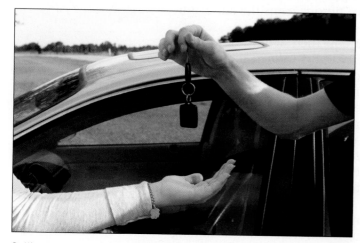

Selling a car benefits both the owner and the buyer.

The Coase Theorem

In 1960, economist Ronald Coase argued that establishing private property rights can close the gap between internal costs and social costs.

Consider an example involving two adjacent landowners, one who raises cattle and another who grows wheat. Because neither landowner has built a fence, the cattle wander onto the neighboring land to eat the wheat. Coase concluded that in this situation both parties are equally responsible for solving the problem. He arrived at that conclusion by considering two possible scenarios.

The first scenario supposes that the wheat farmer has the legal right to expect cattle-free

The cattle are near the wheat to the same extent . . .

. . . that the wheat is near the cattle.

fields. In this scenario, the cattle rancher is liable for the damage caused to the wheat farmer. If the damage is costly and the rancher is liable, the rancher will build a fence to keep the cattle in rather than pay for the damage they cause. The fence internalizes the negative externality and forces the rancher to bear the full cost of the damage. If the cost of the damage to the crop is much smaller than the cost of building a fence, then the rancher is more likely to compensate the wheat farmer for his losses rather than build the fence.

What if the wheat farmer does not have the legal right to expect cattle-free fields? In this scenario, the cattle rancher is not liable for any damages his cattle cause to the wheat farmer. If the damage to the nearby wheat field is large and the rancher is *not* liable, the wheat farmer will build a fence to keep the cattle out. The fence internalizes the negative externality and forces the wheat farmer to bear the full cost of the damage. If the amount of damage is smaller than the cost of a fence, the farmer may accept occasional damage as the lower-cost option.

> The **Coase theorem** states that if there are no barriers to negotiations, and if property rights are fully specified, interested parties will bargain to correct any externalities that exist.

From comparing these two scenarios, Coase determined that whenever the externality is large enough to justify the expense, the externality gets internalized. As long as the property rights are fully specified (and there are no barriers to negotiations; see below), either the cattle rancher or the wheat farmer will build a fence. The fence will keep the cattle away from the wheat, remove the externality, and prevent the destruction of property.

With this in mind, we can now appreciate the **Coase theorem**, which states that if there are no barriers to negotiations, and if property rights are fully specified, interested parties will bargain privately to correct any externalities. As a result, the assignment of property rights, under the law, gives each party an incentive to internalize any externalities. If it is difficult to bargain, because the costs of reaching an agreement are too high, private parties will

A fence internalizes the externality.

be unable to internalize the externality between themselves. Therefore, the Coase theorem also suggests that private solutions to externality problems are not always possible. This implies a role for government in solving complex externality issues.

To think about the case for a government role, consider the difference between the example of a rancher and a farmer with adjacent land and the example of a community-wide problem such as pollution. With two land-owners, a private solution should be possible because the parties can bargain with each other at a low cost. With pollution, though, so many individuals are impacted that the polluting company cannot afford to bargain with each one. Since bargaining costs are high in this case, an intermediary, like the government, may be necessary to ensure that externalities are internalized.

Private and Public Goods

Excludable goods are those that the consumer must purchase before being able to use them.

Rival goods are those that cannot be enjoyed by more than one person at a time.

Private goods have two characteristics: they are both excludable and rival in consumption.

Public goods can be jointly consumed by more than one person, and nonpayers are difficult to exclude.

When we think of private goods, most of us imagine something that we enjoy, like a slice of pizza or a favorite jacket. When we think of public goods, we think of goods provided by the government, like roads, the post office, and the military. The terms "private" and "public" typically imply ownership or production, but that is not how economists categorize private and public goods. To understand the difference between private and public goods, you need to know whether a good is *excludable*, *rival*, or both. An **excludable good** is one that the consumer is required to purchase before being able to use it. A **rival good** is one that cannot be enjoyed by more than one person at a time.

Private Goods

A **private good** is both excludable and rival in consumption. For instance, a slice of pizza is excludable because it must be purchased before you can eat it. Also, a slice of pizza is rival; only one person can eat it. These two characteristics, excludability and rivalry, allow the market to work efficiently in the absence of externalities. Consider a pizza business. The pizzeria bakes pizza pies because it knows it can sell them to consumers. Likewise, consumers are willing to buy pizza because it is a food they enjoy. Since the producer gets to charge a price and the consumer gets to acquire a rival good, the stage is set for mutual gains from trade.

Gains from trade

Public Goods

Markets have no difficulty producing purely private goods, like pizza, since in order to enjoy them you must first purchase them. But when was the last time you paid to see a fireworks display? Hundreds of thousands of people view many of the nation's best displays of fireworks, but only a small percentage of them pay admission to get a preferred seat. Fireworks displays are a **public good** because (1) they can be jointly consumed by more than one person, and (2) it is difficult to exclude nonpayers. Since consumers cannot be easily forced to pay to observe fireworks, they may desire more of the good than is typically supplied. This leads a market economy to underproduce fireworks displays and many other public goods.

Pizza is a private good.

The Case behind the Coase Theorem

The scene is London in the 1870s. The properties of a doctor and candy maker sit next to each other. For years they coexist peacefully, but as both businesses expand, they start using rooms that are separated by only a common wall. The candy-making process in the candy maker's room makes so much noise that the doctor has trouble using his stethoscope. This difficult situation must be resolved. The doctor can file a civil complaint and sue the candy maker, or the two parties can arrive at a solution on their own.

In the Coase Theorem, the clear delineation of property rights is vital to the bargaining of private parties to correct externalities. If it's not clear whether the doctor has the legal right to expect a noise-free office, the case will likely be decided in court.

 If the doctor has the right to a noise-free office, the candy maker must decide what's cheaper: build a soundproof wall, or move?

 But if the doctor does not have the legal right to expect a noise-free office, then it's his choice to make: build the soundproof wall, or move?

This was an actual case! Want to find out what happened? Search online for "Sturges v. Bridgman."

REVIEW QUESTIONS

- What is the negative externality involved in the case above?

- Suppose an agreement can't be reached and that the doctor files a civil complaint against the candy maker. What possible risks or losses does the doctor face when filing the complaint?

World-renowned violinist Joshua Bell performs incognito in the Washington, D.C., Metro.

A **free-rider problem** occurs whenever someone receives a benefit without having to pay for it.

Public goods are often underproduced because people can get them without paying for them. Consider Joshua Bell, one of the most famous violinists in the world. The day after giving a concert in Boston where patrons paid $100 a ticket, he decided to reprise the performance in a Washington, D.C., subway station and just ask for donations.* Any passer-by could listen to the music—it did not need to be purchased to be enjoyed. In other words, it was nonexcludable and nonrival in consumption. But because it is impossible for a street musician to force bystanders to pay, it is difficult for the musician—even one as good as Joshua Bell—to make a living. Suppose he draws a large crowd and the music creates $500 worth of enjoyment among the audience. At the end of the performance, he receives a loud round of applause and then motions to the donation basket. A number of people come up and donate, but when he counts up the contributions he finds only $30—the actual amount he earned while playing in the Metro.

Why did Joshua Bell receive $30, when he created many times that amount in value? This phenomenon, known as a **free-rider problem**, occurs whenever people receive a benefit they do not need to pay for. A street musician provides a public good and must rely on the generosity of the audience to contribute. If very few people contribute, many potential musicians will not find it worthwhile to perform. We tend to see very few street performances because free-riding lowers the returns. This means that the private equilibrium amount of street performances is undersupplied in comparison to the social optimum. When payment cannot be linked to use, the efficient quantity is not produced.

Street performances are just one example of a public good. National defense, lighthouses, streetlights, clean air, and open-source software such as Mozilla Firefox are other examples. Let's examine national defense since it is a particularly clear example of a public good that is subject to a free-rider problem. All citizens value security, but consider the difficulty of trying to organize and provide adequate national defense through private contributions alone. How could you voluntarily coordinate a missile defense system or get enough people to pay for an aircraft carrier and the personnel to operate it? Society would be underprotected because many people would not voluntarily contribute their fair share of the expense. For this reason, defense expenditures are normally provided by the government and funded by tax revenues. Since most people pay taxes, this almost eliminates the free-rider problem in the context of national defense.

Most people would agree that government should provide certain public goods for society including, among others, national defense, the interstate high-

Concerned about security? Only the government is capable of providing adequate national defense.

---

* This really happened! The *Washington Post* and Bell conducted an experiment to test the public's reaction to performances of "genius" in unexpected settings. Our discussion here places the event in a hypothetical context—for the real-life result, see Gene Weingarten, "Pearls before Breakfast," *Washington Post*, April 8, 2007.

way system, and medical and science-related research to fight pandemics. In each case, public-sector provision helps to eliminate the free-rider problem and restore the socially optimal level of activity.

Club Goods and Common-Resource Goods

There are two additional goods that we have not yet introduced. Since *club* and *common-resource goods* have characteristics of both private and public goods, the line between private provision and public provision is often blurred.

Club goods are nonrival in consumption and excludable. Satellite television is an example; it is excludable because you must pay to receive the signal, yet because more than one customer can receive the signal at the same time, it is nonrival in consumption. Since customers who wish to enjoy club goods can be excluded, markets typically provide these goods. However, once a satellite television network is in place, the cost of adding customers is low. Firms are motivated to maximize profits, not the number of people they serve, so the market price is higher and the output is lower than what society desires.

Common-resource goods are rival in consumption but nonexcludable. King crab in the Bering Sea off Alaska is an example. Since any particular crab can be caught by only one boat crew, the crabs are a rival resource. At the same time, exclusion is not possible because any boat crew that wants to brave the elements can catch crab.

We have seen that the market generally works well for private goods. In the case of public goods, however, the market generally needs a hand. In between, club and common-resource goods illustrate the tension between the private and public provision of many goods and services. Table 7.3 highlights each of the four types of goods we have discussed.

© 2006 Bil Keane, Inc.
Dist. by King Features Synd.
www.familycircus.com

"How much would it cost to see a sunset if God decided to charge for it?"

Club goods have two characteristics: they are nonrival in consumption and excludable.

Common-resource goods have two characteristics: they are rival in consumption and nonexcludable.

Satellite television is a club good.

Alaskan king crab is a common-resource good.

TABLE 7.3

The Four Types of Goods

		Consumption	
		Rival	**Nonrival**
Excludable?	**Yes**	*Private goods* are rival and excludable: pizza, watches, automobiles.	*Club goods* are nonrival and excludable: satellite television, education, country clubs.
	No	*Common-resource goods* are rival and not excludable: Alaskan king crab, a large shared popcorn at the movies, congested roads.	*Public goods* are nonrival and not excludable: street performers, defense, tsunami warning systems.

PRACTICE WHAT YOU KNOW

Public Goods: Are Parks Public Goods?

Many goods have the characteristics of a public good, but few goods meet the exact definition.

Question: Are parks public goods?

Answer: We tend to think of public parks as meeting the necessary requirements to be a public good. But not so fast. Have you been to any of America's top national parks on a peak summer weekend? Parks are subject to congestion, which makes them rival. In addition, most national and state parks require an admission fee—translation: they are excludable. Therefore, public parks do not meet the exact definition of a public good.

Not surprisingly, there are many good examples of private parks that maintain, protect, and conserve the environment alongside their public counterparts. For instance, Natural Bridge is a privately owned and operated park in Virginia that preserves a rare natural arch over a small stream. The East Coast is dotted with private parks that predate the establishment of the national park system. Like their public counterparts, private parks are also not public goods.

Natural Bridge in Virginia

What Are the Challenges of Providing Nonexcludable Goods?

Understanding the four types of goods provides a solid foundation for understanding the role of markets and the government in society. Next, we consider some of the special challenges that arise in providing nonexcludable goods.

Cost-Benefit Analysis

To help make decisions about providing public goods, economists turn to **cost-benefit analysis,** a process used to determine whether the benefits of providing a public good outweigh the costs. It is relatively easy to measure the cost of supplying a public good. For instance, if a community puts on a Fourth of July celebration, it will have to pay for the fireworks and labor involved in setting up the event. The costs are a known quantity. But benefits are difficult to quantify. Since people do not need to pay to see the fireworks, it is hard to determine how much benefit the community receives. If asked, people might misrepresent the social benefit in two ways. First, some residents who value the celebration highly might claim that the fireworks bring more benefit than they actually do, because they want the community fireworks to continue. Second, those residents who dislike the crowds and noise might understate the benefit they receive. Since there is no way to know how truthful respondents are when responding to a questionnaire, the actual social benefit of a fireworks show is hard to measure. As a result, there is no way to know the exact amount of consumer and producer surplus generated by a public good like fireworks.

Since people do not pay to enjoy public goods, and since the government provides them without charging a direct fee, determining the socially optimal amount typically takes place through the political system. Generally speaking, elected officials do not get reelected if the populace believes that they have not done a good job with their cost-benefit analyses.

Cost-benefit analysis
is a process that economists use to determine whether the benefits of providing a public good outweigh the costs.

Figuring out the social benefit of a fireworks display is quite difficult.

ECONOMICS IN THE REAL WORLD

Internet Piracy

The digitization of media, and the speed with which it can be transferred across the Internet, has made the protection of property rights very difficult. Many countries either do not have strict copyright standards or fail to enforce them. The result is a black market filled with bootlegged copies of movies, music, and other media.

Since digital "file sharing" is so common these days, you might not fully understand the harm that occurs. Piracy is an illegal form of free-riding. Every song and every movie that is transferred takes away royalties that would have gone to the original artist or the studio. After all, producing content is expensive, and violations of copyright law cost legitimate businesses the opportunity to make a fair return on their investments. However, consumers of content don't often see it this way. Some believe that breaking the copyright encryption is fair game since they "own" the media, or bought it legally, or got it from a friend. The reality is different. One reason copyright law exists is to limit free-riding. When copyrights are fully specified and enforced across international boundaries, content creators receive compensation for their efforts. But if copyrights are routinely violated, revenues to private businesses will decline and the amount of music and movies produced will decrease. In the long run, artists will produce less and society will suffer. (For other benefits of copyright law, see Chapter 10.)

This Boy Scout merit badge signifies a commitment to honoring copyright.

Think about the relationship between artists and the public as reciprocal: each side needs the other. In that sense, the music you buy or the movie you watch is not a true public good, but more of a club good. Copyright laws make the good excludable but nonrival. This means that some people will always have an incentive to violate copyright law, that artists and studios will insist on ever more complicated encryption methods to protect their interests, and that, for the betterment of society as a whole, the government will have to enforce copyright law to prevent widespread free-riding. ✳

Incentives

Common Resources and the Tragedy of the Commons

Tragedy of the commons occurs when a good that is rival in consumption but nonexcludable becomes depleted.

Incentives

Common resources often give rise to the **tragedy of the commons**, a situation that occurs when a good that is rival in consumption but nonexcludable becomes depleted. The term "tragedy of the commons" refers to a phenomenon that the ecologist Garrett Hardin wrote about in the magazine *Science* in 1968. Hardin described the hypothetical use of a common pasture shared by local herders in pastoral communities. Herders know that intensively grazed land will be depleted and that this is very likely to happen to common land. Knowing that the pasture will be depleted creates a strong incentive for individual herders to bring their animals to the pasture as much as possible while it is still green, since every other herder will be doing the same thing. Each herder has the same incentive to overgraze, which quickly makes the pasture unusable. The overgrazing is a negative externality brought about by poorly designed incentives and the absence of clearly defined private property rights.

Even though the concept of common ownership sounds ideal, it can be a recipe for resource depletion and economic disaster. Common ownership, unlike public ownership (like national parks) and private ownership, leads to overuse. With a system of private property rights, an owner can seek damages in the court system if his property is damaged or destroyed. But the same cannot be said for common property, since joint ownership allows any party to use the resource as he or she sees fit. This creates incentives to use the resource now rather than later and to neglect it. In short, common property leads to abuse and depletion of the resource.

As already mentioned, the tragedy of the commons also gives rise to negative externalities. Consider global warming. Evidence points to a connection between the amount of CO_2 being emitted into the atmosphere and the Earth's recent warming. This is a negative externality caused by some but borne jointly by everyone. Since large CO_2 emitters consider only the internal costs of their actions and ignore the social costs, the amount of CO_2 released, and the corresponding increase in global warming, is larger than optimal. The air, a common resource, is being "overused" and degraded.

Private property rights give owners an incentive to maintain, protect, and conserve their property and to transfer it if someone else values it more than the current owner does. How are those incentives different under a system of common ownership? Let's examine a real-world example of the tragedy of the commons: the collapse of cod populations off Newfoundland, Canada, in the 1990s. Over the course of three years, cod hauls fell from over 200,000 tons annually to close to zero. Why did the fishing community allow this to happen? The answer: incentives. Let's consider the incentives associated with common property in the context of the cod industry.

Incentives

1. *The incentive to neglect.* No one owns the ocean. As a result, fishing grounds in international waters cannot be protected. Even fishing grounds within territorial waters are problematic since fish do not adhere to political borders. Moreover, the fishing grounds in the North Atlantic cannot be maintained in the same way that one can, say, check the oil in an automobile. The grounds are too large, and population of cod depends on variations in seawater temperature, salinity, and availability of algae and other smaller fish to eat. The idea that individuals or communities could "maintain" a population of cod in this wild environment is highly impractical.

2. *The incentive to overuse.* Each fishing-boat crew would like to maintain a sustainable population of cod to ensure future harvests. However, conservation on the part of one boat is irrelevant since other boats would catch whatever it leaves behind. Since cod are a rival and finite resource, boats have an incentive to harvest as much as they can before another vessel does. With common resources, no one has the authority to define how much of a resource can be used. Maintaining economic activity at a socially optimal level would require the coordination of thousands of vested interests, each of whom could gain by free-riding. For instance, if a socially responsible boat crew (or country) limits its catch in order to protect the species from depletion, this action does not guarantee that rivals will follow suit. Instead, rivals who disregard the socially optimal behavior stand to benefit by overfishing what remains.

Common resources, such as cod, encourage overuse (in this case, overfishing).

Since cod are a common resource, the incentives we discussed under a system of private ownership do not apply. With common property, resources are neglected and overused.

Solutions to the Tragedy of the Commons

Preventing the tragedy of the commons requires planning and coordination. Unfortunately, in our cod example, officials were slow to recognize that there was a problem with Atlantic cod until it was too late to prevent the collapse. Ironically, just as they placed a moratorium on catching northern cod, the collapse of the fish population became an unprecedented disaster for all of Atlantic Canada's fisheries. Cod populations dropped to 1 percent of their former sizes. The collapse of this and many other species led to the loss of 40,000 jobs and over $300 million in income annually. Because the communities in the affected region relied almost exclusively on fishing, this outcome crippled their economies.

The lesson of the northern cod is a powerful reminder that efforts to avoid the tragedy of the commons must begin before a problem develops. For example, king crab populations off the coast of Alaska have fared much better than cod thanks to proactive management. To prevent the collapse of the king crab population, the state and federal governments enforce several regulations. First, the length of the fishing season is limited so that populations have time to recover. Second, there are regulations that limit how much fishing boats can catch. Third, to promote sustainable populations, only adult males are harvested. It is illegal to harvest females and young crabs, since these are necessary for repopulation. It is important to note that without government enforcement of these regulations, the tragedy of the commons would result.

Trade-offs

Cap and trade
is an approach used to curb pollution by creating a system of pollution permits that are traded in an open market.

Can the misuse of a common resource be foreseen and prevented? If predictions of rapid global warming are correct, our analysis points to a number of solutions to minimize the tragedy of commons. Businesses and individuals can be discouraged from producing emissions through carbon taxes. This policy encourages parties to internalize the negative externality, since the tax acts as an internal cost that must be considered before creating carbon pollution.

What is the best way to curb global warming?

Another solution, known as *cap and trade*, is an approach to emissions reduction that has received much attention lately. The theory behind **cap and trade** policy is to create the conditions for carbon producers to internalize the externality by establishing markets for tradable emission permits. Under cap and trade, the government sets a *cap*, or limit, on the amount of CO_2 that can be emitted. Businesses and individuals are then issued permits to emit a certain amount of carbon each year. Also, permit owners may *trade* permits. In other words, companies that produce fewer carbon emissions can sell the permits they do not use. By establishing property rights that control emissions permits, cap and trade causes firms to internalize externalities and to seek out methods that lower emissions.

Global warming is an incredibly complex process, but this is one tangible step that minimizes free-riding, creates the incentives for action, and promotes a socially efficient outcome.

Cap and trade is a good idea in theory. However, there are negative consequences as well. For example, cap and trade presumes that nations can agree on and enforce emissions limits, but such agreements have proven difficult to negotiate. Without an international consensus, nations that adopt cap and trade policies will experience higher production costs, while nations that ignore them—and free-ride in the process—will benefit. Also, since cap and trade ultimately aims to encourage firms to switch sources of energy, the buying and selling of carbon permits can be seen to act as a kind of tax on businesses that produce carbon emissions. As an indicator of what cap and trade is likely to cost U.S. consumers, consider what other countries are already experiencing. Britain's Treasury, for example, estimates that the average family will pay roughly £25 a year in higher electric bills for carbon-cutting programs. As this example shows, with any policy there are always trade-offs to consider.

Trade-offs

ECONOMICS IN THE REAL WORLD

Deforestation in Haiti

Nothing symbolizes the vicious cycle of poverty in Haiti more than the process of deforestation. Haiti was once a lush tropical island covered with pines and broad-leaf trees. Today, only about 3% of the country has tree cover. A number of factors have contributed to this environmental catastrophe: shortsighted logging and agricultural practices, demand for charcoal, rapid population growth, and increased competition for land. Widespread deforestation caused soil erosion, which in turn caused the fertile topsoil layer to wash away. As a result, land that was once lush and productive became desert-like. Eventually, nearly all remaining trees were cut down. Not enough food could be produced on this impoverished land, which contributed to widespread poverty.

Haiti is an extreme example of the tragedy of the commons. Its tragedy is especially striking because Haiti shares the island of Hispaniola with the Dominican Republic. The starkest difference between the two countries is the contrast between the lush tropical landscape of the Dominican Republic and the eroded, deforested Haitian land. In Haiti, the land was a semi-public resource that was overused and abused and therefore subject to the tragedy of the commons. In the Dominican Republic, property rights preserved the environment. What does this mean for Haiti? The nation would not be as poor today if it had relied more on private property rights. ✳

Haiti, seen on the left in this aerial photo, is deforested. The Dominican Republic, seen on the right, has maintained its environment.

PRACTICE WHAT YOU KNOW

Common Resources: President Obama's Inauguration

Approximately two million people filled the National Mall for President Obama's 2009 inauguration. After the celebration concluded, the Mall was strewn with litter and trash.

Inaugural trash

Question: What economic concept explains why the National Mall was trashed after the inauguration?

Answer: Attendees brought snacks to eat and newspapers to read during the long wait. They also bought commemorative programs. So a lot of trash was generated. Would you throw trash on your own lawn? Of course not. But otherwise conscientious individuals often don't demonstrate the same concern for public property. As a public space, the National Mall is subject to the *tragedy of the commons*. The grass is often trampled, and trash is very common on normal days. No one person can effectively keep the park green and clean so overuse and littering occurs. When two million people filled the space for Obama's inauguration, the result became much more apparent.

Tragedy of the Commons

South Park and Water Parks

If you have ever been to a water park or community pool, you know that the staff checks the pH of the water regularly to make sure it is clean. However, in a 2009 episode of *South Park* everyone is peeing in Pi Pi's water park. The resulting pee concentration ends up being so high that it triggers a disaster-movie-style cataclysm, unleashing a flood of pee that destroys the place.

Why did this happen? Because each person looked at all the water and thought it wouldn't matter if *he* or *she* peed in it. But when *everyone* thought the same way, the water quality was affected. This led to the tragedy of the commons, in which the overall water quality became degraded. Pee-ew.

Thankfully, the real world is cleaner than South Park!

Buying Used Is Good for Your Wallet and for the Environment

Many people waste their hard-earned money buying new. We could do our pocketbooks, and the environment, a favor by opting to buy used instead. Some customers are willing to pay a premium for that "new" feeling—but if you avoid that price markup, you'll save money *and* extend the usable life of a product. Here are a few ideas.

1. **Jewelry**. Would you buy something that immediately depreciates by 70%? When you buy at a retail store, you'll rarely get even a third of it back if you need to sell. If you are comfortable with the risk, search Craigslist or a local pawn shop instead—just be sure to get an appraisal before buying.

2. **Sports equipment**. Let the enthusiasts buy the latest equipment. When they tire of it and switch to the newest golf clubs or buy a new kayak, you can swoop in and make big savings.

3. **Video game consoles and games**. You can buy used and pay half price or less—the catch is you'll have to wait. But the good news is that you'll never find out that your expensive new system isn't as exciting as advertised. Waiting means better information *and* lower prices. That's how you find a good deal.

4. **Automobiles**. The average new car can lose as much as 20% of its value during the first year after purchase. For a $30,000 car, that means $6,000 in depreciation. Let someone else take that hit and buy a used vehicle instead.

5. **Tools and yard equipment**. Think twice before heading to the hardware store. Many tools like hammers and shovels are designed to last—they might not look shiny-new, but they work just as well.

Every time you buy used, you extend the usable life of a product, which helps maximize the value society gets from its resources. This also illustrates the benefit of private property: recall that owners have incentives to (1) maintain, (2) protect, and (3) conserve the products they own so that they can (4) maximize the value when they sell them.

Buying used can save you thousands.

Conclusion

Trade-offs

Although it's tempting to believe that the appropriate response to pollution is always to eliminate it, this is a misconception. As with all things, there are trade-offs. When pollution is taxed or regulated, business activity declines. It's possible to eliminate too much pollution, forcing businesses to shut down, creating undesirably high prices for anything from groceries to gasoline to electronics, and all in all creating an enormous deadweight loss to society. A truly "green" environment without any pollution would leave most people without enough "green" in their wallets. Therefore, the goal for pollution isn't zero—it's an amount that we need to determine through cost-benefit analysis and then attain by correcting market externalities.

In this chapter, we have considered two types of market failure: externalities and public goods. When externalities and public goods exist, the market does not provide the socially optimal amount of the good or service. One solution is to encourage businesses to internalize externalities. This can occur through taxes and regulations that force producers to account for the negative externalities that they create. Similarly, subsidies can spur the production of activities that generate positive externalities. However, not all externalities require active management from the government. Many are too small to matter and do not justify the costs associated with government regulation or taxation.

Likewise, public goods present a challenge for the market. Free-riding leads to the underproduction of goods that are nonrival and nonexcludable. Since not enough is produced privately, one solution is to eliminate free-riding by making involvement compulsory through taxation or regulation. A second problem occurs whenever goods are nonexcludable, as is the case with common-resource goods. This condition gives rise to the tragedy of the commons and can lead to the overuse of valuable resources.

ANSWERING THE BIG QUESTIONS

What are externalities, and how do they affect markets?

* Social costs include the internal costs and the external costs of an activity.
* An externality exists whenever an internal cost (or benefit) diverges from a social cost (or benefit). Third parties experience negative or positive externalities from a market activity.
* When a negative externality exists, government can restore the social optimum by discouraging economic activity that harms third parties. When a positive externality exists, government can restore the social optimum by encouraging economic activity that benefits third parties.
* An externality is internalized when decision-makers must pay for the externality created by their participation in the market.

What are private goods and public goods?

* Private goods, or property, ensures that owners have an incentive to maintain, protect, and conserve their property, and also to trade it to others.
* A public good has two characteristics: it is nonexcludable and nonrival in consumption. This gives rise to the free-rider problem and results in the underproduction of the good in the market.

What are the challenges of providing nonexcludable goods?

* Economists use cost-benefit analysis to determine whether the benefits of providing a type of good outweigh the costs, but benefits can be hard to determine.
* Under a system of common property, the incentive structure causes neglect and overuse.

CONCEPTS YOU SHOULD KNOW

cap and trade (p. 230)
club goods (p. 225)
Coase theorem (p. 221)
common-resource goods (p. 225)
cost-benefit analysis (p. 227)
excludable goods (p. 222)
external costs (p. 212)

externalities (p. 212)
free-rider problem (p. 224)
internal costs (p. 212)
internalize (p. 215)
private goods (p. 222)
private property (p. 220)
property rights (p. 219)

public goods (p. 222)
rival goods (p. 222)
social costs (p. 212)
social optimum (p. 214)
third-party problem (p. 212)
tragedy of the commons
   (p. 228)

QUESTIONS FOR REVIEW

1. Does the market overproduce or underproduce when third parties enjoy positive externalities? Show your answer on a supply and demand graph.

2. Is it possible to use bargaining to solve externality problems involving many parties? Explain your reasoning.

3. Describe all of the ways that externalities can be internalized.

4. Does cost-benefit analysis apply to public goods only? If yes, why? If not, name situa-

tions in which economists would use cost-benefit analysis.

5. What is the tragedy of the commons? Give an example that is not in the textbook.

6. What are the four incentives of private property? How do they differ from the incentives found in common property?

7. Give an example of a good that is nonrival in consumption and nonexcludable. What do economists call goods that share these characteristics?

STUDY PROBLEMS (*solved at the end of the section*)

1. Many cities have noise ordinances that impose especially harsh fines and penalties for early-morning and late-evening disturbances. Explain why this is the case.

2. Indicate whether the following activities create a positive or negative externality:

   a. Late-night road construction begins on a new bridge. As a consequence, traffic is rerouted past your house while the construction takes place.
   b. An excavating company pollutes a local stream with acid rock.
   c. A homeowner whose property backs up on a city park enjoys the sound of kids playing soccer.
   d. A student uses her cell phone discreetly during class.
   e. You and your friends volunteer to plant wildflowers along the local highway.

3. Indicate whether the following are private goods, club goods, common-resource goods, or public goods:

   a. a bacon double cheeseburger
   b. an NHL hockey game between the Detroit Red Wings and Boston Bruins
   c. a Fourth of July fireworks show
   d. a swimming pool
   e. a vaccination for the flu
   f. street lights

4. Can you think of a reason why making cars safer would create negative externalities? Explain.

5. Which of the following activities give rise to the free-rider problem?

   a. recycling programs
   b. biking
   c. studying for an exam
   d. riding a bus

✳ **6.** The students at a crowded university have trouble waking up before 10 a.m., and most work jobs after 3 p.m. As a result, there is a great deal of demand for classes between 10 a.m. and 3 p.m., and classes before and after those hours are rarely full. To make matters worse, the university has a limited amount of classroom space and faculty. This means that not every student can take classes during the most desirable times. Building new classrooms and hiring more faculty are not options. The administration asks for your advice about the best way to solve the problem of demand during the peak class hours. What advice would you give?

7. Two roommates are opposites. One enjoys playing Modern Warfare with his friends all night. The other likes to get to bed early for a full eight hours of sleep. If Coase is right, the roommates have an incentive to solve the noise externality issue themselves. Name at least two solutions that will internalize, or eliminate, the externality.

✳ **8.** Two companies, Toxic Waste Management and Sludge Industries, both pollute a nearby lake. Each firm dumps 1,000 gallons of goo into the lake every day. As a consequence, the lake has lost its clarity and the fish are dying. Local residents want to see the lake restored. But Toxic Waste's production process depends heavily on being able to dump the goo into the lake. It would cost Toxic Waste $10 per gallon to clean up the goo it generates. Sludge can clean up its goo at a cost of $2 per gallon.

a. If the local government cuts the legal goo emissions in half for each firm, what are the costs to each firm to comply with the law? What is the total cost to both firms in meeting the goo-emissions standard?

b. Another way of cutting goo emissions in half is to assign each firm tradable pollution permits that allow 500 gallons of goo to be dumped into the lake every day. Under this approach, will each firm still dump 500 gallons of goo? Why or why not?

9. A study finds that leaf blowers make too much noise, so the government imposes a $10 tax on the sale of every unit to correct for the social cost of the noise pollution. The tax completely internalizes the externality. Before the corrective tax, Blown Away Manufacturing regularly sold blowers for $100. After the tax is in place, the consumer price for leaf blowers rises to $105.

a. Describe the impact of the tax on the number of leaf blowers sold.
b. What is the socially optimal price to the consumer?
c. What is the private market price?
d. What net price is Blown Away receiving after it pays the tax?

10. In most areas, developers are required to submit environmental impact studies before work can begin on new construction projects. Suppose that a commercial developer wants to build a new shopping center on an environmentally protected piece of property that is home to a rare three-eyed toad. The shopping complex, if approved by the local planning commission, will cover ten acres. The planning commission wants the construction to go forward since that means additional jobs for the local community, but it also wants to be environmentally responsible. One member of the commission suggests that the developer relocate the toads. She describes the relocation process as follows: "The developer builds the shopping mall and agrees to create ten acres of artificial toad habitat elsewhere." Will this proposed solution make the builder internalize the externality? Explain.

SOLVED PROBLEMS

6. A flat-fee congestion charge is a good start, since this would reduce the quantity demanded between 10 a.m. and 3 p.m., but such a fee is a blunt instrument. Making the congestion charge dynamic (or varying the price by the hour) will encourage students to move outside the window with the most popular class times in order to pay less. For instance, classes between 11 a.m. and 2 p.m. could have the highest fee. Classes between 10 and 11 a.m. and between 2 and 3 p.m. would be slightly discounted. Classes between 9 and 10 a.m. and between 3 and 4 p.m. would be cheaper still, and those earlier than 9 a.m. and after 4 p.m. would be the cheapest. By altering the price of different class times, the university would be able to offer classes at less popular times and fill them up regularly, thus efficiently using its existing resources.

8.a. If the local government cuts the legal goo emissions in half for each firm, Toxic Waste will cut its goo by 500 gallons at a cost of $10 per gallon, for a total cost of $5,000. Sludge Industries will cut its goo by 500 gallons; at $2 per gallon, the cost is $1,000. The total cost to both firms in meeting the goo-emissions standard is $5,000 + $1,000 = $6,000.

b. It costs Toxic Waste $10 per gallon to clean up its goo. It is therefore more efficient for Toxic to buy all 500 permits from Sludge—which enables Toxic to dump an additional 500 gallons in the lake and saves the company $5,000. At the same time, Sludge could not dump any goo in the lake. Since it costs Sludge $2 per gallon to clean up its goo, it will have to pay $1,000. Since Toxic is saving more than it costs Sludge to clean up the goo, the two sides have an incentive to trade the permits.

The Theory of
THE FIRM

Larger firms have lower costs than their smaller competitors do.
Walmart, the nation's largest retailer, leverages its size to get price breaks on bulk purchases from its suppliers. People commonly believe that this kind of leverage enables larger firms to operate at lower costs than smaller firms do. This is often true; large firms also have broader distribution networks, and they benefit from more specialization and automation compared to their smaller competitors. However, not all industries enjoy lower costs with additional sales the way retailers do. And even Walmart, known for its very low prices, can be undercut by online outlets that have still lower costs and, therefore, better prices. This means that larger firms do not always have the lowest cost.

More generally, in any industry where transportation and advertising costs are high, smaller localized firms are not always at a disadvantage in terms of pricing. In fact, they often have the edge. For instance, in most college towns you will find many pizza shops—the national brands (Pizza Hut, Papa John's, Domino's) and the local shops. Often, the local shop is the one with the cheapest pizza special, while the name brands charge more. By the end of this chapter, you will be able to appreciate the importance of cost and understand why smaller and more nimble firms are sometimes able to undercut the prices of larger companies.

We begin the chapter with a rigorous examination of costs and how they relate to production. After we understand the basics, we will consider how firms can keep their costs low in the long run by choosing a scale of operation that best suits their needs.

A Walmart distribution center speeds goods to its stores.

BIG QUESTIONS

* How are profits and losses calculated?
* How much should a firm produce?
* What costs do firms consider in the short run and the long run?

Profits and losses
are determined by calculating the difference between expenses and revenues.

Total revenue
is the amount a firm receives from the sale of the goods and services it produces.

Total cost
is the amount a firm spends in order to produce the goods and services it produces.

How Are Profits and Losses Calculated?

To determine the potential profits of a business, the first step is to look at how much it will cost to run it. Consider a McDonald's restaurant. While you are probably familiar with the products McDonald's sells, you may not know how an individual franchise operates. For one thing, the manager at a McDonald's must decide how many workers to hire and how many to assign to each shift. Other managerial decisions involve the equipment needed and what supplies to have on hand each day—everything from hamburger patties to paper napkins. In fact, behind each purchase a consumer makes at McDonald's there is a complicated symphony of delivery trucks, workers, and managers.

For a company to be profitable, it is not enough to provide products that consumers want. It must simultaneously manage its costs. In this section, we will discuss how profits and costs are calculated.

The first McDonald's—much like the one pictured here—opened in San Bernardino, California, in 1940.

Calculating Profit and Loss

The simplest way to determine **profit** or **loss** is to calculate the difference between expenses and revenues. Losses occur whenever total revenue is less than total cost. The **total revenue** of a business is the amount the firm receives from the sale of the goods and services it produces. In the case of McDonald's, the total revenue is determined on the basis of the number of items sold and their prices. **Total cost** is the amount that a firm spends in order to produce the goods and services it sells. This is determined by adding the individual costs of the resources used in producing the goods for sale. We can express this relationship as an equation:

(Equation 8.1)

$$\text{Profit (or loss)} = \text{total revenue} - \text{total cost}$$

To calculate total revenue, we look at the dollar amount that the business earns over a specific period. For instance, suppose that in a given day McDonald's sells 1,000 hamburgers for $1.00 each, 500 orders of large fries for $2.00 each, and 100 shakes for $2.50 each. The total revenue is the sum of all of these values, or $2,250. The profit is therefore $2,250 (total revenue) minus the total cost.

Calculating costs, however, is a little more complicated than calculating revenue; we don't simply tally the cost of making each hamburger, order of large fries, and shake. Total cost has two parts—one that is visible and one that is largely invisible. In the next section, we will see that determining total costs is part art and part science.

Explicit Costs and Implicit Costs

Economists break costs into two components: *explicit costs* and *implicit costs*. **Explicit costs** are tangible out-of-pocket expenses. To calculate explicit costs, we add every expense incurred to run the business. For example, in the case of a McDonald's franchise, the weekly supply of hamburger patties is one explicit cost; the owner receives a bill from the meat supplier and has to pay it. **Implicit costs** are the opportunity costs of doing business.

Let's consider an example. Purchasing a McDonald's franchise costs about one million dollars; this is an explicit cost. However, there is also a high opportunity cost—the next-best possibility for investing a million dollars. That money could have earned interest in a bank, been used to open a different business, or been invested in the stock market. Each alternative is an implicit cost.

Implicit costs are hard to calculate and easy to miss. For example, it is difficult to determine how much an investor could have earned from an alternative activity. Is the opportunity cost the 3% interest he might have earned by placing the money in a bank, the 10% he might have hoped to earn in the stock market, or the 15% he might have gained by investing in a different business? We can be sure that there is an opportunity cost for owner-provided capital, but we can never know exactly how much that might be.

In addition to the opportunity cost of capital, implicit costs include the opportunity cost of the owner's labor. Often, business owners do not pay themselves a direct salary. However, since they could have been working somewhere else, it is reasonable to consider the fair value of the owner's time—income

Explicit costs
are tangible out-of-pocket expenses.

Implicit costs
are the opportunity costs of doing business.

TABLE 8.1	
Examples of a Firm's Explicit and Implicit Costs	
Explicit costs	**Implicit costs**
The electricity bill	The labor of an owner who works for the company but does not draw a salary
Advertising in the local newspaper	The capital invested in the business
Employee wages	The use of the owner's car, computer, or other personal equipment to conduct company business

the owner could have earned by working elsewhere—as part of the business's costs.

To fully account for all the costs of doing business, you must calculate the explicit costs, determine the implicit costs, and add them together:

(Equation 8.2)

$$\text{Total cost} = \text{explicit costs} + \text{implicit costs}$$

A simple way of thinking about the distinction between explicit costs and implicit costs is to consider someone who wants to build a bookcase. Suppose that John purchases $30 in materials and takes half a day off from work, where he normally earns $12 an hour. After four hours, he completes the bookcase. His explicit costs are $30, but his total cost is much higher because he also gave up four hours of work at $12 an hour. His implicit cost is therefore $48. When we add the explicit cost ($30) and the implicit cost ($48), we get John's total cost ($78).

Table 8.1 shows examples of a firm's implicit and explicit costs.

Accounting Profit versus Economic Profit

Accounting profit
is calculated by subtracting the explicit costs from total revenue.

Now that you know about explicit and implicit costs, we can refine our definition of profit. In fact, there are two types of profit—*accounting profit* and *economic profit*.

A firm's **accounting profit** is calculated by subtracting only the explicit costs from total revenue. Accounting figures permeate company reports, quarterly and annual statements, and the media.

(Equation 8.3)

$$\textbf{Accounting profit} = \text{total revenues} - \text{explicit costs}$$

Economic profit
is calculated by subtracting both the explicit and the implicit costs of business from total revenue.

As you can see, accounting profit does not take into account the implicit costs of doing business. To calculate the full cost of doing business, we need to consider both implicit and explicit costs. This will yield a firm's *economic profit*. **Economic profit** is calculated by subtracting both the explicit and the

TABLE 8.2

Historical Rates of Return in Stocks, Bonds, and Savings Accounts

Financial instrument	Historical average rate of return since 1928 (adjusted for inflation)
Stocks	6%
Bonds	3%
Savings account at a financial institution	2%

Source: Federal Reserve database in St. Louis (FRED) and author's adjustments. Data from 1928–2011.

implicit costs of business from total revenue. Economic profit gives a more complete assessment of how a firm is doing.

$$\textbf{Economic profit} = \text{total revenues} - (\text{explicit costs} + \text{implicit costs})$$ (Equation 8.4)

Simplifying the equation above gives us:

$$\textbf{Economic profit} = \text{accounting profit} - \text{implicit costs}$$ (Equation 8.5)

Therefore, economic profit is always less than accounting profit.

The difference in accounting profits among various types of firms can be misleading. For instance, if a company with $1 billion in assets reports an annual profit of $10 million, we might think it is doing well. After all, wouldn't you be happy to make $10 million in a year? However, that $10 million is only 1% of the $1 billion the company holds in assets. As you can see in Table 8.2, a 1% return is far less than the typical return available in a number of other places, including the stock market, bonds, or a savings account at a financial institution.

If the return on $1 billion in assets is low compared to what an investor can expect to make elsewhere, the firm with the $10 million accounting profit actually has a negative economic profit. For instance, if the firm had invested the $1 billion in a savings account, according to Table 8.2 it would have earned 2% on $1 billion—that is, $20 million. That would have yielded an economic profit of:

$$
\begin{aligned}
\textbf{Economic profit} &= \text{accounting profit} - \text{implicit costs} \\
&= \$10 \text{ million} - \$20 \text{ million} \\
&= -\$10 \text{ million}
\end{aligned}
$$

As you can see, economic profit is never misleading. If a business has an economic profit, its revenues are larger than the combination of its explicit and implicit costs. The difficulty in determining economic profit lies in calculating the tangible value of implicit costs.

PRACTICE WHAT YOU KNOW

Accounting Profit versus Economic Profit: Calculating Summer Job Profits

Kyle is a college student who works during the summers to pay for tuition. Last summer he worked at a fast-food restaurant and earned $2,500. This summer he is working as a painter and will earn $4,000. To do the painting job, Kyle had to spend $200 on supplies.

How much economic profit do you make from painting?

Question: What is Kyle's accounting profit?

Answer: Accounting profit = total revenues − explicit cost
$$= \$4{,}000 - \$200 = \$3{,}800$$

Question: If working at the fast-food restaurant was Kyle's next-best alternative, how much economic profit will Kyle earn from painting?

Answer: To calculate economic profit, we need to subtract the explicit and implicit costs from the total revenue. Kyle's total revenue from painting will be $4,000. His explicit costs are $200 for supplies, and his implicit cost is $2,500—the salary he would have earned in the fast-food restaurant. So:

$$\text{Economic profit} = \text{total revenues} - (\text{explicit cost} + \text{implicit cost})$$
$$= \$4{,}000 - (\$200 + \$2{,}500) = \$1{,}300$$

Kyle's economic profit will be $1,300.

Question: Suppose that Kyle can get an internship at an investment banking firm. The internship provides a stipend of $3,000 and tangible work experience that will help him get a job after graduation. Should Kyle take the painting job or the internship?

Answer: The implicit costs have changed because Kyle now has to consider the $3,000 stipend and the increased chance of securing a job after graduation versus what he can make painting houses. Calculation of economic profit from painting is now:

$$\text{Economic profit} = \$4{,}000 - (\$200 + \$3{,}000) = \$800$$

But this number is incomplete. There is also the value of the internship experience, so at this point his economic profit from painting would be only $800. If Kyle wants to work in investment banking after graduation, then this is a no-brainer. He should take the internship—that is, unless some investment banks value painting houses more than work experience!

How Much Should a Firm Produce?

Every business must decide how much to produce. In this section, we describe the factors that determine output, and we explain how firms use inputs to maximize their production. Since it is possible for a firm to produce too little or too much, we must also consider when a firm should stop production.

The Production Function

For a firm to earn an economic profit, it must produce a product, known as its **output**, that consumers want. It must also control its costs. To accomplish this, the firm must use resources efficiently. There are three primary components of output, known as the **factors of production**: labor, land, and capital. Each factor of production is an input, or a resource used in the production process, to generate the firm's output. Labor consists of the workers, land consists of the geographic location used in production, and capital consists of all the resources that the workers use to create the final product. Consider McDonald's as an example. The labor input includes managers, cashiers, cooks, and janitorial staff. The land input includes the land on which the McDonald's building sits. And the capital input includes the building itself, the equipment used, the parking lot, the signs, and all the hamburger patties, buns, fries, ketchup, and other foodstuffs.

Output
is the production the firm creates.

Factors of production
are the inputs (labor, land, and capital) used in producing goods and services.

To keep costs down in the production process, a firm needs to find the right mix of these inputs. The **production function** describes the relationship between the inputs a firm uses and the output it creates. As we saw at the beginning of the chapter, the manager of a McDonald's must make many decisions about inputs. If she hires too little labor, some of the land and capital will be underutilized. Likewise, with too many workers and not enough land or capital, some workers will not have enough to do to stay busy. For example, suppose that only a single worker shows up at McDonald's one day. This employee will have to do all the cooking; bag up the meals; handle the register, the drive-thru, and the drinks; and clean the tables. This single worker, no matter how productive, will not be able to keep up with demand. Hungry customers will grow tired of waiting and take their business elsewhere—maybe for good!

The **production function**
describes the relationship between inputs a firm uses and the output it creates.

When a second worker shows up, the two employees can begin to specialize at what they do well. Recall that specialization and comparative advantage lead to higher levels of output (see Chapter 2). Therefore, individual workers will be assigned to tasks that match their skills. For example, one worker can take the orders, fill the bags, and get the drinks. The other can work the grill area and drive-thru. When a third worker comes on, the specialization process can extend

McDonald's needs the correct amount of labor to maximize its output.

even further. This specialization and division of labor is key to the way McDonald's operates. Production per worker expands as long as additional workers become more specialized and there are enough capital resources to keep each worker occupied.

When only a few workers share capital resources, the resources that each worker needs are readily available. But what happens when the restaurant is very busy? The manager can hire more staff for the busiest shifts, but the amount of space for cooking and the number of cash registers, drink dispensers, and tables in the seating area are fixed. Because the added employees have less capital to work with, beyond a certain point the additional labor will not continue to increase the restaurant's productivity at the same rate as it did at first. You might recognize this situation if you have ever gone into a fast-food restaurant at lunchtime. Even though the space behind the counter bustles with busy employees, they can't keep up with the orders. Only so many meals can be produced in a short time and in a fixed space; some customers have to wait.

The restaurant must also maintain an adequate supply of materials. If a shipment is late and the restaurant runs out of hamburger patties, the shortage will impact sales. The manager must therefore be able to (1) decide how many workers to hire for each shift, and (2) manage the inventory of supplies to avoid shortages.

Marginal thinking

Marginal product is the change in output associated with one additional unit of an input.

Let's look more closely at the manager's decision about how many workers to hire. On the left side of Figure 8.1, we see what happens when workers are added, one by one. When the manager adds one worker, output goes from 0 meals to 5 meals. Going from one worker to two workers increases total output to 15 meals. This means that a second worker has increased the number of meals produced from 5 to 15, or an increase of 10 meals. This increase in output is the **marginal product**, which is the change in output associated with one additional unit of an input. In this case, the change in output (10 additional meals) divided by the increase in input (1 worker) gives us a marginal product of $10 \div 1$, or 10. Since the table in Figure 8.1 adds one worker at a time, the marginal product is just the increase in output shown in the third column.

Looking down the three columns, we see that after the first three workers the rate of increase in the marginal product slows down. But the total output continues to expand, and it keeps growing through 8 workers. This occurs because the gains from specialization are slowly declining. By the ninth worker (going from 8 to 9), we see a negative marginal product. Once the cash registers, drive-thru, grill area, and other service stations are fully staffed, there is not much for an extra worker to do. Eventually, extra workers will get in the way or distract other workers from completing their tasks.

The graphs on the right side of Figure 8.1 show (a) total output and (b) marginal product of labor. The graph of total output in (a) uses data from the second column of the table. As the number of workers goes from 0 to 3 on the *x* axis, total output rises at an increasing rate from 0 to 30. The slope of the total output curve rises until it reaches 3 workers at the first dashed line. Between 3 workers and the second dashed line at 8 workers, the total output curve continues to rise, though at a slower rate; the slope of the curve is still positive but becomes progressively flatter. Finally, once we reach the ninth worker, total output begins to fall and the slope becomes negative. At this point, it is not productive to have so many workers.

FIGURE 8.1

The Production Function and Marginal Product

(a) Total output rises rapidly in the green-shaded zone from 0 to 3 workers, rises less rapidly in the yellow zone between 3 and 8 workers, and falls in the red zone after 8 workers. (b) The marginal product of labor rises in the green zone from 0 to 3 workers, falls in the yellow zone from 3 to 8 workers but remains positive, and becomes negative after 8 workers. Notice that the marginal product becomes negative after total output reaches its maximum at 8 workers. As long as marginal product is positive, total output rises. Once marginal product becomes negative, total output falls.

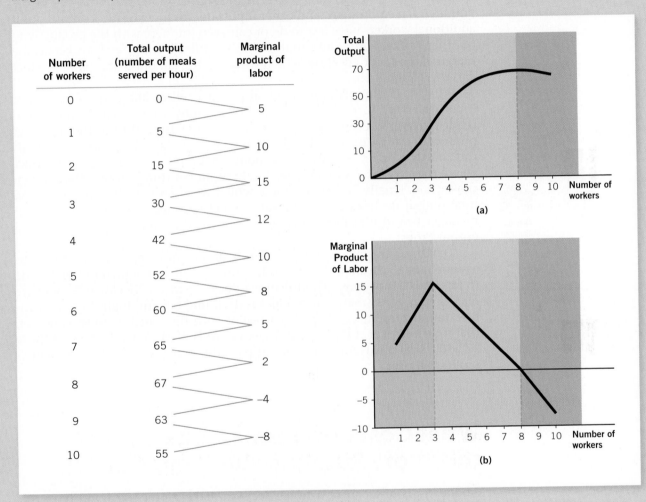

Diminishing Marginal Product

The marginal product curve in Figure 8.1b explains the shape of the total output curve above it. Consider that the marginal productivity of each worker either adds to or subtracts from the overall output of the firm. Marginal product increases from 5 meals served per hour with the first worker to 15 meals per hour with the third worker. From the first worker to the third, each additional worker leads to increased specialization and teamwork. This explains the rapid rise—from 0 to 30 meals—in the total output curve. By the fourth worker, marginal product begins to decline. Looking back to the table, you can see that the fourth worker produces 12 extra meals—3 fewer than the third worker. The point at which successive increases in inputs are associated with a slower rise in output is known as the point of **diminishing marginal product**.

Diminishing marginal product occurs when successive increases in inputs are associated with a slower rise in output.

Why does the rate of output slow? Recall that in our example the size of the McDonald's restaurant is fixed in the short run. Because the size of the building, the equipment, and other inputs do not increase, at a certain point additional workers have less to do or can even interfere with the productivity of other workers. After all inputs are fully utilized, additional workers cause marginal product to decline, which we see in the fall of the marginal product curve in Figure 8.1b.

What does diminishing marginal product tell us about the firm's labor input decision? Turning again to the two graphs, we see that in the green-shaded area as the number of workers increases from 0 to 3, the marginal product and total output also rise. But when we enter the yellow zone with the fourth worker, we reach the point of diminishing marginal product where the curve starts to decline. Total output continues to rise, though at a slower rate. Finally, in the red zone, which we enter with the ninth worker, total output declines and marginal product becomes negative. No rational manager would hire more than 8 workers in this scenario, since the total output drops.

Marginal thinking

A common mistake when considering diminishing marginal product is to assume that a firm should stop production as soon as marginal product starts to fall. This is not true. "Diminishing" does not mean "negative." There are many times when marginal product is declining but still high. In our example, diminishing marginal product begins with the fourth worker. However, that fourth worker still produces 12 extra meals. If McDonald's can sell those 12 additional meals for more than it pays the fourth worker, the company's profits will rise.

What Costs Do Firms Consider in the Short Run and the Long Run?

Production is one part of a firm's decision-making process. If you have run even a simple business—for example, cutting lawns—you know that it requires decision-making. How many lawns do you want to be responsible for? Should you work on different lawns at the same time or specialize by task, with one person doing all the mowing and another taking care of the trimming? These are the kinds of production-related questions every firm must address. The other major component of production is cost. Should you invest in a big industrial-size mower? How much gasoline will you need to run your mowers? What does it cost to hire someone to help get the work done? These are some of the types of cost-related concerns that firms face. Each one may seem like a small decision, but the discovery process that leads to the answers is crucial.

PRACTICE WHAT YOU KNOW

Diminishing Returns: Snow Cone Production

It's a hot day, and customers are lined up for snow cones at your small stand. The following table shows your firm's short-run production function for snow cones.

Number of workers	Total output of snow cones per hour
0	0
1	20
2	50
3	75
4	90
5	100
6	105
7	100
8	90

How many workers are too many?

Question: When does diminishing marginal product begin?

Answer: You have to be careful when calculating this answer. Total output is maximized when you have six workers, but diminishing marginal return begins before you hire that many workers. Look at the following table, which includes a third column showing marginal product.

Number of workers	Total output of snow cones per hour	Marginal product
0	0	0
1	20	20
2	50	30
3	75	25
4	90	15
5	100	10
6	105	5
7	100	−5
8	90	−10

The marginal product is highest when you hire the second worker. After that, each subsequent worker you hire has a lower marginal product. Therefore, the answer to the question is that diminishing marginal product begins after the second worker.

Every firm, whether just starting out or already well established and profitable, can benefit by assessing how much to produce and how to produce it more efficiently. In addition, production and cost consideration are different in the short run and in the long run. We begin with the short run because the majority of firms are most concerned with making the best short-run decisions, and then we extend our analysis to the long run, where planning ahead plays a central role.

Costs in the Short Run

All firms experience some costs that are unavoidable in the short run. These unavoidable costs—for example, a lease on space or a contract with a supplier—are a large part of short-run costs. In the short run, costs can be *variable* or *fixed*.

Variable costs change with the rate of output. Let's see what this means for a McDonald's and further simplify our example by assuming that the McDonald's produces only Big Macs. In this case, the variable costs include the number of workers the firm hires; the electricity the firm uses; the all-beef patties, special sauce, lettuce, cheese, pickles, onions, and sesame-seed buns needed to create the Big Mac; and the packaging. These items are considered variable costs because the restaurant doesn't need them unless it has customers. The amount of these resources varies with the amount of output the restaurant produces.

Fixed costs are unavoidable; they do not vary with output in the short run. For instance, no matter how many hamburgers the McDonald's sells, the costs associated with the building remain the same and the business must pay for them. These fixed costs—also known as overhead—include rent, insurance, property taxes, and so on.

Interpreting Tabular Data

Every business must be able to determine how much it costs to provide the products and services it sells. Table 8.3 lists many different ways to measure the costs associated with business decisions.

Let's begin with total variable cost (TVC) in column 2 and total fixed cost (TFC) in column 3. Notice that when output—the quantity (Q) of Big Macs produced per hour—is 0, total variable cost starts at $0 and rises with production at an uneven rate depending on the productivity of labor and the cost of the ingredients that go into each Big Mac. We attribute this to the simple fact that additional workers and other inputs are needed to generate additional output. In contrast, total fixed cost starts at $100, even when output is 0, and remains constant as output rises. As noted above, fixed costs include overhead expenses such as rent, insurance, and property taxes. For simplicity, we assume that this amount is $100 a day. When we add fixed cost and variable cost together, we get total cost, listed in column 4: TC = TVC + TFC.

Column 5, *average variable cost*, and column 6, *average fixed cost*, enable us to determine the cost of producing a Big Mac by examining the average cost of production. **Average variable cost** (AVC) is the total variable cost

---

Variable costs change with the rate of output.

Fixed costs are unavoidable; they do not vary with output in the short run.

Average variable cost (AVC) is determined by dividing total variable costs by the output.

TABLE 8.3

Measuring Costs

(1) Quantity (Q = Big Macs produced/hour)	(2) Total Variable Cost	(3) Total Fixed Cost	(4) Total Cost	(5) Average Variable Cost	(6) Average Fixed Cost	(7) Average Total Cost	(8) Marginal Cost
Abbreviation:	TVC	TFC	TC	AVC	AFC	ATC	MC
Formula:			TVC + TFC	TVC ÷ Q	TFC ÷ Q	AVC + AFC	ΔTVC ÷ ΔQ
0	$0.00	$100.00	$100.00				
							$3.00
10	30.00	100.00	130.00	$3.00	$10.00	$13.00	
							2.00
20	50.00	100.00	150.00	2.50	5.00	7.50	
							1.50
30	65.00	100.00	165.00	2.17	3.33	5.50	
							1.20
40	77.00	100.00	177.00	1.93	2.50	4.43	
							1.00
50	87.00	100.00	187.00	1.74	2.00	3.74	
							1.30
60	100.00	100.00	200.00	1.67	1.67	3.34	
							2.00
70	120.00	100.00	220.00	1.71	1.43	3.14	
							4.00
80	160.00	100.00	260.00	2.00	1.25	3.25	
							6.00
90	220.00	100.00	320.00	2.44	1.11	3.55	
							8.00
100	300.00	100.00	400.00	3.00	1.00	4.00	

divided by the output produced: AVC = TVC ÷ Q. Notice that the average variable cost declines until 60 Big Macs are produced at an average cost of $1.67. This is the lowest average cost. Why should we care about AVC? Because it can be a useful signal. In this case, total variable costs in column 2 always rise, but the average variable cost falls until 60 Big Macs are produced. The decline in AVC is a powerful signal to the firm to increase its output up to a point.

Average fixed cost (AFC), listed in column 6, is calculated by dividing total fixed cost by the output: AFC = TFC ÷ Q. Since total fixed cost is constant, dividing these costs by the output means that as the output rises, the average fixed cost declines. In other words, higher output levels spread out the total fixed costs across more units. As Table 8.3 shows, average fixed costs are lowest at an output of 100 Big Macs, where:

Average fixed cost (AFC) is determined by dividing total fixed costs by the output.

$$AFC = TFC ÷ Q$$
$$AFC = \$100 ÷ 100$$
$$AFC = \$1$$

What does this example tell a business that wants to lower costs? Since overhead costs such as rent cannot be changed, the best way to lower fixed costs is to raise output.

Average total cost (ATC) is the sum of average variable cost and average fixed cost.

Average total cost (ATC), shown in column 7, is calculated by adding the AVC and AFC. Let's look at the numbers to get a better understanding of what average total cost tells us. Even though the average variable cost rises after 60 Big Macs are produced, from $1.67 to $1.71, the average fixed cost is still falling, from $1.67 to $1.43. The decline in average fixed cost is enough to pull the average total cost down to $3.14. Eventually, increases in variable cost overwhelm the cost savings achieved by spreading fixed cost across more production. We can see this if we compare the average total costs of making 70 Big Macs and 80 Big Macs.

For 70 Big Macs:

$$ATC = AVC + AFC$$
$$ATC = \$1.71 + \$1.43 = \$3.14$$

For 80 Big Macs:

$$ATC = AVC + AFC$$
$$ATC = \$2.00 + \$1.25 = \$3.25$$

At 80 Big Macs, the average variable cost rises from $1.71 to $2.00. And the average fixed cost falls from $1.43 to $1.25. Therefore, the rise in average variable cost—$0.29—is higher than the fall in average fixed cost—$0.18. This finding removes the benefit of higher output. Thus, the most efficient number of Big Macs to produce is between 70 and 80.

Interpreting Data Graphically

Now that we have walked through the numerical results in Table 8.3, it is time to visualize the cost relationships with graphs. Figure 8.2 shows a graph of total cost curves (a) and the relationship between the marginal cost curve and the average cost curves (b).

In panel (a) of Figure 8.2, we see that although the total cost curve continues to rise, the rate of increase in total cost is not constant. For the first 50 Big Macs, the total cost rises at a decreasing rate. This reflects the gains of specialization and comparative advantage that come from adding workers who concentrate on specific tasks. After 50 Big Macs, diminishing marginal product causes the total cost curve to rise at an increasing rate. Since a McDonald's restaurant has a fixed capacity, producing more than 50 Big Macs requires a significantly higher investment in labor, and those workers do not have any additional space to work in—a situation that makes the total cost curve rise more rapidly at high production levels. The total cost (TC) curve is equal to the sum of the fixed cost and variable cost curves, which are shown in panel (a). Total fixed costs (TFC) are constant, so it is the total variable costs (TVC) that give the TC curve its shape.

Marginal thinking

But that is not the most important part of the story. Any manager at McDonald's can examine total costs. Likewise, she can look at the average cost and compare that information to the average cost at other local businesses. But neither the total cost of labor nor the average cost will tell her anything about the cost of making additional units—that is, Big Macs.

A manager can make even better decisions by looking at *marginal cost*. The **marginal cost (MC)** is the increase in extra cost that occurs from producing

Marginal cost (MC) is the increase in cost that occurs from producing additional output.

FIGURE 8.2

The Cost Curves

(a) The total variable cost (TVC) dictates the shape of the total cost (TC) curve. After 50 Big Macs, diminishing marginal product causes the total cost curve to rise at an increasing rate. Notice that the total fixed cost curve (TFC) stays constant, or flat. (b) The marginal cost curve (MC) reaches its minimum before average variable cost (AVC) and average total cost (ATC). Marginals always lead the average either up or down. Average fixed cost (AFC), which has no variable component, continues to fall with increased quantity, since total fixed costs are spread across more units. The minimum point of the ATC curve is known as the efficient scale.

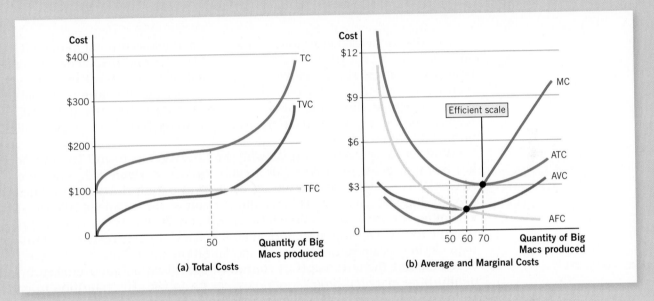

(a) Total Costs

(b) Average and Marginal Costs

additional output. (In column 8 of Table 8.3, this relationship is shown as the change, or Δ, in TVC divided by the change, or Δ, in quantity produced.) For example, in planning the weekly work schedule the manager has to consider how many workers to hire for each shift. She wants to hire additional workers when the cost of doing so is less than the expected boost in profits. In this situation, it is essential to know the marginal cost, or extra cost, of hiring one more worker.

In Table 8.3, marginal cost (MC) falls to a minimum of $1.00 when between 40 and 50 Big Macs are produced. Notice that the minimum MC occurs at a lower output level than average variable cost (AVC) and average total cost (ATC) in panel (b) of Figure 8.2. When output is less than 50 Big Macs, marginal cost is falling because over this range of production the marginal product of labor is increasing on account of better teamwork and more specialization. After the fiftieth Big Mac, MC rises. This acts as an early warning indicator that average and total costs will soon follow suit. Why would a manager care about the last few units being produced more than the average cost of producing all the units? Because marginal cost tells the manager if making one more unit of output will increase profits or not!

Marginal thinking

The MC curve reaches its lowest point before the lowest point of the AVC and ATC curves. For this reason, a manager who is concerned about rising costs would look to the MC curve as a signal that average costs will eventually increase as well. Once marginal cost begins to increase, it continues to pull down average variable cost until sales reach 60 Big Macs. After that point, MC is above AVC and AVC begins to rise as well. However, ATC continues to fall until 70 Big Macs are sold.

Why does average total cost fall while MC and AVC are rising? The answer lies in the average fixed cost (AFC) curve shown in Figure 8.2. Since the ATC = AVC + AFC, and AFC always declines as output rises, ATC declines until 70 Big Macs are sold. This is a direct result of the decline in AFC overwhelming the increase in AVC between 60 and 70 Big Macs. Notice also that the AVC curve stops declining at 60 Big Macs. Variable costs should initially decline as a result of increased specialization and teamwork. However, at some point the advantages of continued specialization are overtaken by diminishing marginal product, and costs begin to rise. The transition from falling costs to rising costs is of particular interest because as long as costs are declining, the firm can lower its costs by increasing its output. Economists refer to the quantity of output that minimizes the average total cost as the **efficient scale**.

The **efficient scale** is the output level that minimizes the average total cost.

Once the marginal costs in Table 8.3 rise above the average total costs, the average total costs begin to rise as well. This is evident if we compare the average total cost of making 70 Big Macs ($3.14) and 80 Big Macs ($3.25) with the marginal cost ($4.00) of making those extra 10 Big Macs. Since the marginal cost ($4.00) of making Big Macs 71 through 80 is higher than the average total cost at 70 ($3.14), the average total cost of making 80 Big Macs goes up (to $3.25).

Marginal costs always lead (or pull) average costs along, no matter what we are considering. The MC eventually rises above the average total cost because of diminishing marginal product. In this case, since the firm has to pay a fixed wage, the cost to produce each hamburger increases as each worker decreases in productivity.

There is, however, one "average" curve that the marginal cost does not affect: average fixed costs. Notice that the AFC curve in panel (b) of Figure 8.2 continues to fall even though marginal costs eventually rise. The AFC curve declines with increased output. Since McDonald's has $100.00 in fixed costs each day, we can determine the average fixed costs by dividing the total fixed cost ($100.00) by the number of Big Macs sold. When 10 Big Macs are sold, the average fixed cost is $10.00 per Big Mac, but this value falls to $1.00 per Big

Costs in the Short Run

ECONOMICS IN THE MEDIA

The Office

The popular TV series *The Office* had an amusing episode devoted to the discussion of costs. The character Michael Scott establishes his own paper company to compete with both Staples and his former company, Dunder Mifflin. He then outcompetes his rivals by keeping his fixed and variable costs low.

In one inspired scene, we see the Michael Scott Paper Company operating out of a single room and using an old church van to deliver paper. This means the company has very low *fixed costs*, which enables it to charge unusually low prices. In addition, Michael Scott keeps *variable costs* to a minimum by hiring only essential employees and not paying any benefits, such as health insurance. But this is a problem, since Michael Scott does not fully account for the cost of the paper he is selling. In fact, he is selling below unit cost!

As we will discover in upcoming chapters, firms with lower costs have many advantages in the market. Such firms can keep their prices lower to attract additional customers. Cost matters because price matters.

Michael Scott doesn't understand the difference between fixed and variable costs.

Mac if 100 burgers are sold. Since McDonald's is a high-volume business that relies on low costs to compete, being able to produce enough Big Macs to spread out the firm's fixed costs is essential.

Costs in the Long Run

We have seen that in the short run, businesses have fixed costs and fixed capacities. In the long run, all costs are variable and can be renegotiated. Thus, firms have more control over their costs in the long run, which enables them to reach their desired level of production. One way that firms can adjust in the long run is by changing the **scale**, or size, of the production process. If the business is expected to grow, the firm can ramp up production. If the business is faltering, it can scale back its operations. This flexibility enables firms to avoid a situation of diminishing marginal product.

A long-run time horizon allows a business to choose a scale of operation that best suits its needs. For instance, if a local McDonald's is extremely

Scale
refers to the size of the production process.

popular, in the short run the manager can only hire more workers or expand the restaurant's hours to accommodate more customers. However, in the long run all costs are variable; the manager can add drive-thru lanes, increase the number of registers, expand the grill area, and so on.

The absence of fixed factors in the long-run production process means that we cannot explain total costs in the long run in the same way that we explained short-run costs. Short-run costs are a reflection of diminishing marginal product, whereas long-run costs are a reflection of scale and the cost of providing additional output. One might assume that since diminishing marginal product is no longer relevant in the long run, costs would fall as output expands. However, this is not the case. Depending on the industry and the prevailing economic conditions, long-run costs can rise, fall, or stay approximately the same.

Three Types of Scale

In this section, we describe three different scenarios for a firm in the long run. A firm may experience *economies of scale*, *diseconomies of scale*, or *constant returns to scale*. In the long run, whether costs fall, remain constant, or rise with increasing output will depend on *scale*, or the amount of output a firm desires to produce. Let's consider each of these in turn.

Economies of scale
occur when costs decline as output expands in the long run.

If output expands and costs decline, businesses experience **economies of scale**. National homebuilders, like Toll Brothers, provide a good example of economies of scale. All builders, whether they are local or national, do the same thing—they build houses. Each builder needs lumber, concrete, excavators, electricians, plumbers, roofers, and many more specialized workers or subcontractors. A big company, such as Toll, is able to hire many specialists and also buy the equipment it needs in bulk. As a result, Toll can manufacture the same home as a local builder at a much lower cost than the local builder can.

Diseconomies of scale
occur when costs rise as output expands in the long run.

But bigger isn't always better! Sometimes a company grows so large that coordination problems make costs rise. For example, as the scale of an enterprise expands, it might require more managers, highly specialized workers, and a coordination process to pull everything together. As the layers of management expand, the coordination process can break down. For this reason, a larger firm can become less effective at holding down costs and experience **diseconomies of scale**, or higher average total costs as output expands.

The problem of diseconomies of scale is especially relevant in the service sector of the economy. For example, large regional hospitals have many layers of bureaucracy. These added management costs and infrastructure expenses can make medical care more expensive beyond a certain point. If you are not convinced, ask yourself why large cities have many smaller competing hospitals rather than one centralized hospital. The answer becomes obvious: bigger doesn't always mean less expensive (or better)!

Building more than one house at a time would represent an economy of scale.

Finally, if the advantages of specialization, mass production, and bulk purchasing are approximately equal, then the long-run costs will remain constant as the firm expands its output. When costs remain constant even as output expands, we say that the firm has **constant returns to scale**. For example, large national restaurant chains like Olive Garden, which specializes in Italian cuisine, compete with local Italian restaurants. In each case, the local costs to hire workers and build the restaurant are the same. Olive Garden does have a few advantages; for example, it can afford to advertise on national television and buy food in bulk. But Olive Garden also has more overhead costs for its many layers of management. Constant returns to scale in the bigger chain mean that a small local Italian restaurant will have approximately the same menu prices as its bigger rivals.

Would you rather see the ER's doctor du jour or your own physician?

Constant returns to scale occur when costs remain constant as output expands in the long run.

Long-Run Cost Curves

Now it is time to illustrate the long-run nature of cost curves. We have seen that increased output may not always lead to economies of scale. Costs can be constant or can even rise with output. Figure 8.3 illustrates each of the three possibilities graphically. The long-run average total cost curve (LRATC) is actually a composite of many short-run average total cost (SRATC) curves, which appear as the faint U-shaped dashed curves drawn in gray. By visualizing the short-run cost curves at any given output level, we can develop a composite of them to create the LRATC. From this, we see that the long-run average total cost curve comprises all the short-run cost curves that the firm may choose to deploy in the long run. In the long run, the firm is free to

Will you find lower prices at the Olive Garden or your local Italian restaurant?

FIGURE 8.3

Costs in the Long Run

In the long run, there are three distinct possibilities: the long-run average total cost curve (LRATC) can exhibit economies of scale (the green curve), constant returns to scale (the purple curve), or diseconomies of scale (the orange curve).

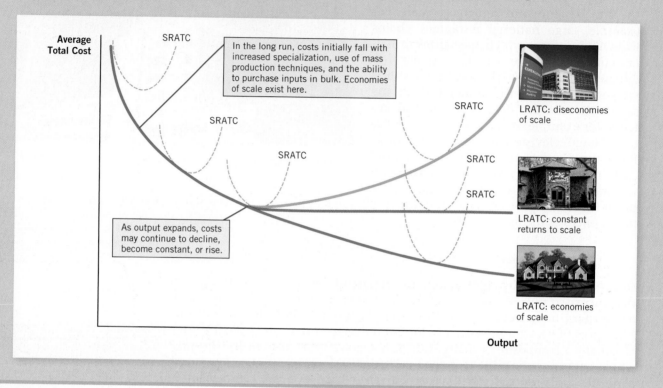

choose any of its short-run curves, so it always picks the output/cost combination that minimizes costs.

In the long run, there are three distinct possibilities: economies of scale, constant returns to scale, and diseconomies of scale. At first, each LRATC exhibits economies of scale as a result of increased specialization, the utilization of mass production techniques, bulk purchasing power, and increased automation. The main question in the long run is whether the cost curve will continue to decline, level off, or rise. In an industry with economies of scale at high output levels—for example, a homebuilder—the cost curve continues to decline, and the most efficient output level is always the largest output: the green curve in Figure 8.3. In this situation, we would expect only one large firm to dominate the industry because large firms have significant cost advantages. However, in an industry with constant returns to scale—for example, restaurants—the cost curve flattens out: the purple line. Once the curve becomes constant, firms of varying sizes can compete equally with one another because they have the same costs. Finally, in the case of diseconomies of scale—for example, big-city hospitals—bigger firms have higher costs: the orange curve.

Bigger Is Not Always Better

Large firms take advantage of economies of scale in many ways, such as buying their inputs at discounted prices. But bigger is not always better. One major problem that confronts large firms is becoming "top-heavy"—that is, having a labor force that requires a large number of managers whose only job is to manage. This lowers the overall productivity of the labor force and increases costs.

■ Owner / Executive manager ■ Division manager ■ Line manager ■ Supervisor ■ Worker

Small Business

10% Reduced productivity

A typical small business might consist of 1 owner and 9 workers.

Mid-Sized Business

12.2% Reduced productivity

A typical mid-sized business might consist of 41 employees, including 1 executive manager and 4 supervisors who oversee 9 workers each.

Large Business

14.9% Reduced productivity

A typical large company might consist of 127 employees: 1 executive manager, 2 division managers, 4 line managers, 12 supervisors, and 108 workers.

REVIEW QUESTIONS

- Calculate the reduced productivity in a company of 1,000 employees when there are 2 executive managers, 6 line managers, and 12 supervisors for every 80 workers.

- Your friend owns a business and is looking to expand. Describe the risks and rewards of such a move using economies of scale and costs.

Economies of Scale

Modern Times

The 1936 comedy *Modern Times* is regarded as one of the top 100 English-language films of all time. The movie features Charlie Chaplin in his final silent film role. Chaplin, who was a master of slapstick comedy, plays a tramp who finds work on an assembly line in a large factory. The company bosses are ruthless taskmasters. For the production process to remain in sync and maximum efficiency to occur, each assembly line worker must complete a small task and pass the product down the line.

As the movie progresses, the bosses introduce a novel product called the Billows Feeding Machine. The idea is simple: if the lunch break were shorter, the workers' downtime would be minimized and production increased. Here is the exact transcript from the film:

Would a feeding machine for workers lower long-run costs?

> May I take the pleasure of introducing Mr. J. Widdecombe Billows, the inventor of the Billows Feeding Machine, a practical device which automatically feeds your men while at work. Don't stop for lunch: be ahead of your competitor. The Billows Feeding Machine will eliminate the lunch hour, increase your production, and decrease your overhead. Allow us to point out some of the features of this wonderful machine: its beautiful, aerodynamic, streamlined body; its smoothness of action, made silent by our electro-porous metal ball bearings. Let us acquaint you with our automaton soup plate— its compressed-air blower, no breath necessary, no energy required to cool the soup. Notice the revolving plate with the automatic food pusher. Observe our counter-shaft, double-knee-action corn feeder, with its synchro-mesh transmission, which enables you to shift from high to low gear by the mere tip of the tongue. Then there is the hydro-compressed, sterilized mouth wiper: its factors of control insure against spots on the shirt front. These are but a few of the delightful features of the Billows Feeding Machine. Let us demonstrate with one of your workers, for actions speak louder than words. Remember, if you wish to keep ahead of your competitor, you cannot afford to ignore the importance of the Billows Feeding Machine.

The company bosses are eager to test the feeding machine, but things go terribly wrong—in a hilarious way—when they select Chaplin as the human guinea pig. Because the machine does not work as promised, the company decides that the feeding machine is not a practical idea.

Although no firm in the real world is likely to try something like the feeding machine, firms do constantly seek efficiency gains. Of course, not all ideas are practical, and sometimes there are insufficient economies of scale to implement an idea. For instance, the assembly line depicted in *Modern Times* is efficient, but it wouldn't make sense for a company to use this process unless it sells a large volume of bolts. This is analogous to production in the automobile industry. Large manufacturers like Toyota and Ford use assembly lines to create economies of scale, whereas a small specialty shop that produces only a handful of vehicles a year builds each car by hand and fails to enjoy the benefits of economies of scale.

PRACTICE WHAT YOU KNOW

Marginal Cost: The True Cost of Admission to Universal Studios

You and your family visit Orlando for a week. While there, you decide to go to Universal Studios. When you arrive, you notice that each family member can buy a day pass for $80 or a two-day pass for $90. Your parents are concerned about spending too much, so they decide to calculate the average cost of a two-day pass to see if it is a good value. The average cost is $90 ÷ 2, or $45 per day. The math is correct, but something you learned in economics tells you that they are not thinking about this in the correct way.

Question: What concept can you apply to make the decision more clear?

Answer: Tell them about *marginal cost*. The first day costs $80, but the marginal cost of going back to the park on the second day is only the extra cost per person, or $90 − $80, which equals $10. Your parents still might not want to spend the extra money, but only spending an extra $10 for the second day

Is one day enough to do it all?

makes it an extraordinary value. Someone who does not appreciate economics might think the second day costs an extra $45 since that is the average cost. But the average cost is misleading. Looking at marginal cost is the best way to weigh these two options.

Conclusion

Do larger firms have lower costs? Not always. When diseconomies of scale occur, costs will rise with output. This result contradicts the common misconception that bigger firms have lower costs than their smaller competitors. Simply put, sometimes a leaner firm with less overhead can beat its larger rivals on cost.

Costs are defined in a number of ways, but marginal cost plays the most crucial role in a firm's cost structure. By observing what happens to marginal cost, you can understand changes in average cost and total cost. This is why economists place so much emphasis on marginal cost. Going forward, a solid grasp of marginal analysis will help you understand many of the most important concepts in microeconomics.

Marginal thinking

You now understand the cost, or supply side, of business decisions. However, to provide a complete picture of how firms operate, we still need to examine how markets work. Costs are only part of the story, and in the next chapter we will take a closer look at profits.

ANSWERING THE BIG QUESTIONS

How are profits and losses calculated?

* Profits and losses are determined by calculating the difference between expenses and revenue.

* There are two types of profit: economic profit and accounting profit. If a business has an economic profit, its revenues are larger than the combination of its explicit and implicit costs.

* Economists break cost into two components: explicit costs, which are easy to calculate, and implicit costs, which are hard to calculate. Since economic profit accounts for implicit costs, the economic profit is always less than the accounting profit.

How much should a firm produce?

* A firm should produce an output that is consistent with the largest possible economic profit.

* In order to maximize production, firms must effectively combine labor and capital in the right quantities.

* In any short-run production process, a point of diminishing marginal product will occur at which additional units of a variable input no longer generate as much output as before. This occurs because each firm has separate fixed and variable costs.

* The marginal cost (MC) curve is the key variable in determining a firm's cost structure. The MC curve always leads the average total cost (ATC) and average variable cost (AVC) curves up or down.

What costs do firms consider in the short run and the long run?

* Firms consider variable and fixed costs, as well as marginal costs. Firms also consider average variable cost (AVC), average fixed cost (AFC), and average total cost (ATC).

* With the exception of the average fixed cost (AFC) curve, which always declines, short-run cost curves are U-shaped. All variable costs initially decline due to increased specialization. At a certain point, the advantages of continued specialization give way to diminishing marginal product, and the MC, AVC, and ATC curves begin to rise.

* Long-run costs are a reflection of scale. They can experience diseconomies, economies, or constant returns to scale depending on the industry.

How Much Does It Cost to Raise a Child?

Raising a child is one of life's most rewarding experiences, but it can be very expensive. According to the U.S. Department of Agriculture, the cost for a middle-income, two-parent family to raise a child from birth to age 18 is more than $250,000—and that does not include college. To determine this number, the government considers all related costs, such as food, clothing, medical care, and entertainment. In addition, the government apportions a share of the costs of the family home and vehicles to each child in the household. To put the cost of raising a child in perspective, the median home value in 2011 was $156,000. Talk about opportunity cost!

What if a family has more than one child? You wouldn't necessarily multiply the cost by two or three because there are economies of scale in raising more children. For example, some things can be shared: the children might share a bedroom and wear hand-me-downs. Also, the family can purchase food in bulk. As a result, families that have three or more children can manage to spend an average of 22% less on each child.

The cost of raising children also forces families to make trade-offs. In many households, both parents must work or work longer hours. When one parent steps out of the workforce, the household loses a paycheck. While this may save in expenses associated with working, including certain clothes, transportation, and childcare, there are also hidden costs. For example, the lack of workplace continuity lowers the stay-at-home parent's future earning power.

Raising a child is an expensive proposition in both the short run and the long run. But don't let this discourage you; it is also one of the most rewarding investments you will ever make.

Daddy Day Care? Childcare expenses add up.

CONCEPTS YOU SHOULD KNOW

accounting profit (p. 244)
average fixed cost (AFC) (p. 253)
average total cost (ATC) (p. 254)
average variable cost (AVC)
  (p. 252)
constant returns to scale (p. 259)
diminishing marginal
  product (p. 250)
diseconomies of scale (p. 258)

economic profit (p. 244)
economies of scale (p. 258)
efficient scale (p. 256)
explicit costs (p. 243)
factors of production (p. 247)
fixed costs (p. 252)
implicit costs (p. 243)
losses (p. 242)
marginal cost (MC) (p. 254)

marginal product (p. 248)
output (p. 247)
production function (p. 247)
profits (p. 242)
scale (p. 257)
variable costs (p. 252)
total cost (p. 242)
total revenue (p. 242)

QUESTIONS FOR REVIEW

1. What is the equation for the profit (or loss) of a firm?

2. Why is economic profit a better measure of profitability than accounting profit? Give an example.

3. What role does diminishing marginal product play in determining the ideal mix of labor and capital a firm should use?

4. Describe what happens to the total product of a firm when marginal product is increasing, decreasing, and negative.

5. Explain why marginal cost is the glue that connects average variable cost and average total cost.

6. Compare the short-run and long-run cost curves. In a few sentences, explain their differences.

7. Name examples of industries that illustrate each of the following: economies of scale, constant returns to scale, and diseconomies of scale. Think creatively; do not use the textbook examples.

STUDY PROBLEMS (✳ solved at the end of the section)

1. Go to www.lemonadegame.com. This free online game places you in the role of a lemonade seller. Nothing could be simpler, right? Not so fast! You still need to control costs and ensure you have the right ingredients on hand to be able to sell. You will need to manage your supply of lemons, sugar, ice, and cups. You will also have to set a price and decide how many lemons and how much sugar and ice to put in each glass of lemonade you produce. This is not a trivial process, so play the game. Your challenge is to make $20 in profit over the first five days. (Your business starts with $20, so you need to have $40 in your account by the end of day 5 to meet the challenge. Are you up to it?)

2. The following table shows a short-run production function for laptop computers. Use the data to determine where diminishing product begins.

Number of workers	Total output of laptop computers
0	0
1	40
2	100
3	150
4	180
5	200
6	205
7	200
8	190

3. A pizza business has the cost structure described below. The firm's fixed costs are $25 per day. Calculate the firm's average fixed costs, average variable costs, average total costs, and marginal costs.

Output (pizzas per day)	Total cost of output
0	$25
10	75
20	115
30	150
40	175
50	190
60	205
70	225
80	250

✳ 4. A firm is considering changing its plant size, so it calculates the average cost of production for various plant sizes below. If the firm is currently using plant size C, is the firm experiencing economies of scale, diseconomies of scale, or constant returns to scale?

Plant size	Average total cost
A (smallest)	$10,000
B	9,500
C	9,000
D	8,800
E	8,800
F (largest)	8,900

5. True or false?
   a. The AFC curve can never rise.
   b. Diminishing marginal product is a long-run constraint that prevents lower costs.
   c. The MC curve intersects the AVC and ATC curves at the minimum point along both curves.
   d. Accounting profit is smaller than economic profit.
   e. Total cost divided by output is equal to marginal cost.

6. Digital media distributed over the Internet often have marginal costs of zero. For instance, people can download music and movies instantly through many providers. Do these products exhibit economies, diseconomies, or constant returns to scale?

7. An airline has a marginal cost per passenger of $30 on a route from Boston to Detroit. At the same time, the typical fare charged is $300. The planes that fly the route are usually full, yet the airline claims that it loses money on the route. How is this possible?

8. Many amusement parks offer two-day passes at dramatically discounted prices. If a one-day pass costs $40 but the two-day pass costs $50, what is the average cost for the two-day pass? What is the marginal cost of the two-day pass?

✳ 9. Suppose that you own a yard care business. You have your own mower, flatbed truck, and other equipment. You are also the primary employee. Why might you have trouble calculating your profits? (**Hint:** think about the difference between accounting profits and economic profits.)

10. Use the information provided in the following table to fill in the blanks.

Output	Total fixed cost	Total variable cost	Total cost	Average fixed cost	Average variable cost	Average total cost	Marginal cost
0	$500	$0	$500	——	——	——	
1	$500	$200	——	——	——	——	——
2	——	——	$800	——	——	——	——
3	——	——	$875	——	——	——	——
4	——	——	$925	——	——	——	——
5	——	——	——	$100	——	——	$25
6	——	$450	——	——	——	——	——

SOLVED PROBLEMS

4. The key to solving this problem is recognizing the direction of change in the average total cost. If the firm were to switch to a smaller plant, like B, its average total cost would rise to $9,500. Since the smaller plant would cost more, plant C is currently enjoying economies of scale. When we compare the average total cost of C ($9,000) to D ($8,800), it continues to fall. Since the average total cost is falling from B to D, we again know that the firm is experiencing economies of scale.

9. When calculating your costs for the mower, truck, and other expenses, you are computing your explicit costs. Subtracting the explicit costs from your total revenue will yield the accounting profit you have earned. However, you still do not know your economic profit because you haven't determined your implicit costs. Because you are the primary employee, you also have to add in the opportunity cost of the time you invest in the business. You may not know exactly what you might have earned doing something else, but you can be sure it exists—this is your implicit cost. This is why you may have trouble computing your profits. You might show an accounting profit only to discover that what you thought you made was less than you could have made by doing something else. If that is the case, your true economic profit is actually negative.

Firms in a Competitive Market

Firms control the prices they charge.

Many people believe that firms set the prices for their products with little concern for the consumer. However, this is incorrect. The

misconception that firms control the prices they charge occurs because many people think that the firm is central to the functioning of the market. However, market forces are much stronger than individual firms. Under the right conditions, markets produce high-quality goods at remarkably low prices, to the benefit of both buyers and sellers. Competition drives prices down, which limits the firm's ability to charge as much as it would like.

In this chapter and the next four, we will look in more detail at how markets work, the profits firms earn, and how market forces determine the price that a firm can charge for its product or service. We begin our sequence on market structure, or how individual markets are interconnected, by examining the conditions necessary to create a competitive market. Although few real markets achieve the ideal market structure described in this chapter, this model provides a benchmark, or starting point, for understanding other market structures. In competitive markets, firms are completely at the mercy of market forces that set the price to be charged throughout the industry.

Our analysis of competitive markets will show that when competition is widespread firms have little or no control over the price they can charge and they make little or no economic profit. Let's find out why this is the case.

Individual vendors in flower markets face stiff competition.

BIG QUESTIONS

* **How do competitive markets work?**
* **How do firms maximize profits?**
* **What does the supply curve look like in perfectly competitive markets?**

How Do Competitive Markets Work?

Competitive markets exist when there are so many buyers and sellers that each one has only a small impact on the market price and output. Recall that in Chapter 3 we used the example of the Pike Place Market, where each fish vendor sells similar products. Because each fish vendor is small relative to the whole market, no single firm can influence the market price. It doesn't matter where you buy salmon because the price is the same or very similar at every fish stall. When buyers are willing to purchase a product anywhere, sellers have no control over the price they charge. These two characteristics—similar goods and many participants—create a highly competitive market where the price and quantity sold are determined by the market conditions rather than by any one firm.

In competitive markets, buyers can expect to find consistently low prices and a wide availability of the good that they want. Firms that produce goods in competitive markets are known as *price takers*. A **price taker** has no control over the price set by the market. It "takes"—that is, accepts—the price determined from the overall supply and demand conditions that regulate the market.

Competitive markets have another feature in common as well: new competitors can easily enter the market. If you want to open a copy shop, all you have to do is rent store space and several copy machines. There are no licensing or regulatory obstacles in your way. Likewise, there is very little to stop competitors from leaving the market. If you decide to close, you can lock the doors, return the equipment you rented, and move on to do something else. When barriers to entry into a marketplace are low, new firms are free to compete with existing businesses, which ensures the existence of competitive markets and low prices. Table 9.1 summarizes the characteristics of competitive firms.

A **price taker** has no control over the price set by the market.

TABLE 9.1

Characteristics of Competitive Firms

- Many sellers
- Similar products
- Free entry and exit
- Price taking

Real-life examples of competitive markets usually fall short of perfection. Examples that are almost perfectly competitive, shown in Table 9.2, include the stock market, farmers' markets, online ticket auctions, and currency trading. When markets are almost perfectly competitive, the benefit to society is still extremely large because markets create consumer and producer surplus (as we saw in Chapter 6).

TABLE 9.2
Almost Perfect Markets

Example	How it works	Reality check
Stock market 	Millions of shares of stocks are traded every day on various stock exchanges, and generally the buyers and sellers have access to real-time information about prices. Since most of the traders represent only a small share of the market, they have little ability to influence the market price.	Because of the volume of shares that they control, large institutional investors, like Pacific Investment Management Company (PIMCO), manage billions of dollars in funds. As a result, they are big enough to influence the market price.
Farmers' markets 	In farmers' markets, sellers are able to set up at little or no cost. Many buyers are also present. The gathering of numerous buyers and sellers of similar products causes the market price for similar products to converge toward a single price.	Many produce markets do not have enough sellers to achieve a perfectly competitive result. Without more vendors, individual sellers can often set their prices higher.
Online ticket auctions 	The resale market for tickets to major sporting events and concerts involves many buyers and sellers. The prices for seats in identical sections end up converging quickly toward a narrow range.	Some ticket companies and fans get special privileges that enable them to buy and sell blocks of tickets before others can enter the market.
Currency trading 	Hundreds of thousands of traders around the globe engage in currency buying and selling on any given day. Since all traders have very good real-time information, currency trades in different parts of the world converge toward the same price.	Currency markets are subject to intervention on the part of governments that might want to strategically alter the prevailing price of their currency.

ECONOMICS IN THE REAL WORLD

Aalsmeer Flower Auction

The world's largest flower auction takes place in Aalsmeer, a small town in the Netherlands. Each week, producers sell over 100 million flowers there. In fact, over one-third of all the flowers sold in the world pass through Aalsmeer. Since the Aalsmeer market serves thousands of buyers and sellers, it is one of the best examples of a competitive market you will ever find. The supply comes from approximately 6,000 growers worldwide. More than 2,000 buyers attend the auction to purchase flowers.

The Aalsmeer flower market is almost perfectly competitive.

Aalsmeer uses a method known as a Dutch auction to determine the price for each crate of flowers sold. Most people think of an auction as a situation in which two or more individuals try to outbid each other. However, in Aalsmeer that process is reversed. As each crate of flowers goes on sale, the price on a huge board starts at 100 euros and then goes down until the lot is sold. This special kind of auction was invented here, and it is a very efficient way of getting the highest price out of the buyer who wants the lot the most.

At Aalsmeer, individual buyers and sellers are small compared to the overall size of the market. In addition, the flowers offered by one seller are almost indistinguishable from those offered by the other sellers. As a result, individual buyers and sellers have no control over the price set by the market. ✳

In the next section, we will examine the profits that competitive firms make. After all, profits motivate firms to produce a product, so knowing how a business can make the most profit is central to understanding how competitive markets work.

How Do Firms Maximize Profits?

All firms, whether they are active in a competitive market or not, attempt to maximize profits. Making a profit requires that a firm have a thorough grasp of its costs and its revenues. In the previous chapter, we learned about the cost structure of the firm. In this section, we examine its revenues. Combining the firm's revenues with its costs enables us to determine how much profit the firm makes.

Profits are the goal of every firm, but they don't always materialize. Sometimes, firms experience losses instead of profits, so we also explore whether a firm should shut down or continue to operate in order to minimize its losses. Once we fully understand the firm's decision-making process, we will better

PRACTICE WHAT YOU KNOW

Price Takers: Mall Food Courts

Your instructor asks you to find an example of a competitive market nearby. Your friend suggests that you visit the food court at a nearby mall.

Question: Do the restaurants in a food court meet the definition of a price taker, thereby signaling a competitive market?

Answer: Most food courts contain a lot of competition. Customers can choose among burgers, sandwiches, salads, pizza, and much more. Everywhere you turn, there is another place to eat and the prices at each place are comparable. Is this enough to make each restaurant a price taker? Not quite, since each restaurant has some market power because it serves different food. This enables the more popular places to charge somewhat more.

Are the restaurants in a food court price takers?

While the restaurants in the court are not price takers, the drinks (both fountain drinks and bottled water) that they sell are essentially the same. Any customer who is only interested in getting something to drink has a highly competitive market to choose from.

comprehend how the entire market functions. To make this process easier, throughout this section we refer to Mr. Plow (from the *Simpsons* episode mentioned in the Economics in the Media box on p. 277) to examine the choices every business must make. We'll look at the price Mr. Plow charges and how many driveways he clears, and then we'll compare his revenues to his costs in order to determine whether he is maximizing his profit.

The Profit-Maximizing Rule

Let's imagine how much revenue Mr. Plow will make if he charges $10 for each driveway he clears. Table 9.3 shows how much profit he might make if he clears up to 10 driveways. As we learned in Chapter 8, total profits (column 4) are determined by taking the total revenue (column 2) and subtracting the total cost (column 3). Mr. Plow's profits start out at −$25 because even if he does not clear any driveways, he incurs a fixed cost of $50,000 to buy a snow plow before he can get started (this cost will enter into other calculations later in the chapter). In order to recover the fixed cost, he needs to generate revenue by clearing driveways. As Mr. Plow clears more driveways, the losses (the negative numbers) shown in column 4 gradually contract; he begins to earn a profit by the time he plows 6 driveways.

TABLE 9.3

Calculating Profit for Mr. Plow

(1)	(2)	(3)	(4)	(5)	(6)	(7)
Quantity (q = driveways cleared)	Total Revenue	Total Cost	Total Profit	Marginal Revenue	Marginal Cost	Change (Δ) in Profit
Abbreviation:	TR	TC	π	MR	MC	Δπ
Formula:			TR − TC	ΔTR	ΔTC	MR − MC
0	$0	$25	−$25			
1	10	34	−24	$10	$9	$1
2	20	41	−21	10	7	3
3	30	46	−16	10	5	5
4	40	49	−9	10	3	7
5	50	51	−1	10	2	8
6	60	54	6	10	3	7
7	70	60	10	10	6	4
8	80	70	10	**10** = **10**		0
9	90	95	−5	10	25	−15
10	100	145	−45	10	50	−40

What does Table 9.3 tell us about Mr. Plow's business? Column 4 shows the company's profits at various output (q) levels. Profits reach a maximum of $10 in a range of 7 to 8 driveways. From looking at this table, you might suppose that the firm can make a production decision based on the data in the profit column. However, firms don't work this way. The total profit (or loss) is typically determined after the fact. For example, Homer may have to fill up with gas at the end of the day, buy new tires for his plow, or purchase liability insurance. His accountant will take his receipts and deduct each expense to determine his profits. All of this takes time. An accurate understanding of Homer's profits may have to wait until the end of the quarter, or even the year, in order to fully account for all the irregular expenses associated with running a business. This means that the information found in the profit column is not available until long after the business decisions have been made. So, in day-to-day operations, the firm needs another way to make production decisions.

Marginal thinking

The key to determining Mr. Plow's profits comes from understanding the relationship between marginal revenue (column 5) and marginal cost (column 6). The marginal revenue is the change (Δ) in total revenue when the firm produces additional units. So, looking down column 5, we see that for every driveway Mr. Plow clears, he makes $10 in extra revenue. The marginal cost (column 6) is the change (Δ) in total cost when the firm produces additional units. Column 7 calculates the difference between the marginal revenue (column 5) and marginal cost (column 6).

Competitive Markets

The Simpsons: Mr. Plow

In this episode, Homer buys a snow plow and goes into the snow removal business. After a few false starts, his business, Mr. Plow, becomes a huge success. Every snowy morning, he looks out the window and comments about "white gold."

The episode illustrates each of the factors that go into making a competitive market. Businesses providing snow removal all offer the *same* service. Since there are many buyers (homeowners) and many businesses (the "plow people"), the market is competitive.

However, Homer's joy, profits, and notoriety are short-lived. Soon his friend Barney buys a bigger plow and joins the ranks of the "plow people." Barney's *entry* into the business shows how easy it is for competitors to enter the market. Then Homer, who has begun to get lazy and rest on his success, wakes

Homer's great idea is about to melt away.

up late one snowy morning to find all the driveways in the neighborhood already plowed. A nasty battle over customers ensues.

When firms can easily enter the market, any higher-than-usual profits that a firm enjoys in the short run will dissipate in the long run due to increased competition. As a result, we can say that this *Simpsons* episode shows an industry that is not just competitive; it is perfectly competitive.

In Chapter 8, we saw that to understand cost structure, a firm focuses on marginal cost. The same is true on the revenue side. To make a good decision on the level of investment, Mr. Plow must use marginal analysis. Looking at column 7, we see that where total profits equal $10, the change in profits, MR − MC, is equal to $0. (See the numbers in red in columns 4 and 7.) At output levels below 7, MR − MC is positive, as indicated by the numbers in green. Expanding output to 7 driveways adds to profits. But as Mr. Plow services more driveways, the marginal cost rises dramatically. For instance, Mr. Plow may have to seek driveways that are farther away and thus incur higher transportation costs for those additional customers. Whatever the cause, increased marginal costs (column 6) eventually overtake the constant marginal revenues (column 5).

Recall that we began our discussion by saying that a firm can't wait for the yearly, or even quarterly, profit statements to make production decisions. By examining the marginal impact, shown in column 7, a firm can make good day-to-day operational decisions. This means that Mr. Plow has to decide whether or not to clear more driveways. For instance, if he is plowing 4 driveways, he may decide to work a little harder the next time it snows and plow 1 more. At 5 driveways, his profits increase by $8. Since he enjoys making this extra money, he could expand again from 5 to 6 driveways. This time, he makes an extra $7. From 6 to 7 driveways, he earns $4 more. However,

If you already own a truck and a plow, starting your own snow plow business is inexpensive.

when Mr. Plow expands from 7 to 8 driveways, he discovers that he does not earn any additional profits, and at 9 driveways he loses $15. This would cause him to scale back his efforts to a more profitable level of output.

Marginal thinking helps Mr. Plow discover the production level at which his profits are maximized. The **profit-maximizing rule** states that profit maximization occurs when a firm expands output until marginal revenue is equal to marginal cost, MR = MC. (This is the point at which 10 = 10 in columns 5 and 6 of Table 9.3.) The profit-maximizing rule may seem counterintuitive, since at MR = MC (where marginal revenue is equal to the extra cost of production) there is no additional profit. However, according to the MR = MC rule, production should stop at the point at which profit opportunities no longer exist. Suppose that Mr. Plow chooses a point at which MR > MC. This means that the cost of producing additional units adds more to revenue than to costs, so production should continue. However, if MR < MC, the cost of producing additional units is more than the additional revenue those units bring in. At that point, production is not profitable. The point at which MR = MC is the exact level of production at which no further profitable opportunities exist and losses have not yet occurred. This is the optimal point at which to stop production. In the case of Mr. Plow, he should stop adding new driveways once he reaches 8.

The **profit-maximizing rule** states that profit maximization occurs when the firm chooses the quantity that causes marginal revenue to be equal to marginal cost, or MR = MC.

Marginal thinking

Deciding How Much to Produce in a Competitive Market

We have observed that a firm in a highly competitive market is a price taker; it has no control over the price set by the market. Since snow removal companies provide the same service, they must charge the price that is determined from the overall supply and demand conditions that regulate that particular market.

To better understand these relationships, we can look at them visually. In Figure 9.1, we use the MR and MC data from Table 9.3 to illustrate the profit calculation. For reference, we also include the average cost curves such as the ones shown in Figure 8.2 on page 255 of Chapter 8. Recall that the marginal cost curve (shown in purple) always crosses the average total cost (ATC) curve and the average variable cost (AVC) curve at their lowest point. Figure 9.1 highlights the relationship between the marginal cost curve (MC) and the marginal revenue curve (MR). Since the price (P) Mr. Plow charges is constant at $10, marginal revenue is horizontal. Unlike MR, MC at first decreases and then rises due to diminishing marginal product. Therefore, the firm wants to expand production as long as MR is greater than MC, and it will stop production at the quantity where MR = MC = $10. When q = 8, MR = MC and profits are maximized. At quantities beyond 8, the MC curve is above the MR curve; marginal cost is higher than marginal revenue, and the firm's profits will fall.

Note: we can use the profit-maximizing rule, MR = MC, to identify the most profitable output in a two-step process:

1. Locate the point at which the firm will maximize its profits: MR = MC. This is the point labeled A in Figure 9.1.
2. Look for the profit-maximizing output: move down the vertical dashed line to the *x* axis at point q. Any quantity greater than, or less than, q would result in lower profits.

FIGURE 9.1

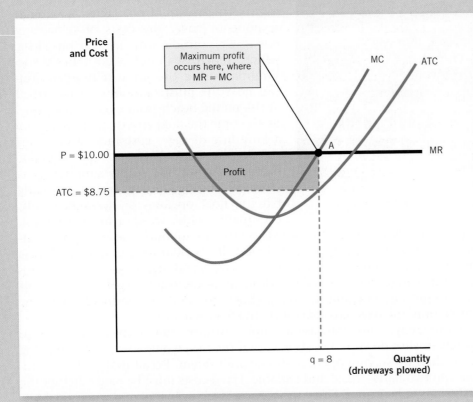

Profit Maximization

Mr. Plow uses the profit-maximizing rule to locate the point at which marginal revenue equals marginal cost, or MR = MC. This determines the ideal output level, q. The firm takes the price from the market; this is shown as the horizontal MR curve where price = $10.00. Since the price charged is higher than the average total cost curve along the dashed line at quantity q, the firm makes the economic profit shown in the green rectangle.

Once we know the profit-maximizing quantity, we can determine the average cost of producing q units. From q, we move up along the dashed line until it intersects with the ATC curve. From that point, we move horizontally until we come to the *y* axis. This tells us the average cost of making 8 units. Since the total cost in Table 9.3 is $70 when 8 driveways are plowed, dividing 70 by 8 gives us $8.75 for the average total cost. We can calculate Mr. Plow's profit rectangle from Figure 9.1 as follows:

Profit = (Price − ATC [along the dashed line at quantity q]) × q

This gives us (10−8.75) × 8 = $10, which is the profit we see in Table 9.3, column 4, in red numbers. Since the MR is the price, and since the price is higher than the average total cost, the firm makes the profit visually represented in the green rectangle.

The Firm in the Short Run

Deciding how much to produce in order to maximize profits is the goal of every business. However, there are times when it is not possible to make a profit. When revenue is insufficient to cover cost, the firm suffers a loss—at which point it must decide whether to operate or temporarily shut down. Successful businesses make this decision all the time. For example, retail

The Ice Cream Float, a cool idea on a hot day at the lake.

stores often close by 9 p.m. because operating overnight would not generate enough revenue to cover the costs of remaining open. Or consider the Ice Cream Float, which crisscrosses Smith Mountain Lake in Virginia during the summer months. You can hear the music announcing its arrival at the public beach from over a mile away. By the time the float arrives, there is usually a long line of eager customers waiting for the float to dock. This is a very profitable business on hot and sunny summer days. However, during the late spring and early fall the float operates on weekends only. Eventually, colder weather forces the business to shut down until the crowds return the following season. This shutdown decision is a short-run calculation. If the float were to operate during the winter, it would need to pay for employees and fuel. Incurring these variable costs when there are so few customers would result in greater total costs than simply dry-docking the boat. When the float is dry-docked over the winter, only the fixed cost of storing the boat remains.

Fortunately, a firm can use a simple, intuitive rule to decide whether to operate or shut down in the short run: if the firm would lose less by shutting down than by staying open, it should shut down. Recall that costs are broken into two parts—fixed and variable. Fixed costs must be paid whether the business is open or not. Since variable costs are only incurred when the business is open, if it can make enough to cover its variable costs—for example, employee wages and the cost of the electricity needed to run the lighting—it will choose to remain open. Once the variable costs are covered, any extra money goes toward paying the fixed costs.

A business should operate if it can cover its variable costs, and it should shut down if it cannot. Figure 9.2 illustrates the decision using cost curves. As long as the MR (marginal revenue) curve of the firm is greater than the minimum point on the AVC (average variable cost) curve—the green- and yellow-shaded areas—the firm will choose to operate. (Note that the MR curve is not shown in Figure 9.2. The colored areas in the figure denote the range of potential MR curves that are profitable or that cause a loss.) Recalling our example of the Ice Cream Float, you can think of the green-shaded area as the months during the year when the business makes a profit and the yellow-shaded area as the times during spring and fall when the float operates even though it is incurring a loss (because the loss is less than if the float were to shut down entirely). Finally, if the MR curve falls below the AVC curve—the red-shaded area—the firm should shut down. Table 9.4 summarizes these decisions.

To make the shut-down decision more concrete, imagine that the Ice Cream Float's minimum ATC (average total cost) is $2.50 and its minimum AVC is $2.00. During the summer, when many customers line up on the dock waiting for it to arrive, it can charge more than $2.50 and earn a substantial profit. However, as the weather cools, fewer people want ice cream. The Ice Cream Float still has to crisscross the lake to make sales, burning expensive gasoline and paying employees to operate the vessel. If the Ice

FIGURE 9.2

When to Operate and When to Shut Down

If the MR (marginal revenue) curve is above the minimum point on the ATC (average total cost) curve, the Ice Cream Float will make a profit (shown in green). If the MR curve is below the minimum point on the ATC curve, $2.50, but above the minimum point on the AVC (average variable cost) curve, the float will operate at a loss (shown in yellow). If the MR curve is below the minimum point on the AVC curve, $2.00, the float will temporarily shut down (shown in red).

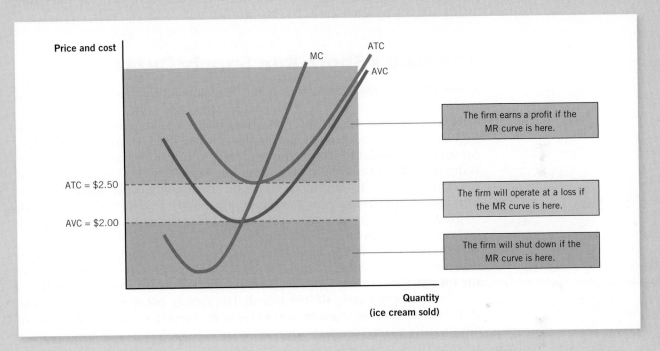

TABLE 9.4

Profit and Loss in the Short Run

Condition	In words	Outcome
P > ATC	The price is greater than the average total cost of production.	The firm makes a profit.
ATC > P > AVC	The average total cost of production is greater than the price the firm charges, but the price is greater than the average variable cost of production.	The firm will operate to minimize loss.
AVC > P	The price is less than the average variable cost of production.	The firm will temporarily shut down.

Cream Float is to keep its revenues high, it needs customers; but cooler weather suppresses demand. If the Ice Cream Float charges $2.25 in the fall, it can make enough to cover its average variable costs of $2.00, but not enough to cover its average total costs of $2.50. Nevertheless, it will continue to operate because it makes enough in the yellow region to pay part of its fixed cost. Finally, it reaches a point at which the price drops below $2.00. Now the business is no longer able to cover its average variable costs. At this point, it shuts down for the winter. It does this because operating when MR is very low causes the business to incur a larger loss.

The Firm's Short-Run Supply Curve

Marginal thinking

Cost curves provide a detailed picture of a firm's willingness to supply a good or service. We have seen that when the MR curve is below the minimum point on the AVC curve, the firm shuts down and production, or output, falls to zero. Another way of stating this is that when revenues are too low, no supply is produced. For example, during the winter the Ice Cream Float is dry-docked, so the supply curve does not exist. However, when the firm is operating, it bases its output decisions on the marginal cost. Recall that the firm uses the profit-maximizing rule, or MR = MC, to determine how much to produce. The marginal cost curve is therefore the firm's short-run supply curve as long as the firm is operating.

Figure 9.3 shows the Ice Cream Float's short-run supply curve. In the short run, diminishing marginal product causes the firm's costs to rise as the quantity produced increases. This is reflected in the shape of the firm's short-run supply curve, shown in red. The supply curve is upward sloping above the minimum point on the AVC curve. Below the minimum point on

FIGURE 9.3

The Firm's Short-Run Supply Curve

The supply curve (S_{SR}) and marginal cost curve (MC) are equivalent when the price is above the minimum point on the average variable cost curve (AVC). Below that point, the firm shuts down and no supply exists.

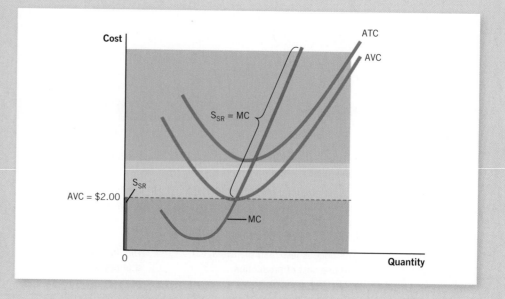

the AVC curve, the short-run supply curve becomes vertical at a quantity of zero, indicating that a willingness to supply the good does not exist below a price of $2.00. At prices above $2.00, the firm will offer more for sale as the price increases.

The Firm's Long-Run Supply Curve

In the long run, a firm's output decision is directly tied to profits. Since the firm is flexible in the long run, all costs are variable. As a result, the firm's long-run supply curve exists only when the firm expects to cover its total costs of production (because otherwise the firm would go out of business).

Returning to the Ice Cream Float example, recall that the boat shuts down over the winter instead of going out of business because demand is low but is expected to return. If for some reason the crowds do not come back, the float would go out of business. Turning to Figure 9.4, we see that at any point below the minimum point, $2.50 on the ATC curve, the float will experience a loss. Since, in the long run, firms are free to enter or exit the market, no firm will willingly produce in the market if the price is less than average total cost (P < ATC). As a result, no supply exists below $2.50. However, if price is greater than cost (P > ATC), the float expects to make a profit and thus will continue to produce.

The firm's long-run supply curve, shown in Figure 9.4 in red, is upward sloping above the minimum point on the ATC curve, which is denoted by ATC on the y axis. The supply curve becomes vertical at a quantity of zero, indicating that a willingness to supply the good does not exist below a price

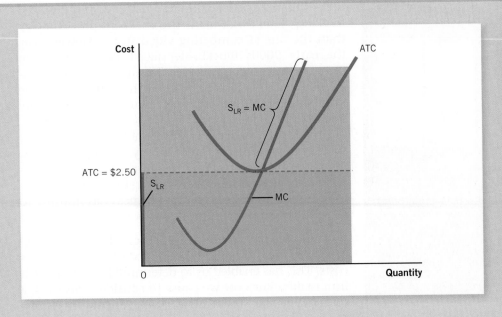

FIGURE 9.4

The Firm's Long-Run Supply Curve

The long-run supply curve (S_{LR}) and marginal cost curve (MC) are equivalent when the price is above the minimum point on the average total cost curve (ATC). Below that point, the firm shuts down and no supply exists.

Incentives

of $2.50. In the long run, a firm that expects price to exceed ATC will continue to operate, since the conditions for making a profit seem favorable. In contrast, a firm that does not expect price to exceed ATC should cut its losses and exit the industry. Table 9.5 outlines the long-run decision criteria.

ECONOMICS IN THE REAL WORLD

Blockbuster and the Dynamic Nature of Change

What happens if your customers do not return? What if you simply had a bad idea to begin with, and the customers never arrived in the first place?

When the long-run profit outlook is bleak, the firm is better off shutting down. This is a normal part of the ebb and flow of business. For example, once there were thousands of buggy whip companies. Today, as technology has improved and we no longer rely on horse-drawn carriages, few buggy whip makers remain. However, many companies now manufacture automobile parts.

Similarly, a succession of technological advances has transformed the music industry. Records were replaced by 8-track tapes, and then by cassettes. Already, the CD is on its way to being replaced by better technology as iPods, iPhones, and MP3 players make music more portable and as web sites such as Pandora and Spotify allow live streaming of almost any selection a listener wants to hear. However, there was a time when innovation meant playing music on the original Sony Walkman. What was cool in the early 1980s is antiquated today. Any business engaged in distributing music has had to adapt or close.

Similar changes are taking place in the video rental industry. Blockbuster was founded in 1982 and experienced explosive growth, becoming the nation's largest video store chain by 1988. The chain's growth was fueled by its large selection and use of a computerized tracking system that made the checkout process faster than the one at competing video stores. However, by the early 2000s Blockbuster faced stiff competition from online providers like Netflix and in-store dispensers like Redbox. Today, the chain has one-quarter the number of employees it once had and its future is very uncertain.

In addition to changes in technology, other factors such as downturns in the economy, changes in tastes, demographic factors, and migration can all force businesses to close. These examples remind us that the long-run decision to go out of business has nothing to do with the short-term profit outlook. ✳

Blockbuster's best days are long gone.

So far, we have examined the firm's decision-making process in the short run in the context of revenues versus costs. This has enabled us to determine the profits each firm makes. But now we pause to consider *sunk costs*, a special type of cost that all firms, in every industry, must consider when making decisions.

TABLE 9.5

The Long-Run Shut-Down Criteria

Condition	In words	Outcome
P > ATC	The price is greater than the average total cost of production.	The firm makes a profit.
P < ATC	The price is less than the average total cost of production.	The firm should shut down.

PRACTICE WHAT YOU KNOW

The Profit-Maximizing Rule: Show Me the Money!

Here is a question that often confuses students.

Question: At what point does a firm maximize profits?

a. where the profit per unit is greatest

b. where total revenue is maximized

c. where the total revenue is equal to the total cost

d. where marginal revenue equals marginal cost

What is the rule for making the most profit?

Answer: Each answer sounds plausible, so the key is to think about each one in a concrete way. To help do that, we will refer back to the Mr. Plow data in Table 9.3.

a. Incorrect. Making a large profit per unit sounds great. However, if the firm stops production when the profit per unit is the greatest—$8 in column 7—it will fail to realize the additional profits—$7 and $4 in column 7—that come from continuing to produce until MR = MC.

b. Incorrect. Recall that total revenue is only half of the profit function, Profit = TR − TC. No matter how much revenue a business brings in, if total costs are more, the firm will experience a loss. Therefore, the firm wishes to maximize profits, not revenue. For example, looking at column 2, we see that at 10 driveways Mr. Plow earns total revenues of $100. But column 3 tells us that the total cost of plowing 10 driveways is $145. With a total profit of −$45, this level of output would not be a good idea.

c. Incorrect. If total revenue and total cost are equal, the firm makes no profits.

d. Correct. Answers (a), (b), and (c) all sound plausible. But a firm maximizes profits where MR = MC, since at this point all profitable opportunities are exhausted. If Mr. Plow clears 7 or 8 driveways, his profit is $10. If he clears 9 driveways, his profits fall from $10 to −$5 since the marginal cost of clearing that ninth driveway, $25, is greater than the marginal revenue he earns of $10.

Sunk Costs

Costs that have been incurred as a result of past decisions are known as **sunk costs**. For example, the decision to build a new sports stadium is a good application of the principle of sunk costs. Many professional stadiums have been built in the past few years, even though the arenas they replaced were built to last much longer. For example, Three Rivers Stadium in Pittsburgh and Veterans Stadium in Philadelphia were built in the early 1970s as multi-use facilities for both football and baseball, each with an expected lifespan of 60 or more years. However, in the early 2000s both were replaced. Each city built two new stadiums with features such as luxury boxes and better seats that generate more revenue than Veterans and Three Rivers did. The additional revenue makes the new stadiums financially attractive even though the old stadiums were still structurally sound.

Stadium implosions are an example of marginal thinking.

Sunk costs
are unrecoverable costs that have been incurred as a result of past decisions.

Demolishing a structure that is still in good working order may sound like a waste, but it can be good economics. When the extra benefit of a new stadium is large enough to pay for the cost of imploding the old stadium and constructing a new one, a city will do just that. In fact, since Pittsburgh and Philadelphia draw significantly more paying spectators with the new stadiums, the decision to replace the older stadiums has made the citizens in both cities better off. This occurs because new stadiums create increased ticket sales, higher tax revenues, and a more enjoyable experience for fans.

Opportunity
cost

Continuing to use an out-of-date facility has an opportunity cost. Thinkers who do not understand sunk costs might point to the benefits of getting maximum use out of what already exists. But good economists learn to ignore sunk costs and focus on marginal value. They compare marginal benefits and marginal costs. If a new stadium, and the revenue it brings in, will create more value than the old stadium, the decision should be to tear the old one down.

What Does the Supply Curve Look Like in Perfectly Competitive Markets?

We have seen that a firm's willingness to supply a good depends on whether the firm is making a short-run or long-run decision. In the short run, a firm may choose to operate at a loss in order to recover a portion of its fixed costs. In the long run, there are no fixed costs, so a firm is willing to operate only if it expects the price it charges to cover total costs.

However, the supply curve for a single firm represents only a small part of the overall supply of a good provided in a competitive market. We will now turn to market supply and develop the short-run and long-run market supply curves.

Sunk Costs: If You Build It, They Will Come

Replacing an old stadium with a new one is sometimes controversial. People often misunderstand sunk costs and argue for continuing with a stadium until it's completely worn down. But economics tells us not to focus on the sunk costs of the old stadium's construction. Instead, we should compare the marginal benefit of a new stadium to the marginal cost of demolition and new construction.

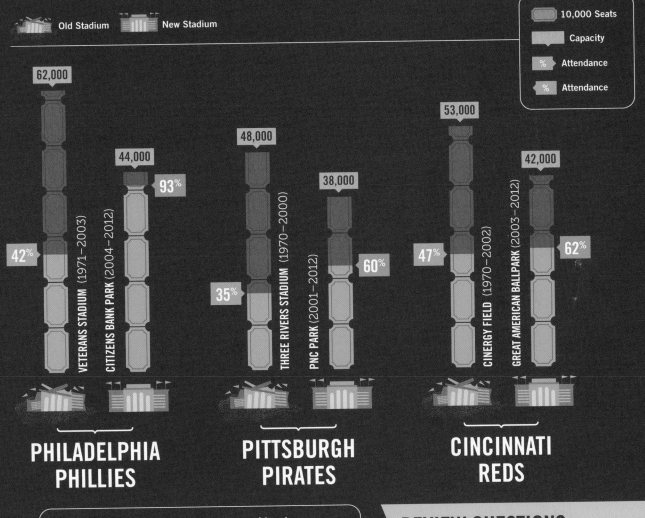

Old Stadium   New Stadium

10,000 Seats
Capacity
% Attendance
% Attendance

PHILADELPHIA PHILLIES

- 62,000 — Veterans Stadium (1971–2003) — 42%
- 44,000 — Citizens Bank Park (2004–2012) — 93%

PITTSBURGH PIRATES

- 48,000 — Three Rivers Stadium (1970–2000) — 35%
- 38,000 — PNC Park (2001–2012) — 60%

CINCINNATI REDS

- 53,000 — Cinergy Field (1970–2002) — 47%
- 42,000 — Great American Ballpark (2003–2012) — 62%

The three new stadiums shown are considered successes. Higher attendance (especially in Philadelphia) and higher revenue per ticket—thanks to luxury boxes and better concessions—make the franchises happy.

An economist's analysis of the stadiums would go beyond attendance, however. The additional revenue generated by the new stadiums must be weighed against the costs of imploding the old stadiums and building new venues.

REVIEW QUESTIONS

- What do you think the smaller size of the new stadiums does to ticket prices, and why?

- Use the idea of sunk costs to analyze switching majors in college.

The Short-Run Market Supply Curve

A competitive market consists of a large number of identical sellers. Since an individual firm's supply curve is equal to its marginal cost curve, if we add together all the individual firm supply curves in a market, we arrive at the short-run market supply curve. Figure 9.5 shows the short-run market supply curve in a two-firm model consisting of Mr. Plow and the Plow King. At a price of $10, Mr. Plow is willing to clear 8 driveways (q_A) and the Plow King is willing to clear 20 driveways (q_B). When we horizontally sum the output of the two firms, we get a total market supply of 28 driveways (Q_{market}), seen in the third graph.

The Long-Run Market Supply Curve

Incentives

Recall that a competitive market is one in which a large number of buyers seek a product that many sellers offer. Competitive markets are also characterized by easy entry and exit. Existing firms and entrepreneurs decide whether to enter and exit a market based on incentives. When existing firms are enjoying profits, there is an incentive for them to produce more and also for entrepreneurs to enter the market. This leads to an increase in the quantity of the good supplied. Likewise, when existing firms are experiencing losses, there is an incentive for them to exit the market; then the quantity supplied decreases. Entry and exit have the combined effect of regulating the amount of profit a firm can hope to make in the long run. As long as profits exist, the quantity supplied will increase and the price will drop. When losses exist, the quantity supplied will decrease and the price will rise. So both profits and losses signal a need for an adjustment in market supply. Therefore, profits and losses act as

FIGURE 9.5

Short-Run Market Supply

The market supply is determined by summing the individual supply of each firm in the market. Although we have only shown this process for two firms, Mr. Plow and Plow King, the process extends to any number of firms in a market.

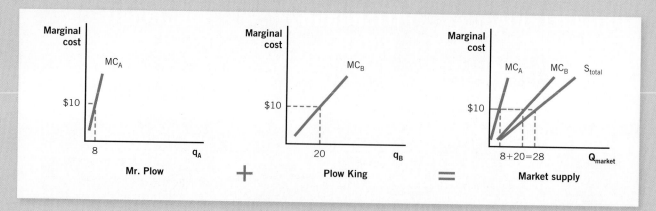

signals for resources to enter or leave an industry. **Signals** convey information about the profitability of various markets.

The only time an adjustment does not take place is when participants in the market make zero economic profit—this is the long-run equilibrium. At that point, existing firms and entrepreneurs are not inclined to enter or exit the market; the adjustment process that occurs through price changes ends.

The benefit of a competitive market is that profits guide existing firms and entrepreneurs to produce more goods and services that society values. Losses serve the same valuable function by encouraging firms to exit and move elsewhere. Without profits and losses acting as signals for firms to enter or exit the market, resources will be misallocated and surpluses and shortages of goods will occur.

Figure 9.6 captures how entry and exit determine the market supply. The profit-maximizing point of the individual firm in panel (a), MR = MC, is located at the minimum point on the ATC curve. The price (P = min. ATC) that existing firms receive is just enough to cover costs, so profits are zero. As a result, new firms have no incentive to enter the market and existing firms have no reason to leave. At all prices above P = min. ATC, firms will earn a profit (the green-shaded area), and at all prices below P = min. ATC firms

The **signals** of profits and losses convey information about the profitability of various markets.

Incentives

FIGURE 9.6

The Market Supply Curve and Entry and Exit

Entry into the market and exit from it force the long-run price to be equal to the minimum point on the average total cost curve (ATC). At all prices above P = min. ATC, firms will earn a profit (the green-shaded area), and at all prices below P = min. ATC, firms will experience a loss (the red-shaded area). This means the long-run supply curve (S_{LR}) must be horizontal at price P = min. ATC. If the price was any higher or lower, firms would enter or exit the market, and the market could not be in a long-run equilibrium.

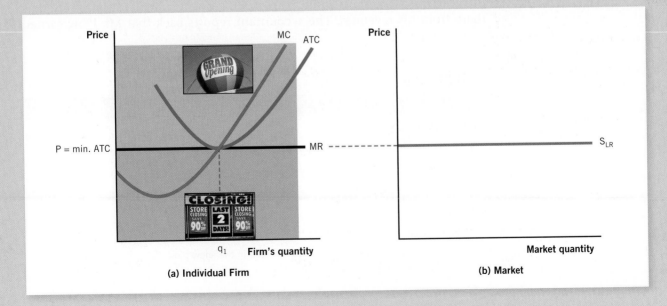

(a) Individual Firm

(b) Market

will experience a loss (the red-shaded area). This picture is consistent for all markets with free entry and exit; zero economic profit occurs at only one price, and that price is the lowest point of the ATC curve.

At this price, the supply curve in panel (b) must be a horizontal line at P = min. ATC. If the price was any higher, firms would enter, supply would increase, and this would force the price back down to P = min. ATC. If the price was any lower, firms would exit, supply would decrease, and this would force the price up to P = min. ATC. Since we know that these adjustments will have time to take place in the long run, the long-run supply curve must also be equal to P = min. ATC in order to satisfy the demand that exists at this price.

A Reminder about Economic Profit

Now that you have learned how perfect competition affects business profits in the long run, you may not think that it is a desirable environment for businesses seeking to earn profits. After all, if a firm cannot expect to make an economic profit in the long run, why bother? It's easy to forget the distinction between accounting profit and economic profit. Firms enter a market when they expect to be reasonably compensated for their investment. And they leave a market when the investment does not yield a satisfactory result. Economic profit is determined by deducting the explicit and implicit costs. Therefore, firms are willing to stay in perfectly competitive markets in the long run when they are breaking even because they are being reasonably compensated for the explicit expenses they have incurred and also for the implicit expenses—like the opportunity costs of other business ventures— that they would expect to make elsewhere.

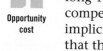

Opportunity cost

For example, if Mr. Plow has the explicit and implicit costs shown in Table 9.6, we can see the distinction between accounting profit and economic profit more clearly. Mr. Plow has revenues of $25,000 during the year.

If Mr. Plow asks his accountant how much the business earned during the year, the accountant adds up all of Mr. Plow's explicit costs and subtracts them from his revenues. The accountant reports back that Mr. Plow earned

TABLE 9.6

Mr. Plow's Economic Profit and the Entry or Exit Decision

Explicit costs per year	
Payment on the loan on his snow plow	$7,000
Gasoline	2,000
Miscellaneous equipment (shovels, salt)	1,000
Implicit costs	
Forgone salary	$10,000
The forgone income that the $50,000 invested in the snow plow could have earned if invested elsewhere	5,000
Total cost	$25,000

$25,000 − $10,000, or $15,000 in profit. Now $15,000 in profit would sound good to a lot of firms, so we would expect many new entrants in the plowing business. But not so fast! We have not accounted for the implicit costs—the money Mr. Plow could have earned by working another job instead of plowing, and also the money he invested in the plow ($50,000) that could have yielded a return ($5,000) elsewhere. If we add in the explicit costs, we find the economic profit, $25,000 − $10,000 − $15,000 = $0. Zero profit sounds unappealing, but it is not. It means that Mr. Plow covered his forgone salary and also his next-best investment alternative. If you could not make any more money doing something else with your time or your investments, you might as well stay in the same place. So Mr. Plow is content to keep on plowing, while others, outside the industry, do not see any profit from entering the industry.

How the Market Adjusts in the Long Run: An Example

We have seen that profits and losses may exist in the short run; in the long run, the best the competitive firm can do is earn zero economic profit. This section looks in more detail at the adjustment process that leads to long-run equilibrium.

We begin with the market in long-run equilibrium, shown in Figure 9.7. Panel (a) represents an individual firm operating at the minimum point on

FIGURE 9.7

The Market in Equilibrium before a Decrease in Demand

When a market is in long-run equilibrium, the short-run supply curve (S_{SR}) and short-run demand curve (D_{SR}) intersect along the long-run supply curve (S_{LR}). When this occurs, the price that the firm charges is equal to the minimum point along the average total cost curve (ATC). This means that the existing firms in the market earn zero economic profit and there is no incentive for firms to enter or exit the market.

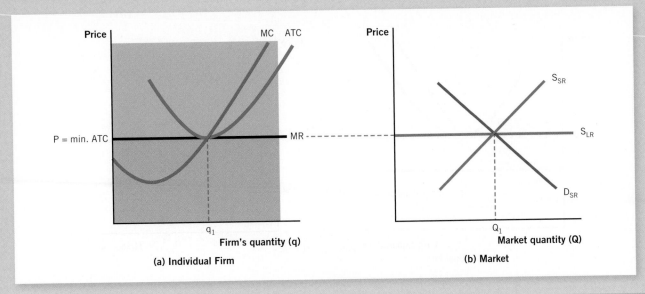

(a) Individual Firm

(b) Market

its ATC curve. In long-run equilibrium, all firms are operating as efficiently as possible. Since the price is equal to the average cost of production, economic profit for the firm is zero. In panel (b), the SR supply curve and the demand curve intersect along the LR supply curve, so the market is also in equilibrium. If, for instance, the SR supply curve and the demand curve happened to inter-sect above the LR supply curve, the price would be higher than the minimum point on the ATC curve. This would lead to short-run profits and indicate that the market was not in long-run equilibrium. The same would be true if the SR supply curve and the demand curve happened to intersect below the LR supply curve, since the price would be lower than the minimum point on the ATC curve. This would lead to short-run shortages, thus causing the price to rise, and then once again the market would be in long-run equilibrium.

Now suppose that demand declines, as shown in Figure 9.8. In panel (b), we see that the market demand curve shifts from D_1 to D_2. When demand falls, the equilibrium point moves from point A to point B. The price drops to P_2 and the market output drops to Q_2. The firms in this industry take their price from the market, so the new marginal revenue curve shifts down from MR_1 to MR_2 at P_2 in panel (a). Since the firm maximizes profits where $MR_2 = MC$, the firm will produce an output of q_2. When the output is q_2 the firm's costs, C_2, are higher than the price it charges, P_2, so it experiences a loss equal to the red-shaded area in panel (a). In addition, since the firm's output is lower, it is no longer producing at the minimum point on its ATC curve, so the firm is not as efficient as before.

FIGURE 9.8

The Short-Run Adjustment to a Decrease in Demand

A decrease in demand causes the price to fall in the market, as shown by the movement from D_1 to D_2 in panel (b). Since the firm is a price taker, the price it can charge falls to P_2. As we see in panel (a), the intersection of MR_2 and MC occurs at q_2. At this output level, the firm incurs the short-run loss shown in (a).

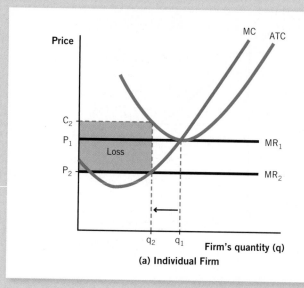

(a) Individual Firm

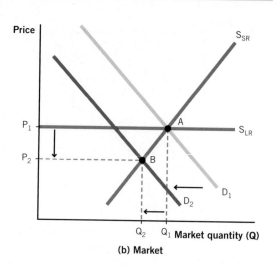

(b) Market

Entry and Exit

I Love Lucy

I Love Lucy was the most watched television comedy of the 1950s. The show featured two couples who are best friends, the Ricardos and the Mertzes, who find themselves in the most unlikely situations.

One particular episode finds Ricky Ricardo disillusioned with show business. After some conversation, Ricky and Fred Mertz decide to go into business together and start a diner. Fred and Ethel Mertz have the experience to run the diner, and Ricky plans to use his name and star power to help get the word out about the restaurant, which they name A Little Bit of Cuba.

If you have seen any of the *I Love Lucy* series, you already know that the business venture is destined to fail. Sure enough, the Mertzes get tired of doing all of the hard work—cooking and serving the customers—while Ricky and Lucy Ricardo meet and greet the guests. Things quickly deteriorate, and the two couples decide to part ways. The only problem is that they are both part owners, and neither can afford to buy out the other. So they decide to split the diner in half right down the middle!

The result is absurd and hilarious. On one side, guests go to A Little Bit of Cuba. On the other side, the Mertzes set up Big Hunk of America. Since both restaurants use the same facilities and sell the same food, the only way they can differentiate themselves is by lowering their prices. This leads to a hamburger price war to attract customers:

> **Ethel:** "Three!"
> **Lucy:** "Two!"
> **Ethel:** "One-cent hamburgers."
> **Fred:** "Ethel, are you out of your mind?" *[Even in the 1950s, a penny was not enough to cover the marginal cost of making a hamburger.]*
> **Ethel:** "Well, I thought this could get 'em."
> **Fred:** "One-cent hamburgers?"

After the exchange, Lucy whispers in a customer's ear and gives him a dollar. He then proceeds to Big Hunk of America and says, "I'd like 100 hamburgers!"

Fred Mertz replies, "We're all out of hamburgers."

How do the falling prices described here affect the ability of the firms in this market to make a profit?

The exchange is a useful way of visualizing how perfectly competitive markets work. Competition forces the price down, but the process of entry and exit takes time and is messy. The Ricardos and Mertzes can't make a living selling one-cent hamburgers—one cent is below their marginal cost—so one of the couples will end up exiting. At that point, the remaining couple would be able to charge more. If they end up making a profit, that profit will encourage entrepreneurs to enter the business. As the supply of hamburgers expands, the price that can be charged will be driven back down. Since we live in an economically dynamic world, prices are always moving toward the long-run equilibrium.

What does it take to produce more mangoes?

Firms in a competitive market can exit the industry easily. Some will do so in order to avoid further losses. Figure 9.9 shows that as firms exit, the market supply contracts from S_{SR1} to S_{SR2} and the market equilibrium moves to point C. At point C, the price rises back to P_1. Market output then drops to Q_3 and the price returns to P_1. The firms that remain in the market no longer experience a short-run loss, since MR_2 returns to MR_1 and costs fall from C_2 to C_1. The end result is that the firm is once again efficient, and economic profit returns to zero.

For example, suppose there is a decline in demand for mangoes due to a false rumor that links the fruit to a salmonella outbreak. The decline in demand causes the price of mangoes to drop. As a consequence, mango producers experience negative economic profit—generating curves like the ones shown in Figure 9.8. In response to the negative profit, some mango growers will exit the industry, the mango trees will be sold for firewood, and the land will be converted to other uses. With fewer mangoes being produced, the supply will contract. Eventually, the smaller supply will cause the price of mangoes to rise until a new long-run equilibrium is reached at a much lower level of output, as shown in Figure 9.9.

FIGURE 9.9

The Long-Run Adjustment to a Decrease in Demand

Short-run losses cause some firms to exit the industry. Their exit shifts the market supply curve to the left in panel (b) until the price returns to long-run equilibrium at point C. This restores the price to P_1 and shifts the MR curve up in panel (a) to MR_1. At P_1 the firm is, once again, earning zero economic profit.

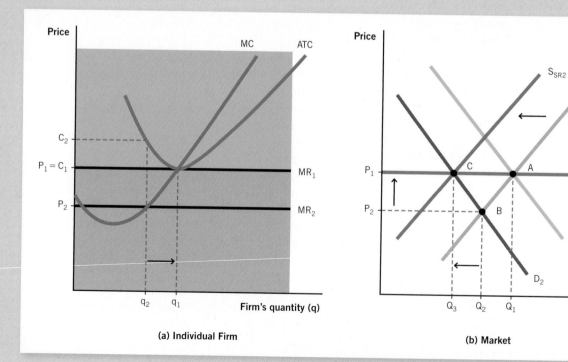

(a) Individual Firm

(b) Market

PRACTICE WHAT YOU KNOW

Long-Run Profits: How Much Can a Firm Expect to Make?

Fill in the blank: In the long run, a firm in a perfectly competitive market earns _____ profits.

(Caution: there may be more than one right answer!)

Calculating profits

a. positive accounting

b. zero accounting

c. positive economic

d. zero economic

Answers:

a. **Correct**. Accounting profits only cover the explicit costs of doing business, so they are positive. But they do not include the implicit costs; once those costs are taken into account, the economic profit will be lower. If the implicit costs are exactly equal to the accounting profits, the firm will earn zero economic profit and the long-run equilibrium will be reached.

b. **Incorrect**. If a firm earns zero accounting profits, the implicit costs will make the economic profit negative. When economic profit is negative, firms will exit the market.

c. **Incorrect**. When a firm earns an economic profit, this sends a signal to firms outside the market to enter. The long-run equilibrium occurs when there is no incentive to enter or exit the market.

d. **Correct**. This answer only makes sense when you recall that *zero* does not mean *nothing*. Zero economic profit means that the firm can cover its explicit (accounting) and implicit (opportunity) costs. It also means that firms inside the market are content to stay and that firms outside the market do not see the value of entering. In the long run, the only condition that would not signal firms to enter or exit would be zero economic profit.

More on the Long-Run Supply Curve

To keep the previous example as simple as possible, we assumed that the long-run supply curve was horizontal. However, this is not always the case. There are two reasons why the long-run supply curve may slope upward. First, some resources needed to produce the product may only be available in limited supplies. As firms try to expand production, they must bid to acquire those resources—a move that causes the average total cost curve to rise. For instance, a mango grower who wants to plant more trees must acquire more suitable land. Since mangoes grow in tropical areas with warm, wet summers, not all land is perfectly adaptable for growing them. The limited supply of land will cause the price of producing mangoes to rise, which will cause the supply curve to be positively sloped.

Opportunity cost

A second reason the long-run supply curve may be upward sloping is the opportunity cost of the labor used in producing the good. If you want to produce more mangoes, you will need more workers to pick the fruit. Hiring extra workers will mean finding people who are both willing and capable. Some workers are better than others at picking mangoes, and some workers have higher opportunity costs. As your firm attempts to expand production, it must increase the wage it pays to attract additional help or accept new workers who are not quite as capable. Either way you slice it, this means higher costs, which would be reflected in a rising long-run supply curve.

This discussion simply means that higher prices are necessary to induce suppliers to offer more for sale. None of it changes the basic ideas we have discussed throughout this section. The entry and exit of firms ensures that the market supply curve is much more elastic in the long run than in the short run.

Conclusion

It is tempting to think that firms control the prices they charge. This is not true in competitive markets, where firms are at the mercy of market forces that set the price charged throughout the industry. Individual firms have no control over the price because they sell the same products as their competitors. In addition, profits and losses help regulate economic activity in competitive markets and also promote economic efficiency. Profits reward producers for producing a good that is valued more highly than the resources used to produce it. This encourages entry into those markets. Likewise, losses penalize producers who operate inefficiently or produce goods that consumers do not want. This encourages exit from the market. The process of entry and exit ensures that resources flow into markets that are undersupplied and away from markets where too many firms exist.

In this chapter, we have studied competitive markets to establish a benchmark that will help us understand how other market structures compare to this ideal. In the next few chapters, we will explore imperfect markets. These markets provide a significant contrast with the results we have just seen. The closer a market is to meeting the criteria of perfect competition, the better the result for consumers and society in general.

ANSWERING THE BIG QUESTIONS

How do competitive markets work?

* The firms in competitive markets sell similar products. Firms are also free to enter and exit the market whenever they wish.
* A price taker has no control over the price it receives in the market.
* In competitive markets, the price and quantity produced are determined by market forces instead of by the firm.

How do firms maximize profits?

* A firm can maximize profits by expanding output until marginal revenue is equal to marginal cost (MR = MC, or the profit-maximizing rule). The profit-maximizing rule is a condition for stopping production at the point where profit opportunities no longer exist.
* The firm should shut down if the price it receives does not cover its average variable costs. Since variable costs are only incurred when operating, if a firm can make enough to cover its variable costs in the short run, it will choose to continue to operate.

What does the supply curve look like in perfectly competitive markets?

* Profits and losses act as signals for firms to enter or leave an industry. As a result, perfectly competitive markets drive economic profit to zero in the long run.
* The entry and exit of firms ensure that the market supply curve in a competitive market is much more elastic in the long run than in the short run.

Tips for Starting Your Own Business

Before you go into business for yourself, you need to devise a plan. Over 80% of all small businesses fail within five years because the businesses were ill conceived or counted on unrealistic sales projections. You don't need a hugely detailed plan as long as it covers these essential points:

Do a cost-benefit analysis, and determine how long it will take you to break even. If you don't do this, you could run out of money and have to close your doors before you start to make a profit. Reaching the break-even point is different from earning an economic profit. Breaking even requires that you cover your explicit expenses with your revenues, or have a positive cash flow. This is especially important if you enter a perfectly competitive market where long-run profits are not possible. You need to be lean and efficient just to survive.

Keep your start-up costs as low as possible. Consider investing as much of your own money as possible. It can be very tempting to take out loans to cover your start-up costs, but if you expect to start immediately paying back your loans with the profits from your new business, think again. It can take years to become profitable. To lessen this problem, you can invest more of your own capital into the business to ensure that loans don't sink you. Also, start small and grow your business slowly in order to avoid overreaching.

Protect yourself from risk. If you are a sole proprietor, you are liable for business debts and judgments, and your creditors can come after your personal assets—like your home and savings accounts. To protect against this possibility, you can

Make sure your plan covers the essential points.

incorporate into what is known as a limited liability corporation, which helps shield business owners from personal liability.

Realize that you need a competitive advantage to attract customers. It could be price, better service, a better product—but it has to be something. Don't expect to be successful unless you can do something better than your rivals!

Hire the right people to help you. Remember what we learned about specialization: embrace it. You don't have to be an expert tax accountant, manager, and marketer. Offload some of these tasks on others who are better at them, and focus on doing what you do best. However, once you find the right people to help, treat them well and provide an environment in which they will thrive and give their all.

CONCEPTS YOU SHOULD KNOW

price taker (p. 272)   signals (p. 289)   sunk costs (p. 286)
profit-maximizing rule (p. 278)

QUESTIONS FOR REVIEW

1. What are the necessary conditions for a perfectly competitive market to exist?

2. Describe the two-step process used to identify the profit-maximizing level of output.

3. Under what circumstances will a firm have to decide whether to operate or to shut down?

4. What is the difference between the decision to go out of business and the decision to operate or to shut down?

5. How do profits and losses act as signals that guide producers to use resources to make what society wants most?

6. What are sunk costs? Give an example from your own experience.

7. Why do competitive firms earn zero economic profit in the long run?

STUDY PROBLEMS (✱ *solved at the end of the section*)

1. Using the definition of a price taker as your guide, for the following industries explain why the outcome does not meet the definition.
   a. the pizza delivery business
   b. the home improvement business
   c. cell phone companies
   d. cereals

2. A local snow cone business sells snow cones in one size for $3 each. It has the following cost and output structure per hour:

Output (cones per hour)	Total cost (per hour)
0	$60
10	$90
20	$110
30	$120
40	$125
50	$135
60	$150
70	$175
80	$225

   a. Calculate the total revenue for the business at each rate of output.

   b. Calculate the total profit for the business at each rate of output.
   c. Is the business operating in the short run or the long run?
   d. Calculate the profit-maximizing rate of output using the MR = MC rule. (**Hint:** to do this, you should first compute the marginal revenue and marginal cost from the table.)

3. Determine whether the following statements are true or false. Explain your answers.
   a. A firm will make a profit when the price it charges exceeds the average variable cost of the chosen output level.
   b. In order to maximize profits in the short run, a firm must minimize its costs.
   c. If economic profit is positive, firms will exit the industry in the short run.
   d. A firm that receives a price greater than its average variable costs but less than its average total costs should shut down.

4. In the table at the top of p. 300, fill in the blanks. After you have completed the entire table, determine the profit-maximizing output.

Output	Price	Total revenue	Marginal revenue	Total cost	Marginal cost	Total profit
1	$20	___	___	$40	___	−$20
2	___	___	___	$50	___	___
3	___	___	___	$60	___	___
4	___	___	___	$65	5	___
5	___	___	___	$85	___	___
6	___	$120	___	$120	___	___

5. Use the graph to answer the questions that follow.

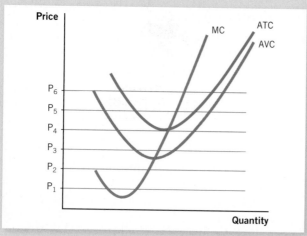

a. At what prices is the firm making an economic profit, breaking even, and experiencing an economic loss?
b. At what prices would the firm shut down?
c. At what prices does the firm's short-run supply curve exist? At what prices does the firm's long-run supply curve exist?

✳ 6. Identify as many errors as you can in the following graph.

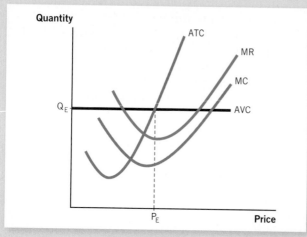

7. A firm is experiencing a loss of $5,000 per year. The firm has fixed costs of $8,000 per year.
   a. Should the firm operate in the short run or shut down?
   b. If the situation persists into the long run, should the firm stay in the industry or go out of business?
   c. Now suppose that the firm's fixed costs are $2,000. How would this change its short-run and long-run decisions?

8. Three students at the same school hear about the success of cookie delivery businesses on college campuses. Each student decides to open a local service. The individual supply schedules are shown below.

Delivery charge	Quantity supplied		
	Esra	Remzi	Camilo
$1	2	3	6
$2	4	6	7
$3	6	9	8
$4	8	12	9
$5	10	15	10
$6	12	18	11

a. Draw the individual supply curves.
b. Sum the individual supply schedules to compute the short-run industry supply schedule.
c. Draw the industry supply curve.

9. Do you agree or disagree with the following statement? "A profit-maximizing, perfectly competitive firm should select the output level at which the difference between the marginal revenue and marginal cost is the greatest." Explain your answer.

10. Barney's snow removal service is a profit-maximizing, competitive firm. Barney clears driveways for $10 each. His total cost each day is $250, and half of his total costs are fixed. If Barney clears 20 driveways a day, should he continue to operate or shut down? If this situation persists, will Barney stay in the industry or exit?

✳ 11. Suppose you are the owner of a firm producing jelly beans. Your production costs are
shown in the table. Initially, you produce 100
boxes of jelly beans per time period. Then a
new customer calls and places an order for an
additional box of jelly beans, requiring you to
increase your output to 101 boxes. She offers
you $1.50 for the additional box. Should you
produce it? Why or why not?

Jelly Bean Production

Boxes	Average cost per box
100	$1.00
101	$1.01
102	$1.02
103	$1.03

SOLVED PROBLEMS

6. Here is the corrected graph with the errors
struck out and some explanation below.

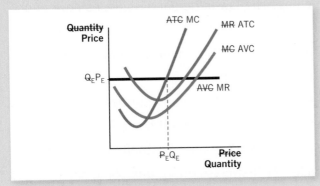

Also, the ATC and AVC curves did not intersect the MC curve at their minimum points.
That is corrected here.

11. This problem requires marginal thinking.
We know the profit-maximizing rule, or
MR = MC. Here all we need to do is compare
the additional costs, or MC, against the additional revenue, or MR, to see if the deal is a
good idea. We know that MR = $1.50, because
that is what the customer is offering to pay for
another box of jelly beans. Now we need to
calculate the marginal cost of producing the
additional box.

Jelly Bean Production

Boxes	Average cost per box	Total cost	Marginal cost
100	$1.00	$100.00	—
101	$1.01	$102.01	$2.01
102	$1.02	$104.04	$2.03
103	$1.03	$106.09	$2.05

First we compute the total cost. To do this,
we multiply the number of boxes, listed in the
first column, by the average cost, shown in the
second column. The results are shown in the total
cost column.

Next we find the marginal cost. Recall that the
marginal cost is the amount that it costs to produce one more unit. So we subtract the total cost
of producing 101 boxes from the total cost of
producing 100. For 101 boxes, MC = $102.01 −
$100.00, or $2.01. Since MR − MC is $1.50 −
$2.01, producing the 101st box would create a
loss of $0.51. Therefore, at a price of $1.50, your
firm should not produce the 101st box.

CHAPTER

10 | Understanding Monopoly

Monopolists always make a profit.

In this chapter, we will explore another market structure: monopoly. Many people mistakenly believe that monopolists always make a profit.

MIS CONCEPTION

This is not true. Monopolists enjoy market power for their specific product, but they cannot force consumers to purchase what they are selling. The law of demand regulates how much a monopolist can charge. This means that when a monopolist charges more, people buy less. It also means that if demand is low, a monopolist may experience a loss instead of a profit.

While pure monopolies are unusual, this market structure is important to study because many markets exhibit some form of monopolistic behavior. Microsoft, the National Football League, the United States Postal Service (for first-class mail), and some small-town businesses are all examples of monopoly. In this chapter, we explore the conditions that give rise to monopolies and also the ways in which monopoly power can erode.

The typical result of monopoly is higher prices and less output than we find in a competitive market. Once we understand the market conditions that give rise to a monopoly, we will consider how governments seek to address the problems that monopolies present, and also how governments can be the cause of monopolies as well.

A small town's sole veterinarian functions as a monopolist.

BIG QUESTIONS

* How are monopolies created?
* How much do monopolies charge, and how much do they produce?
* What are the problems with, and solutions for, monopoly?

How Are Monopolies Created?

As we explained in Chapter 3, a monopoly is characterized by a single seller who produces a well-defined product for which there are no good substitutes. Two conditions enable a single seller to become a monopolist. First, the firm must have something unique to sell. Second, it must have a way to prevent potential competitors from entering the market.

Monopolies occur in many places and for several different reasons. For example, natural gas, water, and electricity are all examples of a monopoly that occurs naturally because of economies of scale. But monopolies can also occur when the government regulates the amount of competition. For example, trash pickup, street vending, taxicab rides, and ferry service are often licensed by local governments. This has the effect of limiting competition and creating **monopoly power**, which measures the ability of firms to set the price for a good.

Monopoly power measures the ability of firms to set the price for a good.

A monopoly operates in a market with high **barriers to entry**, which are restrictions that make it difficult for new firms to enter a market. As a result, monopolists have no competition nor any threat of competition. High barriers to entry insulate the monopolist from competition, which means that many monopolists enjoy long-run economic profits. There are two basic ways that this can happen: through natural barriers and through government-created barriers. Let's look at each.

Barriers to entry are restrictions that make it difficult for new firms to enter a market.

Natural Barriers

Some barriers exist naturally within the market. These include control of resources, problems in raising capital, and economies of scale.

Control of Resources

The best way to limit competition is to control a resource that is essential in the production process. This extremely effective barrier to entry is hard to accomplish. If you control a scarce resource, other competitors will not be able to find enough of it to compete. For example, in the early twentieth century the Aluminum Company of America (ALCOA) made a concerted effort to buy bauxite mines around the globe. Within a decade, the company owned 90% of the world's bauxite, an essential element in making aluminum. This effort enabled ALCOA to crowd out potential competitors and achieve dominance in the aluminum market.

Problems in Raising Capital

Monopolists are usually very big companies that have grown over an extended period. Even if you had a wonderful business plan, it is unlikely that a bank or a venture capital company would lend you enough money to start a business that could compete effectively with a well-established company. For example, if you wanted to design a new operating system to compete with Microsoft, you would need tens of millions of dollars to fund your start-up. Lenders provide capital for business projects when the chance of success is high, but the chance of a new company successfully competing against an entrenched monopoly is not high. Consequently, raising capital to compete against an entrenched monopolist is very difficult.

Economies of Scale

In Chapter 8, we saw that average costs fall as production expands. Low unit costs, and the low prices that follow, give larger firms the ability to drive out rivals. For example, imagine a market for electric power where companies compete to generate electricity and deliver it through their own grids. In such a market, it would be technically possible to run competing sets of wire to every home and business in the community, but the cost of installation and the maintenance of separate lines to deliver electricity would be both prohibitive and impractical. Even if a handful of smaller electric companies could produce electricity at the same cost, each would have to pay to deliver power through its own grid. This would be inefficient.

In an industry that enjoys large economies of scale, production costs per unit continue to fall as the firm expands. Smaller rivals then will have much higher average costs that prevent them from competing with the larger company. As a result, firms in the industry tend to combine over time. This leads to the creation of a **natural monopoly**, which occurs when a single large firm has lower costs than any potential smaller competitor.

A natural monopoly occurs when a single large firm has lower costs than any potential smaller competitor.

Government-Created Barriers

The creation of a monopoly can be either intentional or an unintended consequence of a government policy. Government-enforced statutes and regulations, such as laws and regulations covering licenses and patents, limit the scope of competition by creating barriers to entry.

Licensing

In many instances, it makes sense to give a single firm the exclusive right to sell a good or service. In order to minimize negative externalities, governments establish monopolies, or near monopolies, through licensing requirements. For example, in some communities trash collection is licensed to a single company. The rationale usually involves economies of scale, but there are also costs to consider. Since firms cannot collect trash without a government-issued operating license, opportunities to enter the business are limited, which leaves consumers with a one-size-fits-all level of service. This is the opposite of what we'd expect to see in a competitive market, where there would be many varieties of service at different price points.

Licensing also creates an opportunity for corruption. In fact, in many parts of the world bribery is such a common practice that it often determines which companies receive the licenses in the first place.

Patents and Copyright Law

Another area in which the government fosters monopoly is that of patents and copyrights. For example, when musicians create a new song and copyright their work, they earn royalties over the life of the copyright. The copyright is the government's assurance that no one else can play or sell the work without the artist's permission. Similarly, when a pharmaceutical company develops a new drug, the company receives a patent under which it has the exclusive right to market and sell the drug for as long as the patent is in force. By granting patents and copyrights to developers and inventors, the government creates monopolies. Patents and copyrights create stronger incentives to develop new drugs and produce new music than would exist if market competitors could immediately copy inventions. As a result, pharmaceutical companies invest heavily in developing new drugs and musicians devote their time to writing new music. At least in theory, these activities make our society a healthier and culturally richer place. After the patent or copyright expires, rivals can mimic the invention. This opens up the market and provides dual benefits: wider access to the innovation and more sellers—both of which are good for consumers in the long run.

Incentives

As appealing as the process described in the previous paragraph sounds, nothing works quite as well as advertised. Many economists wonder if patents and copyrights are necessary or have unintended consequences. For instance, illegal file sharing, downloads, and pirated DVDs are common in the music and movie business. At first glance, this appears to be a revenue loss for legitimate companies. But often the companies benefit from the exposure. For example, when a music video goes viral on YouTube, the exposure causes many people to buy the original artist's work. Consider Justin Bieber. He managed to leverage his YouTube fame into a successful album launch, concert tours, and appearance fees that might never have occurred if a music studio had tightly controlled his sound.

Does Justin Bieber need copyright protection to make money?

ECONOMICS IN THE REAL WORLD

Merck's Zocor

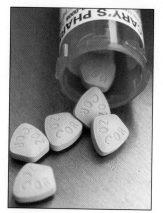

Do you want fries with that cholesterol medication?

In 1985, the pharmaceutical giant Merck released Zocor, the first statin drug for treating high cholesterol. The company spent millions of dollars developing the drug and bringing it to the market. Zocor is highly effective and has probably saved or extended millions of lives. It was also highly profitable for Merck, generating over $4 billion in annual revenues before the patent ran out in 2006. Zocor is now available in an inexpensive generic formulation at a price that is 80 to 90% lower than the original patent-protected price.

Would Zocor have been developed without patent protection? Probably not. Merck would have had little incentive to incur the cost of developing a cholesterol treatment if other companies could immediately copy the drug. In this case, society benefits because of the twofold nature of patents: they give firms the incentive to innovate, but they also limit the amount of time the patent is in place, thereby guaranteeing that competitive forces will govern long-run access to the product. ✳

TABLE 10.1
The Characteristics of Monopolies

- One seller

- A unique product without close substitutes

- High barriers to entry

- Price making

Though market-created and government-created barriers occur for different reasons, they have the same effect—they create monopolies. Table 10.1 summarizes the key characteristics of monopolies. In the next section, we will examine how the monopolist determines the price it charges and how much to produce.

PRACTICE WHAT YOU KNOW

Monopoly: Can You Spot the Monopolist?

Here are three questions to test your understanding of the conditions necessary for monopoly power to arise.

Question: Is Lebron James (an NBA superstar) a monopolist?

Answer: Lebron is a uniquely talented basketball player. Because of his physical gifts, he can do things that other players can't. But that does not mean there are no substitutes for him around the league. So no, Lebron is not a monopolist. Perhaps more important, his near-monopoly power is limited because new players are always entering the league and trying to establish themselves as the best.

Question: Is a sole small-town hairdresser a monopolist?

Answer: For all practical purposes, yes. He or she sells a unique service with inelastic demand. Because the nearest competitor is in the next town, the local hairdresser enjoys significant monopoly power. At the same time, the town's size limits potential competitors from entering the market, since the small community may not be able to support two hairdressers.

Monopoly profits!

Question: Is Amazon a monopolist?

Answer: Amazon is the nation's largest bookseller, with sales that dwarf those of its nearest retail rival, Barnes & Noble. But Amazon's market share does not make it a monopolist. Amazon is a lot like Walmart: it relies on low prices to fend off its rivals.

ECONOMICS IN THE MEDIA

Barriers to Entry

Forrest Gump

In this 1994 movie, Tom Hanks's character, Forrest Gump, keeps his promise to his deceased friend, Bubba, to go into the shrimping business after leaving the army. Forrest invests $25,000 in an old shrimp boat, but the going is tough—he only catches a handful of shrimp because of the competition for space in the shrimping waters. So Forrest tries naming his boat for good luck and brings on a first mate, Lieutenant Dan, who unfortunately is less knowledgeable and resourceful than Forrest. The fledgling enterprise continues to struggle, and eventually Forrest decides to pray for shrimp. Soon after, Forrest's boat, the *Jenny*, is caught out in the Gulf of Mexico during a hurricane. Miraculously, the *Jenny* makes it through the storm while the other shrimp boats, all anchored in the harbor, are destroyed.

Forrest recounts the events to some strangers while sitting on a park bench:

Forrest: After that, shrimping was easy. Since people still needed them shrimps for shrimp cocktails and barbecues and all, and we were the *only* boat left standing, Bubba-Gump shrimp's what they got. We got a whole bunch of boats. Twelve *Jennys*, big old warehouse. We even have hats that say "Bubba-Gump" on them. Bubba-Gump Shrimp. A household name.

Man on the bench: Hold on there, boy. Are you telling me you're the owner of the Bubba-Gump Shrimp Corporation?

Forrest: Yes. We got more money than Davy Crockett.

Man on the bench: Boy, I heard some whoppers in my time, but that tops them all. We were sitting next to a millionaire.

The film suggests that Forrest's good luck—being in the right place at the right time—explains how he became a millionaire. But is this realistic? Let's leave the movie's storyline for a moment and consider the situation in real-world economic terms.

If shrimping were easy, everyone would do it.

Remember, Forrest was able to enter the business simply by purchasing a boat. To be sure, he would catch more shrimp in the short run, while the other boats were docked for repairs. However, once the competitors' boats return, they will catch shrimp and Forrest's short-run profits will disappear. The reason we can be so confident of this result is that shrimping, with low barriers to entry and undifferentiated product, is an industry that closely mirrors a perfectly competitive market. So when profits exist, new entrants will expand the supply produced and profits will return to the break-even level. Having Forrest become a "millionaire" makes for a good movie, but none of the elements are in place to suggest that he could attain a permanent monopoly. Forrest does not control an essential resource; the other shrimp captains will have little difficulty raising capital to repair their boats, and the economies of scale in this situation are small.

How Much Do Monopolies Charge, and How Much Do They Produce?

Both monopolists and firms in a competitive market seek to earn a profit. However, a monopolist is the sole provider of a product and holds market power. Thus, monopolists are *price makers*. A **price maker** has some control over the price it charges. As you learned in Chapter 9, a firm in a competitive market is a price taker.

A **price maker** has some control over the price it charges.

We can see the difference graphically in Figure 10.1. The demand curve for the product of a firm in a competitive market, shown here in panel (a), is horizontal. When individual firms are price takers, they have no control over what they charge. In other words, demand is perfectly elastic—or horizontal— because every firm sells the same product. Demand for an individual firm's product exists only at the price determined by the market, and each firm is such a small part of the market that it can sell its entire output without lowering the price. In contrast, because a monopolist is the only firm—the sole provider—in the industry, the demand curve for its product, shown in panel (b), constitutes the market demand curve. But the demand curve is downward sloping, which limits the monopolist's ability to make a profit. The monopolist would like to exploit its market power by charging a high price to many customers; however, the law of demand, which identifies an inverse relationship between price and

FIGURE 10.1

Comparing the Demand Curves of Perfectly Competitive Firms and Monopolists

(a) Firms in a competitive market have a horizontal demand curve. (b) Since the monopolist is the sole provider of the good or service, the demand for its product constitutes the industry—or market—demand curve, which is downward sloping. So while the perfectly competitive firm has no control over the price it charges, the monopolist gets to search for the profit-maximizing price and output.

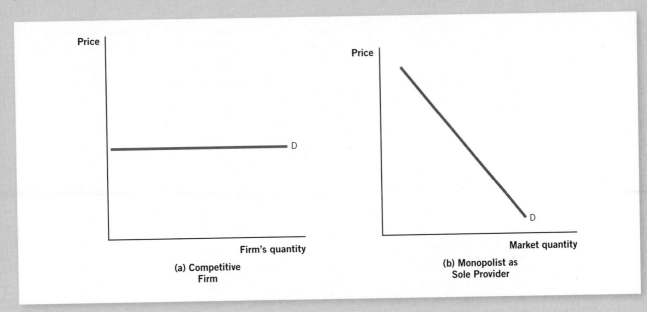

quantity demanded, dictates otherwise. Unlike the horizontal demand curve of a firm in a competitive market, the downward-sloping demand curve of the monopolist has many price-output combinations. If the monopolist charges a high price, only a few customers will buy the good. If it charges a low price, many customers will buy the good. As a result, monopolists get to search for the profit-maximizing price and output.

The Profit-Maximizing Rule for the Monopolist

Marginal thinking

A competitive firm can sell all it produces at the existing market price. But a monopolist, because of the downward-sloping demand curve, must search for the most profitable price. To maximize profits, a monopolist can use the profit-maximizing rule we introduced in Chapter 9: MR = MC. But the monopolist's marginal revenue is computed differently.

Table 10.2 shows the marginal revenue for a cable company that serves a small community. Notice the inverse relationship between output (quantity of customers) and price in columns 1 and 2: as the price goes down, the quantity of customers goes up. Total revenue is calculated by multiplying output by price (TR = Q × P). At first, total revenue rises as the price falls. Once the price becomes too low ($40), total revenue begins to fall. As a result, the total revenue function in column 3 initially rises to $250,000 before it falls off. The final column, marginal revenue, shows the change (Δ) in total revenue. Here we see positive (though falling) marginal revenue associated with prices above $50 (see the green dollar amounts in column 4). Below $50, marginal revenue becomes negative (see the red dollar amounts in column 4).

TABLE 10.2

Calculating the Monopolist's Marginal Revenue

(1) Quantity of customers (Q) Formula:	(2) Price of service (P)	(3) Total revenue (TR) (Q) × (P)	(4) Marginal revenue per 1,000 customers (MR) Δ (TR)
0	$100	$0.00	
1,000	$90	90,000	$90,000
2,000	$80	160,000	70,000
3,000	$70	210,000	50,000
4,000	$60	240,000	30,000
5,000	$50	250,000	10,000
6,000	$40	240,000	−10,000
7,000	$30	210,000	−30,000
8,000	$20	160,000	−50,000
9,000	$10	90,000	−70,000
10,000	$0	0.00	−90,000

Trade-offs

The change in total revenue reflects the trade-off that a monopolist encounters in trying to attract additional customers. To gain additional output, the firm must lower its price. But the lower price is available to both new and existing customers. The impact on total revenue therefore depends on how many new customers buy the good because of the lower price.

Figure 10.2 uses the linear demand schedule from Table 10.2 to illustrate the two separate effects that determine marginal revenue. First, there is a *price effect*, which reflects how the lower prices affect revenue. If the price of service drops from $70 to $60, each of the 3,000 existing customers will save $10. The firm would lose $10 × 3,000, or $30,000 in revenue, represented by the yellow-shaded area on the graph. But dropping the price also has an *output effect*, which reflects how the lower prices affect the number of customers. Since 1,000 new customers buy the product (that is, cable service) when the price drops to $60, revenue increases by $60 × 1,000, or $60,000, represented by the blue-shaded area. The output effect ($60,000) is greater than the price effect ($30,000). When we subtract the $30,000 in lost revenue (the yellow rectangle) from the $60,000 in revenue gained (the blue rectangle), this yields $30,000 in marginal revenue at an output level between 3,000 and 4,000 customers.

Lost revenues associated with the price effect are always subtracted from the revenue gains created by the output effect. Now let's think of this data at the individual level. Since the firm adds 1,000 new customers, the marginal revenue per customer—$30,000 ÷ 1,000 new customers—is $30. Notice that

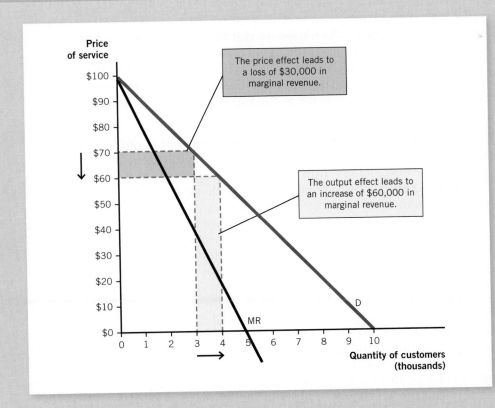

FIGURE 10.2

The Marginal Revenue Curve and the Demand Curve

A price drop has two effects. (1) Existing customers now pay less—this is the price effect. (2) New customers decide to purchase the good for the first time—this is the output effect. The relative size of the two effects, as shown by the yellow and blue rectangles, determines whether the firm is able to increase its revenue by lowering its price.

this is less than the price, $60, that the firm charges. Since there is a price effect whenever the price drops, the marginal revenue curve lies below the demand curve. Therefore the *y* intercept is the same for the demand and marginal revenue curves and the *x* intercept of the MR curve is half of the demand curve's.

At high price levels—where demand is elastic—the price effect is small relative to the output effect. As the price drops, demand slowly becomes more inelastic. At this point, the output effect diminishes and the price effect increases. This means that as the price falls it becomes harder for the firm to acquire enough new customers to make up for the difference in lost revenue. Eventually, the price effect becomes larger than the output effect. When this happens, marginal revenue becomes negative and dips below the *x* axis, as shown by the MR curve in Figure 10.2. When the marginal revenue is negative, the firm cannot be profit-maximizing. This outcome puts an upper limit on the amount that the firm will produce. This is evident in Table 10.2: once the price becomes too low, the firm's marginal revenue is negative.

Marginal thinking

Deciding How Much to Produce

In Chapter 9, we explored the profit-maximizing rule for a firm in a competitive market. This rule also applies to a monopolist: marginal revenue should be equal to marginal cost. However, there is one big difference: a monopolist does not charge a price equal to marginal revenue.

Figure 10.3 illustrates the profit-maximizing decision-making process for a monopolist. We will use a two-step process to determine the monopolist's profit:

1. Locate the point at which the firm will maximize its profits: MR = MC.
2. Set the price. From the point at which MR = MC, determine the profit-maximizing output, Q. From Q, move up along the dashed line until it intersects with the demand curve (D). From that point, move horizontally until you come to the *y* axis. This tells us the price (P) the monopolist should charge.

Using this two-step process, we can determine the monopolist's profit. Locate the average total cost, C, of making Q units along the dashed line. From that point, move horizontally until you come to the *y* axis. This tells us the cost of making Q units. The difference between the price and the cost multiplied by Q tells us the profit (or loss) the firm makes.

Since the price (P) is higher than the average total cost (C), the firm makes the profit shown in the green rectangle. For example, if a small-town veterinarian charges $50 for a routine examination and incurs a cost of $35 for every exam, she earns $15 every time she sees a pet. If she provides 1,000 examinations a year, her total economic profit is $15 × 1,000, or $15,000.

Table 10.3 summarizes the differences between a competitive market and a monopoly. The competitive firm must take the price established in the market. If it does not operate efficiently, it cannot survive. Nor can it make an economic profit in the long run. The monopolist operates very differently. Since high barriers to entry limit competition, the monopolist may be able to earn long-run profits by restricting output. It operates inefficiently from society's perspective, and it has significant market power.

FIGURE 10.3

The Monopolist's Profit Maximization

The firm uses the profit-maximizing rule to locate the point at which MR = MC. This determines the ideal output level, Q. Since the price (which is determined by the demand curve) is higher than the average total cost curve (ATC) along the dashed line at quantity Q, the firm makes the profit shown in the green-shaded area.

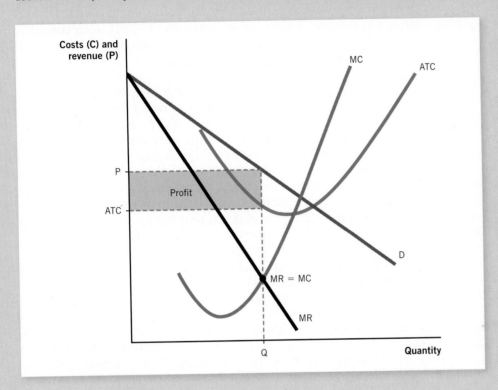

TABLE 10.3

The Major Differences between a Monopoly and a Competitive Market

Competitive market	Monopoly
Many firms	One firm
Produces an efficient level of output (since P = MC)	Produces less than the efficient level of output (since P > MC)
Cannot earn long-run economic profits	May earn long-run economic profits
Has no market power (is a price taker)	Has significant market power (is a price maker)

ECONOMICS IN THE REAL WORLD

The Broadband Monopoly

Many markets in the United States have only a single high-speed Internet provider. The technology race strongly favors cable over competing DSL. In fact, DSL is provided by telephone companies using aging copper wiring, whereas cable companies use the latest fiberoptic technology. When it comes to truly high-speed Internet access, cable companies benefit from considerable barriers to entry. In many places, Comcast effectively owns access to the Internet and can price its service accordingly.

The cable monopoly on high-speed Internet access resonates in two ways. First, consumers increasingly need more bandwidth to stream movies, view YouTube, and load media-rich web sites. A slow connection can make surfing the Internet a chore. In other words, consumer demand is high and very inelastic. Second, businesses rely on bandwidth to maintain web sites and provide services to customers. Companies such as Netflix, which delivers streaming content over the Internet, rely on access to a relatively affordable broadband Internet connection. Therefore, businesses also have high demand that is quite inelastic. For this reason, many people argue that relatively inexpensive access to the Internet is crucial if it is to continue to be an engine of economic growth. And without competition, access will remain expensive.

Our dependence on the Internet invites a larger question. Where the bandwidth is controlled by only one provider, should the government have a role in providing the infrastructure, or cables, in order to allow more access? This is a concern in metropolitan areas served by only one high-speed provider. Meanwhile, small rural communities may have no high-speed access at all. For example, Chireno, Texas, has a population of 413 people and remains off the grid. Cable companies wouldn't make enough profit to connect these low-density areas, but this makes it very difficult for their residents to participate in today's economy. ✳

Does Comcast own the Internet in your area?

PRACTICE WHAT YOU KNOW

Monopoly Profits: How Much Do Monopolists Make?

Question: A monopolist always earns _____ economic profit.

a. a positive

b. zero

c. a negative

d. We cannot be sure about the profit a monopolist makes.

Is there a key profit takeaway?

Answers:

a. Incorrect. A monopolist is a price maker with considerable market power. This usually, but not always, leads to a positive economic profit.

b. Incorrect. Zero economic profit exists in competitive markets in the long run. Since a monopolist, by definition, does not operate in competitive markets, it is protected from additional competition that would drive its profit to zero.

c. Incorrect. Whoa there! Negative profit? There is absolutely no reason to think that would happen. Monopolists sell a unique product without close substitutes in a market that is insulated from competitive pressures. Time to reread the first part of this chapter more carefully!

d. Correct. Since a monopolist benefits from barriers that limit the entry of competitors into the industry, we would expect an economic profit. However, this is not guaranteed. Monopolies do not control the demand for the product they sell. Consequently, in the short run the monopolist may experience either a profit (if demand is high) or a loss (if demand is low).

What Are the Problems with, and Solutions for, Monopoly?

Monopolies can adversely affect society by restricting output and charging higher prices than sellers in competitive markets do. This activity causes monopolies to operate inefficiently, provide less choice, promote an unhealthy form of competition known as *rent seeking* (see below), and make economic profits that fail to guide resources to their highest-valued use. The occurrence of an inefficient output is known as **market failure**. Once we have examined the problems with monopoly, we will turn to the potential solutions for it.

Market failure
occurs when the output level of a good is inefficient.

The Problems with Monopoly

Monopolies result in an inefficient level of output, provide less choice to consumers, and encourage monopoly firms to lobby for government protection. Let's look at each of these concerns.

Inefficient Output and Price

From an efficiency standpoint, the monopolist charges too much and produces too little. This result is evident in Figure 10.4, which shows what happens when a competitive market (denoted by the subscript *c*) ends up being controlled by a monopoly (denoted by the subscript *m*).

First, imagine a competitive fishing industry in which each boat catches a small portion of the fish, as shown in panel (a). Each firm is a price taker that must charge the market price. In contrast, panel (b) depicts pricing and output decisions for a monopoly fishing industry when it confronts the same cost structure as presented in panel (a). When a single firm controls the entire fishing ground, it is the sole supplier; to set its price, it considers the downward-sloping demand and marginal revenue curves that serve the entire market. Therefore, it sets marginal revenue equal to marginal cost. This yields a smaller output ($Q_M < Q_C$) than the competitive industry and a higher price ($P_M > P_C$).

FIGURE 10.4

When a Competitive Industry Becomes a Monopoly

(a) In a competitive industry, the intersection of supply and demand determines the price (P_C) and quantity (Q_C). (b) When a monopoly controls an entire industry, the supply curve becomes the monopolist's marginal cost curve. The monopolist uses MR = MC to determine its price (P_M) and quantity (Q_M). This means that the monopolist charges a higher price and produces a smaller output than when an entire industry is populated with competitive firms.

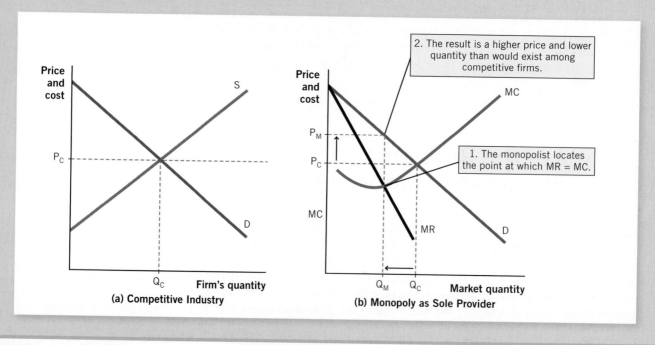

(a) Competitive Industry

(b) Monopoly as Sole Provider

2. The result is a higher price and lower quantity than would exist among competitive firms.

1. The monopolist locates the point at which MR = MC.

FIGURE 10.5

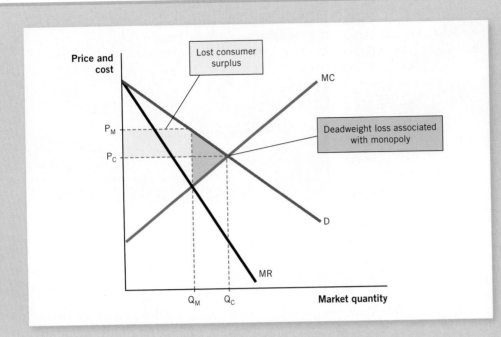

The Deadweight Loss of Monopoly

Since the profit-maximizing monopolist produces an output of Q_M, an amount that is less than Q_C, this results in the deadweight loss shown in the yellow triangle. The blue rectangle is the consumer surplus that is transferred to the monopolist.

The smaller output level is not efficient. In addition, the price the monopolist charges, P_M, is significantly above the marginal cost at the profit-maximizing level of output, which is higher than the price when there are many smaller competing firms.

Figure 10.5 captures the deadweight loss (see Chapter 6) of the monopoly. The monopolist charges too high a price and produces too little of the product, so some consumers who would benefit from a competitive market lose out. Since the demand curve, or the willingness to pay, is greater than the marginal cost between output levels Q_M and Q_C, society would be better off if output expanded to Q_C. But a profit-maximizing monopolist will limit output to Q_M. The result, a deadweight loss equal to the area of the yellow triangle, is inefficient for society. Consumer surplus is also transferred to the monopolist, as shown in the blue rectangle.

Few Choices for Consumers

Another problem associated with monopoly is the lack of choice. Have you ever wondered why cable companies offer their services in bundles? You can buy basic, digital, and premium packages, but the one thing you cannot do is buy just the cable channels you want. This is because cable companies function like monopolies, and monopolies limit consumer choice. Since the monopolist sells a good with few close substitutes, it can leverage its market power to offer product features that benefit itself at the expense of consumer choice. With a monopolist, there is only one outlet: if you do not like the design, features, price, or any other aspect of the good provided, you have few other options. For example, in many small communities there is only one cable television provider. In a hypothetical competitive market, we would expect each company to provide more options to satisfy consumer

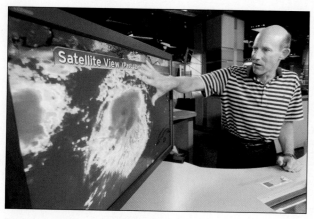

Would you rather watch the Weather Channel . . .

. . . or SportsCenter?

preferences. For instance, in a competitive market you should be able to find a firm willing to sell only ESPN and the Weather Channel. In a monopoly situation, though, the cable company forces you to choose between buying a little more cable than you really need or going without cable altogether. Because the cable company has a good deal of market power, it can restrict your options and force you to buy more in order to get what you want. This is a profitable strategy for the company but a bad outcome for consumers.

Rent Seeking

Rent seeking
occurs when resources are used to secure monopoly rights through the political process.

Trade
creates
value

The attempt to gain monopoly power encourages *rent seeking*. **Rent seeking** occurs when resources are used to secure monopoly rights through the political process. Throughout this text, we have seen the desirable effects of competition: lower prices, increased efficiency, and enhanced service and quality. However, rent seeking is a form of competition that produces an undesirable result. When firms compete to become monopolists, there is one winner without any of the benefits usually associated with competition. Consider the U.S. steel industry, which has been in decline for many years and has lost market share to steel firms in China, Japan, and Europe. If a U.S. steel company is losing money because of foreign competition, it can address the situation in one of two ways. It can modernize by building new facilities and using the latest equipment and techniques. (In other words, it can become competitive with the overseas competition.) Or it can lobby the government to limit imports. The domestic steel industry chose to lobby, and in 2002 the George W. Bush administration imposed tariffs of up to 30% on imported steel. Here is the danger: when lobbying is less expensive than building a new factory, the company will choose to lobby! If politicians give in and the lobbying succeeds, society is adversely affected because the gains from trade are smaller.

A former steel plant in Bethlehem, Pennsylvania.

PRACTICE WHAT YOU KNOW

Problems with Monopoly: Coffee Consolidation

A community has many competing coffee shops.

Question: How can we use the market demand curve to illustrate the consumer and producer surplus created by a competitive market?

Answer:

In a competitive market, supply and demand determine the price and quantity.

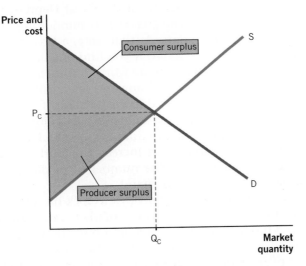

When companies compete, consumers win.

Question: Now imagine that all the independent coffee shops combine under one fictional franchise, known as Harbucks. How can we create a new graph that illustrates the consumer surplus, producer surplus, and deadweight loss that occur when a monopoly takes over the market?

Answer:

In this figure, we see that the consumer surplus has shrunk; the producer surplus has increased; and the higher price charged by Harbucks creates deadweight loss. Allowing a monopolist to capture a market does not benefit consumers and is inefficient for society.

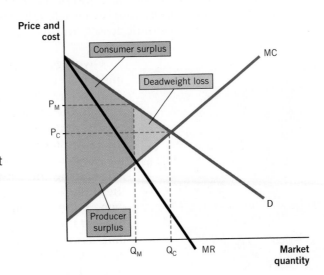

Supply and demand tell us that steel prices will rise in the absence of competition. This outcome is inefficient. Also, instead of pushing for legislation that grants market power, the lobbying resources could have gone into the production of useful products. As a result, the process of rent seeking benefits the rent seeker and yields little direct benefit for society.

ECONOMICS IN THE REAL WORLD

New York City Taxis

In 1932, during the depths of the Great Depression, New York City decided to license taxi cabs. The goal was to standardize fares, operating procedures, and safety requirements. At that time, a taxi cab license, or medallion, was available at no cost. Today, if you find one on the resale market, it costs over $300,000. The medallions are worth so much because the owners often make six-figure incomes from leasing and operating taxis in New York City.

The city did not intend to create an artificial monopoly, but it did. From 1932 until the 1990s, the number of medallions, which represents the supply of taxis, was fixed at approximately 12,000. During the same 60-year period, population growth and an increase in tourism caused the demand for taxi services to rise steeply. The number of medallions would have had to quadruple to keep up with demand.

In recent years, the city of New York has offered three auctions to introduce more medallions into the market. These auctions have netted the city over $100 million in revenue and have raised the number of medallions to slightly more than 13,000. Each of the current medallion holders owns a small part of an artificially created government monopoly. Collectively, the holders of medallions own a monopoly on taxi services worth $13,000 \times \$300,000$, or about $4 billion. Yet demand for the medallions continues to far outpace the supply, and the market price has steadily climbed to an astonishing level.

Imagine what would happen if the city lifted restrictions on the number of available medallions and gave them out to any qualified applicant. Applications for licenses would increase, and profits for cab drivers and cab companies would fall until supply roughly equaled demand. Conversely, if taxi cab drivers experienced economic losses, the number of taxis operating would decline until the losses disappeared.

Owning and operating a taxi has all the makings of an industry with low barriers to entry. The only reason that medallions are worth so much is the artificially created barrier to entry—this protects medallion holders from competition. Restoring competitive markets would make each current medallion holder worse off by reducing the existing barriers to entry into the industry. This would cause the medallion owners' profits to fall. Therefore, it is not surprising that they seek to keep the number of medallions as low as possible. Since monopolists make profits by charging higher prices than firms in competitive markets do, no one who already has a medallion wants the supply to expand. ✳

Medallion owners in New York City are protected from competition.

The Problems of Monopoly

One-Man Band

This Pixar short animation from 2005 tells the story of two street musicians competing for the gold coin of a young peasant girl who wants to make a wish in the town square's fountain.

When the short opens, there is only one street musician in the plaza. He performs a little bit and almost coaxes the girl to place her coin in his tip basket. Just as she is about to give it to him, another street musician starts playing. Since there is no longer a single performer, a spirited rivalry develops between the two very eager musicians vying to win the little girl's attention and money.

This clever story illustrates monopoly and competition in a number of compelling ways. The first street musician plays only halfheartedly in the beginning, when he does not face any competition. Indeed, lack

A little competition goes a long way to reduce monopoly.

of choice is one of the major criticisms of monopoly. But then the second musician's arrival changes the dynamic, inspiring a spirited competition for the gold coin. The "one-man band" is not really a monopolist; he is providing a service that has many good substitutes and lacks the ability to keep imitators from entering the market.

Solutions to the Problems of Monopoly

We have learned that monopolies do not produce as much social welfare as competitive markets do. As a result, public policy approaches attempt to address this problem. The policy solutions include breaking up the monopolist, reducing trade barriers, and regulating markets.

Breaking Up the Monopolist

Eliminating deadweight loss and restoring efficiency can be as simple as promoting competition. From 1913 until 1982, AT&T had a monopoly on the delivery of telephone services. As the years passed, however, it became progressively harder for AT&T to defend its position that having a single provider of phone services was good for consumers. By the early 1980s, AT&T was spending over $300 million to fend off antitrust suits from the states, the federal government, and many private firms. The AT&T monopoly ended in 1982, when enormous pressure from the government led the company to split into eight smaller companies. Suddenly, AT&T had to compete to survive. The newly competitive phone market forced each of the phone companies to expand the services it offered—and sometimes even lower its prices—to avoid losing customers. For example, rates on long-distance calls, which were quite high before the break-up, plummeted.

Incentives

From this example, we see that the government can help to limit monopoly outcomes and restore a competitive balance. This is often accomplished through antitrust legislation. Antitrust laws are designed to prevent monopoly practices and promote competition. The government has exercised control over monopoly practices since the passage of the Sherman Act in 1890, and the task currently falls to the Department of Justice. We will discuss these regulations at greater length in Chapter 13.

Reducing Trade Barriers

Countries use tariffs, which are taxes on imported goods, as a trade barrier to prevent competition and protect domestic business. However, any barrier—

Since 1994, reduced barriers to competition have transformed the Indian airline industry.

be it tariffs, quotas, or prohibitions—limits the possible gains from trade. For monopolists, trade barriers prevent rivals from entering their territory. For example, imagine that Florida could place a tariff on California oranges. For every California orange sold in Florida, the seller would have to pay a fee. Florida orange producers might like this because it would limit competition from California. But California growers would cry foul and reciprocate with a tariff on Florida oranges. Growers in both states would be happy, but consumers would be harmed. For example, if a damaging freeze in Florida depleted the crop, Florida consumers would have to pay more than the demand-driven price for imported oranges from California. If, in contrast, Florida had a bumper crop, the tariff would keep prices artificially high and much of the extra harvest would go to waste.

The United States has achieved tremendous growth by limiting the ability of individual states to place import and export restrictions on goods and services. The Constitution reads, "No State shall, without the consent of Congress, lay any imposts or duties on imports or exports." Rarely have so few words been more profound. With this simple law in place, states must compete on equal terms.

Trade creates value

Reducing trade barriers creates more competition, lessens the influence of monopoly, and promotes the efficient use of resources. For example, prior to 1994 private air carriers accounted for less than 0.5% of the air traffic in India. In 1994, Indian airspace was opened to allow private airlines to operate scheduled service. This move forced the state-owned Air India to become more competitive. These changes in Indian aviation policies had the effect of raising the share of private airline operators in domestic passenger carriage to over 70% by 2012. Two private companies, Jet Airways and IndiGo, are now the largest carriers in India, while Air India—which once controlled the market—has slipped to third place.

Regulating Markets

In the case of a natural monopoly, it is not practical to harness the benefits of competition. Consider the economies of scale that utility companies experience. Breaking up a company that provides natural gas, water, or electricity

The Demise of a Monopoly

A monopoly can be broken up by the courts or by market forces. In the case of Microsoft, only one has worked. In November 1999, a federal judge declared Microsoft a monopoly of computer operating systems. The original decision underwent appeals that continue to this day, making the ruling largely ineffective in breaking up the monopoly. But market forces have had more success. New technologies have made the market much more competitive, meaning Microsoft is rarely considered a monopoly anymore.

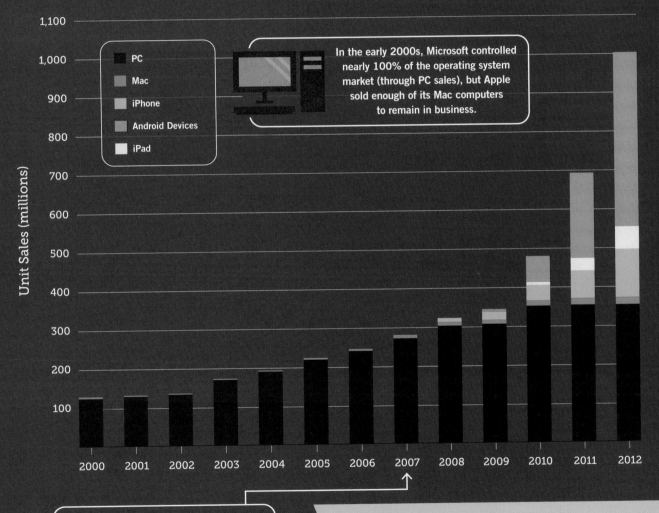

Legend:
- PC
- Mac
- iPhone
- Android Devices
- iPad

In the early 2000s, Microsoft controlled nearly 100% of the operating system market (through PC sales), but Apple sold enough of its Mac computers to remain in business.

Unit Sales (millions) — y-axis: 100, 200, 300, 400, 500, 600, 700, 800, 900, 1,000, 1,100

x-axis: 2000, 2001, 2002, 2003, 2004, 2005, 2006, 2007, 2008, 2009, 2010, 2011, 2012

Since 2007, the explosive growth of smartphone and tablet sales has tilted the operating system market toward Android (owned by Google) and Apple, eating into Microsoft's market share.

REVIEW QUESTIONS

- About what percentage of the operating system market did Microsoft (PC) control in 2012?

- Describe the demise of the Microsoft operating system monopoly using the following terms: competition, innovation, and market power.

would result in higher production costs. For instance, a second water company would have to build infrastructure to each residence or business in a community. Having redundant water lines with only a fraction of the customers would make the delivery of water extremely expensive, such that the final price to the consumer, even with competition, would be higher. Therefore, keeping the monopoly intact would be the best option. In this situation, policymakers might attempt to create a more efficient outcome and maximize the welfare of society by regulating the monopolist's prices. Theoretically, this would be a straightforward process—as we will see below. However, the reality is that few regulators are experts in the fields of electricity, natural gas, water, and other regulated industries, so they often lack sufficient knowledge to make the regulations work as designed.

When a natural monopoly exists, the government may choose to use the marginal-cost pricing rule to generate the greatest welfare for society. This is done by setting P = MC. Since the price is determined along the demand curve, setting P = MC guarantees that the good will be produced as long as the willingness to pay exceeds the additional cost of production. Figure 10.6 shows the difference in pricing and profits for a regulated and an unregulated natural monopoly.

To maximize profits, an unregulated monopolist sets MR = MC and produces Q_M at a price of P_M. Since P_M is greater than the average cost of producing Q_M units, or C_M, the monopolist earns the profit shown in the green rectangle. If the firm is regulated and the price is set at marginal cost, regulators can set P = MC and the output expands to Q_R. (The subscript R denotes the regulated monopolist.) In this example, since the cost of production is subject to economies of scale, the cost falls from C_M to C_R. This is a large improvement in efficiency. The regulated price, P_R, is lower than the unregulated monopo-

FIGURE 10.6

The Regulatory Solution for Natural Monopoly

An unregulated monopolist uses the profit-maximizing rule, MR = MC, and earns a small profit, shown in the green-shaded rectangle. If the monopolist is regulated using the marginal cost pricing rule, P = MC, it will experience the loss shown in the red-shaded rectangle.

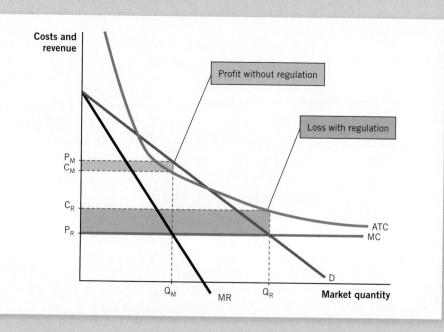

list's price, P_M, and production increases. As a result, consumers are better off. But what happens to the monopoly? It loses profits in the amount of the red rectangle. This occurs since the average costs under the marginal-cost pricing solution, C_R, are higher than the price allowed by regulators, P_R. This outcome is problematic because a firm that suffers losses will go out of business. That outcome is not desirable from society's standpoint, since the consumers of the product will be left without it. There are three possible solutions. First, to make up for the losses incurred at the higher output level, C_R, the government could subsidize the monopolist. Second, the regulated price could be set so that P = ATC at Q_R and the monopoly breaks even. (Remember that ATC is the average total cost.) Third, the government could own and operate the business in lieu of the private firm. This solution, however, has its own challenges, as we will explore in the next section.

Marginal thinking

A Caveat about Government Oversight

Firms with a profit motive have an incentive to minimize the costs of production, since lower costs translate directly into higher profits. Consequently, if the managers of firms do a poor job, they will be fired. The same cannot be said about government managers, or bureaucrats. Government employees are rarely let go, regardless of their performance. As a result, the government oversight and management of monopolies is problematic because there are fewer incentives to keep costs in check.

Consequently, the marginal-cost pricing rule is not as effective as it first seems. Regulated firms and government-owned businesses do not have the same incentives to keep costs down. Without the correct incentives in place, we would expect cost inefficiencies to develop.

Incentives

Public policy can mitigate the power of monopolies. But this outcome is not guaranteed. While monopolies are not as efficient as firms in competitive markets, this is not always the relevant comparison to make. We need to ask how the inefficiency of monopoly compares with the inefficiencies associated with government involvement in the market. Since good economists assess the benefits as well as the costs, when the costs of government involvement are greater than the efficiency gains that can be realized, the best solution to the problem of monopoly might be to do nothing.

Conclusion

It is tempting to believe that monopolies always earn a profit, but that is a misconception. The monopolist controls the supply, not the demand, so monopolies occasionally suffer losses despite the advantages they enjoy. Still, many monopolists do make profits.

In this chapter, we examined the monopoly model and, along the way, compared the result under monopoly with the competitive model that we developed in the previous chapter. While competitive markets generally yield welfare-enhancing outcomes for society, monopolies often do the opposite. Since monopolists do not produce an efficient outcome, government often seeks to limit monopoly outcomes and promote competitive markets.

Competitive markets and monopoly are market structures at opposite extremes. Indeed, we rarely encounter the conditions necessary for either a pure monopoly or a perfectly competitive market. Most economic activity takes place between these two alternatives. In the upcoming chapters, we will examine monopolistic competition and oligopoly—two markets that constitute the bulk of the economy. Fortunately, if you understand the market structures at the extremes, understanding the middle ground is straightforward. As a result, one way to think of how firms operate is to imagine a broad spectrum of industries ranging from those that are highly competitive to those for which competition is nonexistent. As we move forward, we will deploy the same tools we have used to examine monopoly in order to understand monopolistic competition (Chapter 12) and oligopoly (Chapter 13).

ANSWERING THE BIG QUESTIONS

How are monopolies created?

* Monopoly is a market structure characterized by a single seller that produces a well-defined product with few good substitutes.
* Monopolies operate in a market with high barriers to entry, the chief source of market power.
* Monopolies are created when a single firm controls the entire market.

How much do monopolies charge, and how much do they produce?

* Monopolists are price makers who may earn long-run profits.
* Like perfectly competitive firms, a monopoly tries to maximize its profits. To do so, it uses the profit-maximizing rule, MR = MC, to select the optimal price and quantity combination of a good or service to produce.

What are the problems with, and solutions for, monopoly?

* From an efficiency standpoint, the monopolist charges too much and produces too little. Since the monopolist's output is smaller than what would exist in a competitive market, monopolies lead to deadweight loss.
* Government grants of monopoly power encourage rent seeking, or the use of resources to secure monopoly rights through the political process.
* There are three potential solutions to the problem of monopoly. First, the government may break up firms that gain too much market power in order to restore a competitive market. Second, the government can promote open markets by reducing trade barriers. Third, the government can regulate a monopolist's ability to charge excessive prices.
* Finally, there are some circumstances in which it is better to leave the monopolist alone.

Playing Monopoly Like an Economist

Monopoly is the ultimate zero-sum game. You profit only by taking from other players. The assets of its world are fixed in number. The best player drives others into bankruptcy and is declared the winner only after gaining control of the entire board.

Here is some advice on how to play the game like an economist.

Apply some basic economic principles, and you can win big.

- Remember that a monopoly is built on trade. You are unlikely to acquire a monopoly by landing on the color-groups you need; instead, you have to trade properties in order to acquire the ones you need. Since every player knows this, acquiring the last property to complete a color-group is nearly impossible. Your competitors will never willingly hand you a monopoly unless they get something of great value in return.

- Don't wait to trade until it is obvious what you need. Instead, try to acquire as many properties as you can in order to gain trading leverage as the game unfolds. Always pick up available properties if no other player owns one of the same color-group; purchase properties that will give you two or three of the same group; or purchase a property if it blocks someone else from completing a set.

- Think about probability. Mathematicians have determined that Illinois Avenue is the property most likely to be landed on and that B&O is the best railroad to own. Know the odds, and you can weigh the risks and rewards of trade, better than your opponents. This is just like doing market research before you buy: being informed matters in Monopoly and in business.

- When you get a monopoly, develop it quickly. Build as many houses as you can. That's sound advice in the board game and in life. Monopoly power is fleeting—you must capitalize on your advantages as soon as possible.

- Finally, if you gain the upper hand and have a chance to bankrupt a player from the game, do it. Luck plays a key role in Monopoly as it does in life. Although it may sound harsh, eliminating a competitor moves you one step closer to winning the game.

The decisions you make while playing Monopoly are all about cost-benefit analysis. You have limited resources and only so many opportunities to use them to your advantage. The skilled player understands how to weigh the values of tradeable properties, considers the risk-return proposition of every decision, manages money effectively, and eliminates competitors when given a chance.

CONCEPTS YOU SHOULD KNOW

barriers to entry (p. 304)
market failure (p. 315)

monopoly power (p. 304)
natural monopoly (p. 305)

price maker (p. 309)
rent seeking (p. 318)

QUESTIONS FOR REVIEW

1. Describe the difference between a monopoly and a natural monopoly.

2. What are barriers to entry, and why are they crucial to the creation of potential long-run monopoly profits? Give an example of a barrier that can lead to monopoly.

3. Explain why a monopoly is a price maker but a perfectly competitive firm is a price taker.

4. Why is a monopolist's marginal revenue curve less than the price of the good it sells?

5. What is the monopolist's rule for determining the profit-maximizing output? What two steps does the monopolist follow to maximize profits?

6. Why does a monopolist operate inefficiently? Draw a demand curve, a marginal revenue curve, and a marginal cost curve to illustrate the deadweight loss from monopoly.

7. Why is it difficult to regulate a natural monopoly?

STUDY PROBLEMS (*solved at the end of the section)*

1. In the figure below, identify the price the monopolist will charge and the output the monopolist will produce. How do these

two decisions on the part of the monopolist compare to the efficient price and output?

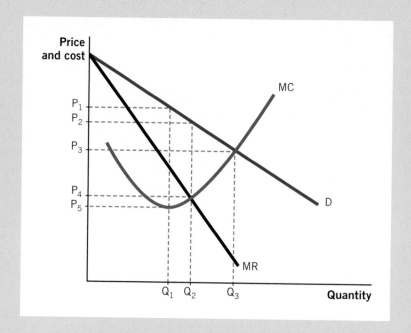

2. Which of the following could be considered a monopoly?

   a. your local water company
   b. Boeing, a manufacturer of airplanes
   c. Brad Pitt
   d. Walmart
   e. the only gas station along a 100-mile stretch of road

3. A monopolist has the following fixed and variable costs:

Price	Quantity	Fixed cost	Variable cost
$10	0	$8	$0
$9	1	8	5
$8	2	8	8
$7	3	8	10
$6	4	8	11
$5	5	8	13
$4	6	8	16
$3	7	8	20
$2	8	8	25

At what level of output will the monopolist maximize profits?

4. The year is 2278, and the starship *Enterprise* is running low on dilithium crystals, which are used to regulate the matter-antimatter reactions that propel the ship across the universe. Without the crystals, space-time travel is not possible. If there is only one known source of dilithium crystals, are the necessary conditions met to establish a monopoly? If the crystals are government-owned or -regulated, what price should the government set for them?

✳ 5. If demand falls, what is likely to happen to a monopolist's price, output, and economic profit?

✳ 6. A new musical group called The Incentives cuts a debut single. The record company determines a number of price points for the group's first single, "The Big Idea."

Price per download	Quantity of downloads
$2.99	25,000
$1.99	50,000
$1.49	75,000
$0.99	100,000
$0.49	150,000

The record company can produce the song with fixed costs of $10,000 and no variable cost.

   a. Determine the total revenue at each price. What is the marginal revenue as the price drops from one level to the next?
   b. What price would maximize the record company's profits? How much would the company make?
   c. If you were the agent for The Incentives, what signing fee would you request from the record company? Explain your answer.

7. Recalling what you have learned about elasticity, what can you say about the connection between the price a monopolist chooses to charge and whether or not demand is elastic, unitary, or inelastic at that price? (**Hint:** examine the marginal revenue curve of a monopolist. Since marginal revenue becomes negative at low prices, this implies that a portion of the demand curve cannot possibly be chosen.)

8. A small community is served by five independent gas stations. Gasoline is a highly competitive market. Use the market demand curve to illustrate the consumer and producer surplus created by the market. Now imagine that the five independent gas stations are all combined under one franchise. Create a new graph that illustrates the consumer surplus, producer surplus, and deadweight loss after the monopoly enters the market.

9. A local community bus service charges $2.00 for a one-way fare. The city council is thinking of raising the fare to $2.50 to generate 25% more revenue. The council has asked for your advice as a student of economics. In your analysis, be sure to break down the impact of the price increase into the price effect and the output effect. Explain why the city council's estimate of the revenue increase is likely to be overstated. Use a graph to illustrate your answer.

10. Suppose that a monopolist's marginal cost curve shifts upward. What is likely to happen to the price the monopolist charges, the quantity it produces, and the profit it makes? Use a graph to illustrate your answer.

SOLVED PROBLEMS

5. There is a two-part answer here. The first graph shows the monopolist making a profit:

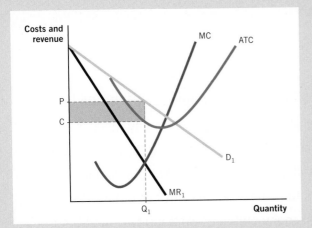

Now we show what happens if demand falls:

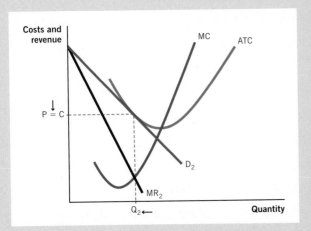

Lower demand causes the price to fall, the output to decline, and the profit to disappear.

6. a.

Price per download	Downloads	Total revenue	Marginal revenue
$2.99	25,000	$74,750	$74,750
$1.99	50,000	99,500	24,750
$1.49	75,000	111,750	12,250
$0.99	100,000	99,000	−12,750
$0.49	150,000	73,500	−25,500

b. Since marginal costs are $0, the firm would maximize its profits at $1.49. The company would make $111,750 − $10,000, or $101,750.

c. The company makes $101,750 from production, so as the agent you could request any signing fee up to that amount. Since determining a fee is a negotiation and both sides have to gain from trade, as the agent you should argue for a number close to $100,000, and you should expect the firm to argue for a much smaller fee.

Price Discrimination

Charging different prices to different people is unfair and harmful.
Have you ever wondered why out-of-state students pay more than
in-state students for the same education at many public universities?
Or why private colleges have high sticker prices and then offer
tuition discounts to some students but not others? Maybe you
have noticed that many clubs let women in without a cover
charge but require men to pay. And why do theaters charge more for
adults and less for children when everyone sees the same movie? In
each of these examples, some customers pay more and others pay less.
Is this unfair and harmful? Not really. When a firm can charge more
than one price, markets work more efficiently.

In this chapter, we examine many real-life pricing situations and how
businesses can make additional profits if they charge more than one
price to different groups of customers. The study of *price discrimination*
adds a layer of complexity to the simple models of perfect competition
and monopoly. A thorough understanding of how price discrimination
works will be especially useful as we complete our study of market
structure with monopolistic competition and oligopoly in the next two
chapters.

Why do some clubs offer no cover charge to women but not to men?

BIG QUESTIONS

✳ **What is price discrimination?**

✳ **How is price discrimination practiced?**

What Is Price Discrimination?

Price discrimination
occurs when a firm sells
the same good at different
prices to different groups of
customers.

Price discrimination occurs when a firm sells the same good at different prices to different groups of customers. The difference in price is not related to differences in cost. Although "price discrimination" sounds like something illegal, in fact it is beneficial to both sellers and buyers. When a firm can charge more than one price, markets work more efficiently. Since price-discriminating firms typically charge a "high" and a "low" price, some consumers are able to buy the product at a low price. Of course, firms are not in business to provide goods at low prices; they want to make a profit. Price discrimination enables them to make more money by dividing their customers into at least two groups: those who get a discount and others who pay more.

We have seen that in competitive markets, firms are price takers. If a competitive firm attempts to charge a higher price, its customers will likely buy elsewhere. To practice price discrimination, a firm must be a price maker: it must have some market power before it can charge more than one price. Both monopolies and non-monopoly companies use price discrimination to earn higher profits. Common examples of price discrimination are movie theater tickets, restaurant menus, college tuition, airline reservations, discounts on academic software, and coupons.

Conditions for Price Discrimination

For price discrimination to take place, two conditions must be met. First, the firm must be able to distinguish groups of buyers with different price elasticities of demand. Second, the firm must be able to prevent resale of the product or service. Let's look at each in turn.

Distinguishing Groups of Buyers

In order to price-discriminate, the firm must be able to distinguish groups of buyers with different price elasticities of demand. Firms can generate additional revenues by charging more to customers with inelastic demand and less to customers with elastic demand. For instance, many restaurants offer lower prices, known as "early-bird specials," to people who eat dinner early. Who are these customers? Many, such as retirees and families with children, are on a limited budget. These early diners not only have less demand but also represent demand that is more elastic; they eat out only if the price is low enough.

Trade-offs

Early-bird specials work for restaurants by separating customers into two groups: one that is price-sensitive and another that is willing to pay full price. This strategy enables the restaurants to serve more customers and generate additional revenue.

Preventing Resale

For price discrimination to be a viable strategy, a firm must also be able to prevent resale of the product or service. In some cases, preventing resale is easy. For example, airlines require that electronic tickets match the passenger's government-issued photo ID. This prevents a passenger who received a discounted fare from reselling it to another passenger who would be willing to pay more. The process works well for airlines and enables them to charge more to groups of flyers with more inelastic demand. It also works well for restaurants offering early-bird specials, since the restaurants can easily distinguish between customers who arrive in time for the specials and those who arrive later.

One Price versus Price Discrimination

A business that practices price discrimination would prefer to differentiate every customer by selling the same good at a price unique to that customer—a situation known as **perfect price discrimination**. To achieve this, a business would have to know exactly what any particular customer would be willing to pay and charge them exactly that price. Many jewelry stores and automobile dealerships attempt to practice perfect price discrimination by posting high sticker prices and then bargaining with each customer to reach a deal. When you enter a jewelry store or a vehicle showroom, the salesperson tries to determine the highest price you are willing to pay. Then he or she bargains with you until that price is reached.

Perfect price discrimination occurs when a firm sells the same good at a unique price to every customer.

In practice, perfect price discrimination is hard to implement. To see why, let's look at a hypothetical example. Consider two small airlines, Flat Earth Air and Discriminating Fliers. Each airline has a monopoly on the route it flies, and each faces the same market demand curves and marginal costs. The costs of running a flight—fuel, pilots, flight attendants, ground crew, and so on—are about the same no matter how many passengers are on board. Both firms fly the same airplane, which seats 200 passengers. So the marginal cost of adding one passenger—the extra weight and the cost of a can of soda or two—is very small. What happens if one of the airlines price-discriminates but the other does not?

In Figure 11.1, Flat Earth Air charges the same price to every passenger, while Discriminating Fliers uses two different price structures. To keep our example easy to work with, the marginal cost (MC) is set at $100, shown as a horizontal line.

Flat Earth sets its price by using the profit-maximizing rule, MR = MC. It charges $300 for every seat and serves 100 customers (that is, passengers). Since the marginal cost is $100, every passenger who gets on the plane generates $200 in marginal revenue. The net revenue, represented by the green rectangle in the graph, is $200 × 100, or $20,000. At 100 passengers, this

Marginal
thinking

FIGURE 11.1

One Price versus Price Discrimination

(a) A firm that charges a single price uses MR = MC to earn a profit. (b) When a firm price-discriminates, it takes in more revenue than a firm that charges a single price. The discriminating firm increases its revenue by charging some customers more and other customers less, as shown in blue. The increase in revenue is partly offset by the loss of revenue from existing customers who receive a lower price, as shown in red.

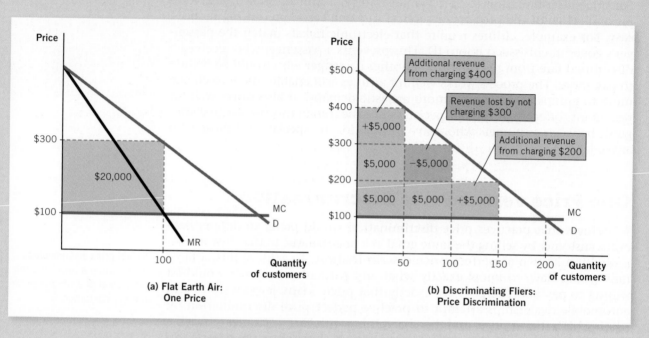

airline has done everything it can to maximize profits at a single price. At the same time, there are plenty of unsold seats in the plane, which holds 200 passengers. Those unfilled seats represent a lost opportunity to earn additional revenue. As a result, in cases like this airlines typically try to fill the plane by discounting the price of some seats.

In contrast, Discriminating Fliers experiments with two prices. It charges $400 for midweek flights or last-minute bookings, and $200 for weekend flights and to customers who book in advance. Let's look at the reasoning behind these two prices.

Since the firm faces a downward-sloping demand curve, the airline cannot sell every seat on the plane at the higher price. So it saves a number of seats, in this case 50, for last-minute bookings to capture customers with less flexibility who are willing to pay $400. These are travelers with inelastic demand, such as those who travel for business. The airline offers the rest of the seats at a low price, in this case $200, to capture customers with more elastic demand. The challenge for the airline is to make sure that the people who are willing to pay $400 do not purchase the $200 seats. To do this, it makes the low fare available to customers who book far in advance, because these customers are typically more flexible and shop for the best deal. It is common for a businessperson who needs to visit a client to make flight arrangements just days before the meeting, which precludes purchasing a $200 ticket available only weeks in advance. The customers who book early fill the seats that would otherwise be empty if the airline had only charged one price, as Flat Earth does. We can see this by comparing the total number of passengers under the two strategies. Discriminating Fliers, with its two-price strategy, serves 150 passengers. Flat Earth's single price brings in 100 passengers.

The net effect of price discrimination is apparent in the shaded areas of Figure 11.1b. By charging two prices, Discriminating Fliers generates more net revenue. The high price, $400, generates additional revenue equal to the upper blue rectangle—$5,000—from passengers who must

Airlines offer lower fares if you are willing to take the red-eye.

pay more than the $300 charged by Flat Earth. Discriminating Fliers also gains additional revenue with its low price of $200. The less expensive tickets attract passengers with more elastic demand, such as college students, vacationers, and retirees. This generates $5,000, as shown by the lower blue rectangle.

Some customers would have paid Discriminating Fliers more if the airline had charged a single price. The group of customers willing to pay $300 is able to acquire tickets on Discriminating Fliers for $200. We see this in the red rectangle, which represents lost revenues equal to $5,000. The $10,000 in revenue represented by the blue rectangles more than offsets the $5,000 in lost revenue represented by the red rectangle. The airline that price-discriminates generates a net revenue of $25,000 in panel (b). The airline that charges a single price generates a net revenue of $20,000 in panel (a).

In reality, airlines often charge many prices. For example, you can find higher prices for travel on Friday and for midday flights. If your stay includes a Saturday night, or if you choose a red-eye flight, the prices will be lower still. Airlines also change prices from day to day and even from hour to hour. All these efforts price-discriminate on multiple fronts.

Since passengers cannot resell their tickets or easily change their plans, airlines can effectively price-discriminate. In fact, if an airline could charge unique prices for every passenger booking a flight, it would transform the entire area under the demand curve and above the marginal cost curve into more revenue.

The Welfare Effects of Price Discrimination

Price discrimination is profitable for the companies that practice it. But it also increases the welfare of society. How, you might ask, can companies make more profit and also benefit consumers? The answer: because a price discriminator charges a high price to some and a low price to others, more consumers are able to buy the good.

To illustrate this point, let's imagine an airline, Perfect Flights, that is able to perfectly price-discriminate. Perfect Flights charges each passenger a price exactly equal to what that passenger is willing to pay. As a result, some customers pay more and others pay less than they would under a single-price system. This is evident in Figure 11.2, where a profit-maximizing firm charges $300. At this price, the firm captures the net revenue in the green rectangle, B. However, Perfect Flights charges each passenger a price based on his or her willingness to pay. Therefore, it earns significantly more net revenue. By charging higher prices to those willing to pay more than $300 ($P_{high}$), the firm is able to capture additional net revenues in the upper blue triangle, A. Likewise, by charging lower prices to those not willing to pay $300 ($P_{low}$), the firm is able to capture additional net revenues in triangle C. As a result, Perfect Flights is making more money and serving more customers.

By charging a different fare to every customer, Perfect Flights can also increase the quantity of tickets sold to 200. This strategy yields two results worth noting. First, in the long run, a perfectly competitive firm would charge a price

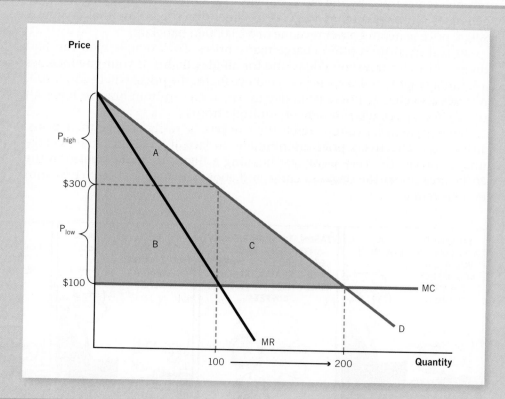

FIGURE 11.2

Perfect Price Discrimination

If the firm charges one price, the most it can earn is the net revenue in the green rectangle. However, if a firm is able to perfectly price-discriminate, it can pick up the additional revenue represented by the blue triangles.

just equal to marginal cost. In the case of Perfect Flights, the last customer who gets on the plane will pay an extraordinarily low price of $100—the price you might find in a competitive market. Second, this outcome mirrors the result of a government-regulated monopolist that uses the marginal-cost pricing rule, P = MC, to enhance social welfare. Perfect Flights is therefore achieving the efficiency noted in a competitive market while also producing the output that a regulated monopolist would choose. This strategy provides the firm with the opportunity to convert the area consisting of the two blue triangles into more revenue. In other words, the process maximizes the quantity sold. The efficiency of the market improves, and the firm generates more revenue.

Comparing Perfect Price Discrimination with Perfect Competition and Monopoly

To understand the welfare effects of perfect price discrimination, we can compare the consumer and producer surplus in three scenarios: a competitive market, a market in which a monopolist charges a single price, and a market characterized by perfect price discrimination. The results, shown in Table 11.1, are derived by examining Figure 11.2.

First, in a "perfectly" competitive market, there are no barriers to entry and no firm has market power. In the long run, the price will be equal to the marginal cost. In our example of airline ticket prices, the price is driven down to $100. At this price, 200 tickets are sold. The entire area above the marginal cost curve (A + B + C) is consumer surplus, since the willingness to pay—as determined along the demand curve—is greater than the price. Because the ticket price is the same as the marginal cost, the producer surplus is zero. Also, since every customer who is willing to pay $100 or more can find a ticket, there is no deadweight loss. Under perfect competition, the market structure clearly favors consumers.

Marginal
thinking

Second, a monopoly holds substantial market power, so the firm sets a price using the profit-maximizing rule, MR = MC, without having to worry about competition driving the price down to marginal cost. The monopolist's profit-maximizing price, or $300 in Figure 11.2, is higher than the $100 price under perfect competition. This higher price reduces the amount of consumer surplus to triangle A and creates a producer surplus equal to rectangle B. In addition, because the number of tickets sold falls to 100, there is now deadweight loss equal to triangle C. Economic activity associated with triangle C

TABLE 11.1

The Welfare Effects of Perfect Price Discrimination

	Perfect competition	A monopolist that charges a single price	Perfect price discrimination
Consumer surplus	A + B + C	A	0
Producer surplus	0	B	A + B + C
Deadweight loss	0	C	0
Total welfare	A + B + C	A + B	A + B + C

ECONOMICS IN THE MEDIA

Perfect Price Discrimination

Legally Blonde

In this 2001 film, Reese Witherspoon stars as Elle Woods, a sun-washed sorority girl who defies expectations. Believing that her boyfriend is about to propose to her, Elle and two friends go shopping to find the perfect dress for the occasion. They enter an exclusive boutique and start trying on dresses.

The saleswoman comments to another associate, "There's nothing I love more than a dumb blonde with daddy's plastic." She grabs a dress off the clearance sale rack and removes the "half price" tag. Approaching Elle, she says, "Did you see this one? We just got it in yesterday." Elle fingers the dress, then the price tag, and looks at the saleswoman with excitement.

Do you know how to look good for the right price?

> **ELLE:** "Is this a low-viscosity rayon?"
> **SALESWOMAN:** "Uh, yes—of course."
> **ELLE:** "With half-loop top-stitching on the hem?"
> **SALESWOMAN** (smiling a lie): "Absolutely. It's one of a kind."
> (Elle hands the dress back to her, no longer pretending to be excited.)
> **ELLE:** "It's impossible to use a half-loop top-stitch on low-viscosity rayon. It would snag the fabric. And you didn't just get this in, because I remember it from the June *Vogue* a year ago, so if you're trying to sell it to me at full price, you picked the wrong girl."

The scene is a wonderful example of an attempt at price discrimination gone wrong. Unbeknownst to the saleswoman, Elle is majoring in fashion merchandising in college and knows more about fashion than the saleswoman does. Her effort to cheat Elle fails miserably.

What makes the scene powerful is the use of stereotypes. When merchants attempt to price-discriminate, they look for clues to help them decide whether the buyer is willing to pay full price or needs an incentive, or discount, in order to make a purchase. In this case, Elle's appearance suggests that she is an uninformed buyer with highly inelastic demand. Consequently, the saleswoman's strategy backfires.

no longer exists, and the total welfare of society is now limited to A + B. From this, we see that monopoly causes a partial transfer of consumer surplus to producers and a reduction in total welfare for society.

Third, a firm that can practice perfect price discrimination is able to charge each customer a price exactly equal to the price that customer is willing to pay. This strategy enables the firm to convert the entire area of consumer surplus that existed under perfect competition into producer surplus (A + B + C). For the firm to capture the entire area of available consumer surplus, it must lower some prices all the way down to marginal cost. At that point, the number of tickets sold returns to 200, the market is once again efficient, and the deadweight loss disappears. Perfect price discrimination transfers the gains from trade from consumers to producers, but it also yields maximum efficiency.

Note that this gives us a better understanding of what economists mean when they use the word "perfect" in connection with a market. It can mean that consumer surplus is maximized, as it is under perfect competition, or that producer surplus is maximized, as it is under perfect price discrimination. It does not specify an outcome from a particular perspective; instead, it describes any market process that produces no deadweight loss. If society's total welfare is maximized, economists do not distinguish whether the benefits accrue to consumers or producers.

ECONOMICS IN THE REAL WORLD

Outlet Malls—If You Build It, They Will Come

Have you ever noticed that outlet malls along major roadways are often located a considerable distance from large population centers? Moreover, every item at an outlet mall can be found closer to home. The same clothes, shoes, and kitchenware are available nearby.

Logic tells us that it would be more convenient to shop locally and forget the time and hassle of getting to an outlet center. But that is not how many shoppers feel.

Discount shopping is a big deal. How big? Here are a few statistics. Potomac Mills, 30 miles south of Washington, D.C., is Virginia's most popular attraction, with nearly 17 million visitors a year. (That figure rivals the number of annual visitors to Disney World's Magic Kingdom!) But Potomac Mills is not

How far would you drive to visit an outlet mall?

unique. Two adjacent outlet malls in San Marcos, Texas, attract over 6 million visitors a year—many more than the number that visit the Alamo. And in Pigeon Forge, Tennessee, over 10 million shoppers go to the outlets annually—more than the number of visitors to nearby Great Smoky Mountains National Park.

Outlet shopping is an example of price discrimination at work. Traditional malls are usually situated in urban settings and offer a wide variety of choices, but not necessarily low prices. If you want convenience, the local shopping mall is right around the corner. But if you want a bargain, shopping at a traditional, local mall is not the best way to go.

Incentives

What makes outlets so attractive are the discounts. Bargain hunters have much more elastic demand than their traditional mall-shopping counterparts who desire convenience. Moreover, the difference in the price elasticity of demand between these two groups means that traditional malls can more easily charge full price, while outlets must discount their merchandise in order to attract customers. This gives merchants a chance to price-discriminate on the basis of location—which is another way of separating customers into two groups and preventing resale at the same time. Retailers can therefore earn additional profits through price discrimination, while price-sensitive consumers can find lower prices at the outlets.

It is noteworthy that the convenience of finding discounts online threatens not only the traditional malls but also the outlets. When savvy shoppers can simply click to find the best deal, will they continue to drive to the outlets? ✳

Opportunity
cost

PRACTICE WHAT YOU KNOW

How much would you pay to fly in a helicopter?

Price Discrimination: Taking Economics to New Heights

Consider the table below, which shows seven potential customers who are interested in taking a 30-minute helicopter ride. The helicopter has room for eight people, including the pilot. The marginal cost of taking on additional passengers is $10.

Customer	Maximum willingness to pay	Age
Amelia	$80	66
Orville	70	34
Wilbur	40	17
Neil	50	16
Charles	60	9
Chuck	100	49
Buzz	20	9

Question: If the company can charge only one price, what should it be?

Answer: First, create an ordered array of the customers, from those willing to pay the most to those willing to pay the least.

Customer	Maximum willingness to pay	Price	TR	MR
Chuck	$100	$100	$100	$100
Amelia	80	$80	160	60
Orville	70	$70	210	50
Charles	60	$60	240	30
Neil	50	$50	250	10
Wilbur	40	$40	240	−10
Buzz	20	$20	140	−100

(CONTINUED)

(CONTINUED)

If the firm charges $100, only Chuck will take the flight. When the firm drops the price to $80, Chuck and Amelia both buy tickets, so the total revenue (TR) is $80 × 2, or $160. Successively lower prices result in higher total revenue for the first five customers. Since the marginal cost is $10, the firm will benefit from lowering its price as long as the increase in marginal revenue is greater than, or equal to, the marginal cost. When the price is $50, five customers get on the helicopter, for a total of $250 in revenue. Adding the fifth passenger brings in exactly $10 in marginal revenue, so $50 is the best possible price to charge. Since each of the five passengers has a marginal cost of $10, the company makes $250 − (5 × $10), or $200 in profit.

Question: If the company could charge two prices, what should they be and who would pay them?

Answer: First, arrange the customers in two distinct groups: adults and children.

Adult customers	Willingness to pay	Age	Price	TR	MR
Chuck	$100	49	$100	$100	$100
Amelia	80	66	$80	160	60
Orville	70	34	$70	210	50

Young customers	Willingness to pay	Age	Price	TR	MR
Charles	$60	9	$60	$60	60
Neil	50	16	$50	100	40
Wilbur	40	17	$40	120	20
Buzz	20	9	$20	80	−40

As you can see, two separate prices emerge. For adults, total revenue is maximized at a price of $70. For children, total revenue is maximized at $40. The company should charge $70 to the adult customers, which brings in $70 × 3, or $210 in total revenue. The company should charge $40 for each child under age 18, which brings in $40 × 3, or $120. Note that if the company lowered the price of a child's ticket to $20 in order to entice Buzz to buy a ticket, it would earn $20 × 4, or $80, a lower total revenue.

Price discrimination earns the company $210 + $120 − (6 × $10), or $270 in profit. This is a $70 improvement over charging a single price. In addition, six passengers are now able to get on the helicopter instead of only five under the single-price model.

How Is Price Discrimination Practiced?

Price discrimination is one of the most interesting topics in economics because each example is slightly different from the others. In this section, we take a closer look at real-world examples of price discrimination at movie theaters and on college campuses. As you will see, price discrimination takes many forms, some that are easy to describe and others that are more nuanced.

Price Discrimination at the Movies

Have you ever gone to the movies early so you can pay less for tickets? Movie theaters price-discriminate based on the time of day, age, student status, and whether or not you buy snacks. Let's examine these pricing techniques to see if they are effective.

Pricing Based on the Time of the Show

Why are matinees priced less than evening shows? To encourage customers to attend movies during the afternoon, theaters discount ticket prices for matinees. This makes sense because customers who can attend matinees (retirees, people on vacation, and those who do not work during the day) either have less demand or are more flexible, or price elastic. Work and school limit the options for many other potential customers. As a result, theaters discount matinee prices to encourage moviegoers who have elastic demand and are willing to watch at a less crowded time. Movie theaters also discount the price of matinee shows since they pay to rent films on a weekly basis—so it is in their interest to show a film as many times as possible. Since the variable cost of being open during the day is essentially limited to paying a few employees relatively low wages, the theater can make additional profits even with a relatively small audience. On weekends, matinees also offer a discount to families that want to see a movie together—adding yet another layer of price discrimination.

Theaters charge two different prices based on show time because they can easily distinguish between high-demand customers and price-sensitive customers who have the flexibility to watch a matinee. Those with higher demand or less flexible schedules must pay higher show prices to attend in the evening.

Pricing Based on Age or Student Status

Why are there different movie prices for children, seniors, students, and everyone else? This is a complex question. Income does not fully explain the discounts that the young, the old, and students receive. Movie attendance is highest among 13- to 24-year-olds and declines thereafter with age. Given the strong demand among

Once the doors open, matinee prices will bring in moviegoers with elastic demand.

teenagers, it is not surprising that "child" discounts are phased out at most theaters by age 12. But did you know that most "senior" discounts begin before age 65? In some places, senior discounts start at age 50. Now you might think that because people in their fifties tend to be at the peak of their earning power, discounting ticket prices for them would be a bad move. However, since interest in going to the movies declines with age, the "senior" discount actually provides an incentive for a population that might not otherwise go to a movie theater. However, as we have seen, age-based price discrimination does not always work perfectly. Theaters do not usually ask for proof of age, and it may be hard to tell the difference between a child who is just under 12 and one who is over 12. Nonetheless, price discrimination works well enough to make age or student status a useful revenue-generating tool.

Concession Pricing

Have you ever wondered why it is so expensive to purchase snacks at the movie theater? The concession area is another arena in which movie theaters practice price discrimination. To understand this, we need to think of two groups of customers: those who want to eat while they watch movies and those who do not. By limiting outside food and drink, movie theaters push people with inelastic demand for snacks to buy from the concession area. Of course, that does not stop some customers with elastic demand from sneaking food into the theater. But as long as some moviegoers are willing to buy concession fare at exorbitant prices, the theater will generate more revenue. Movie theaters cannot prevent smuggling in of snacks, and they don't have to. All they really want to do is separate their customers into two groups: a price-inelastic group of concession-area snackers and a price-elastic group of nonsnackers and smugglers who fill up the remaining empty seats. This is very similar to the problem we examined with airlines. Empty seats represent lost revenue, so it makes sense to price-discriminate through a combination of high and low prices.

If you have ever smuggled food into a movie theater, it is because your demand for movie theater concessions is elastic.

Price Discrimination on Campus

Colleges and universities are experts at price discrimination. Think about tuition. Some students pay the full sticker price, while others enjoy a free ride. Some students receive the in-state rate, while out-of-state students pay substantially more. And once you get to campus, discounts for students are everywhere. In this section, we consider the many ways in which colleges and universities differentiate among their students.

Tuition

Price discrimination begins before you ever set foot on campus, with the Free Application for Federal Student Aid (known as the FAFSA) that most families complete. The form determines eligibility for federal aid. Families that qualify are eligible for grants and low-interest loans, which effectively lower the tuition cost for low- and medium-income families. Therefore, the FAFSA enables colleges to separate applicants into two groups based on income. Since many colleges also use the FAFSA to determine eligibility for their own institutional grants of aid, the FAFSA makes it possible for colleges to precisely target

Resort or college? Sky-high tuition and room and board are one way to help pay for a beautiful campus.

grants and loans to the students who need the most help in order to attend.

Many state institutions of higher education have a two-tiered pricing structure. In-state students get a discount on the tuition, and out-of-state students pay a much higher rate. Part of the difference is attributable to state subsidies that are intended to make in-state institutions more affordable for residents. In-state students pay less because their parents have been paying taxes to the state, often for many years, and the state then uses those tax dollars to support its system of higher education.

This two-tiered pricing structure creates two separate groups of customers with distinctly different elasticities of demand. Students choose an out-of-state college or university because they like what that institution has to offer more than the institutions in their home state. It might be that a particular major or program is more highly rated, or simply that they prefer the location of the out-of-state school. Whatever the reason, they are willing to pay more for the out-of-state school. Therefore, out-of-state students have a much more inelastic demand. Colleges know this and price their tuition accordingly. Conversely, in-state students often view the opportunity to attend a nearby college as the most economical decision. Since price is a big factor in choosing an in-state institution, it is not surprising that in-state demand is more elastic.

Selective private colleges also play the price discrimination game by advertising annual tuition and room and board fees that exceed $50,000. With price discrimination, the "sticker" price is often discounted. Depending on how much the college wants to encourage a particular student to attend, it can discount the tuition all the way to zero. This strategy enables selective private colleges to price-discriminate by offering scholarships based on financial need, while also guaranteeing placements for the children of wealthy alums and others willing to pay the full sticker price.

Student Discounts

The edge of campus is a great place to look for price discrimination. Local bars, eateries, and shops all want college students to step off campus, so student discounts are the norm. Why do establishments do this? Think about the average college student. Price matters to that student. Knowing this, local merchants in search of college customers can provide student discounts without lowering their prices across the board. This means they can charge more to their regular clients, while providing the necessary discounts to get college students to make the trek off campus.

Price discrimination also occurs on campus. For example, students typically receive discounts for campus activities like concerts and sporting events. Since students generally have elastic demand, price discrimination provides greater student access to on-campus events than charging a single price does.

Now Playing: Economics!

Have you ever gone to the movies early so you can pay less for tickets? Movie theaters price-discriminate based on the time of the movie and the age of the customer. In order to be able to practice price discrimination, theaters must be able to identify different groups of moviegoers, where each group has a different price elasticity of demand

MATINEE $9

Demand for matinees is typically low. These showings attract groups with relatively elastic demand, like families and those on a budget, who decide to attend matinees because of lower prices.

EVENING $13

Evening movie showings attract larger crowds that consist mainly of adults and couples on dates. This group has relatively inelastic demand, so price is not the determining factor of when and where they see a movie.

The concession counter also generates profit for the movie theater. The high prices mean that patrons who are price conscious (having relatively elastic demand) skip the counter or smuggle in their own snacks, while those who are more concerned about convenience than price (having relatively inelastic demand) buy snacks at the counter.

REVIEW QUESTIONS

- Does price discrimination hurt all consumers? Think about the example of movie theaters as you craft your response.

- Your local movie theater is thinking about increasing ticket prices for just the opening day of a blockbuster movie. How would you explain the economics behind this price increase to your friends?

PRACTICE WHAT YOU KNOW

Price Discrimination in Practice: Everyday Examples

Question: Test your understanding by thinking about the examples below. Are they examples of price discrimination?

a. **Retail coupons.** Programs such as discount coupons, rebates, and frequent-buyer plans appeal to customers willing to spend time pursuing a deal.

b. **Using Priceline to make hotel reservations.** "Naming your price" on Priceline is a form of haggling that enables users to get hotel rooms at a discount. Hotels negotiate with Priceline to fill unused rooms while still advertising the full price on their web sites.

c. **$5 footlong subs at Subway.** Customers who buy a $5 footlong get more sub at a substantially lower price per inch than a 6-inch sub.

d. **The Dollar Menu at McDonald's.** Customers who order off the Dollar Menu get a variety of smaller menu items for $1 each.

e. **Discounts for early shoppers on Black Friday.** Customers who line up in the early-morning hours after Thanksgiving get first dibs on a limited quantity of reduced-price items at many retailers.

Answers:

a. **Retail coupons.** Affluent customers generally do not bother with the hassle of clipping, sending in, and keeping track of the coupons because they value their time more than the small savings. However, customers with lower incomes usually take the time to get the discount. This means that coupons, rebates, and frequent-buyer programs do a good job of price discriminating.

b. **Using Priceline to make hotel reservations.** Priceline enables hotels to divide their customers into two groups: those who don't want to be bothered with haggling, and those who value the savings enough to justify the time spent negotiating. This is a good example of price discrimination.

c. **$5 footlong subs at Subway.** The $5 price is available to anyone anytime. Therefore, the $5 footlong is catchy marketing, but it does not strictly meet the definition of price discrimination. However, to get the deal customers must buy a 12-inch sub. This is an example of secondary price discrimination—that is, the price per unit varies with the quantity sold. Anyone could conceivably get the deal, but only those with big appetites or a willingness to eat leftovers will choose a footlong. Those with smaller appetites are stuck paying $3.50 for a 6-inch sub.

d. **The Dollar Menu at McDonald's.** Anyone can buy off the Dollar Menu at any time. Since McDonald's does not force customers to buy a large serving in order to get the deal, this is not price discrimination.

e. **Discounts for early shoppers on Black Friday.** The discounts are time-sensitive. Shoppers who arrive before the deadline get a lower price; shoppers who arrive after it do not. This is a clear-cut example of price discrimination.

Price discrimination or not?

Price Discrimination

Extreme Couponing

Most of us use coupons from time to time, when it is convenient. The TV show *Extreme Couponing* showcases a small number of shoppers who plan their trips to the store with military precision. They clip coupons, scout out the stores that offer the best deals, and buy products in enormous quantities to save money. The returns are typically hundreds of dollars in savings each time they visit the store.

While these couponers often get groceries for practically nothing and appear to beat the system, they go to a lot of trouble to secure a deal. Some dive in dumpsters to get the discarded Sunday newspaper coupon sections. Others keep food stashes that take up most of the space in their homes. They use spreadsheets, folders, and calculators to determine how to save as much as possible.

As good economists, we know that getting a really good deal on something doesn't make it free. The amount of time it takes to be an extreme couponer is staggering—equivalent to a part-time job. Clearly, the participants do not fully account for the time

Would you dumpster-dive to get coupons?

they spend on couponing. Saving $200 at the store sounds great unless it takes you 20 hours to do so; that's only $10 an hour. Many of the people on the show might find that they could earn substantially more by putting their organizational skills to use in the workforce. It is this very reason that causes many households not to clip coupons in the first place. After all, time is money.

ECONOMICS IN THE REAL WORLD

Groupon

Groupon is an organization that negotiates sizable discounts (typically 50% or more) with local businesses. It then sends the deals to local subscribers through email, Facebook, or Twitter. If enough subscribers decide they like the deal, Groupon sends—for a fee—a discount coupon to everyone who signed up. Both parties win: Groupon subscribers score a deal on something they might not otherwise purchase, and businesses generate additional revenue through price discrimination.

Does Groupon price-discriminate perfectly? No. Some people who might have been willing to pay full price will occasionally score a discount. But on balance, since Groupon operates in many major cities, there are many residents who want to try something new. In addition, Groupon users tend to be more price-sensitive than nonusers. Because using Groupon requires some effort, not everyone will bother to

If enough people sign up, each one gets a discount.

become a subscriber, sign up for coupons, and remember to use them. This is imperfect price discrimination, but it is still good business. ✳

Conclusion

The word "discrimination" has negative connotations, but not when combined with the word "price." Charging different prices to different groups of customers results in more economic activity and is more efficient than charging a single price across the board. Under price discrimination, many consumers pay less than they would if a firm charged a single price. This has the effect of increasing social welfare, reducing deadweight loss, and creating a more efficient outcome. Perfect price discrimination occurs when a firm is able to charge a different price to every customer. The result is a socially efficient outcome in which most of the gains from exchange accrue to sellers.

Price discrimination also helps us understand how many markets actually function, since instances of highly competitive markets and monopoly are rare.

ANSWERING THE BIG QUESTIONS

What is price discrimination?

✳ Price discrimination occurs when firms have downward-sloping demand curves, can identify different groups of customers with varying price elasticities of demand, and can prevent resale among their customers.

✳ A firm must have some market power before it can charge more than one price.

How is price discrimination practiced?

✳ Under price discrimination, some consumers pay a higher price and others receive a discount. Price discrimination is profitable for the firm, reduces deadweight loss, and helps to restore a higher output level.

Outsmarting Grocery Store Tactics

Throughout this chapter, we have considered the shopping experience in the context of price discrimination. Here we focus on how the typical grocery store is set up to manipulate buyers into spending more. Grocery stores carefully cultivate an enticing, multisensory experience—from the smell of the bread in the bakery, to the colorful cut flowers and fresh produce, to the eat-in restaurants and coffee bars, and the tens of thousands of other items to purchase. You need to be on your game so as not to overspend your budget. Here is some advice to help you save a few dollars.

Understand how grocery stores route you through the store. Have you ever wondered why the produce is displayed in a certain area? Or why most of the stuff you really need is at the back of the store? The grocery store has set things up to entice you to purchase more than you really need. Suppose that you are there to pick up a gallon of milk. In most stores, the refrigerated section is in the back, so that you have plenty of opportunities to impulsively grab something else that looks good.

Notice that popular items are placed at eye level. Believe it or not, supermarkets make more profits from *manufacturers* than from consumers. Manufacturers pay "slotting fees" to have their products placed in desirable locations. But the product you actually want may be on a higher or lower shelf—so it pays to look up and down.

Beware of sales. Stores know that shoppers gravitate to markdowns and sales. However, many shoppers are not very diligent in determining if the sale is a good value. Don't buy something simply because it is "on sale" and located at the end of the aisle. This is one way that groceries make extra money: you end up buying stuff you don't really need.

Find the loss leaders. To draw traffic to the store, groceries compete by offering a few fantastic promotions. Sometimes, the sale items are priced so low that the store actually loses money by selling them.

Grocery stores try to tempt you to buy more than you need.

But the store's management is counting on making up the difference when you buy other items throughout the store. The deal you get on one item should not cause you to let down your guard on other purchases.

Beware of coupons! Coupons aren't always the best deal either. Stores know which manufacturer coupons their customers have, so they rarely reduce the price on those products. If you have to pay full price in order to use a coupon, is it really a good deal? Consider store brands or other brands of the same item before you use a coupon.

Try the store brands. Generally, store brands are cheaper than name brands. The store brand is often exactly the same product as the name brand—it is just repackaged at the manufacturing plant and sold for less. You can save a lot of money by buying store brands.

Finally, get a smaller shopping cart. When their carts fill up, most shoppers instinctively ration the remaining space and become far more selective about what they pick up.

If you are aware of the tactics that grocery stores deploy, you can start beating them at their own game.

CONCEPTS YOU SHOULD KNOW

perfect price discrimination (p. 335)

price discrimination (p. 334)

QUESTIONS FOR REVIEW

1. What two challenges must a firm overcome to effectively price-discriminate?

2. Why does price discrimination improve the efficiency of the market?

3. Why is preventing resale a key to successful price discrimination?

4. If perfect price discrimination reduces consumer surplus to zero, how can this lead to the most socially desirable level of output?

STUDY PROBLEMS (✱ solved at the end of the section)

1. Seven potential customers are interested in seeing a movie. Since the marginal cost of admitting additional customers is zero, the movie theater maximizes its profits by maximizing its revenue.

Customer	Maximum willingness to pay	Age
Allison	$8	66
Becky	11	34
Charlie	6	45
David	7	16
Erin	6	9
Franco	10	28
Grace	9	14

a. What price would the theater charge if it could only charge one price?

b. If the theater could charge two prices, what prices would it choose? Which customers would pay the higher price, and which would pay the lower price?

2. Identify whether each of the following is an example of price discrimination. Explain your answers.

a. A cell phone carrier offers unlimited calling on the weekends for all of its customers.

b. Tickets to the student section for all basketball games are $5.

c. A restaurant offers a 20% discount for customers who order dinner between 4 and 6 p.m.

d. A music store has a half-price sale on last year's guitars.

e. A well-respected golf instructor charges each customer a fee just under the customer's maximum willingness to pay for lessons.

3. At many amusement parks, customers who enter after 4 p.m. receive a steep discount on the price of admission. Explain how this practice is a form of price discrimination.

4. Name three products for which impatience on the part of the consumer enables a firm to price-discriminate.

✱ 5. Prescription drug prices in the United States are often three to four times higher than in Canada, the United Kingdom, and India. Today, pharmacies in these countries fill millions of low-cost prescriptions through the mail to U.S. citizens. Given that the pharmaceutical industry cannot prevent the resale of these drugs, are the industry's efforts to price-discriminate useless? Explain your answer.

✱ 6. Metropolitan Opera tickets are the most expensive on Saturday night. There are often a very limited number of "student rush" tickets, with which a lucky student can wind up paying $20 for a $250 seat. The student rush tickets are available first-come, first-served. Why does the opera company offer these low-cost tickets? How does it benefit from this practice? Why are students, and not other groups of customers, offered the discounted tickets?

SOLVED PROBLEMS

5. Buying prescription drugs outside the United States is increasingly common. Since the pharmaceutical companies charge three to four times more for drugs sold domestically than they do in most other countries, it would seem that the drug industry's efforts to price-discriminate aren't working, but that is not true. Not everyone fills their prescriptions from foreign sources—only a small fraction of U.S. customers go to that much effort. Since most U.S. citizens still purchase the more expensive drugs here, the pharmaceutical companies are benefiting from price discrimination, even though some consumers manage to navigate around their efforts.

6. The Met hopes to sell all of its $250 tickets, but not every show sells out and some tickets become available at the last minute. The student rush tickets benefit both the opera company and the students: the company can fill last-minute seats, and the students, who have elastic demand and low income, get a steep discount. The Met is able to perfectly price-discriminate, since the rush tickets require a student ID. Other groups of operagoers are therefore unable to buy the rush tickets. This practice effectively separates the customer base into two groups: students and nonstudents. Students make ideal rush customers because they are more willing to change their plans in hopes of obtaining last-minute tickets than other groups. Some opera companies also open up the rush tickets to seniors, another group that is easy to identify and generally has significant flexibility.

Monopolistic Competition and Advertising

Advertising increases the price of products without adding value for the consumer.

If you drive down a busy street, you will find many competing businesses, often right next to one another. For example, in most places a consumer in search of a quick bite has many choices, and more fast-food restaurants appear all the time. These competing firms advertise heavily. The temptation is to see advertising as driving up the price of a product, without any benefit to the consumer. However, this misconception doesn't account for why firms advertise. In markets where competitors sell slightly differentiated products, advertising enables firms to inform their customers about new products and services; yes, costs rise, but consumers also gain information to help make purchase decisions.

In this chapter, we look at *monopolistic competition,* a widespread market structure that has features of both competitive markets and monopoly. We also explore the benefits and disadvantages of advertising, which is prevalent in markets with monopolistic competition.

Want something to eat quickly? There are many choices.

BIG QUESTIONS

* **What is monopolistic competition?**
* **What are the differences among monopolistic competition, competitive markets, and monopoly?**
* **Why is advertising prevalent in monopolistic competition?**

What Is Monopolistic Competition?

Some consumers prefer the fries at McDonald's, while others may crave a salad at Panera Bread or the chicken at KFC. Each fast-food establishment has a unique set of menu items. The different products in fast-food restaurants give each seller a small degree of market power. This combination of market power and competition is typical of the market structure known as *monopolistic competition*. Indeed, **monopolistic competition** is characterized by free entry, many different firms, and *product differentiation*. **Product differentiation** is the process firms use to make a product more attractive to potential customers. Firms use product differentiation to contrast their product's unique qualities with competing products. The differences, which we will examine in detail, can be minor and can involve subtle changes in packaging, quality, availability, and promotion.

How does monopolistic competition compare to other market structures we have studied? As Table 12.1 shows, monopolistic competition falls between competitive markets and monopoly.

We have seen that firms in competitive markets do not have any market power. As a result, buyers can expect to find consistently low prices and wide availability. And we have seen that monopolies charge more and restrict availability. In markets that are monopolistically competitive, firms sell differentiated products. This gives the monopolistic competitor some market power, though not as much as a monopolist, who controls the entire market. Monopolistically competitive firms have a small amount of market power that enables them to search for the price that is most profitable.

To understand how monopolistic competition works, we will begin with a closer look at product differentiation.

Monopolistic competition is characterized by free entry, many different firms, and product differentiation.

Product differentiation is the process that firms use to make a product more attractive to potential customers.

TABLE 12.1		
Competitive Markets, Monopolistic Competition, and Monopoly		
Competitive markets	**Monopolistic competition**	**Monopoly**
Many sellers	Many sellers	One seller
Similar products	Differentiated products	A unique product without close substitutes
Free entry and exit	Low barriers to entry and exit	Significant barriers to entry and exit

Product Differentiation

We have seen that monopolistically competitive firms create some market power through product differentiation. Differentiation can occur in a variety of ways, including style, location, and quality.

Style or Type

A trip to a mall is a great way to see product differentiation firsthand. For example, you will find many clothing stores, each offering a unique array of styles and types of clothing. Some stores, such as Abercrombie & Fitch, carry styles that attract younger customers. Others, such as Ann Taylor, appeal to older shoppers. Clothing stores can also vary by the type of clothing they sell, specializing in apparel such as business clothing, plus sizes, or sportswear. Each store hopes to attract a specific type of customer.

When you're ready for lunch at the mall, you can go to the food court, where many different places to eat offer an almost endless variety of choices. Where you decide to eat is a matter of your personal preferences and the price you are willing to pay. Like most consumers, you will select the place that gives you the best combination of choice and value. This makes it possible for a wide range of food vendors to compete side by side with other rivals who provide many good substitutes.

Location

Many businesses attract customers because of their convenient location. Gasoline stations, dry cleaners, barber shops, and car washes provide products and services that customers tend to choose on the basis of convenience of location rather than price. When consumers prefer to save time and to avoid the inconvenience of shopping for a better deal, a firm with a more convenient location will have some pricing power. As a result, producers who sell very similar products can generate some market power by locating their businesses along routes to and from work or in other areas where customers frequently travel.

Quality

Firms also compete on the basis of quality. For instance, if you want Mexican food you can go to Taco Bell, which is inexpensive and offers food cooked

Would you like your Mexican food cheaper . . .   . . . or fresher?

PRACTICE WHAT YOU KNOW

Product Differentiation: Would You Recognize a Monopolistic Competitor?

Is Hollister a monopolistic competitor?

Question: Which of the following are monopolistic competitors?

a. a local apple farm that grows Red Delicious apples

b. Hollister, an apparel store

c. your local water company

Answers:

a. Since Red Delicious apples are widely available at grocery stores, this local apple farm does not have a differentiated product to sell. In addition, it has many competitors that grow exactly the same variety of apples. This apple farm is part of a competitive market; it is not a monopolistic competitor.

b. Hollister has a slightly different mix of clothes than competitors Abercrombie & Fitch and American Eagle Outfitters. This gives the brand some pricing power. Hollister is a good example of a monopolistically competitive firm.

c. Because water is essential and people cannot easily do without it, the local water company has significant monopoly power. Moreover, purifying and distributing water are subject to economies of scale. Your local water company is definitely a monopolist, not a monopolistic competitor.

in advance. In contrast, at Baja Fresh the food is freshly prepared and, as a result, is more expensive. This form of product differentiation serves consumers quite well. Budget-conscious consumers can feast at Taco Bell, while those with a larger budget and a taste for higher-quality Mexican food can consider Baja Fresh as another option.

What Are the Differences among Monopolistic Competition, Competitive Markets, and Monopoly?

Monopolistic competition occupies a place between competitive markets, which produce low prices and an efficient output, and monopoly, which produces high prices and an inefficient output. To help you decide whether monopolistic competition is desirable or not, we consider the outcomes that individual firms can achieve when facing monopolistic competition in the short run and in the long run. Once you understand how monopolistic competition works, we will be able to compare the long-run equilibrium result with that of competitive markets, and then determine if monopolistic competition is desirable from society's standpoint.

Monopolistic Competition in the Short Run and the Long Run

A monopolistically competitive firm sells a differentiated product; this gives it some market power. We see this in the shape of the demand curve for the monopolistic competitor, which is downward sloping. Like a monopolist, the monopolistic competitor uses the profit-maximizing rule, $MR = MC$, and locates the corresponding point on its demand curve to determine the best price to charge and the best quantity to produce. Whether the firm earns a profit, experiences a loss, or breaks even is a function of entry and exit of firms from the market. Recall that entry and exit do not take place in the short run. However, in the long run firms are free to enter an industry when they see a potential for profits, or leave if they are making losses. Therefore, entry and exit regulate how much profit a firm can make in the long run.

Suppose you own a Hardee's fast-food restaurant in Asheville, North Carolina. Your business is doing well and making a profit. Then one day a Five Guys opens up across the street. Some of your customers will try Five Guys and switch, while others will still prefer your fare. But your profit will take a hit. Whether or not you stay in business will depend on how much you lose. To understand how a business owner would make this decision, we now turn to the short-run and long-run implications of monopolistic competition.

Marginal thinking

Monopolistic Competition in the Short Run

Figure 12.1 depicts a firm, like Hardee's, in a monopolistically competitive environment. In 12.1a, the firm makes a profit. Figure 12.1b shows the same firm incurring a loss after a new competitor, like Five Guys, opens nearby. In each case, the firm uses the profit-maximizing rule to determine the best price to charge by locating the point at which marginal revenue equals marginal cost. This calculation establishes the profit-maximizing output along the vertical dashed line. The firm determines the best price to charge (Q_{max}) by locating the intersection of the demand curve with the vertical dashed line.

In Figure 12.1a, we see that because price is greater than cost ($P > ATC$), the firm makes a short-run economic profit. The situation in Figure 12.1b is different. Because $P < ATC$, the firm experiences a short-run economic loss. What accounts for the difference? Since we are considering the same firm, the marginal cost (MC) and average total cost (ATC) curves are identical in both panels. The only functional difference is the location of the demand (D) and marginal revenue (MR) curves. The demand in panel (a) is high enough for the firm to make a profit. In panel (b), however, there is not enough demand; perhaps too many customers have switched to the new Five Guys. So even though the monopolistic competitor has some market power, if demand is too low the firm may not be able to price its product high enough to make a profit.

Monopolistic Competition in the Long Run

In the long run, when firms can easily enter and exit a market, competition will drive economic profit to zero. This dynamic should be familiar to you from our previous discussions of competitive markets. If a firm is making an economic profit, it attracts new entrants to the business. Then the larger supply of competing firms will cause the demand for an individual firm's

FIGURE 12.1

The Monopolistically Competitive Firm in the Short Run

In this figure, we see how a single monopolistic firm may make a profit or incur a loss depending on the demand conditions it faces. Notice that the marginal cost (MC) and average total cost (ATC) curves are identical in both panels, since we are considering the same firm. The only functional difference is the location of the demand (D) and marginal revenue (MR) curves. The demand in (a) is high enough for the firm to make a profit. In (b), however, there is not enough demand, so the firm experiences a loss.

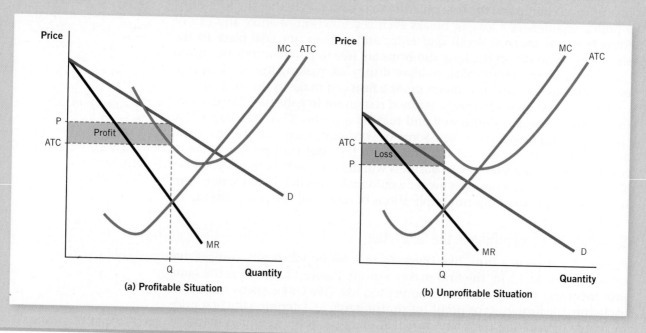

(a) Profitable Situation

(b) Unprofitable Situation

product to contract. Eventually, as more firms enter the market, it will no longer be possible for existing firms to make an economic profit. A reverse process unfolds in the case of a market that is experiencing a loss. In this case, some firms will exit the industry. Then consumers will have fewer options to choose from, and the remaining firms will experience an increase in demand. Eventually, demand will increase to the point at which firms will no longer experience a loss.

Figure 12.2 shows the market after the long-run adjustment process takes place. Price (P) is just equal to the average total cost of production (ATC) at the profit-maximizing rate of output (Q). At this point, firms are earning zero economic profit, as noted by P = ATC along the vertical axis; the market reaches a long-run equilibrium at the point where there is no reason for firms to enter or exit the industry. Note that the demand curve is drawn just *tangent* to the average total cost curve. If demand were any larger, the result would look like Figure 12.1a and firms would experience an economic profit. Conversely, if demand were any lower, the result would look like Figure 12.1b and firms would experience an economic loss. Where entry and exit exist, profits and losses are not possible in the long run. In this way, monopolistic competition resembles a competitive market.

Returning to our example of Hardee's, the firm's success will attract attention and encourage rivals, like Five Guys, to enter the market. As a result, the

FIGURE 12.2

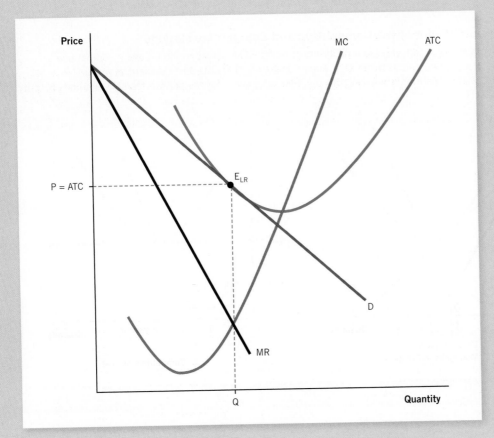

The Monopolistically Competitive Firm in the Long Run

Entry and exit cause short-run profits and losses to disappear in the long run. This means that the price charged (P) must be equal to the average total cost (ATC) of production. At this point, firms are earning zero economic profit, as noted by P = ATC along the vertical axis; the market reaches a long-run equilibrium (E_{LR}) at the point where there is no reason for firms to enter or exit the industry.

short-run profits that Hardee's enjoys will erode. As long as profits occur in the short run, this will encourage other competitors to enter, while short-run losses will prompt some existing firms to close. The dynamic nature of competition guarantees that long-run profits are not possible.

Incentives

Monopolistic Competition and Competitive Markets

We have seen that monopolistic competition and competitive markets are similar; both market structures drive economic profit to zero in the long run. But monopolistic competitors enjoy some market power, which is a crucial difference. In this section, we will compare pricing and output decisions in these two market structures. Then we will look at issues of scale and output.

The Relationship among Price, Marginal Cost, and Long-Run Average Cost

Monopolistically competitive firms have some market power, which enables them to charge slightly more than firms in competitive markets. Figure 12.3 compares the long-run equilibrium between monopolistic competition and

FIGURE 12.3

The Long-Run Equilibrium in Monopolistic Competition and Competitive Markets

There are two primary differences between the long-run equilibrium in monopolistic competition (a) and a competitive market (b). First, monopolistic competition produces markup, since P is greater than MC. In a competitive market, P = MC. Second, the output in monopolistic competition is smaller than the efficient scale. In a competitive market, the firm's output is equal to the most efficient scale.

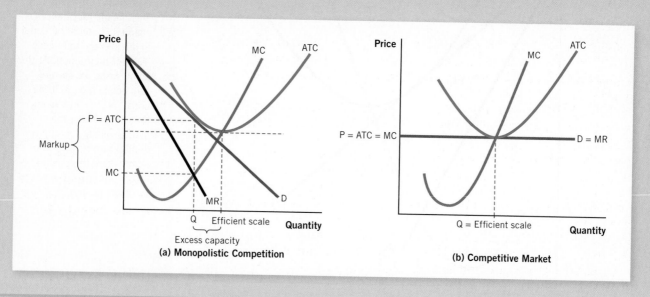

(a) Monopolistic Competition

(b) Competitive Market

Markup
is the difference between the price the firm charges and the marginal cost of production.

a competitive market. Turning first to the firm in a market characterized by monopolistic competition, notice that the price (P) is greater than the marginal cost (MC) of making one more unit. The difference between P and MC is known as the *markup*, which is shown in Figure 12.3a. **Markup** is the difference between the price the firm charges and the marginal cost of production. A markup is possible when a firm enjoys some market power and sells a differentiated product. Products such as bottled water, cosmetics, prescription medicines, eyeglass frames, brand-name clothing, restaurant drinks, and greeting cards all have hefty markups. Let's focus on bottled water. In most cases, it costs just pennies to produce bottled water, but you're unlikely to find it for less than $1; there is a lot of markup on every bottle! Some firms differentiate their product by marketing their water as the "purest" or the "cleanest." Other companies use special packaging. While the marketing of bottled water is unquestionably a successful business strategy, the markup means that consumers pay more. You can observe this result in Figure 12.3a, where the price under monopolistic competition is higher than the price in a competitive market, shown in Figure 12.3b.

Next, look at the ATC curves in both panels. Since a monopolistic competitor has a downward-sloping demand curve, the point of tangency between the demand curve and the ATC curve is different from the same point in a competitive market. The point where P = ATC is higher under monopolistic competition. Panel (b) shows the demand curve just tangent to the ATC curve

at its lowest point in a competitive market. Consequently, we can say that monopolistic competition produces higher prices than a competitive market does. If this result seems odd to you, recall that entry and exit do not ensure the lowest possible price, only that the price is equal to the average total cost of production. In a competitive market, where the demand curve is horizontal, the price is always the lowest possible cost of production. This is not the case under monopolistic competition.

Scale and Output

When a firm produces at an output level that is smaller than the output level needed to minimize average total costs, we say it has **excess capacity**. Turning back to Figure 12.3a, we see excess capacity in the difference between Q and the efficient scale.

This result differs from what we see in Figure 12.3b for a competitive market. In a competitive market, the profit-maximizing output is equal to the most efficient scale of operation. This result is guaranteed because each firm sells an identical product and must therefore set its price equal to the minimum point on the average total cost curve. If, for instance, a corn farmer tried to sell a harvest for more than the prevailing market price, the farmer would not find any takers. In contrast, a monopolistic competitor in a food court enjoys market power because some customers prefer its product. This enables food court vendors to charge more than the lowest average total cost. Therefore, under monopolistic competition, the profit-maximizing output is less than the minimum efficient scale. Monopolistically competitive firms have the capacity to produce more output at a lower cost. However, if they produced more, they would have to lower their price. Because a lower price decreases the firm's marginal revenue, it is more profitable for the monopolistic competitor to operate with excess capacity.

Perrier has a distinctive look—but how different is it from other mineral water?

Excess capacity occurs when a firm produces at an output level that is smaller than the output level needed to minimize average total costs.

Monopolistic Competition, Inefficiency, and Social Welfare

Monopolistic competition produces a higher price and a lower level of output than a competitive market does. Recall that we looked at efficiency as a way to determine whether the decisions of a firm are consistent with an output level that is beneficial to society. Does monopolistic competition display efficiency?

In Figure 12.3a, we observed that a monopolistic competitor has costs that are slightly above the lowest possible cost. So the average total costs of a monopolistically competitive firm are higher than those of a firm in a competitive market. This result is not efficient. To achieve efficiency, the monopolistically competitive firm could lower its price to what we would find in competitive markets. However, since a monopolistic competitor's goal is to make a profit, there is no incentive for this to happen. Every monopolistic competitor has a downward-sloping demand curve, so the demand curve cannot be tangent to the minimum point along the average total cost curve, as seen in Figure 12.3a.

Incentives

Markup is a second source of inefficiency. We have seen that for a monopolistically competitive firm at the profit-maximizing output level, $P > MC$

by an amount equal to the markup. The price reflects the consumer's willingness to pay, and this amount exceeds the marginal cost of production. A reduced markup would benefit consumers by lowering the price and decreasing the spread between the price and the marginal cost. If the firm did away with the markup entirely and set P = MC, the output level would benefit the greatest number of consumers. However, this result would not be practical. At the point where the greatest efficiency occurs, the demand curve would be below the average total cost curve and the firm would lose money. It is unreasonable to expect a profit-seeking firm to pursue a pricing strategy that would benefit its customers at the expense of its own profit.

What if the government intervened on behalf of the consumer? Increased efficiency could be achieved through government regulation. After all, the government regulates monopolists to reduce market power and restore social welfare. Couldn't the government do the same in monopolistically competitive markets? Yes and no! It is certainly possible, but not desirable. Monopolistically competitive firms have a limited amount of market power, so they cannot make a long-run economic profit like monopolists do. In addition, regulating the prices that firms in a monopolistically competitive market can charge would put many of them out of business. Bear in mind that we are talking about firms in markets like the fast-food industry. Doing away with a significant percentage of these firms would mean fewer places for consumers to grab a quick bite. The remaining restaurants would be more efficient, but with fewer restaurants the trade-off for consumers would be less convenience and fewer choices.

Trade-offs

Regulating monopolistic competition through marginal cost pricing, or setting P = MC, would also create a host of problems like those we discussed for monopoly. A good proportion of the economy consists of monopolistically competitive firms—so the scale of the regulatory effort would be enormous. And since implementing marginal cost pricing would result in widespread losses, the government would need to find a way to subsidize the regulated firms to keep them in business. Since the only way to pay for these subsidies would be through higher taxes, the inefficiencies present in monopolistic competition do not warrant government action.

Varying Degrees of Product Differentiation

We have seen that products sold under monopolistic competition are more differentiated than those sold in a competitive market and less differentiated than those sold under monopoly. At one end of these two extremes we have competitive markets where firms sell identical products, have no market power, and face a perfectly elastic demand curve. At the other end we have a monopolist who sells a unique product without good substitutes and faces a steep downward-sloping demand curve indicative of highly inelastic demand. What about the firm that operates under monopolistic competition?

Figure 12.4 illustrates two monopolistic competitors with varying degrees of product differentiation. Firm A enjoys significant differentiation. This occurs when the firm has an especially attractive location, style, type, or quality of product that is in high demand among consumers and that competitors cannot easily replicate. H&M, Urban Outfitters, and Abercrombie & Fitch are good examples. Consumers have strong brand loyalty for the clothes these firms sell, so the demand curve is quite inelastic. The relatively steep slope of

FIGURE 12.4

Product Differentiation, Excess Capacity, and Efficiency

Firm A enjoys more product differentiation. As a result, it has more excess capacity and is less efficient. Firm B sells a product that is only slightly different from its competitors'. In this case, consumers have only weak preferences about which firm to buy from, and consumer demand is elastic. This produces a small amount of excess capacity and a more efficient result.

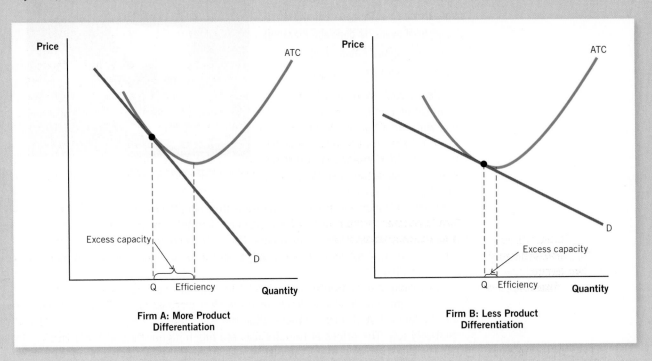

Firm A: More Product Differentiation

Firm B: Less Product Differentiation

the demand curve means that the point of tangency between the demand curve (D) and the average total cost curve (ATC) occurs at a high price. This produces a large amount of excess capacity. In contrast, Firm B sells a product that is only slightly different from its competitors'. Here we can think of T.J.Maxx, Ross, and Marshalls—three companies that primarily sell discounted clothes. In this case, consumers have only weak preferences for a particular firm and consumer demand is elastic. The relatively flat nature of the demand curve means that the point of tangency between demand (D) and average total cost (ATC) occurs at a relatively low cost. This produces a small amount of excess capacity.

Monopolisitic competition leads to substantial product variety and greater selection and choice, all of which are beneficial to consumers. Therefore, any policy efforts that attempt to reduce inefficiency by

Would you want to dress like this every day? Product variety is something consumers are willing to pay for.

PRACTICE WHAT YOU KNOW

Markup: Punch Pizza versus Pizza Hut

Question: Punch Pizza is a small upscale chain in Minnesota that uses wood-fired ovens. In contrast, Pizza Hut is a large national chain. Would one have more markup on each pizza?

Punch Pizza uses wood-fired ovens.

Answer: If you ask people in the Twin Cities about their favorite pizza, you will find a cultlike following for Punch Pizza. That loyalty translates into inelastic demand. Punch Pizza claims to make the best Neapolitan pie. Fans of this style of pizza gravitate to Punch Pizza for the unique texture and flavor. In contrast, Pizza Hut competes in the middle of the pizza market and has crafted a taste that appeals to a broader set of customers. Pizza Hut's customers can find many other places that serve a similar product, so these customers are much more price-sensitive.

The marginal cost of making pizza at both places consists of the dough, the toppings, and wages for labor. At Pizza Hut, pizza assembly is streamlined for efficiency. Punch Pizza is more labor intensive, but its marginal cost is still relatively low. The prices at Punch Pizza are much higher than at Pizza Hut. As a result, the markup—or the difference between the price charged and the marginal cost of production—is greater at Punch Pizza than at Pizza Hut.

lowering the prices that monopolistically competitive firms can charge will have the unintended consequence of limiting the product variety in the market. That sounds like a small price to pay for increased efficiency. But not so fast! Imagine a world without any product differentiation in clothes. Part of the reason why fashions go in and out of style is the desire among consumers to express their individuality. Therefore, consumers are willing to pay a little more for product variety in order to look different from everyone else.

Why Is Advertising Prevalent in Monopolistic Competition?

Advertising is a familiar fact of daily life. It is also a means by which companies compete and, therefore, a cost of doing business in many industries. In the United States, advertising expenditures account for approximately 2% of all economic output annually. Worldwide, advertising expenses are a little

Advertising

Super Bowl Commercials

The be-all of advertising spots is the televised Super Bowl. Because commercial time costs more than $3 million for a 30-second spot, examining the companies that advertise provides a useful barometer of economic activity. In 2013, three of the most popular commercials were by Best Buy, Taco Bell, and Anheuser-Busch. They joined the usual suspects Coca-Cola and Pepsi (soft drinks), Tide (detergent), Paramount (motion pictures), and Volkswagen, Audi, Toyota, Mercedes-Benz, Kia, and Hyundai (autos), in buying advertising time.

Super Bowl ads highlight sectors of the economy that are thriving. In addition, firms that advertise during the Super Bowl build brand recognition, which helps to differentiate their product from the competition.

"Ladies, look at me, now look at your man, now back to me."—Old Spice guy

less—about 1% of global economic activity. While the percentages are small in relative terms, in absolute terms worldwide advertising costs are over half a trillion dollars each year. Is this money well spent? Or is it a counterproductive contest that increases cost without adding value for the consumer? In this section, we will find that the answer is a little of both. Let's start by seeing who advertises.

Why Firms Advertise

No matter the company or slogan, the goal of advertising is to drive additional demand for the product being sold. Advertising campaigns use a variety of techniques to stimulate demand. In each instance, advertising is designed to highlight an important piece of information about the product. Table 12.2 shows how this process works. For instance, the FedEx slogan, "When it absolutely, positively has to be there overnight," conveys reliability and punctual service. Some customers who use FedEx are willing to pay a premium for overnight delivery because the company has differentiated itself from its competitors—UPS, DHL, and (especially) the United States Postal Service.

A successful advertising campaign will change the demand curve in two dimensions: it will shift the demand curve to the right and alter its shape.

TABLE 12.2

Advertising and Demand

Company / Product	Advertising slogan	How it increases demand
Quaker / Life cereal	*He likes it! Hey, Mikey!*	The slogan attempts to convince parents that children will like Life cereal, making it a healthy choice that their children will eat.
John Deere / tractors	*Nothing runs like a Deere.*	The emphasis on quality and performance appeals to buyers who desire a high-quality tractor.
Frito-Lay / Lay's potato chips	*Betcha can't eat just one.*	The message that one potato chip is not enough to satisfy your craving appeals to chip buyers who choose better taste over lower-priced generics.
Energizer / batteries	*He keeps going and going and going.*	The campaign focuses attention on longevity in order to justify the higher prices of top-quality batteries.
FedEx / delivery service	*When it absolutely, positively has to be there overnight*	Reliability and timeliness are crucial attributes of overnight delivery.
Visa / credit card	*It's everywhere you want to be.*	Widespread acceptance and usability are two of the major reasons for carrying a credit card.
Avis / rental cars	*We're number two; we try harder.*	The emphasis on service encourages people to use the company.

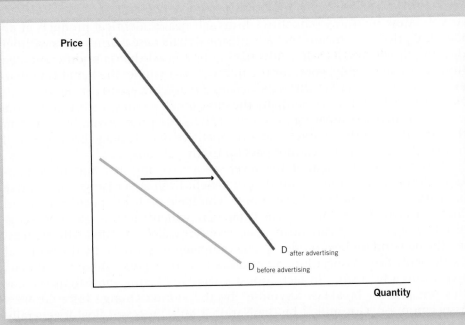

FIGURE 12.5

Advertising and the Demand Curve

A successful advertising campaign increases demand. Advertising also makes the demand curve more inelastic, or vertical, by informing consumers about differences that they care about. After advertising, consumers desire the good more intensely, which makes the demand curve for the firm's product somewhat more vertical.

Turning to Figure 12.5, we see this change. First, the demand curve shifts to the right in response to the additional demand created by the advertising. Second, the demand curve becomes more inelastic, or slightly more vertical. This happens because advertising has highlighted features that make the product attractive to specific customers who are now more likely to want it. Since demand is more inelastic after advertising, the firm increases its market power and can raise its price.

In addition to increasing demand, advertising conveys information that consumers may find helpful in matching their preferences. It tells us about the price of the goods offered, the location of products, and the introduction of new products. Firms also use advertising as a competitive mechanism to underprice one another. Finally, an advertising campaign signals quality. Firms that run expensive advertising campaigns are making a significant investment in their product. It is highly unlikely that a firm would spend a great deal on advertising if it did not think the process would yield a positive return. So a rational consumer can infer that firms spending a great deal on advertising are likely to have a higher-quality product than a competitor who does not advertise.

Advertising in Different Markets

Many firms engage in advertising, but not all market structures find advertising to be equally productive. In our continuum from competitive markets to monopoly, markets that function under monopolistic competition invest the most in advertising.

Advertising in Competitive Markets

As you know by now, competitive firms sell nearly identical products at an identical price. This means that advertising dollars raise a firm's costs without directly influencing its sales. Advertising for a good that is undifferentiated functions like a public good for the industry as a whole: the benefits flow to every firm in the market through increased market demand for the product. However, each firm sells essentially the same good, so consumers can find the product at many competing locations at the same price. An individual firm that advertises in this market is at a competitive disadvantage because it will have higher costs that it cannot pass on to the consumer.

This does not mean that we never see advertising in competitive markets. Although individual firms do not benefit from advertising, competitive industries as a whole can. For example, you have probably heard the slogan "Beef—it's what's for dinner." The campaign, which began in 1992, is recognized by over 80% of Americans and has been widely credited with increasing the demand for beef products. The campaign was funded by the National Cattlemen's Beef Association, an organization that puts millions of dollars a year into advertising. In fact, industry-wide marketing campaigns such as "It's not just for breakfast anymore" by the Florida Orange Juice Growers Association, or "Got milk?" by the National Milk Processor Board, generally

ECONOMICS IN THE MEDIA

Advertising

E.T.: The Extra-Terrestrial

The movie *E.T.* (1982) contains one of the most famous examples of product placement. In the movie, a boy leaves a trail of candy to bring E.T. closer to him. Originally, the filmmakers offered Mars the chance to have M&Ms used in the movie. Mars said no thanks. The filmmakers instead approached Hershey's, the manufacturers of Reese's Pieces—at that time a rival product of M&Ms that was not terribly successful. When *E.T.* became a blockbuster, the demand for Reese's Pieces suddenly tripled and firmly established the product in the minds of many Americans. How much did Hershey's pay for the product placement? It paid $1 million—not bad, considering how successful Reese's Pieces have become.

This is a great example of how firms must think beyond their advertising budgets and consider the

Hungry for a snack?

strategic repercussions of possibly losing market share to a rival. Mars failed to protect its position in the market.

Advertising and the Super Bowl

Super Bowl commercials are watched at least as closely as the football game itself. Fans love these usually creative and comedic ads. But economists pay close attention for different reasons. Who's advertising and what does it say about those industries? Are the ads money well spent, or do they increase business costs without making a noticeable difference in profits? Here we examine advertising over ten recent Super Bowls.

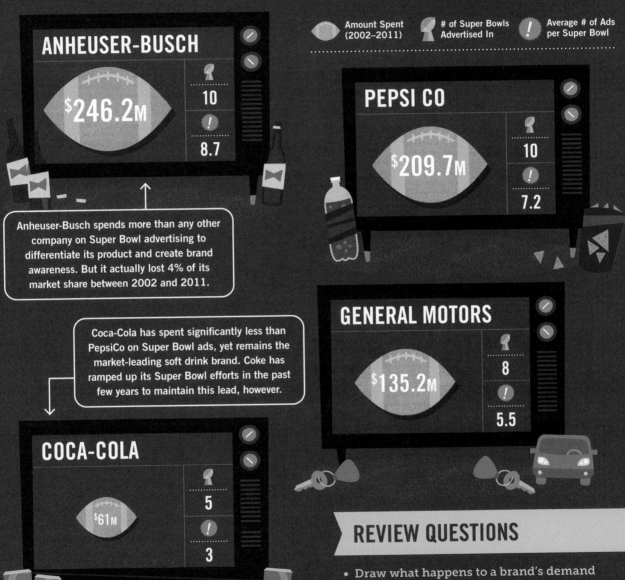

Amount Spent (2002–2011) # of Super Bowls Advertised In Average # of Ads per Super Bowl

ANHEUSER-BUSCH
$246.2M
10
8.7

Anheuser-Busch spends more than any other company on Super Bowl advertising to differentiate its product and create brand awareness. But it actually lost 4% of its market share between 2002 and 2011.

PEPSI CO
$209.7M
10
7.2

Coca-Cola has spent significantly less than PepsiCo on Super Bowl ads, yet remains the market-leading soft drink brand. Coke has ramped up its Super Bowl efforts in the past few years to maintain this lead, however.

GENERAL MOTORS
$135.2M
8
5.5

COCA-COLA
$61M
5
3

Some of these companies, especially Coca-Cola and Pepsi, are considered oligopolists rather than monopolistic competitors. We'll discuss oligopoly in the next chapter.

REVIEW QUESTIONS

- Draw what happens to a brand's demand curve when it successfully achieves product differentiation through advertising.

- Describe the risks and rewards of advertising from the perspective of both the brand and the consumer.

indicate that competitive firms have joined forces to advertise in an effort to increase demand.

Advertising under Monopolistic Competition

Advertising is widespread under monopolistic competition because firms have differentiated products. This is easy to observe if we look at the behavior of pizza companies. Television commercials by national chains such as Domino's, Pizza Hut, Papa John's, and Little Caesars are widespread, as are flyers and advertisements for local pizza places. Since each pizza is slightly different, each firm's advertising increases the demand for its product. In short, the gains from advertising go directly to the firm spending the money. This generates a strong incentive to advertise to gain new customers or to keep customers from switching to other products. Since each firm feels the same way, advertising becomes the norm among monopolistically competitive firms.

Incentives

Monopoly

The monopolist sells a unique product without close substitutes. The fact that consumers have few good alternatives when deciding to buy the good makes the monopolist less likely to advertise than a monopolistic competitor. When consumer choice is limited, the firm does not have to advertise to get business. In addition, the competitive aspect is missing, so there is no need to advertise to prevent consumers from switching to rival products. However, that does not mean that the monopolist never advertises.

The monopolist may wish to advertise to inform the consumer about its product and stimulate demand. This strategy can be beneficial as long as the gains from advertising are enough to cover the firm's cost. For example, De Beers, the giant diamond cartel, controls most of the world's supply of rough-cut diamonds. The company does not need to advertise to fend off competitors, but it advertises nevertheless because it is interested in creating more demand for diamonds. De Beers authored the famous "A diamond is forever" campaign and, more recently, has developed a new marketing campaign that suggests women should purchase a "right-hand ring" for themselves.

The Negative Effects of Advertising

We have seen the benefits of advertising, but there are also drawbacks. Two of the most significant are that advertising raises costs and can be deceitful.

Advertising and Costs

Advertising costs are reflected in the average total cost curve of the firm. Figure 12.6 shows the paradox of advertising for most firms. When a firm advertises, it hopes to increase demand for the product and sell more units—say, from point 1 at Q_1 to point 2 at the higher quantity, Q_2. If the firm can sell enough additional units, it will enjoy economies of scale and the cost will fall from ATC_1 to ATC_2. This return on the advertising investment looks like a good business decision.

However, the reality of advertising is much more complex. Under monopolistic competition, each firm is competing with many other firms selling somewhat different products. Rival firms will respond with advertising of their own. This dynamic makes advertising the norm in monopolistic competition. Each firm engages in competitive advertising to win new customers and keep the old ones. As a result, the impact on each individual firm's demand largely cancels out. This result is evident in the movement from point 1 to point 3 in Figure 12.6. Costs rise from ATC_1 to ATC_3 along the higher LRATC curve, but demand (that is, quantity produced) may remain at Q_1. The net result is that advertising creates higher costs. In this case, we can think of advertising as causing a negative *business-stealing externality* whereby no individual firm can easily gain market share but feels compelled to advertise to protect its customer base.

We have seen that advertising raises costs for the producer. It also raises prices for consumers. In fact, consumers who consistently favor a particular

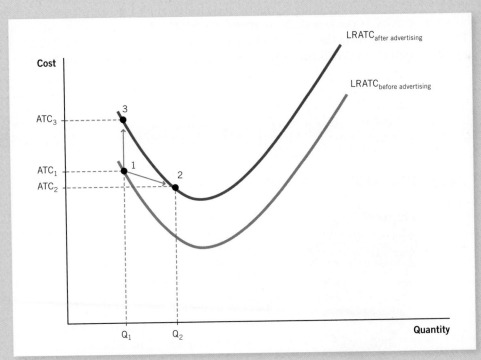

FIGURE 12.6

Advertising Increases Cost

By advertising, the firm hopes to increase demand (or quantity) from point 1 to point 2. In this scenario, the increase in demand from Q_1 to Q_2 is large enough to create economies of scale even though advertising causes the long-range average total cost curve (LRATC) to rise. Since monopolistically competitive firms each advertise, the advertising efforts often cancel each other out. This raises the long-range average total costs without increasing demand much, so the firm may move from point 1 to point 3 instead.

Pearl ear studs are a nice gift, but they are even better when they come in a . . .

. . . blue box.

brand of a product have more inelastic demand than those who are willing to switch from one product to another. Therefore, brand loyalty often means higher prices. Let's look at an example.

Suppose that you buy all your jewelry at Tiffany's. One day, you enter the store to pick up pearl ear studs. You can get a small pair of pearl studs at Tiffany's for $300. But it turns out that you can get studs of the same size, quality, and origin (freshwater) at Pearl World for $43, and you can find them online at Amazon for $19. There are no identifying marks on the jewelry that would enable you, or a seasoned jeweler, to tell the ear studs apart! Why would you buy them at Tiffany's when you can purchase them for far less elsewhere? The answer, it turns out, is that buying ear studs is a lot like consuming many other goods: name recognition matters. So do perception and brand loyalty. Many jewelry buyers also take cues from the storefront, how the staff dresses, and how the jewelry is packaged. Now spending $300 total is a lot of money for the privilege of getting the Tiffany's blue box. Consumers believe that Tiffany's jewelry is better, when all that the store is doing is charging more markup.

PRACTICE WHAT YOU KNOW

Advertising: Brands versus Generics

Why do some frozen pizzas cost more than others, when brands that offer similar quality are only a few feet away in the frozen-foods aisle? To answer that question, consider the following questions:

Question: What would graphs showing price and output look like for DiGiorno and for a generic pizza? What is the markup for DiGiorno?

DiGiorno or generic?

(CONTINUED)

(CONTINUED)

Answer: Here is the graph for DiGiorno.

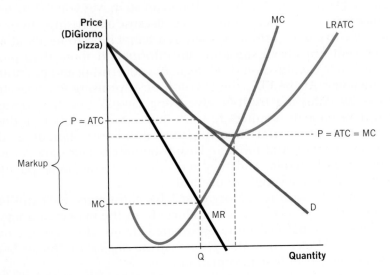

Answer: And here is the graph for the generic pizza.

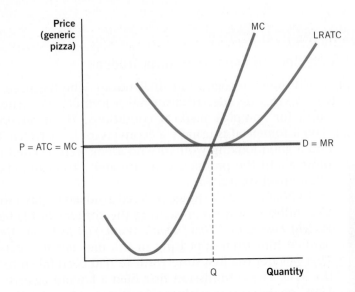

Question: Does DiGiorno or a generic brand have a stronger incentive to maintain strict quality control in the production process? Why?

Answer: DiGiorno has a catchy slogan: "It's not delivery. It's DiGiorno!" This statement tries to position the product as being just as good as a freshly delivered pizza. Some customers who buy frozen pizzas will opt for DiGiorno over comparable generics since they are familiar with the company's advertising claim about its quality. Therefore, DiGiorno has a stronger incentive to make sure that the product delivers as advertised. Since generic, or store-name, brands are purchased mostly on the basis of price, the customer generally does not have high expectations about the quality.

Truth in Advertising

Finally, many advertising campaigns are not just informative—they are designed to produce a psychological response. When an ad moves you to buy or act in a particular way, it becomes manipulative. Because advertising can be such a powerful way to reach customers, there is a temptation to lie about a product. To prevent firms from spreading misinformation about their products, the Federal Trade Commission (FTC) regulates advertising and promotes economic efficiency. At the FTC, the Division of Advertising Practices protects consumers by enforcing truth-in-advertising laws. While the commission does not have enough resources to track down every violation, it does pay particular attention to claims involving food, non-prescription drugs, dietary supplements, alcohol, and tobacco. Unsubstantiated claims are particularly prevalent on the Internet, and they tend to target vulnerable populations seeking quick fixes to a variety of medical conditions.

Of course, even with regulatory oversight, consumers must still be vigilant. At best, the FTC can remove products from the market and levy fines against companies that make unsubstantiated claims. However, the damage is often already done. The Latin phrase *caveat emptor*, or "buyer beware," sums up the dangers of false information.

ECONOMICS IN THE REAL WORLD

The Federal Trade Commission versus Kevin Trudeau

Channel flippers will surely recognize Kevin Trudeau, who has been a staple of infomercials for over a decade. Trudeau has a formula: he writes books about simple cures for complex medical conditions. He is an engaging, smooth talker. The infomercial is usually a "conversation" between Trudeau and a good-looking woman who seems very excited to learn more about the product. Unfortunately, Trudeau's claims are often unsubstantiated.

In 2009, a federal judge ordered Trudeau to pay more than $37 million for misrepresenting the content of his book *The Weight Loss Cure "They" Don't Want You to Know About* and banned him from appearing in infomercials for three years. This was not the first time Trudeau had been taken to task by the FTC. The commission first filed a lawsuit against him in 1998, charging him with making false and misleading claims in infomercials for products that he claimed could cause significant weight loss, cure drug addictions, and improve memory.

More recently, Trudeau has been offering his products for "free." Customers who call in receive a copy of one of his books and one issue of a monthly newsletter at no charge. However, those who fail to cancel the newsletter incur a monthly charge of $9.95 on their credit card. While there is nothing illegal about the 30-day free trial period, and while many other firms use this tactic, it has sparked additional outrage. ✳

Do you trust this guy?

Product Differentiation: Would You Buy a Franchise?

Franchises are valuable in markets where product differentiation matters. McDonald's, Panera Bread, and KFC each has a different take on serving fast food. But what does it mean to own a franchise?

Franchises are sold to individual owners, who operate subject to the terms of their agreement with the parent company. For instance, purchasing a McDonald's franchise, which can cost as much as $2 million, requires the individual restaurant owner to charge certain prices and offer menu items selected by the parent corporation. As a result, customers who prefer a certain type and quality of food know that the dining experience at each McDonald's will be similar. Most franchises also come with non-compete clauses that guarantee that another franchise will not open nearby. This guarantee gives the franchise owner the exclusive right to sell a differentiated product in a given area.

Suppose that you want to start a restaurant. Why would you, or anyone else, be willing to pay as much as $2 million just for the right to sell food? For that amount, you could open your own restaurant with a custom menu and interior, create your own marketing plan, and locate anywhere you like. For example, Golden Corral and Buffalo Wild Wings are two restaurants with high franchising fees that exceed $1 million. Golden Corral is the largest buffet-style restaurant in the country, and Buffalo Wild Wings is one of the top locations to watch sporting events.

How much do different franchises cost?

You might think that it would make more sense to avoid the franchising costs by opening your own buffet or setting up a bank of big-screen TVs. However, failures in the restaurant industry are high. With a franchise, the customer knows what to expect.

Franchise owners are assured of visibility and a ready supply of customers. Purchasing a franchise means that more potential customers will notice your restaurant, and that drives up revenues. Is that worth $2 million? Yes, in some cases. Suppose that you'll do $1 million in annual sales as part of a franchise, but only $0.5 million on your own. That half-million difference over 20 years means $10 million more in revenue, a healthy chunk of which will turn into profits. This is the magic of franchising.

Conclusion

We began this chapter by discussing the misconception that advertising increases the price of goods and services without adding value for the consumer. Advertising does cost money, but that does not mean it is harmful. Firms willingly spend on advertising because it can increase demand, build brand loyalty, and provide consumers with useful information about differences in products. Monopolistic competitors advertise and mark up their products like monopolists, but, like firms in a competitive market, they cannot earn long-run profits. While an economic profit is possible in the short run for all three, only the monopolist, who has significant barriers to entry, can earn an economic profit in the long run. Entry and exit cause long-run profits to equal zero in competitive and monopolistically competitive firms.

Monopolistic competitors are price makers who fail to achieve the most efficient welfare-maximizing output for society. But this observation does not tell the entire story. Monopolistic competitors do not have as much market power or create as much excess capacity or markup as monopolists. Consequently, the monopolistic competitor lacks the ability to exploit consumers. The result is not perfect, but widespread competition generally serves consumers and society well.

In the next chapter, we continue our exploration of market structure with *oligopoly*, which produces results that are much closer to monopoly than monopolistic competition.

ANSWERING THE BIG QUESTIONS

What is monopolistic competition?

* Monopolistic competition is a market characterized by free entry and many firms selling differentiated products.
* Differentiation of products takes three forms: differentiation by style or type, location, and quality.

What are the differences among monopolistic competition, competitive markets, and monopoly?

* Monopolistic competitors, like monopolists, are price makers who have downward-sloping demand curves. Whenever the demand curve is downward sloping, the firm is able to mark up the price above marginal cost. This leads to excess capacity and an inefficient level of output.
* In the long run, barriers to entry enable a monopoly to earn an economic profit. This is not the case for monopolistic competition or competitive markets.

Why is advertising prevalent in monopolistic competition?

* Advertising performs useful functions under monopolistic competition: it conveys information about the price of the goods offered for sale, the location of products, and new products. It also signals differences in quality. However, advertising also encourages brand loyalty, which makes it harder for other businesses to successfully enter the market. Advertising can be manipulative and misleading.

CONCEPTS YOU SHOULD KNOW

excess capacity (p. 363)
markup (p. 362)

monopolistic competition
(p. 356)

product differentiation (p. 356)

QUESTIONS FOR REVIEW

1. Why is product differentiation necessary for monopolistic competition? What are three types of product differentiation?

2. How is monopolistic competition like competitive markets? How is monopolistic competition like monopoly?

3. Why do monopolistically competitive firms produce less than those operating at the most efficient scale of production?

4. Draw a graph that shows a monopolistic competitor making an economic profit in the short run and a graph that shows a monopolistic

competitor making no economic profit in the long run.

5. Monopolistic competition produces a result that is inefficient. Does this mean that monopolistically competitive markets should be regulated? Discuss.

6. Draw a typical demand curve for competitive markets, monopolistic competition, and monopoly. Which of these demand curves is the most inelastic? Why?

7. How does advertising benefit society? In what ways can advertising be harmful?

STUDY PROBLEMS (✻ *solved at the end of the section*)

✻ 1. At your high school reunion, a friend describes his plan to take a break from his florist shop and sail around the world. He says that if he continues to make the same economic profit for the next five years, he will be able to afford the trip. Do you think your friend will be able to achieve his dream in five years? What do you expect to happen to his firm's profits in the long run?

2. Which of the following could be considered a monopolistic competitor?
   a. local corn farmers
   b. the Tennessee Valley Authority, a large electricity producer
   c. pizza delivery
   d. grocery stores
   e. Kate Spade, fashion designer

3. Which of the following produces the same outcome under monopolistic competition and in a competitive market in the long run?
   a. the markup the firm charges
   b. the price the firm charges to consumers
   c. the firm's excess capacity

   d. the average total cost of production
   e. the amount of advertising
   f. the firm's profit
   g. the efficiency of the market structure

4. In competitive markets, price is equal to marginal cost in the long run. Explain why this is not true for monopolistic competition.

5. Econoburgers, a fast-food restaurant in a crowded local market, has reached a long-run equilibrium.
   a. Draw a diagram showing demand, marginal revenue, average total cost, and marginal cost curves for Econoburgers.
   b. How much profit is Econoburgers making?
   c. Suppose that the government decides to regulate burger production to make it more efficient. Explain what would happen to the price of Econoburgers and the firm's output.

✻ 6. Consider two different companies. The first manufactures cardboard, and the second sells books. Which firm is more likely to advertise?

7. In the diagram below, identify the demand
   curve consistent with a monopolistic competitor making zero long-run economic
   profit. Explain why you have chosen that
   demand curve and why the other two demand
   curves are not consistent with monopolistic
   competition.

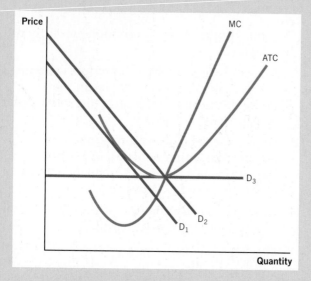

8. Titleist has an advertising slogan, "The #1 ball
   in golf." Consumers can also buy generic golf
   balls. The manufacturers of generic golf balls
   do not engage in any advertising. Assume that
   the average total cost of producing Titleist and
   generic golf balls is the same.
   a. Create a graph showing the price and the
      markup for Titleist.
   b. In a separate graph, show the price and
      output for the generic firms.
   c. Who has a stronger incentive to maintain
      strict quality control in the production
      process—Titleist or the generic firms? Why?

SOLVED PROBLEMS

1. The florist business is monopolistically competitive. This means that firms are free to enter and exit at any time. Firms will enter because your friend's shop is making an economic profit. As new florist shops open, the added competition will drive prices down, causing your friend's profits to fall. In the long run, this means that he will not be able to make an economic profit. He will only earn enough to cover his opportunity costs, or what is known as a fair return on his investment. That is not to say that he won't be able to save enough to sail around the world, but it won't happen as fast as he would like because other firms will crowd in on his success and limit his profits going forward.

6. The cardboard firm manufactures a product that is a component used mostly by other firms that need to package final products for sale. As a result, any efforts at advertising will only raise costs without increasing the demand for cardboard. This contrasts with the bookseller, who advertises to attract consumers to the store. More traffic means more purchases of books and other items sold in the store. The bookstore has some monopoly power and markup. In this case, it pays to advertise. A cardboard manufacturing firm sells exactly the same product as other cardboard producers, so it has no monopoly power and any advertising expenses will only make its cost higher than its rivals'.

Oligopoly and Strategic Behavior

Cell phone companies are highly competitive.

If you have a cell phone, chances are that you receive service from one of four major cell phone carriers in the United States: AT&T, Verizon, Sprint Nextel, or T-Mobile. Together, these firms control 85% of all cellular service. In some respects, this market is very competitive. For example, cell phone companies advertise intensely, and they offer a variety of phones and voice and data plans. Also, there are differences in network coverage and in the number of applications users can access. But despite outward appearances, the cell phone companies are not a good example of a competitive, or even a monopolistically competitive, market. How can we explain this misconception? An important reason is the expense of building and maintaining a cellular network. The largest cell phone companies have invested billions of dollars in infrastructure. Therefore, the cost of entry is very high. And as we learned in Chapter 10, barriers to entry are a key feature of monopolies.

The cell phone industry has features of both competition and monopoly: competition is fierce, but smaller firms and potential entrants into the market find it difficult to enter and compete. This mixture of characteristics represents another form of market structure—*oligopoly*. In this chapter, we will examine oligopoly by comparing it to other market structures that are already familiar to you. We will then look at some of the strategic behaviors that firms in an oligopoly employ; this will lead us into a fascinating subject known as game theory.

Lots of advertising and regular promotions lead most people to view cell phone companies as highly competitive firms—is that true?

BIG QUESTIONS

* What is oligopoly?
* How does game theory explain strategic behavior?
* How do government policies affect oligopoly behavior?
* What are network externalities?

What Is Oligopoly?

Oligopoly
exists when a small number of firms sell a differentiated product in a market with high barriers to entry.

Oligopoly exists when a small number of firms sell a product in a market with significant barriers to entry. An oligopolist is like a monopolistic competitor in that it sells a differentiated product. But, like pure monopolists, oligopolists enjoy significant barriers to entry. Table 13.1 compares the differences and similarities among these three market structures.

We have seen that firms in monopolistically competitive markets usually have a limited amount of market power. As a result, buyers often find low prices and wide availability. In contrast, an oligopoly sells in a market with significant barriers to entry and fewer rivals. This gives the oligopolist more market power than a firm operating under monopolistic competition. However, since an oligopolistic market has more than one seller, no single oligopoly has as much market power as a monopoly.

Our study of oligopoly begins with a look at how economists measure market power in an industry. We will then work through a simplified model of oligopoly to explore the choices that oligopolists make.

Measuring the Concentration of Industries

In markets with only a few sellers, industry output is highly concentrated among a few large firms. Economists use *concentration ratios* as a measure of the oligopoly power present in an industry. The most common measure, known

TABLE 13.1

Comparing Oligopoly to Other Market Structures

Competitive market	Monopolistic competition	Oligopoly	Monopoly
Many sellers	Many sellers	A few sellers	One seller
Similar products	Differentiated product	Typically differentiated product	Unique product without close substitutes
Free entry and exit	Easy entry and exit	Barriers to entry	Significant barriers to entry

TABLE 13.2

Highly Concentrated Industries in the United States

Industry	Concentration ratio of the four largest firms (%)	Top firms
Search engines	98.5	Google, Yahoo, Microsoft
Wireless telecommunications	94.7	Verizon, AT&T, Sprint Nextel, T-Mobile
Satellite TV providers	94.5	DIRECTV, DISH Network
Soda production	93.7	Coca-Cola, PepsiCo, Dr Pepper Snapple
Sanitary paper products	92.7	Kimberly-Clark, Procter & Gamble, Georgia-Pacific
Lighting and bulb manufacturing	91.9	General Electric, Philips, Siemens
Tire manufacturing	91.3	Goodyear, Michelin, Cooper, Bridgestone
Major household appliances	90.0	Whirlpool, Electrolux, General Electric, LG
Automobile manufacturing	87.0	General Motors, Toyota, Ford, Daimler-Chrysler

Source: Highly Concentrated: Companies That Dominate Their Industries, www.ibisworld.com. Special Report, February 2012.

as the four-firm concentration ratio, expresses the sales of the four largest firms in an industry as a percentage of that industry's total sales. Table 13.2 lists the four-firm concentration ratios for highly concentrated industries in the United States. This ratio is determined by taking the output of the four largest firms in an industry and dividing that output by the total production in the entire industry.

In highly concentrated industries like search engines, wireless telecommunications, soda production, and tire manufacturing, the market share held by the four largest firms approaches 100%. At the bottom of our list of most concentrated industries is domestic automobile manufacturing. General Motors, Daimler-Chrysler, Ford, and Toyota (which has eight manufacturing plants in the United States) dominate the domestic automobile industry. These large firms have significant market power.

However, when evaluating market power in an industry, it is important to be aware of international activity. In several industries, including automobile and tire manufacturing, intense global competition keeps the market power of U.S. companies in check. For instance, domestic manufacturers that produce automobiles also must compete globally against cars that are produced elsewhere. This means that vehicles produced by Honda, Nissan, Volkswagen, Kia,

Competition from foreign car companies keeps the market power of the U.S.-based automobile companies in check.

and Volvo, just to name a few companies, limit the market power of domestic producers. As a result, the concentration ratio is a rough gauge of oligopoly power—not an absolute measure.

Collusion and Cartels in a Simple Duopoly Example

In this section, we explore the two conflicting tendencies found in oligopoly: oligopolists would like to act like monopolists, but they often end up competing like monopolistic competitors. To help us understand oligopolistic behavior, we will start with a simplified example: an industry consisting of only two firms, known as a *duopoly*. Duopolies are rare in national and international markets, but not that uncommon in small, local markets. For example, in many small communities the number of cell phone carriers is limited. Imagine a small town where only two providers have cell phone towers. In this case, the cell towers are a sunk cost (see Chapter 9): both towers were built to service all of the customers in the town, so each carrier has substantial excess capacity when the customers are divided between the two carriers. Also, since there is extra capacity on each network, the marginal cost of adding additional customers is zero.

Table 13.3 shows the community's demand for cell phones. Since the prices and quantities listed in the first two columns are inversely related, the data are consistent with a downward-sloping demand curve.

TABLE 13.3

The Demand Schedule for Cell Phones

(1) Price/month (P)	(2) Number of customers (Q)	(3) Total revenue (TR) (P) × (Q)
$180	0	$0
$165	100	16,500
$150	200	30,000
$135	300	40,500
$120	400	48,000
$105	500	52,500
$90	600	54,000
$75	700	52,500
$60	800	48,000
$45	900	40,500
$30	1,000	30,000
$15	1,100	16,500
$0	1,200	0

Column 3 calculates the total revenue from columns 1 and 2. With Table 13.3 as our guide, we will examine the output in this market under three scenarios: competition, monopoly, and duopoly.

Duopoly sits between the two extremes. Competition still exists, but it is not as extensive as you would see in competitive markets, which ruthlessly drive the price down to cost. Nor does the result always mirror that of monopoly, where competitive pressures are completely absent. In an oligopoly, a small number of firms feel competitive pressures and also enjoy some of the advantages of monopoly.

Recall that competitive markets drive prices down to the point at which marginal revenue is equal to the marginal cost. So, if the market is highly competitive and the marginal cost is zero, we would expect the final price of cell phone service to be zero and the quantity supplied to be 1,200 customers—the number of people who live in the small town. At this point, anyone who desires cell phone service would be able to receive it without cost. Since efficiency exists when the output is maximized, and since everyone who lives in the community would have cell phone service, the result would be socially efficient. However, it is unrealistic to expect this outcome. Cell phone companies provide a good that is non-rival and also excludable; in other words, they sell a club good (see Chapter 7). Since these firms are in business to make money, they will not provide something for nothing.

Marginal thinking

At the other extreme of the market structure continuum, since a monopoly faces no competition, price decisions do not depend on the activity of other firms. A monopoly can search for the price that brings it the most profit. Looking at Table 13.3, we see that total revenue peaks at $54,000. At this point, the price is $90 per month and 600 customers sign up for cell phone service. The total revenue is the monopolist's profit since the marginal cost is zero. Notice that the monopolist's price, $90, is more than the marginal cost of $0. In this case, the monopolist's marginal revenue is $1,500. The marginal revenue is determined by looking at column 3 and observing that total revenue rises from $52,500 to $54,000—an increase of $1,500. Since the firm serves 100 additional customers, the marginal revenue is $15 per customer. When the price drops to $75, marginal revenue is −$1,500, since total revenue falls from $54,000 to $52,500. Dividing −$1,500 by 100 yields a marginal revenue of −$15 per customer. The monopolist will maximize profit where MC = MR = 0, and the point closest to this in Table 13.3 is where P = $90. Compared to a competitive market, the monopoly price is higher and the quantity sold is lower. This represents a loss of efficiency.

In a duopoly, the two firms can decide to cooperate—though this is illegal in the United States, as we will discuss shortly. If the duopolists cooperate, we say that they *collude*. **Collusion** is an agreement among rival firms that specifies the price each firm charges and the quantity it produces. The firms that collude can act like a single monopolist to maximize their profits. In this case, the monopoly would maximize its profit by charging $90 and serving 600 customers. If the duopolists divide the market equally, they will each have 300 customers who pay $90, for a total of $27,000 in revenue.

When two or more firms act in unison, economists refer to them as a **cartel**. Many countries prohibit cartels. In the United States, **antitrust laws** prohibit collusion. However, even if collusion were legal, it would probably fail more often than not. Imagine that two theoretical cell phone companies, AT-Phone and Horizon, have formed a cartel and agreed that each will serve

Collusion
is an agreement among rival firms that specifies the price each firm charges and the quantity it produces.

A **cartel** is a group of two or more firms that act in unison.

Antitrust laws
attempt to prevent oligopolies from behaving like monopolies.

Incentives

300 customers at a price of $90 per month per customer. But AT-Phone and Horizon each have an incentive to earn more revenue by cheating while the rival company keeps the agreement. Suppose that AT-Phone believes Horizon will continue to serve 300 customers per their collusive agreement, and AT-Phone lowers its price to $75. Looking at Table 13.3, we see that at this price the total market demand rises to 700 customers. So AT-Phone will be able to serve 400 customers, and its revenue will be 400 × $75, or $30,000. This is an improvement of $3,000 over what AT-Phone made when the market price was $90 and the customers were equally divided.

How would Horizon react? First of all, it would be forced to match AT-Phone's lower price, which would lower the revenue from its 300 customers to $22,500. But put in this position, there's no reason for Horizon to sit on the sideline and do nothing: if it decides to match AT-Phone's market share of 400 customers by lowering its price to $60, it would increase its revenue to 400 × $60, or $24,000. AT-Phone would match that price and make the same revenue, leaving each firm making $3,000 less than when they served only 600 customers.

From what we know about competitive markets, we might expect the competition between the two to cause a price war in which prices eventually fall to zero. But this is not the case. The duopolist will try to gain more market share and then wait to see its competitor's response. Once the market participants understand that a competitor is likely to match their movements, they will stop trying to increase production and end up at the second-best option. (This second-best option, often referred to as the Nash equilibrium, will be discussed in the next section.) For example, if AT-Phone is serving 400 customers and Horizon decides to serve 500 customers, the price of cell phone service will fall to $45. Horizon will make $45 × 500 customers, or $22,500. This is $1,500 less than what the company would have earned if it simply matched its rival's price at $60. As a result, duopolists are unlikely to participate in an all-out price war, and the result of their competition is more efficient than a monopoly's output. In the end, each firm will serve 400 customers, for a total of 800 customers—or 200 more than the monopolist would serve.

Mutual interdependence is a market situation where the actions of one firm have an impact on the price and output of its competitors.

Table 13.4 summarizes the different results under competition, duopoly, and monopoly, using our cell phone example. From this example, we see that a market with a small number of sellers is characterized by **mutual interdependence**, which is a market situation in which the actions of one firm have

TABLE 13.4

Outcomes under Competition, Duopoly, and Monopoly

	Competitive markets	Duopoly	Monopoly
Price	$0	$60	$90
Output	1,200	800	600
Socially Efficient?	Yes	No	No
Explanation	Since the marginal cost of providing cell phone service is zero, the price is eventually driven to zero. Since firms are in business to make a profit, it is unrealistic to expect this result.	Since each firm is mutually interdependent, it adopts a strategy based on the actions of its rival. This leads both firms to charge $60 and serve 400 customers.	The monopolist is free to choose the profit-maximizing output. In the cell phone example, it maximizes its total revenue. As a result, the monopolist charges $90 and serves 600 customers.

an impact on the price and output of its competitors. As a result, a firm's market share is determined by the products it offers, the price it charges, and the actions of its rivals.

ECONOMICS IN THE REAL WORLD

OPEC: An International Cartel

The best-known cartel is the Organization of the Petroleum Exporting Countries, or OPEC, a group of oil-exporting countries that have a significant influence on the world crude oil price and output of petroleum. In order to maintain relatively high oil prices, each member nation colludes to limit the overall supply of oil. While OPEC's activities are legal under international law, collusion is illegal under U.S. antitrust law.

OPEC controls almost 80% of the world's known oil reserves and accounts for almost half of the world's crude production. This gives the cartel's 12 member nations significant control over the world price of oil. OPEC's production is dominated by Saudi Arabia, which accounts for approximately 40% of OPEC's reserves and production. As is the case within any organization, conflict inevitably arises. In the 50 years that OPEC has existed, there have been embargoes (government prohibitions on the exchange of oil), oil gluts, production disputes, and periods of falling prices. As a result, OPEC has been far

What would oil prices be like if OPEC didn't exist?

from perfect in consistently maintaining high prices. In addition, it is careful to keep the price of oil below the cost of alternative energy options. Despite the limitations on OPEC's pricing power, the evidence suggests that OPEC has effectively acted as a cartel during the periods when it adopted output rationing in order to maintain price. ✳

Oligopolists want to emulate the monopoly outcome, but the push to compete with their rivals often makes it difficult to maintain a cartel. Yet the idea that cartels are unstable is not guaranteed. In the appendix to this chapter, we explore two alternative theories that oligopolists will form long-lasting cartels. When a stable cartel is not achieved, firms in oligopoly fall short of fully maximizing profits. But they do not compete to the same degree as firms in competitive markets either. Therefore, when a market is an oligopoly, output is likely to be higher than under monopoly and lower than within a competitive market. As you would expect, the amount of output affects the prices. The higher output (compared to monopoly) makes oligopoly prices generally lower than monopoly prices, and the lower output (compared to a competitive market) makes oligopoly prices higher than those found in competitive markets.

The Nash Equilibrium

As we have discussed in earlier chapters, the market price is the price at which the quantity of a product or service demanded is equal to the quantity supplied. At this price, the market is in equilibrium. In oligopoly, the process

Nash Equilibrium

A Brilliant Madness and *A Beautiful Mind*

A Brilliant Madness (2002) is the story of a mathematical genius, John Nash, whose career was cut short by a descent into madness. At the age of 30, Nash began claiming that aliens were communicating with him. He spent the next three decades fighting paranoid schizophrenia. Before this time, while he was a graduate student at Princeton, Nash wrote a proof about non-cooperative equilibrium. The proof established the Nash equilibrium and became a foundation of modern economic theory. In 1994, Nash was awarded a Nobel Prize in Economics. The documentary features interviews with John Nash, his wife, Alicia, his friends and colleagues, and experts in both game theory and mental illness.

A Brilliant Madness conveys the essentials about Nash without taking liberties with the facts, as Ron Howard did in his 2001 film *A Beautiful Mind*, based on the life of Nash. If you watch *A Brilliant Madness* and then watch the famous bar scene in *A Beautiful Mind*, you should be able to catch the error Ron Howard made in describing how a Nash equilibrium works!

Russell Crowe playing John Nash, who revolutionized modern microeconomics.

that leads to equilibrium may take on a special form referred to as a *Nash equilibrium*, named for mathematician John Nash.

A **Nash equilibrium**, or second-best outcome, occurs when an economic decision-maker has nothing to gain by changing strategy unless it can collude. The theoretical phone example we just explored was an example of a Nash equilibrium. The best strategy for AT-Phone and Horizon is to increase their output to 400 customers each. When both firms reach that level of output, neither has an incentive to change. Bear in mind that the rivals can do better if they collude. Under collusion, each rival serves 300 customers and their combined revenues rise. However, as we saw, if one rival is willing to break the cartel, it will make more revenue if it serves 400 customers ($30,000) while the other firm continues to serve only 300 ($22,500). The firms continue to challenge each other until they reach a combined output level of 800 customers. At this point, the market reaches a Nash equilibrium and neither firm has a reason to change its short-term profit-maximizing strategy.

> A **Nash equilibrium** occurs when an economic decision-maker has nothing to gain by changing strategy unless it can collude.

Oligopoly with More Than Two Firms

We have seen how firms behave in a duopoly. What happens when more firms enter the market? The addition of a third firm complicates efforts to maintain a cartel and increases the possibility of a more competitive result.

We can see this interaction in the cell phone market. The four major companies are not all equal. AT&T and Verizon are significantly larger than Sprint Nextel and T-Mobile. If AT&T and Verizon were the only two providers, the market might have very little competition. However, the smaller Sprint Nextel and T-Mobile play a crucial role in changing the market dynamic. Even though Sprint Nextel and T-Mobile have significantly less market share, they still have developed extensive cellular networks in order to compete. Since Sprint Nextel and T-Mobile have networks with smaller subscriber bases and significant excess capacity, they both aggressively compete on price. As a result, in many respects the entire cell phone industry functions competitively.

To see why this is the case, consider what the addition of a third firm will do to price and output in the market. When the third firm enters the market, there are two effects to consider—price and output. For example, if the third firm builds a cell phone tower, it will increase the overall capacity to provide cell phone service. As we observed in the duopoly example, if the total number of cell phone contracts sold (the supply) increases, all the firms must charge a lower price. This demonstrates the **price effect**, which occurs when the price of a good or service is affected by the entrance of a rival firm in the market. But since the marginal cost of providing cell phone service is

A **price effect** occurs when the price of a good or service is affected by the entrance of a rival firm in the market.

PRACTICE WHAT YOU KNOW

Oligopoly: Can You Recognize the Oligopolist?

Question: Which firm is the oligopolist?

a. Firm A is in retail. It is one of the largest and most popular clothing stores in the country. It also competes with many rivals and faces intense price competition.

b. Firm B is in the airline industry. It is not the largest carrier, but significant barriers to entry enable it to serve a number of very profitable routes.

c. Firm C is a restaurant in a small, isolated community. It is the only local eatery. People drive from miles away to eat there.

Are airlines a good example of an oligopolist?

Answer: Firm A sells clothing, a product with many competing brands and outlets. The competition is intense, which means that the firm has little market power. As a result, firm A is a player in a monopolistically competitive market. It is not an oligopolist. Firm B has market power on a number of routes it flies. Since barriers to entry often prevent new carriers from securing gate space, even smaller airlines are oligopolists—as is Firm B. Firm C is a monopolist. It is the only place to eat out in the isolated community, and no other restaurant is nearby. It is not an oligopolist.

An **output effect** occurs when the entrance of a rival firm in the market affects the amount produced.

essentially zero, the price that each firm charges is substantially higher than the marginal cost of adding a new customer to the network. When the firm sells an additional unit, it generates additional revenues for the firm. This is known as the **output effect**, which occurs when the entrance of a rival firm in the market affects the amount produced.

The price effect and output effect make it difficult to maintain a cartel when there are more than two firms. Generally, as the number of firms grows, each individual firm becomes less concerned about its impact on the overall price level, because any price above marginal cost creates a profit. Therefore, individual firms are more willing to lower prices since this creates a large output effect for the individual firm and only a small price effect in the market.

Of course, not all firms are the same size. Therefore, smaller and larger firms in an oligopolistic market react differently to the price and output effects. Increased output at smaller firms will have a negligible impact on overall prices because small firms represent only a tiny fraction of the market supply. But this is not true for firms with a large market share—decisions at these firms will have a substantial impact on price and output because the overall amount supplied in the market will change appreciably. In other words, in an oligopoly the decisions of one firm directly affect other firms.

How Does Game Theory Explain Strategic Behavior?

Game theory is a branch of mathematics that economists use to analyze the strategic behavior of decision-makers.

Decision-making under oligopoly can be complex. Recall that with a Nash equilibrium, participants make decisions based on the behavior of others around them. This is an example of **game theory**, a branch of mathematics that economists use to analyze the strategic behavior of decision-makers. In particular, the techniques of game theory can help us determine what level of cooperation is most likely to occur. A game consists of a set of players, a set of strategies available to those players, and a specification of the payoffs for each combination of strategies. The game is usually represented by a payoff matrix that shows the players, strategies, and payoffs. It is presumed that each player acts simultaneously or without knowing the actions of the other.

In this section, we will learn about the prisoner's dilemma, an example from game theory that will help us understand how dominant strategies often frame short-run decisions. We will use the idea of the dominant strategy to explain why oligopolists often choose to advertise. Finally, we will come full circle and argue that the dominant strategy in a game may be overcome in the long run through repeated interactions.

Strategic Behavior and the Dominant Strategy

We have seen that in oligopoly there is mutual interdependence: a rival's business choices affect the earnings that the other rivals can expect to make. In order to learn more about the decisions firms make, we will explore a fundamental problem in game theory known as the *prisoner's dilemma*. The dilemma takes its name from a famous scenario devised by pioneer game theorist Al Tucker soon after World War II.

The scenario goes like this: two prisoners are being interrogated separately about a crime they both participated in, and each is offered a plea bargain to cooperate with the authorities by testifying against the other. If both suspects refuse to cooperate with the authorities, neither can be convicted of a more serious crime, though they will have to spend some time in jail. But the police have offered full immunity if one cooperates and the other does not. This means that each suspect has an incentive to betray the other. The rub is that if they both confess, they will spend more time in jail than if they had both stayed quiet. When decision-makers face incentives that make it difficult to achieve mutually beneficial outcomes, we say they are in a **prisoner's dilemma**. This situation makes the payoff for cooperating with the authorities more attractive than the result of keeping quiet. We can understand why this occurs by looking at Figure 13.1, a payoff matrix that shows the possible outcomes in a prisoner's dilemma situation. Starting with the white box in the upper-left-hand corner, we see that if both suspects testify against each other, they each get 10 years in jail. If one suspect testifies while his partner remains quiet—the upper-right and lower-left boxes—he goes free and his partner gets 25 years in jail. If both keep quiet—the result in the lower-right-hand corner—they each get off with one year in jail. This result is better than the outcome in which both prisoners testify.

Since each suspect is interrogated separately, the decision about what to tell the police cannot be made cooperatively; thus, each prisoner faces a

Incentives

The **prisoner's dilemma** occurs when decision-makers face incentives that make it difficult to achieve mutually beneficial outcomes.

FIGURE 13.1

The Prisoner's Dilemma

The two suspects know that if they both keep quiet, they will spend only one year in jail. The prisoner's dilemma occurs because the decision to confess results in no jail time for the one who confesses if the other does not confess. However, this outcome means that both are likely to confess and get 10 years.

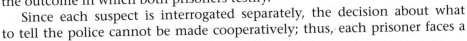

		Tony Montana	
		Testify	Keep quiet
Manny Ribera	Testify	10 years in jail 10 years in jail	25 years in jail goes free
	Keep quiet	goes free 25 years in jail	1 year in jail 1 year in jail

dilemma. The interrogation process makes it a non-cooperative "game" and changes the incentives that each party faces.

Under these circumstances, what will our suspects choose? Let's begin with the outcomes for Tony Montana. Suppose that he testifies. If Manny Ribera also testifies, Tony will get 10 years in jail (the upper-left box). If Manny keeps quiet, Tony will go free (the lower-left box). Now suppose that Tony decides to keep quiet. If Manny testifies, Tony can expect 25 years in jail (the upper-right box). If Manny keeps quiet, Tony will get 1 year in jail (the lower-right box). No matter what choice Manny makes, Tony is always better off choosing to testify. If his partner testifies and he testifies, he gets 10 years in jail as opposed to 25 if he keeps quiet. If his partner keeps quiet and he testifies, Tony goes free as opposed to spending a year in jail if he also keeps quiet. A similar analysis applies to the outcomes for Manny.

A dominant strategy exists when a player will always prefer one strategy, regardless of what his opponent chooses.

When a player always prefers one strategy, regardless of what his opponent chooses, we say it is a **dominant strategy**. We can see this at work in the case of our two suspects. They know that if they both keep quiet, they will spend one year in jail. The dilemma occurs because both suspects are more likely to testify and get 10 years in jail. This choice is obvious for two reasons. First, neither suspect can monitor the actions of the other after they are separated. Second, once each suspect understands that his partner will save jail time if he testifies, he realizes that the incentives are not in favor of keeping quiet.

Incentives

The dominant strategy in our example is a Nash equilibrium. Recall that a Nash equilibrium occurs when economic decision-makers choose the best possible strategy after taking into account the decisions of others. If each suspect reasons that the other will testify, the best response is also to testify. Each suspect may wish that he and his partner could coordinate their actions and agree to keep quiet. However, without the possibility of coordination, neither has an incentive to withhold testimony. So they both think strategically and decide to testify.

Duopoly and the Prisoner's Dilemma

The prisoner's dilemma example suggests that cooperation can be difficult to achieve. To get a better sense of the incentives that oligopolists face when trying to collude, we will use game theory to evaluate the outcome of our cell phone duopoly example.

Recall that our duopolists, AT-Phone and Horizon, produced an output of 800 customers, an amount that was lower than would occur under perfect competition (1,200) but higher than under monopoly (600). Figure 13.2 puts the information from Table 13.3 into a payoff matrix and highlights the revenue that AT-Phone and Horizon could earn at various production levels.

Looking at the bottom two boxes, we see that at high production Horizon can earn either $30,000 or $24,000 in revenue, depending on what AT-Phone does. At a low production level, it could earn either $27,000 or $22,500. The same reasoning is true for AT-Phone. Now look at the right-hand column, and you will see that AT-Phone can earn either $30,000 or $24,000, depending on what Horizon does. At a low production level, it could earn either $27,000 or $22,500. So, once again, the high production levels dominate. The two companies always have an incentive to serve more customers because this strategy yields the most revenue. A high level of production leads to a Nash

Incentives

FIGURE 13.2

The Prisoner's Dilemma in Duopoly

Each company has a dominant strategy to serve more customers because it makes the most revenue even if its competitor also expands production. A high level of production leads to a Nash equilibrium at which both firms make $24,000.

	AT-Phone	
	Low production: 300 customers	High production: 400 customers
Horizon — Low production: 300 customers	$27,000 revenue $27,000 revenue	$30,000 revenue $22,500 revenue
Horizon — High production: 400 customers	$22,500 revenue $30,000 revenue	$24,000 revenue $24,000 revenue

Prisoner's Dilemma

Murder by Numbers

There is an especially compelling example of the prisoner's dilemma at work in *Murder by Numbers* (2002). In this scene, the district attorney's office decides to interrogate two murder suspects. Without a confession, they don't have enough evidence and the two murderers are likely to go free. Each is confronted with the prisoner's dilemma by being placed in a separate room and threatened with the death penalty. In order to get the confession, the detective tells one of the suspects, "Just think of it as a game. Whoever talks first is the winner." The detective goes on to tell one of the suspects that his partner in the other room is "rolling over" (even though the partner is not actually talking) and that the partner will get a

Would you rat on your partner in crime?

lighter sentence because he is cooperating. This places added pressure on the suspect.

equilibrium; both firms make $24,000. However, if the companies operate as a cartel, they can both earn $27,000. Therefore, the Nash equilibrium is their second-best outcome.

Advertising and Game Theory

Incentives

We have seen that oligopolists function like monopolistic competitors in that they sell differentiated products. We know that advertising is commonplace in markets with a differentiated product. In the case of an oligopoly, mutual interdependence means that advertising can create a contest among firms looking to gain customers. This may lead to skyrocketing advertising budgets and little, or no, net gain of customers. Therefore, oligopolists have an incentive to scale back their advertising, but only if the other rivals also agree to scale back. Like all cooperative action among competitors, this is easier said than done.

Figure 13.3 highlights the advertising choices of Coca-Cola and PepsiCo, two fierce rivals in the soft drink industry. Together, Coca-Cola and PepsiCo account for 75% of the soft drink market, with Coca-Cola being the slightly larger of the two firms. Both companies are known for their advertising campaigns, which cost hundreds of millions of dollars. To determine if they gain anything by spending so much on advertising, let's look at the dominant strategy. In the absence of cooperation, each firm will choose to advertise, because the payoffs under advertising ($100 million or $150 million) exceed those of not advertising ($75 million or $125 million). When each firm chooses

FIGURE 13.3

The Prisoner's Dilemma and Advertising

The two companies each have a dominant strategy to advertise. We can see this by observing that Coca-Cola and PepsiCo each make $25 million more profit by choosing to advertise. As a result, they both end up in the upper-left box earning $100 million profit when they could have each made $125 million profit in the lower-right box if they had agreed not to advertise.

		Coca-Cola	
		Advertises	**Does not advertise**
PepsiCo	**Advertises**	$100 million profit $100 million profit	$75 million profit $150 million profit
	Does not advertise	$150 million profit $75 million profit	$125 million profit $125 million profit

Airlines in the Prisoner's Dilemma

American Airlines and Delta Airlines once found themselves in a classic prisoner's dilemma. It all started when Delta wanted to expand its share of the lucrative Dallas-to-Chicago route, where American was the dominant carrier. Delta offered a substantial fare cut on that route to attract new travelers. American threatened a price war by offering its own fare cut on the Delta-dominated Dallas-to-Atlanta route.

Worst

Both airlines had a dominant strategy to cut their fare on the targeted route. Why? If one airline cut its fare and the other did not, the airline that did would gain market share. This was each airline's best possible outcome.

Best

3rd Best

Even if the rival cut its fare too, lowering the price was still the right move—the dominant strategy—for each airline. Why? Because if an airline failed to match the fare of its rival, it would lose market share. This scenario, where both rivals would cut fares and maintain the same market share, was the third-best outcome.

3rd Best

American

Delta

	Discount	No Discount
Discount	3rd Best / 3rd Best (Dallas)	Worst / Best (Chicago)
No Discount	Best / Worst (Dallas)	2nd Best / 2nd Best (Atlanta)

The hallmark of a prisoner's dilemma is when two rivals follow their dominant strategy and the result is the third-best situation for both. It would have been better if no fare discounts were ever considered.

What happened? Fortunately for both airlines, they posted their planned fare cuts on a computer system that allowed them to see what their rival was doing. They each saw the price war starting, backed down, and escaped the prisoner's dilemma!

REVIEW QUESTIONS

- Which expected outcome in the matrix reflects the outcome of this American/Delta pricing war?

- Explain how the ability to communicate can allow two parties to escape a prisoner's dilemma.

to advertise, it generates a profit of $100 million. This is a second-best outcome compared to the $125 million profit each could earn if neither firm advertises. The dilemma is that each firm needs to advertise to market its product and retain its customer base, but most advertising expenditures end up canceling each other out and costing the companies millions of dollars.

ECONOMICS IN THE REAL WORLD

The Cold War

The idea that companies benefit from spending less on advertising has an analogue in warfare. Countries benefit from a "peace dividend" whenever war ends. There is no better example of this than the Cold War between the Soviet Union and the United States that began in the 1950s. By the time the Cold War ended in the late 1980s, both countries had amassed thousands of nuclear warheads in an effort to deter aggression.

The Cold War created a prisoner's dilemma for the United States and the Soviet Union.

This buildup put enormous economic pressure on each country to keep up with the other. During the height of the Cold War, each country found itself in a prisoner's dilemma in which spending more in an arms race was the dominant strategy. When the Soviet Union ultimately dissolved, the United States was able to spend less money on deterrence. In the post–Cold War world of the 1990s, the U.S. military budget fell from 6.5 to 3.5% of gross domestic product (GDP) as the nation reaped a peace dividend. Of course, the prisoner's dilemma cannot account for all military spending: following the terrorist attacks of 2001, U.S. military spending increased again to nearly 5% of GDP by 2004. ✳

Escaping the Prisoner's Dilemma in the Long Run

We have seen how game theory can be a useful tool for understanding strategic decision-making in non-cooperative environments. When you examine the prisoner's dilemma or the Nash equilibrium, the solution represents an outcome that yields the largest gain in the short run. However, many decisions are not made in this way. The dominant strategy does not consider the possible long-run benefits of cooperation.

Game theorist Robert Axelrod decided to examine the choices that participants make in a long-run setting. He ran a sophisticated computer simulation in which he invited scholars to submit strategies for securing points in a prisoner's dilemma tournament over many rounds. All the submissions were collected and paired, and the results were scored. After each simulation, Axelrod eliminated the weakest strategy and re-ran the tournament with the remaining strategies. This evolutionary approach continued until the best strategy remained. Among all strategies, including those that were solely cooperative

ECONOMICS IN THE MEDIA

Prisoner's Dilemma

The Dark Knight

In what is arguably the greatest superhero movie of all time, *The Dark Knight* (2008), the Joker (played by the late Heath Ledger) always seems to be one step ahead of the law. The strategic interactions between the police and the conniving villain are an illustration of game theory in action.

Near the end of the movie, the Joker rigs two full passenger ferries to explode at midnight and tells the passengers that if they try to escape, the bomb will detonate earlier. To complicate matters, one of the ferries is carrying civilian passengers, including a number of children, while the other ferry is transporting prisoners. Each ferry can save itself by hitting a detonator button attached to the other ferry.

The Joker's plan sets up a prisoner's dilemma between the two boats and an ethical experiment. Are the lives of those on the civilian boat worth more than those of the prisoners? The Joker's intention is to have one of the ferries blow up the other and thereby create chaos in Gotham City.

In the payoff matrix, the dominant strategy is to detonate the other boat. Failing to detonate the other boat results in death—either one ferry blows

up at midnight, or the other boat detonates it first. In this scenario, the only chance of survival is if one ferry detonates the other ferry first. As the scene unfolds and the tension builds, the passengers on both boats realize their plight and wrestle with the consequences of their decisions. Gradually, everyone becomes aware that the dominant strategy is to detonate the other boat. What is interesting is how the civilians and prisoners react to this information.

What actually happens? Passengers on each boat decide that they would rather be detonated than willingly participate in the Joker's experiment. Watching the scene as a game theorist will give you a new appreciation for the film.

		Prisoner ferry	
		Detonate other boat	Do not detonate other boat
Civilian ferry	Detonate other boat	Cannot simultaneously happen / Cannot simultaneously happen	Die / Survive
	Do not detonate other boat	Survive / Die	Die / Die

Tit-for-tat
is a long-run strategy that promotes cooperation among participants by mimicking the opponent's most recent decision with repayment in kind.

Incentives

Opportunity cost

or non-cooperative, *tit-for-tat* dominated. **Tit-for-tat** is a long-run strategy that promotes cooperation among participants by mimicking the opponent's most recent decision with repayment in kind. As the name implies, a tit-for-tat strategy is one in which you do whatever your opponent does. If your opponent breaks the agreement, you break the agreement too. If the opponent behaves properly, then you behave properly too.

Since the joint payoffs for cooperation are high in a prisoner's dilemma, tit-for-tat begins by cooperating. In subsequent rounds, the tit-for-tat strategy mimics whatever the other player did in the previous round. The genius behind tit-for-tat is that it changes the incentives and encourages cooperation. Turning back to our example in Figure 13.3, suppose that Coca-Cola and PepsiCo want to save on advertising expenses. The companies expect to have repeated interactions, so they both know from past experience that any effort to start a new advertising campaign will be immediately countered by the other firm. Since the companies react to each other's moves in kind, any effort to exploit the dominant strategy of advertising will ultimately fail. This dynamic can alter the incentives that the firms face in the long run and lead to mutually beneficial behavior.

Tit-for-tat makes it less desirable to advertise by eliminating the long-run benefits. Advertising is still a dominant strategy in the short run because the payoffs with advertising ($100 million or $150 million) exceed those of not advertising ($75 million or $125 million). In the short run, the firm that advertises could earn $25 million extra, but in every subsequent round—if the rival responds in kind—the firm should expect profits of $100 million because its rival will also be advertising. As a result, there is a large long-run opportunity cost for not cooperating. If one firm stops advertising and the other follows suit, they will each find themselves making $125 million in the long run. Why hasn't this happened in the real world? Because Coke and PepsiCo don't trust each other enough to earn the dividend that comes from an advertising truce.

The prisoner's dilemma nicely captures why cooperation is so difficult in the short run. But most interactions in life occur over the long run. For example, scam artists and sketchy companies take advantage of short-run opportunities that cannot last because relationships in the long run—with businesses and with people—involve mutual trust. Cooperation is the default because you know that the other side is invested in the relationship. Under these circumstances, the tit-for-tat strategy works well.

A Caution about Game Theory

Game theory is a decision-making tool, but not all games have dominant strategies that make player decisions easy to predict. Perhaps the best example is the game known as Rock, Paper, Scissors. This simple game has no dominant strategy: paper beats rock (because the paper will cover the rock) and rock beats scissors (because the rock will break the scissors), but scissors beats paper (because the scissors will cut the paper). The preferred choice is strictly a function of what the other player selects. Many situations in life, and business, are more like Rock, Paper, Scissors than the prisoner's dilemma. Winning at business in the long run often occurs because you are one step ahead of the competition, not because you deploy a strategy that attempts to take advantage of a short-run opportunity.

Consider two friends who enjoy playing racquetball together. Both players are of equal ability, so each point comes down to whether the players guess correctly about the direction the other player will hit. Take a look at Figure 13.4. The success of Joey and Rachel depends on how well each one guesses where the other will hit.

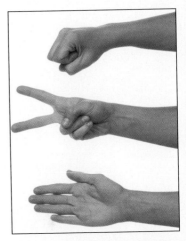

Rock, Paper, Scissors is a game without a dominant strategy.

FIGURE 13.4

No Dominant Strategy Exists

Neither Rachel nor Joey has a dominant strategy that guarantees winning the point. Any of the four outcomes are equally likely on successive points, and there is no way to predict how the next point will be played. As a result, there is no Nash equilibrium here.

		Rachel	
		Guesses to the left	**Guesses to the right**
Joey	**Hits to the left**	Rachel wins the point Joey loses the point	Rachel loses the point Joey wins the point
	Hits to the right	Rachel loses the point Joey wins the point	Rachel wins the point Joey loses the point

In this competition, neither Rachel nor Joey has a dominant strategy that guarantees success. Sometimes Joey wins when hitting to the right; at other times he loses the point. Sometimes Rachel wins when she guesses to the left; at other times she loses. Each player only guesses correctly half the time. Since we cannot say what each player will do from one point to another, there is no Nash equilibrium. Any of the four outcomes are equally likely on successive points, and there is no way to predict how the next point will be played. In other words, we cannot expect every game to include a prisoner's dilemma and produce a Nash equilibrium. Game theory, like real life, has many different possible outcomes.

How Do Government Policies Affect Oligopoly Behavior?

When oligopolists in an industry form a cooperative alliance, they function like a monopoly. Competition disappears, which is not good for society. One way to improve the social welfare of society is to restore competition and limit monopoly practices through policy legislation.

Antitrust Policy

The **Sherman Antitrust Act** was the first federal law limiting cartels and monopolies.

Efforts to curtail the adverse consequences of oligopolistic cooperation began with the **Sherman Antitrust Act** of 1890. This was the first federal law to place limits on cartels and monopolies. The Sherman Act was created in response to the increase in concentration ratios in many leading U.S. industries, including steel, railroads, mining, textiles, and oil. Prior to passage of the Sherman Act, firms were free to pursue contracts that created mutually beneficial outcomes. Once the act took effect, however, certain cooperative actions became criminal. Section 2 of the Sherman Act reads, "Every person who shall monopolize, or attempt to monopolize, or combine or conspire with any other person or persons, to monopolize any part of the trade or commerce among the several States, or with foreign nations, shall be deemed guilty of a felony."

The **Clayton Act** targets corporate behaviors that reduce competition.

The **Clayton Act** of 1914 targets corporate behaviors that reduce competition. Large corporations had been vilified during the presidential election of 1912, and the Sherman Act was seen as largely ineffective in curbing monopoly power. To shore up antitrust policy, the Clayton Act added to the list of activities that were deemed socially detrimental, including:

1. *price discrimination* if it lessens competition or creates monopoly
2. *exclusive dealings* that restrict a buyer's ability to deal with competitors
3. *tying arrangements* that require the buyer to purchase an additional product in order to purchase the first
4. *mergers and acquisitions* that lessen competition, or situations in which a person serves as a director on more than one board in the same industry

As the Clayton Act makes clear, there are many ways to reduce competition.

PRACTICE WHAT YOU KNOW

Dominant Strategy: To Advertise or Not—That Is the Question!

Question: University Subs and Savory Sandwiches are the only two sandwich shops in a small college town. If neither runs a special 2-for-1 promotion, both are able to keep their prices high and earn $10,000 a month. However, when both run promotions, their profits fall to $1,000. Finally, if one runs a promotion and the other does not, the shop that runs the promotion earns a profit of $15,000 and the other loses $5,000. What is the dominant strategy for University Subs? Is there a Nash equilibrium in this example?

How much should a firm charge for this sandwich?

		University Subs	
		Runs a 2-for-1 promotion	Keeps price high
Savory Sandwiches	**Runs a 2-for-1 promotion**	Makes $1,000 / Makes $1,000	Loses $5,000 / Makes $15,000
	Keeps price high	Makes $15,000 / Loses $5,000	Makes $10,000 / Makes $10,000

Answer:

If University Subs runs the 2-for-1 promotion, it will make either $1,000 or $15,000, depending on its rival's actions. If University Subs keeps the price high, it will make either –$5,000 or $10,000, depending on what Savory Sandwiches does. So the dominant strategy will be to run the special, since it guarantees a profit of at least $1,000. Savory Sandwiches has the same dominant strategy and the same payoffs. Therefore, both companies will run the promotion and each will make $1,000. Neither firm has a reason to switch to the high-price strategy since it would lose $5,000 if the other company runs the 2-for-1 promotion. A Nash equilibrium occurs when both companies run the promotion.

Over the past hundred years, lawmakers have continued to refine antitrust policy. Additional legislation, as well as court interpretations of existing antitrust law, have made it difficult to determine whether a company has violated the law. The U.S. Justice Department is charged with oversight, but it often lacks the resources to fully investigate every case. Antitrust law is complex and cases are hard to prosecute, but these laws are essential to maintain a competitive business environment. Without effective restraints on excessive market power, firms would organize into cartels more often or would find other ways to restrict competition. Table 13.5 briefly describes the most influential antitrust cases in U.S. history.

TABLE 13.5

Influential Antitrust Cases in U.S. History

Defendant	Year	Description
Standard Oil	1906	Standard Oil was founded in 1870. By 1897, the company had driven the price down to 6 cents a gallon, which put many of its competitors out of business. Subsequently, Standard Oil became the largest company in the world. In 1906, the U.S. government filed suit against Standard Oil for violating the Sherman Antitrust Act. Three years later, the company was found guilty and forced to break up into 34 independent companies.
ALCOA	1937	The Aluminum Company of America (ALCOA), founded in 1907, maintained its position as the only producer of aluminum in the United States for many years. To keep that position, the company acquired exclusive rights to all U.S. sources of bauxite, the base material from which aluminum is refined. It then acquired land rights to build and own hydroelectric facilities in both the United States and Canada. By owning both the base materials and the only sites where refinement could take place, ALCOA effectively barred other firms from entering the U.S. aluminum market. In 1937, the Department of Justice filed suit against ALCOA. Seven years later, the Supreme Court ruled that ALCOA had taken measures to restrict trade and functioned as a monopoly. ALCOA was not divested because two rivals, Kaiser and Reynolds, emerged soon thereafter.
AT&T	1974	In 1974, the U.S. Attorney General filed suit against AT&T for violating antitrust laws. It took seven years before a settlement was reached to split the company into seven new companies, each serving a different region of the United States. However, five of the seven have since merged to become AT&T Incorporated, which is now one of the largest companies in the world.
Microsoft	1995	When Internet Explorer was introduced in 1995, Microsoft insisted that it was a feature rather than a new Windows product. The U.S. Department of Justice did not agree and filed suit against Microsoft for illegally discouraging competition to protect its software monopoly. After a series of court decisions and appeals, a settlement ordered Microsoft to share application programming interfaces with third-party companies.

Predatory Pricing

While firms have a strong incentive to cooperate in order to keep prices high, they also want to keep potential rivals out of the market. The practice of setting prices deliberately below average variable costs with the intent of driving rivals from the market is known as **predatory pricing**. When this occurs, the firm suffers a short-run loss in order to prevent rivals from entering the market or to drive rival firms out of business in the long run. Once the rivals are gone, the firm should be able to act like a monopolist.

Predatory pricing is illegal, but it is difficult to prosecute. Neither the court system nor economists have a simple rule that helps to determine when a firm steps over the line. Predatory pricing can look and feel like spirited competition. Moreover, the concern is not the competitive aspect or lower prices, but the effect on the market when all rivals fail. To prove that predatory pricing has occurred, the courts need evidence that the firm's prices increased significantly after its rivals failed.

Though Walmart keeps its prices low, there is no evidence that it engages in predatory pricing.

Predatory pricing occurs when firms deliberately set their prices below average variable costs with the intent of driving rivals from the market.

Walmart is often cited as an example of a firm that engages in predatory pricing because its low prices effectively drive many smaller companies out of business. However, there is no evidence that Walmart has ever systematically raised prices after a rival failed. Therefore, its price strategy does not meet the legal standard for predatory pricing. Similarly, Microsoft came under intense scrutiny in the 1990s for giving away its browser, Internet Explorer, in order to undercut Netscape, which also ended up giving away its browser. Microsoft understood that the key to its long-term success was the dominance of the Windows platform. Bundling Internet Explorer with Microsoft Office enabled the company not only to gain over 80% of the browser market but also to keep its leadership with the Windows operating system. Eventually, Microsoft was prosecuted by the government—but not for predatory pricing, which could not be proved because Microsoft never significantly raised the price of Internet Explorer. Instead, the government prosecuted Microsoft for tying the purchase of Internet Explorer to the Windows operating system in order to restrict competition. The Microsoft case lasted over four years, and it ended in a settlement that placed restrictions on the firm's business practices.

What Are Network Externalities?

We end this chapter by considering a special kind of externality that often occurs in oligopoly. A **network externality** occurs when the number of customers who purchase or use a good influences the quantity demanded. This means that firms with many customers often find it easier to attract new customers and to keep their regular customers from switching to other rivals. In the early days of social networking, for example, MySpace and Friendster

A **network externality** occurs when the number of customers who purchase or use a good influences the quantity demanded.

PRACTICE WHAT YOU KNOW

Predatory Pricing: Price Wars

You've undoubtedly encountered a price war at some point. It could be two gas stations, clothing outlets, or restaurants that are charging prices that seem unbelievably low.

Question: Is a price war between two adjacent pizza restaurants evidence of predatory pricing?

Answer: One essential element for proving predatory pricing is evidence of the intent to raise prices after others are driven out of business. That is a problem in this example. Suppose one of the pizza places closes. The remaining firm could then raise its price substantially. But

Predatory pricing? Check out the two competing signs above!

barriers to entry in the restaurant industry are low in most metropolitan areas, so any efforts to maintain high prices for long will fail. Customers will vote with their feet and wallets by choosing another pizza place a little farther away that offers a better value. Or a new competitor will sense that the victor is vulnerable because of the high prices and will open a new pizza parlor nearby. Either way, the market is competitive, so any market power created by driving out one rival will be fleeting.

The aggressive price war is not evidence of predatory pricing. Instead, it is probably just promotional pricing to protect market share. Firms often price some items below their variable costs to attract customers. These firms hope to make up the difference and then some with high profit margins on other items, such as beverages and side dishes.

had many more users than Facebook. How did Facebook gain over 2 billion users when it had to play catch-up? Facebook built a better social network, and MySpace was slow to respond to the threat. By the time MySpace did respond, it was too late: Facebook was on its way. Now the tables are turned, as Facebook is the dominant social-networking platform. Moreover, the sheer size of Facebook makes it a better place to do social networking than MySpace or Google+. However, even though Facebook now enjoys significant network externalities, it must be mindful to keep innovating or else it might end up like MySpace someday.

Most examples of network externalities involve the introduction of new technologies. For instance, some technologies need to reach a critical mass before consumers can effectively use them. Consider that today everyone seems to have a cell phone. However, when cell phones were introduced in the United States in 1983, coverage was quite limited. The first users could not surf the Internet, roam, text, or use many of the applications we enjoy today. Moreover, the phones were large and bulky. How did we get from that situation in 1983 to today? As additional people bought cell phones, networks expanded and manufacturers and telephone companies responded by building more cell towers and offering better phones. The expansion of networks brought more users, and the new adopters benefited from the steadily expanding customer base.

Other technologies have gone through similar transformations. The Internet, fax machines, and Blu-ray disks all depend on the number of users. If you were the only person on the Internet, or the only person with the ability to send and receive a fax, your technical capacity would have little value. Likewise, the owner of a Blu-ray machine depends on the willingness of movie studios to create content in that format. In a world with ever-changing technology, first adopters pave the way for the next generation of users.

Positive network externalities are also generated by the **bandwagon effect**, which arises when a buyer's preference for a product increases as the number of people buying it increases. Fads of all sorts fall into this category. North Face jackets, oversized handbags, Uggs, and Bluetooth headsets are in vogue today, but how long that will remain true is anyone's guess.

In addition to the advantages of forming a larger network, firms find that many of their customers face significant *switching costs* if they leave. **Switching costs** are the costs incurred when a consumer changes from one supplier to another. For instance, the transition from listening to music on CDs to using digital music files involved a substantial switching cost for many users. Today, there are switching costs among the many digital music options. Once a consumer has established a library of MP3s or uses iTunes, the switching costs of transferring the music from one format to another create a significant barrier to change. When consumers face switching costs, the demand for the existing product becomes more inelastic. As a result, oligopolists not only leverage the number of customers they maintain in their network, but also try to make switching to another network more difficult.

There is no better example of the costs of switching than cell phone providers. First, contract termination fees apply to many cell phone agreements if the contract is broken. Second, many providers do not charge for calls inside the network or among a circle of friends. This means that if you switch and your friends do not, you will end up using more minutes on a rival network. These two tactics create high switching costs for many cell phone customers. To reduce switching costs, the Federal Communications Commission in 2003 began requiring that phone companies allow customers to take their cell phone numbers with them when they change to a different provider. This change in the law has reduced the costs of switching from one provider to another and has made the cell phone market more competitive.

Oligopolists are keenly aware of the power of network externalities. As new markets develop, the first firm into an industry often gains a large customer base. When there are positive network externalities, the customer base enables the firm to grow quickly. In addition, consumers are often more

Users of the first-generation cell phone, the Motorola DynaTAC 8000X, created a positive network externality for future users.

The **bandwagon effect** arises when a buyer's preference for a product increases as the number of people buying it increases.

Switching costs are the costs incurred when a consumer changes from one supplier to another.

comfortable purchasing from an established firm. These two factors favor the formation of large firms and make it difficult for smaller competitors to gain customers. As a result, the presence of significant positive network externalities causes small firms to be driven out of business or forces them to merge with larger competitors.

ECONOMICS FOR LIFE

Why Waiting Is Generally a Good Idea

If you are like a lot of people when you hear about something new and cool, you check it out. There is no harm in doing that. But what happens when you decide to purchase the latest gadget or join a new social media web site? You've made an investment of money or time. The fruitfulness of that investment often depends on how many other people do the same thing.

Consider the first people to get a 3D television—the first purchasers paid well over $5,000 for the new technology, but what exactly could they watch? The amount of 3D programming to start was tiny. Those early purchasers had very expensive TVs that they could rarely use to watch 3D because the content was playing catch-up. In contrast, consumers who waited could buy a 3D unit with greater clarity at a lower price, and more content was available to watch. That meant a win-win-win for procrastinators. The early adopters got penalized for paving the way.

The same is true today with many social media sites. Waiting for a web site to gain traction will save you from setting up a profile and investing your time and effort only to find out that other people are not nearly as excited about the features as you are. You end up wasting a lot of time, and because other online users never show up, you don't get the benefits that come from network externalities. If you wait until a platform is already established, then you can be fairly confident that your return on investment will be rewarded. This is certainly true with Facebook, Twitter, and LinkedIn—all of which have come to dominate segments of the social media market.

Google glasses? Should you buy the newest gadget when it comes out?

Network externalities are also important on dating sites. Just consider the overwhelming number of choices in this market: Match.com, Zoosk, eHarmony, OurTime, Chemistry.com, and many other sites. You could sign up for dozens of dating sites or simply choose the largest site, Match.com, because it offers the biggest database. Since dating sites charge member fees, waiting and seeing which sites are more popular is one way to use network externalities to improve your odds of success.

PRACTICE WHAT YOU KNOW

Examples of Network Externalities

Question: In which of these examples are network externalities important?

a. college alumni

b. Netflix

c. a local bakery that sells fresh bread

Does Netflix benefit from network externalities?

Answers:

a. Colleges and universities that have more alumni are able to raise funds more easily than smaller schools, so the size of the alumni network matters. The number of alumni also matters when graduates look for jobs, since alumni are often inclined to hire individuals who went to the same school. For example, Penn State University has the nation's largest alumni base. This means that each PSU graduate benefits from network externalities.

b. Netflix's size enables it to offer a vast array of DVDs and downloads. If it were smaller, Netflix would be unable to make as many obscure titles available. This means that Netflix customers benefit from network externalities by having more DVDs to choose from.

c. The local bakery is a small company. If it attracts more customers, each one will have to compete harder to get fresh bread. Since the supply of bread is limited, additional customers create congestion, and network externalities do not exist.

Conclusion

We opened this chapter with the misconception that cell phone companies are highly competitive—that is, that they compete like firms in competitive markets or monopolistically competitive markets do. The reality is that cell phone companies are oligopolists. Firms in oligopoly markets can compete or collude to create monopoly conditions. The result is often hard to predict. In many cases, the presence of a dominant short-run strategy causes firms to compete on price and advertising even though doing so yields a lower economic profit. In contrast, the potential success of a tit-for-tat strategy suggests that oligopolistic firms are capable of cooperating in order to jointly maximize their long-run profits. Whether oligopoly mirrors the result found in monopolistic competition or monopoly matters a great deal because society's welfare is higher when more competition is present. Since oligopoly is not a market structure with a predictable outcome, each oligopolistic industry must be assessed on a case-by-case basis by examining data and utilizing game theory. This makes the study of oligopoly one of the most fascinating parts of the theory of the firm.

In the next section of the book, we will examine how resource markets work. After all, each firm needs access to resources such as land, labor, and capital to produce goods and services. As a result, understanding how resource markets work will deepen our grasp of the theory of the firm. We will pay special attention to the labor market going forward since it determines workers' job prospects and the amount of income inequality within society.

ANSWERING THE BIG QUESTIONS

What is oligopoly?

* Oligopoly exists when a small number of firms sell a differentiated product in a market with significant barriers to entry. An oligopolist is like a monopolistic competitor in that it sells differentiated products. It is also like a monopolist in that it enjoys significant barriers to entry. The small number of sellers in oligopoly leads to mutual interdependence.
* Oligopolists have a tendency to collude and to form cartels in the hope of achieving monopoly-like profits.
* Oligopolistic markets are socially inefficient since price and marginal cost are not equal. The result under oligopoly falls somewhere between the competitive-market and monopoly outcomes.

How does game theory explain strategic behavior?

* Game theory helps to determine when cooperation among oligopolists is most likely to occur. In many cases, cooperation fails to occur because decision-makers have dominant strategies that lead them to be uncooperative. This can cause firms to compete with price, advertising, or research and development when they could potentially earn more profit by curtailing these activities.
* A dominant strategy ignores the possible long-run benefits of cooperation and focuses solely on the short-run gains. Whenever repeated interaction occurs, decision-makers fare better under tit-for-tat, an approach that maximizes the long-run profit.

How do government policies affect oligopoly behavior?

* Antitrust law is complex, and cases are hard to prosecute. Nevertheless, these laws are essential in providing oligopoly firms an incentive to compete rather than collude.
* Antitrust policy limits price discrimination, exclusive dealings, tying arrangements, mergers, and predatory pricing.

What are network externalities?

* A network externality occurs when the number of customers who purchase a good or use it influences the quantity demanded. The presence of significant positive network externalities can cause small firms to go out of business.

CONCEPTS YOU SHOULD KNOW

antitrust laws (p. 387)
bandwagon effect (p. 407)
cartel (p. 387)
Clayton Act (p. 402)
collusion (p. 387)
dominant strategy (p. 394)

game theory (p. 392)
mutual interdependence (p. 388)
Nash equilibrium (p. 390)
network externality (p. 405)
oligopoly (p. 384)
output effect (p. 392)

predatory pricing (p. 405)
price effect (p. 391)
prisoner's dilemma (p. 393)
Sherman Antitrust Act (p. 402)
switching costs (p. 407)
tit-for-tat (p. 400)

QUESTIONS FOR REVIEW

1. Compare the price and output under oligopoly to that of monopoly and monopolistic competition.

2. How does the addition of another firm affect the ability of an oligopolistic industry to form an effective cartel?

3. What is predatory pricing?

4. How is game theory relevant to oligopoly? Does it help to explain monopoly? Give reasons for your response.

5. What does the prisoner's dilemma indicate about the longevity of collusive agreements?

6. What is a Nash equilibrium? How does it differ from a dominant strategy?

7. What practices do antitrust laws prohibit?

8. What are network externalities? Describe why network externalities matter to an oligopolist.

STUDY PROBLEMS (∗ *solved at the end of the section*)

1. Some places limit the number of hours that alcohol can be sold on Sunday. Is it possible that this sales restriction could help liquor stores? Use game theory to construct your answer. **Hint:** even without restrictions on the hours of operation, individual stores could still limit Sunday sales if they wanted to.

2. Which of the following markets are oligopolistic?
   a. passenger airlines
   b. cereal
   c. fast food
   d. wheat
   e. golf equipment
   f. the college bookstore on your campus

∗ 3. At many local concerts, the crowd stands for some songs and sits for others. You are a fan of the concerts but not of having to stand; you prefer to stay seated throughout concerts. What would be your tit-for-tat strategy to encourage other concertgoers to change their behavior?

4. After teaching a class on game theory, your instructor announces that if every student skips the last question on the next exam, everyone will receive full credit for that question. However, if one or more students answer the last question, all responses will be graded and those who skip the question will get a zero. Will the entire class skip the last question? Explain your response.

5. For which of the following are network externalities important?
   a. gas stations
   b. American Association of Retired Persons (AARP)
   c. eHarmony, an Internet dating site

6. Your economics instructor is at it again (see question 4). This time, you have to do

a two-student project. Assume that you and your partner are both interested in maximizing your grade, but you are both very busy and get more happiness if you can get a good grade with less work.

	Your partner	
	Work hard	**Work less hard**
Work hard	Grade = A, but you had to work 10 hours. Happiness = 7/10.	Grade = A, and you only worked 5 hours. Happiness = 9/10.
You	Grade = A, but you had to work 10 hours. Happiness = 7/10.	Grade = A, but you had to work 15 hours. Happiness = 4/10.
Work less hard	Grade = A, but you had to work 15 hours. Happiness = 4/10.	Grade = B, but you only worked 5 hours. Happiness = 6/10.
	Grade = A, and you only worked 5 hours. Happiness = 9/10.	Grade = B, but you only worked 5 hours. Happiness = 6/10.

a. What is your dominant strategy? Explain.
b. What is your partner's dominant strategy? Explain.
c. What is the Nash equilibrium in this situation? Explain.
d. If you and your partner are required to work together on a number of projects throughout the semester, how might this change the outcome you predicted in parts (a), (b), and (c)?

7. Suppose that the marginal cost of mining gold is constant at $300 per ounce and the demand schedule is as follows:

Price (per oz.)	Quantity (oz.)
$1,000	1,000
$900	2,000
$800	3,000
$700	4,000
$600	5,000
$500	6,000
$400	7,000
$300	8,000

a. If the number of suppliers is large, what would be the price and quantity?
b. If there is only one supplier, what would be the price and quantity?
c. If there are only two suppliers and they form a cartel, what would be the price and quantity?
d. Suppose that one of the two cartel members in part (c) decides to increase its production by 1,000 ounces while the other member keeps its production constant. What will happen to the revenues of both firms?

✳ 8. Trade agreements encourage countries to curtail tariffs so that goods may flow across international boundaries without restrictions. Using the following payoff matrix, determine the best policies for China and the United States in this example.

		China	
		Low tariffs	**High tariffs**
United States	**Low tariffs**	China gains $50 billion / U.S. gains $50 billion	China gains $100 billion / U.S. gains $10 billion
	High tariffs	China gains $10 billion / U.S. gains $100 billion	China gains $25 billion / U.S. gains $25 billion

a. What is the dominant strategy for the United States?
b. What is the dominant strategy for China?
c. What is the Nash equilibrium for these two countries?
d. Suppose that the United States and China enter into a trade agreement that simultaneously lowers trade barriers. Is this a good idea? Explain your response.

9. A small town has only one pizza place, The Pizza Factory. A small competitor, Perfect Pies, is thinking about entering the market. The profits of these two firms depends on whether Perfect Pies enters the market and

whether The Pizza Factory—as a price leader—decides to set a high or a low price. Use the payoff matrix below to answer the questions that follow.

Perfect Pies

	Enter	Stay out
High price	Perfect Pies makes $10,000 The Pizza Factory makes $20,000	Perfect Pies makes $0 The Pizza Factory makes $50,000
Low price	Perfect Pies loses $10,000 The Pizza Factory makes $10,000	Perfect Pies makes $0 The Pizza Factory makes $25,000

The Pizza Factory

a. What is the dominant strategy of The Pizza Factory?

b. What is the dominant strategy of Perfect Pies?

c. What is the Nash equilibrium in this situation?

d. The combined profit for both firms is highest when The Pizza Factory sets a high price and Perfect Pies stays out. If Perfect Pies enters the market, how will this affect the profits of The Pizza Factory? Would The Pizza Factory be willing to pay Perfect Pies not to enter the market? Explain.

SOLVED PROBLEMS

3. Since standing at a concert imposes a negative externality on those who like to sit, the behavior is non-cooperative by nature. When one person, or a group of people, stands up, it forces those who would prefer to sit to have to stand up as well to see the performance. When this happens repeatedly, it diminishes the enjoyment of those who like to sit—especially when others nearby dance, sway, scream, and raise their arms. A concert typically consists of two sets of music with 20 to 25 songs played over the course of a few hours. As a result, your behavior has the potential to influence the behavior of those nearby. Think of this as a game in which you utilize tit-for-tat, or your behavior when the next song is played mimics what the other concertgoers did during the previous song. If you stand, dance, sway, scream, and raise your arms when everyone else is seated, eventually they will get the message that their actions impose a cost on everyone else. Once they understand this and remain seated, you can sit down as well and everyone can see the performance.

8. a. The dominant strategy for the United States is to impose high tariffs, because it always earns more from that strategy than if it faces low tariffs no matter what policy China pursues.
   b. The dominant strategy for China is to impose high tariffs, because it always earns more from that strategy than if it faces low tariffs no matter what policy the United States pursues.
   c. The Nash equilibrium for both countries is to levy high tariffs. Each country will earn $25 billion.
   d. China and the United States would each benefit from cooperatively lowering trade barriers. In that case, each country would earn $50 billion.

Two Alternative Theories of Pricing Behavior

Two alternative theories argue that oligopolists will form long-lasting cartels. These are the kinked demand curve and price leadership.

The Kinked Demand Curve

Imagine that a group of oligopolists has established an output level and price designed to maximize economic profit. The **kinked demand curve** theory states that oligopolists have a greater tendency to respond aggressively to the price cuts of rivals but will largely ignore price increases. When a rival raises prices, the other firms all stand to benefit by holding their prices steady in order to capture those customers who do not want to pay more. In this scenario, the firm that raises its price will see a relatively large drop in sales. However, if any of the rivals attempts to lower the price, other firms in the industry will immediately match the price decrease. The price match policy means that the firm that lowers its price will not gain many new customers. In practice, since a price drop by one firm will be met immediately by a price drop from all the competitors, no one firm will be able to attract very many new customers. This is the case at any price below the agreed-to price.

The firms' behavior creates a demand curve that is more elastic (or flatter) at prices above the cartel price and more inelastic (or steeper) at prices below the cartel price. The junction of the elastic and inelastic segments on the demand curve creates a "kink" that we see in Figure 13A.1.

This illustration begins with each of the firms in the industry charging P and producing Q. Since demand is more elastic above P and less elastic below P, the marginal revenue curve (MR) is discontinuous. The gap is illustrated by the dashed black vertical line. The presence of the gap in marginal revenue means that more than one marginal cost curve intersects marginal revenue at output level Q. This is evident in marginal cost curves MC_1 and MC_2. As a consequence, small changes in marginal cost, like those shown in Figure 13A.1, will not cause the firms to deviate from the established price (P) and quantity (Q).

The **kinked demand curve** theory states that oligopolists have a greater tendency to respond aggressively to the price cuts of rivals but will largely ignore price increases.

Price Leadership

The kinked demand curve explains why firms generally keep the same price, but it cannot explain how prices change. In that regard, the theory of price leadership provides some insight.

FIGURE 13A.1

The Kinked Demand Curve

At prices above P, demand is relatively elastic. At prices below P, demand is relatively inelastic. This creates a kink in the demand curve that causes the marginal revenue curve to become discontinuous. As a result, small changes in marginal cost do not cause firms to change their pricing and output. Therefore, firms are generally slow to adjust to changes in cost.

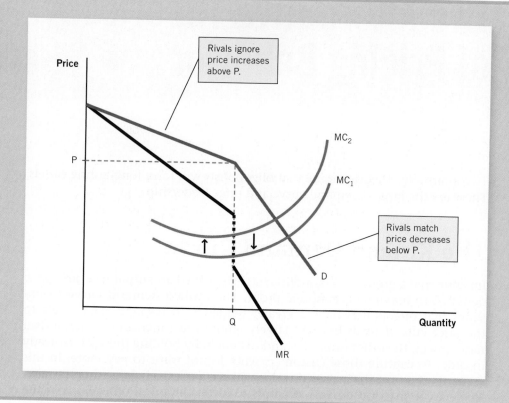

Price leadership
occurs when a dominant firm in an industry sets the price that maximizes profits and the smaller firms in the industry follow.

The airline industry is often cited as a market where price leadership is at work behind the scenes.

In many industries, smaller firms may take a cue from the decisions made by the price leader. **Price leadership** generally occurs when a single firm, known as the price leader, produces a large share of the total output in the industry. The price leader sets the price and output level that maximizes its own profits. Smaller firms then set their prices to match the price leader. Since the impact on price is small to begin with, it makes sense that smaller rivals tend to follow the price leader.

Price leadership is not illegal since it does not involve collusion. Rather, it relies on an understanding that an effort to resist changes implemented by the price leader will lead to increased price competition and lower profits for every firm in the industry. Since the firms act in accordance with one another, this practice is commonly known as *tacit collusion*.

One well-known example of price leadership is pricing patterns in the airline industry. On almost any route with multiple-carrier options, a price search for flights will reveal almost identical prices on basic economy-class flights. This happens even though the firms do not collude to set a profit-maximizing price. Rather, when one firm sets a fare, the other carriers feel compelled to match it. Airlines are very good at matching low prices, just like the model predicts. They are much less successful in implementing across-the-board fare increases, since that involves the leader sticking its neck out and trusting that the other firms will follow suit.

CONCEPTS YOU SHOULD KNOW

kinked demand curve (p. 415)   price leadership (p. 416)

STUDY PROBLEMS

1. A parking garage charges $10 a day. When-
   ever it tries to raise its price, the other parking
   garages in the area keep their prices constant
   and it loses customers to the cheaper garages.
   However, when the parking garage lowers its
   price, the other garages almost always match
   the price reduction. Which type of oligopoly
   behavior best explains this situation? If the
   parking garage business has marginal costs that
   generally vary only a small amount, should it
   change the price it charges when its marginal
   costs change a little?

2. Most large banks charge the same or nearly
   the same prime interest rate. In fact, banks
   avoid changing the rate; they try to do it only
   when market conditions require an adjustment. When that happens, one of the major
   banks announces a change in its rate and other
   banks quickly follow suit. Is this an example of
   price leadership or the kinked demand curve?
   Explain.

PART 4

Labor Markets and
EARNINGS

The Demand and Supply of Resources

Outsourcing is bad for the economy.

When U.S. jobs are outsourced, workers in the United States lose their jobs. People commonly think that this means outsourcing is bad for

MIS **CONCEPTION**

the economy, but that is misleading. Outsourced jobs are relocated from high-labor-cost areas to low-labor-cost areas. Often, a job lost to outsourcing creates more than one job

in another country. In addition, outsourcing lowers the cost of manufacturing goods and providing services. Those lower costs translate into lower prices for consumers and streamlined production processes for businesses. The improved efficiency helps firms compete in the global economy. In this chapter, we will examine the demand and supply of resources throughout the economy. The outsourcing of jobs is a very visible result of these resource flows and an essential part of the market-economy process.

In earlier chapters, we have seen that profit-maximizing firms must decide how much to produce. For production to be successful, firms must combine the right amounts of labor and capital to maximize output while simultaneously holding down costs. Since labor often constitutes the largest share of the costs of production, we will begin by looking at the labor market. We will use the forces of supply and demand to illustrate the role of the labor market in the U.S. economy. We will then extend the lessons learned about labor into the markets for land and capital. In Chapter 15, we will expand our understanding of the labor market by examining income inequality, unemployment, discrimination, and poverty.

If jobs are relocated to low-labor-cost areas like rural India, is it good or bad for the economy?

BIG QUESTIONS

* **What are the factors of production?**
* **Where does the demand for labor come from?**
* **Where does the supply of labor come from?**
* **What are the determinants of demand and supply in the labor market?**
* **What role do land and capital play in production?**

What Are the Factors of Production?

Wages and salaries account for two-thirds of all the income generated by the U.S. economy. The remaining one-third of income goes to the owners of land and capital. Together, labor, land, and capital make up the factors of production, or the inputs used in producing goods and services.

Derived demand is the demand for an input used in the production process.

For instance, let's imagine that Sophia wants to open a Mexican restaurant named Agaves. Sophia will need a dining room staff, cooks, dishwashers, and managers to coordinate everyone else; these are the labor inputs. She also will need a physical location; this is the land input. Finally, she will need a building in which to operate, along with ovens and other kitchen equipment, seating and tableware, and a cash register; these are the capital inputs.

Of course, Sophia's restaurant won't need any inputs if there is no demand for the food she plans to sell. The demand for each of the factors of production that go into her restaurant (land, labor, and capital) is said to be a **derived demand** because the factors are inputs the firm uses to supply a good in another market—in this case, the market for Mexican cuisine. Let's say that Sophia secures the land, builds a building, and hires employees in order to produce the food she will serve. She is willing to spend a lot of money up front to build and staff the restaurant, because she expects there to be demand for the food her restaurant will make and serve.

Derived demand is not limited to the demand for a certain type of cuisine. For example, consumer demand for iPads causes Apple to demand the resources needed to make them. The switches, glass, memory, battery, and other parts have little value alone, but when assembled into an iPad they become a device that many people find very useful. Therefore, when economists speak of derived demand, they are differentiating between the demand for a product or service and the demand for the resources used to make or produce that product or service.

A lack of customers is an ominous sign for restaurant workers.

PRACTICE WHAT YOU KNOW

Derived Demand: Tip Income

Your friend waits tables 60 hours a week at a small restaurant. He is discouraged because he works hard but can't seem to make enough money to cover his bills. He complains that the restaurant does not have enough business and that is why he has to work so many hours just to make ends meet.

Question: As an economist, what advice would you give him?

Answer: Since labor is a derived demand, he should apply for a job at a more popular restaurant. Working at a place with more customers will help him earn more tip income.

Want more tip income? Follow the crowd.

Where Does the Demand for Labor Come From?

As a student, you are probably hoping that one day your education will translate into tangible skills that employers will seek. As you choose a major, you might be thinking about potential earnings in different occupations. Have you ever wondered why there is so much variability in levels of salary and wages? For instance, economists generally earn more than elementary school teachers but less than engineers. Workers on night shifts earn more than those who do the same job during the day. And professional athletes and actors make much more for jobs that are not as essential as the work performed by janitors, construction workers, and nurses. In one respect, the explanation is surprisingly obvious: demand helps to regulate the labor market in much the same way that it helps to determine the prices of goods and services sold in the marketplace.

To understand why some people get paid more than others, we will explore the output of each worker, or what is known as the *marginal product of labor*. In fact, the value that each worker creates for a firm is highly correlated with the demand for labor. Then, to develop a more complete understanding of how the labor market works, we will examine the factors that influence labor demand.

Why do economists generally earn more than elementary school teachers?

The Marginal Product of Labor

To gain a concrete appreciation for how labor demand is determined, let's look at the restaurant business—a market that is highly competitive. In Chapter 8, we saw that a firm determines how many workers to hire by comparing the output of labor with the wages the firm must pay. We will apply this analysis of production to the labor market in the restaurant business. Table 14.1 should look familiar to you; it highlights the key determinants of the labor hiring process.

The **marginal product of labor** is the change in output associated with adding one additional worker.

Let's work our way through the table. Column 1 lists the number of laborers, and column 2 reports the daily numbers of meals that can be produced with differing numbers of workers. Column 3 shows the **marginal product of labor**, or the change (Δ) in output associated with adding one additional worker. For instance, when the firm moves from three employees to four, output expands from 120 meals to 140 meals. The increase of 20 meals is the marginal product of labor for the fourth worker. Note that the values in column 3 decline as additional workers are added. Recall from Chapter 8 that when each successive worker adds less value, this is known as diminishing marginal product.

Marginal thinking

It is useful to know the marginal product of labor because this tells us how much each additional worker adds to the firm's output. Combining this information about worker productivity with the price the firm charges gives us a tool that we can use to explain how many workers the firm will hire. Suppose that Agaves charges $10 for each meal. When the firm multiplies the marginal product of labor in column 3 by the price it charges, $10 per meal, we see the *value of the marginal product* in column 4. The **value of the marginal product (VMP)** is the marginal product of an input multiplied by the price of the output it produces. The firm compares the gain in column 4 with the cost of achieving that gain—the wage that must be paid—in column 5. This reduces the hiring decision to a simple cost-benefit analysis in which the

The **value of the marginal product (VMP)** is the marginal product of an input multiplied by the price of the output it produces.

TABLE 14.1

Deciding How Many Laborers to Hire

(1) Labor (number of workers)	(2) Output (daily meals produced)	(3) Marginal product of labor	(4) Value of the marginal product of labor	(5) Wage (daily)	(6) Marginal profit
Formula:		Δ Output	Price × marginal product of labor		Value of the marginal product of labor − wage
0	0				
		50	$500	$100	$400
1	50				
		40	400	100	300
2	90				
		30	300	100	200
3	120				
		20	200	100	100
4	140				
		10	100	100	0
5	150				
		0	0	100	− 100
6	150				

wage (column 5) is subtracted from the value of the marginal product (column 4) to determine the marginal profit (column 6) of each worker.

You can see from the green numbers that the marginal profit is positive for the first four workers. Therefore, the firm is better off hiring four workers. After that, the marginal profit is zero for the fifth worker, shown in black. The firm would be indifferent about hiring the fifth worker since the marginal cost of hiring that employee is equal to the marginal benefit. The marginal profit is negative for the sixth worker, shown in red. Therefore, the firm would not hire the sixth worker.

Figure 14.1 plots the value of the marginal product (VMP) from Table 14.1. Look at the curve: what do you see? Does it remind you of a demand curve? The VMP is the firm's willingness to pay for each laborer; in other words, it is the firm's labor demand curve.

The VMP curve slopes downward due to diminishing marginal product—which we see in column 3 of Table 14.1. As long as the value of the marginal product is higher than the market wage, shown as $100 a day, the firm will hire more workers. For example, when the firm hires the first worker, the VMP is $500. This amount easily exceeds the market wage of hiring an extra worker and creates a marginal profit of $400. We illustrate this additional profit in Figure 14.1 with the longest green arrow under the demand curve and above the market wage. The second, third, and fourth workers generate additional profit of $300, $200, and $100 respectively, represented by the progressively smaller green arrows. As the value of the marginal product declines, there will be a point at which hiring additional workers will cause profits to fall. This occurs because labor is subject to diminishing marginal product; eventually, the value created by hiring additional labor falls below the market wage.

FIGURE 14.1

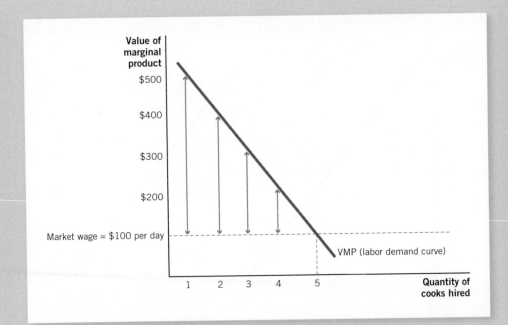

The Value of the Marginal Product

The firm will hire workers as long as the value of the marginal product (VMP) is greater than the wage it must pay. The value of the marginal product is the firm's labor demand curve. When the value of the marginal product is higher than the market wage, the firm will hire more workers. However, since labor is subject to diminishing marginal product, eventually the value created by hiring additional labor falls below the market wage.

Changes in the Demand for Labor

We know that customers desire good food and that restaurants like Agaves hire workers to satisfy their customers. Figure 14.2 illustrates the relationship between the demand for restaurant meals and restaurant workers. Notice that the demand for labor is downward-sloping; this tells us that at high wages Agaves will use fewer workers and that at lower wages it will hire more workers. We illustrate this with the orange arrow that moves along the original demand curve (D_1). Recall from Chapter 3 that this relationship is known as a change in the quantity demanded. In addition, the demand for workers depends on, or is derived from, the number of customers who place orders. So changes in the restaurant business as a whole can influence the number of workers that the restaurant hires. For example, if the number of customers increases, the demand for workers will increase, or shift to D_2. Likewise, if the number of customers decreases, the demand for workers will decrease, or shift to the left to D_3.

Two primary factors shift labor demand: a change in demand for the product that the firm produces, and a change in the cost of producing that product.

Changes in Demand for the Product the Firm Produces

A restaurant's demand for workers is derived from the firm's desire to make a profit. Because the firm is primarily interested in making a profit, it only hires workers when the value of the marginal product of labor is higher than the cost of hiring labor. Consider Agaves. If a rival Mexican restaurant closes down, many of its customers will likely switch to Agaves. Then Agaves will

FIGURE 14.2

The Labor Demand Curve

When the wages of workers change, the quantity of workers demanded, shown by the gold arrow moving along the demand curve, also changes. Changes that shift the entire labor demand curve, shown by the gray horizontal arrows, include changes in demand for the product that the firm produces, in labor productivity, or in innovation.

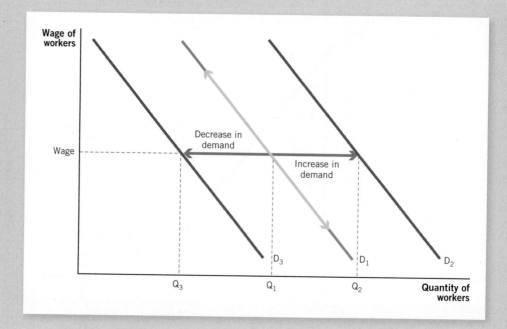

need to prepare more meals, which will cause the entire demand curve for cooks, table clearers, and waitstaff to shift outward to D_2.

Changes in Cost

A change in the cost of production can sometimes be positive, such as when a new technology makes production less expensive. It can also be negative, such as when an increase in the cost of a needed raw material makes production more expensive.

In terms of a positive change for the firm, technology can act as a substitute for workers. For example, microwave ovens enable restaurants to prepare the same number of meals with fewer workers. The same is true with the growing trend of using conveyor belts

A machine at McDonald's helps to fill the drink orders.

and automated systems to help prepare meals or even serve them. Therefore, changes in technology can lower a firm's demand for workers.

In the short run, substituting technology for workers may seem like a bad outcome for the workers and for society in general. However, in the long run that is not typically the case. Consider how the demand for lumberjacks in the forestry business is affected by technological advances. As timber companies invest in new harvesting technology, they can replace traditional logging jobs, which are dangerous and inefficient, with equipment that is safer to use and more efficient. By deploying the new technology, the lumber companies can cut down trees faster and more safely, and the workers are freed up to work in other parts of the economy. In the short run, that means fewer timber jobs; those workers must find employment elsewhere. Admittedly, this adjustment is painful for the workers involved, and they often have difficulty finding jobs that pay as well as the job that they lost. However, the new equipment requires trained, highly skilled operators who can fell more trees in a shorter period than traditional lumberjacks can. As a result, harvester operators have a higher marginal product of labor and can command higher wages.

For every harvester operator employed at a higher wage, there are perhaps ten traditional lumberjacks displaced and in need of a job. But consider what happens after the short-run job losses. Overall production rises because while one worker harvests trees, the nine other workers are forced to move into related fields or do something entirely different. It might take some of these displaced workers many years to find new work, but when they eventually do, society benefits in the long run. What once required ten workers to produce now takes only one, and the nine other workers are able to complete other jobs and grow the economy in different ways.

One John Deere 1270D harvester can replace ten lumberjacks.

PRACTICE WHAT YOU KNOW

Value of the Marginal Product of Labor: Flower Barrettes

Question: Penny can make five flower barrettes each hour. She works eight hours each day. Penny is paid $75.00 a day. The firm can sell the barrettes for $1.99 each. What is Penny's value of the marginal product of labor? What is the barrette firm's marginal profit from hiring her?

Answer: In eight hours, Penny can make 40 barrettes. Since each barrette sells for $1.99, her value of the marginal product of labor, or VMP_{labor} is 40 × $1.99, or $79.60. Since her VMP_{labor} is greater than the daily wage she receives, the marginal profit from hiring her is $79.60 − $75, or $4.60.

How many flower barrettes could you make in an hour?

To summarize, if labor becomes more productive, the VMP curve shifts to the right, driving up both wages and employment. This is what occurs with the demand for harvester operators. There is the potential for substitution as well, causing the demand for traditional labor to fall. This is what has happened to traditional lumberjack jobs, leading to a decrease in those workers' wages.

Where Does the Supply of Labor Come From?

In this section, we examine the connection between the wage rate and the number of workers who are willing to supply their services to employers. Since workers also value leisure, the supply curve is not always directly related to the wage rate. Indeed, at high wage levels some workers may desire to cut back the number of hours that they work. Other factors that influence the labor supply include the changing composition of the workforce, migration, and immigration; we explore these factors below as well.

The Labor-Leisure Trade-off

People work because they need to earn a living. While it is certainly true that many workers enjoy their jobs, this does not mean they would work for nothing. In other words, while many people experience satisfaction in their work, most of us have other interests, obligations, and goals. As a result, the supply of labor depends both on the wage that is offered and on how individuals want to use their time. This is known as the *labor-leisure trade-off*.

Trade-offs

In our society today, most individuals must work to meet their basic needs. However, once those needs are met, a worker might be more inclined to use his or her time in leisure. Would higher wages induce an employee to give up leisure and work more hours? The answer is both yes and no!

At higher wage rates, workers may be willing to work more hours, or substitute labor for leisure. This is known as the **substitution effect**. One way to think about this is to note that higher wages make leisure time more expensive, because the opportunity cost of enjoying more leisure means giving up more income. For instance, suppose that Emeril is a short-order cook at Agaves. He works 40 hours at $10 per hour and can also work 4 hours overtime at the same wage. If Emeril decides to work the overtime, he ends up working 44 hours and earns $440. In that case, he substitutes more labor for less leisure.

The **substitution effect** occurs when laborers work more hours at higher wages, substituting labor for leisure.

Opportunity cost

But at higher wage rates, other workers may work fewer hours, or substitute leisure for labor. This is known as the **income effect**. Leisure is a normal good (see Chapter 3), so as income rises some workers may use their additional income to demand more leisure. As a consequence, at high income levels the income effect may overwhelm the substitution effect and cause the supply curve to bend backward. For example, suppose that Rachael chooses to work overtime for $10 per hour. Her total pay (like Emeril's) will be $10 × 44, or $440. If her wage rises to $11, she may continue to work the overtime at a higher wage. However, if she does not work overtime, she will earn as much as she earned before the wage increase ($11 × 40 = $440), and she might choose to discontinue the overtime. In this case, Rachael enjoys more leisure.

The **income effect** occurs when laborers work fewer hours at higher wages, using their additional income to demand more leisure.

Figure 14.3 shows what can happen to the labor supply curve at high wage levels. When the supply of labor responds directly to wage increases, the wage rises progressively from W_1 to W_2 to W_3, and the number of hours worked increases from Q_1 to Q_2 to Q_3, along the curve labeled S_{normal}. However, at high wage rates workers might experience diminishing marginal utility from the additional income and, thus, might value increased leisure time more than increased income. In this situation, workers might choose to work less. When this occurs, the normal supply curve bends backward beyond W_2 because as the wage goes up, the hours worked go down.

The **backward-bending labor supply curve** occurs when workers value additional leisure more than additional income. This happens when the income effect is large enough to offset the substitution effect that typically causes individuals to work more when the wage rate is higher. Since most workers do not reach wage level W_2 (that is, a wage at which they might begin to value leisure more than labor), we will draw the supply curve as upward-sloping throughout the chapter. Nevertheless, it is important to recognize that the direct relationship we normally observe does not always hold.

A **backward-bending labor supply curve** occurs when workers value additional leisure more than additional income.

Changes in the Supply of Labor

If we hold the wage rate constant, a number of additional factors determine the supply of labor. Immigration, migration, demographic shifts in society, and job characteristics and opportunities all play important roles in determining

FIGURE 14.3

The Labor Supply Curve

At high wage levels, the income effect may become larger than the substitution effect and cause the labor supply curve to bend backward. The backward-bending supply curve occurs when additional leisure time becomes more valuable than additional income.

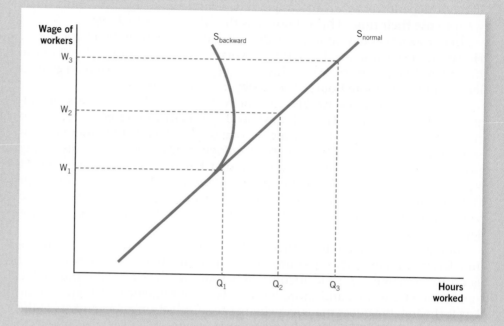

the number of workers who are willing to perform various jobs. In this section, we look beyond the wage rate to other forces that govern the supply of labor.

Turning to Figure 14.4, the gold arrow along S_1 shows that the quantity of workers increases when the wage rate rises. But what will cause a shift in the supply curve? Three primary factors affect the supply curve: other employment opportunities, the changing composition of the workforce, and migration and immigration.

Other Employment Opportunities

The supply of workers for any given job depends on the employment opportunities and prevailing wage in related labor markets. Let's consider the supply of labor at Agaves. Notice that the supply curve for labor in Figure 14.4 is upward-sloping; this tells us that if Agaves offers higher wages, more workers, such as table clearers, would be willing to work there. We illustrate this situation with the gold arrow that moves along the original supply curve (S_1). Moreover, the supply of table clearers also depends on a number of non-wage factors. Since table clearers are generally young and largely unskilled, the number of laborers willing to work is influenced by the prevailing wages in similar jobs. For instance, if the wages of baggers at local grocery stores increase, some of the table clearers at Agaves will decide to bag at local grocery stores instead. This will decrease the supply of table clearers and cause a leftward shift to S_3. If the wages of baggers were to fall, the supply of table clearers would increase, or shift to the right to S_2. These shifts reflect the fact that when jobs that require comparable skills have different wage

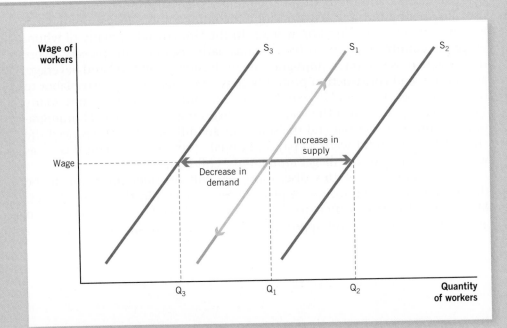

FIGURE 14.4

The Labor Supply Curve

A change in the quantity supplied occurs when the wages of workers changes. This causes a movement along the supply curve S_1, shown by the gold arrow. Changes in the supply of labor (the quantity of workers), shown by the gray horizontal arrows, can occur due to immigration, migration, demographic shifts in the workforce, and other employment opportunities.

rates, the number of workers willing to supply labor for the lower-wage job will shrink and the number willing to supply labor for the better-paid job will grow.

The Changing Composition of the Workforce

Over the last 30 years, the labor force participation rate (as measured by the female/male ratio) has increased significantly in most developed countries. Among that group, as measured by the United Nations Development Programme, the United States saw its female/male ratio rise from 66% to 81%, Switzerland from 67% to 82%, and New Zealand from 65% to 82%. Overall, there are many more women employees in the workforce today than there were a generation ago, and the supply of workers in many occupations has expanded significantly as a result.

Immigration and Migration

Demographic factors, including immigration and migration, also play a crucial role in the supply of labor. For example, immigration—both legal and illegal—increases the available supply of workers by a significant amount each year.

In 2010, over one million people from foreign countries entered the United States through legal channels and gained permission to seek employment. Today, there are over 40 million legal immigrants in the United States. To put this in perspective, the United States accepts more legal immigrants as permanent residents than the total number of legal immigrants accepted into all other nations in the world combined. In addition, illegal immigrants account for close to 20 million workers in the United States, many of whom enter the country to work as hotel maids, janitors, and fruit pickers. Every time a state passes a tough immigration law, businesses in food and beverage, agriculture, and construction protest because they need inexpensive labor to remain competitive, and U.S. citizens are reluctant to work these jobs. Many states have wrestled with the issue, but policies that address illegal immigration remain controversial and the solutions are difficult. The states need the cheap labor but don't want to pay additional costs such as medical care, as well as schooling for the illegal immigrants' children.

For the purposes of this discussion, we will consider migration to be the process of moving from one place to another within the United States. Migration patterns also affect the labor supply. Although the U.S. population grows at an annual rate of approximately 3%, there are significant regional

ECONOMICS IN THE MEDIA

Immigration

A Day without a Mexican

This offbeat film from 2004 asks a simple question: what would happen to California's economy if all the Mexicans in the state suddenly disappeared? The answer: the state economy would come to a halt.

Indeed, the loss of the Mexican labor force would have a dramatic impact on California's labor market. For example, the film makes fun of affluent Californians who must do without low-cost workers to take care of their yards and homes. It also showcases a farm owner whose produce is ready to be picked without any migrant workers to do the job.

In addition, the film adeptly points out that migrants from Mexico add a tremendous amount of value to the local economy through their purchases as well as their labor. One inspired scene depicts a television commercial for a "disappearance sale" put on by a local business after it realizes that most of its regular customers are gone.

A Day without a Mexican illustrates both sides of the labor relationship at work. Because demand and supply are inseparably linked, the disappearance of all of the Mexican workers creates numerous voids that require serious adjustments for the economy.

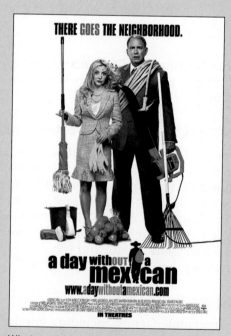

What would happen to an economy if one-third of the workers suddenly disappeared?

differences. Indeed, large population influxes lead to marked regional changes in the demand for labor and the supply of people looking for work. According to the U.S. Census Bureau, in 2010 the 10 fastest-growing states were in the South or West, with some states adding as much as 4% to their population in a single year. States in these areas provided 84% of the nation's population growth from 2000 to 2010, with Nevada, Utah, North Carolina, Idaho, and Texas all adding at least 20% to their populations.

It is worth noting that statewide data can hide significant localized changes. For example, census data from 2010 indicate that a number of counties experienced 50% or more population growth between 2000 and 2010. The biggest population gain was in Kendall County, Illinois, a far-flung suburb of Chicago that grew by nearly 100% between censuses. The county has been transitioning from an agricultural area to a bedroom community. Most of the fastest-growing counties are, like Kendall, relatively distant suburbs of major metropolitan areas. These are areas where new homes are available at comparatively reasonable prices.

PRACTICE WHAT YOU KNOW

The Labor Supply Curve: What Would You Do with a Big Raise?

Question: Your friend is concerned about his uncle, who just received a big raise. Your friend doesn't understand why his uncle wants to take time off from his job to travel. Can you help him understand why his uncle might want to cut back on his hours?

Answer: Ordinarily, we think of the labor supply curve as upward-sloping. When this is the case, higher wages translate into more hours worked and less leisure time. However, when the wage rate becomes high enough, some workers choose to substitute leisure for labor because they feel that enjoying free time is more valuable than earning more

Would you travel the world?

money. When this happens, the labor supply curve bends backward, and the worker spends fewer hours working as his wage rises. Your friend's uncle is reflecting this tendency.

What Are the Determinants of Demand and Supply in the Labor Market?

In earlier chapters, we have seen how markets reconcile the forces of demand and supply through pricing. Now that we have considered the forces that govern demand and supply in the labor market, we are ready to see how the equilibrium wage is established. This will enable us to examine the labor market in greater detail and identify what causes shortages and surpluses of labor, why outsourcing occurs, and what happens when there is a single buyer. The goal of this section is to provide a rich set of examples that help you become comfortable using demand and supply curves to understand how the labor market operates.

How Does the Market for Labor Reach Equilibrium?

We can think about wages as the price at which workers are willing to "rent" their time to employers. Turning to Figure 14.5, we see that at wages above equilibrium (W_E), the supply of workers willing to rent their time exceeds the

---

FIGURE 14.5

Equilibrium in the Labor Market

At high wages (W_{high}), a surplus of workers exists. This drives the wage rate down until the supply of workers and the demand for workers reach the equilibrium. At low wages (W_{low}), a shortage occurs. The shortage forces the wage rate up until the equilibrium wage is reached and the shortage disappears.

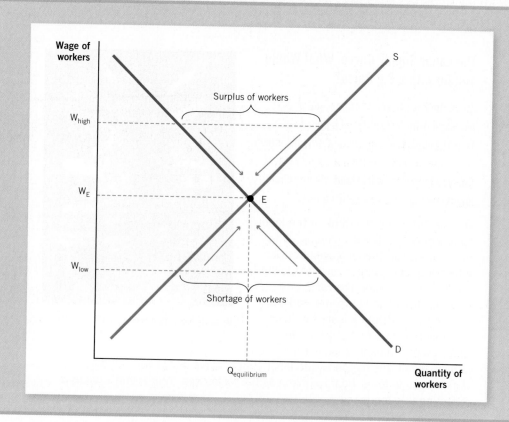

demand for that time. This causes a surplus of available workers. The surplus, in turn, places downward pressure on wages. As wages drop, fewer workers are willing to rent their time to employers. When wages drop to the equilibrium wage, the surplus of workers is eliminated; at that point, the number of workers willing to work in that profession at that wage is exactly equal to the number of job openings that exist at that wage.

A similar process guides the labor market toward equilibrium from low wages. At wages below the equilibrium, the demand for labor exceeds the available supply. The shortage forces firms to offer higher wages in order to attract workers. As a result, wages rise until the shortage is eliminated at the equilibrium wage.

ECONOMICS IN THE REAL WORLD

Where Are the Nurses?

The United States is experiencing a shortage of nurses. A stressful job with long hours, nursing requires years of training. As baby boomers age, demands for nursing care are expected to rise. At the same time, the existing pool of nurses is rapidly aging and nearing retirement. By some estimates, the shortage of nurses in America will approach one million by 2020. This makes nursing the #1 job in the country in terms of growth prospects, according to the Bureau of Labor Statistics.

However, economists are confident that the shortage of nurses will disappear long before 2020. After all, a shortage creates upward pressure on wages. In this case, rising wages also signal that nursing services are in high demand and that wages will continue to rise. This will lead to a surge in nursing school applications and will also cause some practicing nurses to postpone retirement.

Since the training process takes two or more years to complete, the labor market for nurses won't return to equilibrium immediately. The nursing shortage will persist for a few years until the quantity of nurses supplied to the market increases. During that time, many of the tasks that nurses traditionally carry out—such as taking patients' vital signs—will likely be shifted to nursing assistants or technicians.

Entering an occupation with a shortage of workers will result in higher pay.

Economics tells us that the combination of more newly trained nurses entering the market and the transfer of certain nursing services to assistants and technicians will eventually cause the nursing shortage to disappear. Remember that when a market is out of balance, forces are acting on it to restore it to equilibrium. ✳

Change and Equilibrium in the Labor Market

Now that we have seen how labor markets find an equilibrium, let's see what happens when the demand or supply changes. Figure 14.6 contains two graphs: panel (a) shows a shift in labor demand, and panel (b) shows a shift in labor supply. In both cases, the equilibrium wage and the equilibrium quantity of workers employed adjust accordingly.

Let's start with a shift in labor demand, shown in panel (a). Imagine that the demand for medical care increases due to an aging population and that, as a result, the demand for nurses (as we noted in the Economics in the Real World feature) increases and the demand curve shifts from D_1 to D_2. This creates a shortage of workers equal to $Q_3 - Q_1$. The shortage places upward pressure on wages, which increase from W_1 to W_2. As wages rise, nursing becomes more attractive as a profession; additional people choose to enter the field, and existing nurses decide to work longer hours or postpone retirement. Thus, the number of nurses employed rises from Q_1 to Q_2. Eventually, the wage settles at E_2 and the number of nurses employed reaches Q_2.

Turning to panel (b), we see what happens when the supply of nurses increases. As additional nurses are certified, the overall supply shifts from S_1 to S_2. This creates a surplus of workers equal to $Q_3 - Q_1$, which places downward pressure on wages. As a result, the wage rate falls from W_1 to W_2. Eventually, the market wage settles at E_2, the new equilibrium point, and the number of nurses employed reaches Q_2.

Outsourcing

Why would a firm hire someone from outside if it has a qualified employee nearby? This practice, known as *outsourcing,* has gotten a lot of attention in recent years. In this section, we explain how outsourcing works, why companies engage in it, and how it affects the labor market for workers.

Outsourcing of labor
occurs when a firm shifts jobs to an outside company, usually overseas, where the cost of labor is lower.

The **outsourcing of labor** occurs when a firm shifts jobs to an outside company, usually overseas, where the cost of labor is lower. In the publishing industry, for example, page make-up (also known as composition) is often done overseas to take advantage of lower labor costs. This outsourcing has been facilitated by the Internet, which eliminates the shipping delays and costs that used to constitute a large part of the business. Today, a qualified worker can lay out book pages anywhere in the world.

Sometimes, outsourcing occurs when firms relocate within the country to capitalize on cheaper labor or lower-cost resources. For example, when General Motors introduced its Saturn division in 1985, it built an entirely new production facility in Tennessee, where wages were substantially lower than those in Detroit.

When countries outsource, their pool of potential workers expands. But whether a labor expansion is driven by outsourcing, which is an external factor, or by an increase in the domestic supply of workers, those who are already employed in that particular industry find that they earn less. As a result, a rise in unemployment occurs in the occupation that can be outsourced.

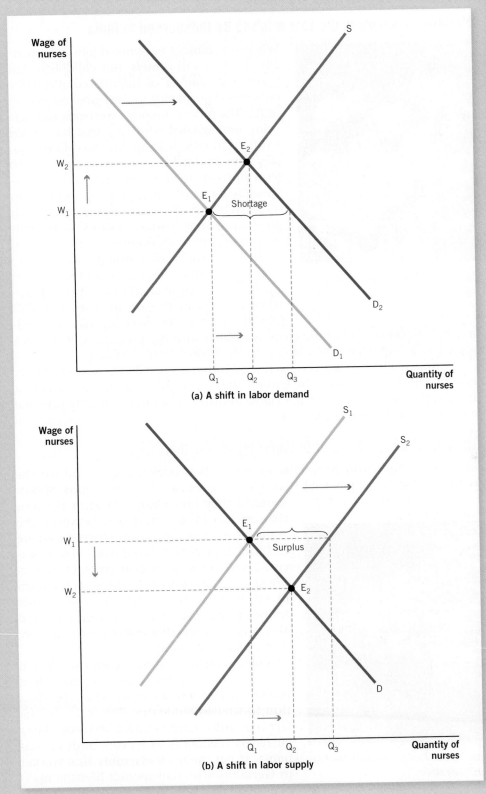

(a) A shift in labor demand

(b) A shift in labor supply

FIGURE 14.6

Shifting the Labor Market Equilibrium

In panel (a), the demand for nurses increases. This creates a shortage of workers equal to Q_3-Q_1, which leads to a higher equilibrium wage (E_2) and quantity of nurses employed (Q_2) than before. In panel (b), the supply of nurses increases. This leads to a surplus of workers equal to Q_3-Q_1, and causes the equilibrium wage to fall (E_2) and the number of nurses employed to rise (Q_2).

ECONOMICS IN THE REAL WORLD

Pregnancy Becomes the Latest Job to Be Outsourced to India

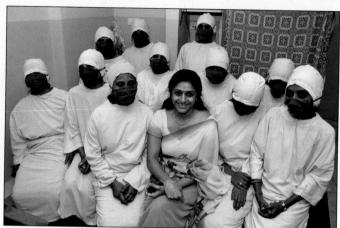

Kaival Hospital in Anand, India, matches infertile couples with local women, such as these surrogate mothers.

When we think of outsourced jobs, we generally think of call centers, not childbirth. But a growing number of infertile couples have outsourced pregnancy to surrogate mothers in India. The process involves surrogate mothers being impregnated with eggs that have been fertilized in vitro with sperm taken from couples who are unable to carry a pregnancy to term on their own. Commercial surrogacy—"wombs for rent"—is a growing industry in India. While no reliable numbers track such pregnancies nationwide, doctors work with surrogates in virtually every major city in India.

In India, surrogate mothers earn roughly $5,000 for a nine-month commitment. This amount is the equivalent of what could take 10 or more years to earn in many low-skill jobs there. Couples typically pay approximately $10,000 for all of the costs associated with the pregnancy, which is a mere fraction of what it would cost in the United States or Europe.

Commercial surrogacy has been legal in India since 2002, as it is in many other countries, including the United States. However, the difference is that India is the leader in making it a viable industry rather than a highly personal and private fertility treatment. ✳

The Global Implications of Outsourcing in the Short Run

Recall our chapter-opening misconception that outsourcing is bad for the economy. Many people hold that opinion because when they think of outsourcing they immediately imagine the jobs that are lost in the short run. However, the reality is more complex. Outsourced jobs are not lost; they are relocated from high-labor-cost areas to low-labor-cost areas. Outsourcing also creates benefits for firms in the form of lower production costs. The lower costs translate into lower prices for consumers and also help the firms that outsource to compete in the global economy.

Outsourcing need not cost the United States jobs. Consider what happens when foreign countries outsource their production to the United States. For example, the German auto manufacturer Mercedes-Benz currently has many of its cars built in Alabama. If you were an assembly line worker in Germany who had spent a lifetime mak-

The Mercedes-Benz plant near Tuscaloosa, Alabama, illustrates that outsourcing is more than just a one-way street.

ing cars for Mercedes, you would likely be upset if your job was outsourced to North America. You would feel just like the American technician who loses a job to someone in India or the software writer who is replaced by a worker in China. Outsourcing always produces a job winner and a job loser. In the case of foreign outsourcing to the United States, employment in this country rises. In fact, the Mercedes-Benz plant in Alabama employs more than 3,000 workers. Those jobs were transferred to the United States because the company felt that it would be more profitable to hire American workers and make the vehicles in the United States rather than constructing them in Germany and shipping them across the Atlantic.

Figure 14.7 shows how outsourcing by foreign firms helps to increase U.S. labor demand. In panel (a), we see the job loss and lower wages that occur in Germany when jobs are outsourced to the United States. As the demand for labor in Germany falls from D_1 to D_2, wages drop to W_2 and employment declines to Q_2. Panel (b) illustrates the corresponding increase in demand for U.S. labor in Alabama. As demand shifts from D_1 to D_2, wages rise to W_2 and employment rises to Q_2.

Since each nation will experience outsourcing flows out of and into the country, it is impossible to say anything definitive about the overall impact of outsourcing on labor in the short run. However, it is highly unlikely that workers who lose high-paying jobs toward the end of their working lives will be able to find other jobs that pay equally well.

The Global Implications of Outsourcing in the Long Run

Although we see mixed results for outsourcing in the short run, we can say that in the long run outsourcing benefits domestic consumers and producers. In fact, outsourcing is a key component in international trade. In earlier chapters, we have seen that trade creates value. When companies and even countries specialize, they become more efficient. The efficiency gains, or cost savings, help producers to expand production. In the absence of trade barriers, lower costs benefit consumers in domestic and international markets through lower prices, and the outsourcing of jobs provides the income for foreign workers to be able to purchase domestic imports. Therefore, the mutually interdependent nature of international trade enhances overall social welfare.

Trade creates value

FIGURE 14.7

Shifting the Labor Market Equilibrium

Outsourcing creates more demand in one market at the expense of the other. In panel (a), the demand for German labor declines from D_1 to D_2, leading to lower wages and less employment. Panel (b) shows the increase in the demand for labor from D_1 to D_2 in Alabama. This leads to higher wages and more employment.

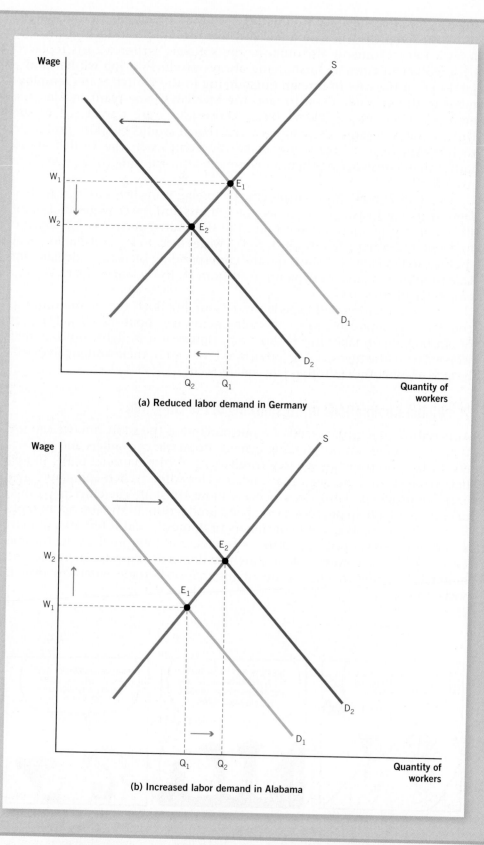

(a) Reduced labor demand in Germany

(b) Increased labor demand in Alabama

Outsourcing

Outsourced

In this film from 2006, an American novelty products salesman from Seattle heads to India to train his replacement after his entire department is outsourced.

Some of the funniest scenes in this charming movie occur in the call center. The Indian workers speak fluent English but lack familiarity with American customs and sensibilities, so they often seem very awkward. In one memorable phone call, an American caller becomes irate when he learns that the product he is ordering was not made in the United States. He gives the voice on the other end of the line an earful about the loss of jobs in America. However, the call center supervisor devises a clever tactic to convince the disgruntled customer to buy the product despite his objections. She tells him that a manufacturer in the United States offers the same product for $20 more. He pauses and after some thought decides that he would rather buy the cheaper, foreign-made product.

Because *Outsourced* humanizes the foreign workers who benefit from outsourced domestic jobs, we learn to appreciate how outsourcing affects consumers, producers, domestic workers, and foreign laborers.

Outsourcing can connect different cultures in positive ways.

Monopsony

In looking at supply, demand, and equilibrium in the labor market, we have assumed that the market for labor is competitive. But that is not always the case. Sometimes, the labor market has only a few buyers or sellers who are able to capture market power. One extreme form of market power is **monopsony**, which occurs when a only single buyer exists. Like a monopolist, a monopsonist has a great deal of market power. As a consequence, the output in the labor market will favor a monopsonist whenever one is present.

In Chapter 10, we examined how a monopolist behaves. Compared to a firm in a competitive market, the monopolist charges a higher price for the product it sells. Likewise, a monopsonist in the labor market can leverage its market power. Because it is the only firm hiring, it can pay its workers less. Isolated college towns are a good example. Workers who wish to live in such college towns often find that almost all the available jobs are through the college. Since it is the chief provider of jobs, it is said to have a monopsony in the labor market. The college can use its market power to hire many local workers at low wage levels.

Monopsony
is a situation in which there is only one buyer.

ECONOMICS IN THE REAL WORLD

Pay and Performance in Major League Baseball

What is the correlation between winning and revenues?

Gerald Scully was the first sports economist. In his seminal work, "Pay and Performance in Major League Baseball," published in 1974 in the *American Economic Review,* Scully used economic analysis to determine the value of the marginal product that each player produced during the season. Scully's work was important because at that time each player's contract had a "reserve clause" stating that the player belonged to the team for his entire career unless he was traded or released.

If a player was unhappy with his contract, his only option was to withdraw from playing. Since most players could not make more than they were earning as baseball players in their next-most-productive job, the teams knew that the players would stay for the wage that the team was willing to pay. Therefore, under the reserve clause each team was a monopsonist. The teams used their market power to suppress wages and increase their profits.

In this context, Scully's work changed everything. He used two baseball statistics—slugging percentage for hitters, and the strikeout-to-walk ratio for pitchers—to evaluate the players' performance and then estimate how much player performance affected winning. Next he examined the correlation between winning and revenues, which enabled him to estimate how many dollars of revenue each player generated for his team. The results were stunning. The top players at that time earned about $100,000 per season but generated nearly $1,000,000 in revenue for their teams, or approximately 10 times more than they were being paid. However, since each player was tied to a particular team through the reserve clause, no matter how good the player was he lacked the leverage to bargain for higher wages.

Scully's work played a key role in the court decisions of two players, Andy Messersmith and Dave McNally, whose cases led to the repeal of the reserve clause in 1975. The reserve clause was struck down because the practice was deemed anti-competitive. Today, because players have gained limited free agency, salaries have steadily increased. Top professional baseball players can earn over $30 million a year, and the average salary is slightly more than $3 million. ✳

Why Do Some Workers Make More Than Others?

While most workers generally spend 35 to 40 hours a week at work, the amount they earn varies dramatically. Table 14.2 presents a number of simple questions that illustrate why some workers make more than others.

The table shows how demand and supply determine wages in a variety of settings. Workers with a high-value marginal product of labor invariably earn more than those with lower-value marginal product of labor. It is important to note that working an "essential" job does not guarantee a high income. Instead, the highest incomes are reserved for jobs that have high demand and a low supply of workers. In other words, our preconceived notions of fairness take a backseat to the underlying market forces that govern pay. In the next chapter, we will consider many additional factors that determine wages, including wage discrimination.

TABLE 14.2

Why Some Workers Make More than Others

Question	Answer
Why do economists generally earn more than elementary school teachers?	Supply is the key. There are fewer qualified economists than certified elementary school teachers. Therefore, the equilibrium wage in economics is higher than it is in elementary education. It's also important to note that demand factors may be part of the explanation. The value of the marginal product of labor of economists is generally higher than that of most elementary school teachers since many economists work in industry.
Why do people who work the night shift earn more than those who do the same job during the day?	Again, supply is the key. Fewer people are willing to work at night, so the wage necessary to attract labor to perform the job must be higher. (That is, night shift workers earn what is called a compensating differential, which we discuss in Chapter 15.)
Why do professional athletes and actors make so much when what they do is not essential?	Now demand takes over. The paying public is willing, even eager, to spend a large amount of income on entertainment. Thus, demand for entertainment is high. On the supply end of the equation, the number of individuals who capture the imagination of the paying public is small, and they are therefore paid handsomely to do so. The value of the marginal product that they create is incredibly high, which means that they can earn huge incomes.
Why do janitors, construction workers, and nurses—whose jobs are essential—have salaries that are a tiny fraction of celebrities' salaries?	Demand again. The value of the marginal product of labor created in these essential jobs is low, so their employers are unable to pay high wages.

PRACTICE WHAT YOU KNOW

Labor Supply: Changes in Labor Supply

Labor is always subject to changes in demand.

Question: A company builds a new facility that doubles its workspace and equipment. How is labor affected?

Answer: The company has probably experienced additional demand for the product it sells. Therefore, it needs additional employees to staff the facility, causing a positive shift in the demand curve. When the demand for labor rises, wages increase and so does the number of people employed.

Question: A company decides to outsource 100 jobs from a facility in Indiana to Indonesia. How is labor affected in the short run?

Answer: This situation leads to two changes. First, a decrease in demand for labor in Indiana results in lower wages there and fewer workers hired. Second, an increase in demand for labor in Indonesia results in higher wages there and more workers hired.

Value of the Marginal Product of Labor

Moneyball

Moneyball, a film based on Michael Lewis's 2003 book of the same name, details the struggles of the Oakland Athletics, a major league baseball team. The franchise attempts to overcome some seemingly impossible obstacles with the help of their general manager, Billy Beane, by applying innovative statistical analysis, known as Sabermetrics, pioneered by Bill James.

Traditional baseball scouts utilize experience, intuition, and subjective criteria to evaluate potential players. However, Beane, formerly a heavily recruited high school player who failed to have a successful professional career, knows firsthand that this method of scouting does not guarantee success. The Oakland A's lack the financial ability to pay as much as other teams. While trying to negotiate a trade with the Cleveland Indians, Beane meets Peter Brand, a young Yale economist who has new ideas about applying statistical analysis to baseball in order to build a better team. Brand explains that evaluating a player's marginal product would be a better tool for recruitment.

In the key scene in the movie, Brand briefly explains his methodology for evaluating players and how the A's can build a championship team:

It's about getting things down to one number. Using the stats the way we read them, we'll find value in players that no one else can see. People are overlooked for a variety of biased reasons and perceived flaws: age, appearance, and personality. Bill James and mathematics cut straight through that. Billy, of the 20,000 notable players for us to consider, I believe that there is a championship team of 25 people that we can afford, because everyone else in baseball undervalues them.

The A's go on to have a remarkable season by picking up "outcasts" that no other team wanted.

Can a young economist's algorithm save the Oakland A's?

Thanks to Kim Holder of the University of West Georgia.

What Role Do Land and Capital Play in Production?

In addition to labor, firms need land and capital to produce goods and services. In this section, we complete our analysis of the resource market by considering how land and capital enter into the production process. Returning to the restaurant Agaves for a moment, we know that the business hires labor to make meals, but to do their jobs the workers need equipment, tables, chairs, registers, and a kitchen. Without a physical location and a host of capital resources, labor would be irrelevant.

The Market for Land

Like the demand for labor, the demand for land is determined by the value of the marginal product that it generates. However, unlike the supply of labor, the supply of land is ordinarily fixed. We can think of it as nonresponsive to prices, or perfectly inelastic.

In Figure 14.8, the vertical supply curve reflects the inelastic supply. The price of land is determined by the intersection of supply and demand. Notice the label on the vertical axis, which reflects the price of land as the rental price necessary to use it, not the price necessary to purchase it. When evaluating a firm's economic situation, we do not count the entire purchase price of the land it needs. To do so would dramatically overstate the cost of land in the production process because the land is not used up, but only occupied for a certain period. For example, consider a car that you buy. You drive it for a year and put 15,000 miles on it. Counting the entire purchase price of the car would overstate the true operating cost for one year of service. The true cost of operating the vehicle includes wear and tear along with operating expenses such as gasoline, maintenance, and service visits. A similar process is at work with land. Firms that own land consider the rent they could have earned if they had rented the land out for the year. This nicely captures the opportunity cost of using the land.

Opportunity cost

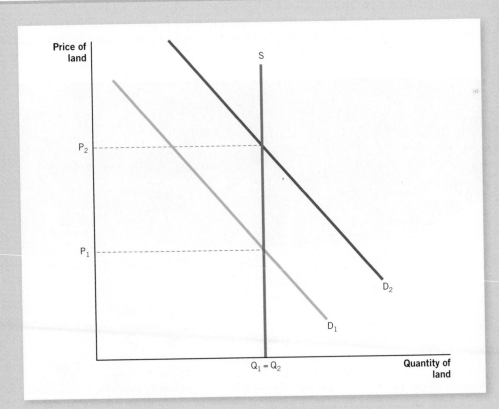

FIGURE 14.8

Supply and Demand in the Market for Land

Since the supply of land is fixed, the price it commands depends on demand. If demand increases from D_1 to D_2, the price will rise from P_1 to P_2.

Since the supply of land is usually fixed, changes in demand determine the rental price. When demand is low—say, at D_1—the rental price received, P_1, is also low. When demand is high—say, at D_2—the rental price of land is high, at P_2. Apartment rentals near college campuses provide a good example of the conditions under which the demand for land is high. Since students and faculty want to live near campus, the demand for land is often much higher there than even a few blocks away. Like labor, the demand for land is derived from the demand for the products that it is used to produce. In this case, the demand for apartments, homes, and retail space near campus is very high. The high demand drives up the rental price of land closer to campus because the marginal product of land there is higher.

When we see the term "rent," most of us think of the rental price of an apartment or a house. But when economists talk about an **economic rent**, they mean the difference between what a factor of production earns and what it could earn in the next-best alternative. Economic rent is different from *rent seeking*. Recall from Chapter 10 that rent seeking occurs when firms compete to seek a monopoly position. In contrast, "rent" here refers to the ability of investors to beat their opportunity cost. For instance, in the case of housing near college campuses, a small studio apartment generally commands a much higher rent than a similar apartment located 10 miles away. This occurs because the rent near campus must be high enough to compensate the property owners for using their land for an apartment instead of in other ways that might also be profitable in the area—for example, for a single residence, a business, or a parking lot. Once you move 10 miles farther out, the number of people interested in using the land for these purposes declines.

More generally, in areas where many people would like to live or work, rental prices are often very high. Many places in the United States have high rental

Marginal thinking

Economic rent is the difference between what a factor of production earns and what it could earn in the next-best alternative.

A satellite photo shows manmade islands in Dubai—an exception to our assumption that the amount of land is fixed.

Outsourcing

Outsourcing, though painful for those whose jobs are outsourced, is simply the application of a fundamental economic principle—keep costs as low as possible. Labor is usually the most expensive input for a business, so all managers must seek to pay the lowest wage that still ensures an effective workforce. Firms seek the right balance of costs and relevant skills when outsourcing jobs. Here is a look at three representative jobs in the United States, Mexico, China, and India, with salaries measured as a percentage of the typical U.S. salary.

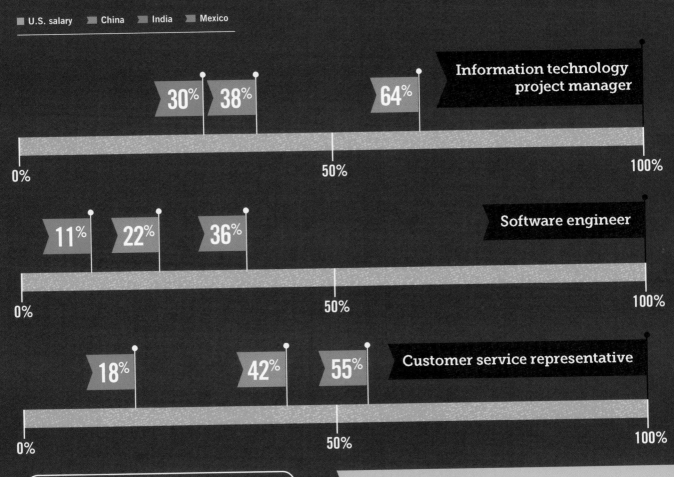

■ U.S. salary ■ China ■ India ■ Mexico

Information technology project manager
30% 38% 64%
0% 50% 100%

Software engineer
11% 22% 36%
0% 50% 100%

Customer service representative
18% 42% 55%
0% 50% 100%

The communications and transportation revolutions, along with the increasing skill level of foreign labor, have created conditions for the outsourcing of millions of U.S. jobs to China, India, and Latin America.

Outsourcing is about comparative advantage. Firms hire foreign workers who hold a comparative advantage and can produce a good or service more cheaply and at a lower opportunity cost than domestic workers.

REVIEW QUESTIONS

- Software engineering jobs are outsourced from the United States to India. Use supply and demand curves to sketch the effects on the American and Indian labor forces.

- Outsourcing is controversial. Describe why by citing effects to the economy both in the short run and in the long run.

prices, but none of those compare with Hong Kong, where an average two-bedroom apartment rents for almost $7,000 a month. That staggering amount makes most apartment rental prices in the United States seem downright inexpensive. While not as high as Hong Kong, owners of property in Moscow, Tokyo, London, and New York all receive more economic rent on properties than those who own similar two-bedroom apartments in Peoria, Idaho Falls, Scranton, or Chattanooga. The ability to earn a substantial economic rent comes back to opportunity costs: since there are so many other potential uses of property in densely populated areas, rents are correspondingly higher.

Opportunity costs

The Market for Capital

Capital, or the equipment and materials needed to produce goods, is a necessary factor of production. The demand for capital is determined by the value of the marginal product that it creates. Like land and labor, the demand for capital is a derived demand: a firm requires capital only if the product it produces is in demand. The demand for capital is also downward-sloping; this reflects the fact the value of the marginal product associated with its use declines as the amount used rises.

When to Use More Labor, Land, or Capital

Firms must evaluate whether hiring additional labor, utilizing more land, or deploying more capital will constitute the best use of their resources. In order to do this, they compare the value of the marginal product per dollar spent across the three factors of production.

Let's consider an example. Suppose that a company pays its employees $15 per hour, the rental rate of land is $5,000 per acre per year, and the rental rate of capital is $1,000 per year. The company's manager determines that the value of the marginal product of labor is $450, the value of the marginal product of an acre of land is $125,000, and the value of the marginal product of capital is $40,000. Is the firm using the right mix of resources? Table 14.3 compares the ratios of the value of the marginal product (VMP) of each factor of production with the cost of attaining that value (this gives us the bang per buck for each resource), or the relative benefit of using each resource.

TABLE 14.3

Determining the Bang per Buck for Each Resource

(1) Factor of production	(2) Value of the marginal product ($)	(3) Wage or rental price ($)	(4) Bang per buck ($)
Labor	$450	$15	$450 ÷ 15 = 30
Land	125,000	5,000	125,000 ÷ 5,000 = 25
Capital	40,000	1,000	40,000 ÷ 1,000 = 40

Looking at these results, we see that the highest bang per buck is the value $40 created by dividing the VMP of capital by the rental price of capital in column 4. When we compare this value for capital, it tells us that the firm is getting more benefit per dollar spent from using capital than it is from using labor ($30) or land ($25). Therefore, the firm would benefit from using capital more intensively. As it does so, the VMP of capital in column 2 will fall due to diminishing returns. When this happens, the bang per buck for capital will drop from $40 in column 4 to a number that is more in line with bang per buck for labor and land. Conversely, the firm is using land ($25) too intensively, and it would benefit from using less. Doing so will raise the VMP it produces and increase its bang per buck for land. By using less land and more capital, and by tweaking the use of labor as well, the firm will eventually bring the value created by all three factors to a point at which the revenue per dollar spent is equal for each of the factors. At that point, the firm will be utilizing its resources efficiently.

Why does all this matter? Because the world is always changing: wages rise and fall, as do property values and the cost of acquiring capital (interest rates). A firm must constantly adjust the mix of land, labor, and capital it uses to get the largest return for its resources. Moreover, the markets for land, labor, and capital are connected. The amount of labor a firm uses is a function not only of the marginal product of labor, but also of the marginal product of land and capital. Therefore, a change in the supply of one factor will alter the returns of all factors. For instance, if wages fall, firms will be inclined to hire more labor. But if they hire more labor, they will use less capital. Capital itself is not any more, or less, productive. Rather, lower wages reduce the demand for capital. In this situation, the demand curve for capital would shift to the left, lowering the rental price of capital as well as the quantity of capital deployed.

Marginal thinking

ECONOMICS IN THE REAL WORLD

The Impact of the 2008 Financial Crisis on Labor, Land, and Capital

The financial crisis of 2008 led to the loss of 40% of all global wealth. By most measures, $10 trillion in wealth was lost in just a few months. The results are evident in the land, labor, and capital markets. Since demand in the factor markets is derived from the demand in the final goods and services market, it is not surprising that the underlying factor markets felt the impact of the crisis. Unemployment rose from under 6% to over 10% due to the drop in demand for labor. Home prices and land values plummeted by more than 30% since the peak in 2007. Finally, the cost of acquiring, or renting, capital dropped to historic lows.

Our understanding of the factor markets teaches us that workers and land-owners alike were vulnerable to systemic changes in the capital markets. As a result, both Main Street and Wall Street shared the pain. ✳

Market analysts know that the land, labor, and capital markets are interconnected.

How are all those dishes going to get clean?

Bang for the Buck: When to Use More Capital or More Labor

Suppose that Agaves is considering the purchase of a new industrial dishwasher. The unit cleans faster, uses less labor and less water, but costs $10,000. Should the restaurant make the capital expenditure, or would it be better off saving the money and incurring higher operating costs? To help decide what Agaves should do, consider this information: the dishwasher has a usable life of five years before it will need to be replaced. It will save the restaurant $300 a year in water and 10 hours of labor each week.

Question: Should Agaves purchase the new dishwasher?

Answer: This is the kind of question every business wrestles with on a regular basis. And the way to answer it is very straightforward. A firm should invest in new capital when the value of the marginal product it creates per dollar spent is greater than the value of the marginal product per dollar spent on the next-best alternative. In other words, a firm should invest in new capital when the bang per buck exceeds that of labor or other investments.

Let's compare the total cost of purchasing the dishwasher with the total savings. The total cost of the dishwasher is $10,000, but the savings are larger.

Item	Amount saved	Total for five years
Water	$300/year	$1,500
Labor	10 hours per week × $8/hour = $80/week × 52 weeks = $4,160/year	20,800
Total		22,300

The total savings over five years is $22,300. This makes the investment in the dishwasher the best choice!

Conclusion

We began this chapter with the misconception that outsourcing is bad for the economy. Indeed, outsourcing destroys some jobs in high-labor-cost areas, but it also creates jobs in low-labor-cost areas. As a result, it lowers the cost of manufacturing goods and providing services. This improved efficiency helps firms that outsource by enabling them to better compete in the global economy.

Throughout this chapter, we have learned that the compensation for factor inputs depends on the interaction between demand and supply. Resource demand is derived from the demand for the final product a firm produces, and resource supply depends on the other opportunities and compensation level that exists in the market. As a result, the equilibrium prices and outputs in the markets for land, labor, and capital reflect, in large part, the opposing tensions between the separate forces of demand and supply.

In the next chapter, we will examine income and poverty. As you will discover, there are many factors beyond the demand for and supply of workers that explain why some workers make more than others. For instance, wages also depend on the amount of human capital required in order to be hired, as well as location, lifestyle choices, union membership, and the riskiness of the profession. Adding these elements will enable us to deepen our understanding of why workers earn what they do.

ANSWERING THE BIG QUESTIONS

What are the factors of production?

* Labor, land, and capital constitute the factors of production, or the inputs used in producing goods and services.

Where does the demand for labor come from?

* The demand for each factor of production is a derived demand that stems from a firm's desire to supply a good in another market. Labor demand is contingent on the value of the marginal product that is produced, and the value of the marginal product is equivalent to the firm's labor demand curve.

Where does the supply of labor come from?

* The supply of labor comes from the wage rate that is offered, and it is determined by each person's goals and other opportunities. At high wage levels, the income effect may become larger than the substitution effect and cause the supply curve to bend backward.

What are the determinants of demand and supply in the labor market?

* Labor markets reconcile the forces of demand and supply into a wage signal that conveys information to both sides of the market. At wages above the equilibrium, the supply of workers exceeds the demand for labor. This causes a surplus of available workers that places downward pressure on wages until they reach the equilibrium wage, at which point the surplus is eliminated. At wages below the equilibrium, the demand for labor exceeds the available supply of workers, and a shortage develops. The shortage forces firms to offer higher wages in order to attract workers. Wages rise until they reach the equilibrium wage, at which point the shortage is eliminated.

* There is no definitive result for outsourcing of labor in the short run. In the long run, outsourcing moves jobs to workers who are more productive.

What role do land and capital play in production?

* Land and capital (as well as labor) are the factors of production across which firms compare the value of the marginal product per dollar spent.

ECONOMICS FOR LIFE

Will Your Future Job Be Outsourced?

When you select an academic major and learn a set of skills, you hope they will enable you to find stable employment. This becomes more challenging in an environment where labor is easily outsourced. So as you seek employment, you need to consider the long-term likelihood that your job could be replaced. To help you think about this, let's consider jobs that are likely to be outsourced and jobs that are more likely to remain in the United States.

Jobs with a high risk of outsourcing

Let's begin with computer programmers, who typically earn $70,000 per year. Programming is not location specific; that is, it can be done from anywhere. This makes programmers susceptible to outsourcing. Similarly, insurance underwriters, who earn approximately $60,000 per year, are increasingly being outsourced because the mathematical algorithms involved in estimating risk can be analyzed from any location. Also at risk are financial analysts. When we think of financial analysts, who make roughly $70,000, we typically think of Wall Street. However, crunching numbers and evaluating prospective stock purchases do not require residence in New York City. As a result, financial positions are increasingly being outsourced. The same is true of biochemists, who make $85,000, and physicists, who make $95,000. Even jobs in architecture, management, and law are under pressure. Having a high-paying job does not guarantee that it is safe from outsourcing.

Jobs with a low risk of outsourcing

Conversely, it is good to be a dentist because fillings, crowns, and root canals have to be done locally. Most jobs in medical care are also safe. Physicians, nurses, technicians, and support staff are all part of the medical delivery process. More broadly, most service-sector jobs are safe from outsourcing because they require someone to be nearby to assist the client. Real estate and construction jobs, which have typical salaries of $40,000 and $45,000 respec-

tively, function in the same way: houses must be built and sold in the local community, so outsourcing is not possible. Also, despite the increase in online courses, education remains primarily a brick-and-mortar enterprise. Likewise, public-sector jobs such as police protection and administration of government programs cannot be outsourced.

More important, the best way to ensure that your future job is not outsourced is to be valuable to your organization. Developing new skills and knowledge is integral to maintaining and increasing the value of the marginal product of your labor. When you are highly valued, it will be difficult to replace you, especially from overseas.

Might your future job be outsourced? Then what would you do?

CONCEPTS YOU SHOULD KNOW

backward-bending labor supply
  curve (p. 429)
derived demand (p. 422)
economic rent
  (p. 446)

income effect (p. 429)
marginal product of labor
  (p. 424)
monopsony (p. 441)
outsourcing of labor (p. 436)

substitution effect (p. 429)
value of the marginal product
  (VMP) (p. 424)

QUESTIONS FOR REVIEW

1. Why is the demand for factor inputs a derived demand?

2. What rule does a firm use when deciding to hire an additional worker?

3. What are the two labor demand shifters? What are the three labor supply shifters?

4. What can cause the labor supply curve to bend backward?

5. If wages are below the equilibrium level, what would cause them to rise?

6. What would happen to movie stars' wages if all major film studios merged into a single firm, creating a monopsony for film actors?

7. If workers become more productive, what would happen to the demand for labor, the wages of labor, and the number of workers employed?

8. How is economic rent different from rent seeking?

STUDY PROBLEMS (*solved at the end of the section*)

1. Maria is a hostess at a local restaurant. When she earned $8 per hour, she worked 35 hours per week. When her wage increased to $10 per hour, she decided to work 40 hours. However, when her wage increased again to $12 per hour, she decided to cut back to 37 hours per week. Draw Maria's supply curve. How would you explain her actions to someone who is unfamiliar with economics?

2. Would a burrito restaurant hire an additional worker for $10.00 an hour if that worker could produce an extra 30 burritos and each burrito made could add $0.60 in revenues?

* 3. Pam's Pretzels has a production function shown in the following table. It costs Pam's Pretzels $80 per day per worker. Each pretzel sells for $3.

Quantity of labor	Quantity of pretzels
0	0
1	100
2	180
3	240
4	280
5	310
6	330
7	340
8	320

a. Compute the marginal product and the value of the marginal product that each worker creates.

b. How many workers should Pam's Pretzels hire?

4. Jimi owns a music school that specializes in teaching guitar. Jimi has a limited supply of rooms for his instructors to use for lessons. As a result, each successive instructor adds less to Jimi's output of lessons. The following table lists Jimi's production function. Guitar lessons cost $25 per hour.

Quantity of labor	Quantity of lessons (hours)
0	0
1	10
2	17
3	23
4	28
5	32
6	35
7	37
8	38

a. Construct Jimi's labor demand schedule at each of the following daily wage rates for instructors: $75, $100, $125, $150, $175, $200.

b. Suppose that the market price of guitar lessons increases to $35 per hour. What does Jimi's new labor demand schedule look like at the daily wage rates listed in part (a)?

5. In an effort to create a health care safety net, the government requires employers to provide health care coverage to all employees. What impact will this increased coverage have in the following labor markets in the short run?

a. the demand for doctors

b. the demand for medical equipment

c. the supply of hospital beds

6. A million-dollar lottery winner decides to quit working. How can you explain this behavior using economics?

7. Illustrate each of the following changes by using a separate labor supply and demand diagram. Diagram the new equilibrium point, and note how the wage and quantity of workers employed changes.

a. There is a sudden migration out of an area.

b. Laborers are willing to work more hours.

c. Fewer workers are willing to work the night shift.

d. The demand for California wines suddenly increases.

✳ 8. A football team is trying to decide which of two running backs (A or B) to sign to a one-year contract.

Predicted statistics	Player A	Player B
Touchdowns	7	10
Yards gained	1,200	1,000
Fumbles	4	5

The team has done a statistical analysis to determine the value of each touchdown, yard gained, and fumble lost to the team's revenue. Each touchdown is worth an extra $250,000, each yard gained is worth $1,500, and each fumble costs $75,000. Player A costs $3.0 million, and Player B costs $2.5 million. Based on their predicted statistics in the table above, which player should the team sign?

9. How does outsourcing affect wages and employment in the short run and the long run?

10. Farmers in Utopia experience perfect weather throughout the entire growing season, and as a result their crop is double its normal size. How will this bumper crop affect the following factors?

a. the price of the crop

b. the marginal product of workers helping to harvest the crop

c. the demand for the workers who help harvest the crop

11. What will happen to the equilibrium wage of crop harvesters in Dystopia if the price of the crop falls by 50% and the marginal product of the workers increases by 25%?

12. Suppose that the current wage rate is $20 per hour, the rental rate of land is $10,000 per

acre, and the rental rate of capital is $2,500. The manager of a firm determines that the value of the marginal product of labor is $400, the value of the marginal product of an acre of land is $200,000, and the value of the marginal product of capital is $4,000. Is the firm maximizing profit? Explain your response.

SOLVED PROBLEMS

3. a.

Quantity of labor	Quantity of pretzels	Marginal product	Value of the marginal product
0	0	0	$0
1	100	100	300
2	180	80	240
3	240	60	180
4	280	40	120
5	310	30	90
6	330	20	60
7	340	10	30
8	320	−20	−60

b. The VMP of the fifth worker is $90 and each worker costs $80, so Pam should hire five workers. Hiring the sixth worker would cause her to lose $20.

8.

Predicted statistics	Player A	VMP of Player A	Player B	VMP of Player B
Touchdowns	7	$1,750,000	10	$2,500,000
Yards gained	1,200	1,800,000	1,000	1,500,000
Fumbles	4	−300,000	5	−375,000
Total value		3,250,000		3,625,000

Player A has a value of $3.25 million and a cost of $3.0 million, so he is worth $0.25 million. Player B has a value of $3.625 million and a cost of $2.5 million, so he is worth $1.125 million. The team should sign Player B.

Income, Inequality, and Poverty

It's unfair that some jobs pay so much more than others.

Many people believe that the structure of compensation in the working world is unfair. After all, why should someone who does backbreaking work

MIS CONCEPTION

digging holes for fence posts make so much less than someone who sits behind a desk on Wall Street? Why do such large differences in income exist? In the last chapter, we learned that

two primary factors govern wage income: productivity and the forces of supply and demand. You may be an outstanding babysitter or short-order cook, but because these jobs are considered unskilled, many other workers can easily replace you. And neither occupation will ever earn much more than the minimum wage. In contrast, even an average neurosurgeon gets paid very well, since few individuals have the skill and training to perform neurosurgery. In addition, society values neurosurgeons more than babysitters because the neurosurgeons are literally saving lives.

If you wish to earn a sizable income, it is not enough to be good at something; that "something" needs to be an occupation that society values highly. What matters are your skills, what you produce, and the supply of workers in your chosen profession. Therefore, how hard you work has little to do with how much you get paid.

In this chapter, we will continue our exploration of labor by examining income and inequality in labor markets, including the characteristics of successful wage earners and the impediments the poor face when they try to escape poverty. Examining those at the top and the bottom of the income ladder will help us to understand the many forces that determine income. In addition, we will explore the reasons for poverty. These include low worker productivity, insufficient training and education, cyclical downturns in the economy, employment discrimination, single-wage earners, and bad luck.

Why do neurosurgeons earn more than short-order cooks?

BIG QUESTIONS

* **What are the determinants of wages?**
* **What causes income inequality?**
* **How do economists analyze poverty?**

What Are the Determinants of Wages?

The reasons why some workers get paid more than others are complex. We learned in Chapter 14 that the forces of supply and demand explain a large part of wage inequality. However, numerous additional factors contribute to earnings differences. Various non-monetary factors cause some occupations to pay higher or lower wages than supply and demand would seem to dictate. In other contexts, wage discrimination on the basis of gender, race, or other characteristics is an unfortunate but very real factor in wages. And in some markets, a "winner-take-all" structure can lead to a small number of workers capturing a large majority of the total earnings.

A **compensating differential** is the difference in wages offered to offset the desirability or undesirability of a job.

The Non-Monetary Determinants of Wages

Some jobs have characteristics that make them more or less desirable. Also, no two workers are exactly alike. Differences in jobs and worker ability affect the supply and demand of labor. In this section, we will examine non-monetary differences including location, stress, working conditions, prestige, and danger.

Incentives

Compensating Differentials

Some jobs are more unpleasant, risky, stressful, inconvenient, or more monotonous than others. If the characteristics of a job make it unattractive, firms must offer more to attract workers. For instance, roofing, logging, and deep-sea fishing are some of the most dangerous occupations in the world. Workers who do these jobs must be compensated with higher wages to offset the higher risk of injury. A **compensating differential** is the difference in wages offered to offset the desirability or undesirability of a job. If a job's characteristics make it unattractive, the compensating wage differential must be positive.

In contrast, some jobs are highly desirable. For example, restaurant critics sample a lot of great food, radio DJs spend the day playing their favorite music, and video game testers try beta versions before they are released. Some jobs are simply more fun, exciting, prestigious, or stimulating than others. In these cases, the compensating differential is negative and the firm

Are you being paid enough to risk a fall?

TABLE 15.1

The Relationship between Education and Pay

Education level	Median annual earnings in 2010 (persons age 25 and over)
Advanced (master's or doctoral) degree	$68,350
Bachelor's degree	52,550
Some college or associate degree	37,700
High school degree (includes GED)	32,650
Less than high school diploma	22,500

Source: Bureau of Labor Statistics, Current Population Survey, April 2012.

offers lower wages. For example, newspaper reporters and radio DJs earn low pay. Video game testing is so desirable that most people who do it are not paid at all.

Education and Human Capital

Many complex jobs require substantial education, training, and industry experience. Qualifying to receive the specialized education required for certain occupations—for example, getting into medical school—is often very difficult. Only a limited number of students are able to pursue these degrees. In addition, such specialized education is expensive, in terms of both tuition and the opportunity cost of forgone income.

The skills that workers acquire on the job and through education are collectively known as **human capital**. Unlike other forms of capital, investments in human capital accrue to the employee. As a result, workers who have high human capital can shop their skills among competing firms. Engineers, doctors, and members of other professions that require extensive education and training can command high wages in part because the human capital needed to do those jobs is high. In contrast, low-skill workers such as ushers, baggers, and sales associates earn less because the human capital required to do those jobs is quite low; it is easy to find replacements.

Table 15.1 shows the relationship between education and pay. Clearly, attaining more education leads to higher earnings. Workers who earn advanced degrees have higher marginal products of labor because their extra schooling has presumably given them additional skills for the job. But they also have invested heavily in education. The higher marginal product of these workers helps to create high demand for their skills. In addition, the time required to complete more advanced degrees limits the supply of workers with a high marginal product. Taken together, the firm's demand for workers with a high marginal product and the limited supply of such workers causes earnings to rise. Higher wages represent a compensating differential that rewards additional education.

Human capital
is the skill that workers acquire on the job and through education.

ECONOMICS IN THE REAL WORLD

Does Education *Really* Pay?

An alternative perspective on the value of education argues that the returns to increased education are not the product of what a student learns, but rather a signal to prospective employers. According to this perspective, the degree itself (specifically, the classes taken to earn that degree) is not evidence of a set of skills that makes a worker more productive. Rather, earning a degree and attending prominent institutions is a signal of a potential employee's quality. That is, prospective employers assume that a student who gets into college must be intelligent and willing to work hard. Students who have done well in college send another signal: they are able to learn quickly and perform well under stress.

It is possible to test the importance of signaling by looking at the returns to earning a college degree, controlling for institutional quality. At many elite institutions, the four-year price tag has reached extraordinary levels. For example, to attend Sarah Lawrence College in Yonkers, New York, the most expensive institution in the country, it cost $61,236 in 2012–2013. Over four years, that adds up to almost a quarter of a million dollars! What type of return do graduates of such highly selective institutions make on their sizable investments? And are those returns the result of a rigorous education or a function of the institution's reputation? This is difficult to determine because the students who attend more selective institutions would be more likely to have higher earnings potential regardless of where they attend college. These students enter college as high achievers, a trait that carries forward into the workplace no matter where they attend school.

Economists Stacy Dale and Alan Krueger used data to examine the financial outcomes for over 6,000 students who were accepted or rejected by a comparable set of colleges. They found that 20 years after graduation, students who had been accepted at more selective colleges but who decided to attend a less selective college earned the same amount as their counterparts from more selective colleges. This finding indicates that actually attending a prestigious school is less important for future career success than the qualities that enable students to get accepted at a prestigious school.

Although Table 15.1 shows that additional education pays, the reason is not simply an increase in human capital. There is also a signal that employers can interpret about other, less observable qualities. For instance, Harvard graduates presumably learn a great deal in their time at school, but they were also highly motivated and likely to be successful even before they went to college. Part of the increase in income attributable to completing college is a function of a set of other traits that the student already possessed independent of the school or the degree. ✳

Does an advanced degree mean you learned more or were simply smarter anyway?

Location and Lifestyle

For most people, sipping margaritas in Key West, Florida, sounds more appealing than living in Eureka, Nevada, along the most isolated stretch of road in the continental United States. Likewise, being able to see a show, visit a museum, or go to a Yankees game in New York City constitutes a different lifestyle from what you'd experience in Dodge City, Kansas. People find some places more desirable than others. So how does location affect wages? Where the climate is more pleasant, all other things being equal, people are willing to accept lower wages because the non-monetary benefits of enjoying the weather act as a compensating differential. Similarly, jobs in metropolitan areas—where the cost of living is significantly higher than in most other places—pay higher wages as a compensating differential. This helps employees to afford a quality of life similar to what they would enjoy if they worked in less expensive areas.

How much more would you pay to live near here?

Choice of lifestyle is also a major factor in determining wage differences. Some workers are not particularly concerned with maximizing their income; instead, they care more about working for a cause. This is true for many employees of nonprofits or religious organizations, or even for people who take care of loved ones. Others follow a dream of being a musician, writer, or actor. And still others are guided by a passion such as skiing or surfing. Indeed, many workers view their pay as less important than doing something they are passionate about. For these workers, lower pay functions as a compensating differential.

Unions

A **union** is a group of workers that bargains collectively for better wages and benefits. Unions are able to secure increased wages by creating significant market power over the supply of labor available to a firm. A union's ability to achieve higher wages depends on a credible threat of a work stoppage, known as a **strike**. In effect, unions can manage to raise wages because they represent labor, and labor is a key input in the production process. Since firms cannot do without labor, an effective union can use the threat of a strike to negotiate higher wages for its workers.

A **union** is a group of workers that bargains collectively for better wages and benefits.

A **strike** is a work stoppage designed to aid a union's bargaining position.

Some unions are prohibited by law from going on strike. These include many transit workers, some public school teachers, law enforcement officers, and workers in other essential services. If workers in one of these industries reach an impasse in wage and benefit negotiations, the employee union is required to submit to the decision of an impartial third party, a process known as binding arbitration. The television show *Judge Judy* is an example of binding arbitration in action: two parties with a small claims grievance agree in advance to accept the verdict of Judith Sheindlin, a noted family court judge.

The effect of unions in the United States has changed since the early days of unionization in the late 1800s. Early studies of the union wage premium found wages to be as much as 30% higher for workers who were unionized. At the height of unionization approximately 60 years ago, one in three jobs was a unionized position. Today, only about one in eight workers is a member of

Does going on strike result in higher wages?

a union. In a 2003 study, David G. Blanchflower and Alex Bryson found the wage premium to be around 16.5%. The demise of many unions has coincided with the transition of the U.S. economy from a manufacturing base to a greater emphasis on the service sector, which is less centralized.

While union membership in the private sector has steadily declined, membership in the public sector has increased to almost 40%. This asymmetry is explained by competitive pressure. In the private sector, higher union labor costs prompt firms to substitute more capital and use more technology in the production process. Higher union labor costs also spur firms to relocate production to places with large pools of non-union labor. These competitive pressures limit unions' success at organizing and maintaining membership, as well as the wage premium they can secure. However, competition in the government sector is largely absent. Federal, state, and local governments can pay employees according to union scale without having to worry about cost containment. As a result, unions are common among public school teachers, police, firefighters, and sanitation workers.

Efficiency Wages

Efficiency wages
are wages higher than equilibrium wages, offered to increase worker productivity.

Incentives

In terms of paying wages, one approach stands out as unique. Ordinarily, we think of wages being determined in the labor market at the intersection of supply and demand. When the labor market is in equilibrium, the wage guarantees that every qualified worker can find employment. However, some firms willingly pay more than the equilibrium wage. **Efficiency wages** exist when an employer pays its workers more than the equilibrium wage. Why would a business do that? Surprisingly, the answer is: to make *more* profit. That hardly seems possible when a firm that uses efficiency wages pays its workers more than its competitors do. But think again. Above-equilibrium wages (1) provide an incentive for workers to reduce slacking, (2) decrease turnover, and (3) increase productivity. If the gains in overall productivity are higher than the increased cost, the result is greater profit for the firm.

Automaker Henry Ford made use of efficiency wages to generate more productivity on the Model T assembly line. In 1914, Ford decided to more than double the pay of assembly-line workers to $5 a day—an increase that his competitors did not match. He also decreased the workday from nine to eight hours. Ford's primary goal was to reduce worker turnover, which was frequent because of the monotonous nature of assembly-line work. By making the job so lucrative, he figured that most workers would not quit so quickly. He was right. The turnover rate plummeted from over 10% per day to less than 1%. As word of Ford's high wages spread, workers flocked to Detroit. The day after the wage increase was announced, over 10,000 eager job seekers lined up outside Ford's Highland Park, Michigan, plant. From this crowd, Ford hired the most productive employees. The resulting productivity increase per worker was more than enough to offset the wage increase. In addition, reducing the length of each shift enabled Ford to add an extra shift, which increased productivity even more.

We have seen that wages are influenced by factors that include compensating differentials, human capital, location and lifestyle, union membership, and the presence of efficiency wages. Table 15.2 summarizes these non-monetary determinants of income differences.

Henry Ford developed a visionary assembly process and also implemented efficiency wages at his plants.

TABLE 15.2

The Key Non-monetary Determinants of Wage Differences

Determinant	Impact on wages	In pictures
Compensating differentials	Some workers are eager to have jobs that are more fun, exciting, prestigious, or stimulating than others. As a result, they are willing to accept lower wages. Conversely, jobs that are unpleasant or risky require higher wages.	
Human capital	Many jobs require substantial education, training, and experience. As a result, workers who acquire additional amounts of human capital can command higher wages.	
Location and lifestyle	When the location is desirable, the compensating wage will be lower. Similarly, when employment is for a highly valued cause, wage is less important. In both situations, the compensating wage will be lower.	
Unions	Since firms cannot do without labor, unions can threaten a strike to negotiate higher wages.	
Efficiency wages	The firm pays above-equilibrium wages to help reduce slacking, decrease turnover, and increase productivity.	

PRACTICE WHAT YOU KNOW

Efficiency Wages: Which Company Pays an Efficiency Wage?

You are considering two job offers. Company A is well known and respected. This company offers a year-end bonus based on your productivity that can substantially boost your income, but its base wage is relatively low. Company B is less well known, but its wages are higher than the norm in your field. This company does not offer a year-end bonus.

Question: Which company, A or B, is the efficiency wage employer?

Answers: Efficiency wages are a mechanism that some companies use to reduce turnover, encourage teamwork, and create loyalty. Company A's bonus plan will reward the best producers, but the average and less-than-average workers will become frustrated and leave. Company A is not paying efficiency wages; it is simply using incentives tied to productivity. Company B is the efficiency wage employer because it pays every worker somewhat higher wages to reduce turnover. You should work for this company.

Forbes magazine calls Google the best company to work for—and not just because you can bring your dog to work.

Wage Discrimination

Wage discrimination occurs when workers of the same ability are not paid the same as others because of their race, ethnic origin, sex, age, religion, or some other group characteristic. Most economic studies of wage discrimination indicate that the amount of discrimination today accounts for only small wage differences. However, less than 40 years ago it was a serious problem. Economists and policymakers continue to study the issue in order to understand its effect in the past and to help address any remaining discrimination today.

Most of us would like to believe that employers no longer pay men more than women for doing the same job. However, wage discrimination does still exist. In 2009, President Obama signed the Lilly Ledbetter Fair Pay Act, which gives victims of wage discrimination more time to file a complaint with the government. The act is named after a former employee of Goodyear who sued the company in 2007. The courts determined that she was paid 15% to 40% less than her male counterparts. The fact that a major U.S. corporation was violating the Equal Pay Act of 1963 almost 50 years after its passage was a poignant reminder that wage discrimination still occurs in our society.

Determining Wage Discrimination

Determining discrimination is no longer as simple or obvious as it once was. Table 15.3 presents median annual earnings in the United States by sex, race or ethnic group, age and experience, and location. Looking at the data, we see large earnings differences across many groups in U.S. society. You might be tempted to conclude that the gap reflects employer discrimination. However, although female workers earn 23% less than their male counterparts, much of this gap reflects compensating differentials and differences in human capital. Let's explore this point in more detail.

The types of jobs that women and men typically work are different. For example, men are more likely to work outdoors. The higher wages offered for jobs such as road work and construction reflect, in part, a compensating differential for exposure to extreme temperatures, bad weather, and other dangers. Also, more women than men take time off from work to raise a family, meaning that they have fewer years of work experience, put in fewer work hours per year, are less likely to work a full-time schedule, and leave the labor force for longer periods. Because of these differences, women generally earn less than men. These factors—the jobs that men and women undertake, experience, and employment history—explain most of the female-male wage gap.

However, the gender gap is shrinking. In 2009, for example, more women than men in the United States received doctoral degrees. The number of women at every level of academia has been rising for decades. Women now hold a nearly 3-to-2 majority in undergraduate and graduate education. Over time, this education advantage will offset some of the other compensating differentials that have kept the wages of men higher than those of women.

For every $1 men make, women make, on average, 77 cents.

Similarly, wide gaps in earnings data by race or ethnic group largely reflect differences in human capital. Asians often have

TABLE 15.3		

Median Annual Earnings by Group

Group	Median earnings in 2011	Percentage difference within each group
Males	$48,202	–
Females	37,118	−23%
White	$55,412	–
Black	32,229	−42
Asian	65,129	18
Hispanic	38,624	−30
Early-career workers (25–34)	$50,774	−19
Mid-career workers (35–54)	62,889	–
Late-career workers (55–64)	55,937	−11
Inside a metropolitan area	$51,574	–
Outside a metropolitan area	40,527	−19

Source: U.S. Bureau of the Census, "Income, Poverty, and Health Insurance Coverage in the United States: 2011," *Current Population Reports*, September 2012.

much higher education levels than whites, who in turn generally have much higher levels than blacks and Hispanics. Much of the difference in educational attainment is related to cultural values: some groups place more emphasis on formal education than others. We would expect the wage disparities among groups to decrease as these cultural differences become less pronounced. Socioeconomic factors also play a significant role. For instance, the low quality of many inner-city schools limits the educational attainment of many minorities.

The earnings gap between mid-career workers and others also reflects differences in human capital. After all, workers who are just starting out have limited experience. As these workers age, they accumulate on-the-job training and experience that make them more productive and enable them to obtain higher wages. However, for older workers the gains from increased experience are eventually offset by diminishing returns. For example, workers nearing retirement are less likely to keep up with advances in technology or learn new approaches. Consequently, wages peak when these workers are in their fifties and then slowly fall thereafter. This pattern, known as the **life-cycle wage pattern**, refers to the predictable effect that age has on earnings over a person's working life.

The **life-cycle wage pattern** refers to the predictable effect that age has on earnings over the course of a person's working life.

As we noted earlier, location is also a source of wage differentials. Workers who live outside metropolitan areas make, on average, 19% less than their counterparts who live in cities (see again Table 15.3). This gap occurs because the cost of living is much higher in metropolitan areas.

Clearly, broad measures of differences in earnings do not provide evidence of wage discrimination. Since no employer will admit to discriminating, researchers can only infer the amount of discrimination after first correcting for observable differences from compensating differentials and differences in human capital. The unobservable differences that remain are presumed to reflect discrimination. Because these unobservable differences are small, estimates generally put discrimination at less than 5% of wage differences.

ECONOMICS IN THE REAL WORLD

The Effects of Beauty on Earnings

According to research that spans the labor market from the law profession to college teaching, and in countries as different as the United States and China, beauty matters. How much? You might be surprised—as related by economist Daniel S. Hamermesh in his book *Beauty Pays*, beautiful people make as much as 10% more than people with average looks, while those whose looks are considered significantly below average may make as much as 25% below normal.

Jennifer Lopez, Zac Efron, and Katie Holmes—three of the decade's most beautiful people.

The influence of beauty on wages can be viewed in two ways. First, it can be seen as a marketable trait that has value in many professions. Actors, fashion models, waiters, and litigators all rely on their appearance to make a living, so it is not surprising to find that beauty is correlated with wages in those professions. If beautiful people are more productive in certain jobs because of their beauty, then attractiveness is simply a measure of the value of the marginal product that they generate. In other words, being beautiful is a form of human capital that the worker possesses.

However, a second interpretation finds evidence of discrimination. If employers prefer "beautiful" people as employees, then part of the earnings increase associated with beauty might reflect that preference. In addition, the success of workers who are more beautiful could also reflect the preferences of customers who prefer to work with more attractive people.

Since it is impossible to determine whether the beauty premium is a compensating differential or the result of overt discrimination, we have to acknowledge the possibility that the truth, in many situations, could be a little bit of both. ✳

Occupational Crowding: How Discrimination Affects Wages

Occupational crowding is the phenomenon of relegating a group of workers to a narrow range of jobs in the economy.

Discrimination is not as overt or widespread today as it was a few generations ago. Today, doors that were once closed are now open, and this trend has helped to equalize wages among qualified workers. Still, the impact of wage discrimination continues. For example, in many jobs *occupational crowding* continues to suppress wages for women. **Occupational crowding** is the phenomenon of relegating a group of workers to a narrow range of jobs in the economy. To understand how this works, imagine a community named Utopia with only two types of jobs: a small number in engineering and a large number in secretarial services. Furthermore, everyone is equally proficient at

TABLE 15.4

Where the Men Aren't

Job	Percentage female
Kindergarten teachers	98%
Dental hygienists	98
Secretaries	98
Childcare workers	97
Nurses	93
Bank tellers	87
Librarians	86
Legal assistants	84
Telephone operators	83

Source: Bureau of Labor Statistics, 2010.

both occupations, and everyone in the community is happy to work either job. Under these assumptions, we would expect the wages for engineers and secretaries to be the same.

Now imagine that not everyone in Utopia has the same opportunities. Suppose that we roll back the clock to a time when women in Utopia are not allowed to work as engineers. Women who want to work can only find employment as secretaries. As a result of this occupational crowding, workers who have limited opportunities (women, in this example) find themselves competing with one another, as well as with the men who cannot get engineering jobs, for secretarial positions. As a result, wages fall in secretarial jobs and rise in engineering. Since only men can work in engineering, they are paid more than their similarly qualified female counterparts, who are crowded into secretarial positions and earn less. Furthermore, since women who want to work can only receive a low wage as a secretary, many decide instead to stay at home and produce non-market services, such as child-rearing, with a higher value to the women than the wages they could earn as secretaries.

Of course, in the real world women today are not restricted to secretarial jobs. However, women still dominate in many of the lower-paying jobs in our society. Table 15.4 shows a number of female-dominated occupations in the United States. Not surprisingly, given the low wages, men have not rushed into these jobs. However, because women have not exited them to the extent one might expect, wages have remained low. Rigidity in changing occupations, social customs, and personal preferences all help to explain why this is the case. The same forces are at work in traditionally male-dominated jobs, where men have enjoyed higher wages due to a lack of female employees. Engineers, auto mechanics, airline pilots—to name a few—are career areas that have begun to admit women in large numbers over the last 20 years. As the supply of workers expands, the net effect will be to lower wages in traditionally male-dominated jobs.

ECONOMICS IN THE MEDIA

Occupational Crowding

Anchorman: The Legend of Ron Burgundy

This film from 2004 depicts the television news industry in the early days of women anchors—the 1970s! Stations were diversifying their broadcast teams and beginning to add women and minorities to previously all-white, all-male lineups.

In one scene, Veronica Corningstone, a news anchor, introduces herself: "Hello, everyone. I just want you all to know that I look forward to contributing to this news station's already sterling reputation."

The added competition for air time does not sit well with Ron Burgundy and his male colleagues: "I mean, come on, Ed! Don't get me wrong. I love the ladies. They rev my engine, but they don't belong in the newsroom! It is anchorman, not anchor lady! And that is a scientific fact!"

Veronica overhears the conversation, and after leaving the office she begins a monologue: "Here we go again. Every station it's the same. Women ask me how I put up with it. Well, the truth is, I don't really

have a choice. This is definitely a man's world. But while they're laughing and carrying on, I'm chasing down leads and practicing my non-regional diction. Because the only way to win is to be the best."

Do you think Veronica's strategy of trying to be the best would help her to be accepted in a real-world work environment?

"You stay classy, San Diego."

Winner-Take-All

In 1930, baseball legend Babe Ruth demanded and received a salary of $80,000 from the New York Yankees. This would be approximately $1,000,000 in today's dollars. Babe Ruth earned a lot more than the other baseball players of his era. When told that President Herbert Hoover earned less than he was asking for, Ruth famously said, "I had a better year than he did." In fact, the annual salary of the president of the United States is far less than that of top professional athletes, movie stars, college presidents, and even many corporate CEOs.

Why does the most important job in the world pay less than jobs with far less value to society? Part of the answer involves compensating differentials. Being president of the United States means being the most powerful person in the world, so compensation is only a small part of the benefit of holding that office. The other part of the answer has to do with the way labor markets function. Pay at the top of most professions is subject to a form of competition known as **winner-take-all**, which occurs when extremely

Winner-take-all
occurs when extremely small differences in ability lead to sizable differences in compensation.

small differences in ability lead to sizable differences in compensation. This compensation structure has been common in professional sports and in the entertainment industry for many years, but it also exists in the legal profession, medicine, journalism, investment banking, fashion design, and corporate management.

In a winner-take-all market, being a little bit better than one's rivals can be worth a tremendous amount. For example, in 2007 baseball player Alex Rodriguez received a 10-year contract worth $275 million, or $27.5 million a year. As good as Rodriguez is, he is not 10 times better than an average major league baseball player, who makes almost $3 million. Nor is he a thousand times better than a typical minor league player, who

Alex Rodriguez has 27.5 million reasons a year to smile, but not all professional baseball players are as fortunate.

earns a few thousand dollars a month. In fact, it is hard to tell the difference between a baseball game played by major and minor leaguers. Minor league pitchers throw just about as hard, the players run almost as fast, and the fielding is almost as good. Yet major league players make hundreds of times more.

Winner-take-all has also found its way into corporate America. For example, exploding CEO pay is a relatively recent phenomenon in U.S. history, growing from an average of 35 times the salary of the average American worker in 1975, to 150 times by 1990. According to some estimates, CEO salaries today are more than 300 times greater than that of the average worker.

Paying so much to a relatively small set of workers may seem unfair, but the prospect of much higher pay or bonuses motivates many ambitious employees to exert maximum effort. If we look beyond the amount of money that some people earn, we can see that winner-take-all creates incentives that encourage supremely talented workers to maximize their abilities while at the same time helping to maximize social welfare.

Incentives

What Causes Income Inequality?

Income inequality occurs when some workers earn more than others. Compensating differentials, discrimination, corruption, and differences in the marginal product of labor all lead to inequality of income. Would it surprise you to learn that we shouldn't want everyone to have the same income? Income inequality is a fact of life in a market economy. In this section, we first examine why income inequality exists. Once we understand the factors that lead to income inequality, we examine how it is measured. Because income inequality is difficult to measure and easy to misinterpret, we explain how observed income inequality statistics are constructed and what they mean. We end by discussing income mobility, a characteristic in many developed nations that lessens the impact of income inequality on the life-cycle wage pattern.

Factors That Lead to Income Inequality

To illustrate the nature of income inequality, we begin with a simple question: what would it take to equalize wages? For all workers to get the same wages, three conditions would have to be met. First, every worker would have to have the same skills, ability, and productivity. Second, every job would have to be equally attractive. Third, all workers would have to be perfectly mobile. In other words, perfect equality of income would require that workers be clones who perform the same job. Be glad we don't live in a world like that! In the real world, some people work harder than others and are more productive. Some people, such as aid workers, missionaries, teachers, and even ski bums, choose to earn less. What makes us unique—our traits, our desires, and our differences—is also part of what leads to income inequality. In fact, income inequality is perfectly consistent with the forces that govern a market economy.

The Role of Corruption in Income Inequality

One notable area of concern is the influence that corruption has on trade. In this section, we examine why corruption slows trade and simultaneously increases income inequality.

Trade
creates
value

All economic systems require trust in order to exact gains from trade. However, some societies value the rule of law more than others. Many less developed countries suffer from widespread corruption. Consider Somalia, a country without a functional central government. This situation has led to lawlessness in which clans, warlords, and militia groups fight for control. The situation is so dire that international aid efforts often require the bribing of government officials to ensure that the aid reaches those in need.

Corruption can play a large role in income inequality. In societies where corruption is common, working hard or being innovative is not enough; getting ahead often requires bribing officials to obtain business permits or to ward off competitors. Moreover, when investors cannot be sure their assets are safe from government seizure or criminal activity, they are less likely to develop a business. Under political systems that are subject to bribery and other forms of corruption, dishonest people benefit at the expense of the poor. Corruption drives out legitimate business opportunities and magnifies income inequality.

 ECONOMICS IN THE REAL WORLD

5th Pillar

Widespread corruption leads to more income inequality.

Recognizing the damage that corruption causes has prompted some people to fight back. For example, 5th Pillar, an independent organization, has developed zero-rupee notes in India, where corruption is rampant. The notes provide a way for persons who are asked for a bribe to indicate that they are unwilling to participate. Presenting a zero-rupee note lets the other person know that you refuse to give or take any money for services required by law or to give or take money for an illegal activity. Since 5th Pillar reports attempted bribery to the authorities, individuals who are brave enough to use them know that they are not alone in fighting corruption. ✳

Measuring Income Inequality

When is income inequality a serious concern, and when is it simply a part of the normal functioning of the market? To answer this question, we begin with income inequality in the United States. Economists study the distribution of household income in the United States by quintiles, or five groups of equal size, ranging from the poorest fifth (20%) of households to the top fifth. Figure 15.1 shows the most recent data available, for the year 2011.

According to the U.S. Bureau of the Census, the poorest 20% of households makes just 3.2% of all income earned in the United States. The next quintile, the second fifth, earns 8.4% of income. This means that fully 40% of U.S. households (the bottom two quintiles) account for only 12% of earned income. The middle quintile earns 14.3%, the second-highest quintile 23.0%, and the top quintile 51.1%. Being a pie chart, Figure 15.1 vividly shows the wide disparity between the percentage of total U.S. income earned by the poorest households (3.3%) and by the richest households (51.1%). If we divide the percentage of income earned by households in the top fifth (51.1%) by the percentage of income earned by households in the bottom fifth (3.3%), we get about 15.8. Looking at the numbers this way, we can say that households in the top fifth have approximately 15.8 times the income of those in the bottom fifth. Viewing that number in isolation makes the amount of income inequality in the United States seem large.

However, to provide some perspective, Table 15.5 compares the income inequality in various other countries. The countries above the dashed line are more developed, and those below are less developed.

As you can see, the U.S. income inequality ratio of 15.8 is high compared to that of other highly developed nations but relatively low compared to that of less developed nations. In general, highly developed nations have lower degrees of income inequality. This occurs because more developed countries

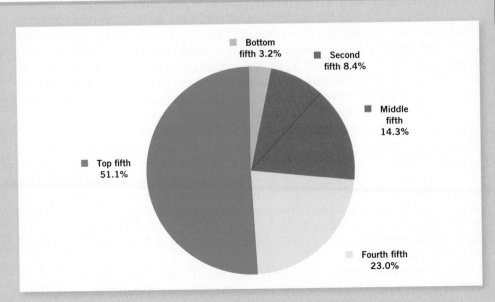

The Distribution of Income in the United States by Quintile

The top fifth of income earners makes 51.1% of all income, an amount equal to the combined income of the four remaining quintiles. Income declines across the quintiles, falling to 3.3% in the lowest fifth.

Source: U.S. Census Bureau.

TABLE 15.5	
Inequality in Selected Countries	
Country	**Inequality ratio** **(richest 20% ÷ poorest 20%)**
Japan	4.1
Germany	6.3
Canada	8.6
United Kingdom	12.7
United States	15.8
Mexico	19.3
Brazil	37.0
Bolivia	85.5
Namibia	98.2

Source: Adapted from United Nations Development Programme, *Human Development Report*, 2009, Table M.

have less poverty, so those individuals who are at the bottom of the income ladder there earn more than those at the bottom in other countries.

Understanding Observed Inequality

Translating income inequality into a number, as we've done with the income quintiles, can mask the true nature of income inequality. In this section, we step back and consider what the income inequality ratio can and cannot tell us.

Since the inequality ratio measures the success of top earners against that of bottom earners, if the bottom group is doing relatively well, then the inequality ratio will be smaller. This explains why many highly developed countries have ratios under 10. However, the United States has an inequality ratio that is close to 15. What is driving the difference? The United States has many highly successful workers and a *poverty rate* that is similar to those found in other highly developed countries. The **poverty rate** is the percentage of the population whose income is below the *poverty threshold*. The **poverty threshold** is the income level below which a person or family is considered impoverished.

According to the Organization for Economic Cooperation and Development (OECD), the United States has a poverty rate that is quite similar to that of Japan, a country with a markedly lower inequality ratio. Given that the poverty rate in the United States is not unusually large compared to Japan's, we cannot explain the higher inequality ratio by pointing to the percentage of poor people. Rather, it is the relative success of the top income earners in the United States that causes the markedly higher inequality ratio. In other words, there are more high income earners in the United States than in Japan. In this case, the inequality ratio is quite misleading because of the success of high-income earners.

High levels of income inequality also occur when the poorest are *really* poor. For example, there are many successful people in Mexico, Brazil, Bolivia, and Namibia. The problem in these countries is that the success of some

The **poverty rate** is the percentage of the population whose income is below the poverty threshold.

The **poverty threshold** is the income level below which a person or family is considered impoverished.

people is benchmarked against the extreme poverty of many others. Therefore, high inequality ratios are a telltale sign of a serious poverty problem. Suppose that the poorest quintile of the population in Bolivia has an average income of $500, while those in the top quintile earn $42,750. The income inequality ratio is $42,750 ÷ $500 ≈ 85.5. By comparison, consider Canada. If the poorest quintile of the population in Canada has an average income of $5,000, while those in the top quintile earn $42,750, the income inequality ratio there is $42,750 ÷ $5,000 = 8.6. In both countries the top quintile is doing equally well, but the widespread poverty problem in Bolivia produces an alarming income inequality ratio. In this example, inequality ratios signal a significant poverty problem.

A high income inequality ratio can occur if people at the bottom earn very little or if the income of high-wage earners is much greater than the income of others. The key point to remember is that even though income inequality ratios give us some idea about the degree of inequality in a society, a single number cannot fully reflect the sources of the underlying differences in income.

Difficulties in Measuring Income Inequality

Not only can income inequality numbers be misinterpreted, but they can often be unreliable. Because inequality data reflects income before taxes, it does not reflect disposable income, which is the portion of income that people actually have to spend. Nor does the data account for **in-kind transfers**—that is, goods and services that are given to the poor instead of cash. Examples of in-kind services are government-subsidized housing and the Subsidized Nutrition Assistance Program that provides food supplements to 35 million low-income citizens in the United States. In addition, the data does not account for unreported or illegally obtained income. Because less developed countries generally have larger underground economies than developed countries do, their income data is even less reliable.

In-kind transfers are transfers (mostly to the poor) in the form of goods or services instead of cash.

Many economists also note that income data alone does not capture the value created from goods and services produced in the household. For example, if you mow your own lawn or grow your own vegetables, those activities have a positive value that is not expressed in your income data. In less developed countries, many households engage in very few market transactions and produce a large portion of their own goods and services. If we do not count these, our comparison of data with other countries will overstate the amount of inequality present in the less developed countries. Finally, the number of workers per household and the median age of each worker differ from country to country. When households contain more workers or those workers are, on average, older and therefore more experienced, comparing inequality across countries is less likely to be accurate.

Individually, none of these shortcomings poses a serious measurement issue from year to year. However, if we try to measure differences in income across generations, the changes are significant enough to invalidate the *ceteris paribus* ("all other things being equal") condition that allows us to assume that outside factors are held constant. In short,

Growing your own vegetables is an activity that is not counted in official income data.

comparing inequality data from this year with last year is generally fine, but comparing inequality data from today with data from 50 years ago is largely meaningless. For instance, we might note that income inequality in the United States increased slightly from 2011 to 2012. However, since this is just a single data point, we must be cautious about interpreting it as a trend. To eliminate that problem, we can extend the time frame from 1962 to 2012. That data shows an unmistakable upward trend in income inequality but also violates *ceteris paribus*; after all, the last 50 years have seen dramatic shifts in the composition of the U.S. labor force, changes in tax rates, a surge in in-kind transfers, a lower birthrate, and an aging population. It is a complex task to determine the impact of these changes on income inequality. A good economist tries to make relevant comparisons by examining similar countries over a relatively short period during which there were no significant socio-economic changes.

Finally, the standard calculations and models that we have discussed assume that the income distribution is a direct reflection of a society's welfare. However, we must be very careful not to infer too much about how well people are living based on their income alone. Indeed, income analysis does not offer a complete picture of human welfare. In Chapter 16, we will see that income is only one factor that determines human happiness and well-being. People also value leisure time, non-wage benefits, a sense of community, safety from crime, and social networks.

Income Mobility

Income mobility
is the ability of workers to move up or down the economic ladder over time.

When workers have a realistic chance of moving up the economic ladder, each person has an incentive to work harder and invest in human capital. **Income mobility** is the ability of workers to move up or down the economic ladder over time. Think of it this way: if today's poor must remain poor tomorrow and 10 years from now, income inequality remains high. However, if someone in the lowest income category can expect to experience enough economic success to move to a higher income quintile, being poor is a temporary condition. Why does this matter? It matters because economic mobility reduces inequality over long periods of time.

The dynamic nature of the U.S. economy is captured by income mobility data. Table 15.6 reports the income mobility in the United States over a series of 10-year periods from 1970 to 2005. We can see that mobility increased through the late 1980s, but thereafter it declined for both the poorest and the

TABLE 15.6

Income Mobility in the United States, 1970–2005

(1) Ten-year period	(2) % Poorest quintile that move up at least one quintile	(3) % Highest quintile that move down at least one quintile	(4) % Poorest quintile that move up at least two quintiles	(5) % Highest quintile that move down at least two quintiles
1970–1980	43.2	48.8	19.1	22.8
1975–1985	45.3	50.9	20.6	24.8
1980–1990	45.2	47.6	21.3	25.7
1985–1995	41.8	45.8	17.8	21.5
1990–2000	41.7	46.7	15.2	20.7
1995–2005	41.9	45.0	15.4	20.2

Source: Katharine Bradbury, *Trends in U.S. Family Income Mobility, 1969–2006,* Working Paper, Federal Reserve Bank of Boston, No. 11-10. Data for 1990–2000 was interpolated.

highest quintiles. Columns 4 and 5 show the percentage of households that moved up or down at least two quintiles.

Mobility data enables us to separate those at the bottom of the economic ladder into two groups: (1) the *marginal poor*, or people who are poor at a particular point in time but have the skills necessary to advance up the ladder, and (2) the *long-term poor*, or people who lack the skills to advance to the next quintile. The differences in income mobility among these two groups provide a helpful way of understanding how income mobility affects poverty.

For the marginal poor, low earnings are the exception. Since most young workers expect to enjoy higher incomes as they get older, many are willing to borrow in order to make a big purchase—for example, a car or a home. Conversely, middle-aged workers know that retirement will be possible only if they save now for the future. As a result, workers in their fifties have much higher savings rates than young workers and workers who are already retired. On reaching retirement, earnings fall; but if the worker has saved enough, retirement need not be a period of low consumption. The life-cycle wage pattern argues that changes in borrowing and saving patterns over one's life smooth out the consumption pattern. In other words, for many people a low income does not necessarily reflect a low standard of living.

Marginal thinking

When we examine how people actually live in societies with substantial income mobility, we see that the annual income inequality data can create a false impression about the spending patterns of young and old. This occurs because the young are generally upwardly mobile, so they spend more than one might expect by borrowing; the middle-aged, who have relatively high incomes, spend less than one might expect because they are saving for retirement; and the elderly, who have lower incomes, spend more than one might expect because they are drawing down their retirement savings.

In the next section, we turn our attention to the long-term poor, who do not have the skills to escape the lowest quintile. Members of this group spend their entire lives near or below the poverty threshold.

PRACTICE WHAT YOU KNOW

The good life: so near, yet so far . . .

Income Inequality: The Beginning and End of Inequality

Consider two communities, Alpha and Omega. Alpha has ten residents: five who earn $90,000, and five who earn $30,000. Omega also has ten residents: five earn $250,000, and the other five earn $50,000.

Question: What is the degree of income inequality in each community?

Answer: To answer this question, we must use quintile analysis. Since there are ten residents in Alpha, the top two earners represent the top quintile and the lowest two earners represent the bottom quintile. Therefore, the degree of income inequality in Alpha using quintiles analysis is $90,000 ÷ $30,000, or 3. In Omega, the top two earners represent the top quintile and lowest two earners represent the bottom quintile. Therefore, the degree of income inequality in Omega is $250,000 ÷ $50,000, or 5.

Question: Which community has the more unequal distribution of income, and why?

Answer: Omega has the more unequal distribution of income because the quintile analysis yields 5, versus 3 for Alpha.

Question: Can you think of a reason why someone might prefer to live in Omega?

Answer: Each rich citizen of Omega earns more than each rich citizen in Alpha, and each poor citizen earns more than each poor citizen of Alpha. Admittedly, there is more income inequality in Omega, but there is also more income across the entire income distribution. So, depending on one's preferences, one could prefer Omega if the absolute amount of income is what matters more, or Alpha if relative equality is what matters more.

How Do Economists Analyze Poverty?

The United States does not have a wealth problem, but it does have a poverty problem. According to the Census Bureau, close to 15% of all households are below the poverty threshold. To help us understand the issues, we begin with poverty statistics. Then, once we understand the scope of the problem, we examine policy solutions.

The Poverty Rate

For the last 50 years, the U.S. Bureau of the Census has been tracking the *poverty rate*, or the percentage of the population whose income is below the *poverty threshold*. The United States sets the poverty threshold at approximately three

Income Inequality around the World

"The rich get richer, and the poor get poorer" is a simple yet profound way to think about income inequality. As top earners make more and bottom earners make less, the inequality rate increases. It's a combination of these factors, not just extreme wealth or extreme poverty, that leads to huge gaps between those at the very top and those at the very bottom.

$$\text{Inequality ratio} = \frac{\text{Wealth controlled by top 20\%}}{\text{Wealth controlled by bottom 20\%}}$$

- Wealth controlled by top 20%
- Wealth controlled by bottom 20%
- Inequality ratio
- Poverty rate

Namibia 98.2

Brazil 37

> Less developed countries, like Namibia, have high rates of inequality. Why? Because the poor are extremely poor and earn just a fraction of the income of the affluent.

United States 15.8

17.3%

> Poverty is not the only factor of inequality, however. When the top earners are highly successful, the gap between rich and poor grows. The United States has a poverty rate similar to Japan's but a top 20% who earn more than Japan's top class.

Japan 4.1

15.7%

REVIEW QUESTIONS

- Suppose the top 20% of Brazilian earners make, on average, the equivalent of $100,000 a year. What does the average earner in the bottom 20% make?

- A friend tells you he wants to live in a world without income inequality. Discuss the pros and cons using at least one of the five foundations of economics from Chapter 1.

Those below the poverty threshold are unable to make ends meet.

times the amount of income required to afford a nutritionally balanced diet. To keep up with inflation, the poverty threshold is adjusted each year for changes in the level of prices. However, an individual family's threshold is calculated to include only the money that represents income earned by family members in the household. It does not include in-kind transfers, nor is the data adjusted for cost-of-living differences in the family's specific geographic area. For these reasons, poverty thresholds are a crude yardstick. Figure 15.2 shows the poverty rate for households in the United States from 1959 to 2011.

In 1964, Congress passed the Equal Opportunity Act and a number of other measures designed to fight poverty. Despite those initiatives, the rate of poverty today is slightly higher than it was 40 years ago. This result is surprising, since the economy's output has roughly doubled in that time. One would have hoped that the economy's progress could be measured at the bottom of the economic ladder, as well as at the top. Unfortunately, the stagnant poverty rate suggests that the gains from economic growth over that period have accrued to households in the middle and upper quintiles, rather than to the poor. Poverty has remained persistent, in part, because many low-income workers lack the necessary skills to earn living wages and, at the same time, investments by firms in automation and technology have reduced the demand for these workers. This situation cannot be easily solved by public-sector jobs initiatives; it will require a long-run investment in education programs targeted at the poor and retraining programs designed to help unemployed workers obtain jobs in growing segments of the economy.

Table 15.7 illustrates that children, female heads of household, and certain minorities disproportionately feel the incidence of poverty. When we combine at-risk groups—for example, black or Hispanic women who are heads of household—the poverty rate can exceed 50%.

FIGURE 15.2

Poverty Rate for U.S. Households, 1959–2011

Poverty rates for households fluctuated from 1959 through 2011. Since 2008, the poverty rate has climbed due to the recession that began in that year.

Source: U.S. Bureau of the Census.

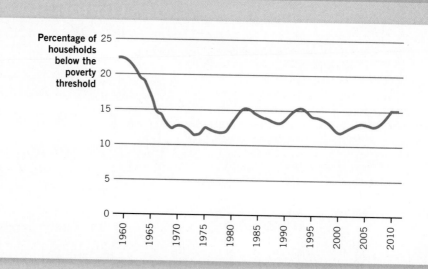

In the next section, we consider how public policy can address the issue of poverty. As Table 15.7 shows, poverty is a wide-ranging and multifaceted problem. Therefore, constructing policies that are targeted at specific groups will be more effective than taking a one-solution-for-all approach.

Poverty Policy

In this section, we outline a number of policies related to the problem of poverty. Because each policy carries both costs and benefits, efforts to help the poor must be considered carefully. Policies do not always distinguish between the truly needy and those who can help themselves. Therefore, in seeking to help the poor, we encounter two conflicting motivations: we want to give generously, but we also want the poor to become self-sufficient and eventually contribute to society. Almost everyone agrees that both goals are vital. Unfortunately, achieving both simultaneously has proven to be almost impossible.

Trade-offs

Welfare

"Welfare" is not a government program, but rather a term that describes a series of initiatives designed to help the poor by supplementing their income. Welfare can take a variety of forms, such as monetary payments, subsidies and vouchers, health services, or subsidized housing. Welfare is provided by the government and by other public and private organizations. It is intended

TABLE 15.7

The Poverty Rate for Various Groups

Group	Poverty rate (percentage)
Age	
Children (under 18)	21.9
Adults (18–64)	13.7
Elderly (65 or older)	8.7
Race/Ethnicity	
White	9.8
Asian	12.3
Hispanic	25.3
Black	27.6
Type of household	
Married couple	6.3
Male head only	15.8
Female head only	31.7

Source: U.S. Bureau of the Census, 2011.

to help the unemployed, those with illnesses or disabilities that prevent them from working, the elderly, veterans, and households with dependent children. An individual's eligibility for welfare is often limited to a set amount of time and is valid only as long as the recipient's income remains below the eligibility cutoff. Some examples of welfare programs include: Temporary Assistance for Needy Families (TANF), which provides financial support to families with dependent children; the Supplemental Security Income (SSI) program, which provides financial support to those who are unable to work; and the Subsidized Nutrition Assistance Program (SNAP), which gives financial assistance to those who need help to purchase basic foods.

In-Kind Transfers

In addition to financial assistance, the poor receive direct assistance in the form of goods and services. Local community food banks, housing shelters, and private charities like Habitat for Humanity and Toys for Tots all provide

ECONOMICS IN THE MEDIA

Welfare

Cinderella Man

The 2005 film *Cinderella Man* portrays the story of James Braddock, a boxing contender in the late 1920s before the stock market crash wiped him out and a busted right hand caused him to lose his license to box. Desperate to earn a living and support his family, Braddock secures a job working on the docks in New Jersey. However, he is unable to make ends meet, and his family is forced to move in with relatives. Braddock swallows his pride and goes to the welfare office, where he receives $19 in relief. Despite the sudden loss of income, separation from his family, and no clear end in sight, Braddock tries to remain upbeat. But the Great Depression begins to defeat him.

At this point, Braddock gets a break to fight in a preliminary match in Madison Square Garden when another fighter cancels the day before. Braddock wins with a stunning knockout, and his comeback begins. As money rolls in, he returns to the relief office and hands the same lady a roll of bills to pay back all that his family had been given.

That gesture might seem like a byproduct of an age of innocence, but there is an important message

Russell Crowe as a reluctant welfare recipient.

that is worth recalling. Welfare assistance represents an ethical obligation from the state to its citizens, but in any meaningful ethical arrangement the process must be two-sided. Welfare recipients also have an ethical obligation to look for work and not exploit welfare assistance.

in-kind benefits to the poor. Moreover, the government gives out food stamps and provides health care to the poor through Medicaid.

The idea behind in-kind transfers is that they protect recipients from the possibility of making poor decisions if they receive cash instead. For example, some recipients may use cash transfers to support drug or alcohol addictions, to gamble, or to spend frivolously on vacations, expensive clothes, or fancy meals. None of those poor decisions will alleviate the recipients' future need for food, clothing, and shelter. To limit the likelihood of such poor decisions, in-kind transfers can be targeted at essential services.

The Earned Income Tax Credit (EITC)

The Earned Income Tax Credit (EITC) is a refundable tax credit designed to encourage low-income workers to work more. At very low income levels, the EITC offers an incentive to work by supplementing earned income with a tax credit that can reduce the amount of taxes owed by as much as $6,000 a year. The amount is determined, in part, by the number of dependent children in the household and the location. Once a family reaches an income level above its earnings threshold, the EITC is phased out, and workers gradually lose the tax credit benefits. Under many welfare and in-kind transfer programs, the qualifying income is a specific cutoff point; an individual or household is either eligible or not. In contrast, the EITC is gradually reduced, which means that workers do not face a sizable disincentive to work as the program is phased out.

The EITC helps over 20 million families, making it the largest poverty-fighting program in the United States. EITC payments are sufficient to lift more than 5 million households out of poverty. In addition, the EITC creates stronger work incentives than those found under traditional welfare and in-kind transfer programs.

Incentives

A **negative income tax** is a tax credit paid to poor households out of taxes received from middle- and upper-income households.

The EITC is a form of *negative income tax*. A **negative income tax** is a tax credit paid to poor households out of taxes collected from middle- and upper-income taxpayers. For example, suppose that a household's tax liability is computed on the basis of the following formula:

$$\text{Taxes owed} = (0.25 \text{ of household taxable income}) - \$10,000$$

Table 15.8 shows taxes that would be owed according to this formula at various income levels.

At any income below $40,000, the government pays a credit. Households with incomes above $40,000 owe taxes. Although taxes in the real world are far more complex, economists have long admired the simple elegance of the negative income tax, and this is essentially how the EITC (with a few extra wrinkles) works in practice.

The Minimum Wage

The minimum wage is often viewed as an anti-poverty measure. However, we learned in Chapter 5 that the minimum wage cannot generate more jobs or guarantee higher pay. Predictably, firms respond to higher minimum wages by hiring fewer workers and utilizing more capital-intensive production processes, such as self-checkout lanes. Since the minimum wage does not guarantee employment, the most it offers to an individual worker is a slightly

TABLE 15.8

How the Negative Income Tax Works

Income	Calculation	Tax owed/Credit
$80,000	($80,000 × 0.25) − $10,000	$10,000
60,000	($60,000 × 0.25) − $10,000	5,000
40,000	($40,000 × 0.25) − $10,000	0
20,000	($20,000 × 0.25) − $10,000	− 5,000
0	($0 × 0.25) − $10,000	− 10,000

larger paycheck. At the same time, a higher minimum wage makes those jobs more difficult to find. Despite rhetoric that trumpets the minimum wage as a potential cure to poverty, the real problem remains: some workers lack skills, motivation, or both. In that case, they cannot improve their earning ability by means of a minimum wage law.

Problems with Traditional Aid

Many welfare programs create work disincentives. In fact, a serious incentive problem arises when we examine the combined effects of welfare and in-kind transfer programs. Many benefits are severely reduced or curtailed altogether at certain income thresholds. This creates an incentive for low-income workers to work less in order to maintain eligibility for government assistance.

To see why this matters, consider a family of five with a combined income of $20,000 a year. Suppose that the family qualifies for public assistance that amounts to another $10,000 in benefits. The family's combined income from employment and benefits thus rises to $30,000. What happens if another family member gets a part-time job and income from wages rises from $20,000 to $30,000? Under the current law, a maximum income of $30,000 disqualifies the family from receiving most of the financial assistance it had been getting. As a result, the family's benefits fall from $10,000 to $2,000 per year. Now the family nets $32,000 total. The person who secured part-time employment may feel that this isn't worth it because even though the family earned an additional $10,000, they lost $8,000 in "welfare" benefits. Since they are only able to raise their net income by $2,000, they have effectively returned $8,000. The loss of those benefits feels like an 80% tax, which creates a large disincentive to work.

Incentives

This is a basic dilemma that poverty-reducing programs face: those that provide substantial benefits discourage participation in the workforce because a recipient who starts to work, in many cases, no longer qualifies for the benefits and loses them. Among the three options we have discussed so far, the EITC does the best job of addressing the work incentive problem by phasing out assistance at a gradual rate.

While few people dispute that welfare programs are well intentioned, many economists are concerned about the programs' unintended consequences. A society that establishes a generous welfare package for the poor will find that it faces a *samaritan's dilemma*. A **samaritan's dilemma** occurs when an act of charity creates disincentives for recipients to take care of themselves. President Bill Clinton addressed this concern in 1996 when he vowed "to end welfare as we know it." As part of the TANF program, Clinton changed the payout structure for federal assistance and encouraged states to require employment searches as a condition for receiving aid. In addition, the TANF program imposed a five-year maximum for the time during which a recipient can receive benefits. This strategy changed welfare from an entitlement under the law into a temporary safety net program, thereby reducing the samaritan's dilemma.

A **samaritan's dilemma** occurs when an act of charity causes disincentives for recipients to take care of themselves.

Incentives

ECONOMICS IN THE REAL WORLD

Muhammad Yunus and the Grameen Bank

One economist, Muhammad Yunus, stands alone. In 2006, he received the Nobel Peace Prize for his work helping poor families in Bangladesh. What did Yunus do to win that honor? He founded the Grameen Bank, which was instrumental in creating a new type of loan that has extended more than $8 billion to poor people in Bangladesh in an effort to eliminate extreme poverty.

The Grameen Bank gives out very small loans, known as *microcredit*, to poor Bangladeshis who are unable to qualify for conventional loans from traditional lenders. The loans are provided without collateral, and repayment is based on an honor system. By conventional standards that sounds preposterous, but it works! The Grameen Bank reports a 99% repayment rate, and according to one survey over 50% of the families of Grameen borrowers have moved above the poverty line.

It all started with just a few thousand dollars. In 1974, Yunus, who was trained as an economist in the United States, returned to Bangladesh and lent $27 to each of 42 villagers who made bamboo furniture. The loans, which were all paid back, enabled the villagers to cut out any middlemen and purchase their own raw materials. A few years later, Yunus won government approval to open the Grameen Bank, named for the Bengali word for "rural."

Yunus had a truly innovative idea. In order to receive a loan, applicants must belong to a five-member group. Once the first two members begin to pay back their loans, the others can get theirs. While there is no group responsibility for returning the loans, the Grameen Bank believes it creates a sense of social responsibility, ensuring that all members will pay back their loans. More important, Yunus trusted that people would honor their commitments, and he was proven right. With just a relatively few dollars, Yunus changed the perception about how to effectively fight poverty in underdeveloped nations—a truly remarkable achievement! ✳

In 2006, Yunus received the Nobel Peace Prize.

PRACTICE WHAT YOU KNOW

Welfare is an economic means of lending a helping hand.

Incentives

Samaritan's Dilemma: Does Welfare Cause Unemployment?

The state you live in is considering two different welfare programs. The first plan guarantees $8,000 for each person. The second plan does not guarantee any payments, but it doubles any income earned up to $12,000.

Question: Which program creates the lesser amount of unemployment?

Answer: Think about incentives. Under the first plan, recipients' benefits are not tied to work. The $8,000 is guaranteed. However, the second plan will pay more if recipients do work. This policy acts as a positive incentive to get a job. For instance, someone who works 20 hours a week and earns $10 per hour would make $200 per week, or about $10,000 a year. Under the second plan, that person would receive an additional $10,000 from the government. Therefore, we can say that the second program reduces the amount of unemployment.

Conclusion

Some jobs pay much more than others, but that is not inherently unfair despite what many people believe. Income inequality is often misunderstood. People and jobs differ in many dimensions, and wages respond accordingly. Wages are determined by supply and demand along with many non-monetary factors, such as compensating differentials, location, and union membership, all of which create significant income inequality. As we have seen, income inequality is neither good nor bad; it simply reflects the way the economic world works. Any effort to equalize incomes would have a very serious unintended consequence: the incentive to work hard would be reduced.

In addition, since the long-term poor are perpetually below the poverty threshold, welfare policies must differentiate between those who are temporarily impoverished and those who need more long-term assistance. The EITC program gives the marginal poor the correct incentives to escape poverty, while welfare and other in-kind transfers provide a safety net for those who need more assistance. The challenge for policymakers is to design aid programs so that they provide a safety net for the long-term poor while creating disincentives for the marginal poor to remain on welfare.

Donating to Charity More Effectively

The samaritan's dilemma is not unique to public assistance; it also applies to private charitable donations. Here the dilemma occurs with the stewardship of the donations. Donors want their gifts to benefit the largest possible set of needs. However, charitable organizations have overhead expenses that limit how much of the gift actually reaches the hands of the needy. In addition, not all charities are aboveboard. Here are a few tips to ensure that your donations make a difference.

1. Ask for a copy of the organization's financial report. Find out how much of your money actually will be used for charitable programs. If the organization is reluctant to share this information upon request, walk away.

2. Be careful of charities with copycat names. Some organizations use names similar to those of well-known organizations in order to confuse donors.

3. Be wary of emotional appeals that talk about problems but do not explain how donated monies will be spent. Do not succumb to high-pressure tactics or solicitations made over the phone; donating should be a reasoned and thoughtfully considered process. Step back, and ask for written materials containing information about the charity.

4. Ask if donations are tax deductible. Do not pay in cash, but instead pay by check so you have proof that you gave if you are ever audited.

5. Finally, after you have done your due diligence, give confidently and generously.

How can you make sure your donation gets to those that need it?

ANSWERING THE BIG QUESTIONS

What are the determinants of wages?

* Supply and demand play a key role in determining wages, along with a number of non-monetary determinants of earnings such as compensating differentials, human capital, location, lifestyle, union membership, and efficiency wages.

* Economic studies of wage discrimination have found that the amount of discrimination is relatively small, accounting for only 3% to 5% of wage differences.

* Despite recent gains, women still earn significantly less than men. Occupational crowding partially explains the wage gap. As long as supply imbalances remain in traditional male and female jobs, significant wage differences will persist.

What causes income inequality?

* Compensating differentials, discrimination, corruption, and differences in the marginal product of labor all lead to income inequality.

* Economic mobility reduces income inequality over long periods. Due to the life-cycle wage pattern, distinct borrowing and saving patterns over an individual's life smooth out his or her spending pattern. Therefore, in societies with substantial income mobility, the annual income inequality data overstates the amount of inequality.

How do economists analyze poverty?

* Economists determine the poverty rate by establishing a poverty threshold.

* The poverty rate in the United States has been stagnant for the last 40 years despite many efforts (welfare, in-kind transfers, and the EITC) to reduce it.

* Efforts to reduce poverty are subject to the samaritan's dilemma because they generally create disincentives for recipients to support themselves.

CONCEPTS YOU SHOULD KNOW

compensating differential
  (p. 458)
efficiency wages (p. 462)
human capital (p. 459)
in-kind transfers (p. 473)
income mobility (p. 474)

life-cycle wage pattern (p. 465)
negative income tax (p. 481)
occupational crowding (p. 466)
poverty rate (p. 472)
poverty threshold (p. 472)
samaritan's dilemma (p. 483)

strike (p. 461)
union (p. 461)
winner-take-all (p. 468)
wage discrimination (p. 464)

QUESTIONS FOR REVIEW

1. Why do garbage collectors make more than furniture movers?

2. What are efficiency wages? Why are some employers willing to pay them?

3. Why is it difficult to determine the amount of wage discrimination in the workplace?

4. Discuss some of the reasons why full-time working women make, on average, 77% as much as full-time working men.

5. How does the degree of income inequality in the United States compare to that in similarly developed countries? How does U.S. income inequality compare with that in less developed nations?

6. Why do high rates of income mobility mitigate income inequality?

7. Which anti-poverty program (welfare, in-kind transfers, or the Earned Income Tax Credit) creates the strongest incentive for recipients to work? Why?

STUDY PROBLEMS (✱ *solved at the end of the section*)

1. Suppose that society restricted the economic opportunities of right-handed persons to jobs in construction, while left-handed persons could work any job.
   a. Would wages in construction be higher or lower than wages for other jobs?
   b. Would left-handed workers make more or less than right-handed workers?
   c. Now suppose that right-handers were allowed to work any job they like. What effect would this change have on the wages of right-handers and left-handers over time?

2. Internships are considered a vital stepping-stone to full-time employment after college, but not all internship positions are paid. Why do some students take unpaid internships when they could be working summer jobs and earning an income? Include a discussion of human capital in your answer.

3. Consider two communities. In Middletown, two families earn $40,000 each, six families earn $50,000 each, and two earn $60,000 each. In Polarity, four families earn $10,000 each, two earn $50,000 each, and four earn $90,000 each. Which community has the more unequal distribution of income? Explain your response.

4. The United States has attracted many highly productive immigrants who work in fields such as education, health, and technology. How do these immigrants affect the income inequality in this country? Is this type of immigration good or bad for the United States, and why? What impact is this type of immigration having on the countries that are losing some of their best workers?

✱5. Suppose that a wealthy friend asks for your advice on how to reduce income inequality. Your friend wants to know if it would be better to give $100 million to poor people who will never attend college or to offer $100 million in financial aid to students who could not otherwise afford to attend college. What advice would you give, and why?

6. What effect would doubling the minimum wage have on income inequality? Explain your answer.

* 7. Suppose that a company has 10 employees. It agrees to pay each worker on the basis of productivity. The individual workers' output is 10, 14, 15, 16, 18, 19, 21, 23, 25, and 30 units, respectively. However, some of the workers complain that they are earning less than the other workers, so they appeal to management to help reduce the income inequality. As a result, the company decides to pay each worker the same salary. However, the next time the company measures each worker's output, they find that 6, 7, 7, 8, 10, 10, 11, 11, 12, and 12 units are produced. Why did this happen? Would you recommend that the company continue the new compensation system? Explain your response.

8. The government is considering three possible welfare programs:
   a. Give each low-income household $10,000.
   b. Give each low-income household $20,000 minus the recipient's income.
   c. Match the income of each low-income household, where the maximum they can receive in benefits is capped at $10,000.

Which program does the most to help the poor? Describe the work incentives under each program.

SOLVED PROBLEMS

5. The return on your wealthy friend's investment will be higher by giving the money to students with the aptitude, but not the income, to afford to go to college. After all, college students earn substantially more than high school graduates do. Therefore, an investment in additional education will raise the marginal revenue product of labor. With the higher earning power that a college degree provides, more people will be lifted out of poverty, thereby reducing the amount of income inequality in society.

7. Begin by calculating the average output when each worker's wage is based on the amount that he or she produces: $10 + 14 + 15 + 16 + 18 + 19 + 21 + 23 + 25 + 30 = 191 \div 10 = 19.1$. Then compute the average output when the company decides to pay each worker the same wage: $6 + 7 + 7 + 8 + 10 + 10 + 11 + 11 + 12 + 12 = 94 \div 10 = 9.4$. The output has dropped by one-half! Why did this happen? The company forgot about incentives. In this case, an attempt to create equal pay caused a disincentive problem (since hard work is not rewarded), and the workers all reduced their work effort. The new compensation system should be scrapped.

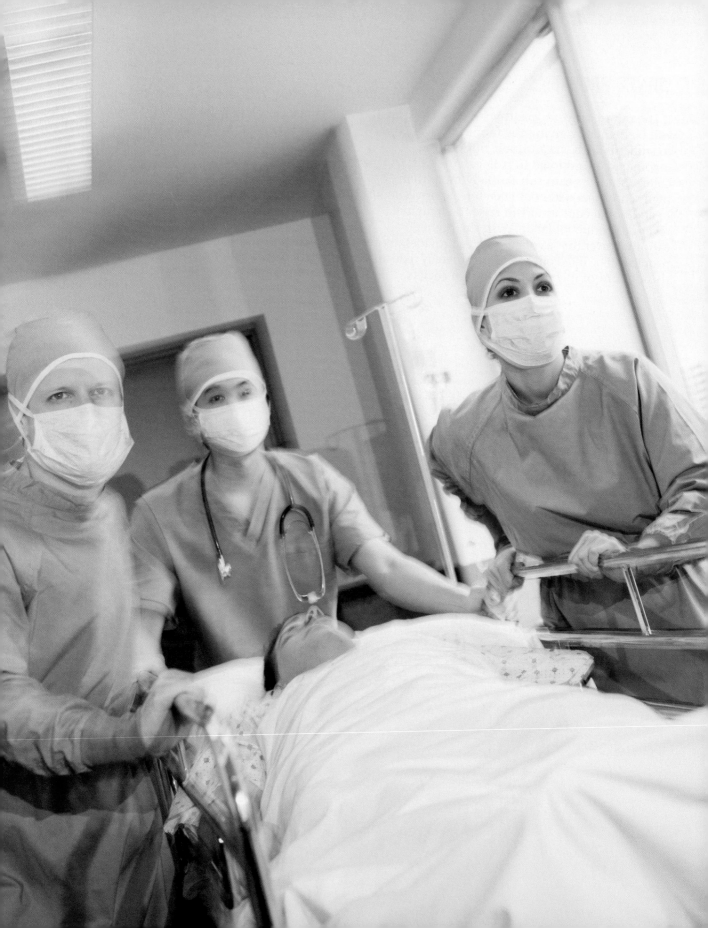

Special Topics in
MICROECONOMICS

Consumer Choice

The more money you have, the happier you'll be.

Did having more money make Ebenezer Scrooge happier? How about Montgomery Burns from *The Simpsons*? Or Mr. Potter from *It's a*

MIS CONCEPTION

Wonderful Life? The answer is *no*. All three fatally flawed characters hoarded money and, in the process, missed out on many of the good things that life has to offer. Then there is Jack Whittaker, a real-life millionaire who won a $315 million Powerball jackpot in 2002. He is now completely broke, is divorced from his wife, has been arrested for DUI, and was robbed on two separate occasions while carrying $500,000. (Who does *that*?) Worst of all, he lost his daughter and granddaughter to drug overdoses. Do you think Jack Whittaker regrets winning the lottery? "If only I could win the lottery" may be one wish you don't want granted.

Money can be used in ways that lift the spirit. For one thing, more money means more opportunities to strengthen your connections with others and contribute to your community. It also means you can afford to travel, experience the diverse wonders of nature, and spend more time with family and friends instead of collecting material possessions. Moreover, saving money for a goal, such as a special trip, can make the experience more rewarding. Money is best spent when it invokes strong positive feelings and creates memories. So can more money buy more happiness? We say yes, but only if you are careful about what you buy and do not become consumed by the pursuit of money.

In this chapter, we will use our understanding of income constraints, price, and personal satisfaction to determine which economic choices yield the greatest benefits.

Can money really buy happiness?

BIG QUESTIONS

* How do economists model consumer satisfaction?
* How do consumers optimize their purchasing decisions?
* What is the diamond-water paradox?

How Do Economists Model Consumer Satisfaction?

Trade-offs

Utility
is a measure of the relative levels of satisfaction that consumers enjoy from the consumption of goods and services.

A **util** is a unit of satisfaction used to measure the enjoyment from consumption of a good or service.

Do you prefer a slice of apple pie . . .

. . . or a fudge brownie?

Imagine that it is a hot afternoon and you decide to make a quick stop at a convenience store for a cold drink. While you're there, you decide to get a snack as well. Brownies are your favorite, but apple pie is on sale and you choose that instead. You may not think about these purchases very carefully, but they involve several trade-offs, including the time you could use to do something else and the money that you could be spending on something else. If brownies are your favorite snack, why do you sometimes choose to eat apple pie? Why do many people pay thousands of dollars for diamond jewelry, which is not essential for life, and yet pay only pennies for water, which is essential for life? These are the kinds of questions we must answer if we are to understand how people make personal buying decisions.

To better understand the decisions that consumers make, economists attempt to measure the satisfaction that consumers get when they make purchases. **Utility** is a measure of the relative levels of satisfaction that consumers enjoy from the consumption of goods and services. Utility theory seeks to measure contentment, or satisfaction. To understand why people buy the goods and services they do, we need to recognize that some products produce more utility than others and that everyone receives different levels of satisfaction from the same good or service; in other words, utility varies from individual to individual. To quantify this idea of relative satisfaction, economists measure utility with a unit they refer to as a **util**.

There is tremendous value in modeling decisions this way. When we understand utility, we can predict what people are likely to purchase. This process is similar to the way we used models in earlier chapters to describe how the firm makes decisions or how the labor market works. We expect the firm to maximize profits, the laborer to accept the best offer, and the consumer to find the combination of goods that gives the most utility. For example, a brownie lover may get 25 utils from her favorite snack, but someone who is less susceptible to the pleasures of chewy, gooey chocolate may rate the same brownie at 10 utils. However, even this is not a completely accurate measurement of relative utility. Who can say whether one person's 25 represents more actual satisfaction than another person's 10? Even if you and a friend agree that you each receive 10 utils from eating brownies, you cannot say that you both experience the same amount of satisfaction or happiness; each of you has a unique personal scale. However, the level of enjoyment one receives can be internally consistent. For example, if you rate a brownie at 25 utils and a slice of apple pie at 15 utils, we know that you like brownies more than apple pie.

Utility, or what most of us think of as happiness, is a balance between economic and personal factors. Even though there is an inherent problem with equating money and happiness, this has not stopped researchers from exploring the connection.

In the next section, we explore the connection between total utility and marginal utility. This connection will help us understand why more money does not necessarily bring more happiness.

ECONOMICS IN THE REAL WORLD

Happiness Index

Since 2006, the Organisation for Economic Co-operation and Development (OECD) has compiled the Better Life Index— popularly called the "happiness index"—that includes social variables alongside economic data for 34 highly developed countries. The OECD measures well-being across these countries, based on 11 topics it has identified as essential in the areas of material living conditions and quality of life.

Which countries are happiest? The OECD doesn't rank them, and the results depend on the relative importance assigned to the different measurements. Giving each category equal weight, Australia currently comes in first, followed closely by Norway and the United States. What makes Australians so happy? It's not their income, which averages only $26,000 per year. However, Australians live to an average age of 82 (two years longer than typical in developed countries), experience low amounts of pollution, display a high degree of civic engagement, and enjoy a very high life satisfaction rating.

"Down under" is a satisfying place to live!

In contrast, the OECD identifies the United States as having the highest income, but it scores substantially lower in work-life balance than many of the other top countries do. At the opposite end of the list, we find Mexico. In Mexico, safety concerns, poor education, and low levels of income combine to produce a very low rating among the countries surveyed. ✳

Total Utility and Marginal Utility

Thinking about choices that consumers make can help us understand how to increase total utility. Consider a person who really likes brownies. In this case, the **marginal utility** is the extra satisfaction enjoyed from consuming one more brownie. In the table on the left-hand side of Figure 16.1, we see that the first brownie eaten brings 25 total utils. Eating additional brownies increases total utility until it reaches 75 utils after eating five brownies.

The graph in panel (a) of Figure 16.1 reveals that while the total utility (the green curve) rises until it reaches 75, the rate of increase slowly falls from 25 utils for the first brownie down to 5 additional utils for the fifth. The marginal utility values from the table are graphed in panel (b), which shows that marginal utility declines steadily as consumption rises.

Marginal utility is the additional satisfaction derived from consuming one more unit of a good or service.

Marginal thinking

FIGURE 16.1

Total Utility and Marginal Utility

The relationship between total utility and marginal utility can be seen by observing the dashed line that connects panels (a) and (b). Since the marginal utility becomes negative after five brownies are consumed, the total utility eventually falls. To the left of the dashed line, the marginal utility is positive in panel (b) and the total utility is rising in panel (a). Conversely, to the right of the dashed line, the marginal utility is negative and the total utility is falling.

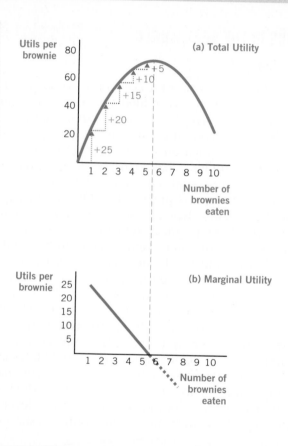

Number of brownies eaten	Total utility (utils per brownie)	Marginal utility (utils per brownie)
0	0	
		25
1	25	
		20
2	45	
		15
3	60	
		10
4	70	
		5
5	75	
		0
6	75	
		−5
7	70	
		−10
8	60	
		−15
9	45	
		−20
10	25	

The relationship between total utility and marginal utility is evident when we observe the dashed line that connects panels (a) and (b). Since the marginal utility becomes negative after five brownies are consumed, the total utility eventually falls. To the left of the dashed line, the marginal utility is positive in panel (b) and the total utility is rising in panel (a). Conversely, to the right of the dashed line, the marginal utility is negative and the total utility is falling.

When marginal utility becomes negative, it means that the consumer is tired of eating brownies. At that point, the brownies are no longer adding to the consumer's utility, and he or she will stop eating them.

Diminishing Marginal Utility

As you can see in Figure 16.1b, the satisfaction that a consumer derives from consuming a good or service declines with each additional unit consumed. Consider what happens when you participate in a favorite activity for an hour and then decide to do something else. **Diminishing marginal utility** occurs when marginal utility declines as consumption increases. The concept of diminishing marginal utility is so universal that it is one of the most widely held ideas in all of economics.

In rare cases, marginal utility can rise—but only temporarily. Consider running. Many people choose to run for recreation because it is both healthy and pleasurable. Often, the first mile is difficult as the runner's body gets warmed up. Thereafter, running is easier—for a while. No matter how good you are at distance running, eventually the extra miles become more exhausting and less satisfying, and you stop. This does not mean that running is not healthy or pleasurable. Far from it! But it does mean that forcing yourself to do more running after you have already pushed your limit yields less utility. Your own intuition should confirm this. If increasing marginal utility were possible, you would find that with every passing second you would enjoy what you were doing more and never want to stop. Since economists do not observe this behavior among rational consumers, we can be highly confident that diminishing marginal utility has tremendous explanatory power.

Table 16.1 highlights how diminishing marginal utility can serve to explain a number of interesting real-world situations.

Diminishing marginal utility occurs when marginal utility declines as consumption increases.

Running is fun for only so long.

PRACTICE WHAT YOU KNOW

Diminishing Marginal Utility

Question: A friend confides to you that a third friend has gradually lost interest in watching *Gossip Girl* with her and has begun saying she's too busy. How would you advise your friend to handle the situation?

Answer: Tell your friend about diminishing marginal utility! Even the best television show runs its course. After a while, the same humor or drama that once made the show interesting no longer seems as interesting. Then suggest to your friend that they mix it up and do something different together. If that doesn't work, it may not be *Gossip Girl* that is the problem—it may be that your friend's friend has grown tired of her.

Would you watch a *Gossip Girl* marathon?

TABLE 16.1

Examples of Diminishing Marginal Utility

	Example	Explanation using diminishing marginal utility
	Discounts on two-day passes to amusement parks	The excitement on the first day is palpable. You run to rides, don't mind waiting in line, and experience the thrill for the first time. By the second day, the enthusiasm has worn off and the lower price entices you to return.
	Discounts on season tickets	Over the course of any season, people anticipate some games and concerts more highly than others. To encourage patrons to buy the entire season package, venues must discount the total price.
	All-you-can-eat buffet	All-you-can-eat buffets offer the promise of unlimited food, but the average diner has a limited capacity. Eating more eventually leads to negative marginal utility. Restaurants assume that diminishing utility will limit how much their customers eat.
	Unlimited night and weekend minutes on cellphone plans	Cellphone companies rely on the diminishing marginal utility of conversation. Because of unused capacity at night and on the weekends, cellphone companies offer "unlimited" plans; they know that consumers will not stay on their phones indefinitely.
	Newspaper vending machines	A person rarely wants a second copy of the same newspaper. Since the value of the second paper is close to zero, most people do not steal additional copies from vending machines. (Sunday papers with money-saving coupons are a possible exception.)
	Nathan's Famous Hot Dog Eating Contest	Many people enjoy eating a hot dog or two or three, but Nathan's Famous Hot Dog Eating Contest is very difficult to watch.

How Do Consumers Optimize Their Purchasing Decisions?

Maximizing utility requires that consumers get the most satisfaction out of every dollar they spend, or what is commonly called "getting the biggest bang for the buck." When this is accomplished, we say that the consumer has optimized his or her purchasing decisions. However, this is easier said than done. Over the course of the year, each of us will make thousands of purchases of different amounts. Our budgets are generally not unlimited, and we try to spend in a way that enables us to meet both our short-run and our long-run needs. The combination of goods and services that maximizes the satisfaction, or utility, we get from our income or budget is the **consumer optimum**. In this section, we examine the decision process that leads to the consumer optimum. We start with two goods and then generalize those findings across a consumer's entire income or budget.

The **consumer optimum** is the combination of goods and services that maximizes the consumer's utility for a given income or budget.

Consumer Purchasing Decisions

Let's begin by imagining a world with only two goods: Pepsi and pizza. This will help us to focus on the opportunity cost of purchasing Pepsi instead of pizza, or pizza instead of Pepsi.

Pepsi is available for $1 per can, and each pizza slice costs $2. Suppose that you have $10 to spend. How much of each good should you buy in order to maximize your satisfaction? Before we can answer that question, we need a rule for making decisions. To reach your consumer optimum, you must allocate your available money by choosing goods that give you the most utility per dollar spent. By attempting to get the biggest bang for your buck, you will end up optimizing your choices. This relationship, shown below in terms of marginal utility (MU), helps quantify the decision. So if you get more for your money by purchasing Pepsi than pizza, then you should buy Pepsi—and vice versa.

$$\frac{MU_{Pepsi}}{Price_{Pepsi}} \quad \textbf{Which is larger?} \quad \frac{Mu_{Pizza}}{Price_{Pizza}}$$

If we divide the marginal utility of a good by its price, we get the utility per dollar spent. Since you wish to optimize your utility, a direct comparison of the marginal utility per dollar spent on Pepsi versus pizza gives you a road map to your consumer satisfaction. Table 16.2 shows the marginal utility for each can of Pepsi (column 2) and the marginal utility for each slice of pizza (column 5).

To decide what to consume first, look at column 3, which lists the marginal utility per dollar spent for Pepsi, and column 6, which lists the marginal utility per dollar spent for pizza. Now it's time to make your first spending decision—whether to drink a Pepsi or eat a slice of pizza. Since the marginal

TABLE 16.2

The Consumer Optimum with Pepsi and Pizza

(1) Pepsi consumed (cans)	(2) Marginal utility (MU Pepsi)	(3) MU Pepsi / Price Pepsi (Pepsi $1/can)	(4) Pizza consumed (slices)	(5) Marginal utility (MU pizza)	(6) MU pizza / Price pizza (pizza $2/slice)
1	9	9/1 = 9	1	20	20/2 = 10
2	8	8/1 = 8	2	16	16/2 = 8
3	7	7/1 = 7	3	12	12/2 = 6
4	6	6/1 = 6	4	8	8/2 = 4
5	5	5/1 = 5	5	4	4/2 = 2
6	4	4/1 = 4	6	0	0/2 = 0
7	3	3/1 = 3	7	−4	−4/2 = −2
8	2	2/1 = 2	8	−8	−8/2 = −4
9	1	1/1 = 1	9	−12	−12/2 = −6
10	0	0/1 = 0	10	−16	−16/2 = −8

utility per dollar spent for the first slice of pizza (10) is higher than the marginal utility for the first can of Pepsi (9), you order a slice of pizza, which costs $2. You have $8 left.

After eating the first slice of pizza, you can choose between having a second slice of pizza, which brings 8 utils per dollar spent, and having the first can of Pepsi, which brings 9 utils per dollar spent. This time you order a Pepsi, which costs $1. You have $7 left.

Now you can choose between having a second slice of pizza, representing 8 utils per dollar spent, and having a second can of Pepsi, also 8 utils per dollar spent. Since the two choices each yield the same amount of utility per dollar spent and you have enough money to afford both, we'll assume you would probably purchase both at the same time. This costs another $3, which leaves you with $4.

Your next choice is between the third slice of pizza at 6 utils per dollar spent and the third can of Pepsi at 7 utils per dollar spent. Pepsi is the better value, so you buy that. This leaves you with $3 for your final choice: between the third slice of pizza at 6 utils per dollar spent, and the fourth can of Pepsi at 6 utils per dollar spent. Since you have exactly $3 left and the items are of equal utility, you end your purchases by buying both.

Let's see how well you have done. Looking at column 2 in Table 16.2, we calculate that the four Pepsis you consumed yielded a total utility of (9 + 8 + 7 + 6) = 30 utils. Looking at column 5, we see that three slices of pizza yielded a total utility of (20 + 16 + 12) = 48 utils. Adding the two together (30 + 48) gives 78 total utils of satisfaction. This is the most utility you can afford with $10. To see why, look at Table 16.3, which reports the maximum utility for every affordable combination of Pepsi and pizza.

The optimum combination of Pepsi and pizza is highlighted in orange. This is the result we found by comparing the marginal utilities per dollar spent in Table 16.2. Notice that Table 16.3 confirms that this process results in the highest total utility. All other affordable combinations of Pepsi and pizza produce less utility. Table 16.3 also illustrates diminishing marginal utility. If you select either pizza or Pepsi exclusively, you would have a much lower total utility: 60 utils with pizza and 45 utils with Pepsi. In addition, the preferred outcome of four Pepsis and three pizza slices corresponds to a modest amount of each good; this avoids the utility reduction associated with excessive consumption.

TABLE 16.3

The Maximum Utility from Different Combinations of Pepsi and Pizza

Affordable combination of pizza and Pepsi	Total utility
5 pizza slices (20 + 16 + 12 + 8 + 4)	60 utils
2 Pepsis (9 + 8) and 4 pizza slices (20 + 16 + 12 + 8)	73 utils
4 Pepsis (9 + 8 + 7 + 6) and 3 pizza slices (20 + 16 + 12)	78 utils
6 Pepsis (9 + 8 + 7 + 6 + 5 + 4) and 2 pizza slices (20 + 16)	75 utils
8 Pepsis (9 + 8 + 7 + 6 + 5 + 4 + 3 + 2) and 1 pizza slice (20)	64 utils
10 Pepsis (9 + 8 + 7 + 6 + 5 + 4 + 3 + 2 + 1 + 0)	45 utils

The OECD Better Life Index

The OECD Better Life Index attempts to measure 11 key factors of material well-being in each of its 34 member countries. The goal of the index is to provide member governments with a snapshot of how its citizens are living, thus providing a road map for future policy priorities. Some factors are objectively measured, such as average household income. Others are more subjective, such as "life satisfaction," and are measured from survey responses. Below is a look at the results in three countries.

Legend	
Housing	Health
Income	Life satisfaction
Jobs	Safety
Community	Work-life balance
Education	Civic engagement
Environment	

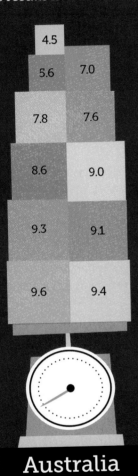

Australia

4.5
5.6 | 7.0
7.8 | 7.6
8.6 | 9.0
9.3 | 9.1
9.6 | 9.4

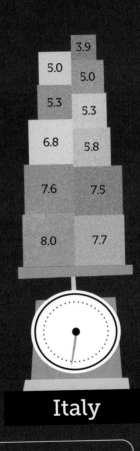

Italy

3.9
5.0 | 5.0
5.3 | 5.3
6.8 | 5.8
7.6 | 7.5
8.0 | 7.7

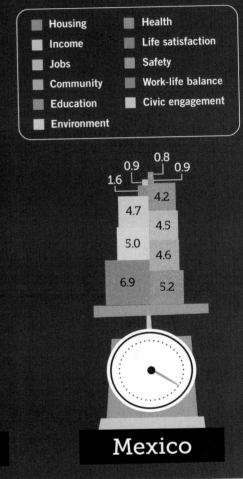

Mexico

1.6 | 0.9 | 0.8 | 0.9
4.7 | 4.2
5.0 | 4.5
| 4.6
6.9 | 5.2

10.0 — Each factor is ranked on a scale of zero to 10, with 10 being the highest. One to three indicators go into each measurement. For instance, "Jobs" is measured through the unemployment rate, job security, and personal earnings.

What do these numbers say about a nation's quality of life? It depends on which factors you think are most important. At www.oecdbetterlifeindex.org you can weight the different categories, create an index, and see how nations compare.

REVIEW QUESTIONS

- Mexico has four glaring challenges to the well-being of its citizens. What are they?

- Visit the OECD website and create your own index. Are any of the 11 factors trade-offs?

**Marginal
thinking**

By thinking at the margin about which good provides the highest marginal utility, you also maximize your total utility. Of course, most people rarely think this way. But as consumers we make choices like this all the time. Instead of adding up utils, we think "that isn't worth it" or "that's a steal." Consumer choice is not so much a conscious calculation as an instinct to seek the most satisfaction. Next we extend our analysis by generalizing the two-good example.

Marginal Thinking with More Than Two Goods

The idea of measuring utility makes our instinctive sense more explicit and enables us to solve simple optimization problems. For instance, when you travel without the aid of GPS you instinctively make choices about which route to take in order to save time. The decision to turn left or right when you come to a stop sign is a decision at the margin: one route will be better than the other. If you consistently make the best choices about which way to turn, you will arrive at your destination sooner. This is why economists focus on marginal thinking.

**Marginal
thinking**

In reality, life is more complex than the simple two-good model implies. When you have $10 to spend, you may choose among many goods. Since you buy many items at all kinds of prices over the course of a year, you must juggle hundreds (or thousands) of purchases so that you enjoy roughly the same utility per dollar spent. Consumer equilibrium captures this idea by comparing the utility gained with the price paid for every item a consumer buys. This means that a consumer's income or budget is balanced so that the ratio of the marginal utility (MU) per dollar spent on every item, from good A to good Z, is equal. In mathematical terms:

$$MU_A \div Price_A = MU_B \div Price_B = \ldots = MU_Z \div Price_Z$$

In the next section, we explore the relationship between changes in price and changes in the consumer optimum.

Left or right? One way will get you to your destination sooner.

Price Changes and the Consumer Optimum

Recall our example of pizza and Pepsi: you reached an optimum when you purchased four Pepsis and three slices of pizza. At that point, the marginal utility per dollar spent for Pepsi and pizza was equal:

$$MU_{pizza} \text{ (12 utils)} \div \$2 = MU_{Pepsi} \text{ (6 utils)} \div \$1$$

In the earlier example, the prices of a slice of pizza ($2) and a can of Pepsi ($1) were held constant. But suppose that the price of a slice of pizza drops to $1.50. This causes the ratio of $MU_{pizza} \div Price_{pizza}$ to change from $12 \div 2$, or 6 utils per dollar, to $12 \div 1.5$, or 8 utils per dollar. The lower price for pizza increases the quantity of slices that the consumer will buy:

$$MU_{pizza} \text{ (12 utils)} \div \$1.50 > MU_{Pepsi} \text{ (6 utils)} \div \$1$$

As a result, we can say that lower prices increase the marginal utility per dollar spent and cause consumers to buy more of a good. Higher prices have

PRACTICE WHAT YOU KNOW

Consumer Optimum

Question: Suppose your favorite magazine, *The Economist*, costs $6 per issue and *People* magazine costs $4 per issue. If you receive 20 utils when you read *People*, how many additional utils would you need to get from reading *The Economist* to cause you to spend the extra $2 it costs to purchase it?

Answer: To answer the question, you first need to equate the marginal utility (MU) per dollar spent for both magazines and solve for the missing variable, the utility from *The Economist*:

$$MU_{\text{The Economist}} \text{ (X utils)} \div \$6 = MU_{\text{People}} \text{ (20 utils)} \div \$4$$
$$X \div \$6 = 20 \div \$4$$
$$X = \$120 \div \$4$$
$$X = 30$$

When the $MU_{\text{The Economist}}$ is equal to 30 utils, you are indifferent between purchasing either of the two magazines. Since the question asks how many additional utils are needed to justify purchasing *The Economist*, you should then subtract the utils from *People*, or 20, to get the difference, which is 30 − 20, or 10 utils.

---

the opposite effect by lowering the marginal utility per dollar spent. If that sounds an awful lot like the law of demand, it is! We have just restated the law of demand in terms of marginal utility.

We know that according to the law of demand (see Chapter 3), the quantity demanded falls when the price rises, and the quantity demanded rises when the price falls—all other things being equal. If we think of consumer desire for a particular product as demand, it makes sense to find a connection among the prices that consumers pay, the quantity that they buy, and the marginal utility that they receive.

When a price changes, there are two effects. First, because the marginal utility per dollar spent is now higher, consumers substitute the product that has become relatively less expensive—a behavior known as the **substitution effect**. Second, at the same time, a price change can also change the purchasing power of income—that is, the **real-income effect**. (For a basic discussion of the trends behind these effects, see Chapter 3).

Let's go back to our Pepsi and pizza example to separate these two effects. A lower price for a slice of pizza makes it more affordable. If slices are $2.00 each, a consumer with a budget of $10.00 can afford five slices. If the price drops to $1.50 per slice, the consumer can afford six slices and still have $1.00 left over.

When the price of a slice of pizza is $2.00, your optimum is three slices of pizza and four Pepsis. If we drop the price of a slice of pizza to $1.50, you save $0.50 per slice. Since you are purchasing three slices, you save $1.50—which

The **substitution effect** occurs when consumers substitute a product that has become relatively less expensive as the result of a price change.

The **real-income effect** occurs when there is a change in purchasing power as a result of a change in the price of a good.

is enough to buy another slice. Looking back at column 5 in Table 16.2, we see that the fourth slice of pizza yields an additional 8 utils. Alternatively, you could use the $1.50 you saved on pizza to buy a fifth can of Pepsi—which has a marginal utility of 5—and still have $0.50 left over.

The lower price of pizza may cause you to substitute pizza for Pepsi since it has become relatively less expensive. This is a demonstration of the substitution effect. In addition, you have more purchasing power through the money you save from the lower-priced pizza. This is the real-income effect.

The real-income effect only matters when prices change enough to cause a measurable effect on the purchasing power of the consumer's income or budget. For example, suppose that a 10% price reduction in peanut butter cups occurs. Will there be a substitution effect, a real-income effect, or both? The secret to answering this question is to consider how much money is saved. Most candy bars cost less than a dollar, so a 10% reduction in price would be less than 10 cents. The lower price will motivate some consumers to switch to peanut butter cups—a substitution effect that can be observed through increased purchases of peanut butter cups. However, the income effect is negligible. The consumer has saved less than 10 cents. The money saved could be used to purchase other goods; but very few goods cost so little, and the enhanced purchasing power is effectively zero. Thus, the answer to the question is that there will be a modest substitution effect and essentially no real-income effect.

What Is the Diamond-Water Paradox?

The **diamond-water paradox** explains why water, which is essential to life, is inexpensive while diamonds, which do not sustain life, are expensive.

Now that you understand the connection between prices and utility, we can tackle one of the most interesting puzzles in economics—the diamond-water paradox. First described by Adam Smith in 1776, the **diamond-water paradox** explains why water, which is essential to life, is inexpensive while diamonds, which do not sustain life, are expensive. Many people of Smith's era found the paradox perplexing. Today, we can use consumer choice theory to answer the question.

Essentially, the diamond-water paradox unfairly compares the amount of marginal utility a person receives from a small quantity of something rare (the diamond) with the marginal utility received from consuming a small amount of additional water after already consuming a large amount.

We know that marginal utility is captured in the law of demand and, therefore, by the price. For example, when the price of diamonds increases, the quantity demanded declines. Moreover, total utility is determined by the amount of consumer surplus enjoyed from a transaction. We learned in Chapter 6 that when thinking graphically the consumer surplus is the area under the demand curve and above the price, or the gains from trade that a consumer enjoys. Therefore, if the price of diamonds rises, consumers will enjoy less surplus from buying them.

Figure 16.2 contrasts the demand and supply equilibrium in both the market for water and the market for diamonds. Notice that the consumer surplus is the area highlighted in light green for water and the triangular area highlighted in dark green for diamonds. The light green area of total utility for water (TU_w) is much larger than the dark green area of total utility for diamonds (TU_d)

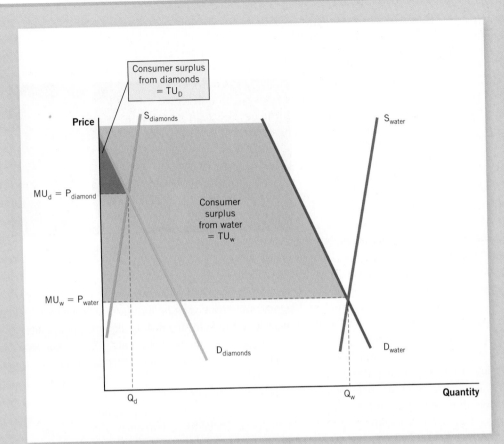

FIGURE 16.2

The Diamond-Water Paradox

The diamond-water paradox exists because people fail to recognize that demand and supply are both equally important in determining the value a good creates in society. The demand for water is large, while the demand for diamonds is small. If we look at the amount of consumer surplus, we observe that the light green area (TU_w) is much larger than the dark green area (TU_d), because water is essential for life. As a result, water creates significantly more total utility (TU) than diamonds. However, since water is abundant in most places, the price, P_{water}, is low. In contrast, diamonds are rare and the price, $P_{diamond}$, is high.

because water is essential for life. Therefore, water creates significantly more total utility than diamonds do. However, in most places in the United States water is very plentiful, so people take additional units of it for granted. In fact, it is so plentiful that if someone were to offer you a gallon of water right now, you would probably hesitate to take it. But what if someone offered you a gallon-size bucket of diamonds? You bet you would take that! Therefore, it should not surprise you that something quite plentiful, water, would yield less marginal utility than something rare, diamonds ($MU_w < MU_d$).

Let's consider how we use water. We bathe in it, cook with it, and drink it. Each of those uses has high value, so the marginal utility of water is high. But we also use it to water our lawns and fill our fish tanks. Those uses are not nearly as essential, so the marginal utility of water for these uses is much lower. The reason we use water in both essential and non-essential ways is that its price is relatively low, so low-value uses, like filling fish tanks, yield enough utility to justify the cost. Since water is abundant in most places, the price (P_{water}) is low. In contrast, diamonds are rare and their price ($P_{diamond}$) is high. The cost of obtaining a diamond means that a consumer must get a great deal of marginal utility from the purchase of a diamond to justify the expense. This explains why diamonds are given as gifts for extremely special occasions.

The Diamond-Water Paradox

Super Size Me

What would happen if you ate all your meals at McDonald's for an entire month—without ever exercising? *Super Size Me*, a 2004 documentary by Morgan Spurlock, endeavored to find out. It is the absurd nature of Spurlock's adventure that pulls viewers in. No one would *actually* eat every meal at the same restaurant for a month, because diminishing marginal utility would cause the utility from the meals to plunge. (This is especially true with McDonald's, which is not known for quality.)

Why did Spurlock take aim at McDonald's, and more generally the fast-food industry? His aim was to reveal how unhealthy fast food really is, but the documentary also happens to unintentionally offer a modern parallel to the diamond-water paradox.

The key is the business model that many fast-food restaurants follow. These restaurants provide filling food at low cost, a combination that encourages consumers to eat more than they would if the price was higher. Eating a lot of food causes diminishing marginal utility; often, the last bite of a sandwich or fries, or the last gulp of a 32-ounce drink, brings very little additional utility, so it is not uncommon for consumers to discard the excess.

In contrast, consider fine dining. Fancy establishments serve smaller portions by design. A five-course meal is meant to be savored, and the experience trumps price. What makes someone willing to pay

A Big Mac a day for 30 days! What could possibly go wrong?

significantly more when dining out at such places? Upscale restaurants are creating high marginal utility by making every bite mouthwatering. They do not want to diminish the marginal value through overeating.

To summarize, McDonald's is a lot like water in the diamond-water paradox. It is easy to find a McDonald's restaurant almost anywhere, and the chain serves close to 50 million customers a day. Therefore, the total utility the chain creates is high, despite the fact that the marginal utility of an individual bite is low. Upscale restaurants are a lot like diamonds: they are uncommon, and the number of customers they serve is small. The total utility that upscale restaurants create is low compared to McDonald's, but the marginal utility of an individual bite at an upscale restaurant is quite high.

Conclusion

Does having more money make people much happier? The answer is no. More money enables people to buy more goods, but because of diminishing marginal utility the increases in happiness from being able to buy more goods, or higher-quality goods, become progressively smaller with rising income. So we could say that having more money makes people somewhat happier. But it seems more appropriate to add that the relationship between quality of life and money is not direct. More money sometimes leads to more utility, and at other times more money means more problems.

As we have seen in this chapter, prices play a key role in determining utility. Since consumers face a budget constraint and wish to maximize their utility, the prices they pay determine their marginal utility per dollar spent. Comparing the marginal utility per dollar spent across many goods helps us to understand individuals' consumption patterns. Diminishing marginal utility also helps to describe consumer choice. Since marginal utility declines with additional consumption, consumers do not exclusively purchase their favorite products; instead, they diversify their choices in order to gain more utility. In addition, changes in prices have two different effects: one on income, and a separate substitution effect that determines the composition of the bundle of goods that are purchased.

In the next chapter, we will question how much individuals use consumer choice theory to make their decisions. An alternative approach, known as behavioral economics, argues that decision-makers are not entirely rational about the choices they make.

Finally, in the appendix that follows we refine consumer theory by discussing indifference curves. Please read the appendix to get a glimpse into how economists model consumer choice in greater detail.

ANSWERING THE BIG QUESTIONS

How do economists model consumer satisfaction?

* Economists model consumer satisfaction by examining utility, which is a measure of the relative levels of satisfaction that consumers enjoy from the consumption of goods and services.

* An important property of utility is that it diminishes with additional consumption. This property limits the amount of any particular good or service that a person will consume.

How do consumers optimize their purchasing decisions?

* Consumers optimize their purchasing decisions by finding the combination of goods and services that maximizes the level of satisfaction from a given income or budget. The consumer optimum occurs when a consumer balances income or budget, so that the marginal utility per dollar spent on every item in the budget is equal to that of every other item.

* Changes in price have two distinct effects on consumer behavior. If the price falls, the marginal utility per dollar spent will be higher. As a result, consumers will substitute the product that has become relatively less expensive. This move reflects a substitution effect. If the lower price also results in substantial savings, it causes an increase in purchasing power known as the real-income effect.

What is the diamond-water paradox?

* The diamond-water paradox explains why water, which is essential to life, is inexpensive, while diamonds, which do not sustain life, are expensive. Many people of Adam Smith's era, in the eighteenth century, found the paradox perplexing. We can solve the diamond-water paradox by recognizing that the price of water is low because its supply is abundant and, at the same time, the price of diamonds is high because their supply is low. If water were as rare as diamonds, there is no doubt that the price of water would exceed the price of diamonds.

ECONOMICS FOR LIFE

The Economic Calculus of Romance: When Do You Know You've Found the "Right" Person?

We all know that finding your soul mate can create more happiness in your life than anything else. Being with the right person can bring you joy, meaning, and a sense of personal strength. But—if you'll forgive us for being a bit unromantic—isn't there also something to say about all this happiness in terms of utility? In this box, we give some "economic" advice about love and marriage.

1. Recognize that your choice in a partner is being made in a market (the dating market), but the market doesn't use money, it uses barter. You offer someone the qualities that they're looking for—love, support, shared life goals—and hope that they are willing to trade those things back to you. (And that they don't get a better offer from someone else!) You find someone you want who feels the same way about you.

2. Partnerships often work best when the partners have characteristics and skills that are quite different from one another. Maybe one person manages the household finances while the other takes care of the yard. In other words, a couple can make gains from trade by using their comparative advantages in the production of household services.

3. Consumption complementarities also exist in a strong relationship. When doing things together makes them more enjoyable than doing them alone, you've found someone special. It can be as simple as taking walks, making dinner together, having a common passion for animals, or belonging to the same religious organization. A beneficial partnership isn't just about getting more done through gains from trade. It's also about having more fun because each partner enjoys "consuming" life more when the other one is around.

4. Finally, when you think of marriage, think of a business contract between two people about how they will organize their lives together. As with any contract, you'll need to set some terms. Will you both need to work to support your lifestyle together? Where will you live, and will you plan to have children? How will you organize your financial affairs—will you use separate or joint bank accounts? How much will you set aside for retirement? The effort you make to understand decisions like these is time and energy well spent, because you can avoid serious conflicts later.

There you have it. All you need to do is to find someone who is willing to enter into a binding contract with you. Or in the words of this chapter, you just need to find someone with a consumer optimum that matches yours!

Do you suppose this couple has found their consumer optimum in the market for romance?

CONCEPTS YOU SHOULD KNOW

consumer optimum
  (p. 498)
diamond-water paradox
  (p. 504)

diminishing marginal utility
  (p. 497)
marginal utility
  (p. 495)

real-income effect (p. 503)
substitution effect (p. 503)
util (p. 494)
utility (p. 494)

QUESTIONS FOR REVIEW

1. After watching a movie, you and your friend both indicate that you liked it. Does this mean that each of you received the same amount of utility? Explain your response.

2. What is the relationship between total utility and marginal utility?

3. How is diminishing marginal utility reflected in the law of demand?

4. What does it imply when we say that the marginal utility per dollar spent is equal for two goods?

STUDY PROBLEMS (*solved at the end of the section*)

1. A local pizza restaurant charges full price for the first pizza but offers 50% off on a second pizza. Using marginal utility, explain the restaurant's pricing strategy.

2. Suppose that the price of trail mix is $4 per pound and the price of cashews is $6 per pound. If you get 30 utils from the last pound of cashews you consume, how many utils would you have to get from the last pound of trail mix to be in consumer equilibrium?

3. Fill in the missing information in the table below:

Number of cookies	Total utility of cookies	Marginal utility of cookies	Number of pretzels	Total utility of pretzels	Marginal utility of pretzels
0	0	25	0	0	—
1	—	15	1	10	—
2	—	10	2	18	—
3	—	5	3	24	4
4	—	—	4	—	2
5	55	—	5	—	0
6	50		6	—	

4. Use the table in problem 3. Suppose that you have a budget of $8 and that cookies and pretzels (in problem 3 above) cost $1 each. What is the consumer optimum?

5. Use the table in problem 3. What is the consumer equilibrium if the price of cookies rises to $1.50 and the price of pretzels remains at $1.00?

6. You are considering either dining at Cici's, an all-you-can-eat pizza chain, or buying pizza by the slice at a local pizzeria for $2 per slice. At which restaurant are you likely to obtain the most marginal utility from the last slice you eat? Explain your response.

7. In consumer equilibrium, a person buys four cups of coffee at $2 per cup and two muffins at $2 per muffin each day. If the price of a cup of coffee rises to $3, what would you expect to happen to the amount of coffee and muffins this person consumes?

8. How do dollar stores survive when *none* of the items sold brings a high amount of total utility to consumers?

* **9.** Imagine that the total utility from consuming five tacos is 10, 16, 19, 20, and 17 utils, respectively. When does marginal utility begin to diminish?

10. You and your friends are considering vacationing in either Cabo San Lucas or Cancun for spring break. When you first researched the cost of your hotel and flights, the total price was $1,000 to each destination. However, a sale has lowered the total cost of going to Cancun to $800. Does this change create a substitution effect, a real-income effect, or both? Explain.

* **11.** Everyone wears underwear, but comparatively few people wear ties. Why are ties so much more expensive than underwear if the demand for underwear is so much greater than the demand for ties?

SOLVED PROBLEMS

9. The key to answering this question is to realize that the data is expressed in total utils. The first taco brings the consumer 10 utils. Consuming the second taco yields $16 - 10$, or 6 additional utils. Since there are fewer extra utils from the second taco (6) than the utils from the first taco (10), diminishing marginal utility begins after the first taco.

11. Recall that demand is only half of the market. The other half is supply. Far fewer ties are produced than items of underwear. The supply of ties also plays a role in determining the price. In addition, ties are a fashion statement. This makes ties a luxury good, whereas underwear is a necessity. As a result, ties are a lot like diamonds: there is a small overall market, and prices are high. Underwear is a lot like water: there is a very large overall market, and prices are low. The fact that ties generally cost more does not mean that ties are more valuable to society. Rather, people get more marginal utility from purchasing the "perfect" tie as opposed to finding the "perfect" underwear.

16A | Indifference Curve Analysis

There is much more to economic analysis than the simple supply and demand model can capture. Chapter 16 considered how consumers can get the biggest bang for their buck, or the greatest utility out of their purchases. Here we explore the question in more detail, using the tool of indifference curve analysis. The purpose of this appendix is to get you thinking at a deeper level about the connections between price changes and consumption decisions.

Indifference Curves

Indifference curves are a tool that economists use to describe the trade-offs that exist when consumers make decisions.

> An **indifference curve** represents the various combinations of two goods that yield the same level of satisfaction, or utility.

> A **maximization point** is the point at which a certain combination of two goods yields the most utility.

An **indifference curve** represents the various combinations of two goods that yield the same level of satisfaction, or utility. The simplest way to think about indifference curves is to envision a topographical map on which each line represents a specific elevation. When you look at a topographical map, you see ridges, mountains, valleys, and the subtle flow of the land. An indifference curve conveys the same complex information about personal satisfaction. Indifference curves visually lead upward to a top called the **maximization point**, or the point at which utility is maximized. The only limitation of this analysis is that this book is a two-dimensional space that we use to illustrate a three-dimensional concept. Let's set this concern aside and focus on achieving the maximization point, where total utility is highest.

Returning to our example of pizza and Pepsi, recall that you had $10 to spend and only two items to purchase: Pepsi at $1 per can, and pizza at $2 per slice. Like all consumers, you will optimize your utility by maximizing the marginal utility per dollar spent, so you select four Pepsis and three slices of pizza. But what happens if your budget is unlimited? If you're free to spend as much you like, how much pizza and Pepsi would you want?

A topographical map and indifference curve analysis share many of the same properties.

Economic "Goods" and "Bads"

To answer the question posed above, we'll start with another question. Are Pepsi and pizza always economic goods? This may seem like a strange question, but think about your own consumption habits. Would you keep eating something after you felt full? Would you continue to eat even if your stomach ached? At some point, we all stop eating and drinking. In this sense, economic goods, like Pepsi and pizza, are "good" only up to a point. Once we are full, however, the utility from attaining another unit of the good becomes negative—a "bad."

Each indifference curve represents lines of equal satisfaction. For simplicity, Figure 16A.1 shows the indifference curve as circles around the point of maximum satisfaction. The closer the indifference curve is to the maximization point, the higher the consumer's level of satisfaction.

Indifference curves are best seen as approaching the maximization point from all directions (like climbing up a mountain on four different sides). In any hike, some paths are better than others. Figure 16A.1 illustrates four separate ways to reach the maximization point. However, only one of the paths makes any sense. In quadrants II, III, and IV, either pizza or Pepsi is a "bad," or both are "bads" (because at those levels of consumption one or both of them make the consumer feel too full or sick). Since the consumer must pay to acquire pizza and Pepsi, and since at least one of them is reducing their utility,

FIGURE 16A.1

Indifference Curves

The maximization point indicates where a consumer attains the most utility. In quadrant I, both Pepsi and pizza are "goods" (because their consumption involves the reactions of either tasting great or getting full), so attaining more of each will cause utility to rise toward the maximization point. In quadrants II, III, and IV, either pizza or Pepsi is a "bad," or both are (because at those levels of consumption they make the consumer feel either too full or sick). Since the consumer must pay to acquire pizza and Pepsi, and since at least one of the items is reducing the consumer's utility in quadrants II, III, and IV, the most affordable path to the highest utility—that is, the maximization point—is quadrant I. (Notice that the labels are qualitative and reflect decreasing utility with additional consumption.)

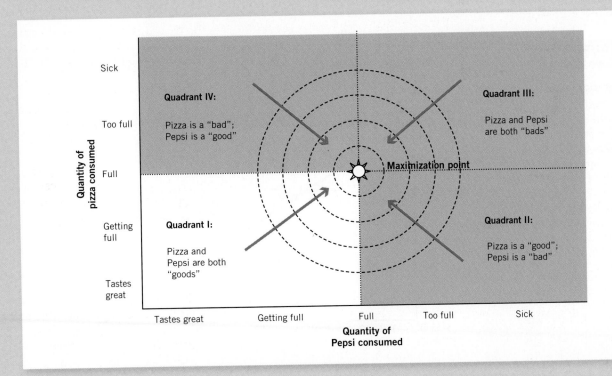

the consumer's satisfaction will increase by purchasing less of the "bad." In other words, why would anyone willingly pay in order to feel worse? Quadrants II, III, and IV are highlighted in red because people are unlikely to choose an option that makes them feel too full or sick. That leaves quadrant I as the preferred path to the highest utility. In quadrant I, increasing amounts of pizza and Pepsi produce more utility. (Notice that the labels in Figure 16A.1 are qualitative and reflect decreasing utility with additional consumption.)

The Budget Constraint

The **budget constraint** is the set of consumption bundles that represent the maximum amount the consumer can afford.

Figure 16A.1 illustrates the choices facing a consumer with an unlimited budget and no opportunity costs. However, in real life the money spent on Pepsi and pizza cannot be spent elsewhere. We need to account for a person's budget and the cost of acquiring each good. The amount a person has to spend is the **budget constraint**, or the set of consumption bundles that represent the maximum amount the consumer can afford. If you have $10 to spend on pizza ($2 per slice) and Pepsi ($1 per can), you could choose to purchase ten cans of Pepsi and forgo the pizza. Alternatively, you could purchase five slices of pizza and do without the Pepsi. Or you could choose a number of different combinations of pizza and Pepsi, as we saw in Chapter 16. The budget constraint line in Figure 16A.2 delineates the affordable combinations of pizza and Pepsi.

There are many different affordable combinations of the two goods. Let's take the pairs along the budget constraint line first. If you spend your entire $10 on Pepsi, the combination of coordinates would be the point (10,0), which represents 10 cans of Pepsi and 0 slices of pizza. If you spend your

The Budget Constraint
The budget constraint line shows the set of affordable combinations of Pepsi and pizza with a budget of $10. Any point inside the budget constraint—for example (2,2)—is also affordable. Points beyond the budget constraint—for example (10,5)—are not affordable.

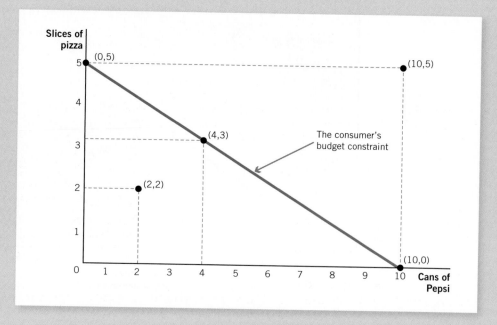

entire budget on pizza, the coordinates would be (0,5). These two points are the extreme outcomes. By connecting these two points with a line—the budget constraint—we can see the many combinations that would fully exhaust $10. As a consumer, your goal is to pick the combination that maximizes your satisfaction, subject to your budget constraint. One possibility would be to spend the $10 on four slices of pizza and three cans of Pepsi (4,3), which happens to be the point of utility maximization we discovered in the chapter (see Table 16.3).

What about the points located below and above the budget constraint? For example, looking again at Figure 16A.2, at the point (2,2) you would be spending $6—that is, $2 on Pepsi and $4 on pizza. You would still have $4 to spend on more of either good. Since both goods are desirable, spending the leftover money in your budget will increase your level of satisfaction. So the combination (2,2) represents a failure to maximize utility. On the other side of the budget constraint line, we find the point (10,5). This combination, which would cost you $20 to attain, represents a lack of funds in your budget. Since you only have $10, you cannot afford that combination. From this example, you can see that the budget constraint is a limiting set of choices, or a constraint imposed by scarcity.

In the next section, we examine the indifference curve in greater detail. Once we fully understand the properties that characterize indifference curves, we can join them with the budget constraint to better describe how consumers make choices.

Properties of Indifference Curves

It is useful to keep in mind several assumptions about indifference curves. The properties described below help to ensure that our model is logically consistent.

Indifference Curves Are Typically Bowed Inward

A rational consumer will only operate in quadrant I in Figure 16A.1. Within that quadrant, the higher indifference curves (those nearer the utility maximization point) are preferred to the lower ones (nearer the origin). Also, nonsatiation, or the idea that consumers cannot get too much of a good thing, requires that indifference curves bow inward with respect to the origin. This convex shape eliminates any outcome in quadrants II through IV by requiring that goods be "good," not "bad." Non-satiation is modeled here because economists assume that people make rational decisions. Since quadrants II through IV result in less utility and greater expenditures, no rational consumer would ever willingly operate in these regions.

Figure 16A.3 shows an indifference curve that reflects the trade-off between two goods. Since the indifference curve bows inward, the **marginal rate of substitution**, or the rate at which a consumer is willing to trade one good for another, varies. This is reflected in the slope of the indifference curve in the figure. Points A and B are both on the same indifference curve, so

Trade-offs

The **marginal rate of substitution** is the rate at which the consumer is willing to purchase one good instead of another.

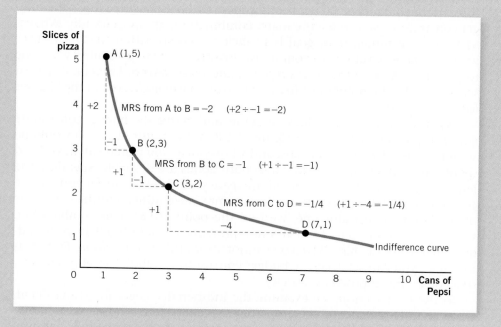

FIGURE 16A.3

The Marginal Rate of Substitution

The marginal rate of substitution (MRS) along an indifference curve varies. This is reflected in the slope of the indifference curve. Since Pepsi and pizza are both subject to diminishing marginal utility, it takes more of the plentiful good to keep the consumer indifferent when giving up another good that is in short supply.

Marginal thinking

the consumer finds the combinations (1,5) and (2,3) to be equally attractive. Between points A and B, the consumer must receive two slices of pizza to compensate for the loss of a can of Pepsi. We can see this in the figure by observing that the consumer chooses only two cans of Pepsi and three slices of pizza at (2,3). Since the marginal utility from consuming Pepsi is high when the amount consumed is low, giving up an additional Pepsi requires that the consumer receive back two slices of pizza to reach the point (1,5). Therefore, the marginal rate of substitution (MRS) is 2 to −1, or −2 (because +2 ÷ −1 = −2).

However, if we examine the same indifference curve between points C and D, we see that the consumer is also indifferent between the combinations (3,2) and (7,1). However, this time the consumer is willing to give up four cans of Pepsi to get one more slice of pizza, so the MRS is 1 to −4, or −1/4 (because +1 ÷ −4 = −1/4). Why is there such a big difference between (3,2) and (7,1) compared to (2,3) and (1,5)? At (7,1), the consumer has a lot of Pepsi and very little pizza to enjoy it with. As a result, the marginal utility of the second pizza is so high that it is worth four Pepsis! We can see the change in the marginal rate of substitution visually, since the slope between points A and B is steeper than it is between points C and D.

What explains why Pepsi is more valuable between points A and B? The consumer starts with only two cans. Pizza is more valuable between points C and D because the consumer starts with only two slices of pizza. Since Pepsi and pizza are both subject to diminishing marginal utility, it takes more of the plentiful good to keep the consumer indifferent when giving up another good that is in short supply.

Indifference Curves Cannot Be Thick

Another property of indifference curves is that they cannot be thick. If they could be thick, then it would be possible to draw two points inside an indifference curve where one of the two points was preferred to the other. Therefore, a consumer could be indifferent between those points. This is evident in Figure 16A.4. Points A, B, and C are all located on the same (impossible) indifference curve. However, points B and C are both strictly preferred to point A. Why? Because point B has one extra slice of pizza compared to point A, and point C has two extra cans of Pepsi compared to point A. Since non-satiation is assumed, more pizza and Pepsi adds to the consumer's utility, and the consumer cannot be indifferent among these three points.

Indifference Curves Cannot Intersect

Indifference curves, by their very nature, cannot intersect. To understand why, let's look at a hypothetical case. Figure 16A.5 shows two indifference curves crossing at point A. Points A and B are both located along the light orange curve (IC_1), so we know that those two points bring the consumer the same utility. Points A and C are both located along the darker orange curve (IC_2), so those two points also yield the same utility for the consumer. Therefore, the utility at point A equals the utility at point B, and the utility at point A also equals the utility at point C. This means that the utility at point B should also equal the utility at point C, but that cannot be true. Point B is located at (1,3), and point C is located at (2,4). Since (2,4) strictly dominates (1,3), point C is preferred to point B. Therefore, we can say that indifference

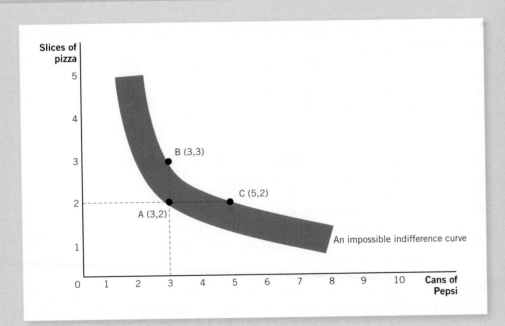

Indifference Curves Cannot Be Thick

If indifference curves could be thick, it would be possible to draw two points inside the curve in a way that indicates that one of the two points is preferred to the other. Point B has one extra slice of pizza and point C has two extra cans of Pepsi compared to point A. Therefore, the consumer cannot be indifferent among these three points, and the indifference curve cannot be thick.

FIGURE 16A.5

Indifference Curves Cannot Intersect

The utility at point B should equal the utility at point C, but that cannot be true even though the utility at point B is equal to the utility at point A (along IC_1) and the utility at point C is equal to the utility at point A (along IC_2). Point B is located at (1,3) and point C is located at (2,4). Since (2,4) strictly dominates (1,3), point C is preferred to point B.

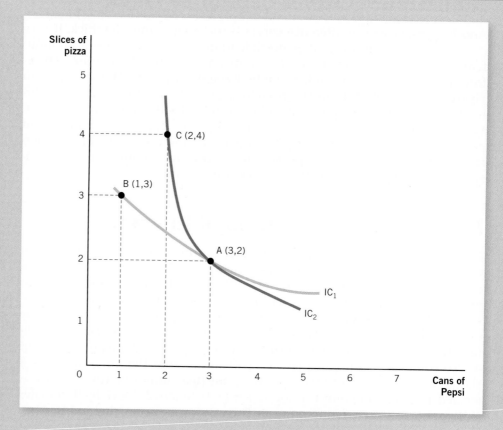

curves cannot intersect without violating the assumption that consumers are rational utility maximizers.

We have seen that indifference curves have three properties: they are inward-sloping, or convex with respect to the origin; they cannot be thick; and they cannot intersect. These properties guarantee that they take the general shape shown in quadrant I of Figure 16A.1.

Extreme Preferences: Perfect Substitutes and Perfect Complements

As we saw above, indifference curves typically are convex and bow inward toward the origin. However, there are two exceptions: *perfect substitutes* and *perfect complements*. These are found on either side of the standard-shaped, convex indifference curve.

A **perfect substitute** exists when a consumer is completely indifferent between two goods. Suppose that you cannot taste any difference between Aquafina and Evian bottled water. You would be indifferent between drinking one additional bottle of Aquafina or one additional bottle of Evian. Turning to Figure 16A.6a, you can see that the indifference curves (IC_1, IC_2, etc.) for these two goods are straight, parallel lines with a marginal rate of substitution, or

A **perfect substitute** exists when the consumer is completely indifferent between two goods, resulting in straight-line indifference curves.

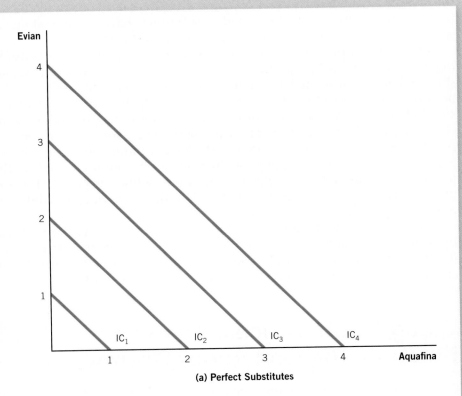

(a) Perfect Substitutes

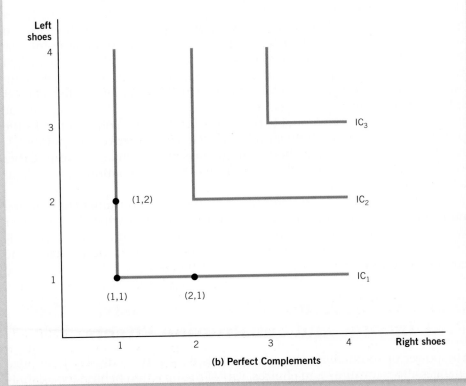

(b) Perfect Complements

FIGURE 16A.6

Perfect Substitutes and Perfect Complements

(a) Since perfect substitutes have a marginal rate of substitution that is constant, they are drawn as straight lines. In this case, the MRS, or slope, is −1 everywhere along the lines, or curves.

(b) Perfect complements are drawn as right angles. A typical indifference curve that reflects the trade-off between two goods that are not perfect substitutes or perfect complements has a marginal rate of substitution that falls between these two extremes.

slope, of -1 everywhere along the curve. However, it's important to note that the slope of an indifference curve of perfect substitutes need not always be -1; it can be any constant rate. Since perfect substitutes have a marginal rate of substitution with a constant rate, they are drawn as straight lines.

A **perfect complement** exists when a consumer is interested in consuming two goods in fixed proportions. Shoes are an excellent example. We buy shoes in pairs because the left or right shoe is not valuable by itself; we need both shoes to be able to walk comfortably. This explains why shoes are not sold individually. An extra left or right shoe has no marginal value to the consumer, so the indifference curves are right angles. For instance, left and right shoes are needed in a 1:1 ratio. Let's look at indifference curve IC_1 in Figure 16A.6b. This curve forms a right angle at the point (1,1) where the person has one left and one right shoe. Now notice that the points (1,2) and (2,1) are also on IC_1. Since an extra left or right shoe does not add utility, the points (1,2), (1,1), and (2,1) are all connected.

Perfect complements can also occur in combinations other than 1:1. For instance, an ordinary chair needs four legs for each seat. In that case, the indifference curve is still a right angle, but the additional chair legs do not enhance the consumer's utility unless they come in groups of four.

A **perfect complement** exists when the consumer is interested in consuming two goods in fixed proportions, resulting in right-angle indifference curves.

Using Indifference Curves to Illustrate the Consumer Optimum

Figure 16A.7 shows the relationship between indifference curves and the budget constraint. As the indifference curves move higher, the consumer moves progressively closer to the maximization point—that is, the point at which he or she has reached the consumer optimum. At some point, the consumer will run out of money. Therefore, the area bounded by the budget constraint (shaded in purple) represents the set of possible choices. The highest indifference curve that can be attained within the set of possible choices is IC_3, where the budget constraint is just tangent to IC_3. Even though all the points on IC_4 are more desirable than those on IC_3, the consumer lacks the purchasing power to reach that level of satisfaction. Moreover, the point (4,3) is now clearly the preferred choice among the set of possible decisions. Other choices that are also affordable—for example, the combination (2,4)—fall on a lower indifference curve.

Progressively higher indifference curves bring the consumer closer to the maximization point. Since the budget constraint limits what the consumer can afford, the tangency of the budget constraint with the highest indifference curve represents the highest affordable level of satisfaction—that is, the consumer optimum.

Using Indifference Curves to Illustrate the Real-Income and Substitution Effects

The power of indifference curve analysis is its ability to display how price changes affect consumption choices. Part of the intuition behind the analysis involves understanding when the substitution effect is likely to dominate the real-income effect, and vice versa.

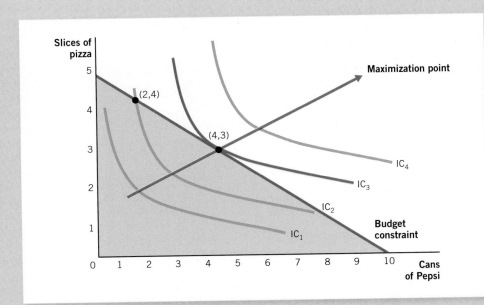

Consumer Optimum
Progressively higher indifference curves bring the consumer closer to the maximization point. Since the budget constraint limits what the consumer can afford, the tangency of the budget constraint with the highest indifference curve represents the highest level of affordable satisfaction—that is, the consumer optimum. In this case, the point (4,3) represents the consumer's preferred combination of Pepsi and pizza.

In our example you have only $10, so when the price of Pepsi increases from $1 to $2 per can, it represents a financial burden that significantly lowers your real purchasing power. However, we can easily think of cases in which a change in the price of Pepsi wouldn't matter. Suppose yours is a typical American household with a median annual income of $50,000. While out shopping, you observe that a local Toyota car dealer is offering 10% off new cars and a nearby grocery store is selling Pepsi at a 10% discount. Since the percentage saved on each product is the same, the substitution effect will be of an equal magnitude: more people will buy Toyotas instead of Hondas, and more people will buy Pepsi instead of Coca-Cola. However, the real-income effects will be quite different. Saving 10% on the price of a new car could easily amount to a savings of $3,000 or more. In contrast, saving 10% on a 2-liter bottle of Pepsi will only save a couple of dimes. In the case of the new car, there is a substantial real-income effect, while in contrast the amount you save on the Pepsi is almost immaterial.

Changes in prices can have two distinct effects. The first is a substitution effect, under which changes in price will cause the consumer to substitute toward a good that becomes relatively less expensive. In our example, suppose that the price of Pepsi rises to $2 per can. This price increase reduces your marginal utility per dollar of consuming Pepsi. As a result, you would probably buy fewer Pepsis and use the remaining money to purchase more pizza. In effect, you would substitute the relatively less expensive good (pizza) for the relatively more expensive good (Pepsi).

However, this is not the only effect at work. The change in the product price will also alter the purchasing power of your money, or income. And a change in purchasing power generates a real-income effect. In this case, your $10 will not go as far as it used to. In Figure 16A.8, we can see that the inward rotation of the budget constraint along the x axis from BC_1 to BC_2 is a result of the rise in the price of Pepsi. At $2 per can, you can no longer afford to buy

How a Change in Price Rotates the Budget Constraint

The inward rotation of the budget constraint along the x axis from BC_1 to BC_2 is a result of the rise in the price of Pepsi. At $2 a can, you can no longer afford to buy ten cans; the most you can purchase is five. Therefore, the budget constraint moves inward along the x axis to five units (causing utility to fall from IC_1 to IC_2) while remaining constant along the y axis (since the price of pizza slices did not change).

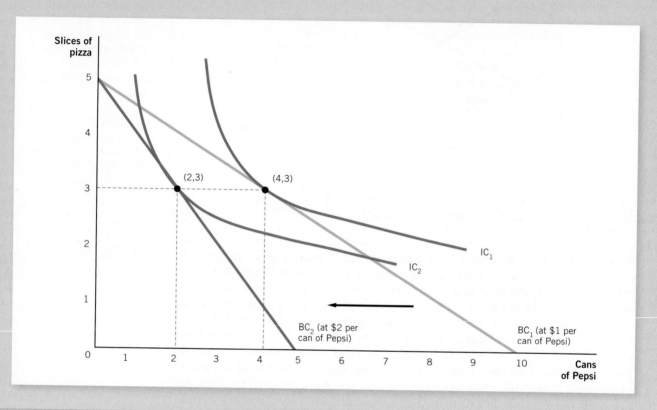

ten cans; the most you can purchase is five. Therefore, the budget constraint moves inward along the x axis to five units while remaining constant along the y axis (since the price of pizza did not change). As a result, the combination (4,3) is no longer affordable. This produces a new consumer equilibrium at (2,3) along IC_2. The end result is predictable: a rise in the price of Pepsi causes you to purchase less Pepsi and yields a lower level of satisfaction at IC_2 than your former point on IC_3 did, which is no longer possible. (See Figure 16A.7 for your former point on IC_3.)

Separating the Substitution Effect from the Real-Income Effect

Sometimes, the substitution effect and the real-income effect reinforce each other; at other times, they work against each other. In this section, we separate the substitution effect from the real-income effect.

Breaking down the movement from IC_3 to IC_2 into the separate real-income effect and substitution effect enables us to see how each effect impacts the consumer's choice. Imagine that you were given just enough money to attain IC_2 in Figure 16A.9 with the original prices of pizza and Pepsi intact. The new budget constraint ($BC_{real\ income}$) will now be parallel to BC_1 but just tangent to IC_2. The change from BC_1 to $BC_{real\ income}$ separates the real-income effect from the substitution effect. Since the slope of the new budget constraint, $BC_{real\ income}$, is less steep than that of BC_2, the point of tangency between $BC_{real\ income}$ and IC_2, point A, is lower. Furthermore, since the slopes of $BC_{real\ income}$ and BC_1 are equal, we can think of the movement from (4,3) to point A as a function of the real-income effect alone. This occurs because we have kept the slope of the budget constraint constant. Keeping the slope constant reflects the fact that the consumer has less money to spend, while the prices of Pepsi and pizza are held constant. The subsequent movement along IC_2 from point A to (2,3) results from the substitution effect exclusively,

FIGURE 16A.9

Separating the Substitution Effect from the Real-Income Effect

Breaking down the movement from IC_3 to IC_2 into the real-income effect and the substitution effect enables us to see how each effect impacts the consumer's choice. The real-income effect causes the budget constraint to shift to $BC_{real\ income}$, and the loss of purchasing power lowers the consumption of both Pepsi and pizza, as noted by the green arrows. At the same time, the substitution effect reduces the amount of Pepsi consumed and increases the consumption of pizza, as noted by the orange arrows.

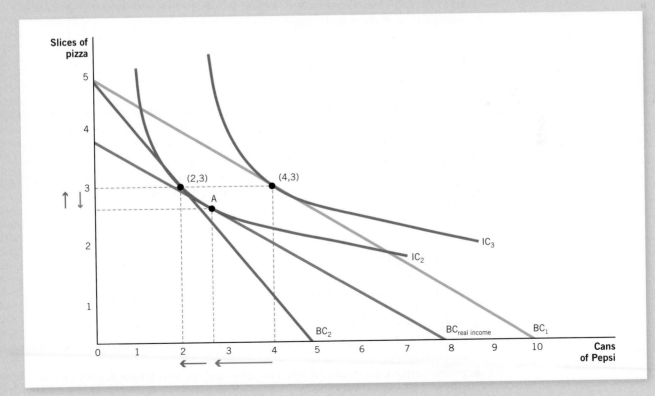

and it occurs because the price of Pepsi is now higher. This outcome causes BC_2 to become steeper.

Beginning with the real-income effect, we see that the impact of a loss of purchasing power lowers consumption of both Pepsi and pizza. The green arrows in Figure 16A.9 highlight this outcome. At the same time, the substitution effect reduces the amount of Pepsi consumed and increases the consumption of pizza. The orange arrows in the figure highlight this outcome. Since Pepsi is now relatively more expensive, you reallocate your consumption toward pizza. Overall, your consumption of Pepsi falls dramatically while your consumption of pizza remains constant.

More generally, whenever the price of a good increases (as Pepsi does in this example), this will lead to a reduction in the amount consumed since both the income and substitution effects (as represented by the orange and green arrows along the x axis) move in the same direction. However, since the real-income effect and substitution effect move in opposite directions with respect to the good whose price has not changed (pizza in this example), the result is ambiguous for that good (pizza), and any change in consumption depends on which effect—the substitution effect or the real-income effect—is greater.

In our example, when the price of Pepsi rose to $2 per can, it produced a large real-income effect (the green arrow along the x axis). Prior to the price increase, you were spending $4 out of your $10 budget on Pepsi, so Pepsi expenditures represented 40% of your budget. When the price doubled, it was like finding out that your rent just doubled from $800 a month to $1,600 a month! Since Pepsi is a big component of your budget, a doubling of its price causes a sizable real-income effect. This is not always the case, however. For example, if the price of a candy bar were to double, the typical household would barely notice this change. When this happens, the real-income effect is negligible and the substitution effect tends to dominate.

Conclusion

Economists use indifference curve analysis to gain additional insights into consumer behavior. This analysis extends the basic understanding found in supply and demand by incorporating utility theory. Because indifference curves are lines of equal utility, we can impose a budget constraint in order to describe the bundle of goods that maximizes utility. This framework enables us to illustrate the effect of price changes and budget constraints on the decisions that consumers make.

Summary

- The point of maximum consumer satisfaction is found at the point of tangency between an indifference curve and the budget constraint line.
- Indifference curves share three properties: they are inward-sloping with respect to the origin (non-satiation), they cannot be thick, and they cannot intersect.
- Indifference curves can be used to separate the substitution effect from the real-income effect.

CONCEPTS YOU SHOULD KNOW

budget constraint (p. 514)
indifference curve
  (p. 512)

marginal rate of substitution
  (p. 515)
maximization point (p. 512)

perfect complement
  (p. 520)
perfect substitute (p. 518)

QUESTIONS FOR REVIEW

1. If your budget increases, what generally happens to the amount of utility you experience?

2. If your budget increases, is it possible for your utility to fall? Explain your response.

3. What is the difference between an economic "good" and an economic "bad"?

4. Describe what happens to your budget constraint if the price of one item in your budget becomes less expensive. Show this on a graph.

5. A friend mentions to you that the campus coffee shop offers a 10% discount each Thursday morning before 10 a.m. Is this more likely to cause a significant substitution effect or a significant real-income effect? Explain.

STUDY PROBLEMS

1. Kate has $20. Fish sandwiches cost $5, and a cup of espresso costs $4. Draw Kate's budget constraint. If espresso goes on sale for $2 a cup, what does her new budget constraint look like?

2. When you head home for dinner, your mother always sets the table with one spoon, two forks, and one knife. Draw her indifference curves for forks and knives.

3. Frank's indifference curves for movies and bowling look like this:

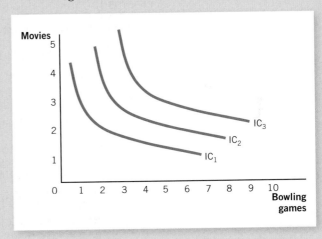

Each game of bowling costs $4, and each movie costs $8. If Frank has $24 to spend, how many times will he go bowling? How many times will he go to the movies?

CHAPTER 17

Behavioral Economics and Risk Taking

People always make rational decisions.

In this textbook, we have proceeded as if every person were *Homo economicus*, or a rationally self-interested decision-maker. *Homo economicus* is acutely aware of opportunities in the environment and strives to maximize the benefits received from each course of action while minimizing the costs. What does *Homo economicus* look like? If you are a fan of *Star Trek: The Next Generation*, you'll recall Data, the android with perfect logic. Data was not capable of human emotion and didn't face the complications that it creates in making decisions.

We don't want to leave you with the misconception that we're all like this! As human beings, we love, laugh, and cry. Sometimes, we seek revenge; at other times, forgiveness. We can be impulsive and shortsighted, and we can fail to see the benefits of pursuing long-run gains. Each of these behaviors is real, although they do not fit squarely within our economic models. Human decision-making is far more complex than the standard economic model of behavior implies. In this chapter, we step back and consider why people don't always make rational decisions. To fold the broadest possible set of human behavior into economic analysis, we must turn to the field of *behavioral economics*, which will enable us to capture a wider range of human motivations than the rational-agent model alone affords.

Data, the android in *Star Trek: The Next Generation*, exemplifies fully rational behavior.

BIG QUESTIONS

* How can economists explain irrational behavior?
* What is the role of risk in decision-making?

How Can Economists Explain Irrational Behavior?

The study of psychology, like economics, endeavors to understand the choices that people make. One key difference is that psychologists do not assume that people always behave in a fully rational way. As a result, psychologists have a much broader toolbox at their disposal to describe human behavior. **Behavioral economics** is the field of economics that draws on insights from experimental psychology to explore how people make economic decisions.

Until relatively recently, economists have ignored many human behaviors that do not fit their models. For example, because traditional economic theory assumed that people make optimal decisions like robots, economic theorists did not try to explain why people might make an impulse purchase. Behavioral economists, however, understand that many behaviors contradict standard assumptions about rationality. They employ the idea of **bounded rationality**, which proposes that although decision-makers want a good outcome, either they are not capable of performing the problem-solving that traditional theory assumes, or they are not inclined to do so.

Bounded rationality, or limited reasoning, can be explained in three ways. First, the information that the individual uses to make the decision may be limited or incomplete. Second, the human brain has a limited capacity to process information. Third, there is often a limited amount of time in which to make a decision. These limitations prevent the decision-maker from reaching the results predicted under perfect rationality.

For example, suppose you're about to get married and find yourself at Kleinfeld Bridal with your bridesmaids. You enter the store to begin your search for the perfect wedding dress. You find a dress that you like, but it's for a price higher than you were planning to spend. Do you make the purchase or not? The decision to buy depends on whether you believe that the value is high enough to justify the expense. But there is a problem: you have a limited amount of information. In a fully rational world, you would check out alternatives in other stores and on the Internet and then make the decision to purchase the dress only after you were satisfied that it is the best possible choice. Full rationality also assumes that your brain is able to recall the features of every dress. However, a dress you tried on at one location often blurs into another dress you tried on elsewhere. Wedding dresses are selected under

Behavioral economics is the field of economics that draws on insights from experimental psychology to explore how people make economic decisions.

Bounded rationality proposes that although decision-makers want a good outcome, either they are not capable of performing the problem-solving that traditional theory assumes, or they are not inclined to do so.

Will you say "yes" to the dress?

a binding deadline. This means that you, the bride, must reach a decision quickly. Collectively, these three reasons often prevent a bride from achieving the result that economists' rational models predict. In reality, you walk into a store, see something you love, and make the purchase using partial information. Whenever people end up making decisions without perfect information, the decisions reflect bounded rationality.

We will continue our discussion of behavioral economics by examining various behaviors that do not fit assumptions about fully rational behavior. These include misperceptions of probabilities, inconsistencies in decision-making, and judgments about fairness when making decisions. The goal in this section is to help you recognize and understand many of the behaviors that lead to contradictions between what economic models predict and what people actually do.

Misperceptions of Probabilities

Economic models that assume rationality in decision-making do not account for the way people perceive the probability of events. Low-probability events are often over-anticipated, and high-probability events are often under-anticipated. To understand why this is the case, we will consider several familiar examples, including games of chance, difficulties in assessing probabilities, and seeing patterns where none exist.

Games of Chance

Playing games of chance—for example, a lottery or a slot machine—is generally a losing proposition. Yet even with great odds against winning, millions of people spend money to play games of chance. How can we explain this behavior?

For some people, the remote chance of winning a lottery offers hope that they will be able to purchase something they need but cannot afford, or even to escape from poverty. In many cases, people have incomplete information about the probabilities and prize structures. Most lottery players do not calculate the exact odds of winning. Lottery agencies typically highlight winners, as if the game has a positive expected value, which gets people excited about playing. Imagine how sobering it would be if every headline trumpeting the newest lottery millionaire was followed by all the names of people who lost. In fact, almost all games of chance have negative expected values for the participants, meaning that players are not likely to succeed at the game.

Players often operate under the irrational belief that they have control over the outcome. They are sure that playing certain numbers or patterns (for example, birthdays, anniversaries, or other lucky numbers) will bring success. Many players also feel they must stick with their favorite numbers to avoid regret; everyone has heard stories about players who changed from their lucky pattern only to watch it win.

In contrast, some gaming behaviors are rational. For example, the film *21* depicts how skilled blackjack players, working in tandem, can beat the casinos by betting

Many games of chance only return about 50 cents for every dollar played.

Incentives

strategically and paying close attention to the cards on the table. In fact, some individuals are able to win at blackjack by counting the cards that have been dealt. Anytime the expected value of a gamble is positive, there is an incentive to play. For instance, if a friend wants to wager $10.00 on the flip of a coin and promises you $25.00 if you guess right, the expected value is half of $25.00, or $12.50. Since $12.50 is greater than the $10.00 you are wagering, we say that the gamble has a positive expected value. In other words, the more you play, the more you are likely to make.

Gambles can also make sense when you have very little to lose or no other options. And some people find the thrill of gambling enjoyable as entertainment whether they win or lose. However, most gambling behaviors do not have rational motivations.

The Difficulties in Assessing Probabilities

In our discussion of games of chance, we saw that people who gamble do not usually evaluate probabilities in a rational way. But this irrational decision-making also happens with many other behaviors besides gambling. For example, on a per mile basis, traveling by airplane is approximately 10 times safer than traveling by automobile. However, millions of people who refuse to fly because they are afraid of a crash do not hesitate to get into a car. Driving seems to create a false sense of control over one's surroundings.

The 1970s television game show *Let's Make a Deal* provides a well-known example of the difficulties in assessing probabilities accurately. At the end of the show, the host asked a contestant to choose one of three curtains. Behind each curtain was one of three possible prizes: a car; a nice but less expensive item; or a worthless joke item. Contestants could have maximized their chances of winning the car if they had used probability theory to make a selection. However, contestants rarely chose in a rational way.

Opportunity cost

Suppose that you are a contestant on a game show like *Let's Make a Deal*. You pick curtain number 3. The host, who knows what is behind the curtains, opens a different one—say, curtain number 1, which has a pen filled with chickens (the joke prize). He then offers you the opportunity to switch your choice to curtain number 2. According to probability theory, what is the right thing to do? Most contestants would stay with their original choice because they figure that now they have a 50/50 chance of winning the car. But the probability of winning with your original choice remains 1/3 because the chance that you guessed correctly the first time is unchanged. Equally, the chance that one of the other curtains contains the car is still 2/3–but with curtain number 1 revealed as the joke prize, that 2/3 probability now belongs entirely to curtain number 2. Therefore, the contestant should take the switch, because it upgrades their chance of winning the car from 1/3 to 2/3. Few do, though. Almost all contestants think that each of the two remaining unopened curtains has an equal probability of holding the car, so they decide not to switch for fear of regretting their decision. Not switching indicates a failure to understand the opportunity costs involved in the decision.

If you were a contestant, would you make a rational choice?

The difficulty in recognizing the true underlying probabilities, combined with an irrational fear of regret, leads to many poor decisions. Understanding these tendencies helps economists to evaluate why some decisions are difficult to get right.

Seeing Patterns Where None Exist

Two fallacies, or false ways of thinking, help to explain how people make decisions: the *gambler's fallacy* and the *hot hand fallacy*.

The **gambler's fallacy** is the belief that recent outcomes are unlikely to be repeated and that outcomes that have not occurred recently are due to happen soon. For example, studies examining state lotteries find that bets on recent winning numbers decline. Because the selection of winning numbers is made randomly, just like flipping coins, the probability that a certain number will be a winner in one week is not related to whether the number came up in the previous week. In other words, someone who uses the gambler's fallacy believes that if many "heads" have occurred in a row, then "tails" is more likely to occur next.

The **hot hand fallacy** is the belief that random sequences exhibit a positive correlation. The classic study in this area examined perceptions about the game of basketball. Most sports enthusiasts believe that a player who has scored several baskets in a row—one with a "hot hand"—is more likely to score a basket with his next shot than he might be at another time. However, the study found no positive correlation between success in one shot and success in the next shot.

Don't let your emotions fool you. There is no such thing as a "hot hand" in sports.

The **gambler's fallacy** is the belief that recent outcomes are unlikely to be repeated and that outcomes that have not occurred recently are due to happen soon.

The **hot hand fallacy** is the belief that random sequences exhibit a positive correlation.

ECONOMICS IN THE REAL WORLD

How Behavioral Economics Helps to Explain Stock Price Volatility

Let's examine some of the traps that people fall into when they invest in the stock market. In a fully rational world, the gambler's fallacy and the hot hand fallacy would not exist. However, in the real world, people are prone to seeing patterns in data even when there are none. Investors, for example, often believe that the rise and fall of the stock market is driven by specific events and by underlying metrics such as profitability, market share, and return on investment. But, in fact, investors often react with a herd mentality by rushing into stocks that appear to be doing well—reflecting the hot hand fallacy—and selling off stocks when a downward trend seems to be occurring. Similarly, there are times when investors believe the stock market has run up or down too rapidly and they expect its direction to change soon—reflecting the gambler's fallacy.

Some segments of the market are driven by investor psychology instead of metrics that measure valuation. Research has also shown that mood matters: believe it or not, there is a small correlation between the weather and how the stock market trades on a particular day. The market is more likely to move higher when it is sunny on Wall Street than when it is cloudy! The very fact that the weather outside in Lower Manhattan could have anything to do with how the overall stock market performs is strong evidence that some market participants are not rational. ✳

The stock market can give investors a wild ride.

PRACTICE WHAT YOU KNOW

Gambler's Fallacy or Hot Hand Fallacy? Patterns on Exams

Your instructor is normally conscientious and makes sure that exam answers are randomly distributed. However, you notice that the first five answers on the multiple choice section are all C. Unsure what this pattern means, you consider the next question. You do not know the answer and are forced to guess. You decide to avoid C because you figure that C cannot happen six times in a row.

Do you ever wonder what it means when the same answer comes up many times in a row?

Question: Which is at work: the gambler's fallacy or the hot hand fallacy?

Answer: According to the gambler's fallacy, recent events are less likely to be repeated again in the near future. So it is the gambler's fallacy at work here in your decision to avoid marking another C. If you had acted on the hot hand fallacy, you would have believed that random sequences exhibit a positive correlation and therefore would have marked the next answer as C.

Inconsistencies in Decision-Making

Trade-offs

If people were entirely rational, they would always be consistent. So the way a question is asked should not alter our responses, but research has shown that it does. Likewise, rational decision-making requires the ability to take the long-run trade-offs into account: if the returns are large enough, people should be willing to sacrifice current enjoyment for future benefits. Yet many of us make shortsighted decisions. In this section, we examine a variety of decision-making mistakes, including *framing effects, priming effects, status quo bias*, and *intertemporal decision-making*.

Framing and Priming Effects

Framing effects
occur when people change their answer (or action) depending on how the question is asked.

We have seen a number of ways in which economic models do not entirely account for the behavior of real people. One common mistake that people make involves the **framing effect**, which occurs when an answer is influenced by the way a question is asked or a decision is influenced by the way alternatives are presented. Consider an employer-sponsored retirement plan. Companies can either (1) ask employees if they want to join or (2) use an automatic enrollment system and ask employees to let them know if they do not wish to participate. Studies have shown that workers who are asked if they want to join tend to participate at a much lower rate than those who are automatically enrolled and must say they want to opt out. Surely, a rational economic decision-maker would determine whether to participate by evaluating

Misperceptions of Probabilities

π

This psychological thriller from 1998 tries to make sense out of chaos. The title refers to the mathematical constant π (pi). In the film, Max Cohen is using his supercomputer to find predictable patterns within the stock market. What makes the film especially interesting are the three assumptions that rule Max's life:

1. Mathematics is the language of nature.
2. Everything around us can be represented and understood from numbers.
3. If you graph the numbers in any system, patterns emerge.

Based on these assumptions, Max attempts to identify a mathematical pattern that will predict the behavior of the stock market. As he gets closer to uncovering the answer, he is pursued by two parties: a Wall Street firm that wishes to use Max's discovery to manipulate the market, and a religious

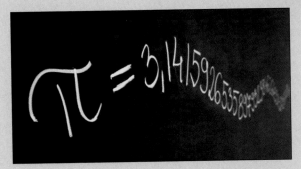

Can we use mathematical patterns to predict what will happen next?

person who believes that the pattern is a code sent from God.

Max's quest reminds us that the average investor lacks full information, but nevertheless irrationally believes that he or she knows more than others. As a result, widespread investor misperceptions about the true probability of events can lead to speculative bubbles and crashes in the stock market.

---

the plan itself, not by responding to the way the employer presents the option to participate. However, people are rarely that rational!

Another decision-making pitfall, known as the **priming effect**, occurs when the order of questions influences the answers. For example, consider two groups of college students. The first group is asked "How happy are you?" followed by "How many dates have you had in the last year?" The second group is asked "How many dates have you had in the last year?" followed by "How happy are you?" The questions are the same, but they are presented in reverse order. In the second group, students who had gone out on more dates reported being much happier than similar students in the first group! In other words, because they were reminded of the number of dates first, those who had more dates believed they were happier.

Priming effects
occur when the ordering of the questions that are asked influences the answers.

Status Quo Bias

When people want to maintain their current choices, they may exhibit what is known as the **status quo bias**. This bias leads decision-makers to try to protect what they have, even when an objective evaluation of their circumstances suggests that a change would be beneficial. In behavioral economics,

Status quo bias
exists when people want to maintain their current choices.

Are you on Team Dollar Bill or Team Dollar Coin?

Loss aversion
occurs when individuals place more weight on avoiding losses than on attempting to realize gains.

the status quo bias is often accompanied by **loss aversion**, which occurs when a person places more value on avoiding losses than on attempting to realize gains.

Loss aversion causes people to behave conservatively. The cost of this behavior is missed opportunities that could potentially enhance welfare. For example, a loss-averse individual would maintain a savings account with a low interest rate instead of actively shopping for better rates elsewhere. This person would lose the potential benefits from higher returns on savings.

Status quo bias also explains why new products and ideas have trouble gaining traction: many potential customers prefer to leave things the way they are, even if something new might make more sense. Consider the $1 coin. It is far more durable than the $1 bill. It is also easier to tell the $1 coin apart from the other coins and bills in your wallet, and if people used the coin, the government would save about $5 billion in production costs over the next 30 years. That sounds like a slam-dunk policy change, but it is not. Americans like their dollar bills and rarely use the $1 coin in circulation even though they repeatedly use nickels, dimes, and quarters to make change, to feed parking meters, and to buy from vending machines. Introducing more of the $1 coin and eliminating the $1 bill would be rational, but the status quo bias has prevented the change from happening.

 ECONOMICS IN THE REAL WORLD

Are You An Organ Donor?

More than 25,000 organ transplants take place every year in the United States, with the vast majority coming from deceased donors. Demand greatly exceeds supply. Over 100,000 people are currently on organ-donation waiting lists. Most Americans are aware of the need, and 90% of all Americans say they support donation. But only 30% know the essential steps to take to be a donor.

There are two main donor systems: the "opt-in" system and the "opt-out" system. In an opt-in system, individuals must give explicit consent to be a donor. In an opt-out system, anyone who has not explicitly refused is considered a donor.

In the United Kingdom, organ donors must opt in.

In the United States, donors are required to opt in. Since opting in generally produces fewer donors than opting out, many states have sought to raise donation awareness by allowing consent to be noted on the individual driver's licenses.

In Europe, many countries have opt-out systems, where consent is presumed. The difference is crucial. After all, in places with opt-in systems, many people who would be willing to donate organs never actually take the time to complete the necessary steps to opt in. In countries like France and Poland, where people must opt out, over 90% of citizens do not explicitly opt out, which means they give consent. This strategy yields organ donation rates that are significantly higher than those of opt-in programs.

According to traditional economic analysis, opting in or opting out should not matter—the results should be the same. The fact that we find strong evidence to the contrary is a compelling illustration of the framing effect. ✳

Opt-Out Is Optimal

Some of the most successful applications of behavioral economics are "opt-out" programs, which automatically enroll eligible people unless they explicitly choose not to participate. The incentives and freedom of choice are exactly the same as in "opt-in" programs, where members must choose to participate, but enrollments are significantly higher under opt-out. Here's a look at three remarkable results.

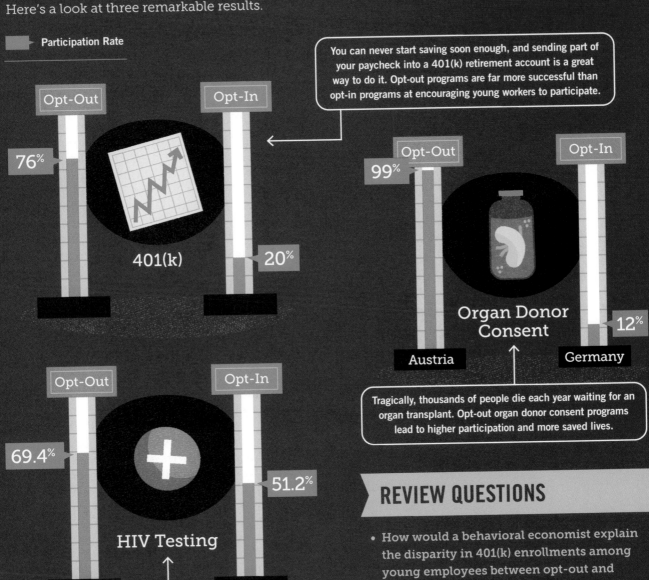

Participation Rate

Opt-Out — 76%
Opt-In — 20%

401(k)

You can never start saving soon enough, and sending part of your paycheck into a 401(k) retirement account is a great way to do it. Opt-out programs are far more successful than opt-in programs at encouraging young workers to participate.

Opt-Out — 99%
Opt-In — 12%

Organ Donor Consent

Austria — Germany

Tragically, thousands of people die each year waiting for an organ transplant. Opt-out organ donor consent programs lead to higher participation and more saved lives.

Opt-Out — 69.4%
Opt-In — 51.2%

HIV Testing

HIV screening remains a crucial public health need. Evidence from one study indicates that opt-out consent at emergency rooms leads to substantially more individuals agreeing to be tested.

REVIEW QUESTIONS

- How would a behavioral economist explain the disparity in 401(k) enrollments among young employees between opt-out and opt-in programs?

- Opt-in and opt-out programs ask us to make the same decisions, but achieve different results. Use the concepts of the framing effect and non-rational behavior to explain why.

Intertemporal Decision-Making

Intertemporal decision-making involves planning to do something over a period of time; this requires valuing the present and the future consistently.

Intertemporal decisions occur across time. **Intertemporal decision-making—** that is, planning to do something over a period of time—requires the ability to value the present and the future consistently. For instance, many people, despite their best intentions, do not end up saving enough for retirement. The temptation to spend money today ends up overwhelming the willpower to save for tomorrow. In a perfectly rational world, a person would not need outside assistance to save enough for retirement. In the real world, however, workers depend on 401(k) plans and other work-sponsored retirement programs to deduct funds from their paycheck so that they don't spend that portion of their income on other things. It may seem odd that people would need an outside agency to help them do something that is in their own long-term interest, but as long as their intertemporal decisions are likely to be inconsistent, the additional commitment helps them to achieve their long-run objectives.

The ability to resist temptation is illustrated by a classic research experiment conducted at a preschool at Stanford University in 1972. One at a time, individual children were led into a room devoid of distractions and were offered a marshmallow. The researchers explained to each child that he or she could eat the marshmallow right away or wait for 15 minutes and be rewarded with a second marshmallow. Very few of the 600 children in the study ate the marshmallow immediately. Most tried to fight the temptation. Of those who tried to wait, approximately one-third held out long enough to earn the second marshmallow. That finding is interesting by itself, but what happened next is truly amazing. Many of the parents of the children in the original study noticed that the children who had delayed gratification seemed to perform better as they progressed through school. Researchers have tracked the participants over the course of 40 years and found that the delayed-gratification group had higher SAT scores, more savings, and larger retirement accounts.

Can you resist eating one marshmallow now, in order to get a second one later?

Judgments about Fairness

The pursuit of fairness is another common behavior that is important in economic decisions but that standard economic theory cannot explain. For example, fairness is one of the key drivers in determining tax rate structure for income taxes. Proponents of fairness believe in progressive taxation, whereby the rich pay a higher tax rate on their income than those in lower income brackets do. Likewise, some people object to the high pay of chief executive officers or the high profits of some corporations because they believe there should be an upper limit to what constitutes fair compensation.

The **ultimatum game** is an economic experiment in which two players decide how to divide a sum of money.

While fairness is not normally modeled in economics, behavioral economists have developed experiments to determine the role of fairness in personal decisions. The **ultimatum game** is an economic experiment in which two players decide how to divide a sum of money. The game shows how fairness enters into the rational decision-making process. In the game, Player 1 is given a sum of money and is asked to propose a way of splitting it with Player 2. Player 2 can either accept or reject the proposal. If Player 2 accepts, the sum is split according to the proposal. However, if Player 2 rejects the proposal, neither player gets anything. The game is played only once, so the first player does not have to worry about reciprocity.

Consider an ultimatum game that asks Player 1 to share $1,000 with Player 2. Player 1 must decide how fair to make the proposal. The decision tree in Figure 17.1 highlights four possible outcomes to two very different proposals—what the figure shows as a fair proposal and an unfair proposal.

Traditional economic theory presumes that both players are fully rational and wish to maximize their income. Player 1 should therefore maximize his gains by offering the minimum, $1, to Player 2. The reasoning is that Player 2 values $1 more than nothing and so will accept the proposal, leaving Player 1 with $999. But real people are not always economic maximizers because they generally believe that fairness matters. Most of the time, Player 2 would find such an unfair division infuriating and reject it.

Player 1 knows that Player 2 will definitely accept an offer of $500; this division of the money is exactly equal and, therefore, fair. Thus, the probability of a 50/50 agreement is 100%. In contrast, the probability of Player 2 accepting an offer of $1 is close to 0%. Offering increasing amounts from $1 to $500 will continue to raise the probability of an acceptance until it reaches 100% at $500.

Player 2's role is simpler: her only decision is whether to accept or reject the proposal. Player 2 desires a fair distribution but has no direct control over the division. To punish Player 1 for being unfair, Player 2 must reject the proposal altogether. The trade-off of penalizing Player 1 for unfairness is a complete loss of any prize. So while Player 2 may not like any given proposal, rejecting it would cause a personal loss. Player 2 might therefore accept a number of unfair proposals because she would rather get something than nothing.

Trade-offs

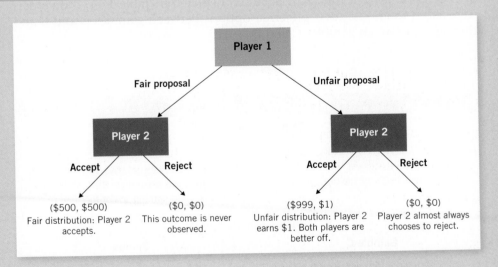

FIGURE 17.1

The Decision Tree for the Ultimatum Game

The decision tree for the ultimatum game has four branches. If Player 1 makes a fair proposal, Player 2 will accept the distribution and both players will earn $500. However, if Player 1 makes an unfair proposal, Player 2 may reject the distribution even though this means receiving nothing.

Each of the ideas that we have presented in this section, including misperceptions of probability, inconsistency in decision-making, and judgments about fairness, represent a departure from the traditional economic model of rational maximization. In the next section, we focus on risk taking. As you will soon learn, not everyone evaluates risk in the same way. This fact has led economists to reconsider their models of human behavior.

What Is the Role of Risk in Decision-Making?

In this section, we examine the role that risk plays in decision-making. The standard economic model of consumer choice assumes that people are consistent in their risk-taking preferences. However, people's risk tolerances actually vary widely and are subject to change. Thus, risk-taking behavior is not nearly as simple, or predictable, as economists once believed. We begin with a phenomenon known as a *preference reversal*. We then consider how negative surprises can cause people to take more risk, which is explained by *prospect theory*.

Preference Reversals

Risk-averse people
prefer a sure thing over a gamble with a higher expected value.

Risk-neutral people
choose the highest expected value regardless of the risk.

Risk takers
prefer gambles with lower expected values, and potentially higher winnings, over a sure thing.

As you know, trying to predict human behavior is not easy. Maurice Allais, the recipient of the 1988 Nobel Prize in Economics, noticed that people's tolerance for risk appeared to change in different situations. This observation did not agree with the standard economic model, which assumes that an individual's risk tolerance is constant and places the individual into one of three distinct groups: **Risk-averse people** prefer a sure thing over a gamble with a higher expected value. **Risk-neutral people** choose the highest expected value regardless of the risk. **Risk takers** prefer gambles with lower expected values, and potentially higher winnings, over a sure thing.

Allais developed a means of assessing risk behavior by presenting the set of choices (known as the Allais paradox) depicted in Table 17.1. Individuals were asked to choose their preferred options between gambles A and B and then again between gambles C and D.

TABLE 17.1

The Allais Paradox

Choose gamble A or B	
Gamble A	**Gamble B**
No gamble—receive $1 million in cash 100% of the time.	A lottery ticket that pays $5 million 10% of the time, $1 million 89% of the time, and nothing 1% of the time.

Choose gamble C or D	
Gamble C	**Gamble D**
A lottery ticket that pays $5 million 10% of the time.	A lottery ticket that pays $1 million 11% of the time.

Economic science predicts that people will choose consistently according to their risk preference. As a result, economists understood that risk-averse individuals would choose the pair A and D. Likewise, the pair B and C makes sense if the participants wish to maximize the expected value of the gambles. Let's see why.

1. *Risk-Averse People:* People who select gamble A over gamble B take the sure thing. If they are asked to choose between C and D, we would expect them to try to maximize their chances of winning something by selecting D, since it has the higher probability of winning.

2. *Risk-Neutral People:* Gamble B has a higher expected value than gamble A. We know that gamble A always pays $1 million since it occurs 100% of the time. Calculating gamble B's expected value is more complicated. The expected value is computed by multiplying each outcome by its respective probability. For gamble B, this means that the expected value is ($5 million × 0.10) + ($1 million × 0.89), which equals $1.39 million. So a risk-neutral player will select gamble B. Likewise, gamble C has a higher expected value than gamble D. Gamble C has an expected value of ($5 million × 0.10), or $0.5 million. Gamble D's expected value is ($1 million × 0.11), or $0.11 million. Therefore, a risk-neutral player who thinks at the margin will choose gambles B and C in order to maximize his or her potential winnings from the game.

Marginal Thinking

PRACTICE WHAT YOU KNOW

Risk Aversion: Risk-Taking Behavior

Question: In the following situations, are the choices evidence of risk aversion or risk-taking?

1. You have a choice between selecting heads or tails. If your guess is correct, you earn $2,000. But you earn nothing if you are incorrect. Alternatively, you can simply take $750 without the gamble. You decide to take the $750.

Answer: The expected value of a 50/50 outcome worth $2,000 is $1,000. Therefore, the decision to take the sure thing, which is $250 less, is evidence of risk aversion.

2. You have a choice between (a) predicting the roll of a six-sided die, with a $3,000 prize for a correct answer, or (b) taking a sure $750. You decide to roll the die.

Answer: The expected value of the roll of the die is 1/6 × $3,000, or $500. Therefore, the $750 sure thing has an expected value that is $250 more. By rolling the die, you are taking the option with the lowest expected value and also the most risk. This indicates that you are a risk taker.

How do you handle risky decisions?

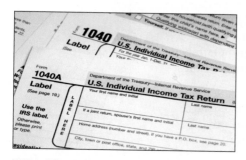

Withholding too much in the previous year and then paying your accountant to file for a rapid refund is a good example of a preference reversal.

A **preference reversal** occurs when risk tolerance is not consistent.

While we would expect people to be consistent in their choices, Allais found that approximately 30% of his research population selected gambles A and C, which are contrasting pairs. Gamble A is the sure thing; however, gamble C, even though it has the higher expected value, carries more risk. This scenario illustrates a *preference reversal*. A **preference reversal** occurs when risk tolerance is not consistent. Allais argued that a person's risk tolerance depends on his or her financial circumstances. Someone who chooses gamble A over gamble B prefers the certainty of a large financial prize—the guarantee of $1 million over the uncertainty of the larger prize. Choosing gamble A could be seen as similar to purchasing insurance: you pay a fee, known as a premium, in order to protect your winnings. In this case, you forfeit the chance to win $5 million. In contrast, gambles C and D offer small chances of success, and therefore the choice is more like playing the lottery.

People who play games of chance are more likely to participate in games with large prizes—for example, Powerball—because the winnings will measurably improve their financial status. Allais showed that people care about how much they might win and also how much they stand to lose. This distinction causes people to choose gambles A and C. By establishing that many people behave this way, Allais reshaped traditional economists' view of risk-taking behavior.

It turns out that preference reversals are more common than economists once believed. For example, approximately 80% of all income tax filers expect to get a refund because they overpaid in the previous year. This behavior is odd, since there is an opportunity cost of waiting to get money back from the government when it didn't need to be paid in the first place. Employees could have asked their employers to withhold less and enjoyed their money sooner. Individuals who choose to wait to receive their money later are said to have a time preference that is weakly positive. In most circumstances, people have strongly positive time preferences: they prefer to have what they want sooner rather than later. So what do these taxpayers do when they learn the amount of their refund? In many cases, they pay their tax preparers an additional fee to have their refunds sent to their bank accounts electronically so they can receive the money sooner! Traditional economic analysis is unable to explain this behavior; but armed with Allais's insights, we now see this behavior as a preference reversal.

Deciding when to take the "deal" makes the show compelling.

Prospect Theory

The television game show *Deal or No Deal* provides an opportunity for economists to examine the risk choices that contestants make in a high-stakes setting. *Deal or No Deal* has created particular excitement among researchers who study game shows because it involves no skill whatsoever. Taking skill out of the equation makes it easier to analyze the contestants' strategy choices. Other TV game shows, such as *Jeopardy!* and *Who Wants to Be a Millionaire?*, require skill to win prizes. Highly skilled players may have different risk tolerances than their less-skilled

Preference Reversals

"Mine"

The music video for Taylor Swift's 2010 hit begins with Swift walking into a coffee shop. When she sits down, she notices a couple arguing at a nearby table. This reminds Swift about her parents arguing when she was very young. Just then, the waiter drops by to take Swift's order. She looks up and dreams of what life would be like with him: we see them running together in the waves at the beach, then unpacking boxes as they move in together. Later, the two argue, resulting in Swift running away from their house and crying, just like she did when she was young and saw her parents arguing. Her boyfriend follows her, and they reconcile. They get married and have two sons. The video ends with Swift re-emerging from her dream and ordering her food at the coffee shop.

In the song's refrain, Swift sings, "You made a rebel of a careless man's careful daughter." Think about that line, keeping in mind that a "rebel" is a risk-taker. Does that remind you of a concept from this chapter? It should—this is a preference reversal. The entire song is about someone (Swift) who is normally risk averse but falls for this guy so hard that she lets her guard down and acts differently. Instead

Taylor's dream illustrates one version of a preference reversal.

of running away when it comes time to fall in love, she stays in the relationship. In other words, the song is about finding someone who would make you believe in love, so much that you were willing to take a chance for the first time in your life.

counterparts. As a result, part of the beauty of studying *Deal or No Deal* is that the outcome is a pure exercise in probability theory.

For those who are unfamiliar with *Deal or No Deal,* here is how the show works. Each of 26 models holds a briefcase that contains a sum of money, varying from one cent to $1 million. The contestant picks one briefcase as her own and then begins to open the other 25 briefcases one at a time, slowly revealing a little more about what her own case might hold. Suspense builds, and the contestant's chance of a big payoff grows as small sums are eliminated and the $1 million case and other valuable cases remain unopened. As cases are eliminated, a "banker" periodically calls the host to offer the contestant a "deal" in exchange for quitting the game.

At the start of the game, the expected value (EV) of the chosen briefcase is determined as follows:

$$\text{EV}_{\text{briefcase}} = \$.01 \times (1/26) + \$1 \times (1/26) + \$5 \times (1/26) + \cdots + \$1\text{M} \times (1/26)$$

This value computes to approximately $131,000. As the game progresses and cases are opened, the "banker" offers a settlement based on whether the expected value of the briefcase has increased or decreased.

Some contestants behave as the traditional model of risk behavior predicts: they maximize the expected value of the briefcase while remaining risk neutral. Since contestants who are risk neutral don't make for exciting television, the "banker" typically offers a "deal" that is far less than the expected value of the remaining cases throughout the early part of the game. This move encourages contestants to play longer so that the excitement and tension have a chance to build.

But not all contestants do what the traditional model expects them to do. For example, some contestants take more risks if they suffer setbacks early in the game, such as opening the $1 million briefcase. This behavior is consistent with *prospect theory* from psychology. **Prospect theory**, developed by Daniel Kahneman and Amos Tversky, suggests that people weigh decisions according to subjective utilities of gains and losses. The theory implies that people evaluate the risks that lead to gains separately from the risks that lead to losses. This result is useful because it explains why some investors try to make up for losses by taking more chances rather than by maximizing the utility they receive from money under a rigid calculation of expected value.

Prospect theory suggests that individuals weigh the utilities and risks of gains and losses differently.

ECONOMICS IN THE REAL WORLD

Why Are There Cold Openings at the Box Office?

The line for tickets is long. Do you suppose this movie was cold-opened?

Movie studios generally make a film available for review if the screenings are expected to generate a positive buzz. Also, access to movie reviews provides moviegoers with a measure of a film's quality. So a rational moviegoer should infer that if a movie studio releases a film without reviews, it is signaling that the movie is not very good: the studio didn't want to risk negative reviews, so it didn't show the movie to reviewers.

Economists Alexander L. Brown, Colin F. Camerer, and Dan Lovallo studied 856 widely released movies and found that cold openings—movies withheld from critics (that is, not screened) before their release—produced a significant increase (15%) in domestic box office revenue compared with poor films that were reviewed and received predictably negative reviews. Most movie openings are accompanied by a marketing campaign to increase consumer demand. As a consequence, cold openings provide a natural field setting to test how rational moviegoers are. Their results are consistent with the hypothesis that some moviegoers do not infer low quality from a cold opening as they should.

The authors showed that cold-opened movies earned more than pre-screened movies after a number of characteristics were controlled for in the study. An important point is that the researchers also found that cold-opened films did not fare better than expected once they reached foreign film or video rental markets. In both of those cases, movie reviews were widely available, which negated any advantage from cold-opening the films. This finding is consistent with the hypothesis that some moviegoers fail to realize that no advance review is a signal of poor quality. The fact that moviegoer ratings from the Internet Movie Database are lower for movies that were cold-opened also suggests that in the absence of information, moviegoers overestimate the expected quality.

Over time, distributors have learned that there is a certain amount of moviegoer naiveté, especially among teenagers. As a result, distributors have overcome their initial reluctance and have cold-opened more movies in recent years.

These findings provide evidence that the best movie distribution strategy does not depend entirely on generating positive movie reviews. Cold openings work because some people are unable to process the negative signal implied by incomplete information, despite what traditional economic analysis would lead us to expect. ✳

Bounded Rationality: How to Guard Yourself against Crime

Suppose that a recent crime wave has hit your community and you are concerned about your family's security. Determined to make your house safe, you consider many options: an alarm system, bars on your windows, deadbolts for your doors, better lighting around your house, and a guard dog. Which of these solutions will protect you from a criminal at the lowest cost? All of them provide a measure of protection—but there's another solution that provides deterrence at an extremely low cost.

The level of security you need depends, in part, on how rational you expect the robber to be. A fully rational burglar would stake out a place, test for an alarm system before breaking in, and choose a home that is an easy target. In other words, the robber would gather full information. But what if the burglar is not fully rational?

Since criminals look for the easiest target to rob, they will find a house that is easy to break into without detection. If you trim away the shrubs and install floodlights, criminals will realize that they can be seen approaching your home. A few hundred dollars spent on better lighting will dramatically lower your chances of being robbed. However, if you believe in bounded rationality, there is an even better answer: a criminal may not know what is inside your house, so a couple of prominently displayed "Beware of dog!" signs would discourage the robber for less than $10! In other words, the would-be thief has incomplete infor-

Beware of dog!

mation and only a limited amount of time to select a target. A quick scan of your house would identify the "Beware of dog!" signs and cause him to move on.

This is an example of bounded rationality since only limited, and in this case unreliable, information is all that is easily available regarding possible alternatives and their consequences. Knowing that burglars face this constraint can be a key to keeping them away.

Conclusion

Behavioral economics helps to dispel the misconception that people always make rational decisions. Indeed, behavioral economics challenges the traditional economics model and invites a deeper understanding of human behavior. Armed with the insights from behavioral economics, we can answer questions that span a wider range of behaviors. We have seen this in the examples in this chapter, which include the "opt in" or "opt out" debate, the economics of risk-taking, the effects of question design, and the status quo bias. These ideas do not fit squarely into traditional economic analysis. You have learned enough at this point to question the assumptions we have made throughout this book. In the next chapter, we will apply all of the tools we have acquired to examine one of the most important sectors of the economy—health care and health insurance.

ANSWERING THE BIG QUESTIONS

How can economists explain irrational behavior?

* Economists use a number of concepts from behavioral economics to explain how people make choices that display irrational behavior. These concepts include bounded rationality, misperceptions of probabilities, the status quo bias, intertemporal decision-making, judgments about fairness, and prospect theory.

* Folding the behavioral approach into the standard model makes economists' predictions about human behavior much more robust.

What is the role of risk in decision-making?

* Risk influences decision-making since people can either be risk averse, risk neutral, or risk takers.

* In the traditional economic model, risk tolerances are assumed to be constant. If an individual is a risk taker by nature, he or she would take risks in any circumstance. Likewise, if an individual does not like to take chances, he or she would avoid risk.

* Maurice Allais proved that many people have inconsistent risk preferences, or what are known as preference reversals. Moreover, he showed that simply because some people's preferences are not constant does not necessarily mean that their decisions are irrational.

  Prospect theory suggests that individuals place more emphasis on gains than on losses, and they are therefore willing to take on additional risk to try to recover losses caused by negative shocks.

CONCEPTS YOU SHOULD KNOW

behavioral economics (p. 528)
bounded rationality (p. 528)
framing effects (p. 532)
gambler's fallacy (p. 531)
hot hand fallacy (p. 531)

intertemporal decision-making (p. 536)
loss aversion (p. 534)
preference reversal (p. 540)
priming effects (p. 533)
prospect theory (p. 542)

risk-averse people (p. 538)
risk-neutral people (p. 538)
risk takers (p. 538)
status quo bias (p. 533)
ultimatum game (p. 536)

QUESTIONS FOR REVIEW

1. What is bounded rationality? How is this concept relevant to economic modeling?

2. What are the hot hand fallacy and the gambler's fallacy? Give an example of each.

3. How does the status quo bias reduce the potential utility that consumers enjoy?

4. Economists use the ultimatum game to test judgments of fairness. What result does economic theory predict?

5. What is prospect theory? Have you ever suffered a setback early in a process (for example, seeking a job or applying for college) that caused you to alter your behavior later on?

STUDY PROBLEMS (✳ *solved at the end of the section*)

✳ 1. You have a choice between taking two jobs. The first job pays $50,000 annually. The second job has a base pay of $40,000 with a 30% chance that you will receive an annual bonus of $25,000. You decide to take the $50,000 job. On the basis of this decision, can we tell if you are risk averse or a risk taker? Explain your response.

2. Suppose that Danny Ocean decides to play roulette, one of the most popular casino games. Roulette is attractive to gamblers because the house's advantage is small (less than 5%). If Danny Ocean plays roulette and wins big, is this evidence that Danny is risk averse or a risk taker? Explain.

3. Many voters go to the polls every four years to cast their ballot for president. The common refrain from those who vote is that their vote "counts" and that voting is important. A skeptical economist points out that with over 100 million ballots cast, the probability that any individual's vote will be decisive is close to 0%. What idea, discussed in this chapter, explains why so many people actually vote?

4. Your instructor is very conscientious and always makes sure that exam answers are randomly distributed. However, you notice that the first five answers on the true/false section are all "true." Unsure what this pattern means, you consider the sixth question. However, you do not know the answer. What answer would you give if you believed in the gambler's fallacy? What answer would you give if you believed in the hot hand fallacy?

✳ 5. Suppose that a university wishes to maximize the response rate for teaching evaluations. The administration develops an easy-to-use online evaluation system that each student can complete at the end of the semester. However, very few students bother to complete the survey. The Registrar's Office suggests that the online teaching evaluations be linked to course scheduling. When students access the course scheduling system, they are redirected to the teaching evaluations. Under this plan, each student could opt out and go directly to the course scheduling system. Do you think this plan will work to raise the response rate on teaching evaluations? What would traditional economic theory predict? What would behavioral economics predict?

6. Ray likes his hamburgers with American cheese, lettuce, and ketchup. Whenever he places an order for a burger, he automatically orders these three toppings. What type of behavior is Ray exhibiting? What does traditional utility theory say about Ray's preferences? What would a behavioral economist say?

7. Many people give to charity and leave tips. What prediction does utility theory make about each of these activities? (Hint: think of the person's narrow self-interest.) What concept from behavioral economics explains this behavior?

8. Given a choice of an extra $1,000 or a gamble with the same expected value, a person prefers the $1,000. But given a choice of a loss of $1,000 or a gamble with the same expected value, the same person prefers the gamble. How would a behavioral economist describe this decision?

SOLVED PROBLEMS

1. The first job pays $50,000 annually, so it has an expected value of $50,000. The second job has a base pay of $40,000 with a 30% chance that you will receive an annual bonus of $25,000. To determine the expected value of the second job, the calculation looks like this: $40,000 + (0.3 × $25,000) = $40,000 + $7,500 = $47,500. Since you decided to take the job with higher expected value, we cannot tell if you are a risk taker or risk averse.

5. Since students who access the course scheduling system are redirected to the teaching evaluations, they are forced to opt out if they do not wish to evaluate the instructors. As a result, behavioral economists would predict that the new system will raise the teaching evaluation response rate. Traditional economic theory predicts that the response rate will not change simply based on whether or not students opt in or opt out.

Health Insurance and Health Care

Providing national health care would be a simple solution to the healthcare crisis.

We have come a long way in our exploration of microeconomics. In this chapter, we will apply our economic tool kit to one particular industry—

health care. The goal of this chapter is not to sway your opinion but to provide you with a simple set of tools to help focus your thinking about how medical care can best serve individuals and society as a whole.

The debate over healthcare spending is at the core of the healthcare crisis in this country. Many people believe that national health care (also called universal health care) would be the solution to the healthcare crisis because it would help to control costs. For example, the Affordable Care Act (or the federal healthcare law) passed under President Obama argues that expanding healthcare coverage will lower healthcare costs. But can we really get more coverage for less? Supporters and opponents vehemently disagree.

The healthcare debate is about trade-offs. The misconception that national health care will solve our healthcare crisis ignores the complex trade-offs that society faces and that drive the healthcare debate. In this chapter, we describe how the healthcare industry works and how the government and the market can each make the delivery of health care more efficient. We will consider how health care is delivered, who pays, and what makes the provision of medical care unlike the delivery of services in any other sector of the economy. Then we will use supply and demand analysis to look at how the medical market functions. One important aspect of medical care is the role that information plays in the incentive structure for patients and providers. Finally, we will

The healthcare debate has many sides.

examine a number of case studies to pull all this information together so you can decide for yourself where you stand on one of the most important issues of the twenty-first century.

Health care is big business. If you add the education and automobile sectors together, they represent about 10% of national economic output. But health care alone accounts for more than 17% of the nation's economic output. That's 1 out of every 6 dollars spent annually in the United States—more than $2 trillion, or almost $8,000 for every citizen. No matter how you slice it, that is a lot of money!

BIG QUESTIONS

* What are the important issues in the healthcare industry?
* How does asymmetric information affect healthcare delivery?
* How do demand and supply contribute to high medical costs?
* How do incentives influence the quality of health care?

What Are the Important Issues in the Healthcare Industry?

In this section, we examine the key issues in health care: how much is spent on it, where the money goes, and who the key players in the industry are. The goal is to give you a sense of how the sector functions. Then we will turn our attention to supply and demand. First, though, we take a brief look at how health care has changed over the past hundred or so years.

At the start of the twentieth century, life expectancy in the United States was slightly less than 50 years. Now life expectancy is close to 80 years—a longevity gain that would have been unthinkable a few generations ago. Let's go back in time to examine the way medical care was delivered and see some of the advances that have improved the human condition.

Early in the twentieth century, infectious diseases were the most common cause of death in the United States. Typhoid, diphtheria, gangrene, gastritis, smallpox, and tuberculosis were major killers. Today, because of antibiotics, they have either been completely eradicated or are extremely rare. Moreover, the state of medical knowledge was so dismal that a cure was often far worse

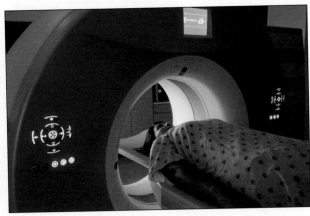

Cutting-edge medical equipment: then . . .   . . . and now.

than the condition it was supposed to treat. For instance, tobacco was recommended for the treatment of bronchitis and asthma, and leeches were used to fight laryngitis. Throughout the first half of the twentieth century, a trip to the doctor was expensive and painful, and it rarely produced positive results.

Since 1950, advances in cellular biology and discoveries in biochemistry have led to a better understanding of the disease process and more precise diagnostic tests. In addition, discoveries in biomedical engineering have led to the widespread use of imaging techniques such as ultrasound, computerized axial tomography (CAT scans), and nuclear magnetic resonance imaging (MRI). These and other procedures have replaced the medical practices of the past and made medical care safer, gentler, and more effective. In addition, pharmaceutical companies have developed a number of "miracle" drugs for fighting many conditions, including high blood pressure, leukemia, and bad cholesterol, thereby limiting the need for more invasive treatments. Each of these amazing medical advances costs money—sometimes, lots of money. As a society, we have made a trade-off: in exchange for a dramatically longer life expectancy, we now devote much more of our personal and government budgets to health care.

Trade-offs

Healthcare Expenditures

We have noted that health expenditures in the United States are more than 17% of economic output. As you can see in Table 18.1, this is quite a bit higher than similar expenditures in Canada and Mexico. Canada spends about 11% of its economic output on health care, and Mexico spends slightly more than 6%.

The United States spends significantly more on health care than our neighbors to the north or south, but life expectancy in the United States is lower than that in Canada. How does Canada achieve a higher life expectancy while spending less money? And why doesn't Mexico, which spends only about one-tenth of what we do on health care, trail farther behind the United States than it does? To answer those questions, consider the usual assumption of *ceteris paribus*, or other things being constant. We all agree that increased healthcare expenditures are making people healthier, probably happier (since they feel better), and more productive—this is true for most

TABLE 18.1			
Selected Health Care Facts			
Country	Total expenditure on health (percentage of economic output)	Per capita expenditure on health (in U.S. dollars)	Life expectancy at birth, total population (in years)
Mexico	6.2%	$916	75.5
Canada	11.4%	$4,445	80.8
U.S.	17.6%	$8,223	78.7

Source: OECD Health Division, *Health Data 2012: Frequently Requested Data.*

countries. However, longevity is also a function of environmental factors, genetics, and lifestyle choices—variables that are not constant across countries. The question we should be asking is not how much money we are spending, but whether we are getting our money's worth. In other words, what concerns economists in this context are the impediments to the efficient delivery of medical care.

Why does health care take up so much of our budget? There are a number of reasons. Health insurance plays a contributing role. When private insurance covers most treatment costs, many patients agree to tests or medical visits that they wouldn't be willing to pay for out of pocket. Also, doctors are more willing to order tests that might not be necessary if they know the patient isn't paying directly. Medicare and Medicaid, the two government-sponsored forms of health insurance, add to the overall demand for medical services by providing medical coverage to the elderly and poor. And we know that anytime there is more demand for services, the market price rises in response.

Another reason for high healthcare costs is the number of uninsured—close to 50 million in the United States. When uninsured people need immediate medical treatment, they often seek care from emergency rooms and clinics. This raises costs in two ways. First, emergency care is extraordinarily expensive—much more so than routine care. Second, waiting until one has an acute condition that requires immediate attention often requires more treatment than would occur with preventative care or an early diagnosis. For example, an insured person who develops a cough with fever is likely to see a physician. If the patient has bronchitis, a few days of medicine and rest will be all it takes to feel better. However, an uninsured person who develops bronchitis is less likely to seek medical help and risks the possibility of a worsening condition, such as pneumonia, which can be difficult and costly to treat.

Medical demand is quite inelastic, so when competition is absent (which is usually the case), hospitals and other providers can charge what they want and patients will have to pay. In addition, people are not usually proactive about their health. Many health problems could be dramatically reduced and costs contained if people curbed habits such as cigarette use, excessive alcohol consumption, and overeating, and if they exercised more. Finally, heroic end-of-life efforts are extraordinarily expensive. These efforts may extend life for a few months, days, or hours, and they come at a steep price.

Diminishing Returns

In the United States, it has become the norm to spare no expense in efforts to extend life for even a few days. However, providing more medical care is subject to diminishing returns, as we can see in Figure 18.1. The purple curve shows a society's aggregate health production function, a measure of health reflecting the population's longevity, general health, and quality of life. This function initially rises rapidly when small amounts of health care are provided, but the benefits of additional care are progressively smaller. This is made evident by looking at points A and B. At point A, only a small amount of medical care is provided (Q_A), but this has a large impact on health. The slope at point A represents the marginal product of medical care. However, by the time we reach point B at a higher amount of care provided (Q_B), the marginal product of medical care (the slope) is much flatter, indicating that diminishing returns have set in.

Marginal
Thinking

Higher medical care expenditures, beyond some point, are unlikely to measurably improve longevity and quality of life. This is because many other factors—for example, disease, genetics, and lifestyle—also play a key role in determining health, quality of life, and longevity. As we move out along the medical production function, extending life becomes progressively more difficult, so it is not surprising that medical costs rise appreciably. Given this pattern, society must answer two questions. First, what is the optimal mix of expenditures on medical care? Second, could society get more from each dollar spent by reallocating dollars away from heroic efforts to extend life, and allocating monies toward prevention and medical research instead?

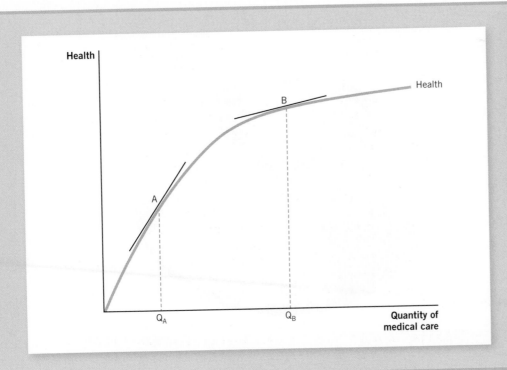

FIGURE 18.1

Health Production Function

The marginal product of medical care, indicated by the slope of the health production function, is higher at point A than at point B.

Figure 18.2 shows where the typical health dollar goes. Hospital care, physicians, and clinics account for half of all medical expenses. After that, prescription drugs, dental care, home health care, and nursing homes each represent smaller parts of healthcare expenditures. Here we note a paradox. On the one hand, medical care has become much more efficient as medical records are increasingly computerized and many procedures that required days of hospitalization a generation ago can now take place on an outpatient basis. Thus, reducing medical costs through efficiency gains is ongoing. Yet, on the other hand, costs continue to rise. What is going on? In the next section, we examine the incentives that patients, providers, and insurance companies face when making medical decisions and how the incentive structure contributes to escalating costs.

Who's Who in Health Care

Incentives

Healthcare consumption is different from that of most other goods and services. Like the others, healthcare services have consumers and producers; but because of intermediaries, such as insurance companies, the two rarely interact directly. This situation generates a unique set of incentives and leads to distortions in the standard supply and demand analysis. It is important to understand how medical care is delivered and paid for, as well as the incentives that patients, medical providers, and insurers face when making decisions.

FIGURE 18.2

The Nation's Health Dollar

Hospital care, physicians, and clinics make up over half of all healthcare expenditures, which totaled $2.6 trillion in 2010. (Dollar amounts shown in parentheses are in billions.)

Source: Centers for Medicare and Medicaid Services, Office of the Actuary, National Health Statistics Group. See "National Health Expenditure Data," cms.gov.

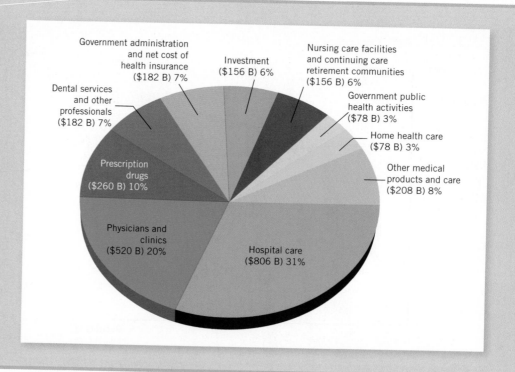

Consumers

The two biggest consumers of medical care are patients and the government. Patients demand medical care to prevent and treat illness. The federal government runs Medicare, a program that provides medical assistance to the elderly, and Medicaid, a program that provides medical assistance to the poor. Medicare and Medicaid are social insurance programs that each serve over 40 million enrollees. The two programs account for approximately one-third of all medical spending in the United States and represent about one-fifth of all U.S. government expenditures.

Producers

The medical care industry employs millions of workers, including doctors, nurses, psychologists, technicians, and many more. There are also over 500,000 medical facilities in this country, including small medical offices, large regional hospitals, nursing homes, pharmacies, and stores that supply medical equipment. In addition, pharmaceutical companies generate over $300 billion in annual sales in the United States.

Intermediaries

Intermediaries—for example, insurance companies—cover certain medical expenses in exchange for a set monthly fee, known as a premium. Medical insurance enables consumers to budget their expenses and limit what they will have to pay out-of-pocket in the event of a serious condition.

In addition to the premium, a *co-payment* or *deductible* is typically required. **Co-payments** are fixed amounts that the insured pays when receiving a medical service or filling a prescription. Insurance companies use co-payments in part to share expenses with the insured. In addition to covering a small portion of the costs, the co-pay serves to prevent most people from seeking care for common conditions that are easy to treat at home. **Deductibles** are fixed amounts that the insured must pay before most of the policy's benefits can be applied. Deductibles are sometimes subject to exceptions, such as a necessary visit to the emergency room or preventative physician visits and tests. Some policies also require **co-insurance payments**, or a percentage that the insured pays after the insurance policy's deductible is exceeded up to the policy's contribution limit. These services vary with each type of plan. Like co-insurance, co-payments and deductibles work to encourage consumers to use medical services judiciously.

Insurance companies use the premiums, co-payments, deductibles, and co-insurance they receive from their customers to pay medical suppliers. For example, you may not need an appendectomy this year, but a predictable number of insured customers will. Using statistical techniques, an insurance company with millions of customers can accurately predict how many of its customers will visit the doctor and require hospitalization and other services. This enables the company to estimate its costs in advance and set premiums that generate a profit for the company.

Many people receive medical care through *health maintenance organizations*, or HMOs—another example of an intermediary. HMOs provide managed care

Co-payments
are fixed amounts that the insured must pay when receiving a medical service or filling a prescription.

Deductibles
are fixed amounts that the insured must pay before most of the policy's benefits can be applied.

Co-insurance payments
are a percentage of costs that the insured must pay after exceeding the insurance policy's deductible up to the policy's contribution limit.

for their patients by assigning them a primary care physician who oversees their medical care. The HMO then monitors the primary care provider to ensure that unnecessary care is not prescribed. HMOs earn revenue from premiums, co-payments, deductibles, and co-insurance.

Another kind of insurance company sells insurance against medical malpractice, or negligent treatment on the part of doctors. The doctor pays a set fee to the insurer, which in turn pays for the legal damages that arise if the doctor faces a malpractice claim. By analyzing statistics about the number of malpractice cases for each type of medical procedure performed each year, insurers can estimate the probability that a particular physician will face a malpractice claim; the insurers then incorporate that risk into the fee they charge.

Pharmaceutical Companies

Constituting another major player in the healthcare industry are the many pharmaceutical companies that develop the drugs used to treat a wide variety of conditions. Global pharmaceutical sales are almost $1 trillion—that's a lot of prescriptions! Pharmaceutical companies spend billions of dollars developing and testing potential drugs, which can take years for even just one drug. Once a drug is developed, it must receive approval by the Food and Drug Administration before it can be sold. The development cost, time required, and risk that a drug may turn out to be problematic or ineffective combine to make the development of new drugs an expensive proposition.

Medical Costs

Incentives

To understand why medical costs are so high, we must look at the incentives that drive the decisions of the major players. Consumers want every treatment to be covered, providers want a steady stream of business and don't want to be sued for malpractice, and the insurance companies and pharmaceutical companies want to make profits. This dynamic showcases the inherent conflict that exists among consumers, producers, and intermediaries, and it helps explain the difficulty of containing medical care at a reasonable cost.

Since patient co-payments are only a tiny fraction of the total cost of care, the effective marginal cost of seeking medical treatment is quite low. This causes consumers to increase the quantity of medical care they demand. Some physicians prescribe more care than is medically necessary in order to earn more income and to avoid malpractice lawsuits. Meanwhile, insurance companies, which are caught in the middle between patients and medical providers, do their best to contain costs, but they find that controlling the behavior of patients and providers is difficult. Consequently, escalating costs result from a system with poorly designed incentive mechanisms. In the case of Medicare and Medicaid, the government attempts to control costs by setting caps on the reimbursements that are paid to providers for medical treatments. An unintended consequence of government price-setting is that it forces physicians and medical centers to raise costs for other procedures that are not covered by Medicare and Medicaid.

PRACTICE WHAT YOU KNOW

Physical Fitness

Question: You go in for a physical, and your doctor suggests that you get more exercise. So you decide to start working out. The increased physical activity has a big payoff and soon you feel much better, so you decide to double your efforts and get in even better shape. However, you notice that the gains from doubling your workout effort do not make you feel much better. What economic concept explains this effect?

Answer: More of a good thing isn't always better. Physical activity extends longevity and increases quality of life up to a point. This occurs because working out is subject to *diminishing returns*. In other words, a small amount of physical activity has a big payoff, but lifting more weights or running more miles, after a certain point, does not increase your overall health—it simply maintains your health.

"I work out . . ."

How Does Asymmetric Information Affect Healthcare Delivery?

We have seen that incentives play an important role in the delivery of medical care. Another important element is the information and lack of information available to participants. Imbalances in information, known as **asymmetric information**, occur whenever one party knows more than the other. Asymmetric information has two forms: *adverse selection* and the *principal-agent problem*.

Asymmetric information is an imbalance in information that occurs when one party knows more than the other.

Adverse Selection

Most of us know very little about medicine. We know when we don't feel well and that we want to feel better, so we seek medical attention. Because we know very little about the service we are buying, we are poor judges of quality. For example, how can you know your provider is qualified or better than another provider? **Adverse selection** exists when one party has information about some aspect of product quality that the other party does not have. As a result, the party with the limited information should be concerned that the other party will misrepresent information to gain an advantage.

Adverse selection exists when one party has information about some aspect of product quality that the other party does not have.

When one side knows more than the other, the only way to avoid an adverse outcome is to gather better information. Suppose that you are new in town and need medical care. You haven't had a chance to meet anyone and find out whom to see or where to go for care. Fortunately, there is a way to avoid the worst doctors and hospitals: websites like ratemds.com and ratemyhospital .com provide patient feedback on the quality of care that they have received. Armed with knowledge from sources like these, you can request to be treated by doctors who you know to be competent and at facilities that have strong reputations. This helps prevent new residents from unknowingly receiving below-average care. More generally, it is important for patients to take charge of their own health care and learn all they can about a condition and its treatment so they are prepared to ask questions and make better decisions about treatment options. When patients are better informed, adverse selection is minimized.

Adverse selection also applies when buyers are more likely to seek insurance if they are more likely to need it. Consider a life insurance company. The company wants to avoid selling an inexpensive policy to someone who is likely to die prematurely, so before selling a policy to that applicant, the insurance company has to gather additional information about the person. It can require a medical exam and delay eligibility for full benefits until it can determine that the applicant has no pre-existing health conditions. As a result, the process of gathering information about the applicant is crucial to minimizing the risk associated with adverse selection. In fact, the process is similar for automobile insurance, in which drivers with poor records pay substantially higher premiums and safe drivers pay substantially lower ones.

The Principal-Agent Problem

Patients generally trust doctors to make good treatment decisions on the basis of medical welfare. Unfortunately, in our current medical system, *the principal-agent problem* means this is not always the case. A **principal-agent problem** arises when a principal entrusts an agent to complete a task and the agent does not do so in a satisfactory way. Some non-medical examples should be familiar to you. When parents (the principal) hire a babysitter (the agent), she might talk on the phone instead of watching the children. A company manager (the agent) might try to maximize his own salary instead of working to increase value for the shareholders (the principal). Finally, a politician (the agent) might be more likely to grant favors to interest groups than to focus on the needs of his constituents (the principal).

In a medical setting, the principal-agent problem occurs whenever patients cannot directly observe how medical providers and insurers are managing their (the patients') interests. The lack of oversight on the part of patients gives their agents, the physicians and insurance companies, some freedom to pursue other objectives that do not directly benefit patients. In the case of medicine, doctors and hospitals may order more tests, procedures, or visits to specialists than are medically necessary. The physician or the hospital may be more concerned about making profits or avoiding medical malpractice lawsuits than ensuring the patient's health and well-being. At the same time, insurance companies may desire to economize on treatment costs in

A **principal-agent problem** arises when a principal entrusts an agent to complete a task and the agent does not do so in a satisfactory way.

order to maximize the bottom line. In both cases, the patient's desire for the best medical care conflicts with the objectives of the agents who deliver their care.

Moral Hazard

Moral hazard occurs when a party that is protected from risk behaves differently from the way it would behave if it were fully exposed to the risk. Moral hazard does not necessary mean "immoral" or "unethical." But it does imply that some people will change their behavior when their risk exposure is reduced and an "it's insured" mentality sets in. This can lead to inefficient outcomes, such as visiting the doctor more often than necessary. Likewise, physicians may prescribe more care than is medically necessary if they stand to make more money from insurance company payouts.

In each of the examples mentioned above, there is a moral hazard problem that can be lessened by restructuring the incentives. For the patient, a higher co-payment will discourage unnecessary visits to the doctor. For the physician, a hospital might tie a portion of the doctor's salary to periodic performance evaluations.

To solve a moral hazard problem in medical care, it is necessary to fix the incentive structure. Many health insurance companies address moral hazard by encouraging preventative care, which lowers medical costs. They also impose payment limits on treatments for preventable conditions, such as gum disease and tooth decay.

Moral hazard
occurs when a party that is protected from risk behaves differently from the way it would behave if it were fully exposed to the risk.

Incentives

Moral Hazard

"King-Size Homer"

In this episode of *The Simpsons*, a new corporate fitness policy is intended to help the power plant workers to become healthier. Morning exercises are instituted, and the employees are whipped into shape. But Homer hates working out, so he decides to gain a lot of weight in order to claim disability and work at home. In order to qualify, he must weigh at least 300 pounds. This means that he must go on an eating binge. Of course, his behavior is not what the designers of the fitness policy had in mind.

This amusing episode is a good example of moral hazard, and it showcases how well-intentioned policies can often be abused.

Moral hazard makes Homer decide to gain weight.

ECONOMICS IN THE MEDIA

Asymmetric Information

Question: In each of the following situations, is adverse selection, the principal-agent problem, or moral hazard at work?

Is she for real, or has she been Photoshopped?

1. You decide to use an online dating site, but you are not entirely sure if the posted picture of your date is accurate.

Answer: Adverse selection is at work. The person you are interested in knows more about himself than you do. He can, and probably would, post a picture of himself that is flattering. When you finally meet him, you are likely to be disappointed.

2. You hire a substitute tutor for your sister and agree to pay $40 up front. Later, you find out that the tutor spent more time texting on his phone than helping your sister.

Answer: Since you paid up front for a one-time session, the substitute tutor has much less incentive to help compared to your sister's regular tutor, who expects repeat business and a tip. The poor outcome is a result of moral hazard.

3. You hire a friend to feed your cat and change the litter twice a day while you are on spring break. However, your friend only visits your apartment every other day, and your cat shows his disapproval by using your bedspread as a litter box.

Answer: This is a principal-agent problem. Since you are out of town, there is no way to tell how often your friend goes to your house. Your friend knows that cats are largely self-sufficient and figures that you won't be able to tell how often she changed the litter.

How Do Demand and Supply Contribute to High Medical Costs?

Now that we have a basic understanding of how the healthcare industry functions and who the key players are, we can examine the way demand and supply operate in the market for health care. On the demand side, we consider what makes healthcare demand stubbornly inelastic. Health care, when you need it, is not about the price—it is about getting the care you need. When you consider this fact and the presence of third-party payments, or payments made by insurance companies, you can begin to understand why medical expenses have risen so rapidly. On the supply side, medical licensing requirements help to explain why the supply of medical services is limited. The combination of strongly inelastic demand and limited supply pushes up prices for medical services.

Healthcare Demand

Health care is usually a necessity, without many good alternatives. This explains why the demand for health care is typically inelastic. For example, going without a heart transplant when you need one isn't an option. In fact, a 2002 RAND Corporation study found that health care has an average price elasticity coefficient of −0.17. This means that a 1% increase in the price of health care will lead to a 0.17% reduction in healthcare expenditures. Recall that as an elasticity coefficient approaches zero, demand becomes more inelastic. So we can say that the demand for medical care is quite inelastic. (For a refresher on elasticity, see Chapter 4.)

But there are some situations in which healthcare expenditures can be reduced. For example, otherwise healthy people with minor colds and other viruses can use home remedies, such as drinking fluids and resting, rather than making an expensive visit to the doctor. So the price elasticity of demand depends on the severity of the medical need and the sense of urgency involved in treatment. Urgent needs have the most inelastic demand. As the time horizon expands from the short run to the long run, the demand for health care becomes progressively more elastic. Non-emergency long-term treatments have the greatest price elasticity. For instance, a significant portion of the adult population postpones routine dental visits, despite the obvious benefits. Later, when a tooth goes bad, some people choose extractions, which are less expensive (though less attractive) than root canals and crowns.

In recent years, demand for health care has grown. As people live longer, demand rises for expensive medical goods and services, including hearing aids, replacement joints, assisted living and nursing home facilities, and so on. In an aging population, the incidence of certain illnesses and conditions—for example, cancer and Alzheimer's disease—rises. In addition, new technologies have made it possible to treat medical conditions for which there previously was no treatment. While these medical advances have improved the quality of life for many consumers, they drive up demand for more advanced medical procedures, equipment, and specialty drugs.

Third-Party Participation

People who are risk averse (see Chapter 17) generally choose to purchase health insurance because it protects them against the possibility of extreme financial hardship in the case of severe illness or other medical problems. But when people have insurance, it may distort their idea of costs and cause them to change their behavior, which creates a potential moral hazard problem. For example, if an insurance policy does not require the patient to pay anything, or requires very little, to see the doctor, the patient may wind up seeing the doctor more often than necessary.

Inelastic Healthcare Demand

John Q

The 2002 feature film *John Q* follows John Quincy Archibald's quest to help his son receive a heart transplant. His son suddenly collapses while playing baseball and is rushed to the emergency room. Doctors inform John Q (played by Denzel Washington) that his son's only hope is a transplant. Since the child will die without the transplant, John Q's demand for this surgery is perfectly inelastic. Unfortunately, due to an involuntary work reduction at his job, John Q's insurance won't cover his son's transplant.

The tagline of the film is "give a father no options and you leave him no choice." This statement summarizes the dilemma that many people without insurance face. However, it does not stop the uninsured from demanding medical care when the situation is life threatening. This is problematic on two fronts. First, when those without insurance turn to the emergency room as their only source of medical care, their medical conditions are treated in the most expensive manner possible. Second, hospitals transfer the cost of treating the uninsured by raising fees for the other services that they provide. As a result, society picks up the tab for the uninsured indirectly through higher insurance premiums.

Inelastic demand for his son's heart transplant drives John Q to take desperate steps.

No one wants to risk a child possibly dying because his family lacks health insurance. After exploring every available financial option, John Q takes matters into his own hands and takes the emergency room staff hostage until the hospital agrees to do the transplant. Of course, this plot line sensationalizes the problem, but it also makes a very powerful point about the costs and benefits of life-saving care.

Consider how this situation affects two patients. Abigail does not have insurance and therefore must pay the full cost of medical care out-of-pocket. Brett has an insurance policy that requires a small co-payment for medical care. Figure 18.3 illustrates the difference between how Abigail (point A) and Brett (point B) might react. Let's suppose that they both get sick five times during the year. Because Abigail pays the full cost of seeking treatment ($100 per physician office visit), she will only go to the doctor's office three times. She ends up paying $300. Brett pays $10 per visit, so he will go to the doctor's office five times for a total cost to him of $50. The insurance company picks up the rest of the cost for Brett, or $90 per visit.

The overall impact of a $10 co-payment on healthcare costs is large. In the scenario described above, since each visit costs $100, total healthcare costs for the office visit are only $300 when a patient is uninsured, but they increase

FIGURE 18.3

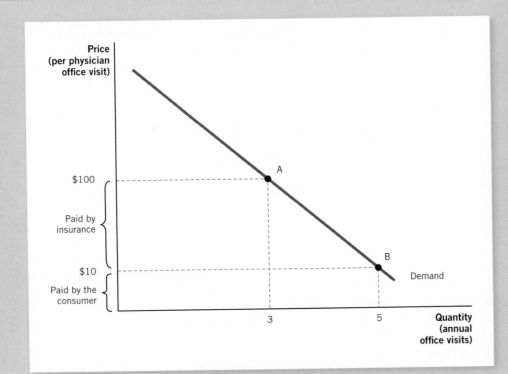

Price and the Quantity Demanded of Medical Care Services

Without insurance, the consumer bears the entire cost of an office visit, or $100. At this amount, the consumer might think twice about whether the medical care is truly necessary. As a result of these costs, the consumer makes 3 office visits per year, represented by point A. However, when a consumer has insurance and pays only a $10 co-payment per visit, the marginal price drops and the quantity demanded increases. This consumer makes 5 office visits per year, represented by point B.

to $500 with healthcare coverage—a $200 increase in total healthcare costs just for the initial office visit. Since in our example the insurance companies are paying 90% of the cost, the consumer has little reason not to seek medical attention, even for minor problems that will respond to home treatment. The two extra visits per year illustrate a change in consumer behavior as a result of the lower co-payment. This demonstrates one simple reason insurance costs are so high.

Healthcare Supply

While consumers worry about the price, or premium, they pay for health insurance, producers are concerned about profits. As much as we might like to think that medical providers care only about our health, we must acknowledge that they are providing a service for which they expect to be paid. Therefore, it is more accurate to think of healthcare providers in the same way we think of any other producers: when the price rises, they are willing to supply additional health care. Producers of medical care such as physicians and hospitals also enjoy significant market power. In this section, we consider how licensing requirements limit the supply of certain healthcare providers and the effect this has on the market.

Becoming a skilled medical provider is a lengthy process that requires extensive training, education, and certification. Physicians must secure licenses from
a medical board before they can practice, and nurses must become registered.
Thus, restrictions associated with entering the medical profession limit the
supply of workers. This point is captured in Figure 18.4, which illustrates how
barriers to entry limit the number of physicians and nurses and the impact
that this outcome has on their wages.

Barriers to entry in the medical profession restrict the supply of physicians
and nurses. The subsequent decrease in the supply of these medical workers
(from Q_1 to Q_2) causes their wages to increase (from W_1 to W_2). In addition, many medical facilities do not face direct competition. For example,
many small communities have only one hospital. In these cases, familiarity, the need for immediate care, and convenience make the nearest hospital
the default option for most patients. Since economies of scale are important in the provision of medical care, even large metropolitan areas tend to
have only a few large hospitals rather than many smaller competitors. As the
population base expands, larger hospitals can afford to offer a wider set of
services than smaller hospitals do. For instance, the need for pediatric care
units, oncology centers, organ transplant centers, and a host of other services
require that the hospital develop a particular expertise. The availability of
specialized care is, of course, a good thing. However, as hospitals become

FIGURE 18.4

**Barriers to Entry Limit
the Supply of Certain
Medical Workers**

Restrictions associated
with entering the medical
profession limit the supply
of certain workers. This
causes a decrease in the
supply of physicians and
nurses from Q_1 to Q_2 and
an increase in wages from
W_1 to W_2.

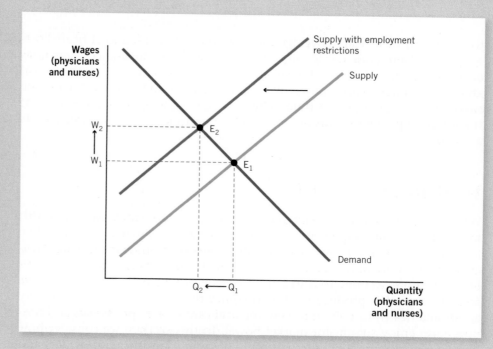

larger and more highly specialized, competitive pressures subside and they are able to charge higher fees.

The market power of suppliers is held in check to some extent by insurance companies and by the Medicare and Medicaid programs. Also, some services are not reimbursed by insurance. And the insurance companies push back against certain other medical charges by limiting the amount they reimburse, as do Medicare and Medicaid for certain treatments. In contrast, elective medical services, such as Lasik eye surgery, are typically not reimbursed by insurance plans. As a result, consumer demand is quite elastic. Still, overall medical costs have continued to rise.

ECONOMICS IN THE REAL WORLD

Medical Tourism

Medical tourism has grown explosively over the last 20 years as the quality of medical care around the globe has improved rapidly and international travel has become more convenient. Today, it is possible for a patient to have cardiac surgery in India, a hip replacement in Egypt, and a face-lift in Rio de Janeiro. Supply and demand helps explain the rapid growth of medical tourism. People seek medical care abroad for two reasons: costs and wait times.

Recovery from surgery doesn't get any better than this!

First, the cost of medical care is as much as 90% lower in a developing country than in a developed country such as the United States. This is a function of lower costs of living, less administrative overhead, a favorable currency exchange rate, and lower malpractice premiums. Also, health insurance is not readily available in many locations, which leads to a policy of cash payment for healthcare services and also suppresses demand. Second, there are long wait times for certain procedures in countries with universal health care. Avoiding long wait times is the leading factor for medical tourism from the United Kingdom and Canada.

In the United States, the main reason for medical tourism is the lower cost. Indeed, many procedures performed abroad cost a fraction of the price in developed countries. For example, a liver transplant in the United States can cost more than $250,000, but it costs less than $100,000 in Taiwan. Some insurance plans offer incentives to have orthopedic surgery, such as knee and hip replacements, performed in Panama and Costa Rica, where the cost of the surgery is a quarter of the cost in the United States. Patients agree to leave the country for this type of surgery because their insurance company will pay all their travel-related expenses and waive the typical out-of-pocket expenses that would be incurred from co-pays and deductibles.

Medical tourism has even led to the creation of medical "safaris," where patients go to South Africa or South America for cosmetic surgery, stay in luxurious accommodations, and take in the savanna or rain forest while recuperating. ✳

PRACTICE WHAT YOU KNOW

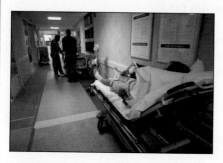

Increased demand for services might mean that "Hurry up and wait" becomes a common experience for most patients.

Demand for Health Care: How Would Universal Health Care Alter the Demand for Medical Care?

Question: Suppose that the United States scraps its current healthcare system and citizens are 100% covered for all medical care with no co-payments or deductibles. How would the new system affect the demand for medical care? Illustrate your answer on a graph.

Answer: Without any co-payment or deductibles, each patient's out-of-pocket expense would be zero. Society would pick up the tab through taxes. As a result, the quantity of medical care demanded by each patient would increase from point A to point B.

At point B, demand is no longer contingent on price, so this represents the largest potential quantity of care demanded.

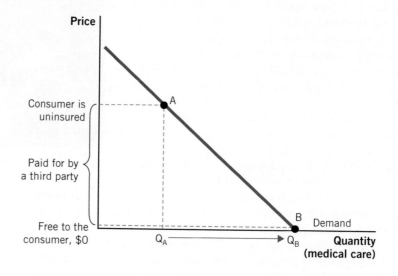

How Do Incentives Influence the Quality of Health Care?

Incentives

In this section, we apply what we've learned about health care. First, we look at the universal healthcare debate by comparing the healthcare systems in the United States and Canada. Then we examine the shortage of human organs available for transplant. By considering these two issues, we can see how incentives influence the quality of health care that patients receive.

Single-Payer versus Private Health Care

Rationing is a fact of life because we live in a world of scarcity. The simplest way of thinking about the health-care issue is to understand how different rationing mechanisms are used in medical care. In the United States, the primary rationing mechanism is the consumer's ability to pay. One consequence of using prices to ration medical care is that close to 50 million U.S. citizens forgo some medical care because they lack insurance or the means to pay for care on their own. In Canada, no citizen lacks the means to pay because medical care is paid for by taxes.

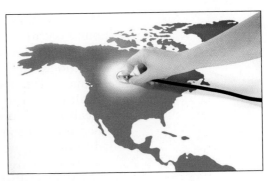

What country has the best health care?

This does not mean that medical care there is unlimited, however. In Canada, rationing occurs through wait times, fewer doctors, and limited availability of certain drugs.

As in almost all things economic, there is a trade-off. No medical system creates the perfect set of incentives. In the United States, a large majority of citizens have the means to pay for medical care, have access to some of the best medical facilities in the world, and face relatively short wait times. However, under the current U.S. system, the poorest members of the society have reduced access to health care.

In Canada, each citizen is treated equally, but access to immediate medical treatment is more restricted. We have seen in Table 18.1 that Canada spends far less than the United States per capita ($4,363 versus $7,960). How does Canada provide medical care to every citizen at approximately half the price of the U.S. system? There are several ways. First, the government sets the rates that are paid to medical providers. Second, physicians are not permitted to have private practices. Third, to eliminate outside competition and to prevent wages from rising with the market, physicians' salaries are capped. Fourth, hospitals receive grants from the government to cover the costs of providing care. This system, in which there is only a *single payer*, makes the government the single buyer, or monopsonist, of most medical care. (See Chapter 14 for a discussion of monopsony.) In other words, in a **single-payer system** the government covers the cost of providing most health care, and citizens pay their share through taxes.

The Canadian government uses its leverage as a monopsonist to set compensation levels for physicians below the competitive market wage rate. Under Canada's Health Act, government funding is required for medically necessary care, but only if that care is delivered in hospitals or by certified physicians. This means that the Canadian government funds about 70% of all medical expenses, with the remaining 30% of costs being generated by prescription medications, long-term care, physical therapy, and dental care. In these areas, private insurance operates in much the same way it does in the United States.

Predictably, cost containment measures have an influence on physician flows. Medical schools in the United States produce a relatively constant number of physicians each year, but the new supply is not enough to keep up with the demand in the United States. In fact, U.S. demand exceeds the supply by approximately 30% annually. As a result, physicians flow into the

In a **single-payer system**, the government covers the cost of providing most health care, and citizens pay their share through taxes.

United States each year from beyond its borders, and one of the major suppliers is Canada.

Patients seeking medical care in Canada are also far more likely to seek additional care in the United States than U.S. patients are to seek care in Canada. This fact might strike you as odd. After all, Canada has national health care, and health services there are covered under the Canadian Health Act. However, there is a difference between access and availability. Because Canada keeps tight control over medical costs, people with conditions that are not urgently life-threatening often face extended waits. Ironically, closely related services that are not regulated—for example, veterinarian visits—provide access to medical care without waiting. Dogs in Canada have no trouble getting MRIs and chemotherapy quickly—unlike their human counterparts, who have to wait—but of course the pet owner has to pay the full expense.

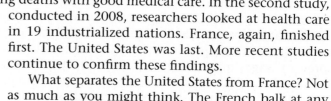

ECONOMICS IN THE REAL WORLD

Health Care in France

In 2000, the World Health Organization (WHO) ranked every country's healthcare system.* France came in first. The United States finished 37 out of 191 nations. When the WHO study was questioned, researchers in London decided to control for longevity by separating out deaths caused by accidents and homicides from those by natural causes to determine how effective each system was at preventing deaths with good medical care. In the second study, conducted in 2008, researchers looked at health care in 19 industrialized nations. France, again, finished first. The United States was last. More recent studies continue to confirm these findings.

What separates the United States from France? Not as much as you might think. The French balk at any notion that they have socialized health care. France, like the United States, relies on both private insurance and government insurance. In both countries, people generally get private insurance through their employer. Both healthcare systems value choice, and patients can choose preferred providers and specialists. The chief difference is that 99.9% of French citizens have health insurance, as opposed to 85% in the United States. This occurs because in France there is mandatory national health insurance, alongside supplemental private insurance that most people purchase.

Another difference between the French and U.S. systems is in the way coverage works for the sickest patients. In France, the most serious conditions

France is #1 in health care, according to the World Health Organization.

---

* Material adapted from Joseph Shapiro, "Healthcare Lessons from France," *National Public Radio,* July 11, 2008. Transcript available at www.npr.org.

are 100% covered. In contrast, in the United States patients' out-of-pocket expenses for the most serious conditions often require supplemental insurance, and experimental procedures and drugs are rarely covered. As a result, the French report that they are quite satisfied with their healthcare system, while similar surveys in the United States find a much more mixed reaction, with roughly half the population happy and the other half concerned.

Of course, none of this is inexpensive. In France, the average person pays slightly over 20% of his or her income to support the national healthcare system. Since French firms must pick up a large chunk of the healthcare tab, they are more reluctant to hire workers. In the United States, workers do not pay as much in taxes, but they do pay more for medical care than the French do when we add in the costs of private insurance and higher out-of-pocket expenses. The lower overall costs of providing medical care in France can be traced to the government control of the amount of compensation that hospitals and providers receive. In other words, the French do a better job of using monopsony power to control costs. Nevertheless, healthcare costs in France have risen rapidly, which has led to cuts in services in order to keep the system solvent. ✳

The Human Organ Shortage

Many altruistic people donate blood each year to help save the lives of tens of thousands of other people. Their generosity makes transplants and other surgeries possible. Unfortunately, the same cannot be said for organ donations. The quantity of replacement organs demanded exceeds the quantity of replacement organs supplied each year, resulting in thousands of deaths. Many of these deaths would be preventable if people were allowed to sell organs. However, the National Organ Transplant Act of 1984 makes it illegal to do so in the United States. Restrictions do not cover the entire body: people can sell platelets, sperm, and ova. In those markets, prices determine who donates. With blood, kidneys, livers, and lungs, the donors are not paid. This discrepancy has created two unintended consequences. First, many people die unnecessarily: in the United States, more than 6,000 patients on transplant waiting lists die each year. Second, the demand for human organs has created a billion-dollar-a-year black market.

Let's consider the market for kidneys. Figure 18.5 illustrates how the supply and demand for human kidneys works. Almost everyone has two kidneys, and a person's life can continue almost normally with only one healthy kidney. Of course, there are risks associated with donation, including complications from the surgery and during recovery, as well as no longer having a backup kidney. However, since there are roughly 300 million "spare" kidneys in the United States (because the population is 300 million), there is a large pool of potential donors who are good matches for recipients awaiting a transplant.

Since kidneys cannot be legally bought and sold, the supply curve shown in Figure 18.5 does not respond to price. As a result, the curve becomes a vertical line at point Q_s (quantity supplied). Notice that the quantity supplied is not zero. This is because many people donate kidneys to friends and family members in need, and others participate in exchange programs under which they donate a kidney to someone they don't know in exchange

FIGURE 18.5

The Supply and Demand for Human Kidneys

Restrictions on selling kidneys limit the supply of organs as shown by $S_{restricted}$ and cause the shortage noted between Q_d and Q_s. A black market develops with an illegal price of $125,000.

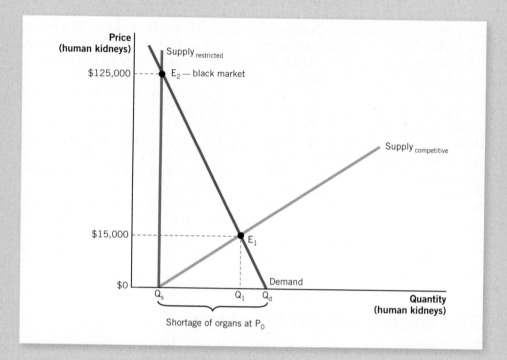

Trade creates value

for someone else agreeing to donate a kidney to a friend or family member. (Exchange programs help to provide better matches so that the recipient is less likely to reject the kidney transplant.) Moreover, a few altruistic persons donate their kidneys to complete strangers. Nevertheless, the quantity supplied still falls short of the quantity demanded, since $Q_d > Q_s$ at a price of $0.

Markets would normally reconcile a shortage by increasing prices. In Figure 18.5, an equilibrium market price of $15,000 is shown ($E_1$). Economists have estimated that this would be the market price if the sale of kidneys were legal in the United States. Since it is illegal, the nation faces the shortage illustrated in Figure 18.5. Over 3,000 people die each year in this country waiting for a kidney transplant. Many others have a low quality of life while waiting to receive a kidney. Because patients waiting for human organs eventually die without a transplant, a black market for kidney transplants has developed outside the United States. However, the price—typically, $125,000 or greater—requires doctors, hospitals, staff, and patients to circumvent the law. As a consequence, the black market price (at E_2) is much higher than it would be if a competitive market for human kidneys existed.

Health: United States vs. Canada

Is the healthcare dollar being spent as efficiently as possible to maintain the health of Americans? To answer this question, it's helpful to compare our situation to other countries, such as Canada. The United States and Canada have very different healthcare systems. Canada's is primarily a publicly funded, single-payer system with the government paying 71% of all health-related expenses. The United States' is primarily a privately funded, multi-payer system with the government paying 48% of all health-related expenses.

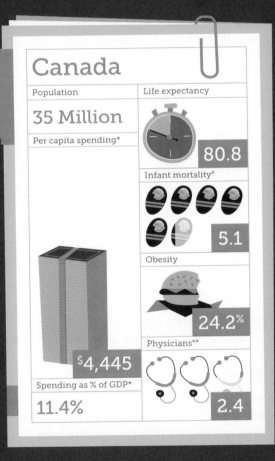

CANADA

Canada

Population	Life expectancy

35 Million

Per capita spending*

Life expectancy: 80.8

Infant mortality°: 5.1

Obesity: 24.2%

$4,445

Physicians°°: 2.4

Spending as % of GDP*

11.4%

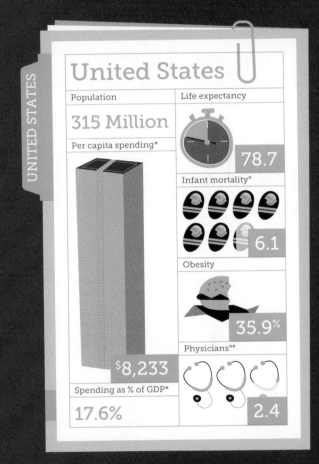

UNITED STATES

United States

Population	Life expectancy

315 Million

Per capita spending*

Life expectancy: 78.7

Infant mortality°: 6.1

Obesity: 35.9%

$8,233

Physicians°°: 2.4

Spending as % of GDP*

17.6%

* Total expenditure, public and private   ° Per 1,000 live births   °° Per 1,000 people

Both countries achieve similar health outcomes, but health care is a clear example of trade-offs. The Canadian system cuts costs, while patients in the United States benefit from shorter wait times for care and the best medical facilities in the world.

REVIEW QUESTIONS

- How do you think the obesity level in the United States contributes to healthcare costs?

- What are the benefits and costs of a private versus a public healthcare system?

ECONOMICS IN THE REAL WORLD

"Baby, baby, baby, oh."

Selling Ova to Pay for College

Did you know that young, bright, American women with college loans can help pay off their debts by donating their ova? The process is relatively simple. The donor is paid to travel to a fertility clinic, and several weeks of hormone treatments are begun. After this, pairs of the donor's ova are removed surgically, then fertilized in a laboratory and implanted inside the womb of a woman who is infertile. With careful lab work and a little luck, the procedure works. The donor receives between $5,000 and $15,000, depending on her track record as a donor. Those whose ova have been successfully implanted and led to the birth of a healthy child are in high demand.

The procedure is not without risks, including rare but potentially serious complications for donors and a high incidence of multiple births among recipients; additionally, long-term risks are not well understood. And, clearly, volunteering for elective surgery isn't a choice everyone would feel comfortable making. But that said, the existence of a market allows a trade that can benefit both the donor and recipient greatly. ✳

PRACTICE WHAT YOU KNOW

Human Organ Shortage: Liver Transplants

Most liver transplants make use of organs from cadavers. However, liver transplants are also possible from live donors, who give a portion of their liver to a needy recipient. Donating a live liver involves major surgery that lasts between 4 and 12 hours. The complication rate for the donor is low, but the recovery time is typically two to three months. Not surprisingly, there is still a shortage of live livers for transplant.

Question: What solutions can you think of that would motivate more people to donate part of their liver to help save the life of someone else?

Answer: One answer would be to repeal the National Organ Transplant Act. This move would create a market for livers and establish a price that would eliminate the shortage. Other ways to increase donations would be to allow donors to claim a tax deduction equal to the value of the liver donated, or to receive scholarships for themselves or members of their family.

The Human Organ Black Market

Law & Order: Special Victims Unit

In one episode of *Special Victims Unit*, the officers try to track down a sleazy kidney dealer. What makes the episode compelling is the tension between doing what the law requires—stopping an illegal kidney transplant mid-surgery—and subsequently wrestling with watching the patient suffer as a result. In addition, the officers interview the dealer, the physician, patients on kidney waiting lists, and an administrator of the national kidney wait list. Their opinions, which run a wide gamut, allow the viewer to experience all of the emotions and arguments for and against the purchase of kidneys.

Each character tugs on viewers' emotions in a different way. The sleazy dealer proudly proclaims that he is making his customers happy and that the officers wouldn't be so judgmental if one of their own family members needed a kidney. The physician who does the transplant explains that he is not driven by making money but by saving lives. The patients all know where they can get an illegal kidney, but most accept their fate within the

On the track of a black-market kidney dealer.

current system. The administrator of the wait list argues that "they have enough trouble getting people to volunteer as it is. What would happen if donors learned that we had made an exception and approved the transplant of an illegally purchased kidney?" By the end of the episode, we see that the economic and ethical dimensions of the issue are not clear-cut.

Despite the success of ova donations, concerns about equity and ethics have made the sale of many vital organs illegal. In its simplest form, the issue is essentially this: why should the affluent, who can afford to pay for organ transplants, continue to live, while the poor, who also need organ transplants, die? That hardly seems fair. Unfortunately, altruism alone has not provided enough organs to meet demand, leading to a shortage of many vital organs. Since we continue to experience shortages of human organs, the supply must be rationed. Whether the rationing takes place through markets, waiting in line, or via some other mechanism is a matter of efficiency. As a result, using markets, in some form, may be one way to prevent avoidable deaths. However, the ethical considerations are significant. For example, if organs can be bought and sold, what would prevent the use of coercion to force people to sell their organs?

Of course, the ethical dilemma becomes moot if viable artificial organs can be created. And in fact, in this regard medical science is making progress toward someday solving the organ shortage. In the meantime, if you are uncomfortable with markets determining the price, remember that relying solely on altruism is not enough. If we really want to increase the supply

Getting the Right Insurance

Many young people go without health insurance after they age out of their parents' plans, figuring that their health will continue to be good. You might be one of these young people. But what happens if, for example, you break a wrist on a weekend ski trip? Do you have $8,000 to pay the medical bill? Going without medical insurance is a high-risk proposition. As an alternative, high-deductible health insurance policies provide a middle ground for healthier consumers who want to insure against catastrophic illness but can handle out-of-pocket expenses for minor treatments. Likewise, going without life insurance is also a high-risk decision once you have a family.

Life insurance protects your family in the event of your death. Most people try to purchase enough life insurance to provide financial security for the family they leave behind. Typically, this means buying enough insurance to pay off the mortgage on the house they own, set up a fund so their children will be able to attend college, and provide a reserve fund for other expenses.

Buying the right life insurance is usually presented as a choice between term insurance and whole life insurance. But don't be fooled. You should buy term insurance. Let's review the differences between these two types of policies.

A term policy includes only life insurance, whereas a whole life policy combines a term policy with an investment component. The term policy provides a fixed benefit upon the death of the insured and covers a specific term that may range up to 30 years, after which the policy expires. A whole life policy buys a specific amount of coverage that does not expire and combines this insurance with an investment component. Whole life policies are typically sold as investment vehicles that the insured can tap into if it becomes necessary to borrow cash later in life. This option may sound appealing, but it is a bad idea because commission rates and fees are very high. If you want to invest your money, you can look on your own to find stock and bond funds with far lower fees and, correspondingly, much higher rates of return.

Premiums for term insurance are low for anyone in good health before age 50. Beyond age 50, the

Wouldn't you want to protect your family's financial future?

premiums rise quickly as the rate of death for any given age group rises. By the time you reach age 65, term insurance is very expensive.

We can illustrate the real value of term insurance by making a direct comparison. Suppose you are a 30-year-old in great health. You can purchase a $1 million policy for a 20-year term for under $1,000 annually or a $1 million whole life policy for $10,000 annually. If you invest the difference, or $9,000, your investment will grow faster than it would as part of a whole life policy. After 20 years, you would have an extra $75,000 saved up due to lower fees alone! If you are also making smart moves by paying down your mortgage and saving for your children's college expenses, there will come a point at which you will need less insurance. In a sense, you will become self-insured. Term insurance is the least expensive bridge to that point. Whole life forces you to save; for some people, that commitment mechanism may be worth pursuing. For others, though, term insurance is the path to greater long-term wealth.

of organs, we need to try incentives. Some proposals along this line include allowing people to receive tax deductions, college scholarships, or guaranteed health care in exchange for donating an organ. All these suggestions would reduce the ethical dilemma while still harnessing the power of incentives to save lives.

Incentives

Conclusion

When people speak about health care, they often debate the merits of universal health care versus private medical care as if the issue involved just those two factors. That misconception, which frames the political debate about health care, obscures the important economic considerations at work on the micro level. The reality is that the healthcare debate exists on many margins and requires complex trade-offs. The way the various participants deal with different healthcare issues affects how well our nation's overall healthcare system functions. Supply and demand works just fine in outlining the incentives that participants face when considering healthcare options; what complicates the analysis is the impact of third parties on the incentives that patients face.

Health care straddles the boundary between microeconomic analysis, which focuses on individual behavior, and macroeconomics, in which society's overarching concern is how to best spend so large an amount of money. Moreover, health decisions are an unavoidable part of our individual lives. Medical expenditures account for one out of every six dollars spent in the United States. Therefore, understanding the micro forces that lead to fundamental changes to the healthcare system will have a large impact—a macro effect—on our economy.

ANSWERING THE BIG QUESTIONS

What are the important issues in the healthcare industry?

* The healthcare debate is about efficiency and cost containment. Increases in longevity and quality of life are subject to diminishing returns and require choices with difficult trade-offs.

* The widespread use of insurance alters the incentives that consumers and producers face when making healthcare decisions. Consumers pay premiums up front and much smaller deductibles and co-payments when seeking medical care. Producers receive the bulk of their revenue from intermediaries such as insurance companies. The result is a system in which consumers demand more medical care because they are insured and many providers have an incentive to order additional tests or procedures that may not be absolutely necessary.

How does asymmetric information affect healthcare delivery?

✳ Asymmetric information (adverse selection, moral hazard, and the principal-agent problem) complicates the way medical insurance is structured. Insurance companies try to structure their plans to align the patient's incentives to seek care only when it is needed and also to seek preventative care. The companies can achieve this by making many preventative care visits free and establishing deductibles and co-payments that are high enough to discourage unnecessary trips to the doctor or the seeking of additional procedures.

✳ Inelastic demand for many medical services, combined with third-party payments that significantly lower out-of-pocket expenses to consumers, gives rise to a serious moral hazard problem in which patients demand more medical care than is medically advisable. As a consequence of the way health care is structured and the moral hazard it creates, the United States devotes a far larger share of its national output to health care than is optimal. To solve a moral hazard problem, it is necessary to fix the incentive structure. This explains why many insurance companies encourage preventative care: it lowers medical costs. This also explains why insurance companies impose payment limits on preventable conditions.

How do demand and supply contribute to high medical costs?

✳ Inelastic demand and third-party payments help explain why medical expenses have risen so rapidly, while licensing helps explain why the supply of medical services is limited. The combination of third-party payments and inelastic demand for medical care increase the quantity of medical care demanded; both factors also result in increased expenditures. As we learned previously, more demand means higher prices.

✳ In addition, licensing requirements limit the supply of key healthcare providers. This provides a supply-side explanation leading to increased medical expenditures. In addition, hospital charges are rarely subject to competitive pressures. In many small communities, there is only one local hospital, clinic, or specialist nearby. This gives providers market power, which they can use in setting prices.

How do incentives influence the quality of health care?

✳ The demand for many replacement organs exceeds the supply made available each year. However, because of the National Organ Transplant Act of 1984, it is illegal to sell most organs in the United States. This restriction results in thousands of deaths annually, many of which would be preventable if people were allowed to sell organs in legal markets.

✳ A single-payer system makes the government the single buyer, or monopsonist, of most medical care. The government uses its leverage as a monopsonist to set compensation levels for providers below the competitive market wage rate.

✳ Single-payer systems ration medical services through increased wait times, whereas private healthcare systems ration medical care through prices.

CONCEPTS YOU SHOULD KNOW

adverse selection (p. 557)
asymmetric information
  (p. 557)

co-insurance payments (p. 555)
co-payments (p. 555)
deductibles (p. 555)

moral hazard (p. 559)
principal-agent problem (p. 558)
single-payer system (p. 567)

QUESTIONS FOR REVIEW

1. What is asymmetric information? Why does it matter for medical care?

2. Give one example each of adverse selection, moral hazard, and the principal-agent problem.

3. For each of the examples you gave in question 2, discuss a solution that lessens the asymmetric information problem.

4. Describe why the marginal product of medical care declines as medical expenditures rise.

5. What are two primary reasons why healthcare demand has increased dramatically over the last 20 years?

6. What is a supply-related reason for high medical care costs?

7. What are the two primary ways in which health care is rationed?

STUDY PROBLEMS (✷ solved at the end of the section)

1. Suppose that a medical specialist charges $300 per consultation. If your insurance charges you a $25 co-pay, what is the marginal cost of your consultation? Suppose that a second patient has a different policy that requires a 25% co-insurance payment, but no co-pay. What is the second patient's marginal cost of the consultation? Which patient is more likely to see the specialist?

✷ 2. Newer automobiles have many safety features, including antilock brakes, side air bags, traction control, and rear backup sensors, to help prevent accidents. Do these safety features lead the drivers of newer vehicles to drive more safely? In your answer, consider how an increased number of safety features affects the problem of moral hazard.

3. A customer wants a new health insurance policy. Even though the customer's medical records indicate a good health history, the insurance company requires a physical exam before coverage can be extended. Why would the insurance company insist on a physical exam?

4. Describe whether the following medical services have elastic or inelastic demand.

  a. an annual physical for someone between the ages of 20 and 35
  b. an MRI used to detect cancer
  c. the removal of a non-cancerous mole on your back
  d. seeing a physician when your child has a 104-degree temperature

5. Most people have two working kidneys, but humans need only one working kidney to survive. If the sale of kidneys was legalized, what would happen to the price and the number of kidneys sold in the market? Would a shortage of kidneys continue to exist? Explain your response.

✷ 6. An isolated community has one hospital. The next closest hospital is two hours away. Given what you have learned about monopoly, what prices would you expect the hospital to charge? How much care would you expect it to provide? Compare the prices and amount of care provided to those of a comparably sized hospital in a major metropolitan area where competition is prevalent.

7. One insurance plan costs $100 a month and has a $50 co-payment for all services. Another insurance plan costs $50 a month and requires patients to pay a 15% co-insurance. A customer is trying to decide which plan to purchase. Which plan would the customer select with an anticipated $200 per month in medical bills? What about $600 per month in medical bills? Set up an equation to determine the monthly amount of medical expenses at which the consumer would be indifferent between the two plans.

8. For each of the following situations, determine whether adverse selection, moral hazard, or the principal-agent problem is at work.

   a. You decide to buy a scalped ticket before a concert, but you are not entirely sure the ticket is legitimate.
   b. A contractor takes a long time to finish the construction work he promised after you gave him his final payment.
   c. You hire a neighborhood teenager to mow your grass once a week over the summer while you are traveling. The teenager mows your grass every three weeks instead.

SOLVED PROBLEMS

2. When drivers feel safer, they drive faster—not more safely. The higher speed offsets the safety gain from safety features that help prevent accidents or make them survivable. Drivers of vehicles who feel especially safe are more likely to take on hazardous conditions and become involved in accidents. In other words, they alter their behavior when driving a safer car. The change in behavior is evidence of a moral hazard problem.

6. Since the demand for medical care is quite inelastic, an isolated hospital with significant monopoly power will charge more and will offer fewer services. In contrast, a comparably sized hospital in a major metropolitan area where competition is prevalent is forced to charge the market price and offer more services to attract customers.

SOLVED PROBLEMS

4. a. If people expect 0% inflation, any positive inflation will stimulate the economy and lower the unemployment rate.

b. If people form their inflation expectations adaptively, they will not anticipate inflation in an election year because it would be a break from their recent experience. Therefore, inflation in election years will consistently lower the rate of unemployment.

c. If expectations are formed rationally, then people will consider the incentives of policymakers during election years. Therefore, they will anticipate higher inflation in those years, and the inflation rate will have no effect on the unemployment rate.

5. a. The increase in inflation is likely a surprise, which means that it stimulates the economy and reduces the unemployment rate to a level below the natural rate.

b. The decrease in inflation is likely a surprise, which means that it slows the economy and increases the unemployment rate to a level above the natural rate.

c. Here there are no inflationary surprises, so the inflation rate does not influence the unemployment rate. Therefore, all else being equal, we should expect the unemployment rate to be near the natural rate.

d. Even though the inflation rate increases, it is not a surprise, so all prices have time to adjust. Therefore, all else being equal, we should expect the unemployment rate to be near the natural rate.

				アルバック	ミツミ
				909	554
11618.53	安	11562.10		+9	+9
部 1624.57	2部	15.96		6752/T	6770/T
11600		+190		パナソニック	アルプス
11630	安	11550		687	608
11600		+195		+16	+3
979.26		+15.78		6753/T	6773/T
981.80	安	976.21		シャープ	パイオニア
1611.68		42		291	195
1612.68	安	1606.60		−19	+5
4.68		0.18		6754/T	6796/T
124.05-15		−0.98		アンリツ	クラリオン
96.66-72		−0.83		1349	125
14000.57		+119.95		47	+4
3161.82		+30.33		6756/T	6841/T
22806.34		+23.90		日立国際	榑河電
				801	987
				+10	+45
				6758/T	6857/T
				ソニー	アドバンテ
				1329	1296

International
ECONOMICS

International Trade

A nation should never trade for goods and services that it can produce itself.

It is generally assumed that nations should try to produce their own goods and services. In particular, it seems intuitive that if the United

MIS CONCEPTION

States can produce a particular good more efficiently than any other nation can produce that good, then the United States should definitely produce that good for itself. But this assumption is not necessarily true. Economics helps us understand that we may be better off letting another nation produce the good and then trading for it later. When we do this, the trade enables us to specialize in production for another good that we can produce best. In addition, it means that a growth in international trade is probably beneficial to nations.

Over the past few decades, the level of trade among the world's nations has risen dramatically. To help illustrate the extent of international trade, we begin this chapter with a look at global trade data. We then consider how international trade affects an economy. Finally, we examine trade barriers and the reasons for their existence.

Imports come into the United States from all over the globe. But do the contents of these shipping containers harm our economy?

BIG QUESTIONS

* Is globalization for real?
* How does international trade help the economy?
* What are the effects of tariffs and quotas?

Is Globalization for Real?

Over the past 70 years, nations all over the world have increased both imports and exports. What this means for you and me is that we now can buy fresh Peruvian strawberries (in February!), roses from Kenya, cars made in Mexico, and electronics produced in South Korea. But the United States also exports more now than in any earlier era. Imports and exports are both up, and this activity indicates that economies around the globe are becoming ever more integrated or interdependent. This is what we mean by *globalization*, and it is changing not only what you purchase but also your future job prospects.

Consider a single popular item: the iPhone. Inside the iPhone are parts made in Germany, Japan, Korea, and the United States. The phone is famously "designed by Apple in California," but it is assembled in China. This single item requires thousands of miles of global shipping before anyone ever receives a call on it.

The modern trade explosion has occurred for many reasons. Among these are lower shipping costs, reduced trade barriers, and increased specialization in world economies. Total world exports of goods and services are now about

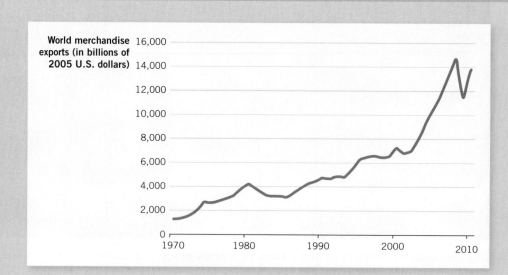

FIGURE 32.1

Real Value of World Merchandise Trade, 1970–2010

Over 40 years, world merchandise trade increased tenfold in real terms, from $1.3 trillion in 1970 to over $13 trillion in 2010. Between 2001 and 2010, merchandise trade doubled.

Source: World Trade Organization.

How many borders does an iPhone cross before it is sold?

one-fourth the size of world GDP. In this section, we look first at the growth in total world trade and then at trends in U.S. trade.

Growth in World Trade

"Globalization" is a buzzword that has gained traction in the past two decades as people have sensed a deeper integration of world economies. In this section, we look at the trade data that confirms this general sentiment. We start with a look at total world exports over time. Figure 32.1 shows total world trade in merchandise (goods) from 1970 to 2010. This data, which is adjusted for inflation, indicates that world trade in goods grew from $1.3 trillion to over $13 trillion. That's a tenfold increase in just 40 years. Furthermore, since 2000, world goods trade has doubled.

World trade has grown, but not just in market value. It has also grown as a percentage of total world output. That is, not only are nations trading more, but they are also trading a greater portion of their GDP. Figure 32.2 shows merchandise trade as a percentage of world GDP. This too has expanded dramatically, more than doubling over 40 years. The data in Figures 32.1 and 32.2 tell us that international trade is now a significant portion of the world economy.

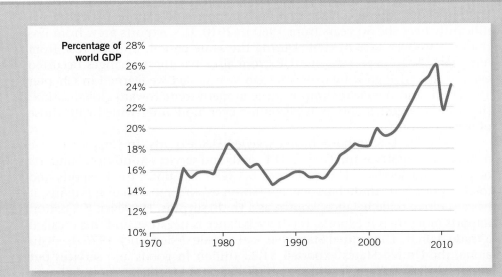

FIGURE 32.2

World Trade as a Percentage of World GDP, 1970–2010

Even as a percentage of world GDP, trade has grown significantly. It more than doubled from 11% in 1970 to over 24% in 2010.

Sources: World Trade Organization; World Bank.

ECONOMICS IN THE REAL WORLD

Nicaragua Is Focused on Trade

Nicaragua, the second-poorest nation in the Western Hemisphere, is trying to escape poverty through international trade. Between 2003 and 2011, its real exports grew from $1.2 trillion to $3.5 trillion.

Trade with Nicaragua is growing in part because the country has established "free zones," where companies can produce goods for export and avoid standard corporate tax rates. Typical Nicaraguan companies pay a myriad of sales taxes, value-added taxes, corporate profit taxes, and dividend taxes. But these do not apply to output that a company exports to other nations. U.S. companies that have taken advantage of production in these free zones include Levi's, Under Armour, and Nike.

All else equal, market-driven international trade certainly helps nations to prosper. Yet while the free zones are increasing exports, the effect on domestic consumers in Nicaragua may not be entirely positive. Because the goods have to be exported in order for the manufacturers to take advantage of the tax breaks, there is very little incentive to produce goods for domestic purchase. ✳

The Levi-Strauss company produces many of its blue jeans in Nicaragua.

Trends in U.S. Trade

The United States is the world's biggest economy. A huge amount of trade takes place among the individual states *inside* the country. For example, residents of Michigan buy oranges from Florida, and Floridians buy cars from Michigan. Still, even with the ability to produce and trade so much within U.S. borders, the nation's participation in international trade rose dramatically in recent years. Figure 32.3 shows U.S. imports and exports as a percentage of GDP from 1960 to 2010.

As you look at the data presented in Figure 32.3, note three features. First, in panel (a) you can see that both imports and exports increased significantly over the 50 years from 1960 to 2010. U.S. exports grew from less than 5% to over 12% of GDP. During the same period, imports rose from less than 5% to over 16% of GDP. Note also that these changes occurred even as real GDP grew by over 3% each year (a fact we learned in Chapter 19). This is another clear glimpse at the modern trend toward globalization: the world's largest economy is becoming ever more intertwined with those of other nations.

Since 1975, U.S. imports have exceeded U.S. exports. In Chapter 19, we defined net exports as total exports of goods and services minus total imports of goods and services. The difference between a nation's total exports and total imports is its **trade balance**. If a nation exports more than it imports, it has a positive trade balance, known as a **trade surplus**. However, if a nation imports more than it exports, the trade balance is negative, and this is called a **trade deficit**. The United States has had a trade deficit since 1975. In 2010 alone, the United States exported $1.83 trillion in goods and services but imported $2.83 trillion, leading to a trade deficit of $1 trillion—no small sum. We will cover this subject further in Chapter 33.

A nation's **trade balance** is the difference between its total exports and total imports.

A **trade surplus** occurs when exports exceed imports, indicating a positive trade balance.

A **trade deficit** occurs when imports exceed exports, indicating a negative trade balance.

(a) Total Goods and Services

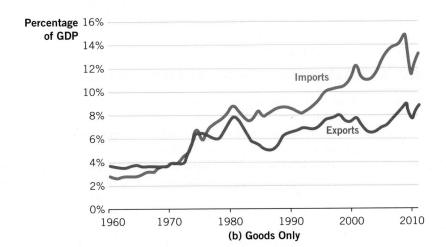

(b) Goods Only

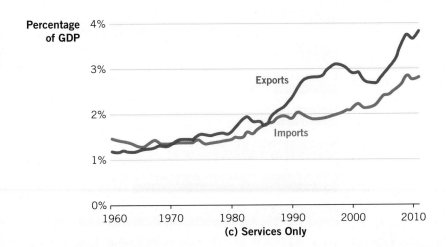

(c) Services Only

FIGURE 32.3

U.S. Exports and Imports, 1960–2010 (as a percentage of GDP)

(a) Both imports and exports are rising in the United States. In addition, the trade balance is becoming more negative over time, as exports are exceeding imports by an increasingly wider margin. This trade deficit grows larger during periods of economic growth and shrinks during recessions (shaded bars).

(b) The trade deficit is driven by a merchandise (goods) deficit, because (c) the United States enjoys a trade surplus in services.

Source: U.S. Bureau of Economic Analysis, *U.S. International Transactions.*

Foreign students who purchase their education in the United States are a picture of one type of U.S. service exports.

Panels (b) and (c) of Figure 32.3 reveal a little-known fact about U.S. trade: while the merchandise (goods) trade deficit is large and growing, the United States actually has a service trade surplus. Popular service exports of the United States include financial, travel, and education services. To put a face on service exports, think about students in your classes who are not U.S. citizens (perhaps this even includes you!). In 2010, the United States exported over $21 billion worth of education services.

Finally, notice how the business cycle affects international trade. During recessionary periods (indicated by the vertical blue-shaded bars in Figure 32.3a), imports generally drop. As the economy recovers, imports begin to rise again. In addition, while exports often drop during recessions, the trade deficit tends to shrink during downturns. Part of this fluctuation reflects the way imports and exports are calculated, which we will discuss in Chapter 33. For now, note the strong relationship between trade and economic activity: trade expands during economic expansions and contracts during recessions.

Major Trading Partners of the United States

In 2011, the United States imported goods and services from 238 nations. However, 60% of goods imports came from just seven nations. Figure 32.4 shows the value of imports from and exports to these top seven trading partners of the United States.

In the past, our closest neighbors—Canada and Mexico—were our chief trading partners. From Canada we get motor vehicles, oil, natural gas, and

---

FIGURE 32.4

Major Goods Trading Partners of the United States, 2011 (in billions of dollars)

Fully 60% of all U.S. goods imports come from the seven nations shown here. We export more to Canada and Mexico than to other nations, but we import more from China. The U.S. trade deficit with China is almost $300 billion.

Source: U.S. Bureau of Economic Analysis.

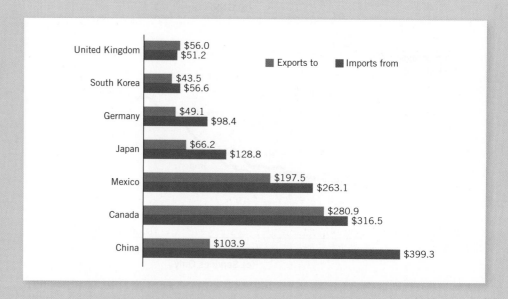

■ Exports to   ■ Imports from

Nation	Exports to	Imports from
United Kingdom	$56.0	$51.2
South Korea	$43.5	$56.6
Germany	$49.1	$98.4
Japan	$66.2	$128.8
Mexico	$197.5	$263.1
Canada	$280.9	$316.5
China	$103.9	$399.3

PRACTICE WHAT YOU KNOW

Trade in Goods and Services: Deficit or Surplus?

The United States imports many goods from Japan, including automobiles, electronics, and medical instruments. But we also export many services to Japan, such as financial and travel services. The table below presents trade data between the United States and Japan in 2011. (All figures are in billions of U.S. dollars.)

	Exports to Japan	Imports from Japan
Goods	$66	$129
Services	$47	$25

Sony PlayStations are a popular U.S. import from Japan.

Question: Using the data shown above, how would you compute the U.S. goods trade balance with Japan? Is the balance a surplus or a deficit?

Answer: The U.S. goods trade balance equals:

goods exports − goods imports
$$= \$66 \text{ billion} - \$129 \text{ billion} = -\$63 \text{ billion}$$

This is a deficit, since imports exceed exports and the trade balance is negative.

Question: Now how would you compute the U.S. service trade balance with Japan? Is the balance a surplus or a deficit?

Answer: The U.S. services trade balance equals:

service exports − service imports
$$= \$47 \text{ billion} - \$25 \text{ billion} = \$22 \text{ billion}$$

This is a surplus, since exports exceed imports and the trade balance is positive.

Question: Finally, how would you compute the overall U.S. trade balance with Japan, which includes both goods and services? Is this overall trade balance a surplus or a deficit?

Answer: The overall U.S. trade balance equals:

goods and service exports − goods and service imports
$$= \$113 \text{ billion} - \$154 \text{ billion} = -\$41 \text{ billion}$$

This is a deficit, since imports exceed exports and the trade balance is negative.

Data source: Office of the United States Trade Representative.

Is there anything in this picture *not* produced in China?

many other goods and services. From Mexico we get coffee, computers, household appliances, and gold. Recently, transportation costs have decreased and we are trading in volume with other countries. For example, total imports from China alone are now roughly $400 billion, up from $105 billion (adjusted for inflation) a decade ago. Popular Chinese imports include electronics, toys, and clothing.

Canada and Mexico buy the most U.S. exports. To Canada we export cars, car parts, computers, and agricultural products. To Mexico we export cars, car parts, computers, and meat, among many other items. Financial and travel services are major U.S. exports to all our major trading partners.

How Does International Trade Help the Economy?

Trade creates value

In this section, we explain how comparative advantage and specialization make it possible to achieve gains from trade among nations. To keep the analysis simple, we will assume that two trading partners—the United States and Mexico—only produce two items, clothes and food. This will enable us to demonstrate that trade creates value in the absence of any restrictions.

Comparative Advantage

In Chapter 2, we saw that trade creates value and that comparative advantage makes this possible. Gains arise when a nation specializes in production and exchanges its output with a trading partner. In other words, each nation should produce the good it is best at making and trade with other nations for the goods they are best at making. When this happens, the transaction leads to lower costs of production and maximizes the combined output of all nations involved.

For example, assume that the U.S. workforce is generally more skilled than that of Mexico and that the United States has much more farmland. Mexico has a less skilled workforce and tends to produce products that require more labor than capital. Therefore, Mexico has a comparative advantage in producing labor-intensive goods such as clothing, and the United States has a comparative advantage in producing capital-intensive goods such as food.

In Figure 32.5, we see the production possibilities frontier (the PPF curve) for each country when it does *not* specialize and trade. In panel (a), Mexico can produce at any point along its PPF. This means that it could produce 900 million (M) units, or articles, of clothing if it does not make any food, or 300 million tons of food if it does not make any clothing. Neither extreme is especially desirable since it would mean that Mexico would have to do without either clothing or food. As a result, Mexico will choose to operate somewhere in between the two extremes. In panel (a), we show Mexico operating along its production possibilities frontier at 450 million articles of clothing and 150 tons of food. Panel (b) shows that the United States could produce 400 million articles of clothing if it does not make any food, or 800 million tons of food if it does not make any clothing. Like Mexico, the United States will choose to operate somewhere in between—for example, at 300 million articles of clothing and 200 million tons of food.

To see whether gains from trade are able to make both countries better off, we must first examine the opportunity cost that each country faces when making these two goods. In Mexico, producing 150 million tons of food means giving up the production of 450 million articles of clothing ($900 - 450 = 450$). Thus, each ton of food incurs an opportunity cost of three articles of clothing, yielding a ratio of 1:3, or one ton of food per three articles of clothing. In the United States, producing 200 million tons of food means giving up production of 100 million articles of clothing ($400 - 300 = 100$). Each ton of food incurs an opportunity cost of one-half an article of clothing, yielding a ratio of 2:1. Table 32.1 shows the initial production choices and the opportunity costs for both nations.

As long as the opportunity cost of the production of the two goods differs between the two countries, as it does here, trade has the potential to benefit both. The key to making trade mutually beneficial in this case is to find a trading ratio between 1:3 and 2:1. For instance, if Mexico and the United States establish a 1:1 trading ratio, it would enable Mexico to acquire food at a lower cost from the United States than the cost of producing food itself. At the same time, the United States would be able to acquire clothing from Mexico at a lower cost than the cost of producing the clothing itself.

FIGURE 32.5

The Production Possibilities Frontier for Mexico and the United States without Specialization and Trade

(a) Mexico chooses to operate along its production possibilities curve at 450 million articles of clothing and 150 tons of food. Each ton of food incurs an opportunity cost of three articles of clothing—a ratio of 1:3.

(b) The United States chooses to operate along its production possibilities curve at 300 million articles of clothing and 200 million tons of food. Each ton of food incurs an opportunity cost of one-half an article of clothing—a ratio of 2:1.

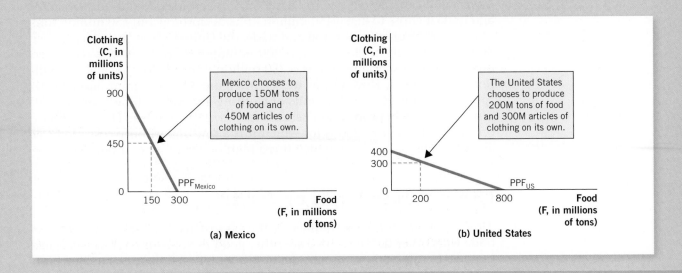

TABLE 32.1

Output and Opportunity Costs for Mexico and the United States

	Chosen output level		Opportunity cost	
	Food (millions of tons)	Clothing (millions of units)	Food (F)	Clothing (C)
Mexico	150	450	3 C	⅓ F
United States	200	300	½ C	2 F

Figure 32.6 shows the effects of a 1:1 trade agreement on the joint production possibilities frontier for each country. If the two countries trade, each can specialize in its comparative advantage. This means that the United States produces food and Mexico produces clothing.

Notice that specialization and trade benefits both countries. Let's begin with Mexico as shown in panel (a). Mexico specializes in the production of clothing, producing 900 million units. It then exports 400 million units of clothing to the United States and imports 400 million tons of food from the United States in return—this is the 1:1 trade ratio we identified previously. Therefore, Mexico ends up at point M_2 with 500 million units of clothing and 400 million tons of food. Notice that Mexico's production without trade (at point M_1) was 450 million units of clothing and 150 tons of food. Therefore, specialization and trade have made Mexico better off by 50 million units of clothing and 250 million tons of food.

Now let's look at the United States in panel (b). The country specializes in the production of food, producing 800 million tons. It exports 400 million tons of food to Mexico and imports 400 million units of clothing from Mexico in return. Therefore, the United States ends up at point US_2 with 400 million units of clothing and 400 million tons of food. Notice that U.S. production without trade (at point US_1) was 300 million units of clothing and 200 tons of food. Therefore, specialization and trade have made the United States better off by 100 million units of clothing and 200 million tons of food.

The combined benefits that Mexico and the United States enjoy are even more significant. As we saw in Figure 32.5, when Mexico did not specialize and trade it chose to make 450 million units of clothing and 150 million tons of food. Without specialization and trade, the United States chose to produce 300 million units of clothing and 200 million tons of food. The combined output without specialization was 750 million units of clothing and 350 million tons of food. However, as we see in Figure 32.6, the joint output with specialization is 900 million units of clothing and 800 million tons of food. Trade is a win-win proposition because each country is able to (1) concentrate on the production of goods for which it is a low-opportunity-cost producer and (2) trade for goods for which it is a high-opportunity-cost producer.

Other Advantages of Trade

Although comparative advantage is the biggest reason that many nations trade with other nations, there are other good reasons for nations to engage in trade. In this section, we consider how international trade encourages both economies of scale and increased competition, and how these factors can help an economy to grow.

Economies of Scale

When a nation specializes its production, it can take advantage of lower production costs that can accompany large-scale production processes. This is especially important for smaller nations that do not have a workforce big enough to support the domestic production of large-scale items such as automobiles, television sets, steel, and aluminum. However, once a smaller nation has free access to larger markets, it can effectively specialize in what it does best and generate low per-unit costs through exports.

In Figures 32.5 and 32.6, the production possibilities frontier is shown as a straight line. This makes the computation of the ratios fairly simple and holds the opportunity cost constant. However, in the real world, access to new markets can create economies of scale and, therefore, lower per-unit costs as production expands. Increased production gives companies the opportunity to economize on distribution costs and marketing, and to utilize assembly lines and other forms of automation.

Consider how a small textile company based in Mexico fares under this arrangement. With international trade, the company can expand its sales into the United States—a much larger market. This move creates additional

FIGURE 32.6

The Joint Production Possibilities Frontier for Mexico and the United States with Specialization and Trade

(a) After Mexico specializes in clothing and trades with the United States, it is better off by 50 million units of clothing and 250 million tons of food (compare points M_1 and M_2).

(b) After the United States specializes in food and trades with Mexico, it is better off by 100 million units of clothing and 200 million tons of food (compare points US_1 and US_2).

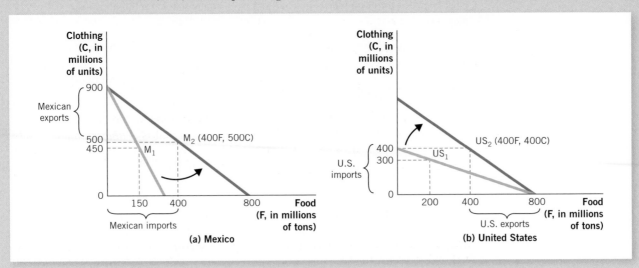

PRACTICE WHAT YOU KNOW

Does China enjoy a comparative advantage in textile production?

Opportunity Cost and Comparative Advantage: Determining Comparative Advantage

U.S. trade with mainland China has exploded in the past decade, with goods imports reaching $400 billion a year and exports up to $100 billion. In this question, we consider a hypothetical production possibilities frontier for food and textiles in both China and the United States.

The table below presents daily production possibilities for a typical worker in both China and the United States, assuming these are the only goods produced in both countries. (The numbers represent units of food and units of textiles.)

	Output per worker per day	
	Food	Textiles
China	1	2
United States	9	3

Question: What are the opportunity costs of food production for both China and the United States?

Answer: The opportunity cost of food production in China is the amount of textile production that is foregone for a single unit of food output. Since a Chinese worker can produce 2 textile units in a day and 1 unit of food, the opportunity cost of 1 unit of food is *2 textiles*.

In the United States, a worker can produce 3 textile units in one day or 9 units of food. Thus, the opportunity cost of 1 unit of food is just ⅓ *textile unit*.

Question: What are the opportunity costs of textile production for both China and the United States?

Answer: The opportunity cost of textile production in China is the amount of food production that is foregone for a single textile produced. Since a Chinese worker can produce 1 unit of food in a day and 2 textile units, the opportunity cost of 1 textile unit is *½ unit of food*.

In the United States, a worker can produce 9 units of food in one day or 3 textile units. Thus, the opportunity cost of 1 textile unit is *3 units of food*.

Question: Which nation has a comparative advantage in food production? Which nation has a comparative advantage in textile production?

Answer: The United States has a lower opportunity cost of food production (⅓ versus 2 textile units), so its comparative advantage is in food production. China has a lower opportunity cost of textile production (½ versus 3 units of food), so it has a comparative advantage in textile production.

demand, which translates into added sales. A larger volume of sales enables the textile firm's production, marketing, and sales to become more efficient. The firm can purchase fabrics in bulk, expand its distribution network, and use volume advertising.

Increased Competition

Another largely unseen benefit from trade is increased competition. In fact, increased competition from foreign suppliers forces domestic firms to become more innovative and to compete in terms of both price and quality. Competition also gives consumers more options to choose from, which enables consumers to purchase a broader array of products that better match their needs. For example, many cars are produced in the United States, but foreign automobiles offer U.S. consumers greater variety and help to keep the prices of domestically made cars lower than they would be otherwise.

Trade Agreements and the WTO

Because trading is so beneficial, nations often reach trade agreements that specify the conditions of free trade. For example, the North American Free Trade Agreement (NAFTA), which was signed in 1992, eliminated nearly all trade restrictions among Canada, Mexico, and the United States. Currently, the United States has trade agreements with 20 nations.

Even though trade agreements often stipulate protections for particular industries (most notably, agriculture), they still increase trade among nations. For example, as a result of NAFTA, real U.S. imports and exports of goods with Canada and Mexico have both doubled. In 1993 the United States exported $183 billion worth of goods to Canada, but by 2010 this amount rose to $350 billion. Over the same period, exports to Mexico grew from $80 billion to $201 billion. Imports from both nations also expanded: imports from Canada grew from $180 billion to $332 billion, and imports from Mexico grew from $76 billion to $260 billion. The reduction in trade barriers has enabled all three nations to move toward the production of goods and services for which they enjoy a comparative advantage.

The World Trade Organization (WTO) is an international organization that facilitates trade agreements among nations. The WTO also works to resolve trade disputes. For example, in 2012 the WTO helped to end a 20-year disagreement between Latin American banana exporters and the European Union over a tax on imported bananas.

NAFTA created a broad, geographically connected network of lower trade barriers, fostering growth across much of North America.

What Are the Effects of Tariffs and Quotas?

Despite the benefits of free trade, significant trade barriers such as import taxes often exist. For example, almost every shoe purchased in the United States is made overseas; but with few exceptions, the U.S. government taxes each pair of shoes that comes across its borders to be sold. In fact, many

Major U.S. Trade Partners

Though the United States imports goods from over 230 nations in the world, just 7 of those countries account for over 60% of these imports. These same 7 countries buy more U.S. goods exports than any other country as well. Clearly, our major trade partners produce numerous items that Americans demand, and the United States produces numerous items that these countries desire.

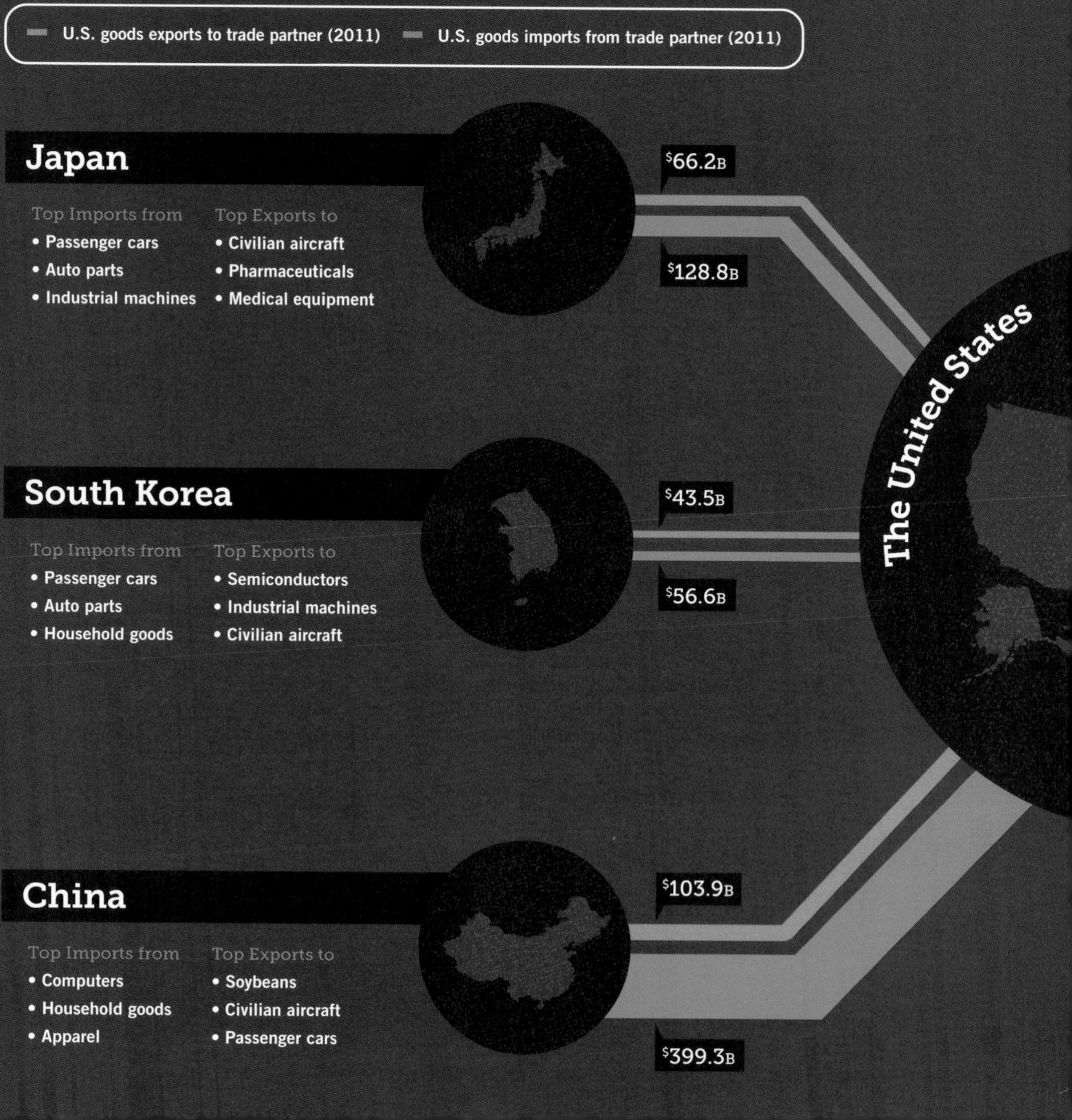

▬ U.S. goods exports to trade partner (2011) ▬ U.S. goods imports from trade partner (2011)

Japan

Top Imports from	Top Exports to
• Passenger cars	• Civilian aircraft
• Auto parts	• Pharmaceuticals
• Industrial machines	• Medical equipment

$66.2B

$128.8B

South Korea

Top Imports from	Top Exports to
• Passenger cars	• Semiconductors
• Auto parts	• Industrial machines
• Household goods	• Civilian aircraft

$43.5B

$56.6B

The United States

China

Top Imports from	Top Exports to
• Computers	• Soybeans
• Household goods	• Civilian aircraft
• Apparel	• Passenger cars

$103.9B

$399.3B

- What U.S. industry generates the most universal demand from our trading partners?

- Based on the list of U.S. imports, how would you finish this sentence? "Americans sure love their _____!"

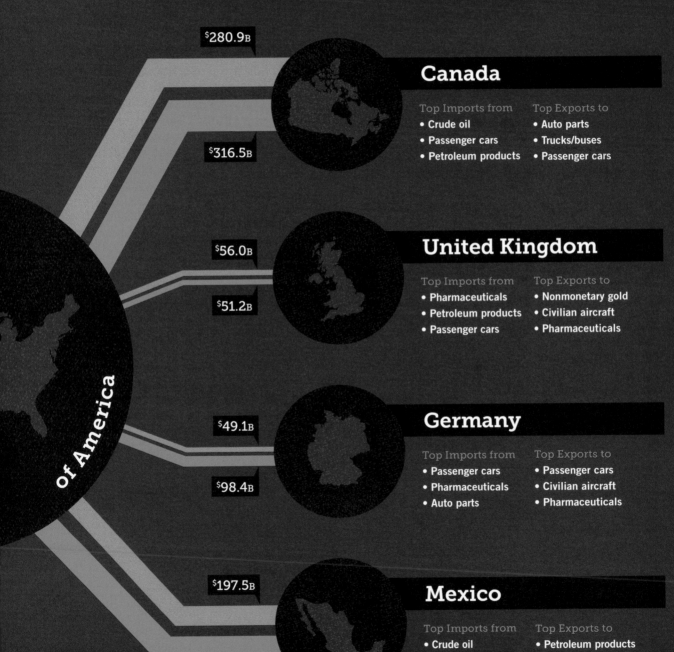

$280.9B

$316.5B

Canada

Top Imports from	Top Exports to
• Crude oil	• Auto parts
• Passenger cars	• Trucks/buses
• Petroleum products	• Passenger cars

$56.0B

$51.2B

United Kingdom

Top Imports from	Top Exports to
• Pharmaceuticals	• Nonmonetary gold
• Petroleum products	• Civilian aircraft
• Passenger cars	• Pharmaceuticals

$49.1B

$98.4B

Germany

Top Imports from	Top Exports to
• Passenger cars	• Passenger cars
• Pharmaceuticals	• Civilian aircraft
• Auto parts	• Pharmaceuticals

$197.5B

$263.1B

Mexico

Top Imports from	Top Exports to
• Crude oil	• Petroleum products
• Passenger cars	• Auto parts
• Auto parts	• Computer accessories

of America

imported shoes are taxed by 37.5% of their value. For example, a new pair of Nike tennis shoes imported from Vietnam is subject to a 20% import tax. If these shoes are valued at $100, the importer has to pay a $20 tax on them.

Import taxes like those on footwear are not unusual. In this section, we explore two of the most common types of trade barriers: *tariffs* and *quotas*. Once you understand how these barriers function, we will look more closely at common economic and political justifications for restricting international trade and determine whether or not they are effective.

Tariffs

Tariffs
are taxes levied on imported goods and services.

Tariffs are taxes levied on imported goods and services. A tariff is paid by the producer of the imported good when the good arrives in a foreign country. Figure 32.7 illustrates the impact of a tariff on foreign shoes. In order to assess how a tariff affects the market price of shoes in the United States, we observe the relationship between domestic demand and domestic supply.

We begin by noting that domestic supply and demand would be in equilibrium at $140 per pair of shoes. However, this is not the market price if free trade prevails. If trade is unrestricted, imports are free to enter the domestic market, so that supply increases; this reduces the domestic price (P_D) to the world price (P_F with $_F$ representing "foreign"), which is $100. At $100, the total quantity demanded is Q_F. Part of this quantity is produced domestically (Q_{D1}), and part is imported from foreign sources ($Q_F - Q_{D1}$).

FIGURE 32.7

The Impact of a Tariff
Without a tariff, the domestic market is dominated by imports. However, when a tariff is imposed, the price rises and domestic production expands from Q_{D1} to Q_{D2}. At the same time, imports fall to $Q_T - Q_{D2}$. Tariffs also create deadweight loss (shaded areas A and B), revenue for the government (area T), and increased producer surplus for domestic firms (area C).

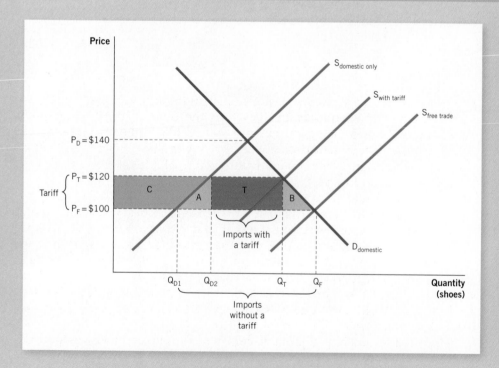

The tariff, T, is added to the world price for any firm wishing to import shoes into the United States. This requirement pushes the domestic price up from $100 to $120 (represented as P_T, reflecting the price with tariff). Foreign producers must pay the tariff, but domestic producers do not have to pay it. One consequence of this situation is that the amount imported drops to $Q_T - Q_{D2}$. At the same time, the amount supplied by domestic producers rises along the supply curve from Q_{D1} to Q_{D2}. Since domestic suppliers are now able to charge $120 and also sell more, they are better off.

We can see this outcome visually by noting that suppliers gain producer surplus equal to the shaded area marked C. The government also benefits from the tariff revenue, shown as shaded area T. The tariff is a pure transfer from foreign suppliers to the government. In addition, there are two areas of deadweight loss, A and B. These harm consumers because the price is higher and some people are forced to switch from foreign brands to domestic shoes. Areas A and B represent the efficiency loss associated with the tariff—or the unrealized gains from trade.

Consider for a moment just how damaging a tariff is. Foreign producers are the lowest-cost producer of shoes, but they are limited in how much they can sell. This situation makes little sense from an import/export standpoint. If foreign shoe manufacturers cannot sell as many shoes in the United States, they will acquire fewer dollars to use in purchasing U.S. exports. So not only does this mean higher shoe prices for U.S. consumers, but it also means fewer sales for U.S. exporters. We will explore the financial implications in more detail in Chapter 33.

The effect of a country's tariff is like moving the country further away from other countries, thereby increasing transportation costs. Both tariffs and transportation costs add to the total cost of selling shoes in the domestic market. With a tariff, a nation isolates itself from others around the globe—on purpose.

Quotas

Sometimes, instead of taxing imports, governments use *import quotas* to restrict trade. **Import quotas** are limits on the quantity of products that can be imported into a country. Quotas function like tariffs with one crucial exception: the government does not receive any tax revenue. In the United States today, there are quotas on many products, including milk, tuna, olives, peanuts, cotton, and sugar.

Import quotas are limits on the quantity of products that can be imported into a country.

One famous example of quotas comes from the automobile industry of the 1980s and 1990s. During that period, Japan agreed to a "voluntary" quota on the number of vehicles it would export to the United States. Why would any group of firms agree to supply less than it could? The answer involves politics and economics. By limiting supply, foreign producers avoid having a tariff applied to their goods. Also, since the supply is somewhat smaller than it would otherwise be, foreign suppliers can charge higher prices. The net result is that a "voluntary" quota makes financial sense if it helps a producing nation to avoid a tariff.

Figure 32.8 shows how a quota placed on foreign-made shoes would work. The figure looks quite similar to Figure 32.7, and this is not an accident. If we set the quota amount on foreign shoes equal to the imports after the tariff illustrated in Figure 32.7, the result is exactly the same with one notable exception: the green tariff rectangle, T, in Figure 32.7 has been replaced with a blue rectangle, F.

The quota is a strict limit on the number of shoes that may be imported into the United States. This limit pushes up the domestic price of shoes from $100 to $120 (represented as P_Q, reflecting the price under a quota). Because foreign producers must abide by the quota, one consequence is that the amount imported drops to $Q_Q - Q_{D2}$ (where Q_Q represents the total quantity supplied after the imposition of the quota). The smaller amount of imports causes the quantity supplied by domestic producers to rise along the supply curve from Q_{D1} to Q_{D2}. Since domestic suppliers are now able to charge $40 more and also sell more, they are better off. We can see this visually by noting that suppliers gain producer surplus equal to shaded area C (as we observed in Figure 32.7). As a result, domestic suppliers are indifferent between a tariff and a quota of equal magnitude. So, like before, there are two areas of deadweight loss, A and B, in which consumers lose because the price is higher and some people are forced to switch from foreign brands to domestic ones.

As you can see in the deadweight loss in shaded areas A and B, a quota suffers the same efficiency loss as a tariff. Even though domestic suppliers are indifferent between a tariff and a quota system, foreign producers are not. Under a quota, they are able to keep the revenue generated in the blue rectangle, F. Under a tariff, the equivalent rectangle, T, shown in Figure 32.7, is the tax revenue generated by the tariff.

FIGURE 32.8

The Impact of a Quota

Without a quota, the domestic market is dominated by imports. However, when a quota is imposed, the price rises and domestic production expands from Q_{D1} to Q_{D2}. At the same time, imports fall to $Q_Q - Q_{D2}$. Quotas create deadweight loss (shaded areas A and B), a gain for foreign suppliers (area F), and increased producer surplus for domestic firms (area C).

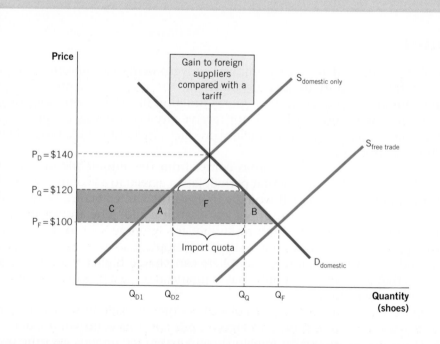

ECONOMICS IN THE REAL WORLD

Inexpensive Shoes Face the Highest Tariffs

Overall, U.S. tariffs average less than 2%, but inexpensive shoes face a tariff 20 times that amount. What makes inexpensive imported shoes so "dangerous"? To help answer this question, a history lesson is in order.

Just 40 years ago, shoe manufacturers in the United States employed 250,000 workers. Today, the number of shoe workers is less than 3,000—and none of those workers assemble cheap shoes. Most of the shoe jobs have moved to low-labor-cost countries. But the shoe tariff, which was enacted to save domestic jobs, remains the same. Not a single sneaker costing less than $3 a pair is made in the United States, so the protection isn't saving any jobs. In contrast, goods such as cashmere sweaters, snakeskin purses, and silk shirts face low or no import tariffs. Other examples range from the 2.5% tariff on cars, to duty-free treatment for cell phones, and tariffs of 4% and 5% for TV sets.

Shoppers who buy their shoes at Walmart and Payless shoe stores face the impact of shoe tariffs that approach 50% for the cheapest shoes, about 20% for a pair of name-brand running shoes, and about 9% for designer shoes from Gucci or Prada. This situation has the unintended consequence of passing along the tax burden to those who are least able to afford it, making the shoe tariff easily one of the most regressive taxes.

Why do cheap imported shoes face such a high tariff?

One could reasonably argue that the shoe tariff is one of the United States' worst taxes. First, it failed to protect the U.S. shoe industry—the shoe jobs disappeared a long time ago. Second, consumers who are poor pay a disproportionate amount of the tax. Third, families with children pay even more because they have more feet that need shoes. ✳

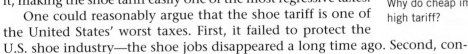

Reasons Given for Trade Barriers

Considering all that we have discussed about the gains from trade and the inefficiencies associated with tariffs and quotas, you might be surprised to learn that trade restrictions are quite common. In this section, we consider some of the reasons for the persistence of trade barriers. These include national security, protection of infant industries, retaliation for *dumping*, and favors to special interests.

National Security

Many people believe that certain industries, such as weapons, energy, and transportation, are vital to our nation's defense. They argue that without the ability to produce its own missiles, firearms, aircraft, and other strategically significant assets, a nation could find itself relying on its enemies. Thus, people often argue that certain industries should be protected in the interest of national security.

On the one hand, it is certainly important for any trade arrangement to consider national security. On the other hand, in practice this argument has been used to justify trade restrictions on goods and services from friendly nations with whom we have active, open trade relations. For example, in 2002 the United States imposed tariffs on steel imports. Some policymakers argued

Free Trade

Star Wars Episode I: The Phantom Menace

The Phantom Menace (1999) is an allegory about peace, prosperity, taxation, and protectionism. As the movie opens, we see the Republic slowly falling apart. Planetary trade has been at the heart of the galactic economy. Interplanetary trade could support a local economy, but in many cases the high levels of economic interaction and the massive scale of exchange required for an advanced society could only be funded by exports. The central conflict in the movie is the Trade Federation's attempt to enforce its franchise by trying to intimidate a small planet, Naboo, which believes in free trade and peace.

The leader of the Naboo, Queen Amidala, refuses to pursue any path that might start a war. Her country is subjected to an excessive tariff and blockade, so she decides to appeal to the central government for help in ending the trade restrictions. However, she discovers that the Republic's Galactic Senate is ineffectual, so she returns home and prepares to defend her country.

Meanwhile, two Jedi who work for the Republic are sent to broker a deal between Naboo and the Trade Federation, but they get stranded on Tatooine, a desert planet located in the Outer Rim. In the Outer Rim, three necessary ingredients for

Disruptive, barriers to trade are!

widespread trade—the rule of law, sound money, and honesty—are missing. As a consequence, when the Jedi try to purchase some new parts for their ship, they find out that no one accepts the credit-based money of the Republic. The Jedi are forced to barter, a process that requires that each trader have exactly what the other wants. This situation results in a complicated negotiation between one of the Jedi and a local parts dealer. The scenes on Tatooine show why institutions, economies of scale, and competition matter so much for trade to succeed.

We encourage you to watch *The Phantom Menace* again with a fresh set of eyes trained on the economics behind the special effects!

---

that the steel tariffs were necessary because steel is an essential resource for national security. But, in fact, most imported steel comes from Canada and Brazil, which are traditional allies of the United States.

Infant Industries

The **infant industry argument** states that domestic industries need trade protection until they are established and able to compete internationally.

Another argument in support of steel tariffs in the United States was that the U.S. steel industry needed some time to implement new technologies that would enable it to compete with steel producers in other nations. This reflects what is known as the **infant industry argument**, which states that domestic industries need trade protection until they are established and able to compete internationally. According to this point of view, once the fledgling industry gains traction and can support itself, the trade restrictions can be removed.

However, reality doesn't work this way. Firms that lobby for protection are often operating in an established industry. For example, the steel industry in the United States is over 100 years old. Establishing trade barriers is often politically popular, but finding ways to remove them is politically difficult. There was a time when helping to establish the steel, sugar, cotton, or peanut industries might have made sense based on the argument for helping new industries. But the tariffs that protect those industries have remained, in one form or another, for over 100 years.

Anti-Dumping

In 2009, the U.S. government imposed tariffs on radial car tires imported from China. These tariffs began at 35% and then gradually decreased to 25% before being phased out after three years. The argument in support of this tariff was that Chinese tire makers were *dumping* their tires in U.S. markets. **Dumping** occurs when a foreign supplier sells a good below the price it charges in its home country. As the name implies, dumping is often a deliberate effort to gain a foothold in a foreign market. It can also be the result of subsidies within foreign countries.

In this case, the WTO allows for special countervailing duties to offset the subsidies. In essence, the United States places a tariff on the imported tires to restore a level playing field. Or, in other words, anytime a foreign entity decides to charge a lower price in order to penetrate a market, a firm, or a nation, the country that is dumped on is likely to respond by imposing a tariff or quota in order to protect its domestic industries from foreign takeover.

Special Interests

The imposition of trade barriers is often referred to as "protection." This term raises the questions *Who is being protected?* and *What are they being protected from?* We have seen that trade barriers drive up domestic prices and lead to a lower quantity of goods or services in the market where they are imposed. This situation does not protect consumers. In fact, tariffs and quotas protect domestic producers from international competition. Steel tariffs were put in place to help domestic steel producers, and tire tariffs were put in place to help domestic tire producers.

When we see trade barriers, the publicly stated reason is generally one of the three reasons we have already discussed: national security, infant industry protection, or anti-dumping. But we must also recognize that these barriers may be put in place as a favor to special interest groups that have much to gain at the expense of domestic consumers. For example, due to sugar import regulations, U.S. consumers pay twice as much for sugar as the rest of the world does. Thus, while sugar tariffs and quotas protect U.S. sugar producers from international competition, they cost U.S. consumers nearly $4 billion in 2011 alone. This outcome represents a special-interest gain at the expense of U.S. consumers. If it were a tax that was transferred from consumers to producers, it would likely not persist. However, this kind of favor doesn't appear in the federal budget.

Which of these, the infant or the adult, is a better representation of the U.S. steel industry?

Dumping
occurs when a foreign supplier sells a good below the price it charges in its home country.

PRACTICE WHAT YOU KNOW

Tariffs and Quotas: The Winners and Losers from Trade Barriers

In 2009, the United States imposed a tariff of 35% on radial car tire imports from China. The result of this tariff was a drop in imports of these tires from 13 million tires to just 5.6 million tires in one quarter. In addition, within a year, average radial car tire prices rose by about $8 per tire in the United States: the average price of Chinese tires rose from $30.79 to $37.98, while the average price of tires from all other nations rose from $53.94 to $62.05.

Why should we penalize Chinese tire imports?

Question: Who were the winners and losers from this tire tariff?

Answer: The primary winners were the producers of tires from everywhere except China. Since this tariff was targeted at a single nation, it did not affect tire producers in other nations. Non-Chinese tire producers realized an average of $8 more per tire. In addition, given that the tire tariff is a tax, it also produced some tax revenue.

The primary losers were U.S. tire consumers, who saw prices rise by about $8 per tire, or $32 for a set of four tires.

Data source: Gary Clyde Hufbauer and Sean Lowry, "U.S. Tire Tariffs: Saving Few Jobs at High Cost," Policy Brief (Washington, D.C.: Peterson Institute for International Economics, April 9, 2012).

Conclusion

We began this chapter with the misconception that nations should not trade for goods and services that they can produce for themselves. The concept of comparative advantage contradicts this misconception by showing that nations can gain by (1) specializing in the production of goods and services for which they have the lowest opportunity cost, and then (2) trading for the other goods and services that they wish to consume.

International trade is expanding all over the world. The United States now imports and exports more than at any time in its history. Increased trade is generally positive for all nations involved. Trade barriers still exist around the globe for various reasons, but these barriers are eroding worldwide.

In Chapter 33, we will take a close look at exchange rates, which influence trade flows, and also at a nation's balance between imports and exports.

ANSWERING THE BIG QUESTIONS

Is globalization for real?

* Since 1970, world exports have grown from 11% to about 25%. In the United States, imports and exports have both grown rapidly since World War II. There's no doubt that the world economy is becoming more integrated.

How does international trade help the economy?

* Gains from trade occur when a nation specializes in production and exchanges its output with a trading partner. For this arrangement to work, each nation must produce goods for which it is a low-opportunity-cost producer and then trade the goods that it has produced in exchange for goods for which it is a high-opportunity-cost producer.

* In addition, trade benefits nations' economies through economies of scale and international competition.

What are the effects of tariffs and quotas?

* Trade restrictions such as tariffs and quotas are surprisingly common. Tariffs are a tax on imports; quotas are a quantity restriction on imports.

* Proponents of trade restrictions often cite the need to protect defense-related industries and fledgling firms, and fend off dumping. But protectionist policies can also serve as political favors to special interest groups.

CONCEPTS YOU SHOULD KNOW

dumping (p. 1013)
import quota
  (p. 1009)

infant industry argument
  (p. 1012)
tariff (p. 1008)

trade balance (p. 996)
trade deficit (p. 996)
trade surplus (p. 996)

REVIEW QUESTIONS

1. What are three problems with trade restrictions? What are three reasons often given for trade restrictions?

2. What would happen to the standard of living in the United States if all foreign trade were eliminated?

3. How might a nation's endowment of natural resources, labor, and climate shape the nature of its comparative advantage?

4. Why might foreign producers voluntarily agree to a quota rather than face an imposed tariff?

5. Tariffs reduce the volume of imports. Do tariffs also reduce the volume of exports? Explain your response.

STUDY PROBLEMS (*solved at the end of the section)

1. Consider the following table for the neighboring nations of Quahog and Pawnee. Assume that the opportunity cost of producing each good is constant.

Product	Quahog	Pawnee
Meatballs (per hour)	4,000	2,000
Clams (per hour)	8,000	1,000

a. What is the opportunity cost of producing meatballs in Quahog? What is the opportunity cost of producing clams in Quahog?
b. What is the opportunity cost of producing meatballs in Pawnee? What is the opportunity cost of producing clams in Pawnee?
c. Based on your answers in parts (a) and (b), which nation has a comparative advantage in producing meatballs? Which nation has a comparative advantage in producing clams?

2. Let's think about how imports affect official GDP statistics. Recall from Chapter 19 that GDP is computed as:

$$GDP = Y = C + I + G + NX$$

Assume that originally U.S. GDP is $10 trillion, but that the economy is closed and there are no imports or exports. Now the nation of Bataslava begins selling high-quality automobiles in the United States but charges a very low price—say, $5 each. Assume that U.S. consumers use this opportunity to substitute out of U.S. produced automobiles and into automobiles from Bataslava, and that spending on other U.S. goods does not change.

a. What happens to U.S. GDP going forward?
b. Is this a positive or negative development for the United States? Why?
c. What would be an argument for a tariff on the Bataslavian cars?

3. Suppose that the comparative-cost ratios of two products—mangoes and sardines—are as follows in the hypothetical nations of Mangolia and Sardinia:

Mangolia: 1 mango = 2 cans of sardines

Sardinia: 1 mango = 4 cans of sardines

In what product should each nation specialize? Explain why the terms of trade of 1 mango =

3 cans of sardines would be acceptable to both nations.

4. What are the two trade restriction policies we discussed in this chapter? Who benefits and who loses from each of these policies? What is the new outcome for society?

＊5. Germany and Japan both produce cars and beer. The table below lists production possibilities per worker in each country (for example, one worker in Germany produces 8 cars or 10 cases of beer).

	Labor force	Cars (C)	Beer (B)
Germany	200	8	10
Japan	100	20	14

a. Which nation has an absolute advantage in car production? Which one has an absolute advantage in beer production? Explain your answers.
b. Which nation has a comparative advantage in car production? Which one has a comparative advantage in beer production? Explain your answers.

＊6. Continuing with the example given in the previous problem, assume that Germany and Japan produce their own cars and beer and allocate half their labor force to the production of each.

a. What quantities of cars and beer does Germany produce? What quantities does Japan produce?

Now suppose that Germany and Japan produce only the good for which they enjoy a comparative advantage in production. They also agree to trade half of their output for half of what the other country produces.

b. What quantities of cars and beer does Germany produce now? What quantities does Japan produce?
c. What quantities of cars and beer does Germany consume now? What quantities does Japan consume?
d. People often act as if international trade is a zero-sum game. State this book's foundational principle that contradicts this idea.

SOLVED PROBLEMS

5. a. Japan has an absolute advantage in both because 20 > 8 and 14 > 10.
   b. Japan has a comparative advantage in car production since its opportunity cost is less than Germany's (0.7 < 1.2). Germany has a comparative advantage in beer production since its opportunity cost is less than Japan's (0.8 < 1.4).

6. a. Germany: (C, B) = (800, 1,000); Japan: (C, B) = (1,000, 700)
   b. Germany: (C, B) = (0, 2,000); Japan: (C, B) = (2,000, 0)
   c. Germany: (C, B) = (1,000, 1,000); Japan: (C, B) = (1,000, 1,000)
   d. Trade creates value.

International Finance

Trade deficits are harmful to an economy.

Since 1975, the United States has had a trade deficit with the rest of the world—we import more than we export. Many people believe that

MIS CONCEPTION

trade deficits are bad for an economy. After all it seems unfair that we are buying goods from other nations but they are not buying goods from us. And the news media often perpetuates these beliefs by reporting trade deficit data in alarmist tones. After all, the word "deficit" never sounds good. Most economists are not bothered by trade deficits. A trade deficit does not indicate economic weakness. In fact, a trade deficit usually accompanies a strong and growing economy. A relatively wealthy economy can afford to buy goods and services from all over the world. But are trade deficits really something to worry about?

In this chapter, we explore the two most important topics in international finance: exchange rates and trade balances. We begin by explaining the determinants of exchange rate levels in both the short run and the long run, and then we come back to the topic of international trade balances.

These books that fill an Amazon warehouse are produced all over the world. Is the U.S. economy worse off if most of these books come into the United States and contribute to our trade deficit?

BIG QUESTIONS

✳ **Why do exchange rates rise and fall?**

✳ **What is purchasing power parity?**

✳ **What causes trade deficits?**

Why Do Exchange Rates Rise and Fall?

An **exchange rate** is the price of foreign currency, indicating how much a unit of foreign currency costs in terms of another currency.

Have you ever tried to exchange one currency for another? Perhaps you've seen exchange rates displayed on a sign at a bank or in an airport. If so, you've seen national flags and a lot of confusing numbers. Each of these numbers represents an *exchange rate*. An **exchange rate** is the price of foreign currency. This price tells how much a unit of foreign currency costs in terms of another currency. For example, the price of a single Mexican peso in terms of U.S. dollars is about $0.08, or eight cents. This is the exchange rate between the peso and the dollar.

A key message from Chapter 32 is that the world economy is becoming ever more integrated: globalization is real and increasing. As more goods and services flow across borders, exchange rates become more important. One goal of this chapter is to explain the reasons why exchange rates rise and fall.

Exchange rates matter because they affect the relative prices of goods and services. Any good that crosses a border has to pass through a foreign exchange market on its way to sale. For example, the price you pay in the United States for a Samsung television built in South Korea depends on the exchange rate between the U.S. dollar and the won, the currency of South Korea.

Zooming out to the macro view, exchange rates affect the prices of all imports and exports—and therefore GDP. The more integrated the world economy becomes, the more closely economists watch exchange rates since they affect both what nations produce and what nations consume.

Our approach to exchange rates is straightforward: *exchange rates are prices*. For example, the exchange rate between the U.S. dollar and the won is the dollar price of one won, or the number of dollars required to buy one won. It is just like the price of other goods that we buy. Exchange rates are prices that are determined in world currency markets. Just as there are global markets where people buy and sell commodities such as sugar, wheat, and roses, there are also world markets where people buy and sell currencies. These markets, often called foreign exchange markets, are places where people buy and sell international currencies.

Exchange rates are determined by the demand for and supply of currency in foreign exchange markets. Thus, if we want to explore the factors that make exchange rates rise and fall, we must consider the factors that affect the demand for

Are you planning a trip abroad? If so, you'd better figure out how to use signs like this to exchange currency.

and the supply of foreign currency. In this section, we look at some special characteristics of foreign exchange markets and then consider the demand for and supply of foreign currency. When we have finished, we will be able to consider why exchange rates rise and fall.

Characteristics of Foreign Exchange Markets

In a foreign exchange market, the good in question is a foreign currency. Very likely, you've held foreign currency at some point in your life—perhaps because a friend or relative saved some as a souvenir from a trip abroad, or perhaps because you were fortunate to vacation or study in a foreign country. People purchase a foreign currency in order to buy goods or services produced in the foreign country that uses that specific currency. Don't lose sight of this simple truth, because it is at the core of our entire conversation about exchange rate determination.

The demand for foreign currency is a *derived demand*. **Derived demand** is demand for a good or service that derives from the demand for another good or service. For example, if you travel to Belgium, you will probably want to buy some Belgian chocolates. But first you must buy euros, since the euro is the currency of Belgium. The euro is an unusual currency because it is used by 23 separate European nations, including Belgium, Germany, France, Spain, and Portugal. The demand for euros in world markets is derived from the demand for Belgian chocolates and many other goods, services, and financial assets produced in those 23 nations.

Derived demand is demand for a good or service that derives from the demand for another good or service.

Today, it is easier to buy goods in foreign countries because you can often just use your credit or debit card to make foreign purchases; you don't have to physically buy foreign currency. This approach works because your bank or card company is willing to buy the foreign currency for you. To you, it feels like you are paying in U.S. dollars, since you use the same card all over the world and you see deductions from your bank account in dollars. But your bank literally takes dollars from your account and then exchanges them for foreign currency so that it can pay foreign companies in their own currency. Your bank charges a fee for this service, but it certainly makes the transaction simpler for you.

Exchange Rates Are the Price of Foreign Currency

In this section, we look more closely at exchange rates. First, we clarify how exchange rates are quoted; then we consider how appreciation and depreciation—two new terms—affect exchange rates.

Table 33.1 shows some actual exchange rates from December 2012. Exchange rates can be viewed from either side of the exchange. For example, the exchange rate between the U.S. dollar and the Japanese yen can be viewed as either of the following:

1. the number of yen required to buy one U.S. dollar (¥ per $)

2. the number of U.S. dollars required to buy one yen ($ per ¥)

While these two rates communicate the same information, they are not usually the same number, since they are reciprocals of each other. For consistency, we exclusively use the second option—the number of U.S. dollars

TABLE 33.1

Exchange Rates between the U.S. Dollar and Other Currencies, December 2012

	Units of foreign currency you can buy with one U.S. dollar	Number of U.S. dollars required to buy one unit of foreign currency
Chinese yuan	6.227	0.1606
Euro	0.769	1.300
Indian rupee	54.348	0.018
Japanese yen	82.645	0.012
Mexican peso	12.953	0.077
Turkish lira	1.788	0.559
U.K. pound	0.624	1.602

Source: Google Public Data.

Currency appreciation occurs when a currency becomes more valuable relative to other currencies.

Currency depreciation occurs when a currency becomes less valuable relative to other currencies.

required to buy one unit of foreign currency. This is represented in the last column in Table 33.1. We choose this option because it is the way we quote all other prices. If you walk into Starbucks and look at the prices posted on the wall, they indicate the number of dollars it takes to buy different coffee drinks. So when we refer to exchange rates in this textbook, we're always talking about the number of dollars required to buy one unit of foreign currency.

If a currency becomes more valuable in world markets, its price rises, and this increase is called an *appreciation*. **Currency appreciation** occurs when a currency increases in value relative to other currencies. In contrast, **currency depreciation** occurs when a currency decreases in value relative to other currencies. If the dollar depreciates, it is less valuable in world markets.

FIGURE 33.1

Exchange Rates and Currency Appreciation and Depreciation

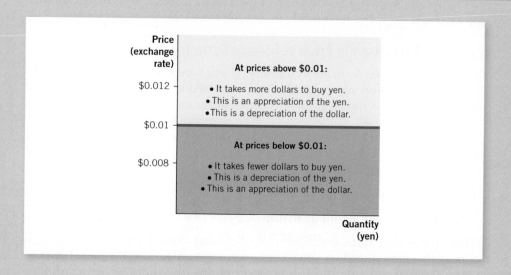

Figure 33.1 illustrates appreciation and depreciation with the exchange rate between the U.S. dollar and the yen. The exchange rate starts at $0.01. If the exchange rate rises above $0.01, it will take more dollars to buy a yen, which signals an appreciation of the yen and a depreciation of the dollar. If, instead, the price falls below $0.01, it will take fewer dollars to buy a yen, which signals a depreciation of the yen and an appreciation of the dollar.

Some Historical Perspective

When exchange rates rise, foreign currencies become more expensive relative to the dollar. This means that imports become more expensive. But it also means that U.S. exports become less expensive, so foreigners around the globe can afford to buy more goods and services from the United States. These are the reasons why exchange rates are important macroeconomic indicators to watch.

The recent past offers a mixed picture of the world value of the dollar. Figure 33.2 plots exchange rates for the currencies of two different trading partners of the United States: one that uses the euro and one that uses the yen (Japan). The vertical axis in each panel measures the dollar price of one unit of the relevant foreign currency. Panel (a) shows the exchange rate with

FIGURE 33.2

Two Foreign Exchange Rates

These exchange rates are reported as the number of U.S. dollars required to purchase a unit of foreign currency. (a) In looking at the exchange rate with the euro from 2007 to 2012, we see that the price of a euro rose from $1.30 to well over $1.50, but eventually it dropped back down to $1.30. (b) The Japanese yen became increasingly expensive over the period shown. This increase has made Japanese goods more expensive for Americans.

Source: Oanda.com.

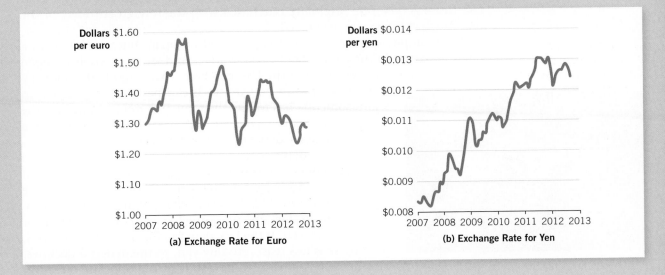

(a) Exchange Rate for Euro

(b) Exchange Rate for Yen

the euro. The euro exchange rate fluctuated wildly over the six years pictured, rising from $1.30 to almost $1.60 during the recession year of 2008. This rise indicates a sharp decline in the value of the dollar. But then, over the next three years, the exchange rate seesawed back down to the $1.30 range.

In contrast, as panel (b) shows, the exchange rate with the Japanese yen climbed fairly steadily from 2007 to 2013. The rise in the price of the yen means that Japanese goods are now more expensive in the United States and U.S. goods are now less expensive in Japan.

The Demand for Foreign Currency

In this section, we discuss the factors that affect the demand side of the market for foreign currency. We distinguish three primary factors: the price of the currency (the exchange rate), the demand for foreign goods and services, and the demand for foreign financial assets.

Price of Foreign Currency

The law of demand holds in foreign currency markets. When the price of the yen falls, goods and services produced in Japan (such as Sony televisions or Toyota SUVs) are less expensive relative to goods and services produced in the United States. Therefore, if the price of the yen falls, the quantity demanded increases. If, instead, price of the yen rises, it becomes more expensive to purchase Japanese goods, and the quantity demanded falls.

Demand for Foreign Goods and Services

As we emphasized earlier, you purchase foreign currency so that you can buy goods or services produced in foreign countries. Perhaps you are thinking, "But wait, I buy goods from other countries quite often without purchasing foreign currency." This is true: you can buy imported TVs, cars, fruits, and clothing without ever touching a coin or bill of foreign currency. But in fact those goods were originally purchased with the foreign currency of the nation where they were produced.

For example, a Sony television is produced in Japan, but you buy it in a retail store here in the United States. The workers and factory owners in Japan are paid in yen. This means that the U.S. company that imports the Sony TV from Japan has to buy yen so it can pay for the product. In short, someone has to buy the foreign currency to pay for the TV, even if it is not you. For this reason, the demand for a nation's currency depends on the demand for its exports.

When the demand for a nation's exports rises, the demand for its currency rises as well. For example, if the U.S. demand for Japanese TVs increases, the demand for yen will increase at all prices. Figure 33.3 illustrates changes in demand for yen. An increase in demand for Sony TVs shifts the demand for yen from D_1 to D_2. If the U.S. demand for Sony TVs decreases, then there is less reason to buy yen, so the demand declines. This decline is illustrated as a shift in the opposite direction from D_1 to D_3.

If you want to snorkel in Mexico, you'd better buy some pesos.

Demand for Foreign Financial Assets

Another reason to purchase foreign currency is to buy financial assets in a foreign nation. To buy stocks or bonds in a foreign country, you have to convert to the local currency. Even to establish a foreign bank account, you must first buy the currency of that country. Likewise, if people from other nations want to buy U.S. stocks or bonds, they exchange their currency for U.S. dollars first.

A primary reason why foreigners demand U.S. dollars is to buy U.S. stocks, bonds, and real estate. Relative to the rest of the world, the United States is often seen as a stable, low-risk economy. Although U.S. stability weakened during the financial turmoil associated with the Great Recession of 2007–2009, the long-term productivity of U.S. firms still attracts foreign funds. For this reason, there is still a stable demand for U.S. dollars.

Along these lines, one key factor in foreign exchange markets is interest rates across nations. If interest rates rise in one country (relative to rates in the rest of the world), the demand for its currency will increase, since there is a greater demand for the assets with higher returns. For example, if interest rates in Japan rise relative to those in the rest of the world, it means that Japanese bonds provide a higher return than previously, and demand for these bonds will rise right along with the interest rate. In Figure 33.3, this move is indicated as a shift from D_1 to D_2. When interest rates fall, there is reduced demand for the nation's currency. We see this outcome in Figure 33.3 as a shift from D_1 to D_3.

The Supply of Foreign Currency

In Chapter 30, we talked about modern money, which is fiat currency. This kind of currency is printed and supplied by governments. From a market standpoint, it is fixed in quantity at any one time. Governments increase and

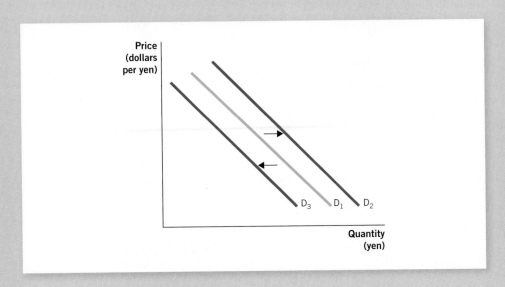

FIGURE 33.3

Shifts in the Demand for Foreign Currency

Increases in the demand for foreign currency derive from an increased demand (D_2) for foreign goods and services and/or foreign financial assets. Decreases in the demand for foreign currency derive from a decreased demand (D_3) for foreign goods and services and/or foreign financial assets. Here we illustrate these relationships with the U.S. dollar and the Japanese yen.

decrease the supply of fiat currency very often, and when they do, the supply curve shifts, as Figure 33.4 shows. For example, consider the possible actions of the Bank of Japan (BOJ), which is the central bank of Japan, the agency that determines monetary policy for the country. Initially, the supply of yen is vertical at S_1. If the BOJ increases the supply of yen relative to the supply of dollars, the supply curve shifts outward to S_2. If, instead, the BOJ reduces the supply of yen relative to the supply of dollars, the supply curve shifts in the opposite direction to S_3.

Applying Our Model of Exchange Rates

In this section, we consider some applications of our model of exchange rates. In reality, exchange rates fluctuate daily, and these prices affect the prices of all imports and exports. These fluctuations are the result of shifts in demand, supply, or both. We start with changes in demand.

Changes in Demand

In most of the world, car shoppers can choose from many cars; these include Toyotas produced in Japan and Jeeps produced in the United States. In micro-

How are exchange rates affected when consumers choose Toyotas over Jeeps?

economics, you might study the impact on the auto manufacturers from a shift in consumer preferences away from Jeeps and toward Toyotas. But these kinds of demand changes, which occur quite frequently, also affect the market for foreign currency. For example, if consumer preferences in the United States shift away from Jeeps and toward Toyotas, the demand for the yen rises.

Figure 33.5 shows the results of a shift toward Toyotas. Initially, the market (for yen) is in equilibrium with supply of S and demand of D_1. The initial equilibrium exchange rate is $0.010. Then, after U.S. consumers demand more Toyotas, the demand for yen shifts outward to D_2. This shift causes the exchange rate to rise to $0.012.

FIGURE 33.4

Shifts in the Supply of Foreign Currency

The supply of any foreign nation's currency is determined by the government of that nation. If the Bank of Japan increases the supply of yen relative to the supply of dollars, the supply curve shifts from S_1 to S_2. If the supply of yen decreases relative to the supply of dollars, the curve shifts in the opposite direction to S_3.

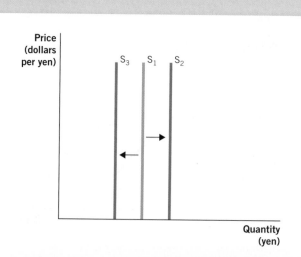

If the cause of the shift were an increase in the demand for Japanese financial assets, the result would be the same. Thus, if interest rates in Japan rise, this sends a signal to investors around the globe to buy financial assets in Japan. The increase in the demand for yen leads to an increase in the exchange rate. The higher exchange rate implies an appreciation of the yen and, by comparison, a depreciation of the dollar. People want more yen, so its value rises in relation to the dollar.

If, instead, global demand for goods, services, and financial assets moves away from Japan and toward the United States, the demand for yen will fall (shifting to D_3) as people move toward dollars. In this case, the exchange rate falls and the yen depreciates, but the dollar appreciates.

These shifts in demand occur naturally in a global economy in which consumers across different nations choose among products produced in a wide variety of countries. Even just focusing on cars, we can choose to buy from the United States, Germany, Japan, South Korea, the United Kingdom, Canada, and Italy, to name a few. But as international demanders' product preferences change, exchange rates are affected. Table 33.2 summarizes how shifts in demand affect foreign exchange rates.

However, there are also "unnatural" changes in exchange rates, caused by intentional actions of government monetary authorities all over the globe. To understand these, we look at shifts in currency supply.

Changes in Supply

The supply side of currency markets is determined by government changes to the supply of currency. Figure 33.6 illustrates a scenario in which the Bank of Japan increases the supply of yen. This move shifts supply from S_1 to S_2 and causes the exchange rate to fall from $0.010 to $0.008. The drop in the exchange rate means that the yen depreciates relative to the dollar—a direct

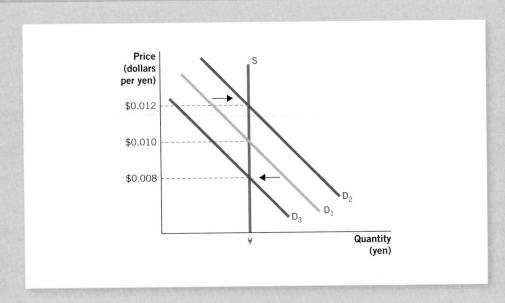

FIGURE 33.5

How Demand Shifts Affect the Exchange Rate

An increase in the demand for foreign currency leads to an increase in the exchange rate from $0.010 to $0.012. This signals a depreciation of the U.S. dollar relative to the yen. A decrease in the demand for foreign currency leads to a decrease in the exchange rate from $0.010 to $0.008. This signals an appreciation of the U.S. dollar relative to the yen.

TABLE 33.2		
Shifts in Demand for Foreign Currency		
Cause	**Demand for foreign currency**	**Exchange rate change**
Increase in demand for foreign goods and services or financial assets	Demand increases.	Exchange rate rises.
Decrease in demand for foreign goods and services or financial assets	Demand decreases.	Exchange rate falls.

result of the increase in yen. The BOJ action means that there are now more yen per dollar, so yen are worth less in relative terms.

The scenario pictured in Figure 33.6 is actually quite common. Government monetary authorities often intervene in markets to drive down their exchange rates. **Exchange rate manipulation** occurs when a national government intentionally adjusts its money supply to affect the exchange rate of its currency.

It may seem odd that a government would take action to purposefully depreciate the value of its own currency. After all, don't we typically want the value of our assets to *appreciate*? If you learned that the value of your car depreciated drastically in the last year, would you take that as good news? What if the value of your parents' home depreciates; is that good news? No, these are both bad news. However, nations depreciate their own currency in order to make their exports more affordable to buyers worldwide. If the yen falls in value, then each dollar buys more yen. And a devalued yen makes

Exchange rate manipulation occurs when a national government intentionally adjusts its money supply to affect the exchange rate of its currency.

FIGURE 33.6

How Supply Shifts Affect the Exchange Rate

All else being equal, an increase in the quantity of yen shifts the supply of yen to the right, to ¥₂. This shift cases the exchange rate to decrease from $0.010 to $0.008. Thus, the yen depreciates and the dollar appreciates.

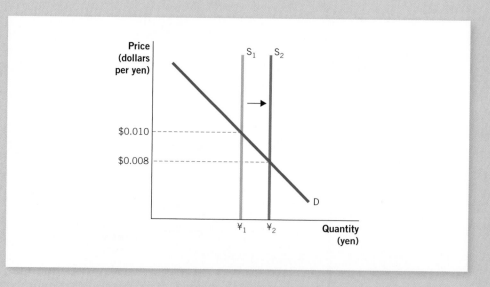

Japanese products more affordable. All else being equal, the demand for Japanese products will rise in the United States.

Currency devaluation, through increasing the quantity of currency, can certainly have a short-run impact on aggregate demand. But to see how this affects the Japanese economy, we need to consider it in the context of the aggregate supply–aggregate demand model. In Chapter 26, we included the value of domestic currency among the factors that shift aggregate demand. We noted that a decrease in the value of domestic currency (depreciation) causes an increase in aggregate demand.

Let's now consider this observation in the context of our present discussion. If the Bank of Japan acts to depreciate the yen, then aggregate demand for Japanese goods and services increases, as shown in Figure 33.7 as a shift from AD_1 to AD_2. In the short run, this shift leads to greater real GDP (Y_1) and lower unemployment. This happens because some prices are inflexible in the short run. But when all prices adjust, output returns to its earlier level, leaving only inflation as the result of the increased quantity of yen—the price level rises from 100 to 110. In the end, yen are less expensive; but because of inflation, it takes more yen to buy Japanese goods. In the long run, there are no real effects from the action: the LRAS curve remains at Y^*.

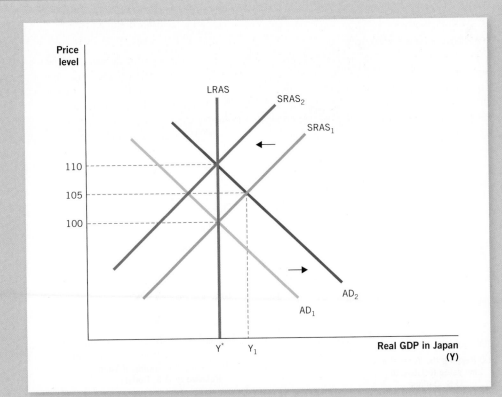

FIGURE 33.7

Increase in Aggregate Demand in Japan Arising from Yen Depreciation

A depreciation of the yen increases aggregate demand for Japanese goods and services. In the short run, real GDP increases and unemployment (not pictured here) decreases, due to some sticky prices. In the long run, when prices adjust fully, there are no real effects, just inflation, because prices rise from 100 to 110.

Pegging Exchange Rates

Panel (a) of Figure 33.8 plots the U.S. dollar exchange rate with the Chinese yuan. Notice the flat period between 2008 and 2010, then the gradual evenly paced increases after that. This pattern is not due to natural market forces; it is because the Chinese government has chosen to maintain a *pegged exchange rate* with the dollar. **Pegged exchange rates** are exchange rates that are fixed at a certain level through the actions of a government. The alternative to pegged, or fixed, exchange rates is *flexible*, or *floating*, exchange rates. **Flexible exchange rates**, also known as **floating exchange rates**, are exchange rates that are determined by the market forces of supply and demand for currency. Previously in this chapter, our discussions have assumed flexible exchange rates.

Many exchange rates today, such as those we have already considered, are flexible. However, China pegs its currency, the yuan, to the U.S. dollar. The yuan has been consistently pegged at a value below that which would prevail if the exchange rate were allowed to be flexible; the market-determined rate would be well above $0.160. For instance, the yuan was pegged at $0.147 between 2008 and 2010, as you can see in the flat part of the graph in panel (a) of Figure 33.8. But countries cannot pass a law that pegs the exchange rate, because world markets are not subject to the laws of other nations. Instead, the Chinese government maintains the peg by adjusting its supply of yuan in world markets.

Pegged exchange rates are exchange rates that are fixed at a certain level through the actions of a government.

Flexible exchange rates, also known as **floating exchange rates,** are exchange rates that are determined by the supply of and demand for currency.

FIGURE 33.8

How China Pegs the Yuan and Increases Its Supply

The Chinese government controls the exchange rate for its nation's currency, pegging the yuan to a particular value relative to the U.S. dollar. Panel (a) shows that from mid-2008 until mid-2010 the pegged rate was set at $0.147; after this, it was allowed to rise but was still kept below the value that world markets would dictate. Panel (b) shows how the Chinese government keeps the exchange rate below the natural market rate. The government uses yuan to buy U.S. dollars and other U.S. assets in world markets. This strategy increases the supply of yuan, which shifts the supply curve to the right.

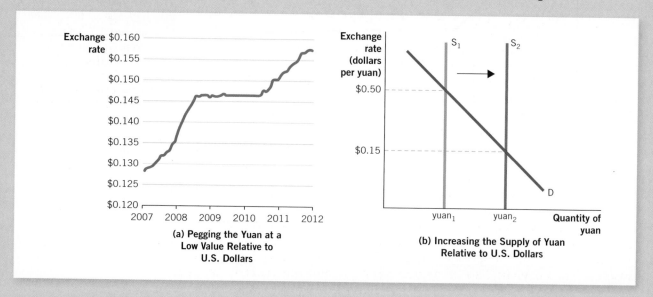

(a) Pegging the Yuan at a Low Value Relative to U.S. Dollars

(b) Increasing the Supply of Yuan Relative to U.S. Dollars

To change its supply of yuan, the Chinese government increases the supply of yuan relative to the supply of dollars. Panel (b) in Figure 33.8 illustrates how an increase in supply drives down the price of the yuan. In practice, the Chinese government buys U.S. dollars and U.S. Treasury securities in world markets. Notice the word "buy" in the last sentence. That's right: the Chinese government has to buy these, and when it buys them with newly minted yuan, the supply of yuan shifts to the right, to S_2. This action causes the Chinese currency to depreciate. Essentially, the Chinese government is conducting open market operations by purchasing U.S. Treasury securities. Ironically, this is exactly how the U.S. Federal Reserve enacts expansionary monetary policy for the United States.

The Chinese government devalues the yuan so that Chinese goods and services become less expensive on world markets. The government wants Chinese exports to be very affordable because it is trying to build the nation's economy through exports. The Chinese view this as a long-term strategy that will help their economy to develop into an industrial economy. Since 2010, the Chinese government has been letting the yuan slowly rise in value, but, as the report described below shows, recently the government seems to be having second thoughts.

ECONOMICS IN THE REAL WORLD

Chinese Export Growth Slows

An October 2011 Bloomberg news article noted that Chinese exports grew by just 17% from a year earlier. While this growth is substantial, it is relatively small compared to China's export growth rates from earlier years. The Bloomberg report goes on to say that the Chinese government might plan to stop letting the yuan appreciate versus the dollar (recall the upward climb in Figure 33.8).

According to the report, "China may move to restrain the yuan, which has gained the most against the dollar among 25 emerging-market currencies in the past four years." The idea is that the appreciating yuan makes it more expensive for Americans to buy Chinese goods. Therefore, since the Chinese government wants Americans to buy more Chinese goods, it may move to slow the appreciation of the nation's currency.

Will the Chinese government continue to keep the value of the yuan down so that Americans can buy these toys at reduced prices?

In one sense, it is clear that the Chinese economy has been growing at historically large rates over the past two decades. This seems to indicate that the devaluation strategy is helping the Chinese economy overall, not just the export sector. Perhaps this is true, but let's be careful. After all, many other changes have taken place in China over the past two decades. Recall from Chapters 24 and 25 that institutional changes (especially the introduction of private property rights) have significantly altered production incentives in China. Therefore, it is inaccurate to pin China's success on currency devaluation alone.

In addition, the devaluation of the Chinese currency has other side effects. In particular, devaluation harms Chinese workers, who are paid in yuan. When the government devalues the currency, this move effectively gives the workers a real pay cut. Part of the reason why Chinese exports are so inexpensive is that the nation's labor costs are very low. But this is not always a positive outcome for the wage earners. ✳

PRACTICE WHAT YOU KNOW

The Bahamian Dollar is Pegged to the U.S. Dollar

While the Chinese government keeps the dollar–yuan exchange rate artificially low to encourage exports, other nations peg their currency to the dollar to guarantee stability. In fact, as of 2011 there were 66 nations that pegged their currency to the U.S. dollar. Not all the exchange rates are held artificially low with their dollar peg.

This might not look like three U.S. dollars, but that's what it basically is.

Question: Assume that the Bahamian government wants to peg its currency to the U.S. dollar at a 1:1 ratio (one U.S. dollar = one Bahamian dollar). But the current exchange rate is at 90 cents (10 cents below the official peg). What must the Bahamian central bank do to return to the $1 exchange rate?

Answer: In this case, as illustrated below, the initial supply and demand curves intersect at $0.90 before the government intervenes to enforce the peg. Thus, the Bahamian central bank should reduce the supply of Bahamian dollars from S_1 to S_2 to increase the exchange rate to $1.00.

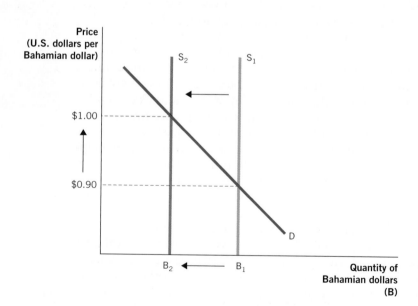

What Is Purchasing Power Parity?

As we have noted, the world economy is becoming ever more integrated. This affects both suppliers and demanders of goods and services. Suppliers can often choose where they wish to sell their output, and demanders can often choose where they want to buy their output—even if doing so requires a little extra shipping.

In this section, we discuss the theory of how exchange rates are determined in the long run. We begin by examining how market exchanges determine the price of a particular good at different locations. Next we extend this discussion to the prices of all goods and services in different nations. Finally, we come back and consider limitations to the theory. We begin with the *law of one price*.

The Law of One Price

Let's consider a simplified example of trade within the borders of one country: Florida oranges are consumed in Michigan and many other states. What happens if the price of Florida oranges is different in Michigan and Florida? Figure 33.9 illustrates two different markets for Florida oranges—one in Florida and one in Michigan. Initially, as we see in panel (a), the price of a pound of oranges in Florida is $1.80; as we see in panel (b), the price of a pound of

FIGURE 33.9

The Law of One Price

(a) Initially, the price of a pound of oranges in Florida is $1.80, while (b) the same oranges sell for $2.20 per pound in Michigan. Thus, orange suppliers reduce supply in Florida and increase supply in Michigan. If transportation costs are zero, these supply changes will take place until the price is the same in both locations.

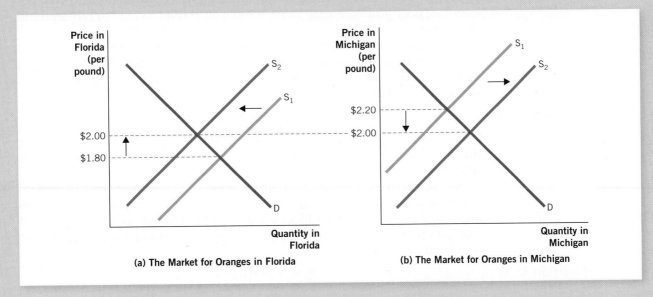

(a) The Market for Oranges in Florida

(b) The Market for Oranges in Michigan

the same oranges in Michigan is $2.20. Assume for now that there are no transportation costs and no trade barriers. In this case, sellers in Florida have an incentive to sell their oranges in Michigan, where the price is 40 cents higher. Thus, the supply in Florida will decline and the supply in Michigan will increase. These supply shifts will lead to an increased price in Florida and a decreased price in Michigan. The adjustment will continue until the prices are the same in both locations.

The **law of one price** says that after accounting for transportation costs and trade barriers, identical goods sold in different locations must sell for the same price.

(Equation 33.1)

This adjustment process is the logic behind the **law of one price**, which says that after accounting for transportation costs and trade barriers, identical goods sold in different locations must sell for the same price. We can state this in equation form, where p_A is the price of a good in location A and p_B is the price of the same good in location B:

$$p_A = p_B$$

The law of one price also holds across international borders. For example, If Florida oranges are sold in Japan, the price should be the same once we account for the costs of shipping and trade barriers. But when oranges ship across international borders, a new issue arises because different nations generally use different currencies. We take up this issue in the next section.

Purchasing Power Parity and Exchange Rates

Purchasing power parity (PPP) is the idea that a unit of currency should be able to buy the same quantity of goods and services in any country.

In Japan, the medium of exchange is the yen. The exchange rate between the U.S. dollar and the yen is about $0.01. Therefore, since each yen is worth about a penny, the law of one price implies that it should take about 100 times as many yen to buy oranges in Japan as it does to buy the same oranges in the United States. Thus, if the price of a pound of oranges in the United States is $2, the price in Japan should be ¥200. This extension of the law of one price is the idea behind *purchasing power parity* (PPP).

Purchasing power parity (PPP) is the idea that a unit of currency should be able to buy the same quantity of goods and services in any country. For example, once you exchange $2 for ¥200, you should be able to buy a pound of oranges.

PPP is an extension of the law of one price. If, after converting currencies, oranges cost more in Japan than they do in Florida, then supply to Japan increases and supply in Florida decreases until the prices are equal. We can also represent this in equation form:

(Equation 33.2)

$$p_A = \text{exchange rate} \times p_B$$

In the short run, PPP may not hold perfectly, and we explain the reasons for this in the next section. But in the long run, after all the adjustments have taken place, PPP holds.

So far, we have considered a single good—oranges. But we can extend purchasing power parity to all final goods and services in order to derive an important implication regarding exchange rates. If Equation 33.2 holds for all final goods and services, then the price levels (P) in different nations should be related as follows:

(Equation 33.3)

$$P_A = \text{exchange rate} \times P_B$$

Impossible Exchange Rates

Eurotrip

In this movie from 2004, four American high school graduates travel to Europe and end up in Bratislava, the capital of Slovakia. They are particularly concerned when they pool their remaining money and find they have just $1.83. But Slovakia is an impoverished country, and it turns out that the U.S. dollar is extremely valuable there. Using this small amount of money, the four friends are able to have an amazing night on the town. At one point, they tip a busboy just five cents, but this is so valuable that the man promptly retires from his job to enjoy his wealth.

An appreciating and strong U.S. dollar is good news to people who are paid in U.S. dollars. The stronger your home currency, the more you can buy around the globe.

But purchasing power parity means that the kind of wild overvaluation of the dollar that we see in *Eurotrip* is not possible in the real world. If the dollar were really this strong in some nation, any

These friends don't have to look far to find a bargain when their dollars are strong relative to the local currency.

nation, tourists would flood in with dollars and then drive the prices up to a more reasonable level. The movie's story makes for entertaining theater, but the law of one price and purchasing power parity mean that these kinds of bargains can't last long in the real world.

In Equation 33.3, P_A is the price level in nation A and P_B is the price level in nation B. We can rewrite Equation 33.3 to derive a key implication of PPP:

$$\text{exchange rate} = P_A \div P_B \qquad \text{(Equation 33.4)}$$

This equation is a direct extension of the law of one price to international trade in all goods and services. We can use Equation 33.4 to learn what causes big swings in exchange rates over time. For example, we have noted that the exchange rate between the U.S. dollar and the Japanese yen has consistently risen in recent years (see Figure 33.2), which means that the dollar has depreciated relative to the yen. In 2007, each yen cost approximately $0.008, but the rate had risen to $0.013 by 2012. This long-run change reflects shifts in relative price levels over the period 2007–2012. While inflation in the United States averaged just 2.7% from 2007 to 2011, the price level in Japan actually declined over the same period, falling by 2.1%. These changing price levels led to an increase in the exchange rate, since $P_{US} \div P_{Japan}$ increased between 2007 and 2011. Thus, in the long run, exchange rate fluctuations are driven by relative changes in price levels.

ECONOMICS IN THE REAL WORLD

The Big Mac Index

Is the price of this McDonald's sandwich the same all over the world?

We have said that purchasing power parity is a condition that should hold in the long run. *The Economist* magazine has devised a creative way to test PPP at any given point in time. It compares the price of a McDonald's Big Mac sandwich across many nations. The Big Mac is a good choice because it is roughly the same good all over the world. For example, in July 2012 the price of a Big Mac in the United States was $4.33. Given that the exchange rate between the U.S. dollar and the euro was about $1.3 in 2012, we can use Equation 33.2 to find the implied price of the Big Mac in Europe:

$$4.33 = 1.3 \times P_{\text{Europe}}$$

Solving for the price in Europe, we find that $4.33 \div 1.3 = 3.33$ euros. In fact, the actual price was 3.58 euros, so the PPP formula worked fairly well in this case.

But PPP doesn't always hold perfectly in the short run. Table 33.3 shows the Big Mac price across seven different nations, along with the price implied by PPP. The first column of numbers gives the actual price of the Big Mac in terms of the domestic currency for each nation. The third column is the price in domestic currency that is implied by PPP. This price is computed by using Equation 33.2, exactly as we used it above in determining the PPP Big Mac price for Europe. The last column shows the actual price of the Big Mac converted into U.S. dollars using the exchange rate. If PPP held perfectly, the prices in the last column would all be $4.33, the price of a Big Mac in the United States.

The Big Mac index is an intuitive illustration of PPP. It also helps us see which currencies are valued close to their long-run equilibrium levels relative to the dollar. For example, the British pound, the euro, and the Turkish lira are all very close to the level implied by PPP. But some prices are off significantly. For example, PPP implies a Big Mac price of 241 rupees in India, but the actual price is just 89 rupees. There is a good reason for this discrepancy: the Indian version of the Big Mac, called the Maharaja Mac, substitutes chicken patties for the customary beef patties.

In the next section, we examine why PPP might not hold exactly in the short run. One of the key reasons is that the food must be identical across nations. ✳

Why PPP Does Not Hold Perfectly

When we looked at the Big Mac index, we saw that PPP does not always hold perfectly. There are five reasons why PPP may not hold in the short run.

First, in order for the law of one price and PPP to hold, the goods or services sold in different locations must be identical. We have already noted that the Indian version of the Big Mac is not even a hamburger; it is a chicken sandwich. Thus, we should not expect the prices to be the same.

Second, some goods and services are not tradable. One example is a haircut. Haircuts in China typically cost less than $5 (and often include a massage), whereas haircuts in the United States almost always cost more than $20. But

TABLE 33.3				

The Big Mac Index, July 2012

	Actual price in domestic currency	Exchange rate	Price implied by PPP	Actual price in U.S. dollars
U.S. dollar	4.33	1.000	4.33	$4.33
Chinese yuan	15.65	0.161	26.961	$2.51
Euro	3.58	1.300	3.331	$4.65
Indian rupee*	89.00	0.018	240.556	$1.60
Japanese yen	320.00	0.012	360.833	$3.84
Mexican peso	37.00	0.077	56.234	$2.85
Turkish lira	8.25	0.559	7.746	$4.61
U.K. pound	2.69	1.602	2.703	$4.31

Source: *The Economist.*

*In India, the Big Mac is not sold; the closest comparison is with the Maharaja Mac, which substitutes chicken for beef.

we cannot import a "haircut produced in China"; you'd have to travel to China to buy that service. Therefore, the supply of foreign haircuts cannot adjust to force PPP to hold. This is the case for all non-tradeable goods and services.

Third, trade barriers inhibit the trade of goods across some international borders. If goods cannot be traded, or if tariffs and quotas add to the costs of trade, then prices will not equalize and PPP will not hold. The higher the trade barriers are, the higher the price of a good in the foreign country will be. For example, tariffs and quotas on Florida oranges imported to Japan would lead to higher prices in Japan than in Florida.

Fourth, shipping costs keep prices from completely equalizing. In fact, higher shipping costs will lead to higher prices of the same good in a foreign nation. The greater the shipping costs, the bigger the difference in prices that can persist.

Finally, we have emphasized consistently throughout this book that some prices take longer to adjust than others. PPP is a theory about long-run price adjustments across nations—with prices reacting to changes in demand and supply. The theory is by definition a long-run theory, which only holds after all prices have completely adjusted. Therefore, it will not typically hold perfectly in the short run.

In sum, PPP is a theory that teaches us a lot about the level of exchange rates in the long run—why exchange rates rise and fall over long periods of time. But in the real world, given these limitations, PPP typically does not hold perfectly at any point in time.

What Causes Trade Deficits?

At the beginning of this chapter, we noted that many people think trade deficits are harmful. In this section, we consider why this is a misconception. We also look at the specific causes of trade deficits.

PRACTICE WHAT YOU KNOW

The Law of One Price: What Should the Price Be?

The Ikea furniture company sells Swedish bookshelves all over the world. One popular model is called the BILLY bookcase. According to the Bloomberg news agency, the 2011 price of the BILLY bookcase in the United States was $59.99, while the price in the United Kingdom was £29.90.

BILLY bookcases from Ikea can be shipped all over the world.

Question: In 2011, the exchange rate between the U.S. dollar and the British pound sterling was about $1.60. Using this figure, how would you determine the 2011 price implied by PPP for the BILLY bookcase in the United Kingdom? To be clear, we are asking for the price in British pounds sterling that is equal to the $59.99 price in the United States.

Answer: From Equation 33.2, we know that PPP implies:

price in the United States = exchange rate × price in the United Kingdom

Therefore, substituting in the price in the United States and the exchange rate, we have:

$59.90 = $1.60 × price in the United Kingdom

Solving this equation, we get:

$$\frac{59.90}{1.60} = £37.44$$

Question: The 2011 price implied by PPP was £37.44, but the actual price in the United Kingdom at that time was £29.90. What are possible reasons why the price was relatively low in the United Kingdom?

Answer: Two reasons seem particularly likely. First, shipping costs to the United Kingdom may have been lower than shipping costs to the United States. In addition, there were likely lower trade barriers across Europe than between Europe and the United States.

Data source: Kristian Siedenburg, "Ikea Billy Bookshelf Index," Bloomberg.com, Sept. 15, 2010.

A trade deficit means that more goods and services are coming in than are going out. On a micro level, individuals can have trade deficits with other individuals or business firms. Think about your favorite place to eat lunch. Perhaps you go there once a week. You have a trade deficit with that restaurant; unless you also happen to work there, you buy more from it than it buys from you. Does this make you worse off or indicate weakness on your part? No. In fact, the wealthier you are, the more you may eat at your favorite restaurant and the more your trade deficit with the restaurant may increase. If voluntary trade creates a trade deficit for you, it doesn't mean that you are worse off. Remember: trade creates value.

When we extend this concept to the entire economy, the result is the same: we are not worse off when more goods and services flow in. In fact, historical data reveal that the U.S. trade deficit often increases during periods of economic growth. Figure 33.10 shows the U.S. trade balance (exports – imports) with recessionary periods shaded as vertical blue bars; the solid blue horizontal line is drawn where exports exactly equal imports. As the orange graph line becomes increasingly negative, it indicates a bigger trade deficit. Notice that the trade deficit widens during periods of expansion and then shrinks during recessions. The data shows us that trade deficits are often a byproduct of positive economic periods.

Before we can explore the various causes of trade deficits, we need to discuss more about the accounting of international trade and financial flows. For this, we turn to the balance of payments.

Your trade deficit with a local lunch spot does not make you worse off.

trade
creates
value

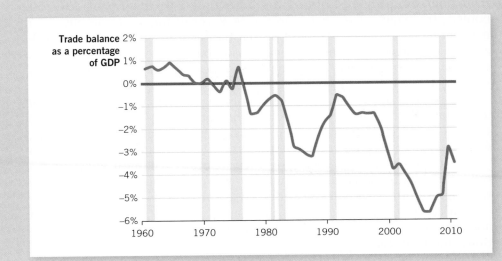

Trade balance as a percentage of GDP

FIGURE 33.10

U.S. Trade Balance and Recessions

Since 1975, the U.S. trade balance has been a deficit, with the deficit growing larger over time. The trade deficit typically grows during economic expansions and shrinks during recessions, which are indicated here with vertical blue bars.

Source: U.S. Bureau of Economic Analysis, *U.S. International Transactions*.

TABLE 33.4	
Current Account Transactions versus Capital Account Transactions	
Account and categories	**Examples**
Current account	
Goods	Domestically produced computer is exported; foreign-produced shoes are imported.
Services	U.S. airline transports foreign passengers; foreign call center offers technical advice.
Income receipt or payment	U.S. citizen earns income from a job in a foreign nation; foreign citizen earns dividends on ownership of shares of stock in a U.S. company.
Gifts	U.S. citizen donates for disaster relief in a foreign country; foreign citizen donates to charity in the United States.
Capital account	
Financial assets	U.S. citizen buys shares of stock in a foreign company; foreign government buys U.S. Treasury securities.
Real assets	U.S. citizen buys a vacation home in another country; foreign citizen buys an office building in United States.

Balance of Payments

In this section, we introduce the terminology of international transactions accounts—the accounts used to track transactions that take place across borders. For a while, it may seem like we have left economics to study accounting. But we need to clarify how international transactions are recorded before we can fully explain the causes of trade deficits and surpluses.

The **balance of payments (BOP)** is a record of all payments between one nation and the rest of the world.

A nation's **balance of payments (BOP)** is a record of all payments between that country and the rest of the world. Anytime a payment is made across borders, the payment is tracked in the BOP. For example, if you buy a car made in Japan, the dollar amount of that transaction is recorded in the balance of payments. If someone from Canada buys shares of stock in a U.S. corporation, that payment is also tracked in the U.S. balance of payments, as well as Canada's.

The balance of payments is divided into two major accounts: the *current account* and the *capital account*. Different types of transactions are entered into each account. The **current account** tracks payments for goods and services, gifts, and current income from investments. When we import TVs from Japan or strawberries from Peru (goods), or when we utilize technical advice from a call center in Mumbai, India (a service), or when we supply international aid to refugees in the Middle East (a gift), these transactions are recorded in the current account. Table 33.4 shows the major categories of both the current and the capital accounts, along with some examples of the types of transactions entered in each.

The **current account** is the BOP account that tracks all payments for goods and services, current income, and gifts.

A **capital account** tracks payments for real and financial assets between nations and extensions of international loans.

The **capital account** tracks payments for real and financial assets between nations. When residents of one nation buy financial securities such as stocks and bonds from another nation, these payments are recorded in the capital

TABLE 33.5				
U.S. Balance of Payments, 2011				
Current account (millions of dollars)		**Capital account** (millions of dollars)		
Goods and services		Real and financial assets		
Exports	$2,103,367	U.S.-owned assets abroad	−$483,653	
Imports	−$2,663,247	Foreign-owned assets in United States	$1,000,990	
Income				
Receipts	$744,621	Net financial derivatives	$39,010	
Payments	−$517,614			
Gifts	−$133,053	Statistical discrepancy	−$90,421	
Balance	−$465,926		$465,926	

Source: United States Bureau of Economic Analysis.

account. When the Chinese government buys U.S. Treasury securities, this transaction is recorded in the capital account. If someone from the United States deposits funds into a Swiss bank account, this transaction is recorded in the capital account. Even if you trade for the currency of another nation, your transaction is recorded in the capital account.

Purchases of real assets also enter in the capital account. If you buy a vacation home in Cozumel, Mexico, it counts as an outgoing payment in the capital account. When the Abu Dhabi Investment Council purchased the Chrysler Building in New York City, the transaction was recorded in the capital account as an incoming payment.

Since much of the activity in the capital account is in financial securities, it is sometimes called the *financial account*.

Table 33.5 shows actual values for the U.S. current and capital accounts in 2011. Goods and services are by far the largest entry in the current account, representing about 80% of total current account activity. For this reason, we focus primarily on goods and services when we discuss the current account.

The dollar amounts in this table represent changes in the various accounts during 2011. For example, on the current account side, the figures indicate that the United States exported about $2.1 trillion worth of goods and services but imported about $2.7 trillion. This trade deficit accounts for most of the current account deficit. On the capital account side, U.S. individuals (and government) purchased about $500 billion worth of assets from abroad, but foreigners bought about $1 trillion in U.S. assets in 2011. In the short run, statistical discrepancies are common. We know that in the long run the two accounts sum to zero by definition.

When we evaluate the trade balance, we are really focusing on the current account. In fact, when you read about a "trade deficit," you are likely reading about a *current account deficit*. An **account deficit** exists when more payments are flowing out of an account than into the account. Generally, this means that we are importing more goods and services than we are exporting. Table 33.5 shows that the U.S. current account deficit in 2011 was $465,926 million—or almost $500 billion.

Did it hurt the U.S. economy when the Abu Dhabi Investment Council bought the Chrysler Building in New York City?

An **account deficit** exists when more payments are flowing out of an account than into the account.

Banana imports are recorded with other goods and services in the current account.

An **account surplus** exists when more payments are flowing into an account than out of the account.

An **account surplus** exists when more payments are flowing into than out of an account. Since goods and services constitute most of the current account, a surplus of the current account would be driven by a trade surplus. Table 33.5 shows a capital account surplus of $465,926 for the United States in 2011. You will notice that this surplus is exactly the same size as the current account deficit. This is no coincidence, and we explain the relationship in the next section.

The Key Identity of Balance of Payments

To talk about the major causes of trade deficits, we need to clarify the link between the current and capital accounts. Basically, when one of the accounts increases, the other decreases. We begin with an example before we state an important identity.

Let's say you are shopping for a new car, and you decide on a Toyota that is manufactured in Japan. Let's assume the following:

- Before you buy a Japanese car, the U.S. trade is completely balanced: imports = exports.
- Before you buy the car, the U.S. capital account is also balanced: U.S. ownership of foreign assets = foreign ownership of U.S. assets.
- The car costs $40,000.

Now when you buy the car, there are two sides to the exchange: from your perspective, you are trading dollars for an imported good; from the perspective of Toyota, the company is trading its car for a U.S. financial asset (dollars). Thus, the exchange is recorded twice in the U.S. balance of payments. First, it is recorded as an import in the current account, and this leads to a current account deficit of $40,000. Second, it is recorded as the purchase of U.S. currency, a U.S. financial asset, in the capital account, and this transaction implies a surplus in the capital account of $40,000. These are entries of equal but offsetting magnitude, which is the principle behind the *balance* of payments.

Now we arrive at an important principle with regard to the balance of payments, which we call the *key identity of the balance of payments*: while either account can be in deficit or surplus, together they sum to zero. A positive balance in the current account means there must be a negative balance in the capital account, and vice versa. We can also write this in equation form:

(Equation 33.5)   current account balance + capital account balance = 0

Thus, if the current account is in deficit, the capital account is in surplus. If the current account is in surplus, the capital account is in deficit.

Before moving on, let's consider two other scenarios within our Japanese car example. First, what happens if the new foreign owners of the $40,000 in U.S. currency decide to use it to buy Microsoft software manufactured in the United States? This transaction involves $40,000 worth of U.S. exports, so the current account deficit disappears, as does the capital account surplus.

Finally, what happens if, instead, the Japanese owners of $40,000 in U.S. currency use it to purchase shares of Microsoft stock? In this case, the

TABLE 33.6

An Example of Balance of Payments

Example: A U.S. citizen buys a Japanese car for $40,000.

Scenario I: The Japanese company holds on to the $40,000.

$$\text{U.S. current account: } -\$40{,}000$$
$$\text{U.S. capital account: } +\$40{,}000$$
$$\text{Total} \qquad 0$$

Scenario II: The Japanese company buys $40,000 worth of U.S.-produced Microsoft software.

$$\text{U.S. current account: } -\$40{,}000 + \$40{,}000 = 0$$
$$\text{U.S. capital account: } +\$40{,}000 - \$40{,}000 = 0$$
$$\text{Total} \qquad 0$$

Scenario III: The Japanese company buys $40,000 worth Microsoft Corporation stock.

$$\text{U.S. current account: } -\$40{,}000$$
$$\text{U.S. capital account: } +\$40{,}000$$
$$\text{Total} \qquad 0$$

U.S. current account deficit stays at $40,000 and the capital account surplus stays at $40,000, because the Japanese have simply shifted to a different U.S. financial asset. These three scenarios are summarized in Table 33.6. In all cases, the current account changes are offset by opposite capital account changes.

We can see this identity when we examine actual balance of payments data for a nation. Figure 33.11 illustrates the identity with real historic data from the United States. The orange line is the U.S. current account balance—clearly, in deficit since 1991. Along with this, we plot the balance of the capital account, which is clearly in surplus. Notice that when the capital account surplus grows, it accompanies a larger current account deficit. As the current account deficit exceeded $750 billion in 2006, the capital account surplus also exceeded $750 billion. The two lines are very close to mirror images, which they should be, based on Equation 33.5.

This identity is important for practical purposes because it shows us that anything that affects the capital account also affects the current account. Thus, if we are interested in the major causes of trade deficits, we need to examine not only what causes a current account deficit to increase but also what causes a capital account surplus to increase, since the two are essentially mirror images.

The Causes of Trade Deficits

People who are concerned about trade deficits often think about trade in terms of fairness. After all, if our economy is buying goods from nations around the globe, shouldn't these nations be buying goods from us? The way we calculate GDP seems to reinforce this point of view. Recall that GDP is the sum of four components—consumption (C), investment (I), government expenditures (G), and net exports (NX):

$$\text{GDP} = Y = C + I + G + NX$$

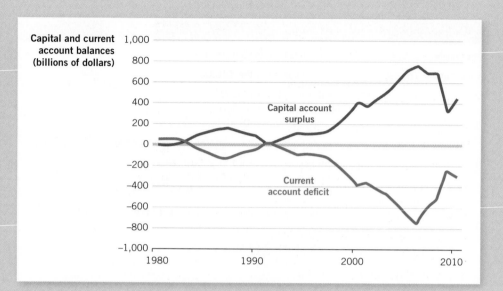

FIGURE 33.11

U.S. Current and Capital Account Balances since 1980

The current account and the capital account are essentially mirror images of each other. If we say that the United States has a current account deficit, we are also saying that it has a capital account surplus.

Source: United States Bureau of Economic Analysis.

The fourth piece is net exports. All else being equal, the net exports component falls when a nation imports more goods. In this sense, the greater current account deficit implies lower GDP. While that implication might make you think that nations are better off with fewer imports or more exports, you shouldn't jump to this conclusion.

There are several causes of deficits in the current account. Although the United States has consistently had a current account deficit since 1975, the cause has varied over time. We consider three primary causes of current account deficits: strong economic growth, lower personal savings rates, and fiscal policy.

Strong Economic Growth

One cause of current account deficits is strong domestic growth. A nation that is growing and increasing in wealth relative to the rest of the world is also a nation that can afford to import significant quantities of goods and services.

Think of this first in terms of individuals. Imagine that you open a coffee shop and your business does very well. You earn significant profits, and your personal wealth grows. This new wealth enables you to purchase many goods and services that you would not be able to afford if you were less well off. With your new wealth, you'll likely develop trade deficits with many stores and restaurants in your town. You might even establish trade deficits with ski resorts, golf courses, and car dealerships. Bill Gates has personal trade deficits all over the world simply because he buys large quantities of goods and services.

This type of scenario also applies to nations. During periods of rapid economic expansion in the United States, our current account deficit has grown. The prime example of this is the late 1990s. Look again at Figure 33.11. In the long (unshaded) period during the late 1990s, the economy was growing and the current account deficit was growing as well. U.S. wealth was increasing,

Bill Gates seems to enjoy his trade deficits.

PRACTICE WHAT YOU KNOW

Current Account versus Capital Account Entries

If a foreign student buys a ticket on a U.S. airline, how does this transaction affect the balance of payments?

Question: Would the following international transactions be recorded in the U.S. current account or the capital account?

a. the purchase of a Canadian government bond by a resident of Pennsylvania

b. the sale of a U.S. Treasury bond to a resident of Ontario, Canada

c. the purchase of a condominium in Cancun, Mexico, by a U.S. resident

d. the purchase of a Samsung television by Best Buy (a U.S. company)

e. the purchase of an airplane ticket from United Airlines (a U.S. company) by a resident of Chengdu, China, to come to the United States to attend college

Answers:

a. This would be recorded in the capital account, since it is the purchase of a financial asset.

b. This would be recorded in the capital account, since it is the sale of a financial asset.

c. This would be recorded in the capital account, since it is the purchase of a real asset.

d. This would be recorded in the current account, since it is the purchase of a good.

e. This would be recorded in the current account, since it is the purchase of a service.

---

and this enabled us to afford more imports from around the globe. The reverse occurs during economic downturns. When U.S. wealth falls, we are less able to afford imports, and the current account deficit shrinks.

Certain distinct effects cause the trade deficit to grow during economic expansion. The first is in the current account: wealthy domestic consumers can afford to import more goods and services. The second is in the capital account: growing economies offer higher investment returns, so funds from around the globe flow in to take advantage of high rates of return. Table 33.7 summarizes these two complementary effects.

When an economy is growing rapidly relative to the rest of the world, the firms in that economy are willing to pay more for investment funds. This causes the demand for loanable funds to shift to the right and leads to higher interest rates. Subsequently, international funds flow in to take advantage of these interest rates.

TABLE 33.7		
Why Strong Growth Leads to a Balance of Payments Deficit		
Primary account	**Explanation**	**Result**
Current account	The growing economy leads to wealthier consumers who import more goods and services from around the world.	Net exports fall, which leads to a greater BOP deficit.
Capital account	The growing economy offers greater returns, which attracts international funds for investment.	The capital account surplus increases, which reinforces the greater BOP deficit.

To clarify, let's return to the example where your coffee shop business is doing very well. One way to expand your business is to offer shares of stock in the business. People buy this stock, hoping to get in on the financial success of your great new business. The stock purchases represent a capital inflow for your business. It works in exactly the same way for nations that are growing relatively quickly: funds from around the globe flow in to take advantage of the high returns.

For a macro example, consider the case of China. In recent years, China has periodically experienced a current account deficit, largely owing to its rapid economic growth. This result seems almost counterintuitive, as the rapid Chinese growth has largely been in the area of manufacturing exports. Yet the income surge has also enabled Chinese citizens to import goods and services from all over the globe. In addition, greater returns have brought an influx of global investment funds. These effects were so strong that by late 2010 China was recording current account deficits.

Lower Personal Savings Rates

A second major cause of current account deficits is low domestic savings rates. When households are not saving much, funds can flow in from overseas to supplement domestic investment.

Let's return to the example of a coffee shop. Your business is doing well, and you are considering expansion. You decide you want to open another location for your coffee shop. If you have been frugal and saved a portion of your income, you can use your own savings to expand the business. However, if you have spent your income, you'll need to rely on the savings of others to pay for your expansion. You'll have to borrow from a bank, or issue some bonds, or perhaps sell shares of stock in your coffee shop business. The purchase of financial assets in your firm is analogous to capital account purchases in the balance of payments.

We can extend the analysis to a macroeconomy. If individuals and governments save a significant portion of their income, the savings can be used to fund investment. In contrast, if savings falls, investment must be funded with outside sources. In the United States, personal savings rates have dropped significantly since the early 1990s (see Figure 22.8). So while the U.S economy was growing throughout the 1990s and into the first decade of this century, the necessary financing was coming from savers around the globe. This activity increased the capital account surplus. Of course, any increase in the capital account surplus implies an increase in the current account deficit.

TABLE 33.8

Causes of Current Account Deficits

Cause	Explanation
Rapid domestic growth	Domestic buyers are able to afford imports given the increase in wealth, which widens the current account deficit. At the same time, foreign funds are attracted to higher rates of return in the growing economy, which increases the capital account surplus.
Declining domestic savings	Falling domestic savings leaves a finance gap for investment. The gap is filled with foreign funds, which increases the capital account surplus.
Government budget deficits	Increased government borrowing means greater competition for investment funds. All else being equal, more foreign funds are needed to lend to government, and this activity widens the capital account surplus.

As we discussed in Chapter 22, the influx of funds from around the globe was instrumental in keeping interest rates low in the United States and enabling firms to fund expansion. These funds were critical as U.S. savings rates fell, but they did contribute to the widening current account deficit.

Fiscal Policy

Large budget deficits also contribute to current account deficits. This is part of the reason for large U.S. current account deficits in the 1980s and then again after 2000. Large government budget deficits devour both domestic and foreign funds. Recall this important principle from Chapter 22: *Every dollar borrowed requires a dollar saved.* So when the U.S. government borrows trillions each year, this is similar to a further reduction in personal savings—the government is using funds that could have been used for private investment. Recall that in Chapter 29 we introduced this concept as crowding-out.

Domestic savings are not enough to fund the budget deficit. International funds also flow in for this purpose. The influx of international funds increases the capital account surplus and thus increases the trade deficit.

Table 33.8 summarizes these different causes of trade deficits. The bottom line is that many factors cause trade deficits, some that don't even seem related to goods and services. The past few decades of U.S. experience offer examples of all three. The 1980s was a time of large budget deficits, and the trade deficit widened. Beginning around 1990, personal savings rates fell and the economy grew rapidly; the trade deficit widened, even as the federal government balanced its budget. Finally, a recent return to historically large budget deficits has added to the pressure for capital inflows, reducing any prospects for elimination of the trade deficit in the near future.

Conclusion

We began this chapter with the misconception that trade deficits are harmful to an economy. But we have seen that there are many factors that affect a trade balance, and typically a trade deficit means that the domestic economy

To Peg or Not to Peg?

Most of the US's major trading partners allow their currency to "float," which means the market forces of supply and demand are allowed to determine the currency's exchange rate versus another. However, the United States' second-largest trading partner and the second-largest economy in the world—China—does not allow its currency to float. Rather, it "pegs" it to a specific value of the U.S. dollar. This activity has been very controversial—let's see why.

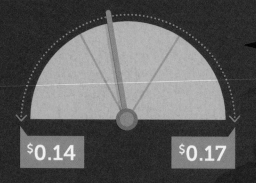

$0.14   **$0.17**

Step 1

In recent years, the yuan has had an exchange rate of between $0.14 and $0.17. If the Chinese government were not pegging the yuan, the exchange rate would be much higher.

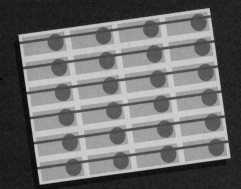

Step 2

When the Chinese government observes the value of the yuan rising against the dollar, they print more yuan.

Step 3

The newly minted yuan are then used to purchase U.S. dollars and Treasury securities on world markets. These actions reduce the value of the yuan relative to the dollar, since the supply of yuan on the currency market increases while the supply of dollars decreases. Note that China has not declared a new exchange rate for the yuan—which is impossible for them to do— but rather has adjusted the supply of currency so that the market creates the outcome they desired.

- Create a simple supply and demand graph showing how the Chinese purchase of U.S. dollars on currency markets reduces the value of the yuan.

- How do U.S. citizens benefit from the fact that China pegs its currency?

Lower prices for Chinese exports

The lower value of the yuan means a higher value of the dollar, and so Americans can afford to buy more Chinese goods and services. This stimulates the quantity of Chinese exports demanded.

Lower real wages for Chinese citizens

The main drawback for China is that the real wages of Chinese citizens decline, since the devalued yuan can purchase fewer goods worldwide.

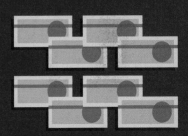

For Rent

Higher prices for U.S. exports

China's actions reduce the quantity of U.S. exports demanded, which hurts domestic industries. This effect is what makes the Chinese monetary policy is actually doing well. Goods and service flows are interrelated with real and financial asset flows. Given this relationship, changes in personal savings rates and government budget deficits can affect trade balances.

We also studied exchange rates in this chapter and considered them as market prices that depend on the supply of, and the demand for, foreign currency. But exchange rates are also subject to manipulation by governments. Depreciating a currency makes exports less expensive but doesn't always help all the residents of a nation, even though some nations' governments have followed this strategy explicitly in recent years.

ANSWERING THE BIG QUESTIONS

Why do exchange rates rise and fall?

* An increase in the exchange rate indicates a depreciation of the domestic currency. This occurs when there is an increase in demand for foreign goods, services, and financial assets relative to the demand for domestic goods, services, and financial assets.

* The exchange rate also increases when there is a decline in the supply of foreign currency relative to the domestic currency.

* A decrease in the exchange rate indicates an appreciation of the domestic currency. This occurs when there is a decrease in demand for foreign goods, services, and financial assets relative to domestic goods, services, and financial assets.

* The exchange rate also falls when there is an increase in the supply of foreign currency relative to the supply of domestic currency.

What is purchasing power parity?

* Purchasing power parity (PPP) is a theory about the determinants of long-run exchange rates. In particular, PPP implies that the exchange rate between two nations is determined by a ratio of relative price levels in the two nations. If a nation experiences more inflation than its trading partners do, its exchange rate will rise, indicating a depreciation of its currency.

* PPP is based on the law of one price.

What causes trade deficits?

* Trade deficits are essentially synonymous with current account deficits. As such, they increase when the current account deficit or the capital account surplus widens.

* Economic growth increases the current account deficits as wealthier residents demand more imports. It also works through the capital account, as higher rates of return attract foreign funds.

* A second cause is lower personal savings rates.

* A third cause is larger government budget deficits.

CONCEPTS YOU SHOULD KNOW

account deficit (p. 1041)
account surplus (p. 1042)
balance of payments (BOP)
 (p. 1040)
capital account (p. 1040)
currency appreciation (p. 1022)
currency depreciation (p. 1022)

current account (p. 1040)
derived demand (p. 1021)
exchange rate (p. 1020)
exchange rate manipulation
 (p. 1028)
flexible (floating) exchange
 rates (p. 1030)

law of one price (p. 1034)
pegged exchange rates
 (p. 1030)
purchasing power parity (PPP)
 (p. 1034)

QUESTIONS FOR REVIEW

1. The United States imports Molson beer from Canada. Assume that Canada and the United States share the same currency and that a bottle of Molson beer costs $2 in Toronto, Canada, but just $1 in Chicago.

   a. What market adjustments will ensue in this case, assuming no shipping costs or trade barriers?
   b. If Canadians really like Molson beer more than the residents of the United States do, can a price differential persist? Why or why not?

2. The United States currently has a current account deficit. How would each of the following events affect this deficit, assuming no other changes?

   a. U.S. economic growth slows relative to the rest of the world.
   b. U.S. personal savings rates increase.
   c. U.S. federal budget deficits decline.
   d. Foreign rates of return (in financial assets) rise relative to rates of return in the United States.

3. Why are current account balances generally mirror images of capital account balances?

4. Sometimes, official government reserves are singled out in the balance of payments accounts. For example, when China buys U.S. financial assets (currency and Treasury securities), this purchase is classified as "Official Government Reserves." On which side of the balance of payments should such purchases be reflected—the current account or the capital account? Explain your logic.

5. What are three factors that might make a capital account surplus grow?

6. Is a trade deficit a sign of economic weakness? Why or why not?

7. The rate of inflation in India from 2007 to 2011 was 8%. Over the same period, the inflation rate in the United States was 2.7%.

   a. What is the implication of these inflation rates for the exchange rate between the dollar and the rupee? In particular, does the PPP condition imply a rise or a fall in the exchange rate? Explain your answer.
   b. Is this an appreciation or a depreciation of the dollar? Is this an appreciation or a depreciation of the rupee?

STUDY PROBLEMS (✻ *solved at the end of the section*)

1. If interest rates in India rise relative to interest rates around the world, how does this affect the world value of the rupee? Illustrate these effects in the market for rupees.

2. From Chapter 21, we know that the primary cause of inflation is expansion of the money supply. In this chapter, we find an additional side effect of monetary expansion. What is this effect? Use demand and supply of foreign currency to illustrate your answer.

3. Explain the numerical effects on both the U.S. current and capital accounts from each of these examples.

   a. In the United States, the Best Buy company purchases $1 million worth of TVs from the Samsung corporation, a Korean firm, using U.S. dollars. In addition, Samsung keeps the U.S. dollars.

   b. Best Buy purchases $1 million worth of TVs from the Samsung corporation, using U.S. dollars. Samsung then trades its dollars to a third party for won, the Korean currency.

   c. Best Buy trades $1 million for Korean won and then uses the won to buy TVs from Samsung.

4. The price of a dozen roses in the United States is about $30. Use this information, along with the exchange rates given in Table 33.1 (see p. 1022), to answer the following questions.

   a. Assuming that PPP holds perfectly, what is the price of a dozen roses in Turkey? Express your answer in units of Turkish lira.

   b. If the actual price in Turkey costs more lira than the answer you found in part (b), how might you account for the discrepancy?

✻5. Explain why the supply curve for foreign currency is vertical. Let's say you return from a trip to Mexico with 1,000 pesos. If you decide to exchange these pesos for dollars, does your action shift the supply of pesos?

✻6. For each of the following transactions, determine whether (a) it will be recorded in the U.S. current account or capital account, and (b) whether the entry will be positive or negative.

   a. A resident of the United States buys an airplane ticket to England on Virgin Atlantic Airways, a British company.

   b. The government of England buys U.S. Treasury securities.

   c. A U.S. citizen buys shares of stock in a Chinese corporation.

SOLVED PROBLEMS

5. The supply curve is vertical because the supply is completely controlled by the government and is invariant to changes in price. Your exchange does not shift the supply of pesos; only the government can do that. Instead, it signals a reduction in demand for pesos.

6. a. This is a purchase of a service, so it enters the current account. It enters negatively because it is an import; thus, funds are flowing out of the U.S. current account.

   b. This is a purchase of financial assets in the United States, so it is entered in the U.S. capital account. The entry is positive because funds are flowing into the capital account.

   c. This is a purchase of financial assets abroad, so it enters the U.S. capital account. It enters negatively because funds are flowing out.

GLOSSARY

absolute advantage: the ability of one producer to make more than another producer with the same quantity of resources

account deficit: condition existing when more payments are flowing out of an account than into the account

account surplus: condition existing when more payments are flowing into an account than out of the account

accounting profit: calculated by subtracting a firm's explicit costs from total revenue

active monetary policy: the strategic use of monetary policy to counteract macroeconomic expansions and contractions

adaptive expectations theory: theory holding that people's expectations of future inflation are based on their most recent experience

adverse selection: phenomenon existing when one party has information about some aspect of product quality that the other party does not have

aggregate demand: the total demand for final goods and services in an economy

aggregate production function: the relationship among all the inputs used in the macroeconomy and the total output (GDP) of that economy

aggregate supply: the total supply of final goods and services in an economy

antitrust laws: attempts to prevent oligopolies from behaving like monopolies

assets: the items that a firm owns

asymmetric information: an imbalance in information that occurs when one party knows more than the other

austerity: policy involving strict budget regulations aimed at debt reduction

automatic stabilizers: government programs that automatically implement countercyclical fiscal policy in response to economic conditions

average fixed cost (AFC): determined by dividing a firm's total fixed costs by the output

average tax rate: the total tax paid divided by the amount of taxable income

average total cost (ATC): the sum of average variable cost and average fixed cost

average variable cost (AVC): determined by dividing a firm's total variable costs by the output

backward-bending labor supply curve: supply curve occurring when workers value additional leisure more than additional income

balance of payments: a record of all payments between one nation and the rest of the world

balance sheet: an accounting statement that summarizes a firm's key financial information

bandwagon effect: condition arising when a buyer's preference for a product increases as the number of people buying it increases

bank: a private firm that accepts deposits and extends loans

bank run: event occurring when many depositors attempt to withdraw their funds at the same time

barriers to entry: restrictions that make it difficult for new firms to enter a market

barter: the trade of a good or service without a commonly accepted medium of exchange

behavioral economics: the field of economics that draws on insights from experimental psychology to explore how people make economic decisions

black markets: illegal markets that arise when price controls are in place

bond: a security that represents a debt to be paid

bounded rationality: concept proposing that although decision-makers want a good outcome, either they are not capable of performing the problem-solving that traditional theory assumes, or they are not inclined to do so

budget constraint: the set of consumption bundles that represent the maximum amount the consumer can afford

budget deficit: condition occurring when government outlays exceed revenue

budget surplus: condition occurring when government revenue exceeds outlays

business cycle: a short-run fluctuation in economic activity

cap and trade: an approach used to curb pollution by creating a system of pollution permits that are traded in an open market

capital account: the balance of payments account that tracks payments for real and financial assets between nations and extensions of international loans

capital gains taxes: taxes on the gains realized by selling an asset for more than its purchase price

capital goods: goods that help produce other valuable goods and services in the future

cartel: a group of two or more firms that act in unison

causality: condition existing when one variable influences another

ceteris paribus: the concept under which economists examine a change in one variable while holding everything else constant

chained CPI: a measure of the consumer price index in which the typical consumer's "basket" of goods considered is updated monthly

checkable deposits: deposits in bank accounts from which depositors may make withdrawals by writing checks

classical economists: economists who stress the importance of aggregate supply and generally believe that the economy can adjust back to full employment equilibrium on its own

Clayton Act: law of 1914 targeting corporate behaviors that reduce competition

club goods: goods with two characteristics: they are nonrival in consumption and excludable

Coase theorem: theorem stating that if there are no barriers to negotiations, and if property rights are fully specified, interested parties will bargain to correct any externalities that exist

co-insurance payments: a percentage of costs that the insured must pay after exceeding the insurance policy's deductible up to the policy's contribution limit

collusion: an agreement among rival firms that specifies the price each firm charges and the quantity it produces

commodity money: the use of an actual good in place of money

commodity-backed money: money that can be exchanged for a commodity at a fixed rate

common-resource goods: goods with two characteristics: they are rival in consumption and nonexcludable

comparative advantage: the situation where an individual, business, or country can produce at a lower opportunity cost than a competitor can

compensating differential: the difference in wages offered to offset the desirability or undesirability of a job

competitive market: one in which there are so many buyers and sellers that each has only a small impact on the market price and output

complements: two goods that are used together; when the price of a complementary good rises, the demand for the related good goes down

constant returns to scale: condition occurring when costs remain constant as output expands in the long run

consumer goods: goods produced for present consumption

consumer optimum: the combination of goods and services that maximizes the consumer's utility for a given income or budget

consumer price index (CPI): a measure of the price level based on the consumption patterns of a typical consumer

consumer surplus: the difference between the willingness to pay for a good and the price that is paid to get it

consumption: the purchase of final goods and services by households, excluding new housing

consumption smoothing: behavior occurring when people borrow and save in order to smooth consumption over their lifetime

contractionary fiscal policy: a decrease in government spending or increase in taxes meant to slow economic expansion

contractionary monetary policy: a central bank's action to decrease the money supply

convergence: the idea that per capita GDP levels across nations will equalize as nations approach the steady state

co-payments: fixed amounts that the insured must pay when receiving a medical service or filling a prescription

cost-benefit analysis: a process that economists use to determine whether the benefits of providing a public good outweigh the costs

countercyclical fiscal policy: fiscal policy that seeks to counteract business-cycle fluctuations

CPI: see *consumer price index*

creative destruction: the introduction of new products and technologies that leads to the end of other industries and jobs

cross-price elasticity of demand: measurement of the responsiveness of the quantity demanded of one good to a change in the price of a related good

crowding-out: phenomenon occurring when private spending falls in response to increases in government spending

currency: the paper bills and coins that are used to buy goods and services

currency appreciation: a currency's increase in value relative to other currencies

currency depreciation: a currency's decrease in value relative to other currencies

current account: the balance of payments account that tracks all payments for goods and services, current income, and gifts

cyclical unemployment: unemployment caused by economic downturns

deadweight loss: the decrease in economic activity caused by market distortions

debt: the sum total of accumulated budget deficits

deductibles: fixed amounts that the insured must pay before most of the policy's benefits can be applied

default risk: the risk that a borrower will not pay the face value of a bond on the maturity date

deflation: condition occurring when overall prices fall

demand curve: a graph of the relationship between the prices in the demand schedule and the quantity demanded at those prices

demand schedule: a table that shows the relationship between the price of a good and the quantity demanded

depreciation: a fall in the value of a resource over time

derived demand: (1) the demand for an input used in the production process; (2) demand for a good or service that derives from the demand for another good or service

diamond-water paradox: concept explaining why water, which is essential to life, is inexpensive while diamonds, which do not sustain life, are expensive

diminishing marginal product: condition occurring when successive increases in inputs are associated with a slower rise in output

diminishing marginal utility: condition occurring when marginal utility declines as consumption increases

direct finance: activity in the loanable funds market when borrowers go directly to savers for funds

discount loans: loans from the Federal Reserve to private banks

discount rate: the interest rate on the discount loans made by the Federal Reserve to private banks

discouraged workers: those who are not working, have looked for a job in the past 12 months and are willing to work, but have not sought employment in the past 4 weeks

discretionary outlays: government spending that can be altered when the government is setting its annual budget

diseconomies of scale: condition occurring when costs rise as output expands in the long run

dissaving: behavior occurring when people withdraw funds from their previously accumulated savings

Dodd-Frank Act: the primary regulatory response to the financial turmoil that contributed to the Great Recession, enacted in 2010

dominant strategy: in game theory, a strategy that a player will always prefer, regardless of what his opponent chooses

double coincidence of wants: condition occurring when each party in an exchange transaction happens to have what the other party desires

dumping: behavior occurring when a foreign supplier sells a good below the price it charges in its home country

economic contraction: a phase of the business cycle during which the economy is growing more slowly than usual

economic expansion: a phase of the business cycle during which the economy is growing faster than usual

economic growth: the percentage change in real per capita GDP

economic profit: calculated by subtracting both the explicit and the implicit costs of business from a firm's total revenue

economic rent: the difference between what a factor of production earns and what it could earn in the next-best alternative

economic thinking: a purposeful evaluation of the available opportunities to make the best decision possible

economics: the study of how people allocate their limited resources to satisfy their nearly unlimited wants

economies of scale: condition occurring when costs decline as output expands in the long run

efficiency: an allocation of resources that maximizes total surplus

efficiency wages: wages higher than equilibrium wages, offered to increase worker productivity

efficient scale: the output level that minimizes a firm's average total cost

elasticity: a measure of the responsiveness of buyers and sellers to changes in price or income

endogenous factors: the variables that can be controlled for in a model

endogenous growth: growth driven by factors inside the economy

equilibrium: condition occurring at the point where the demand curve and the supply curve intersect

equilibrium price: the price at which the quantity supplied is equal to the quantity demanded; also known as the *market-clearing price*

equilibrium quantity: the amount at which the quantity supplied is equal to the quantity demanded

equity: the fairness of the distribution of benefits within the society

excess capacity: phenomenon occurring when a firm produces at an output level that is smaller than the output level needed to minimize average total costs

excess reserves: any reserves held by a bank in excess of those required

exchange rate: the price of foreign currency, indicating how much a unit of foreign currency costs in terms of another currency

exchange rate manipulation: a national government's intentional adjustment of its money supply to affect the exchange rate of its currency

excise taxes: taxes levied on a particular good or service

excludable goods: goods that the consumer must purchase before being able to use them

exogenous factors: the variables that cannot be controlled for in a model

exogenous growth: growth that is independent of any factors in the economy

expansionary fiscal policy: an increase in government spending or decrease in taxes meant to stimulate the economy toward expansion

expansionary monetary policy: a central bank's action to increase the money supply in an effort to stimulate the economy

explicit costs: tangible out-of-pocket expenses

external costs: the costs of a market activity paid by people who are not participants

externalities: the costs or benefits of a market activity that affect a third party

face value: the value of a bond at maturity—the amount due at repayment; also called *par value*

factors of production: the inputs (labor, land, and capital) used in producing goods and services

federal funds: deposits that private banks hold on reserve at the Federal Reserve

federal funds rate: the interest rate on loans between private banks

fiat money: money that has no value except as the medium of exchange; there is no inherent or intrinsic value to the currency

final good: a good sold to final users

financial intermediaries: firms that help to channel funds from savers to borrowers

fiscal policy: the use of government's budget tools, government spending, and taxes to influence the macroeconomy

Fisher equation: equation stating that the real interest rate equals the nominal interest rate minus the inflation rate

fixed costs: costs that do not vary with a firm's output in the short run

flexible exchange rates: exchange rates that are determined by the supply of and demand for currency; also called *floating exchange rates*

floating exchange rates: see *flexible exchange rates*

fractional reserve banking: a system in which banks hold only a fraction of deposits on reserve

framing effects: a phenomenon seen when people change their answer (or action) depending on how the question is asked

free-rider problem: phenomenon occurring when someone receives a benefit without having to pay for it

frictional unemployment: unemployment caused by delays in matching available jobs and workers

full employment output: the output level produced in an economy when the unemployment rate is equal to its natural rate

gambler's fallacy: the belief that recent outcomes are unlikely to be repeated and that outcomes that have not occurred recently are due to happen soon

game theory: a branch of mathematics that economists use to analyze the strategic behavior of decision-makers

GDP: see *gross domestic product*

GDP deflator: a measure of the price level that includes prices of the final goods and services included in gross domestic product

GNP: see *gross national product*

government outlays: the part of the government budget that includes both spending and transfer payments

government spending: spending by all levels of government on final goods and services

Great Recession: the U.S. recession lasting from December 2007 to June 2009

gross domestic product (GDP): the market value of all final goods and services produced within a country during a specific period

gross national product (GNP): the output produced by workers and resources owned by residents of the nation

hot hand fallacy: the belief that random sequences exhibit a positive correlation

human capital: (1) the skill that workers acquire on the job and through education; (2) the resource represented by the quantity, knowledge, and skills of the workers in an economy

immediate run: a period of time when there is no time for consumers to adjust their behavior

imperfect market: one in which either the buyer or the seller has an influence on the market price

implicit costs: a firm's opportunity costs of doing business

import quotas: limits on the quantity of products that can be imported into a country

incentives: factors that motivate a person to act or exert effort

incidence: the burden of taxation on the party who pays the tax through higher prices, regardless of whom the tax is actually levied on

income effect: phenomenon occurring when laborers work fewer hours at higher wages, using their additional income to demand more leisure

income elasticity of demand: measurement of how a change in income affects spending

income mobility: the ability of workers to move up or down the economic ladder over time

indifference curve: a graph representing the various combinations of two goods that yield the same level of satisfaction, or utility

indirect finance: activity in the loanable funds market when savers deposit funds into banks, which then loan these funds to borrowers

infant industry argument: the idea that domestic industries need trade protection until they are established and able to compete internationally

inferior good: a good purchased out of necessity rather than choice

inflation: the growth in the overall level of prices in an economy

in-kind transfers: transfers (mostly to the poor) in the form of goods or services instead of cash

inputs: the resources (labor, land, and capital) used in the production process

institution: a significant practice, relationship, or organization in a society

interest rate: a price of loanable funds, quoted as a percentage of the original loan amount

interest rate effect: effect occurring when a change in the price level leads to a change in interest rates and, therefore, in the quantity of aggregate demand

intermediate good: a good that firms repackage or bundle with other goods for sale at a later stage

internal costs: the costs of a market activity paid by an individual participant

internalization: condition occurring when a firm takes into account the external costs (or benefits) to society that occur as a result of its actions

international trade effect: effect occurring when a change in the price level leads to a change in the quantity of net exports demanded

intertemporal decision-making: decision-making that involves planning to do something over a period of time; this requires valuing the present and the future consistently

investor confidence: a measure of what firms expect for future economic activity

investment: (1) the process of using resources to create or buy new capital; (2) private spending on tools, plant, and equipment used to produce future output

Keynesian economists: economists who stress the importance of aggregate demand and generally believe that the economy needs help in moving back to full employment equilibrium

kinked demand curve: theory stating that oligopolists have a greater tendency to respond aggressively to the price cuts of rivals but will largely ignore price increases

labor force: those who are already employed or actively seeking work

labor force participation rate: the percentage of the population that is in the labor force

Laffer curve: an illustration of the relationship between tax rates and tax revenue

law of demand: the law that, all other things being equal, quantity demanded falls when prices rise, and rises when prices fall

law of increasing relative cost: law stating that the opportunity cost of producing a good rises as a society produces more of it

law of one price: law stating that after accounting for transportation costs and trade barriers, identical goods sold in different locations must sell for the same price

law of supply: the law that, all other things being equal, the quantity supplied of a good rises when the price of the good rises, and falls when the price of the good falls

law of supply and demand: the law that the market price of any good will adjust to bring the quantity supplied and the quantity demanded into balance

liabilities: the financial obligations a firm owes to others

life-cycle wage pattern: the predictable effect that age has on earnings over the course of a person's working life

loanable funds market: the market where savers supply funds for loans to borrowers

long run: a period of time when consumers have time to fully adjust to market conditions

loss: the result of total revenue being less than total cost

loss aversion: phenomenon occurring when individuals place more weight on avoiding losses than on attempting to realize gains

M1: the money supply measure that is essentially composed of currency and checkable deposits

M2: the money supply measure that includes everything in M1 plus savings deposits, money market mutual funds, and small-denomination time deposits (CDs)

macroeconomic policy: government acts to influence the macroeconomy

macroeconomics: the study of the overall aspects and workings of an economy

mandatory outlays: government spending that is determined by ongoing long-term obligations

marginal cost (MC): the increase in cost that occurs from producing additional output

marginal product: the change in output associated with one additional unit of an input

marginal product of labor: the change in output associated with adding one additional worker

marginal propensity to consume: the portion of additional income that is spent on consumption

marginal rate of substitution: the rate at which the consumer is willing to purchase one good instead of another

marginal tax rate: the tax rate paid on an individual's next dollar of income

marginal thinking: the evaluation of whether the benefit of one more unit of something is greater than its cost

marginal utility: the additional satisfaction derived from consuming one more unit of a good or service

market: a system that brings buyers and sellers together to exchange goods and services

market demand: the sum of all the individual quantities demanded by each buyer in the market at each price

market economy: an economy in which resources are allocated among households and firms with little or no government interference

market failure: condition occurring when the output level of a good is inefficient

market supply: the sum of the quantities supplied by each seller in the market at each price

market-clearing price: see *equilibrium price*

markup: the difference between the price the firm charges and the marginal cost of production

maturity date: on a bond, the date on which the loan repayment is due

maximization point: the point at which a certain combination of two goods yields the most utility

Medicare: a mandated federal program that funds health care for U.S. citizens age 65 or older

medium of exchange: what people trade for goods and services

menu costs: the costs of changing prices

microeconomics: the study of the individual units that make up the economy

minimum wage: the lowest hourly wage rate that firms may legally pay their workers

monetary neutrality: the idea that the money supply does not affect real economic variables

monetary policy: the government's adjustment of the money supply to influence the macroeconomy

money illusion: the interpretation of nominal changes in wages or prices as real changes

monopolistic competition: a situation characterized by free entry, many different firms, and product differentiation

monopoly: condition existing when a single company supplies the entire market for a particular good or service

monopoly power: measurement of the ability of firms to set the price for a good

monopsony: a situation in which there is only one buyer

moral hazard: phenomenon seen when a party that is protected from risk behaves differently from the way it would behave if it were fully exposed to the risk

mutual interdependence: a market situation where the actions of one firm have an impact on the price and output of its competitors

Nash equilibrium: in game theory, a phenomenon occurring when a decision-maker has nothing to gain by changing strategy unless it can collude

natural monopoly: a situation when a single large firm has lower costs than any potential smaller competitor

natural rate of unemployment: the typical rate of unemployment that occurs when the economy is growing normally

negative correlation: condition occurring when two variables move in the opposite direction

negative income tax: a tax credit paid to poor households out of taxes received from middle- and upper-income households

net exports: exports minus imports of final goods and services

net investment: investment minus depreciation

network externality: condition occurring when the number of customers who purchase or use a good influences the quantity demanded

new classical critique: critique of fiscal policy asserting that increases in government spending and decreases in taxes are largely offset by increases in savings

nominal GDP: gross domestic product measured in current prices, and not adjusted for inflation

nominal interest rate: the interest rate before it is corrected for inflation

nominal wage: a worker's wage expressed in current dollars

normal good: a good consumers buy more of as income rises, holding other things constant

normative statement: an opinion that cannot be tested or validated; it describes "what ought to be"

occupational crowding: the phenomenon of relegating a group of workers to a narrow range of jobs in the economy

oligopoly: condition existing when a small number of firms sell a differentiated product in a market with high barriers to entry

open market operations: the purchase or sale of bonds by a central bank

opportunity cost: the highest-valued alternative that must be sacrificed in order to get something else

output: the production the firm creates

output effect: phenomenon occurring when the entrance of a rival firm in the market affects the amount produced

outsourcing of labor: a firm's shifting of jobs to an outside company, usually overseas, where the cost of labor is lower

owner's equity: the difference between a firm's assets and its liabilities

par value: see *face value*

passive monetary policy: a central bank's purposeful decision to only stabilize money and price levels through monetary policy

pegged exchange rates: exchange rates that are fixed at a certain level through the actions of a government

per capita GDP: GDP per person

perfect complements: two goods the consumer is interested in consuming in fixed proportions, resulting in right-angle indifference curves

perfect price discrimination: the practice of a firm selling the same good at a unique price to every customer

perfect substitutes: goods that the consumer is completely indifferent between, resulting in straight-line indifference curves

Phillips curve: curve indicating a short-run inverse relationship between inflation and unemployment rates

positive correlation: condition occurring when two variables move in the same direction

positive statement: an assertion that can be tested and validated; it describes "what is"

poverty rate: the percentage of the population whose income is below the poverty threshold

poverty threshold: the income level below which a person or family is considered impoverished

PPP: see *purchasing power parity*

predatory pricing: the practice of a firm deliberately setting its prices below average variable costs with the intent of driving rivals from the market

preference reversal: phenomenon arising when risk tolerance is not consistent

price ceilings: legally established maximum prices for goods or services

price controls: an attempt to set prices through government involvement in the market

price discrimination: the practice of a firm selling the same good at different prices to different groups of customers

price effect: phenomenon seen when the price of a good or service is affected by the entrance of a rival firm in the market

price elasticity of demand: a measure of the responsiveness of quantity demanded to a change in price

price elasticity of supply: a measure of the responsiveness of the quantity supplied to a change in price

price floors: legally established minimum prices for goods or services

price gouging laws: temporary ceilings on the prices that sellers can charge during times of emergency

price leadership: phenomenon occurring when a dominant firm in an industry sets the price that maximizes profits and the smaller firms in the industry follow

price level: an index of the average prices of goods and services throughout the economy

price maker: a firm with some control over the price it charges

price taker: a firm with no control over the price set by the market

priming effects: phenomenon seen when the ordering of the questions that are asked influences the answers

principal-agent problem: a situation in which a principal entrusts an agent to complete a task and the agent does not do so in a satisfactory way

prisoner's dilemma: a situation in which decision-makers face incentives that make it difficult to achieve mutually beneficial outcomes

private goods: goods with two characteristics: they are both excludable and rival in consumption

private property: provision of an exclusive right of ownership that allows for the use, and especially the exchange, of property

private property rights: the rights of individuals to own property, to use it in production, and to own the resulting output

producer surplus: the difference between the willingness to sell a good and the price that the seller receives

product differentiation: the process that firms use to make a product more attractive to potential customers

production function: description of the relationship between inputs a firm uses and the output it creates

production possibilities frontier: a model that illustrates the combinations of outputs that a society can produce if all of its resources are being used efficiently

profit: total revenue minus total cost; a negative result is a *loss*

profit-maximizing rule: the rule stating that profit maximization occurs when the firm chooses the quantity that causes marginal revenue to be equal to marginal cost, or MR = MC

progressive income tax system: one in which people with higher incomes pay a larger portion of their income in taxes than people with lower incomes do

property rights: an owner's ability to exercise control over a resource

prospect theory: a theory suggesting that individuals weigh the utilities and risks of gains and losses differently

public goods: goods that can be jointly consumed by more than one person, and from which nonpayers are difficult to exclude

purchasing power parity (PPP): the idea that a unit of currency should be able to buy the same quantity of goods and services in any country

quantitative easing: the targeted use of open market operations in which the central bank buys securities specifically targeted in certain markets

quantity demanded: the amount of a good or service that buyers are willing and able to purchase at the current price

quantity supplied: the amount of a good or service that producers are willing and able to sell at the current price

rational expectations theory: theory holding that people form expectations on the basis of all available information

real GDP: gross domestic product adjusted for changes in prices

real interest rate: the interest rate that is corrected for inflation

real wage: the nominal wage adjusted for changes in the price level

real-income effect: a change in consumption when there is a change in purchasing power as a result of a change in the price of a good

recession: a short-term economic downturn

rent control: a price ceiling that applies to the housing market

rent seeking: behavior occurring when resources are used to secure monopoly rights through the political process

required reserve ratio: the portion of deposits that banks are required to keep on reserve

reserves: the portion of bank deposits that are set aside and not lent out

resources: the inputs used to produce goods and services; also called *factors of production*

reverse causation: condition occurring when causation is incorrectly assigned among associated events

risk takers: those who prefer gambles with lower expected values, and potentially higher winnings, over a sure thing

risk-averse people: those who prefer a sure thing over a gamble with a higher expected value

risk-neutral people: those who choose the highest expected value regardless of the risk

rival goods: goods that cannot be enjoyed by more than one person at a time

rule of 70: rule stating that if the annual growth rate of a variable is x%, the size of that variable doubles approximately every 70 ÷ x years

samaritan's dilemma: a situation in which an act of charity causes disincentives for recipients to take care of themselves

savings rate: personal saving as a portion of disposable (after-tax) income

scale: the size of the production process

scarcity: the limited nature of society's resources, given society's unlimited wants and needs

scatterplot: a graph that shows individual (x,y) points

secondary markets: markets in which securities are traded after their first sale

securitization: the creation of a new security by combining otherwise separate loan agreements

security: a tradable contract that entitles its owner to certain rights

service: an output that provides benefits without the production of a tangible product

Sherman Antitrust Act: the first federal law limiting cartels and monopolies

shoeleather costs: the resources that are wasted when people change their behavior to avoid holding money

short run: a period of time when consumers can partially adjust their behavior

shortage: market condition when the quantity supplied of a good is less than the quantity demanded

signals: information conveyed by profits and losses about the profitability of various markets

simple money multiplier: the rate at which banks multiply money when all currency is deposited into banks and they hold no excess reserves

single-payer system: government coverage of most healthcare costs, with citizens paying their share through taxes

slope: the change in the rise along the *y* axis (vertical) divided by the change in the run along the *x* axis (horizontal)

social costs: the internal costs plus the external costs of a market activity

social optimum: the price and quantity combination that would exist if there were no externalities

Social Security: a government-administered retirement funding program

social welfare: see *total surplus*

spending multiplier: a formula to determine the total impact on spending from an initial change of a given amount

stagflation: the combination of high unemployment rates and high inflation

status quo bias: condition existing when decision-makers want to maintain their current choices

steady state: the condition of a macroeconomy when there is no new net investment

stocks: ownership shares in a firm

store of value: a means for holding wealth

strike: a work stoppage designed to aid a union's bargaining position

structural unemployment: unemployment caused by changes in the industrial makeup (structure) of the economy

substitutes: goods that are used in place of each other; when the price of a substitute good rises, the quantity demanded falls and the demand for the related good goes up

substitution effect: (1) the decision by laborers to work more hours at higher wages, substituting labor for leisure; (2) a consumer's substitution of a product that has become relatively less expensive as the result of a price change

sunk costs: unrecoverable costs that have been incurred as a result of past decisions

supply curve: a graph of the relationship between the prices in the supply schedule and the quantity supplied at those prices

supply schedule: a table that shows the relationship between the price of a good and the quantity supplied

supply shock: a surprise event that changes a firm's production costs

supply-side fiscal policy: policy that involves the use of government spending and taxes to affect the production (supply) side of the economy

surplus: market condition when the quantity supplied of a good is greater than the quantity demanded

switching costs: the costs incurred when a consumer changes from one supplier to another

tariffs: taxes levied on imported goods and services

technological advancement: the introduction of new techniques or methods so that firms can produce more valuable outputs per unit of input

technology: the knowledge that is available for use in production

third-party problem: a situation in which those not directly involved in a market activity nevertheless experience negative or positive externalities

time preferences: the fact that people prefer to receive goods and services sooner rather than later

tit-for-tat: a long-run strategy that promotes cooperation among participants by mimicking the opponent's most recent decision with repayment in kind

total cost: the amount a firm spends in order to produce the goods and services it produces

total revenue: (1) the amount that consumers pay and sellers receive for a good; (2) the amount a firm receives from the sale of the goods and services it produces

total surplus: the sum of consumer surplus and producer surplus; also known as *social welfare*

trade: the voluntary exchange of goods and services between two or more parties

trade balance: the difference between a nation's total exports and total imports

trade deficit: condition occurring when imports exceed exports, indicating a negative trade balance

trade surplus: condition occurring when exports exceed imports, indicating a positive trade balance

tragedy of the commons: the depletion of a good that is rival in consumption but nonexcludable

transfer payments: payments made to groups or individuals when no good or service is received in return

Treasury securities: the bonds sold by the U.S. government to pay for the national debt

ultimatum game: an economic experiment in which two players decide how to divide a sum of money

underemployed workers: those who have part-time jobs but who would prefer to work full-time

unemployment: condition occurring when a worker who is not currently employed is searching for a job without success

unemployment insurance: a government program that reduces the hardship of joblessness by guaranteeing that unemployed workers receive a percentage of their former income while unemployed

unemployment rate: the percentage of the labor force that is unemployed

union: a group of workers that bargains collectively for better wages and benefits

unit of account: the measure in which prices are quoted

util: a unit of satisfaction used to measure the enjoyment from consumption of a good or service

utility: a measure of the relative levels of satisfaction that consumers enjoy from the consumption of goods and services

value of the marginal product (VMP): the marginal product of an input multiplied by the price of the output it produces

variable: a quantity that can take on more than one value

variable costs: costs that change with the rate of output

wage discrimination: unequal payment of workers because of their race, ethnic origin, sex, age, religion, or some other group characteristic

wealth: the value of one's accumulated assets

wealth effect: the change in the quantity of aggregate demand that results from wealth changes due to price-level changes

welfare economics: the branch of economics that studies how the allocation of resources affects economic well-being

willingness to pay: the maximum price a consumer will pay for a good

willingness to sell: the minimum price a seller will accept to sell a good or service

winner-take-all: phenomenon occurring when extremely small differences in ability lead to sizable differences in compensation

CREDITS

The Economics in the Real World feature in Chapter 5, pp. 165–66, reprints "Efforts Meant to Help Workers Squeeze South Africa's Poorest," by Celia W. Dugger. From *The New York Times*, Sept. 26, 2010. © 2010 The New York Times. All rights reserved. Used by permission and protected by the Copyright Laws of the United States. The printing, copying, redistribution, or retransmission of this content without express written permission is prohibited.

The Economics in the Real World feature in Chapter 20, pp. 625-26, is republished with permission of Dow Jones Company from "Employment, Italian Style," *The Wall Street Journal*, June 25, 2012; permission conveyed through Copyright Clearance Center, Inc. © 2012 Dow Jones, Inc.

The authors thank Courtney Fox for the concept of Figure 24.1 on p. 739, and Bill Russell for the layout.

Figure 24.3 on p. 753 is reprinted from *Geography and Economic Development* by John Luke Gallup and Jeffrey D. Sachs, with Andrew Mellinger. Courtesy of Gallup, Sachs, and Mellinger.

SOURCES FOR SNAPSHOT GRAPHICS

Chapter 4, p. 133: Elasticity values from H. S. Houthakker and Lester D. Taylor, *Consumer Demand in the United States: Analyses and Projections* (Cambridge, MA: Harvard University Press, 1970), and Joachim Moller, "Income and Price Elasticities in Different Sectors of the Economy: An Analysis of Structural Change for Germany, the UK and the USA," in *The Growth of Service Industries: The Paradox of Exploding Costs and Persistent Demand*, edited by Thjis ten Raa and Ronald Schettkat (Northampton, MA: Edward Elgar Publishing, 2001).

Chapter 5, p. 169: Minimum wages as of January 2013, from "Minimum Wage Laws in the States," U.S. Department of Labor, www.dol.gov/whd/minwage/america.htm.

Chapter 6, p. 201: Adapted from "The 10 Strangest State Taxes," *U.S. News and World Report*, money.usnews.com/money/personal-finance/slideshows/the-10-strangest-state-taxes. For British window tax, see the original tax act at British History Online, www.british-history.ac.uk/report.aspx?compid=46825#s1.

Chapter 7, p. 223: The original account is in R. H. Coase, "The Problem of Social Cost," *Journal of Law and Economics* Vol. 3 (1960): 1–44, available at www.jstor.org/stable/724810.

Chapter 9, p. 287: Stadium capacities are approximate. All stadium capacities and attendance records from Baseball Almanac, www.baseball-almanac.com.

Chapter 10, p. 323: All Apple product sales figures from Bare Figures, barefigur.es. PC and Android sales figures from Gartner, Inc., www.gartner.com.

Chapter 12, p. 371: Data from 24/7 Wall St., "Eight Brands That Wasted the Most on the Super Bowl," 247wallst.com/2012/02/01/the-eight-brands-that-wasted-the-most-on-the-super-bowl/2/.

Chapter 13, p. 397: Adapted from an example in David McAdams, *The Game Changer* (New York: W. W. Norton, 2014).

Chapter 14, p. 447: Data from SourcingLine, www.sourcingline.com/country-data/cost-competitiveness.

Chapter 15, p. 477: Income inequality data adapted from United Nations Development Programme, Human Development Report, 2009, Table M. Poverty rates for United States and Japan calculated by OECD as households earning <50% of national median income, for late 2000s: see "Income Distribution—Poverty," at OECD.StatExtracts, http://stats.oecd.org/Index.aspx?DatasetCode=POVERTY.

Chapter 16, p. 501: Adapted from the OECD Better Life Index, www.oecdbetterlifeindex.org (accessed April 2013).

Chapter 17, p. 535: 401(k) data from Robert Strauss, "How Opt Out Keeps People In," *Business Week*, Aug. 23, 2012, www.businessweek.com/articles/2012-08-23/how-opt-out-keeps-people-in. Organ donation numbers from Richard Thaler, "Opting In vs. Opting Out," *New York Times*, Sep. 26, 2009, www.nytimes.com/2009/09/27/business/economy/27view.html. HIV screening data from Rob Goodier, "'Opt-Out' Program for HIV Screening in the ED Gets More

Patients Tested," Oct. 16, 2012, at Modern Medicine, www.modernmedicine.com/legacy/article/793039.

Chapter 18, p. 571: All data from OECD Health Division, *Health Data 2012: Frequently Requested Data*.

Chapter 19, pp. 604–5: Data from the U.S. Bureau of Economic Analysis.

Chapter 20, pp. 638–39: Data from the U.S. Bureau of Labor Statistics, labor force statistics from the Current Population Survey.

Chapter 21, pp. 658–59: Data from the U.S. Bureau of Labor Statistics.

Chapter 23, pp. 722–23: Data from Dow Jones & Company.

Chapter 24, pp. 750–51: Average annual growth rates are calculated as the compound growth rate implied by 1950 and 2008 real per capita GDP for each nation. Data from Angus Maddison, *Statistics on World Population, GDP and Per Capita GDP, 1–2008 AD*. All per capita GDP figures are given in 2010 U.S. dollars. Human welfare data from the World Bank.

Chapter 26, pp. 816–17: Real GDP growth data (quarterly) from the U.S. Bureau of Economic Analysis; unemployment data (monthly) from the U.S. Bureau of Labor Statistics.

Chapter 27, pp. 848–49: Real GDP data (annual) from the U.S. Bureau of Economic Analysis; unemployment data (monthly) from the U.S. Bureau of Labor Statistics.

Chapter 28, pp. 882–83: Data from the U.S. Office of Management and Budget.

Chapter 29, pp. 898–99: Real GDP growth data (quarterly) from the U.S. Bureau of Economic Analysis; unemployment data (monthly) from the U.S. Bureau of Labor Statistics.

Chapter 30, pp. 950–51: Money supply data from the Federal Reserve, Money Stock Measures.

Chapter 31, pp. 982–83: Real GDP growth data (quarterly) from the U.S. Bureau of Economic Analysis; unemployment and inflation data from the U.S. Bureau of Labor Statistics.

Chapter 32, pp. 1006–7: Data from the U.S. Bureau of Economic Analysis.

PHOTOGRAPHS

p. 2: © Pancaketom | Dreamstime.com; **p. 5:** John Lund/Stephanie Roeser/Getty Images; **p. 6 left:** © Phang Kim Shan | Dreamstime.com; **p. 6 right:** © Nguyen Thai | Dreamstime.com; **p. 8:** Visions of America, LLC / Alamy; **p. 9:** © Haywiremedia | Dreamstime.com; **p. 12:** PARAMOUNT / The Kobal Collection/Art Resource, NY; **p. 13:** © Linqong | Dreamstime.com; **p. 14 top:** Joe Robbins/Getty Images; **p. 14 bottom:** © Seanyu | Dreamstime.com; **p. 15:** © Yusputra | Dreamstime.com; **p. 16:** Jacqueline Larma / AP Photo; **p. 18:** Stockbyte/Getty Images; **p. 20:** © Andres Rodriguez | Dreamstime.co; **p. 25:** Wizards of the Coast and Magic: The Gathering are trademarks of Wizards of the Coast LLC. Images used with permission of Wizards of the Coast LLC; **p. 27:** Archive Holdings Inc. /The Image Bank/Getty Images; **p. 28:** M.L. Watts / Wikimedia Commons; **p. 29:** © Nikolai Sorokin | Dreamstime.com; **p. 30:** Paul Springett / Alamy; **p. 36:** Lou-Foto / Alamy; **p. 44:** © Philcold | Dreamstime.com; **p. 45:** DREAMWORKS / Album/Newscom; **p. 46 left:** Teraberb | Dreamstime.com; **p. 46 right:** Yuri Arcurs | Dreamstime.com; **p. 48:** © Globe photos/ ZUMAPRESS.com/Newscom; **p. 49:** © Monkeybusiness | Dreamstime.com; **p. 50:** © Boeing; **p. 66:** Bruce Lonngren/iStockphoto.com; **p. 69:** AP Photo/The Day, Sean D. Elliot; **p. 70:** All Canada Photos / Alamy; **p. 71 top:** Getty Images/First Light; **p. 71 bottom:** Peter Horree/Alamy; **p. 72:** © William Perry | Dreamstime.com; **p. 74:** Maren Caruso/Photodisc/Getty Images; **p. 78:** © Edith Layland | Dreamstime.com; **p. 80:** © John DeFeo/ iStockphoto.com; **p. 81 left:** Radius Images / Alamy; **p. 81 right:** © Showface | Dreamstime.com; **p. 83:** POLYGRAM/WARNERS/SILVER PICTURES/THE KOBAL COLLECTION/JAMES BRIDGES/Art Resource, NY; **p. 87:** © Lucian Coman | Dreamstime.com; **p. 89:** AP Photo/Ted S. Warren; **p. 91:** AP Photo/IBM; **p. 92:** Stockbyte/Getty Images; **p. 95:** CRANKSHAFT(NEW) © 2005 MEDIAGRAPHICS, INC. NORTH AMERICA SYNDICATE; **p. 97:** © R. Gino Santa Maria | Dreamstime.com; **p. 106:** © Hugoht | Dreamstime.com; **p. 109:** AP Photo/Reed Saxon; **p. 110:** © Columbia Pictures/courtesy Everett Collection; **p. 111:** Allstar Picture Library/Alamy; **p. 112 top:** Evan-Amos/Wikimedia Commons; **p. 112 bottom:** © Cobalt88 | Dreamstime.com; **p. 113:** © Seanyu | Dreamstime.com; **p. 114 top:** © Wisconsinart | Dreamstime.com; **p. 114 second from top:** © Oleksiy Mark | Dreamstime.com; **p.114 second from bottom:** Lisa Thornberg/iStockphoto .com; **p. 114 bottom:** IFCAR/Wikimedia Commons; **p. 115:** © 20th Century Fox Film Corp. All rights reserved. Courtesy: Everett Collection; **p. 117:** © Mathew Hayward | Dreamstime.com; **p. 118 top left:** © Mathew Hayward | Dreamstime.com; **p. 118 top right:** © Rick Rhay/iStockphoto.com; **p. 118 bottom left:** © Johnfoto | Dreamstime.com;

INDEX

Page numbers where key terms are defined are in **boldface**.